FEDERAL LAND RESOURCES

FEDERAL LAND RESOURCES

QUINTIN R. TELLES
EDITOR

Nova Science Publishers, Inc.
New York

For permission to use material from this book please contact us:
Telephone 631-231-7269; Fax 631-231-8175
Web Site: http://www.novapublishers.com

LIBRARY OF CONGRESS CATALOGING-IN-PUBLICATION DATA

Available upon request.

ISBN : 978-1-60692-130-2

Published by Nova Science Publishers, Inc. ✢ New York

CONTENTS

PREFACE

The federal land resources include; national parks, monuments, and recreational areas; national trails; public lands; forests, wetlands, and wildlife. They are administered by the Department of the Interior, Department of Agriculture, National Park Service, Fish and Wildlife Service, Forest Service, Environmental Protection Agency, and others. This new book brings together important chapters on a variety of topics relevant to federal land resources.

Chapter 1 - In November 2000, Congress passed and President Clinton signed the Energy Act of 2000 (also referred to as the Energy Policy and Conservation Act [EPCA]). The Act directed the Secretary of the Interior, in consultation with the Secretaries of Agriculture and Energy, to conduct an inventory of oil and natural gas resources beneath onshore Federal lands.

The inventory shall identify:

(1) the United States Geological Survey estimates of oil and gas resources underlying these lands;
(2) the extent and nature of any restrictions or impediments to the development of the resources, including—
    (A) impediments to the timely granting of leases;
    (B) post-lease restrictions, impediments, or delays on development for conditions of approval, applications for permits to drill, or processing of environmental permits...

The EPCA marked the first time that Congress asked the Department of the Interior to conduct a study of restrictions.

On October 11, 2001, Congress provided its sense of priority for this study:

. . . in light of recent attacks on the United States that have underscored the potential for disruptions to America's energy supply, the managers believe this project should be considered a top priority for the Department.

In August 2005, Congress passed and President Bush signed the Energy Policy Act of 2005 (EPAct 2005). Section 364 of this Act amends the inventory requirements of EPCA.[2]

This release presents a large majority of the inventory of public oil and gas resources requested by Congress. The EPCA Phase II inventory is a comprehensive review of Federal oil and gas resources and constraints on their development within 11 geologic provinces across the United States. It is cumulative in that it incorporates the Phase I areas (geologic provinces of the Interior West). Further, it represents an expansion of the inventory to include previously unstudied areas in the Interior West, Northern Alaska and several Eastern basins (Figure ES-1).

The EPCA requires that all onshore Federal lands be inventoried. Areas addressed in the Phase II inventory contain approximately 76 percent of the onshore natural gas and oil under Federal ownership. The inventory will be expanded in the future to include all Federal lands and resources.

For the Federal agencies that manage public land (principally the Department of the Interior's Bureau of Land Management [BLM] and the U.S. Department of Agriculture's Forest Service [USDA-FS]) and the citizens they serve, this inventory will serve primarily as a planning tool. It provides public land managers with additional information to help them develop management plans for the lands under their jurisdiction. It enables them to identify areas of high oil or gas potential and to evaluate the effectiveness of mitigating stipulations and conditions of approval in balancing the responsible development of those resources with the protection of other valuable resources in the area. The inventory also allows resource managers to identify areas of low oil and gas potential, but high potential for other resources (e.g., wildlife habitat) or uses (e.g., recreation). In these situations, resource managers and oil and gas operators can consider applying land management strategies that promote increased protection of other valuable resources or uses that might ordinarily conflict with oil or gas development. This chapter is a critical step in evaluating whether the documented impediments and restrictions are appropriate, or are unnecessarily interfering with oil and gas development.

Chapter 2 - Oil shale is prevalent in the western states of Colorado, Utah, and Wyoming. The resource potential of these shales is estimated to be the equivalent of 1.8 trillion barrels of oil in place. Retorted oil shale yields liquid hydrocarbons in the range of middle-distillate fuels, such as jet and diesel fuel. However, because oil shales have not proved to be economically recoverable, they are considered a contingent resource and not true reserves. It remains to be demonstrated whether an economically significant oil volume can be extracted under existing operating conditions. In comparison, Saudi Arabia reportedly holds proved reserves of 267 billion barrels.

Federal interest in oil shale dates back to the early 20th Century, when the Naval Petroleum and Oil Shale Reserves were set aside. Out of World War II concerns for a secure oil supply, a Bureau of Mines program began research into exploiting the resource. Commercial interest followed during the 1960s. After a second oil embargo in the 1970s, Congress created a synthetic fuels program to stimulate large- scale commercial development of oil shale and other unconventional resources. The federal program proved short-lived, and commercially backed oil shale projects ended in the early 1980s when oil prices began declining.

The current high oil prices have revived the interest in oil shale. The Energy Policy Act of 2005 (EPACT) identified oil shale as a strategically important domestic resource, among others, that should be developed. EPACT also directed the Secretary of Defense to develop a separate strategy to use oil shale in meeting Department of Defense (DOD) requirements when doing so is in the national interest. Tapping unconventional resources, such as oil shale, has been promoted as a means of reducing dependence on foreign oil and improving national security.

Opponents of federal subsidies for oil shale argue that the price and demand for crude oil should act as sufficient incentives to stimulate development. Projections of increased demand and peaking petroleum production in the coming decades tend to support the price-and-supply incentive argument in the long term.

The failure of oil shale has been tied to the perennially lower price of crude oil, a much less risky conventional resource. Proponents of renewing commercial oil shale development might also weigh whether other factors detract from the resource's potential. Refining industry profitability is overwhelmingly driven by light passenger vehicle demand for motor gasoline, and oil-shale distillate does not make ideal feedstock for gasoline production. Policies that discourage the wider use of middle- distillates as transportation fuels indirectly discourage oil shale development. Because the largest oil shale resources reside on federal lands, the federal government would have a direct interest and role in the development of this resource.

Chapter 3 - The development of offshore oil, gas, and other mineral resources in the United States is impacted by a number of interrelated legal regimes, including international, federal, and state laws. International law provides a framework for establishing national ownership or control of offshore areas, and domestic federal law mirrors and supplements these standards.

Governance of offshore minerals and regulation of development activities are bifurcated between state and federal law. Generally, states have primary authority in the three geographical mile area extending from their coasts. The federal government and its comprehensive regulatory regime governs those minerals located in federal waters, which extend from the states' offshore boundaries out to at least 200 nautical miles from the shore. The basis for most federal regulation is the Outer Continental Shelf Lands Act (OCSLA), which provides a system for offshore oil and gas development planning, leasing, exploration, and ultimate development. Regulations run the gamut from health, safety, and environmental standards to requirements for production based royalties and, when appropriate, royalty relief and other development incentives.

Several contentious legal issues remain the subject of national debate and legislative proposals. Before adjournment, the 109th Congress passed a bill that would allow new offshore drilling in the Gulf of Mexico in an area known as Lease Area 181. This measure was incorporated into H.R. 6111, a broad bill passed in the final days of the 109th Congress. President Bush signed the bill into law (P.L. 109- 432) on December 20, 2006.

At the same time, the role of the coastal states in deciding whether to lease in areas adjacent to their shores has also received recent attention, with some legislative proposals granting significant decisional authority to state governments while others would direct the Secretary of the Interior to lease specific areas, limiting the state role to what is provided under existing statutes.

In addition to these legislative efforts, there has also been significant litigation related to offshore oil and gas development. Cases handed down over a number of years have clarified the extent of the Secretary's discretion in deciding how leasing and development are to be conducted.

The development of offshore oil, gas, and other mineral resources in the United States is impacted by a number of interrelated legal regimes, including international, federal, and state laws. International law provides a framework for establishing national ownership or control of offshore areas, and United States domestic law has, in substance, adopted these internationally recognized principles. U.S. domestic law further defines U.S. ocean resource jurisdiction and ownership of offshore minerals, dividing regulatory authority and ownership between the states and the federal government based on the resource's proximity to the shore. This chapter[1] explains the nature of U.S. authority over offshore areas pursuant to international and domestic law. It also describes the laws, at both the state and federal levels, governing the development of offshore oil and gas and the litigation that has flowed from development under the current legal regimes. Also included is an outline of the recent changes to the authorities regulating offshore development wrought by the Energy Policy Act of 2005 and subsequent legislation enacted by the 109th Congress prior to adjournment. Finally, this chapter discusses legislation under consideration by the 110th Congress that might also amend existing law in this area.

Chapter 4 - In a plan released today, the Bureau of Land Management (BLM) announced that it would make land available for leasing in the Northeast portion of the National Petroleum Reserve in Alaska (NPR-A) that could yield nearly 3 billion barrels of oil, equaling one quarter of the oil produced over the last 31 years by North America's largest oilfield in Prudhoe Bay. The lands could also provide trillions of cubic feet of gas for shipment to North American markets through gas pipelines currently in the planning stages.

The BLM would not open 219,000 acres of Teshekpuk Lake and its islands to oil and gas leasing according to the preferred alternative selected by the agency in its Supplemental Final Integrated Activity Plan/Environment Impact Statement (IAP/EIS). The plan's preferred alternative would also defer leasing for 10 years on 430,000 acres north and east of Teshekpuk Lake that are currently unavailable for leasing.

In: Federal Land Resources
Editors: Quintin R. Telles

ISBN: 978-1-60692-130-2

Chapter 1

SCIENTIFIC INVENTORY OF ONSHORE FEDERAL LANDS' OIL AND GAS RESOURCES AND THE EXTENT AND NATURE OF RESTRICTIONS OR IMPEDIMENTS TO THEIR DEVELOPMENT*

U.S. Departments of the Interior, Agriculture and Energy

EXECUTIVE SUMMARY

The Mandate from Congress

In November 2000, Congress passed and President Clinton signed the Energy Act of 2000 (also referred to as the Energy Policy and Conservation Act [EPCA]). The Act directed the Secretary of the Interior, in consultation with the Secretaries of Agriculture and Energy, to conduct an inventory of oil and natural gas resources beneath onshore Federal lands:[1]

The inventory shall identify:

(3) the United States Geological Survey estimates of oil and gas resources underlying these lands;
(4) the extent and nature of any restrictions or impediments to the development of the resources, including—
    (C) impediments to the timely granting of leases;
    (D) post-lease restrictions, impediments, or delays on development for conditions of approval, applications for permits to drill, or processing of environmental permits...

The EPCA marked the first time that Congress asked the Department of the Interior to conduct a study of restrictions.

---

* This is an edited, reformatted and augmented edition of a United States Departments of the Interior, Agriculture and Energy Report dated 2006..

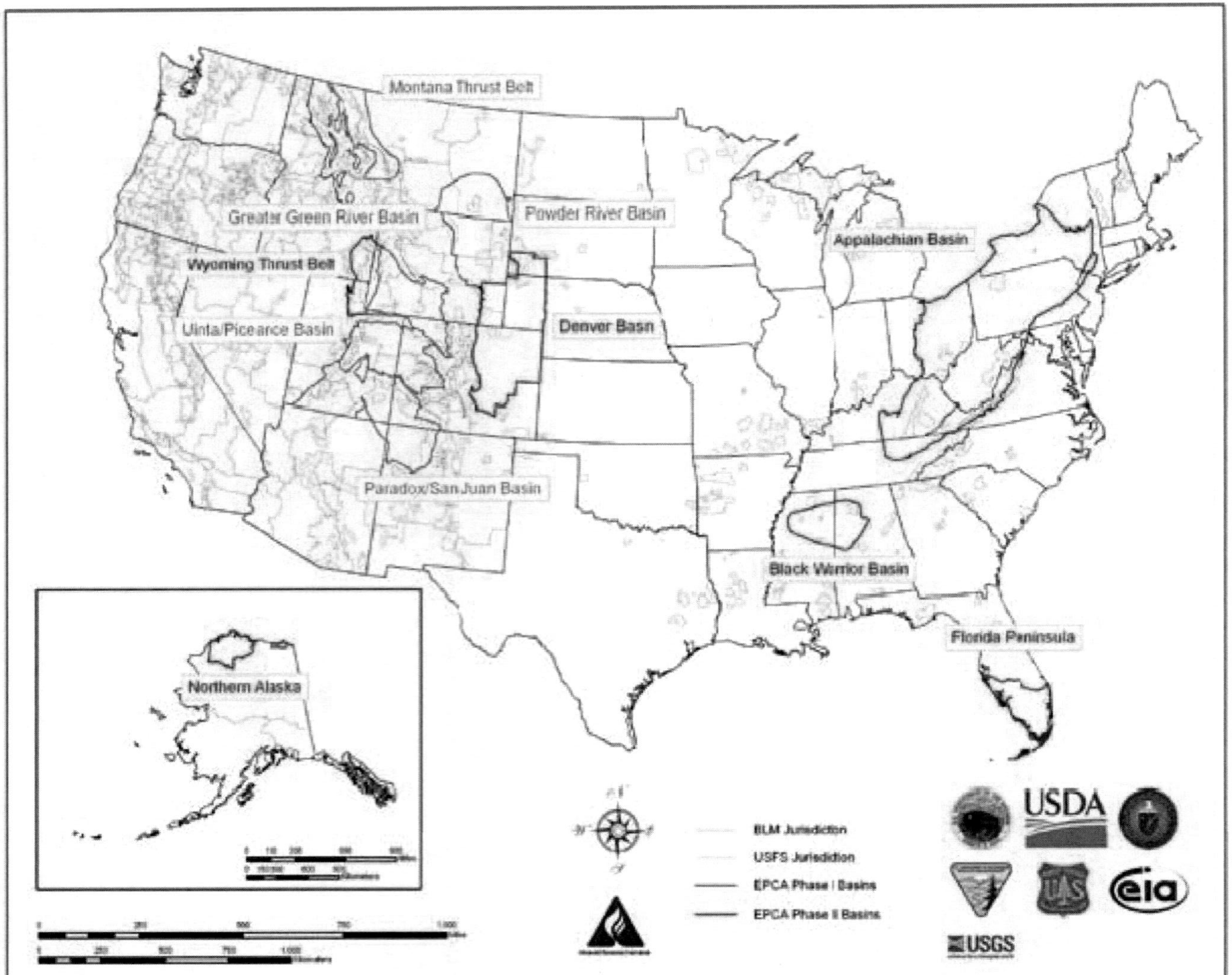

Figure ES-1. Study Area Locations

On October 11, 2001, Congress provided its sense of priority for this study:

> . . . in light of recent attacks on the United States that have underscored the potential for disruptions to America's energy supply, the managers believe this project should be considered a top priority for the Department.

In August 2005, Congress passed and President Bush signed the Energy Policy Act of 2005 (EPAct 2005). Section 364 of this Act amends the inventory requirements of EPCA.[2]

This release presents a large majority of the inventory of public oil and gas resources requested by Congress. The EPCA Phase II inventory is a comprehensive review of Federal oil and gas resources and constraints on their development within 11 geologic provinces across the United States. It is cumulative in that it incorporates the Phase I areas (geologic provinces of the Interior West). Further, it represents an expansion of the inventory to include previously unstudied areas in the Interior West, Northern Alaska and several Eastern basins (Figure ES-1).

The EPCA requires that all onshore Federal lands be inventoried. Areas addressed in the Phase II inventory contain approximately 76 percent of the onshore natural gas and oil under Federal ownership. The inventory will be expanded in the future to include all Federal lands and resources.

For the Federal agencies that manage public land (principally the Department of the Interior's Bureau of Land Management [BLM] and the U.S. Department of Agriculture's Forest Service [USDA-FS]) and the citizens they serve, this inventory will serve primarily as a planning tool. It provides public land managers with additional information to help them develop management plans for the lands under their jurisdiction. It enables them to identify areas of high oil or gas potential and to evaluate the effectiveness of mitigating stipulations and conditions of approval in balancing the responsible development of those resources with the protection of other valuable resources in the area. The inventory also allows resource managers to identify areas of low oil and gas potential, but high potential for other resources (e.g., wildlife habitat) or uses (e.g., recreation). In these situations, resource managers and oil and gas operators can consider applying land management strategies that promote increased protection of other valuable resources or uses that might ordinarily conflict with oil or gas development. This chapter is a critical step in evaluating whether the documented impediments and restrictions are appropriate, or are unnecessarily interfering with oil and gas development.

The President's National Energy Policy Directives

In May 2001, President Bush's National Energy Policy directed that the EPCA inventory be expedited and that constraints to Federal oil and gas leasing be reassessed and modified "where opportunities exist (consistent with the law, good environmental practice, and balanced use of other resources)." The National Energy Policy further directed that any reassessment of constraints be conducted "with full public consultation, especially with people in the region." This inventory provides information regarding the geographical relationship between oil and gas resources and the constraints that govern their development. It is not a reassessment of any stipulations or conditions of approval on the development of oil and gas resources. The public's opportunity to participate in any change of restrictions on oil and gas activities will occur during the land use planning or legislative process. This inventory provides some basic information for any such process. Additional information may be available from monitoring and scientific studies incorporated into adaptive management processes.

The National Energy Policy provides an overview of the U.S. energy situation and alternatives available to increase energy efficiency and conservation, increase energy supplies, and protect the environment. At the direction of Congress, the present study focuses on the traditional energy resources of oil and natural gas beneath Federal lands.[3]

This inventory was prepared under the lead of the Bureau of Land Management. Senior professionals from the Department of the Interior's BLM and United States Geological Survey (USGS), the USDA-FS; the Department of Energy (DOE)-Office of Fossil Energy, and the Energy Information Administration (EIA) were the major contributors. The USGS provided the assessment of undiscovered technically recoverable oil and natural gas resources beneath Federal lands based on commercially available data. The EIA contributed the analysis of reserves growth and proved reserves for Federal lands. The DOE provided technical expertise to guide the design and analysis process for the inventory. Field offices of the BLM and the USDA-FS contributed their land use planning information regarding oil and natural gas availability and leasing stipulations for the lands under their respective jurisdictions.

Methodology

This inventory is based on information that has been previously developed through the scientific and planning processes of the contributing Federal agencies. This information has in large part been provided to the public for its review and use and is the best that is commercially and scientifically available. It has been compiled and analyzed by experts from the contributing agencies. The analytical methods and protocols used in the supporting studies have been subjected to rigorous review. The present study necessarily incorporates the assumptions, conditions, and limitations of the supporting scientific information as discussed in this chapter. This inventory is significant because it builds upon the process established in the EPCA Phase I inventory. It examines oil and gas (undiscovered technically recoverable resources and reserves growth) in context with information about constraints on their development.

The Phase II inventory examines six geologic provinces in addition to the five areas examined within the Interior West in the Phase I inventory. These six provinces are Northern Alaska (the National Petroleum Reserve in Alaska [NPR-A] and the Arctic National Wildlife Refuge [ANWR] Section 1002 only); the Wyoming Thrust Belt in Wyoming, Utah, and Idaho; the Denver Basin in Colorado, Wyoming, Nebraska, and South Dakota; the Florida Peninsula; the Black Warrior Basin in Mississippi and Alabama; and the Appalachian Basin in Tennessee, Kentucky, West Virginia, Virginia, Maryland, Ohio, Pennsylvania, New Jersey, and New York. These areas were selected for Phase II of the inventory because, as a group, they include Alaska, a state containing important oil and gas resources, and contain a large portion of the inventoried onshore Federal oil and gas resources in the lower-48 states relative to the EPCA Phase I study areas. In addition, especially in the West, the Federal lands within these areas are becoming increasingly important for recreation, livestock grazing, open space, wildlife habitat, cultural resources, and mining, as well as oil and gas and other energy production.

The Phase II inventory encompasses 295 million acres, of which about 99 million acres are under Federal management. This acreage includes split estate lands where private surface lands are underlain by Federal mineral rights.

This analysis of constraints to development centers on two factors that affect access to oil and gas resources on Federal lands. These factors are (1) whether the lands are "open" or "closed" to leasing, and (2) the degree of access afforded by lease stipulations and other conditions on "open" lands (some leasable lands may in effect be "closed" if no drilling can occur). All oil and gas leases are subject to a baseline level of constraint governed by statutory and regulatory requirements. These stipulations serve many purposes, ranging from the protection of environmental, social, historical, or cultural resources or values to the payment of rentals and royalties.

The Phase II inventory finds that approximately 2,130 individual lease stipulations are being applied by the land managing agencies in the areas analyzed. To focus the analysis of constraints on oil and gas development, the inventory evaluates the onshore Federal lands: (1) where leasing is permitted under standard stipulations; (2) where leasing is permitted with varying limitations on access, principally seasonal occupancy restrictions; and (3) where oil and gas leasing is precluded or prohibited. The inventory also considers exceptions to stipulations that are granted after a review of on-theground conditions and the use of modern technologies such as directional drilling. The impact of conditions of approval (COAs) attached to Federal drilling permits is also analyzed, which gives a more complete assessment of access constraints. A total of 175 unique COAs were identified and their effects on development evaluated. The nine categories of constraints analyzed in this chapter include the complete range of access restrictions associated with oil and gas leasing.

Results

The results of this cumulative Phase II inventory are unique for each of the eleven areas examined. The aggregate results for all of the areas (Table ES-1, Figure ES-2, and Figure ES-3) are summarized below.

- Total Federal lands, including split estate, total 99.2 million acres.
- Undeveloped oil resources under these Federal lands total 21.2 billion barrels, comprising 20.6 billion barrels of undiscovered technically recoverable resources and 593 million barrels of reserves growth.
- Undeveloped gas resources under these Federal lands total 186.9 trillion cubic feet, comprising 181.9 trillion cubic feet of undiscovered technically recoverable resources and 4.98 trillion cubic feet of reserves growth.
- Total proved reserves under these Federal lands total 444 million barrels of oil and 26.3 trillion cubic feet of natural gas.
- Approximately 24 percent of the Federal land in these areas (23.8 million acres) is accessible under standard lease terms. Based on resource estimates, these lands

contain 3 percent of the oil (743 million barrels) and 13 percent of the gas (25.2 trillion cubic feet).

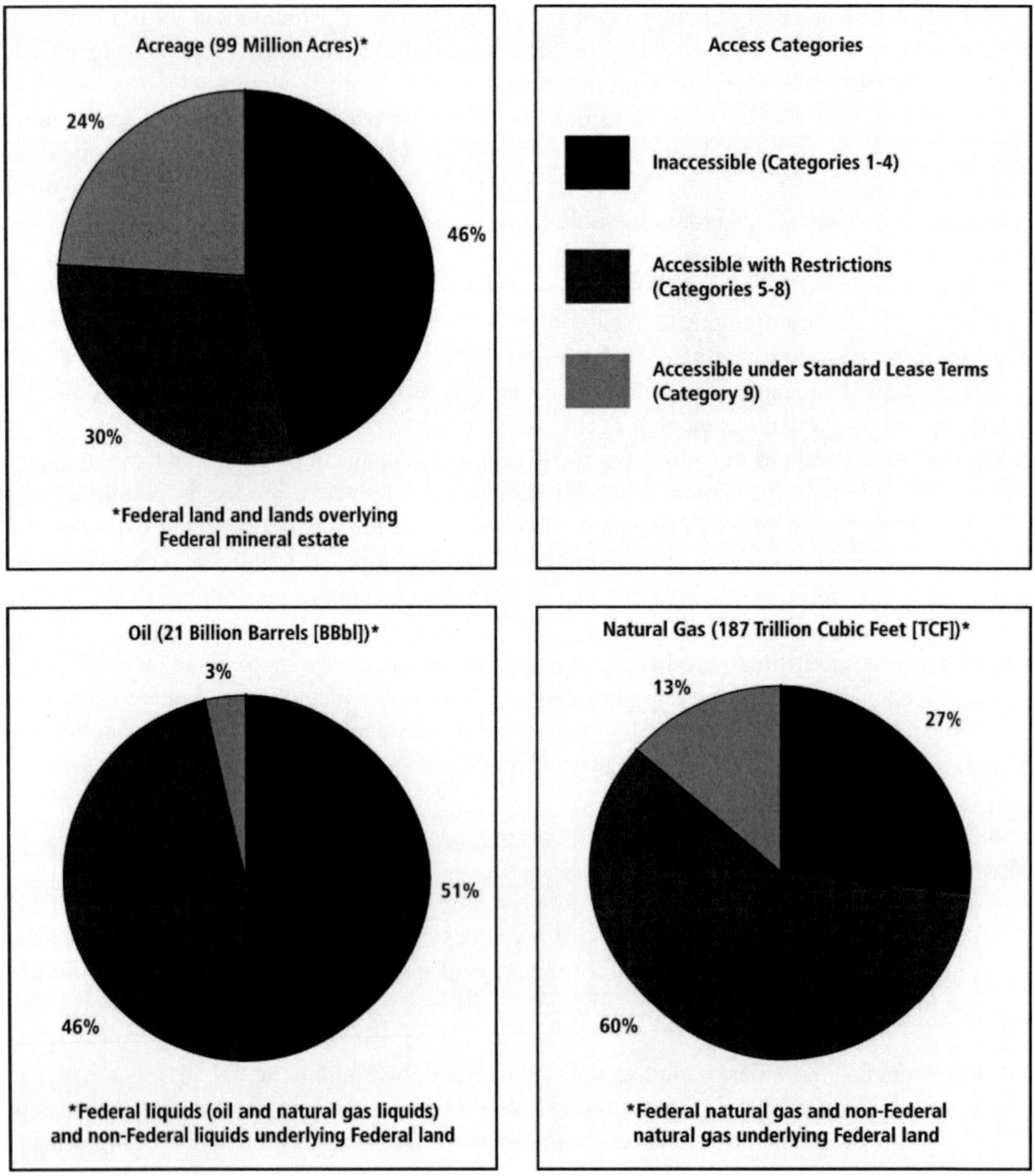

Figure ES-2. Simplified Results; Summary of All Phase II Study Areas—Total Federal Land and Resources by Accessibility

- Approximately 30 percent (30.0 million acres) of the Federal land is accessible with restrictions on oil and gas operations beyond standard stipulations. Based on resource estimates, these lands contain 46 percent of the oil (9.7 billion barrels) and 60 percent of the gas (111.5 trillion cubic feet).

- Approximately 46 percent (45.5 million acres) of the Federal land is inaccessible. Based on resource estimates, these lands contain about 51 percent of the oil (10.8 billion barrels) and 27 percent of the natural gas (50.1 trillion cubic feet).

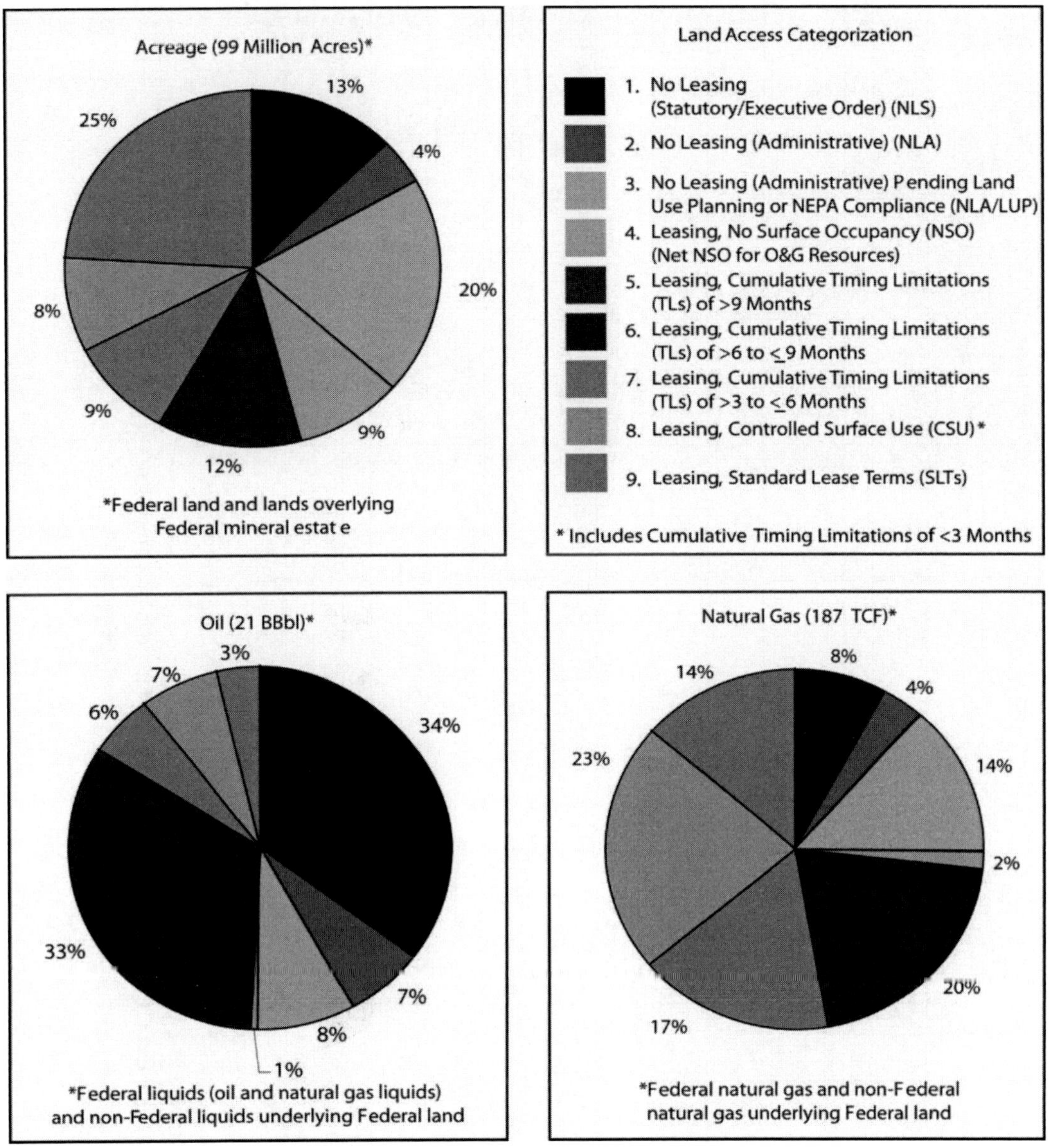

Figure ES-3. Results; Summary of All Phase II Study Areas—Total Federal Land and Oil and Natural Gas Resources by Access Category

Overall the study shows that oil and gas resources are concentrated in Northern Alaska and the Interior West. Figure ES-4 summarizes the accessibility of these resources (on a trillion cubic feet-equivalent basis).

Table ES-1. Summary of All EPCA Inventory Areas—Total Federal Land and Oil and Natural Gas Resources by Access Category

Access Category			Area		Resourcesa			
					Total Oilb		Total Gasc	
			(acres x 1000)	Percent of Federal	(MMbbls)d	Percent of Federal	(BCF)e	Percent of Federal
Less Constrained More Constrained (↑)	1.	No Leasing (Statutory/Executive Order) (NLS)	12,601	12.7%	7,510	35.4%	14,867	8.0%
	2.	No Leasing (Administrative) (NLA)	4,161	4.2%	1,405	6.6%	6,891	3.7%
	3.	No Leasing (Administrative) Pending Land Use Planning or NEPA Compliance (NLA/LUP)	19,680	19.8%	1,727	8.1%	25,444	13.6%
	4.	Leasing, No Surface Occupancy (NSO) (Net NSO for O&G Resources)	9,025	9.1%	135	0.6%	2,923	1.6%
	5.	Leasing, Cumulative Timing Limitations (TLs) of >9 Months	88	0.1%	3	0.0%	14	0.0%
	6.	Leasing, Cumulative Timing Limitations (TLs) of >6 to <9 Months	12,252	12.4%	7,059	33.3%	37,893	20.3%
	7.	Leasing, Cumulative Timing Limitations (TLs) of >3 to <6 Months	9,271	9.3%	1,184	5.6%	31,188	16.7%
	8.	Leasing, Controlled Surface Use (CSU)f	8,374	8.4%	1,451	6.8%	42,428	22.7%
	9.	Leasing, Standard Lease Terms (SLTs)	23,751	23.9%	743	3.5%	25,210	13.5%
Total, Federal Lands including Split Estate			99,203	100%	21,216	100%	186,857	100%
Total Non-Federal			196,204		4,802		156,603	
Total Inventory Area			295,406		26,018		343,460	
Summary								
Inaccessible (Categories 1-4)			45,467	46%	10,776	51%	50,125	27%
Accessible with Restrictions (Categories 5-8)			29,985	30%	9,697	46%	111,522	60%
Accessible under Standard Lease Terms (Category 9)			23,751	24%	743	3%	25,210	13%
Total, Federal Lands Including Split Estate			99,203	100%	21,216	100%	186,857	100%

a Undiscovered technically recoverable resources and reserves growth

b Including oil, natural gas liquids (NGLs) and liquids associated with natural gas reservoirs

c Including associated dissolved and nonassociated natural gas

d Million barrels **e** Billion cubic feet **f** Includes Cumulative Timing Limitations of <3 months

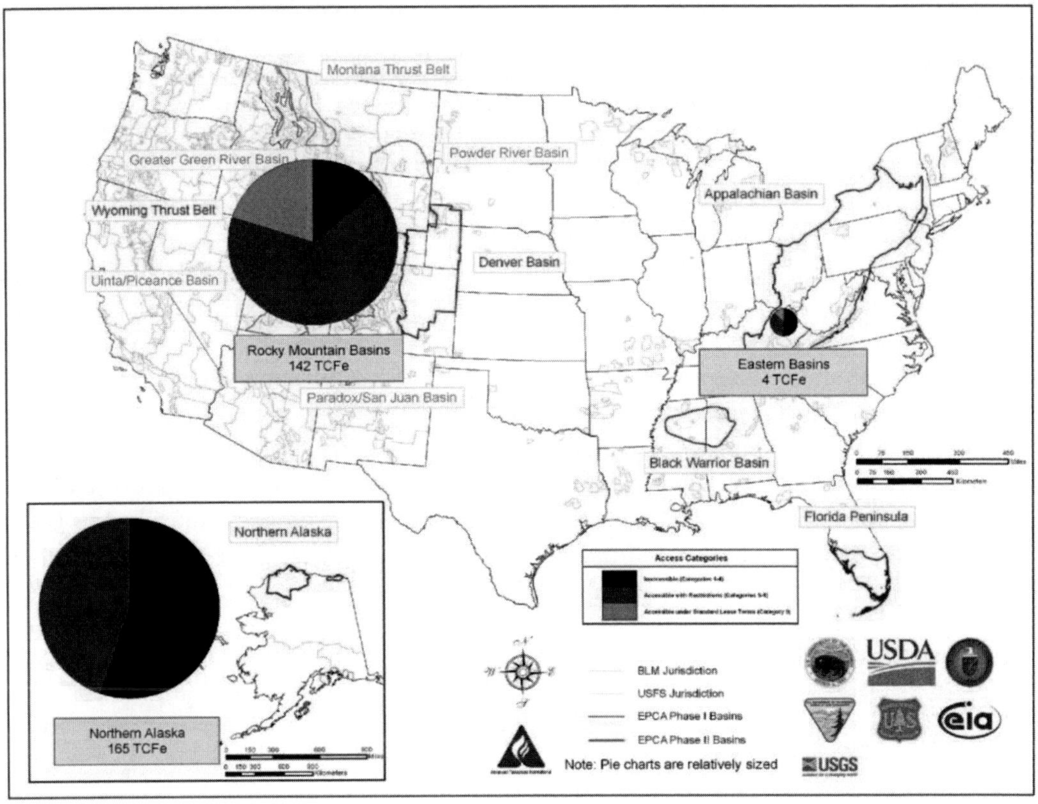

Figure ES-4. Regional Char

Compliance with the Law

All oil and gas leases on Federal land, including those issued with only the standard lease terms, are subject to full compliance with all environmental laws and regulations. These laws include, but are not limited to, the National Environmental Policy Act, Clean Water Act, Clean Air Act, Endangered Species Act, and National Historic Preservation Act. While compliance with these laws may delay, modify, or prohibit oil and gas activities, these laws represent the values and bounds Congress believes appropriate to place on Federal land managers for their stewardship of Federal lands. The present study was conducted at the request of Congress to provide information for forthcoming deliberations on the role of Federal lands in the U.S. energy supply.

It is important to emphasize that this inventory was prepared at the direction of Congress. It is not a decision-making document. The inventory identifies areas of varying oil and gas potential and the nature of constraints to the development of those resources in eleven areas across the U.S. Any reassessment of restrictions on oil and gas activities will occur as part of the public land use planning or legislative processes, both of which are fully open to public participation and debate about the appropriate balance between resource protection and resource development.

1. INTRODUCTION

As the energy needs of the nation continue to grow, the onshore sedimentary basins of the United States become increasingly significant oil and natural gas sources to help meet these needs, especially for natural gas. In 2005, the U.S. consumed about 22 trillion cubic feet (TCF) of natural gas, produced approximately 18 TCF of that consumption domestically, and imported the remaining 4 TCF. Onshore Federal lands produced about 16% of the 2005 domestic consumption. The Energy Information Administration (EIA) in its *Annual Energy Outlook 2006* Reference Case predicts that the demand for natural gas will rise to nearly 27 TCF by 2025, of which over 5 TCF will be imported.[4]

Based on recent U.S. Geological Survey (USGS)[5] and Minerals Management Service (MMS)[6] assessments, the nation's undiscovered natural gas resources[7] total approximately 1,040 TCF. The largest potential source for domestic natural gas production is the Outer Continental Shelf (OCS) with approximately 40 percent of the nation's undiscovered natural gas resources. However, EIA data indicate that OCS natural gas production peaked in 1996 at 4.7 TCF and is forecast to be 4.3 TCF per year in 2025, based largely on production from the Gulf of Mexico.

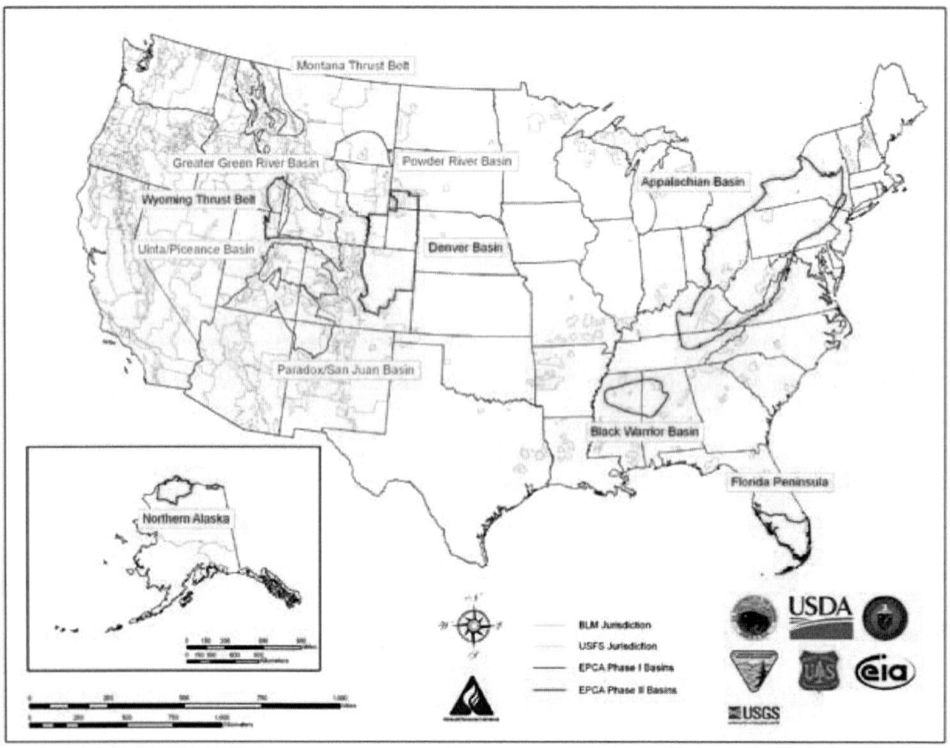

Figure 1-1. Study Area Locations

The nation's second largest natural gas source is the nonfederal onshore lands and state waters, containing about 35 percent of the total.[8] Onshore Federal lands contain the remaining 25 percent. This inventory analyzes onshore Federal natural gas resources in 11 areas, totaling

187 TCF. This 187 TCF would be sufficient to meet the nation's current residential consumption for nearly 39 years.

A full set of acronyms used in this chapter, as well as a glossary, can be found in Appendices 1 and 2, respectively.

Similarly, the U.S. consumed about 7.6 billion barrels (Bbbls) of oil in 2005. About 60% of this oil was imported. Onshore Federal lands produced about 5% of the 2005 domestic consumption. The EIA predicts that the nation will consume 9.5 Bbbls in 2025.

The nation's undiscovered oil resources total slightly over 133 Bbbls. Of that total, the MMS estimates that 86 Bbbls are offshore under the OCS, comprising 64 percent of the nation's resources. Federal onshore oil resources are the second largest potential source of production (20 percent) followed by state waters and nonfederal onshore resources (16 percent).

This inventory estimates that, in the 11 areas examined, there are 21.2 Bbbls of oil resources on Federal onshore lands. Of that total, 17.1 Bbbls occur within just two areas of Northern Alaska: the National Petroleum Reserve–Alaska (NPR-A) and the Arctic National Wildlife Refuge (ANWR) 1002 area.

It is clear that Federal lands will be an important future energy supply source. According to the EIA, the Rocky Mountain region was poised in 2005 to eclipse the Gulf Coast as the single largest supplier of natural gas to the nation. The sedimentary basins in the Interior West are particularly significant future sources of natural gas, and the Alaska North Slope is similarly noteworthy with respect to both oil and gas. Considerable natural gas supply would become available to the lower 48 states with the building of an Alaskan natural gas pipeline.

Congress directed the Secretary of the Interior to inventory the nation's Federal onshore oil and gas resources in relation to Federal actions that inhibit access to these resources. The purpose of this inventory is to add clarity to the debate and assist energy policymakers and Federal land managers in making decisions concerning oil and gas development.

The Phase II inventory examines areas extending from Alaska to Florida (Figure 1-1). Of the more than 295 million acres within these study areas, over 99 million acres of Federal lands (including split estate) were analyzed.

1.1 Background

Access to Federal lands is probably the most oft-cited issue affecting onshore domestic oil and gas exploration and production. The restrictions and impediments that constrain access to Federal lands are frequently a complex patchwork of requirements that can preclude drilling or increase costs and delay activity. They include areas unavailable for leasing and areas where the minerals can be leased, but the surface of the land may not be occupied thereby affecting recovery of those resources. There are also limitations on drilling activities due to a variety of environmental considerations, typically manifested as lease stipulations and drilling permit conditions of approval (COAs).

Recent attempts to understand the impacts of Federal land management decisions on access to oil and gas resources began with a 1999 National Petroleum Council (NPC) study.[9] The NPC is an advisory committee to the Secretary of Energy.

One of the objectives of the NPC study was to collect and analyze data on land use and natural gas resources for Federal lands to identify opportunities for increasing natural gas supply from this area. The NPC identified the Interior West as a significant future source of gas supply to help meet the anticipated growing demand. The NPC also estimated that about 40 percent (137 TCF) of the potential supply from this region is currently unavailable for leasing or is subject to surface-use access restrictions because of competing uses or environmental considerations. This analysis was based on a limited sample of Federal lands in the region. The report was developed through a cooperative effort of Federal agencies, including the Department of Energy (DOE), the Bureau of Land Management (BLM), and the U.S. Department of Agriculture's Forest Service (USDA-FS) and the oil and gas industry. Representatives from state and local governments and other stakeholders also participated.

In response to the NPC recommendation, DOE, with the cooperation of the Department of the Interior (DOI) and the U.S. Department of Agriculture (USDA), embarked on an effort to assess the relationship between gas resources and land use restrictions on Federal lands. The first area studied was the Greater Green River Basin (GGRB) of Wyoming and Colorado. DOE released its report in May 2001, which showed that 53 percent of the GGRB's natural gas resources were either closed to development or available with restrictions.[10]

Both the NPC and DOE studies were substantially less comprehensive than the present Phase II inventory. While the DOE study was being conducted, EPCA was signed into law in November of that year. Section 604 of this act required a similar study, to be led by DOI in cooperation with the USDA and DOE, which was to include an analysis of undiscovered oil and natural gas resources and proved oil and gas reserves for all onshore Federal lands in the United States. The text of Section 604 and the related conference report are given below.

1.2 The EPCA as Amended by the EPAct 2005

Sec. 604. Scientific Inventory of Oil and Gas Resources[11]

(a) In General

The Secretary of the Interior, in consultation with the Secretaries of Agriculture and Energy, shall conduct an inventory of all onshore Federal lands. The inventory shall identify—

(1) the United States Geological Survey estimates of the oil and gas resources underlying these lands;
(2) the extent and nature of any restrictions or impediments to the development of the resources, including—
  (A) impediments to the timely granting of leases;
  (B) post-lease restrictions, impediments, or delays on development for conditions of approval, applications for permits to drill, or processing of environmental permits; and
  (C) permits or restrictions associated with transporting the resources for entry into commerce; and
(3) the quantity of resources not produced or introduced into commerce because of the restrictions.';

(b) Regular Update

Once completed, the USGS resource estimates and the surface availability data as provided in subsection (a)(2) shall be regularly updated and made publicly available.

(c) Inventory

The inventory shall be provided to the Committee on Resources of the House of Representatives and to the Committee on Energy and Natural Resources of the Senate within two years after the date of enactment of this section.

(d) Assessments

Using the inventory, the Secretary of Energy shall make periodic assessments of economically recoverable resources accounting for a range of parameters such as current costs, commodity prices, technology, and regulations.

Congress further emphasized the importance of this inventory during the appropriation process:

Conference Report on H.R. 2217, Department of Interior and Related Agencies Appropriations Act, 2002

Joint Explanatory Statement of the Committee of Conference

The managers agree to the following:

> ... In light of recent attacks on the United States that have underscored the potential for disruptions to America's energy supply, the managers believe this project should be considered a top priority for the Department.[12]

1.3 The National Energy Policy, May 2001

The President's comprehensive National Energy Policy, issued in May 2001, outlines more than 100 recommendations to diversify and increase energy supplies, encourage conservation, and improve energy distribution. The policy recommends a balanced approach that emphasizes renewable energy production, conservation, and traditional fossil fuel production. Oil and natural gas is a major component of the President's policy; in particular, examining ways to increase access to these resources. The Policy notes that some Federal lands otherwise available for leasing, have been legislatively or administratively withdrawn from leasing. The Vice-President's National Energy Policy Development Group recommended:

> ...that the President direct the Secretary of the Interior to examine land status and lease stipulation impediments to Federal oil and gas leasing, and review and modify those where opportunities exist (consistent with the law, good environmental practice, and balanced use of other resources).

Expedite the ongoing Energy Policy and Conservation Act study of impediments to Federal oil and gas exploration and development, and

Review public lands withdrawals and lease stipulations, with full public consultation, especially with the people in the region, to consider modifications where appropriate.[13]

1.4 The EPCA Phase I Inventory, 2003

Completed in January 2003, the Phase I inventory focused on basins of the Interior West, where most Federal onshore oil and gas resources in the lower 48 states are located.[14] The Phase I inventory covered the Uinta-Piceance, Paradox/San Juan, Powder River, and Greater Green River Basins and the Montana Thrust Belt. The methodologies used in the EPCA Phase I inventory and this inventory are similar and modified data from Phase I are incorporated into this study (see Section 2).

1.5 The National Petroleum Council Report, 2003

Also completed in 2003, the NPC provided an update to its 1999 natural gas study.[15] The revised study shows a fundamental shift in the natural gas supply-and-demand balance resulting in higher prices and greater price volatility. Further, the study finds that despite increasing energy efficiency and greater conservation efforts, the traditional North American producing areas can only meet 75 percent of long-term U.S. natural gas needs, leaving the balance to be supplied by imports. To solve some of these problems, the NPC made four recommendations, of which the second was:

Recommendation 2: Increase supply diversity

- Increase Access and Reduce Permitting Impediments to Development of Lower-48 Natural Gas Resources
- Enact Enabling Legislation ... for an Alaska Gas Pipeline

With respect to Federal land access, the NPC examined Conditions of Approval (COAs) in addition to lease stipulations. The study found that the COAs are more of an impediment to development than leasing stipulations. For example, in the Green River Basin, the 2003 NPC study determined that 9 percent of the resource was unavailable for leasing with an additional 31 percent "effectively" off-limits to development due to prohibitive COAs. The NPC study noted that, in addition to making leasable areas unavailable, the COAs added significant costs and delays to development. Further, it estimated that of the 238 TCF undiscovered, technically recoverable natural gas resources in the Rocky Mountain region, 69 TCF are unavailable for development while the remaining 56 TCF are impacted by access-related regulatory requirements.

1.6 Approach

Similar to the Phase I inventory, the Steering Committee, composed of representatives from the participating agencies, was responsible for overseeing the completion of the Phase II inventory. Subsequent to the Phase I inventory, the Steering Committee identified the next six major oil and gas geologic provinces:

- Northern Alaska (NA; NPR-A and ANWR 1002)
- Wyoming Thrust Belt (WTB)
- Denver Basin (DEN)
- Florida Peninsula (FLP)
- Black Warrior Basin (BWB)
- Appalachian Basin (APB).

As with the Phase I inventory, each of these study areas is defined by the aggregation of the USGS oil and gas resource plays for each area. The energy resource, Federal land status, and oil and gas constraints data for these areas have been incorporated into a Geographic Information System (GIS) that allows derivative mapping and statistical analysis. The results presented in this chapter are cumulative as the Phase II inventory incorporates and supersedes Phase I.

1.7 Roles of the Agencies

Section 604 of EPCA designated responsibility for preparing the inventory to the Department of the Interior, in consultation with the Departments of Agriculture and Energy. The Interagency Steering Committee is responsible for providing guidance for conducting the studies, recommending direction to the contractor,[16] making decisions concerning critical parameters, reviewing the methodologies and results, and publishing the report.

The Secretary of the Interior designated the BLM as the lead agency for the inventory. The BLM maintains the oil and gas lease stipulation information and well files containing COAs for lands under its jurisdiction, and land status data for all Federally owned lands within the United States.

The USGS, also a bureau of the DOI, conducts assessments of undiscovered technically recoverable oil and natural gas. The primary source of the oil and gas resource information used in this study is the USGS National Assessment of United States Oil and Gas Resources.

The Secretary of Agriculture designated the USDA-FS, its primary land management agency, to contribute its information regarding oil and gas lease availability and leasing stipulations for lands within the National Forest System.

The DOE, as author of the above-mentioned GGRB report, contributes its expertise and experience in guiding the design and analysis process for the inventory. DOE's EIA contributes its analysis of proved reserves estimates and reserves growth for Federal lands.

Table 1-1. BLM and Forest Service Offices Participating in the Inventory

Jurisdiction	Study Area*
National Forests in Alabama	BWB
Albuquerque, NM, BLM Field Office	PDX/SJ
Allegheny NF	APB
Arapaho and Roosevelt NF and Pawnee NG	DEN
Ashley NF	UP, GGRB
Beaverhead-Deerlodge NF	MTB
Big Cypress NP	FLP
Big Horn NF	PRB
Billings, MT, BLM Field Office	MTB, PRB
Bitterroot NF	MTB
Black Hills NF	PRB, DEN
Bridger-Teton NF	WTB, GGRB
Buffalo, WY, BLM Field Office	PRB
Butte, MT, BLM Field Office	MTB
Caribou-Targhee NF	WTB
Carson NF	PDX/SJ
Casper, WY, BLM Field Office	PRB, DEN
Cedar City, UT, BLM Field Office	PDX/SJ
Cibola NF	PDX/SJ
Custer NF	PRB
Daniel Boone NF	APB
Dillon, MT, BLM Field Office	MTB
Dixie NF	PDX/SJ
Fairbanks, AK, BLM Field Office	NA
Farmington, NM, BLM Field Office	PDX/SJ
Fillmore, UT, BLM Field Office	UP
Finger Lakes NF	APB
Fish and Wildlife Service lands in Florida	FLP
Fishlake NF	UP, PDX/SJ
Flathead NF	MTB
Gallatin NF	MTB
George Washington and Jefferson NF	APB
Glenwood Springs, CO, BLM Field Office	UP, GGRB
Grand Junction, CO, BLM Field Office	UP, PDX/SJ
Grand Mesa Uncompahgre/Gunnison NF	UP, PDX/SJ
Gunnison, CO, BLM Field Office	UP
Helena NF	MTB
Idaho Falls, ID, BLM Field Office	WTB
Jackson, MS, BLM Field Office	FLP, BWB, APB
Kanab, UT, BLM Field Office	PDX/SJ
Kemmerer, WY, BLM Field Office	WTB, GGRB
Kootenai NF	MTB
Lander, WY, BLM Field Office	GGRB
Lewis and Clark NF	MTB, eastern portions only
Lewistown, MT, BLM Field Office	MTB
Little Snake, CO, BLM Field Office	UP, GGRB
Lolo NF	MTB
Manti La Sal NF	UP, PDX/SJ
Medicine Bow-Routt NF; Thunder Basin NG	UP, PRB, GGRB
Miles City, MT, BLM Field Office	PRB
Milwaukee, WI, BLM Field Office	APB
National Forests in Mississippi	BWB

Missoula, MT, BLM Field Office	MTB
Moab, UT, BLM Field Office	UP, PDX/SJ
Monongahela NF	APB
Monticello, UT, BLM Field Office	PDX/SJ
Nebraska NF and Oglala, Buffalo Gap NG	PRB, DEN
Newcastle, WY, BLM Field Office	PRB, DEN
Pike-San Isabel NF	DEN
Pinedale, WY, BLM Field Office	WTB, GGRB
Pocatello, ID, BLM Field Office	WTB
Price, UT, BLM Field Office	UP, PDX/SJ
Rawlins, WY, BLM Field Office	GGRB, DEN
Richfield, UT, BLM Field Office	UP, PDX/SJ
Rock Springs, WY, BLM Field Office	GGRB
Royal Gorge, CO, BLM Field Office	DEN
Salt Lake, UT, BLM Field Office	UP, WTB
San Juan Public Lands Center, USFS/BLM	PDX/SJ
Santa Fe NF	PDX/SJ
South Dakota BLM Field Office	PRB, DEN
St. George, UT, BLM Field Office	PDX/SJ
Tennessee Valley Authority	BWB, APB
Uinta NF	UP
Uncompahgre, CO, BLM Field Office	UP, PDX/SJ
Vernal, UT, BLM Field Office	UP
Wasatch-Cache NF	WTB
Wayne NF	APB
White River, CO, BLM Field Office	UP
White River NF	UP, GGRB

During the course of this study, members of the Steering Committee and contract personnel visited field offices within the various basins. BLM and USDA-FS personnel from more than 80 offices (Table 1-1) participated in these visits. The purpose of these visits was to inform BLM and USDA-FS officials about the studies and to solicit input concerning lease stipulations, COAs, and other issues of concern regarding oil and gas development. As described in Section 2, parameter input from these officials was critical to the study. Data were collected during and following the field visits.

1.8 Intended Use

This inventory is designed to be useful to a wide range of interests. In a broad sense, it gives a picture of where oil and natural gas is estimated to occur and a quantification of what statutory and administrative constraints limit exploration and development. Agencies can use this inventory data to identify areas of high resource potential and to examine Federal land management decisions affecting access to energy resources. This inventory provides both the public and Federal land managers with information about the potential magnitude of oil and natural gas resources unavailable for development due to access limitations. This information can be used in conjunction with information about other resource values and the environment.

The highly detailed Federal land access data along with the oil and gas resource data is available for additional analyses by Congress, industry, environmental organizations, and other interested parties. Land withdrawals, oil and gas lease stipulations, and COAs protect or mitigate adverse impacts to other valuable land resources. Land management agencies can analyze this information together with existing policies and procedures to identify opportunities for improving and enhancing decisions in their land use planning, leasing, and permitting processes. Agencies can use this information to prioritize the need for additional data and analyses, and to identify opportunities for improving access to oil and gas resources. Overall, this inventory provides fundamental information to help resolve development issues.

A fundamental product of this inventory is the GIS database containing numerous layers of geographic data referenced by longitude and latitude. While the surface data used in the inventory is accurate, an important caution applies to the use and interpretation of the undiscovered energy resources data: the *precise* locations of recoverable accumulations of undiscovered oil and natural gas resources on Federal lands are unknown. For the purpose of this inventory, it was assumed that there is a uniform distribution of the resources within a given play or assessment unit.

Over the last several decades, the USGS methodology has been the government's standard for oil and gas resource estimation. The USGS assessment process estimates the volume of undiscovered oil, natural gas, and natural gas liquids that have the potential to be added to reserves during a thirty-year forecast period. Assessment results are based on known or estimated geologic input parameters provided by knowledgeable geologists–parameters such as trapping mechanism, source rock, reservoir quality and size of known accumulations. Because of the uncertainty about the input parameters, the assessment result is expressed as a probability distribution of potential resources in the assessment unit or geologic play. For these reasons this inventory does not imply that the locations of accumulations of undiscovered oil and gas resources are known to occur under specific land parcels.

1.9 Products/Future Direction

The tables, data, maps (GIS products), and this summary report, describing the methodology, applied standards, results, and land access issues, are available on DVD and on the BLM (http://www.blm.gov/) website.

Section 604 of EPCA requires that all Federal lands of the onshore United States be inventoried. With the completion of this Phase II report, an estimated 76 percent of the onshore Federal oil and gas resources have been inventoried. For the Phase III/IV release, the inventory has been redesigned by the Steering Committee to cumulatively analyze 18 geologic provinces comprehensively, and to extrapolate the access constraints for the small portion of remaining resources (estimated to be about 10 percent) in the rest of the U.S. For subsequent releases, the information and analysis for previously studied areas will be updated as the availability of new data and developments in technology warrant.

In addition, the recently passed Energy Policy Act of 2005 (EPAct 2005) Section 364, modifies the scope of this inventory to require the evaluation of additional Federal constraints associated with granting permits, post-lease restrictions, and barriers to transportation. The EPAct 2005 also requires the DOE, using this inventory, to make periodic assessments of economically recoverable resources. The inclusion of the impact of COAs on Federal oil and gas accessibility in this Phase II release represents a partial fulfillment of these additional requirements.

2. METHODOLOGY

The Phase II inventory examines the following geologic provinces:[17]

- Northern Alaska (NA; NPR-A and ANWR 1002 only)
- Uinta-Piceance Basin (UP)
- Paradox/San Juan Basins (PDX/SJ)
- Montana Thrust Belt (MTB)
- Powder River Basin (PRB)
- Wyoming Thrust Belt (WTB)
- Greater Green River Basin (GGRB)
- Denver Basin (DEN)
- Florida Peninsula (FLP)
- Black Warrior Basin (BWB)
- Appalachian Basin (APB).

The study areas were delineated by aggregating oil and/or natural gas resource plays[18] within the provinces as defined by the USGS National Assessment of Oil and Gas Resources. Resource play boundaries and oil and gas resource estimates within the plays were obtained in GIS format from the USGS. These plays were then aggregated in a GIS to create a resource density map layer for each study area.

Where play boundaries span more than a single geologic province, one province was selected over the other in order to preserve geographic uniqueness. For example, at the boundary of the PDX/SJ and UP study areas, the UP was defined by the outline of Uinta plays even though these plays overlap plays from the Paradox Basin. The Uinta/Piceance study area thus contains some Paradox Basin resources and reserves. Likewise, the WTB and GGRB study areas were defined by the GGRB USGS boundaries and the DEN and PRB study areas by the PRB USGS province boundaries.

Federal land status was generated using the "Status" dataset from the BLM's Legacy Rehost 2000 (LR-2000) system to create GIS maps. Oil and gas leasing stipulation and COA data were obtained for each jurisdiction from BLM field offices and USDA-FS offices in the study areas. Most of the stipulation data were available in GIS format; some existed only as hardcopy and had to be digitized to create GIS digital map files.

Stipulations and COAs are additional requirements that are attached to Federal oil and gas leases and drilling permits for environmental protection and other reasons and are subject to change over time. This inventory represents a "snapshot" of the conditions within the study areas at the time of data collection. The stipulations used in the inventory are those applied when new oil and gas leases are issued and are those contained primarily in National Forest Plans (FPs) and BLM Resource Management Plans (RMPs) in effect as of August 2002 (for the UP, PDX/SJ, MTB, PRB, and GGRB study areas), March 2005 (for the WTB, DEN, FLP, BWB, and APB study areas) and January 2006 (NA study area). Some stipulations are not maintained in an automated system and may not have been available for use in this inventory (see Section 2.1.2 for further discussion).

The analyses entailed the spatial intersection (in a GIS) of oil and gas resource information with data on Federal land status and access constraints. The inventory also takes into account how leasing stipulations are implemented in practice by Federal land managers by considering the effect of directional drilling and the general frequency with which exceptions to the stipulations are granted.

To the extent that current leases were issued under and are stipulated according to an existing land use plan, the inventory accurately reflects the access situation. Older leases issued before the effective date of the relevant plans may not be stipulated accordingly. It is reasonably accurate, however, to consider the plan stipulations as a proxy because the environmental conditions that necessitate stipulations often are the driver for COAs that are attached to drilling permits on the older unstipulated leases to achieve the needed environmental protection.

Additional factors exist that affect oil and gas exploration and development on Federal lands and cannot be quantified geographically prior to the receipt of a specific drilling application. The factors include:

- Protection for threatened, endangered, and sensitive species. Surveys are sometimes required to determine whether a lease contains habitat for such species.
- Archaeological surveys required by the National Historic Preservation Act, along with related issues involving cultural resources, including consultation with Native American tribes.
- Air quality impacts and resulting restrictions on activities that may affect air quality.
- Visual impacts of oil and gas operations.
- Noise from oil and gas operations.
- Suburban encroachment on oil and gas fields and county government restrictions.

Section 4 of this chapter presents these issues in greater detail. Many of these requirements manifest themselves as COAs attached to drilling permits following a specific analysis under the National Environmental Policy Act (NEPA). These requirements can delay or modify a planned oil and gas development activity at the permit stage and in some cases preclude it altogether. Site-specific COAs have been incorporated into the inventory.

The rest of this section provides a more detailed description of the inventory methodology.

2.1 Procedures for Collecting and Preparing Land Status and Oil and Gas Access Constraints

2.1.1 Federal Land Status

This section briefly presents the process for determination of land status. See Appendix 3 for a more detailed description.

2.1.1.1 Sources of Land Status Data

In contrast to the Phase I inventory, which exclusively examined basins in the Interior West, Federal lands status determination was much more complex for the Eastern study areas included in the Phase II inventory (FLP, BWB, and APB). For the Eastern study areas the mapping of Federal lands was completed based upon detailed research of multiple sources of information that describe the nature and extent of Federal surface and mineral interests. The primary source of Federal land status data outside of the Eastern areas was the BLM's LR-2000 Status Dataset, which was supplemented by other records from Federal, state, and county governments.

2.1.1.2 Land Status Data Preparation

These data, which are often stored in alphanumeric format, were converted as necessary for this inventory into a GIS layer by using commercially available software. The software interpolated the legal descriptions contained in the Status Dataset against a public land survey GIS layer derived from either the BLM's Geographic Coordinate Database (GCDB) or other sources such as digitized USGS 7-1/2 minute quadrangle maps.

Maps of the Federal land status for the study areas are presented in Figures 2-1 through 2-11.

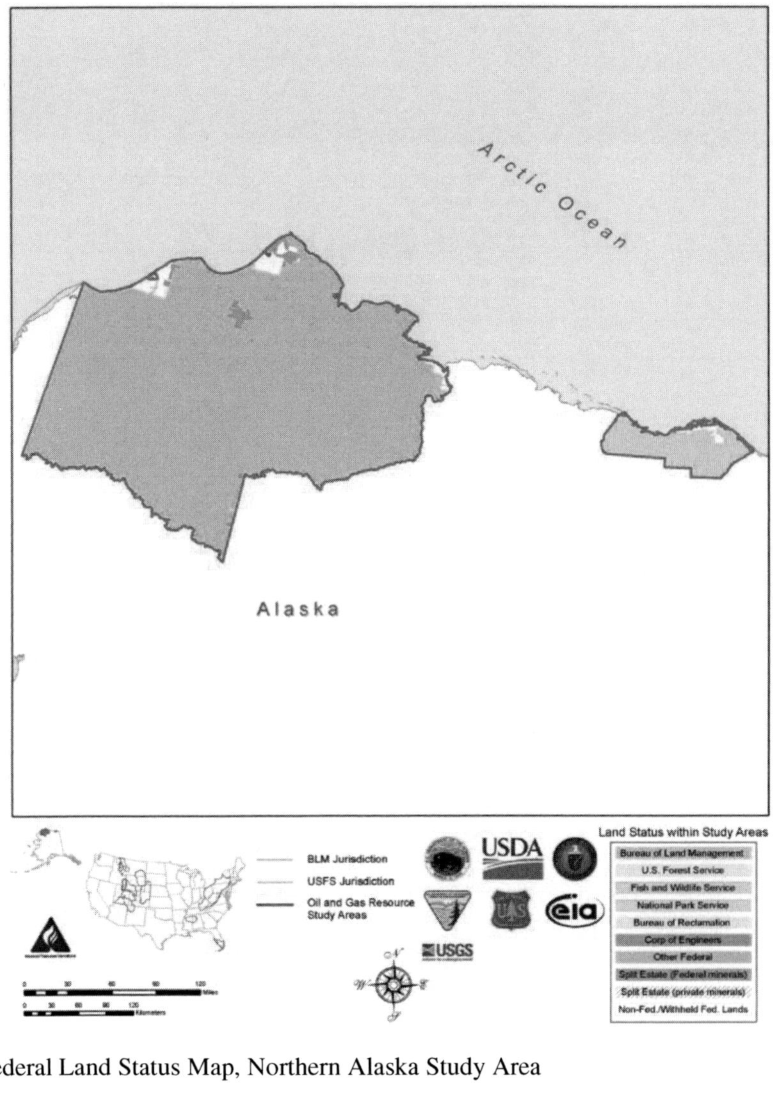

Figure 2-1. Federal Land Status Map, Northern Alaska Study Area

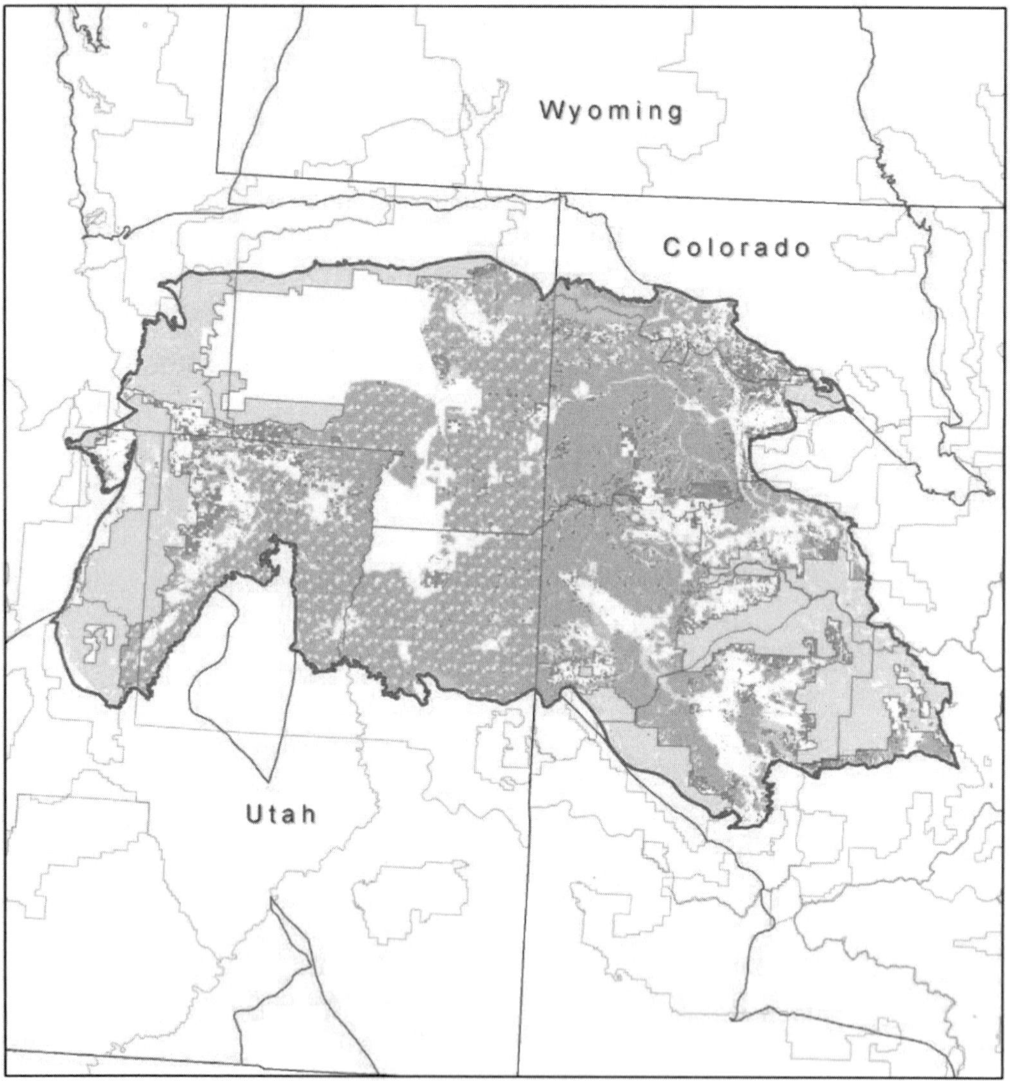

Figure 2-2. Federal Land Status Map, Uinta-Piceance Basin Study Area

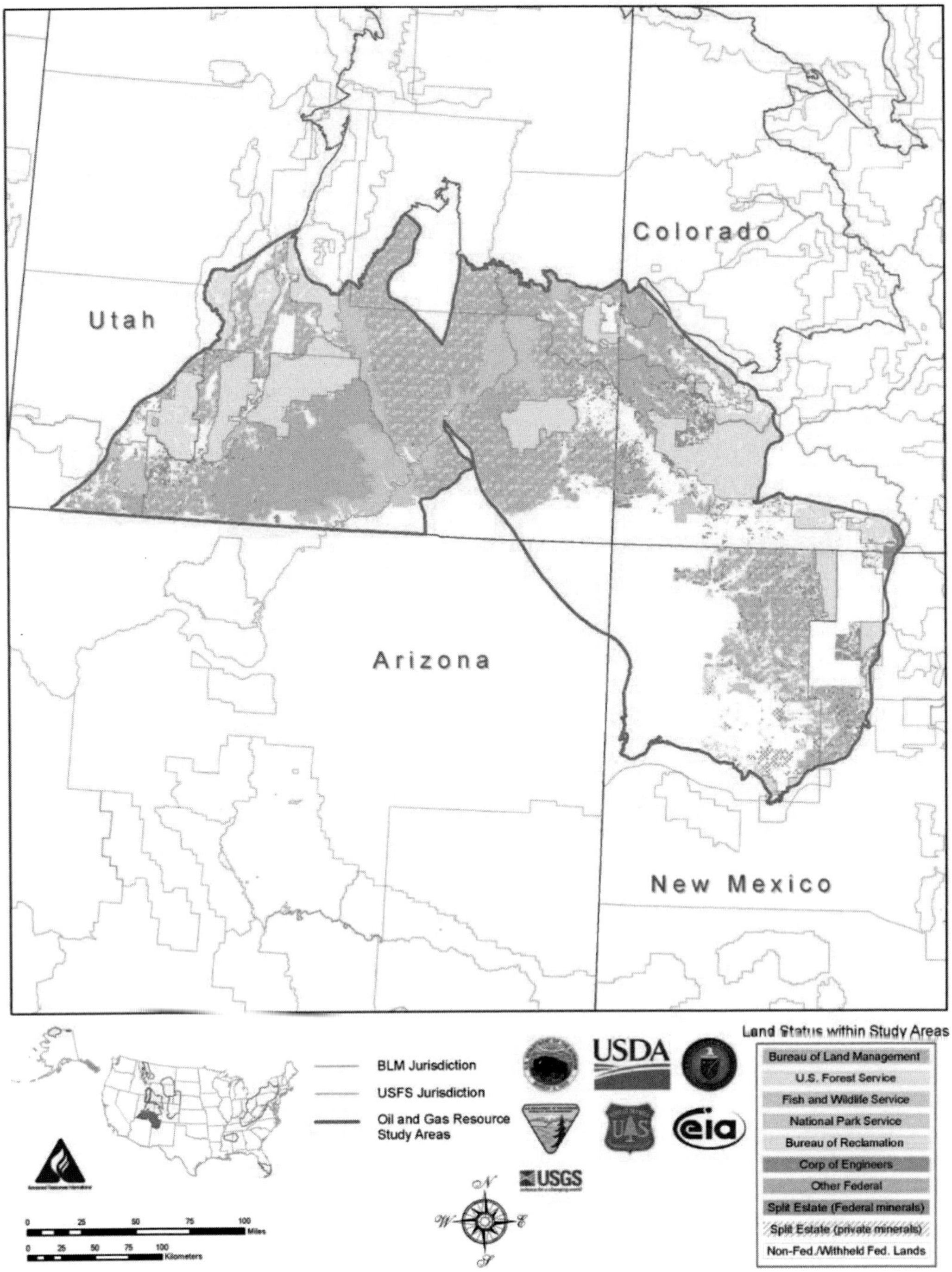

Figure 2-3. Federal Land Status Map, Paradox/San Juan Basins Study Area

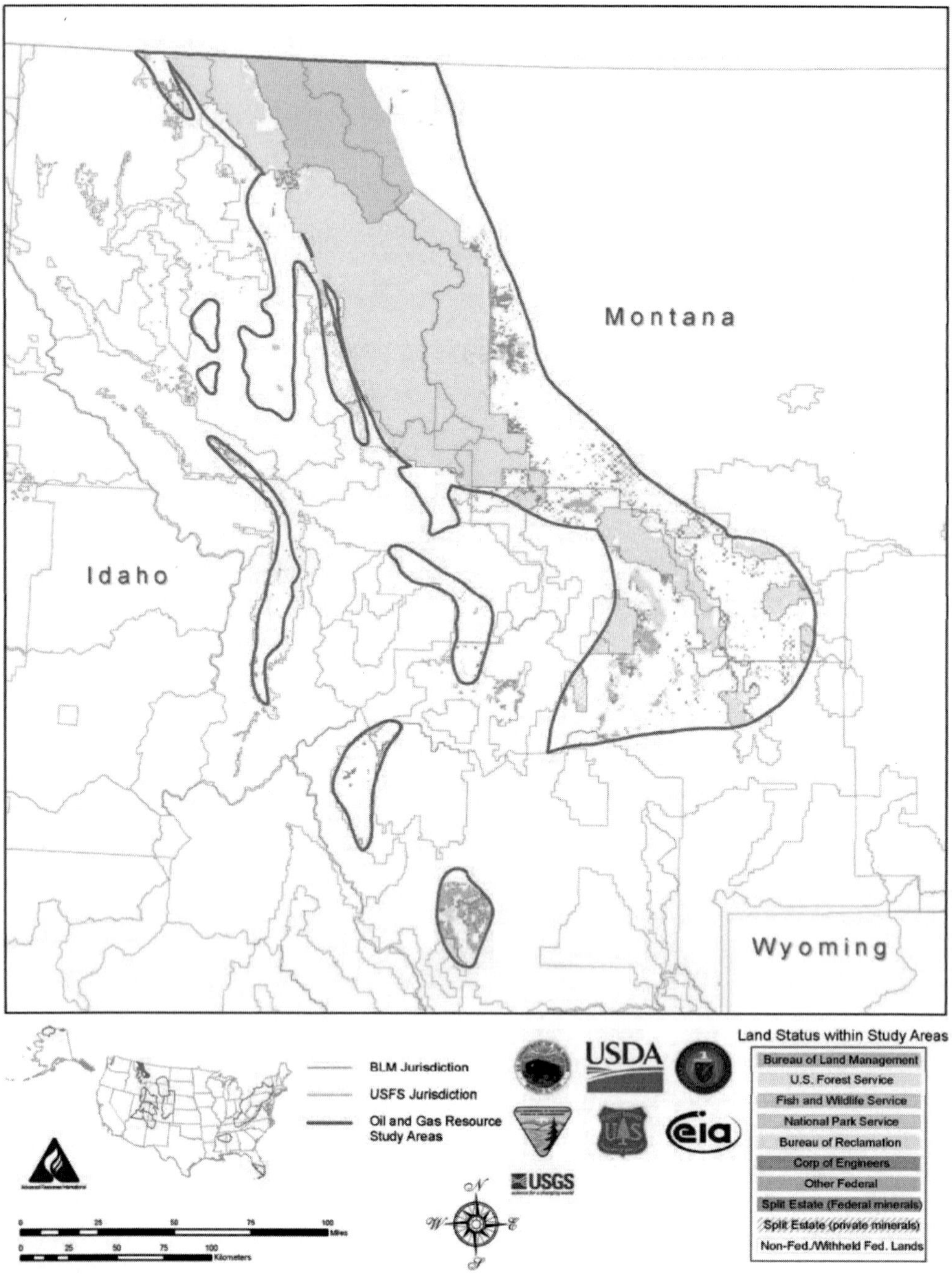

Figure 2-4. Federal Land Status Map, Montana Thrust Belt Study Area

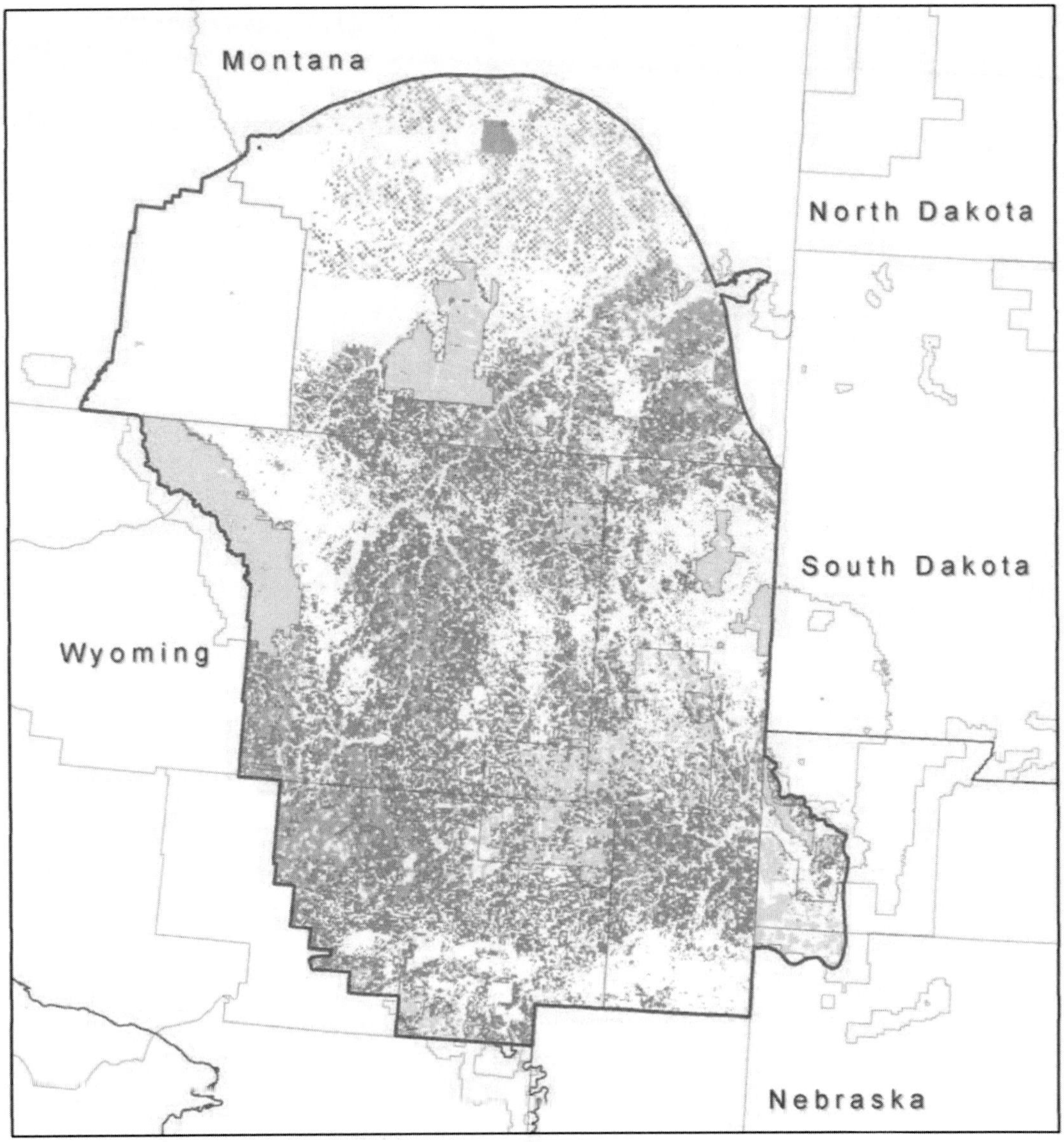

Figure 2-5. Federal Land Status Map, Powder River Basin Study Area

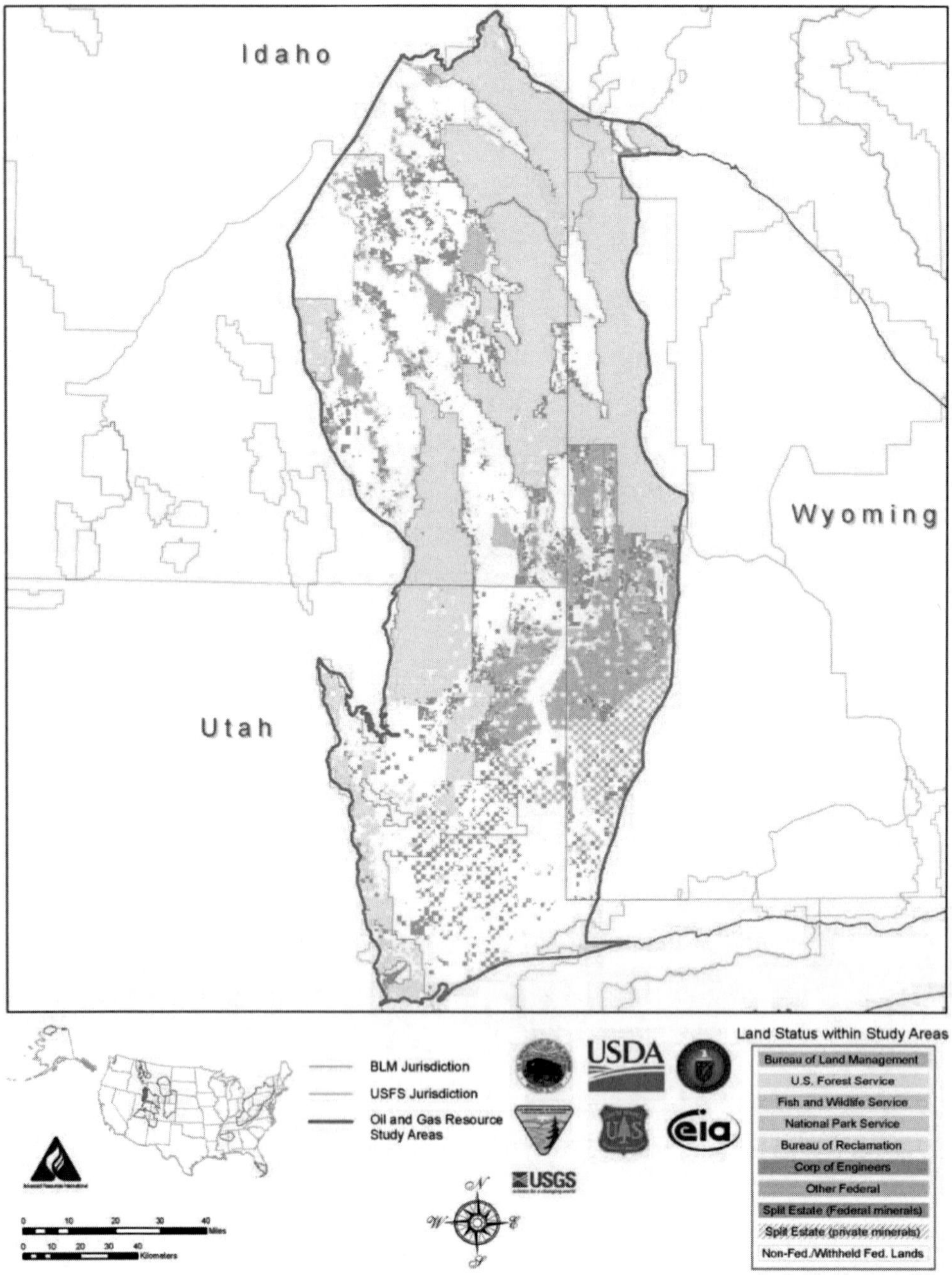

Figure 2-6. Federal Land Status Map, Wyoming Thrust Belt Study Area

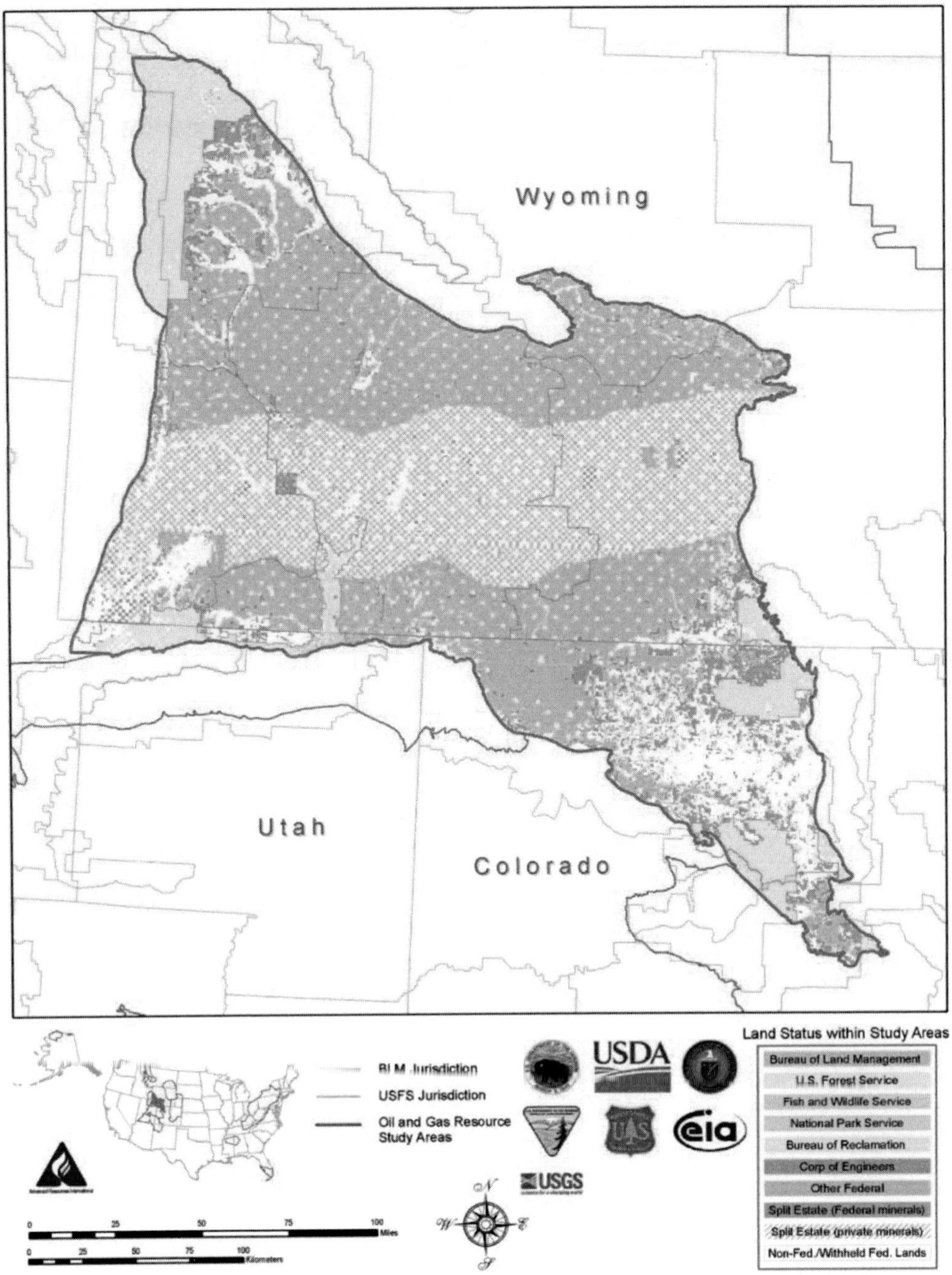

Figure 2-7. Federal Land Status Map, Greater Green River Basin Study Area

Figure 2-8. Federal Land Status Map, Denver Basin Study Area

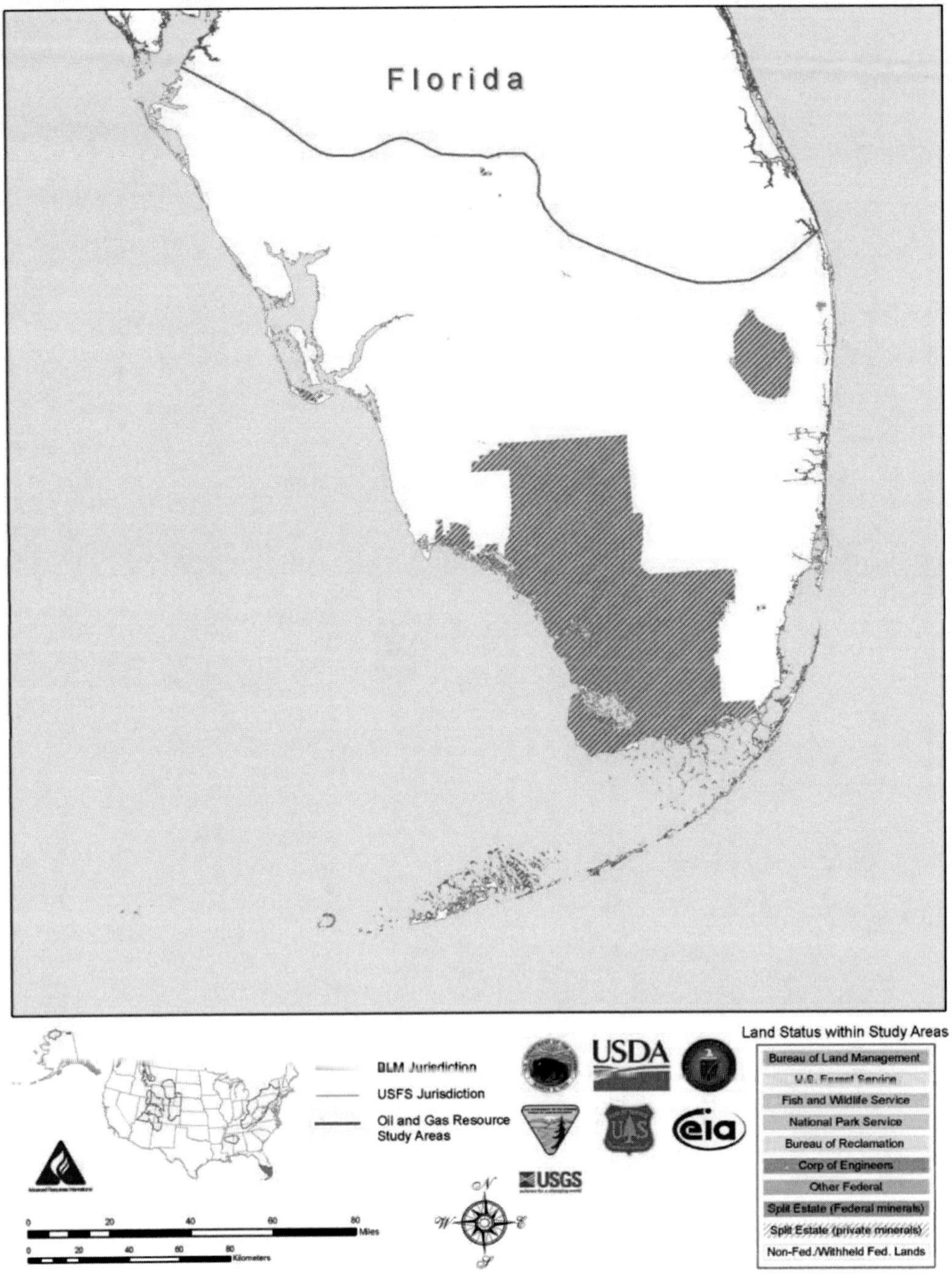

Figure 2-9. Federal Land Status Map, Florida Peninsula Study Area

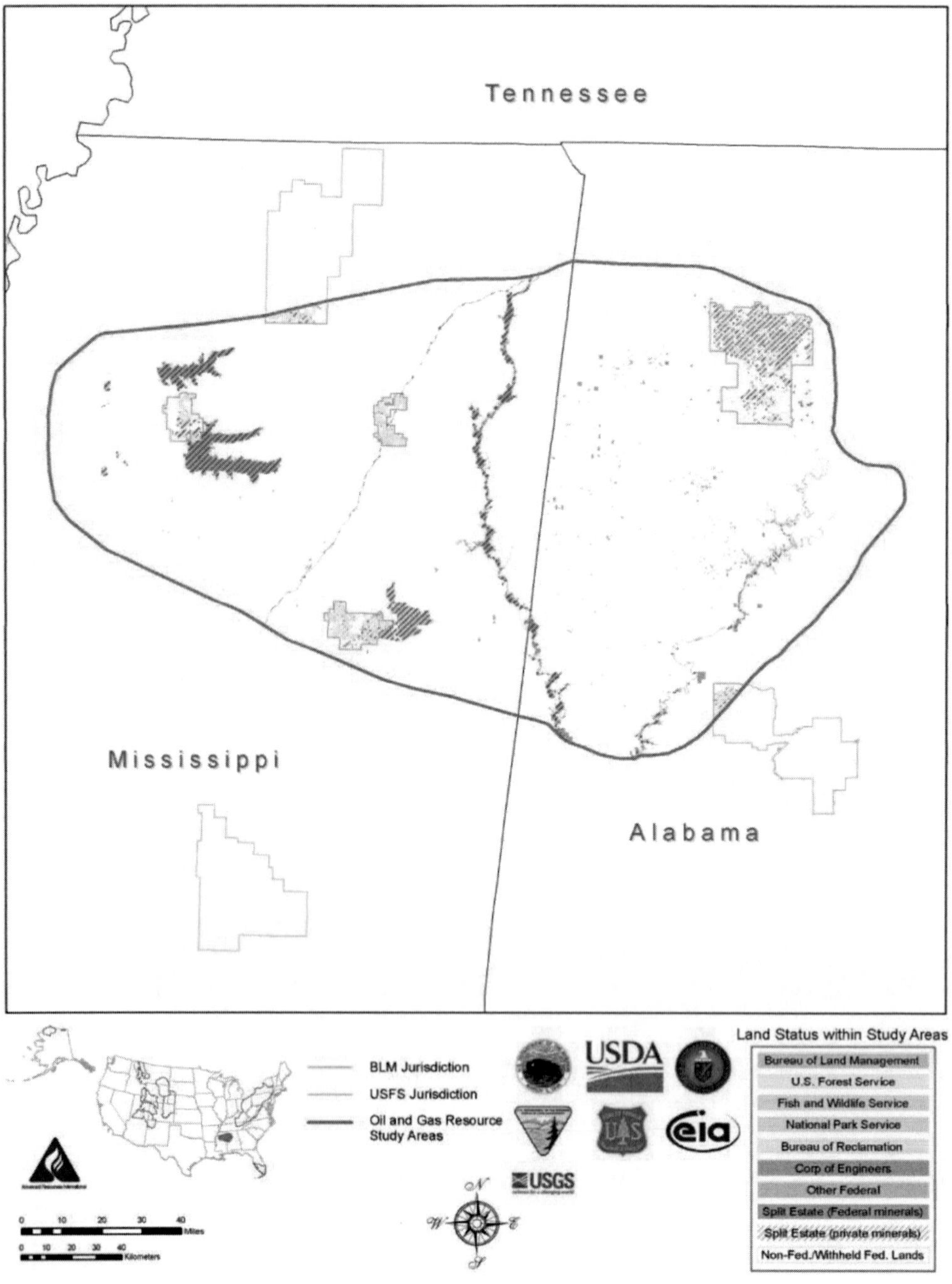

Figure 2-10. Federal Land Status Map, Black Warrior Basin Study Area

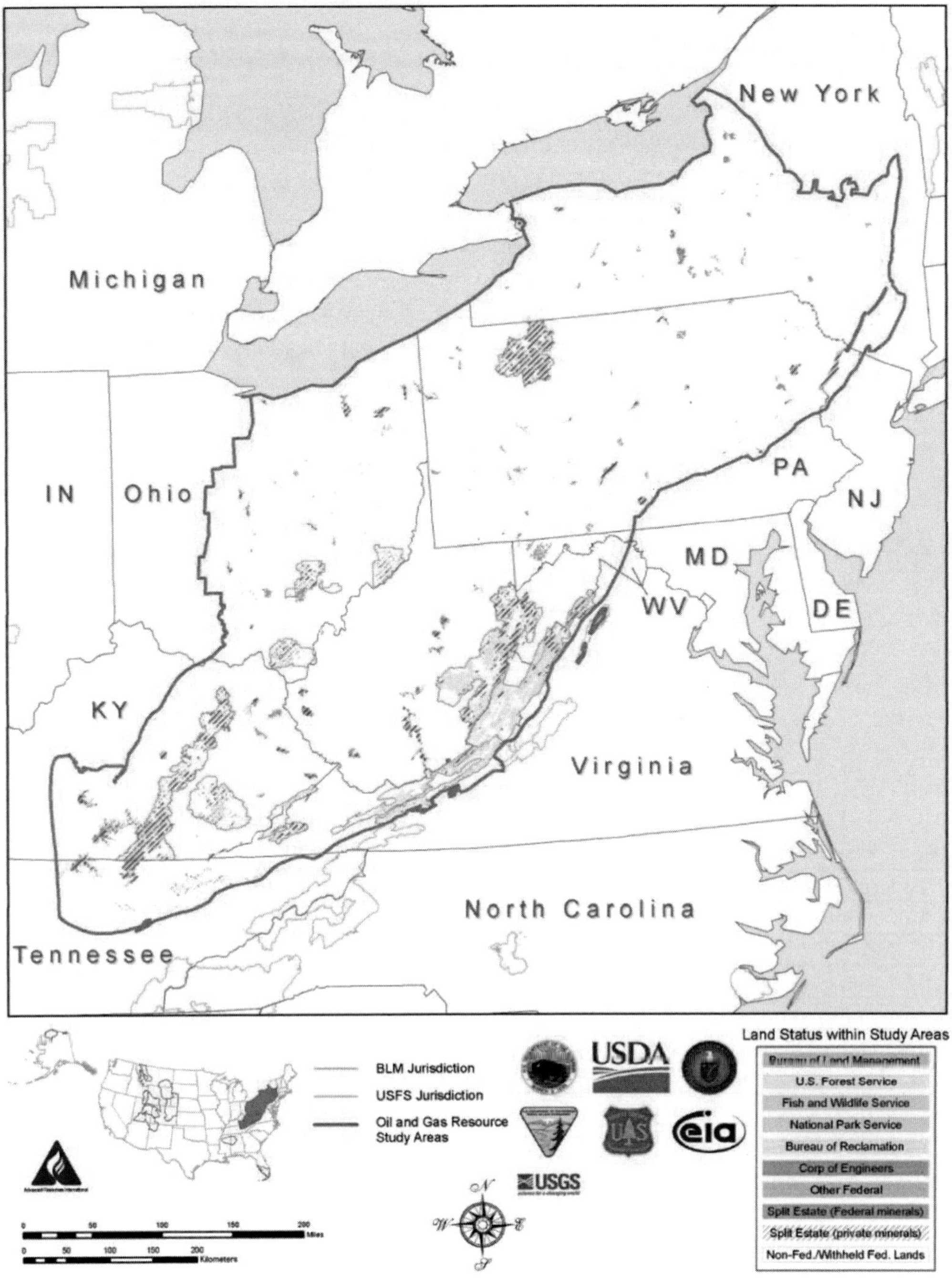

Figure 2-11. Federal Land Status Map, Appalachian Basin Study Area

2.1.1.3 Land Status Data-Related Caveats

The following precautions are advised when reviewing this inventory:

- The land status data are generally spatially accurate down to 40 acres. The data vintage is August 2002 for the Phase I basins and March 2005 for the Phase II basins.
- The GIS files, created using the processes described in detail in Appendix 3, were interpolated from the legal land descriptions contained in the BLM's LR-2000 database. If a legal description referenced a small survey lot or tract by number, a nominal location was mapped through a process that referenced the Legal Land Description dataset. This dataset is limited to a 40-acre description and therefore carries a minor degree of generalization in complex areas. Isolated parcels of less than 40 acres, particularly in the Eastern study areas, were not included in the inventory.
- This mapping process uses public land survey data derived from various sources. The spatial location of the land status parcels so derived matches the accuracy of the survey data.
- Some land status GIS data are restricted from the public domain by agency request. Such data were used in the analyses presented in this chapter, but are not contained in the public datasets.

For purposes of this inventory, Federal lands include split estate. In cases of split estate where the Federal government holds a partial interest in the oil and gas mineral estate, the Federal government was assumed to hold total mineral interest.

Table 2-1. Federal Land Acreage by Surface Management Agency

Federal Surface Management Agency	Phase II Inventory Acreage
Bureau of Land Management (including split estate)	65,872,000
USDA - Forest Service	24,050,000
National Park Service	5,669,000
Army Corps of Engineers	1,911,000
Fish and Wildlife Service	890,000
Bureau of Reclamation	399,000
Department of Defense	329,000
Department of Agriculture	57,000
Tennessee Valley Authority	51,000
Miscellaneous	29,000

Table 2-2. Land Use Plans by Study Area

Study Area	Land Use Plan	Year Published
Northern Alaska	Alaska-NE NPRA Final Integrated Activity Plan/EIS -- Amendment	2006
	Alaska-NW NPRA Final Integrated Activity Plan/EIS	2003
Uinta/Piceance Basin	Ashley NF Stipulation for Lands of the NF System	1992
	Glenwood Springs Resource Area Plan Amendment	1999
	GMUG–Oil and Gas Leasing File EIS ROD	1993
	Grand Junction Resource Area Management Plan and ROD	1987
	Routt NF Land and RMP Revision	1997
	Thunder Basin Nat. Grassland Land and RMP	2002
	Land and RMP–Manti-La Sal NF	1986
	Book Cliffs RMP ROD and Rangeland Program (combine with Diamond Mtn into Vernal RMP)	1985
	Lopez Project, Utah State BLM Statewide Stipulations, Book Cliffs RMP	1985
	Lopez Project, Utah State BLM Statewide Stipulations, Isotract MFP, Randolph MFP	1985/1980
	Leasing Stipulations, Craig-Little Snake BLM	1991
	Land and RMP Revision–Uinta NF	2003
	San Juan/San Miguel RMP Amendment (San Miguel updated with Uncomphagre RMP)	1991
	San Juan/San Miguel RMP Amendment (San Juan RMP revision)	1991
	Diamond Mountain Recreation Area ARMP/ROD Cliffs into Vernal RMP) (combine with Book	1994
	White River Resource Area RMP	1997
	White River RMP, Oil and Gas Final EIS/ROD	1993
Paradox/San Juan Basins	Rio Puerco RMP (Now the Albuquerque FO. Update Document 2001. RMP revision TBD)	1992
	New Mexico BOR–Navajo Reservoir (Draft EA Navajo Reservoir Area RMP)	2005
	Carson NF Plan (Valle Vidal amendments in progress)	1986
	Cedar Beaver Garfield Antimony RMP	1986
	Cibola NF Plan (Grasslands RMP under revision)	1985
	Cibola NF Plan (Forests RMP revision to start 2007)	1985
	Farmington Oil and Gas Leasing Amendment	1991
	Lopez Project, Utah State BLM Statewide Stipulations	
	Santa Fe NF Plan Amendment, O&G EA NM 85795	1996
	St. George FO-ROD and RMP	1999
Montana Thrust Belt	Beaverhead NF EIS	1996
	Headwaters RMP/EIS (South Headwaters update will be part of new Butte FO RMP)	1984
	Headwaters RMP/EIS (North Headwaters RMP revision)	
	Helena NF Plan and ROD	1984
	Lewis and Clark NF, Oil and Gas Leasing Final EIS	1986
	Garnet RMP	1997
	Black Hills NF Plan of Land and RMP	1986
Powder River Basin	Montana State BLM Office-Billings	1991
	Wyoming BLM Mitigation Guidelines for Surface-disturbing and Disruptive Activities	
	Platte River RMP Revised & Updated Decisions (renamed Casper RMP)	
	Miles City BLM Oil and Gas Amendment (Miles City RMP Revision 2007	2001
	Nebraska NF Revised Land and RMP FEIS/RD	1994
	Newcastle FO, ROD & Approved RMP	2002
	Targhee NF Revised Forest Plan	2000
Wyoming Thrust Belt	Pocatello & Medicine Lodge Resource Areas RMP (Pocatello RMP pending)	2000
	Bridger-Teton NF Land and RMP	1988

Table 2-2. (Continued)

Study Area	Land Use Plan	Year Published
Greater Green River Basin	Kemmerer RMP/ROD (Draft EIS available in 2006)	1990
	Lander RMP	1986
	Medicine Bow NF Revised Land and RMP	1987
	Pinedale RMP amended 2000 for oil & gas; RMP revision start 2002 end 2006	2003
	Lease Stipulations, Rawlins BLM	2000
	Lease Stipulations, Rock Springs BLM	2001
	Wasatch-Cache NF, Revised Forest Plan	1997
	Bureau of Reclamation Wyoming Special Stipulations	2003
	Arapaho-Roosevelt NFs, Pawnee NG Revision of the Land and Resource Management Plan	
Denver Basin	Nebraska RMP	1997
	Pike & San Isabel NF, Cimarron & Comanche NG, O&G Leasing Final EIS (Grasslands)	1992
	Pike & San Isabel NF, Cimarron & Comanche NG, O&G Leasing Final EIS (Forests)	1992
	Royal Gorge RMP and NE Royal Gorge RMP	1992
	Florida RMP/ROD	1991
Florida Peninsula	Big Cypress General Management Plan/ Final EIS (update in progress)	1995
	Alabama NFs–Revised Land and RMP	1991
Black Warrior Basin	Mississippi EA report–O&G leasing on the NFs	2004
	Allegheny NF Land and RMP	1976
Appalachian Basin	Mosquito Creek Lake DR	1986
	Berlin Lake Project DR; Conemaugh River Lake Project EA	2000
	Daniel Boone NF Revised Land and RMP	1985
	Seneca Army Depot and Sampson State Park	2004
	George Washington NF–Final revised Land and RMP	1993
	Jefferson NF–Revised Land and RMP	1993
	Monongahela NF and Amendments Land and RMP	2004
	Wayne NF Land and RMP	1986

2.1.2 Federal Oil and Gas Availability for Leasing and Lease Stipulations

All onshore Federal oil and gas leases contain terms and conditions as specified on the standard lease form (BLM Form 3100-11).[19] Some of these terms and conditions govern land use and resource development to a certain extent. Environmental and other considerations, which are identified during the land use planning process, determine the need for additional terms and conditions, also known as lease stipulations. For example, a lease may contain a stipulation that prohibits surface disturbance during certain time periods for wildlife. Such stipulations on land use and timing may constrain exploration and development of oil and natural gas on Federal lands.

Some Federal lands are unavailable for leasing. See Table A9-2 in Appendix 9 for a listing of agencies and Federal designations that generally prohibit oil and gas leasing.

The Federal government does not issue oil and gas leases for areas where it has surface ownership but no mineral rights. In such instances, the Federal government, while allowing access to the subsurface resources owned by another party, typically uses surface occupancy restrictions (SORs) to protect surface resources. From the standpoint of the EPCA inventory, SORs and lease stipulations have similar impacts. Thus, for the purposes of this study, the term "stipulations" is used generically to include SORs.

2.1.2.1 Sources of Lease Stipulation Data

Oil and gas lease stipulations are derived from the Federal surface management agency's land use plans, e.g., Resource Management Plans (RMPs) for the BLM and Forest Plans (FPs) for the Forest Service. These plans are produced and maintained by their respective agencies on a field office jurisdictional basis (in the case of the BLM), or on a National Forest/Grassland basis (in the case of the USDA-FS). Land use planning documents are revised every ten to fifteen years, or on an as-needed basis, but may be amended to address specific land use issues. Table 2-2 lists the land use planning documents used for this inventory.

Hardcopy and digital data showing the mapped lease stipulation areas were collected from BLM and Forest Service offices within the study areas (see Table 1-1). During office visits, copies of guidance documents, such as RMPs and FPs, were also obtained.

Most of the lease stipulation data are maintained by the agencies as GIS data layers (digital map files). Some offices, particularly where the planning effort pre-dated the widespread availability of GIS technology, maintain this information in the form of hardcopy maps. For this inventory, these maps were digitized, stored, and analyzed as GIS layers. The digitized maps were then returned to the originating field offices for review and future use.

For some BLM and USDA-FS plans, maps are not available for some stipulations either in GIS or hardcopy form. Stipulations for which GIS data are not available or could not be generated from other data sources are annotated on the stipulations lists accompanying this chapter.[20]

Data for this study were collected during the two phases of the inventory. For the UP, PDX/SJ, PRB, and MTB study areas, data were collected in the winter of 2001-2002. For the GGRB study area, data were used from the DOE's Federal lands analysis[21] collected during the fall and winter of 2000-2001; these data were verified with the local BLM and USDA-FS offices and were current as of August 2002. The data for NA were collected in the fall of 2003. Data for the WTB, DEN, BWB, FLP and APB were collected during 2004. These data were verified with the local BLM and USDA-FS offices and were current as of March 2005.

2.1.2.2 Lease Stipulation Data Preparation

Most of the lease stipulation data preparation consisted of the gathering, digitizing, and compiling of the gathered data in multi-layered digital map files. Federal Geographic Data Committee Standards (FGDC)-compliant supporting documentation (metadata) for the resulting GIS layers was also created.[22]

This inventory concerns only Federal lands within the aggregate resource play boundaries of the study areas, which are based on geology as defined in the USGS National Assessment of Oil and Gas Resources. Consequently, the land status and stipulation digital map files, which correspond to Federal land management agency jurisdiction boundaries, were clipped using GIS to fit within each of the study area boundaries. Data contained within the compiled digital map files were then queried for unique leasing stipulation values. The results were saved as separate map files. Each digital map file represents a unique stipulation value.

For a description of the specific data preparation steps, see Appendix 4.

2.1.2.3 Lease Stipulation Data-Related Caveats

The following precautions are advised when reviewing this study:

- All stipulations for which GIS data were available from the Federal land management agencies were used in the analysis. Most of the stipulations within the study areas were available in GIS data formats; however, supporting documentation was not generally provided with GIS files. Although this can lead to inaccuracies due to undocumented differences in technical parameters, such errors are minor in terms of the scope of the inventory.
- Many stipulations not available in GIS format were digitized. Any resulting inaccuracies due to this process are likely to have insignificant impacts upon the analysis.
- Neither hardcopy nor digital maps were available for some stipulations (see Section 2.3.1.1 for further discussion).
- The lease stipulation data are generally accurate to a minimum of 40 acres.
- Some lease stipulation GIS data are restricted from the public domain by agency request. Such data were used in the Phase II analysis but are not contained in the public datasets.

2.1.3 Federal Drilling Permit Conditions of Approval

As described in section 2.1.2, a Federal oil and gas lease conveys only the right to develop such resources on the leased land subject to reasonable regulations as determined by the land managing agency. After lease issuance, and prior to approval of any drilling activities, the operator must submit an Application for Permit to Drill (APD). An APD provides operational and geologic information as well as the applicant's proposal for use of the surface. COAs are post-lease requirements that are attached to an approved APD for environmental protection, safety, conservation of resource. COAs have been developed over a number of years as mitigation for surface disturbing activities and are based upon lease notices and/or administrative policy actions.

The Phase I inventory evaluated the impact of lease stipulations on access to oil and gas resources on Federal lands, but did not explicitly address the effects of COAs, assuming that they were implicitly covered by lease stipulations that would be issued for future leases. Subsequent to the Phase I inventory, the 2003 NPC study examined COAs as a complement to lease stipulations and concluded that COAs are a greater impediment to development than leasing stipulations.

Partially in response to the 2003 NPC study, and in anticipation of the inventory amendments contained in EPAct 2005, the effects of COAs on oil and gas accessibility have been incorporated into the Phase II analysis. The purpose of the inclusion of COAs is to enhance the land access constraints analysis and thus provide a more complete assessment of the onshore Federal lands' availability for oil and gas exploration and development.

COAs arise from a variety of controlling authorities, but the most significant and wide-ranging are those governed by four Federal laws; specifically, the Federal Land Policy and Management Act (FLPMA), the National Environmental Policy Act (NEPA), the Endangered Species Act (ESA) and the National Historic Preservation Act (NHPA). The COAs attached to each APD can be general in nature or site-specific, and thus vary from one BLM Field Office (FO) to another.

Some COAs can be identified as "best management practices" while others are included as a standard set by the approving office. In the Phase II study areas, approximately 175 types of COAs provide mitigation for surface-disturbing activities. For example, COAs can address:

- Big game winter range
- Protection of wildlife habitat
- Protection of archeological and paleontological sites
- Noise reduction
- Road construction and maintenance tanks and pits for fluid storage
- Pipeline and power line construction
- Wildfire suppression
- Management of noxious weeds
- Reclamation
- Erosion control
- Fertilizer application

COAs and stipulations beyond the standard lease terms often occur together. Prior to this inventory, there has not been a comprehensive method to characterize their impact on Federal land access. The National Petroleum Council, in its 2003 report (see Section 1.5) crafted an ingenious method to estimate the effect that COAs have on Federal land accessibility. However, the NPC did not have access to the actual well files containing COAs, but instead used publicly available wildlife data as a proxy to estimate their impact. In examining COAs and their effects upon land access for this inventory, it was necessary for the BLM to review extensively the APD well records in its Field Offices. The methodology for the assessment of COAs is described in Appendix 5.

2.1.3.1 Sources of Conditions of Approval Data

For the Phase II inventory, a number of APDs for all study areas were sampled. The APDs were selected by applying a stratified random sampling protocol to a list of all APDs approved during fiscal years 1999-2004. The sample represents approximately 10 percent of the total population of APDs. BLM Field Offices were visited and information on site-specific COAs was abstracted from the hardcopy well files. A summarized version of the COAs and stipulations that affected oil and gas access in each selected APD was noted.

In addition, information was obtained from BLM Field Office personnel to qualitatively assess the extent of negotiations that occur prior to the submission of an APD, including adjustments at the time of well staking and are presented in Appendix 5.

2.1.3.2 Conditions of Approval Data Preparation

The COAs data preparation consisted of compiling the collected information into spreadsheets and spatial GIS displays. The abstracted information was grouped into general classes that were assigned unique codes. Table 2-3 presents a list by BLM office. Appendix 5 contains details on the data preparation task.

Table 2-3. COAs by BLM Field Office

BLM FO	Well Population	Sample Size	Sample Wells w/ COAs
Albuquerque	48	30	4
Buffalo	5,077	200	69
Casper	170	30	25
Farmington	2,713	200	74
Glenwood Springs	349	53	16
Grand Junction	40	30	22
Kemmerer	96	30	22
Lander	11	11	7
Little Snake	63	30	23
Miles City	93	30	30
Milwaukee	14	14	2
Moab	23	23	10
Monticello	9	9	3
New Castle	76	30	8
Pindale	710	107	72
Rawlins	714	107	50
Rock Springs	173	30	15
Royal Gorge	39	30	23
San Juan	35	30	22
Uncompahgre	7	7	7
Vernal	861	130	35
White River	320	48	22
Total	11,641	1,209	561

2.1.3.3 Conditions of Approval Data-Related Caveats

The APDs examined were randomly sampled. To the extent that the sample is not representative of the population, extrapolation of sample results could introduce error.

Because of the large number of approved Federal APDs, the sample for the inventory was restricted to represent a portion of the total number of APDs, but has been improved by means of a stratified sampling protocol explained in Appendix 5. This method reduces the impact of potential inaccuracies introduced due to extrapolation of results to general areas. Some field offices had small populations of wells (<30), which can lead to relatively poor samples. In such cases, all wells in an office were sampled.

2.2 Procedures for Collecting and Preparing Oil and Gas Resource, Reserves Growth and Reserves Data

2.2.1 Undiscovered Oil and Gas Resources

2.2.1.1 Sources of Oil and Gas Resources Data

In conformance with 42 USC §6217, the volumes of undiscovered technically recoverable oil and gas resources in each oil and gas play are supplied exclusively by the USGS.

Editor's note–insert sidebar ("Oil and gas resources occur in four categories:") at this point

Undiscovered technically recoverable resources are those hydrocarbon resources that, on the basis of geologic information and theory, are estimated to exist outside of known producing fields. These resources can be produced using current technology without regard to economic profitability. Technically recoverable resources are a subset of the total resource-in-place that could be expected to be recovered over an exploration and development life cycle measured in decades.

Oil and gas resources occur in four categories:

The In-place resource is the total volume of oil and gas thought to exist (both discovered and yet-to-be discovered) without regard to the ability to either access or produce it. Although the in-place resource is primarily a ?xed, unchanging volume, the current understanding of that volume is continually changing as geologic knowledge and technology improves.

Technically recoverable resources are a subset of the in-place resource that includes only that oil and gas (both discovered and undiscovered) that is expected to be producible given available technology with no regard to current economics. Technically recoverable resources are therefore dynamic, and change in response to our increased understanding of both the in-place resource as well as the likely nature of future technology.

Economically recoverable resources are a subset of the technically recoverable that includes only that oil and gas that is expected to be producible at a pro?t. This is a very dynamic category, changing not only with the increasing knowledge and technology but also with the rapid and sometimes unpredictable changes in economic conditions, prices, markets, and regulation.

Reserves are oil and gas that has been proven by drilling and is available for pro?table production. Reserves are also subject to economic conditions.

The USGS assesses oil and gas resources in geologic "plays" or "assessment units." A play is a set of known or postulated oil and gas accumulations defined by common geological conditions (source rock, migration, timing, charge, traps, seals, etc.) that characterize a group of hydrocarbon accumulations in the subsurface. An assessment unit is defined as a mappable volume of rock within a total petroleum system that encompasses accumulations (discovered and undiscovered) that share similar geologic traits and socio-economic factors. Accumulations within an assessment unit should constitute a sufficiently homogeneous population such that the chosen methodology of resource assessment is applicable. A total petroleum system might equate to a single assessment unit. If necessary, a total petroleum system can be subdivided into two or more assessment units so that each unit is sufficiently homogeneous to assess individually.

The USGS assesses two resource play types: conventional and continuous. Conventional plays contain discrete hydrocarbon accumulations often associated with hydrocarbon/water contacts. Continuous plays are pervasive hydrocarbon accumulations that can cross rock unit

boundaries, lack discrete structural boundaries, and exhibit other atypical reservoir properties (Figure
2-12). They include tight gas sands, gas shales, and coalbed natural gas (also referred to as coal gas, coalbed gas or coalbed methane). Compared to conventional plays, continuous accumulations typically are more geographically extensive. Most of the resources in the study areas in the lower-48 states are of the continuous type.

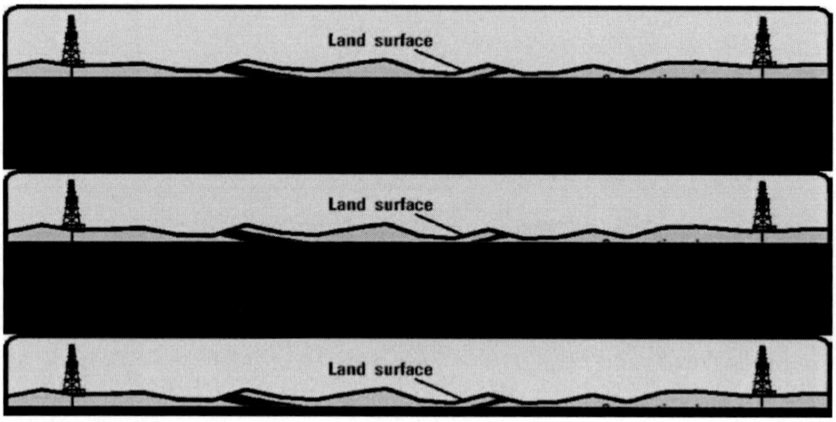

Figure 2-12. Conventional vs. Continuous Accumulations

The USGS has identified 150 discrete oil and natural gas resource plays in the Phase II study areas. The probabilistic mean estimate of hydrocarbon resource volumes for each USGS-defined play was utilized for this inventory (Table 2-4) The assessed resources include oil, natural gas liquids (NGLs), associated dissolved (AD) natural gas, non-associated natural gas (NAG) and liquids in gas reservoirs. Oil is a natural liquid of mostly hydrocarbon molecules. NGLs are liquid when produced to the surface but exist in the gas phase in the subsurface. Natural gas is a mixture of hydrocarbon gases consisting primarily of methane. Associated dissolved natural gas is that produced from oil fields, whereas non-associated natural gas is that produced from gas fields. The USGS assesses technically recoverable resources for each of these resource types, and these volumes were provided for the inventory. While modeled discretely in this analysis, for purposes of presentation in this inventory, undiscovered oil, NGLs, and liquids associated with natural gas reservoirs were subsequently aggregated into a single "Total Oil" resource category. Similarly, AD and non-associated natural gases were combined as "Total Natural Gas."

Table 2-4. Undiscovered Technically Recoverable Resources by Play

USGS Province Name	USGS Code	USGS Play or Assessment Unit Name	Play Type	Total Liquidsa (MMbbl)	Total Natural Gasb (Bcf)
Northern Alaska	npra001	Torok Structural	Conventional	35	17,905
Northern Alaska	npra002	Thrust Belt	Conventional	6	1,521
Northern Alaska	npra003	Ellesmerian Ivishak	Conventional	84	106
Northern Alaska	npra004	Ellesmerian Structural	Conventional	-	1,990
Northern Alaska	npra005	Ellesmerian Lisburne Total	Conventional	29	668
Northern Alaska	npra006	Ellesmerian Endicott Total	Conventional	3	1,073

Northern Alaska	npra007	Ellesmerian Echooka Total	Conventional	7	512
Northern Alaska	npra008	Brookian Topset Structural	Conventional	137	10,606
Northern Alaska	npra009	Brookian Topset	Conventional	239	192
Northern Alaska	npra010	Brookian Clinoform	Conventional	2,787	12,272
Northern Alaska	npra011	Beaufortian Upper Jurassic Topset	Conventional	7,035	10,357
Northern Alaska	npra012	Beaufortian Lower Jurassic Topset	Conventional	83	793
Northern Alaska	npra013	Beaufortian Cretaceous Topset Total	Conventional	103	2,534
Northern Alaska	npra014	Beaufortian Clinoform	Conventional	12	822
Northern Alaska	anwr001	Wedge	Conventional	509	259
Northern Alaska	anwr002	Undeformed Franklin	Conventional	134	353
Northern Alaska	anwr003	Turbidite	Conventional	1,680	1,400
Northern Alaska	anwr004	Topset	Conventional	6,196	1,704
Northern Alaska	anwr005	Thompson	Conventional	420	691
Northern Alaska	anwr006	Thin-Skinned Thrust Belt	Conventional	1,172	1,787
Northern Alaska	anwr007	Niguanak-Aurora	Conventional	411	532
Northern Alaska	anwr008	Kermik	Conventional	63	129
Northern Alaska	anwr009	Ellesmerian Thrust Belt	Conventional	18	876
Northern Alaska	anwr010	Deformed Franklin	Conventional	92	860
Uinta-Piceance Basin	50200101	Conventional Ferron Sandstone Gas	Conventional	<.5	40
Uinta-Piceance Basin	50200161	Deep (6,000 feet plus) Coal and Sandstone Gas	Continuous Gas	-	59
Uinta-Piceance Basin	50200181	Northern Coal Fairway/Drunkards Wash	Coalbed Gas	-	752
Uinta-Piceance Basin	50200182	Central Coal Fairway/Buzzards Bench	Coalbed Gas	-	537
Uinta-Piceance Basin	50200183	Southern Coal Fairway	Coalbed Gas	-	153
Uinta-Piceance Basin	50200184	Joes Valley and Messina Grabens	Coalbed Gas–Not quantitatively assessed	-	-
Uinta-Piceance Basin	50200185	Southern Coal Outcrop	Coalbed Gas	-	11
Uinta-Piceance Basin	50200201	Uinta-Piceance Basin Conventional Gas	Conventional	1	66
Uinta-Piceance Basin	50200261	Uinta Basin Continuous Gas Mesaverde TPS	Continuous Gas	11	7,391
Uinta-Piceance Basin	50200262	Uinta Basin Transitional Gas	Continuous Gas	2	1,493
Uinta-Piceance Basin	50200263	Piceance Basin Continuous Gas Mesaverde TPS	Continuous Gas	9	3,064
Uinta-Piceance Basin	50200264	Piceance Basin Transitional Gas	Continuous Gas	1	302
Uinta-Piceance Basin	50200281	Uinta Basin Blackhawk Coalbed Gas	Coalbed Gas	-	499
Uinta-Piceance Basin	50200282	Mesaverde Group Coalbed Gas	Coalbed Gas	-	368
Uinta-Piceance Basin	50200361	Piceance Basin Continuous Gas Mancos/Mowry TPS	Continuous Gas	2	1,653
Uinta-Piceance Basin	50200362	Uinta Basin Continuous Gas Mancos/Mowry TPS	Continuous Gas	6	3,111
Uinta-Piceance Basin	50200363	Uinta-Piceance Transitional and Migrated Gas	Continuous Gas	2	1,755
Uinta-Piceance Basin	50200401	Hanging Wall	Conventional	5	28
Uinta-Piceance Basin	50200402	Paleozoic/Mesozoic	Conventional	8	50

Table 2-4. (Continued).

Uinta-Piceance Basin	50200501	Uinta Green River Conventional Oil and Gas	Conventional	11	29
Uinta-Piceance Basin	50200502	Piceance Green River Conventional Oil	Conventional–Not quantitatively assessed	-	-
Uinta-Piceance Basin	50200561	Deep Uinta Overpressured Continuous Oil	Continuous Oil	43	64
Paradox Basin	2101	Buried Fault Blocks, Older Paleozoic	Conventional	62	292
Paradox Basin	2102	Porous Carbonate Buildup	Conventional	192	482
Paradox Basin	2103	Fractured Interbed	Continuous	242	194
Paradox Basin	2104	Permian-Pennsylvanian Marginal Clastics	Conventional	3	56
Paradox Basin	2105	Salt Anticline Flank	Conventional	20	396
Paradox Basin	2106	Permo-Triassic Unconformity	Conventional	21	2
Paradox Basin	2107	Cretaceous Sandstone	Conventional	1	58
San Juan Basin	50220101	Tertiary Conventional Gas	Conventional	1	80
San Juan Basin	50220161	Pictured Cliffs Continuous Gas	Continuous Gas	17	5,640
San Juan Basin	50220181	Fruitland Fairway Coalbed Gas	Coalbed Gas	-	3,981
San Juan Basin	50220182	Basin Fruitland Coalbed Gas	Coalbed Gas	-	19,595
San Juan Basin	50220261	Lewis Continuous Gas	Continuous Gas	31	10,177
San Juan Basin	50220302	Gallup Sandstone Conventional Oil and Gas	Conventional	2	<.5
San Juan Basin	50220303	Mancos Sandstones Conventional Oil	Conventional	14	58
San Juan Basin	50220304	Dakota-Greenhorn Conventional Oil and Gas	Conventional	3	22
San Juan Basin	50220361	Mesaverde Central-Basin Continuous Gas	Continuous Gas	5	1,317
San Juan Basin	50220362	Mancos Sandstones Continuous Gas	Continuous Gas	76	5,116
San Juan Basin	50220363	Dakota-Greenhorn Continuous Gas	Continuous Gas	16	3,929
San Juan Basin	50220381	Menefee Coalbed Gas	Coalbed Gas	-	664
San Juan Basin	50220401	Entrada Sandstone Conventional Oil	Conventional	3	6
Montana Thrust Belt	50270101	Thrust Belt Conventional Gas and Oil	Conventional	134	5,761
Montana Thrust Belt	50270102	Sawtooth Range Structure Conventional Oil and Gas	Conventional	18	795
Montana Thrust Belt	50270103	Frontal Structures Conventional Oil and Gas	Conventional	68	1,192
Montana Thrust Belt	50270201	Helena Salient Conventional Oil and Gas	Conventional	15	639
Montana Thrust Belt	50270401	Blacktail Salient Conventional Oil and Gas	Conventional	6	16
Montana Thrust Belt	50270561	Marias River Shale Continuous Oil	Continuous Oil	33	111
Montana Thrust Belt	50270701	Tertiary Basins Oil and Gas	Conventional	73	124
Powder River Basin	3301	Basin Margin Subthrust	Conventional	21	20
Powder River Basin	3302	Basin Margin Anticline	Conventional	7	4

Powder River Basin	3303	Leo Sandstone	Conventional	81	5
Powder River Basin	3304	Upper Minnelusa Sandstone	Conventional	522	31
Powder River Basin	3305	Lakota Sandstone	Conventional	55	22
Powder River Basin	3306	Fall River Sandstone	Conventional	200	115
Powder River Basin	3307	Muddy Sandstone	Conventional	88	449
Powder River Basin	3309	Deep Frontier Sandstone	Conventional	58	193
Powder River Basin	3310	Turner Sandstone	Conventional	25	32
Powder River Basin	3312	Sussex-Shannon Sandstone	Conventional	72	54
Powder River Basin	3313	Mesaverde-Lewis	Conventional	62	58
Powder River Basin	50330101	Eastern Basin Margin Upper Fort Union Sandstone	Conventional	-	27
Powder River Basin	50330181	Wasatch Formation	Coalbed Gas	-	1,934
Powder River Basin	50330182	Upper Fort Union Formation	Coalbed Gas	-	12,132
Powder River Basin	50330183	Lower Fort Union-Lance Formations	Coalbed Gas	-	198
Powder River Basin	50330261	Mowry Continuous Oil Assessment Unit	Continuous Oil	209	198
Powder River Basin	50330361	Niobrara Continuous Oil Assessment Unit	Continuous Oil	240	227
Powder River Basin	50330461	Shallow Continuous Biogenic Gas Assessment Unit	Continuous Gas	-	787
Wyoming Thrust Belt	au360101	Thrust Belt Conventional	Conventional	96	557
Wyoming Thrust Belt	au360281	Frontier-Adaville-Evanstone Coalbed Gas	Continuous	-	361
Southwestern Wyoming	50370101	Sub-Cretaceous Conventional Oil and Gas	Conventional	58	1,383
Southwestern Wyoming	50370201	Mowry Conventional Oil and Gas	Conventional	12	206
Southwestern Wyoming	50370401	Hilliard-Baxter-Mancos Conventional Oil and Gas	Conventional	1	15
Southwestern Wyoming	50370501	Mesaverde Conventional Oil and Gas	Conventional	3	56
Southwestern Wyoming	50370601	Mesaverde-Lance-Fort Union Conventional Oil and Gas	Conventional	17	320
Southwestern Wyoming	50370701	Lewis Conventional Oil and Gas	Conventional	8	195
Southwestern Wyoming	50370801	Lance-Fort Union Conventional Oil and Gas	Conventional	2	246
Southwestern Wyoming	50370361	Niobrara Continuous Oil	Continuous Oil	107	62
Southwestern Wyoming	50370261	Mowry Continuous Gas	Continuous Gas	171	8,543
Southwestern Wyoming	50370461	Hilliard-Baxter-Mancos Continuous Gas	Continuous Gas	752	11,753
Southwestern Wyoming	50370561	Almond Continuous Gas	Continuous Gas	200	13,350
Southwestern Wyoming	50370562	Rock Springs-Ericson Continuous Gas	Continuous Gas	146	12,178
Southwestern Wyoming	50370661	Mesaverde-Lance-Fort Union Continuous Gas	Continuous Gas	614	13,635
Southwestern Wyoming	50370761	Lewis Continuous Gas	Continuous Gas	541	13,536

Table 2-4. (Continued).

Southwestern Wyoming	50370861	Lance-Fort Union Continuous Gas	Continuous Gas	76	7,583
Southwestern Wyoming	50370581	Mesaverde Coalbed Gas	Coalbed Gas	-	249
Southwestern Wyoming	50370681	Mesaverde Coalbed Gas	Coalbed Gas	-	27
Southwestern Wyoming	50370682	Fort Union Coalbed Gas	Coalbed Gas	-	81
Southwestern Wyoming	50370881	Lance Coalbed Gas	Coalbed Gas	-	165
Southwestern Wyoming	50370882	Fort Union Coalbed Gas	Coalbed Gas	-	943
Southwestern Wyoming	50370981	Wasatch-Green River Coalbed Gas	Coalbed Gas	-	65
Denver Basin	au390181g	Denver Formation Coals	Coalbed Gas–Not quantitatively assessed	-	-
Denver Basin	au390182g	Laramie Formation Coals	Coalbed Gas–Not quantitatively assessed	-	-
Denver Basin	au390201g	Fractured Niobrara Limestone Transitional	Conventional	1	1
Denver Basin	au390261g	Fractured Niobrara Limestone (Silo Field Area)	Continuous Oil	8	8
Denver Basin	au390361g	Fractured Pierre Shale	Continuous Oil–Not quantitatively assessed	-	-
Denver Basin	au390401g	Dakota Group and D Sandstone	Conventional	39	45
Denver Basin	au390402g	Subthrust Structural	Conventional	17	41
Denver Basin	au390501g	Permian-Pennsylvanian Reservoirs	Conventional	11	5
Denver Basin	au390601g	Pierre Shale Sandstones	Conventional	3	18
Denver Basin	au390661g	Niobrara-Codell (Wattenberg Area)	Continuous Oil	64	322
Denver Basin	au390662g	Dakota Group Basin-Center Gas	Continuous Gas	11	1,095
Denver Basin	au390761g	Niobrara Chalk	Continuous Gas	-	984
Florida Peninsula	au500101g	Lower Cretaceous Shoal-Reef Oil	Conventional	274	29
Florida Peninsula	au500201g	Pre-Punta Gorda Dolomite Gas and Oil	Conventional	152	1,629
Black Warrior Basin	au650281g	Black Warrior Basin AU	Continuous	-	7,056
Black Warrior Basin	au650102g	Carboniferous Sandstones AU	Conventional	8	368
Black Warrior Basin	au650101g	Pre-Mississippian Carbonates AU	Conventional	6	1,087
Appalachian Basin	au670581g	Pocahontas Basin	Continuous	-	3,577
Appalachian Basin	au670362g	Clinton-Medina Transitional Northeast	Continuous	16	1,619
Appalachian Basin	au670461g	Greater Big Sandy	Continuous	63	6,323
Appalachian Basin	au670582g	Eastern Dunkard Basin	Continuous	-	4,823
Appalachian Basin	au670361g	Clinton-Medina Basin Center	Continuous	108	10,833
Appalachian Basin	au670363g	Clinton-Medina Transitional	Continuous	141	11,771
Appalachian Basin	au670463g	Devonian Siltstone and Shale	Continuous	31	1,294
Appalachian Basin	au670301g	Lower Paleozoic	Conventional	3	302

		Carbonates in Thrust Belt			
Appalachian Basin	au670304g	Lockport Dolomite	Conventional	2	207
Appalachian Basin	au670404g	Mississippian Sandstones	Conventional	6	113
Appalachian Basin	au670403g	Greenbrier Limestone	Conventional	4	128
Appalachian Basin	au670402g	Oriskany Sandstone-Stratigraphic	Conventional	1	65
Appalachian Basin	au670364g	Tuscarora Basin Center	Continuous	10	2,620
Appalachian Basin	au670462g	Northwestern Ohio Shale	Continuous	53	2,654
Appalachian Basin	au670466g	Berea Sandstone	Continuous	163	6,800
Appalachian Basin	au670465g	Catskill Sandstones and Siltstones	Continuous	235	11,741
Appalachian Basin	au670401g	Oriskany Sandstone-Structural	Conventional	2	386
Appalachian Basin	au670101g	Rome Trough	Conventional	4	616
Appalachian Basin	au670464g	Marcellus Shale	Continuous	12	1,925
Appalachian Basin	au670303g	Black River-Trenton Hydrothermal Dolomite	Conventional	35	1,919
Appalachian Basin	au670302g	Knox Unconformity	Conventional	36	574
All values are mean resource values from the USGS National Assessment of Oil and Gas Resources. Note that the resource values presented here			Total Resources	28,382	337,039

[a]Comprising oil, NGLs, and liquids associated with natural gas reservoirs.
[b]Comprising associated dissolved and nonassociated natural gas

2.2.1.2 Oil and Gas Resource Data Preparation

The geometry of an oil and gas play is defined by its geology and extends horizontally and vertically in the subsurface. Figure 2-13 is an idealized block diagram showing how three different plays can occur in a single area. Plays are commonly "stacked" in the subsurface so that a given surface land parcel can overlie numerous plays.

For this inventory, a homogeneous distribution of resource within a play boundary is assumed because of the lack of more geographically specific information. In fact, the USGS indicates that resources are generally not homogeneously distributed within a play. This is particularly true for conventional accumulations, and less so for continuous accumulations. Despite the assumption of homogeneous distribution of resources in the plays, various oil and gas densities can be mapped as a result of play stacking.

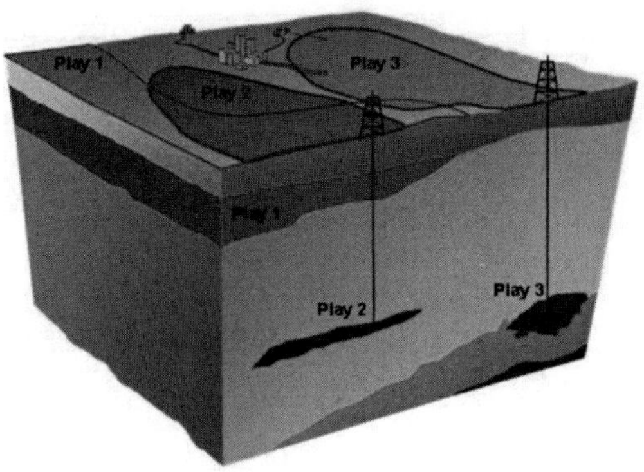

Figure 2-13. Conceptual Block Diagram of Oil and Gas Plays

2.2.1.3 Oil and Gas Resource Data-Related Caveats

The estimation of undiscovered technically recoverable resources is inherently uncertain, as reflected by the fact that the USGS develops cumulative probability distributions of the estimated resources for each play. These distributions are used to derive 95 percent probable resource (a 19-in-20 chance of that volume or more), 5 percent probable resource (a 1-in-20 chance of that much or more), and mean resource volumes. The mean volume, used in this inventory, represents the arithmetic average of all possible resource outcomes weighted by their probability of occurrence. The analytical results in the inventory use the mean and therefore do not explicitly reflect the range of uncertainty in the resource assessments.

Not all of the resource plays recognized by the USGS within the boundaries of this inventory have been evaluated. The USGS has identified hypothetical plays that lack sufficient data to estimate undiscovered resources. To the extent that hypothetical plays contain significant resources, the results presented here would be an underestimate.

It should be understood that all resource assessments change over time. Not only is it difficult to assess accurately the resource at any one point in time, but the recoverable portion of the resource changes in response to advances in technology, and changes in other conditions under which extraction occurs. Nonetheless, accurate and up-to-date assessments of the potential resources must be continually provided to ensure that public policy decisions are conducted with the best information possible.

For this inventory, the assumption is made that the estimated oil and gas volumes are evenly distributed under the surface area of each play. A resource density map for each basin was created in the GIS by using a spatial summation of the oil and gas volumes contributed by each play. The densities are expressed as millions of cubic feet (MMCF) of gas per square mile and thousands of barrels (Mbbls) of oil per square mile.

2.2.2 Proved Ultimate Recovery Growth (Reserves Growth)

The EIA's role in this inventory is to provide data and analysis relevant to proved reserves and reserves growth of crude oil, natural gas, and natural gas liquids that are associated with already discovered fields underlying Federal onshore lands. This responsibility involves:

- Providing estimates of proved reserves for these fields at the highest possible level of detail consistent with a legal requirement to protect the confidentiality of field operators' proprietary data.
- Estimating future ultimate recovery appreciation for currently producing fields.
- Providing inputs to estimate additional land access constraints that may result from expected ultimate recovery appreciation.

The estimation of proved reserves is necessary for developing reserves growth estimates.

The proved ultimate recovery (PUR) of an oil or gas field is the estimated volume of oil or gas that will ultimately be produced from the field. At any point in time, the PUR is the sum of a field's estimated proved reserves and its cumulative production. The estimated PUR for a new oil or gas field generally increases with time, as a result of new geologic and engineering knowledge gained during operation of the field.

This phenomenon is variously termed "reserves growth," "reserves appreciation," "ultimate recovery appreciation" or "proved ultimate recovery growth." Proved ultimate recovery growth (PURG), the term preferred by the EIA, has been recognized since 1960 and currently accounts for the majority of annual additions to domestic proved reserves. Owing to its importance to present and future domestic oil and gas supply, EIA has been highlighting PURG in the overview section of its annual reserves reports since 1992. Since 1976 PURG has grown in all but one year for both oil plus lease condensate and natural gas. From 1976 through 1994 only 12 percent of proved reserves additions of crude oil and lease condensate and 11 percent of proved reserve additions of wet natural gas were booked as new field discoveries. The rest came from the proved reserves categories related to the proved ultimate recovery appreciation process.[23]

The proved ultimate recovery for an individual field or group of fields in a basin "grows" with time due to such factors as:

- Delineation and development drilling that extends the area of known reservoirs
- Discovery of new producing zones (deeper or shallower)
- Application of improved reservoir management and well completion practices and technologies
- Economic factors that increase wellhead prices or reduce operating costs thus extending the economic life of producing fields.

Initial estimates of PUR are usually conservative owing to the small knowledge base available at that time regarding a field's performance. Annual estimates of a field's PUR normally increase significantly in the early post-discovery years as the field is delineated. In later years, PUR continues to grow due to such factors as installation of improved recovery technology, increased knowledge of field performance, and infill drilling, although generally the annual rate of growth slows. Consequently, the growth factors are large during the early years of field development and then often decline as PUR asymptotically approaches a maximum value, i.e., reserves growth usually slows as field development matures.

For the Phase II study areas, the EIA estimated remaining proved ultimate recovery growth (RPURG), the future reserves growth resource. The resources attributed to future reserves growth are 973 million barrels of oil and 10.55 TCF of gas. See Appendix 7 for a detailed explanation of the estimation methodology.

The EIA's selected RPURG estimates covering Federal and nonfederal lands are provided in Table 2-5. Not all of the Phase II study areas could be evaluated owing to insufficient data.

2.2.2.1 Sources of Remaining Proved Ultimate Recovery Data

The EIA compiled the historical increase in estimates of PUR for oil and gas fields in each study area and extrapolated these data to estimate the PUR of the fields at abandonment. RPURG is the estimated future portion of the growth in PUR from 2003 to the time of field abandonment.

Table 2-5. Remaining Proved Ultimate Recovery Growth (Reserves Growth) by Study Area (Federal and Nonfederal)

Study Area	Selected Model	Remaining Ultimate Recovery Growth – "Reserves Growth"
Oil		*(MMbbl)*
Uinta-Piceance Basin	Hyperbolic	99
Paradox/San Juan Basins	Exponential	162
Powder River Basin	Exponential	28
Wyoming Thrust Belt	Exponential	11
Greater Green River Basin	Exponential	659
Denver Basin	Exponential	14
Black Warrior Basin	Exponential	-
Total		973
Natural Gas		*(Bcf)*
Uinta-Piceance Basin	Exponential	1,247
Paradox/San Juan Basins	Hyperbolic	4,996
Powder River Basin	Exponential	16
Wyoming Thrust Belt	Exponential	281
Greater Green River Basin	Hyperbolic	2,539
Denver Basin	Exponential	95
Black Warrior Basin	Exponential	1,380
Total		10,554

For each study area, the EIA created a database containing field names, field discovery dates, annual oil and gas production for each field, estimated cumulative production, and annual estimates of oil and gas proved reserves for each field.[24] Each field in a study area was assigned to a vintage year according to its date of first production or its date of discovery. The annual proved reserves estimates were usually available only from 1977 to present. The resulting files contained vintage year, number of fields in each vintage (in barrels of oil equivalent), PUR for each field vintage, annual natural gas PUR for each vintage, and annual liquid PUR for each vintage.

Many field names and codes had to be altered, corrected, and matched across the multiple data sources in order to accumulate properly the field data. Obvious major errors were corrected, but many apparent data discontinuities and variations within vintages were mostly accepted "as-is." Reserves data were used as reported by the field operators unless very obvious errors were found. Specific vintages that did not fit the trend of most of the data for a basin were excluded from the extrapolation. Attempts to divide the data within a basin into conventional reservoirs, tight formation, and coal gas resources were largely unsuccessful because of the limited number of vintages, the short histories available for some of the fields, and frequent inability to separate the data by reservoir type within a field.

The EIA used two models to estimate RPURG for each study area and resource type, an exponential cumulative growth factor model and a hyperbolic incremental growth factor model. The exponential model depends on annual average cumulative growth factors for a basin. The hyperbolic model depends on incremental growth factors by vintage, or age of the fields in the basin. Both are asymptotic functions that use time as the sole driver. Although other potential drivers such as drilling rates or wellhead prices are not directly used, these factors have affected the historical data that feed into the models. The application of both models for estimating PURG for a basin over time is described in Appendix 7.

Results of the two models were compared for each study area and hydrocarbon type and a preferred model result was selected based on the EIA modeling team's best judgment. The exponential model results were selected most of the time. Appendix 7 provides a detailed report of EIA's methodology and results.

There were insufficient data from the Appalachian Basin and Montana Thrust Belt for a PURG analysis. Separate estimates for tight reservoirs were not made for the Denver Basin, Black Warrior Basin and the Wyoming Thrust Belt owing to a combination of data anomalies and data interpretation concerns. In all study areas, the available coalbed natural gas data were deemed not to be dependable for establishing PURG and are therefore not separately reported. Tight formation results using the exponential model were reported for the Uinta-Piceance and Paradox/San Juan Basins, but were not carried forward into the analysis for the sake of consistency.

2.2.2.2 Remaining Proved Ultimate Recovery Data Preparation

The estimated remaining proved ultimate recovery or "reserves growth" resources for each study area were incorporated into the inventory by adding a "reserves growth resource" layer to the USGS undiscovered technically recoverable resources. As with the undiscovered resource layer, the inventory assumes that the reserves growth resources are homogeneously distributed within the geographic boundaries of the reserves growth resource layer. This is a simplifying assumption, which may be modified in the future as new reserves growth methodologies and findings become available.

The geographic boundary of the reserves growth resource layer was created for each study area from a union of the field boundaries of all the producing oil and gas fields identified by the EIA within the study area. The individual field boundaries were extended an additional mile in all directions prior to the union, so the geographic boundary of the reserves growth resource layer extends a mile beyond the 2003 boundaries of the actual fields incorporated into the layer. This was done to approximate future extensions to the proved area of producing fields, which contributes to reserves growth. Next, the total reserves growth resource estimated for each study area was homogenously distributed within the geographic boundary of the reserves growth resource layer for the study area. Lastly, the two resource layers, the USGS undiscovered technically recoverable resource layer and the EIA RPURG resource layer, were combined to create the oil and natural gas resource maps shown in Section 2.2.3.

2.2.2.3 Remaining Proved Ultimate Recovery Estimate Data-Related Caveats

The estimated reserves growth resources for the Phase II study areas are lower than generally would be expected, especially compared to previously published reserves growth estimates including the USGS 1995 National Assessment[25], the NPC[26], the Potential Gas Committee (PGC),[27] as well as some operators' not necessarily representative anecdotal reports of estimated reserves growth for fields in some study areas.[28] Appendix 7 (Table A7-2) contains a side-by-side comparison of this inventory's reserves growth estimates to other relevant estimates. Reserves growth in most of the study areas ranged from 3 percent to 25 percent of current proved reserves. However, the Black Warrior Basin reserves growth was estimated to be 110 percent of proved reserves.

It is unlikely that there is a single cause of the differences with other studies. Certainly there are some significant differences in methodology and input data. For example, the PGC uses a non-statistical, reservoir-specific approach that relies on expert judgment to estimate the probable resources associated with the additional development of an already discovered reservoir. Historically, the most successful estimates of reserves growth have relied on the use of reservoir level data, rather than the more aggregate field level data on which this inventory's estimates are based. This is not particularly surprising since most factors that affect the reserves growth phenomenon are reservoir- specific and will not necessarily apply to an entire field when it consists of multiple reservoirs as many fields do.[29] Unfortunately, reservoir level proved reserves data are only rarely available for onshore United States fields and the RPURG estimation must therefore be done using the field level data that are available. It should also be noted that this is, insofar as we know, the first time that field level RPURG analysis has been attempted on a scale comparable to that of this inventory.

The Energy Information Administration methodology used for the Phase II study areas and the methodology used by the U.S. Geological Survey to estimate reserves growth for the most recent National Assessment are both statistical extrapolations of historical reserves growth and are subject to the same inherent limitations,[30] although the methodologies differ in detail. These limitations introduce substantial uncertainty into the final results, which the USGS is currently addressing in an ongoing review of their reserves growth estimation methodology (see below). In a recent test, the USGS found that two different statistical extrapolation methodologies produce reserves growth estimates that differed by approximately 25 percent and were as much as 60 percent higher than actual volumetric data.[31] The results shown in Table A7-1 should be interpreted with these limitations in mind:

- Inherent uncertainty in the underlying data (for example, 'reserves' are defined differently by different operators and different commercial/private databases; fields and reservoirs are inconsistently defined).
- Current statistical methodologies rely on field age (since field discovery) as a surrogate for field development effort. Other factors such as reserves recognition practices, differential application of new technology and production monitoring practices, different operating environments, and access to markets may not be adequately represented by field age alone.
- Large fields have more weight in the analysis, which may bias the results toward the development histories of the largest fields in a basin or study area. Large fields may be more likely than smaller fields to receive consistently applied development efforts and new technology applications, and be less sensitive to economic factors.
- Uncertainties are not addressed directly, such as variance of the input data and uncertainties in the underlying assumed field development scenarios.

Table 2-6, which shows the range of RPURG results using the two different models, exponential and hyperbolic, illustrates the uncertainty surrounding the reserves growth estimates. The model fits of the field growth factors (provided as figures in Appendix 7) appear to be very conservative in some cases and inconclusive in others, so that the resulting extrapolation of proved ultimate recovery may be too low. The datasets for some of the study areas may simply be too small to support adequately the extrapolation of remaining proved ultimate recovery. There are many apparent anomalies and errors in the available field-level proved reserves data series that doubtless affect the estimates and that, at present, would require a very labor-intensive effort to isolate, characterize, and correct.

Table 2-6. Range of EIA Estimated Remaining Proved Ultimate Recovery Growth ("Reserves Growth") for Selected Study Areas

Study Area	Type	2003 PUR	RPURG (Exponential Model)	RPURG (Hyperbolic Model)
Uinta-Piceance Basin	Liquids, MMbbl	782	654	99
	Gas, Bcf	5,838	747	1,631
	Gas – Tight, Bcf	1,700	50	n.a.
Paradox/San Juan Basins	Liquids, MMbbl	903	35	453
	Liquids – Tight, MMbbl	124	127	n.a.
	Gas, Bcf	5,157	8,910	1,208
	Gas – Tight, Bcf	18,783	3,788	n.a.
Montana Thrust Belt	Not analyzed; insufficient data			
Powder River Basin	Liquids, MMbbl	3,458	28	237
	Gas, Bcf	3,925	16	502
Wyoming Thrust Belt	Liquids, MMbbl	351	11	15
	Gas, Bcf	4,788	281	319
Greater Green River Basin	Liquids, MMbbl	1,059	659	53
	Gas, Bcf	31,995	19,284	2,539
Denver Basin	Liquids, MMbbl	1,290	14	12
	Gas, Bcf	7,730	95	85
Black Warrior Basin	Liquids, MMbbl	16	-	-
	Gas, Bcf	4,756	1,380	347
Appalachian Basin	Not analyzed; insufficient data			

Note: Liquids include oil and gas condensate for Federal lands only

A phenomenon observed in the 1995 USGS National Assessment may also be operating, in which the estimated reserves growth based on a dataset for the lower-48 states as a whole produced greater reserves growth estimates than the sum of reserves growth estimated independently for individual regions. In October 2005, the USGS commenced a one-year scoping project to evaluate possible improvements to existing reserves growth methodology, identify alternative methodologies, and recommend a robust reserves growth methodology that can be universally applied.[32] The EIA is investigating whether it might be possible to develop improved, less labor-intensive means of cleansing the field level data of its apparent anomalies and errors and whether the estimates can be improved by moving to a multi-parameter estimation methodology. The findings and recommendations of the USGS reserves growth scoping project will be incorporated into the reserves growth assessment for subsequent phases of this inventory. Consequently, the reserves growth volumes estimated for this chapter are likely to be re-evaluated and are subject to change.

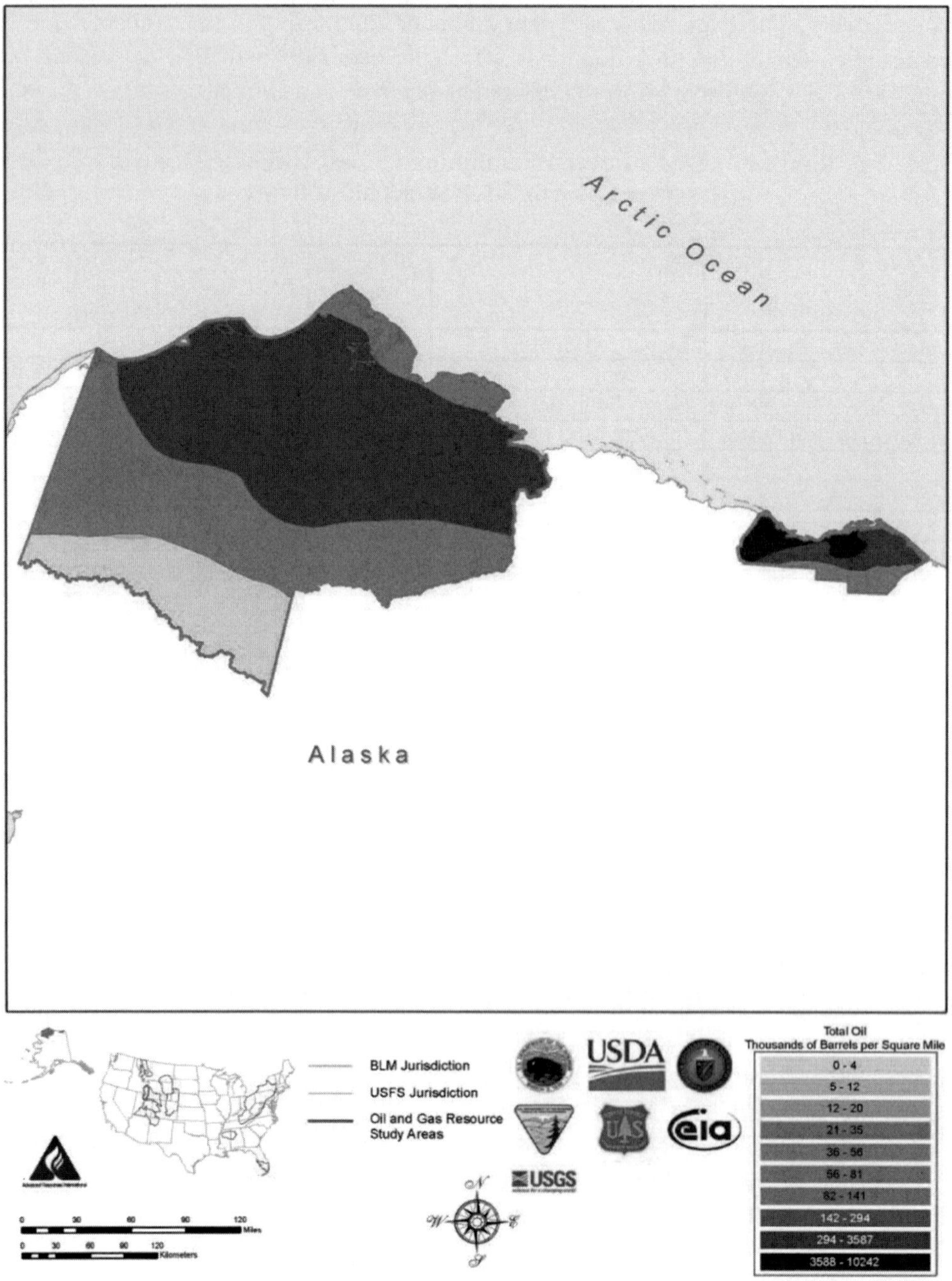

Figure 2-14. Total Oil Map, Northern Alaska Study Area

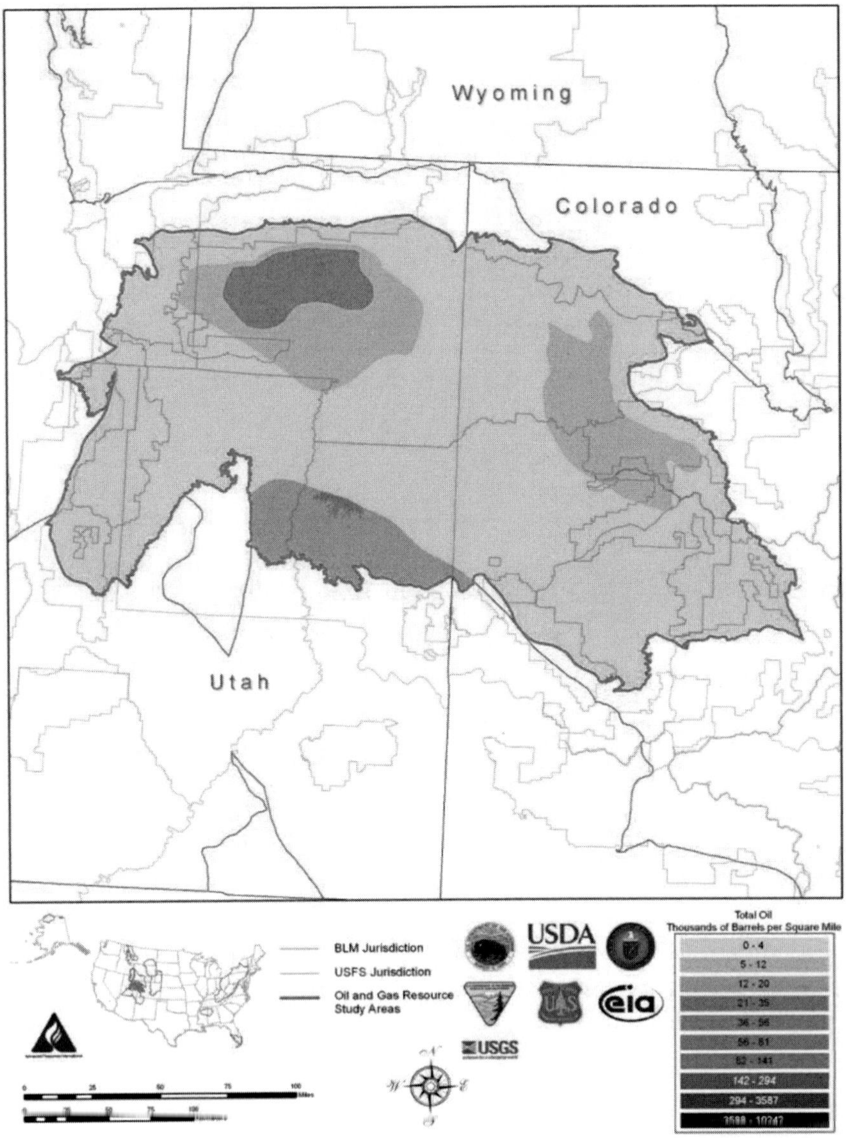

Figure 2-15. Total Oil Map, Uinta-Piceance Basin Study Area

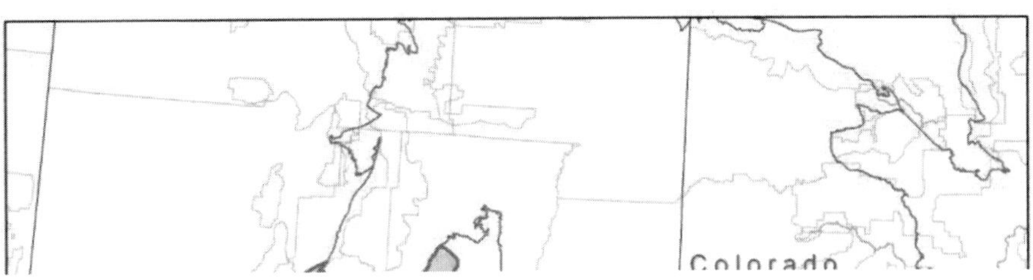

Figure 2-16. Total Oil Map, Paradox/San Juan Basins Study Area

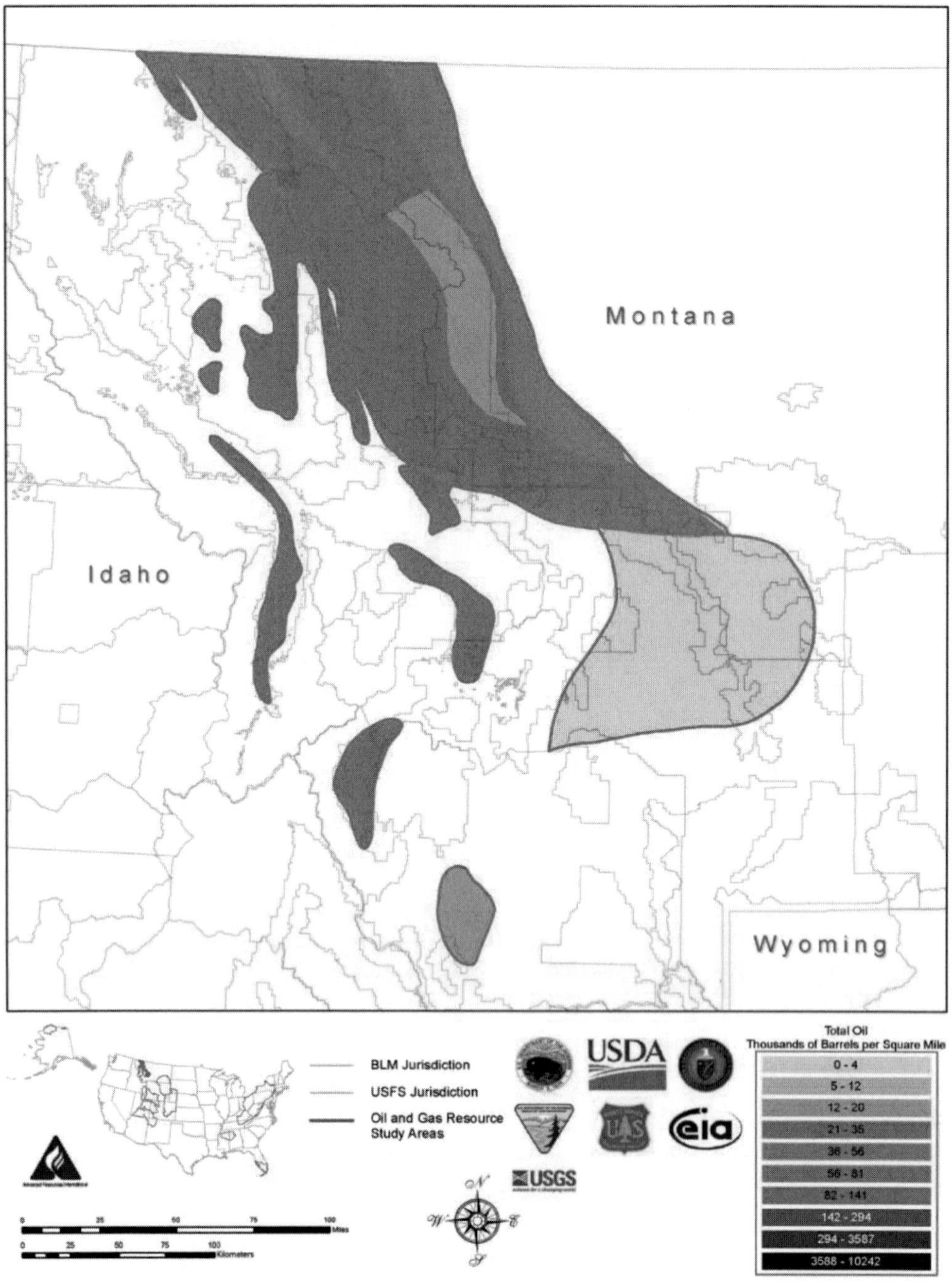

Figure 2-17. Total Oil Map, Montana Thrust Belt Study Area

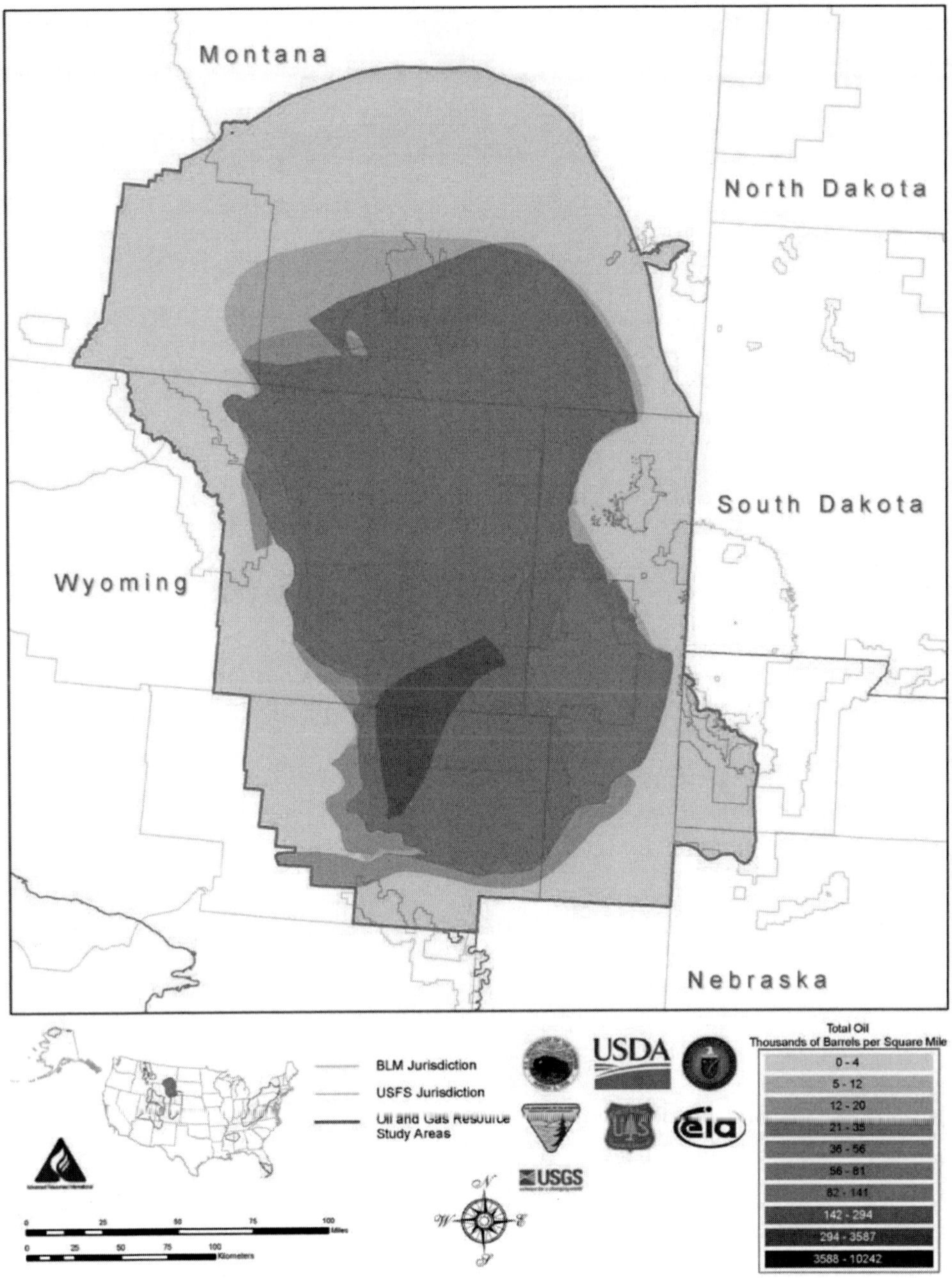

Figure 2-18. Total Oil Map, Powder River Basin Study Area

Figure 2-19. Total Oil Map, Wyoming Thrust Belt Study Area

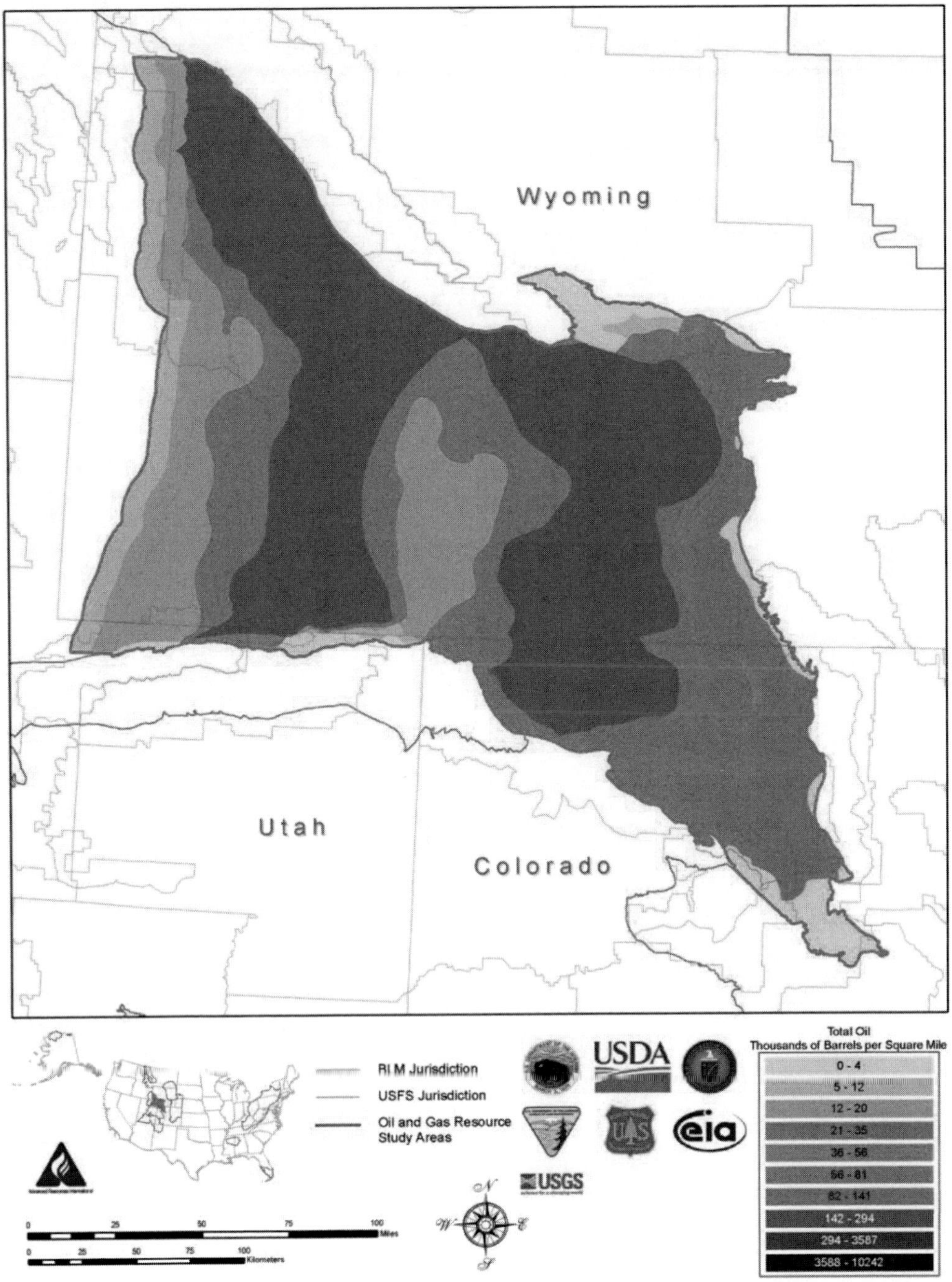

Figure 2-20. Total Oil Map, Greater Green River Basin Study Area

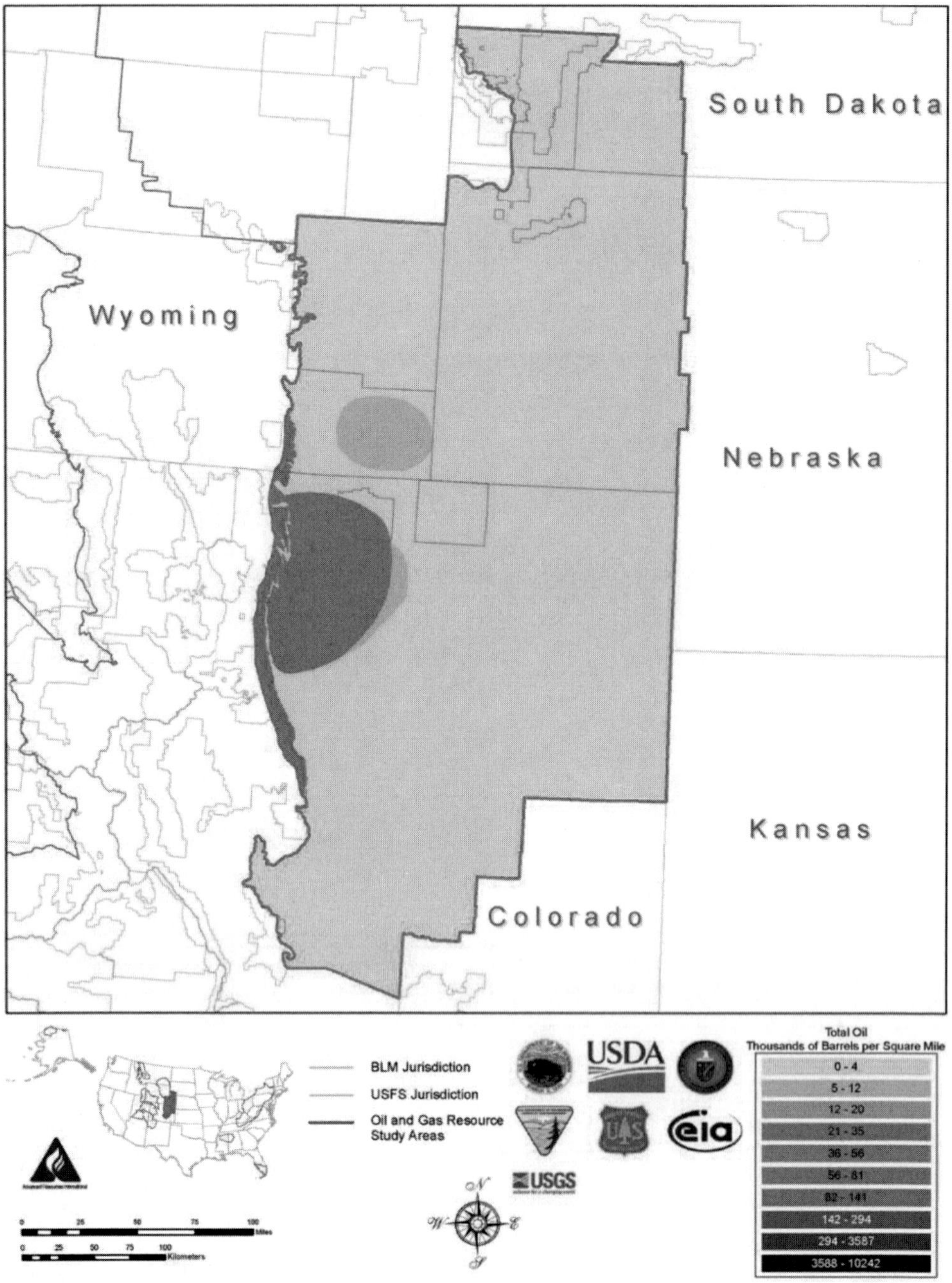

Figure 2-21. Total Oil Map, Denver Basin Study Area

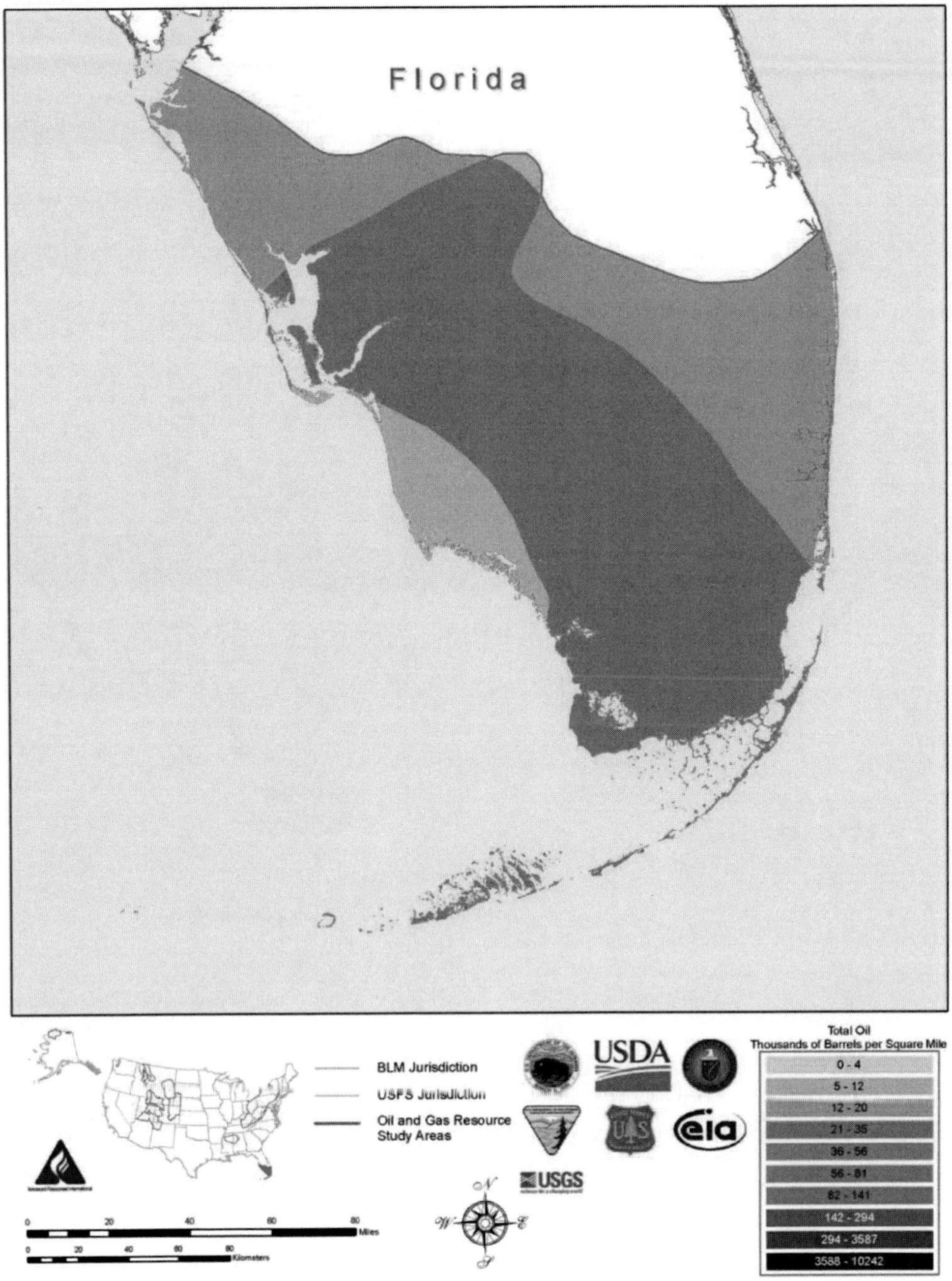

Figure 2-22. Total Oil Map, Florida Peninsula Study Area

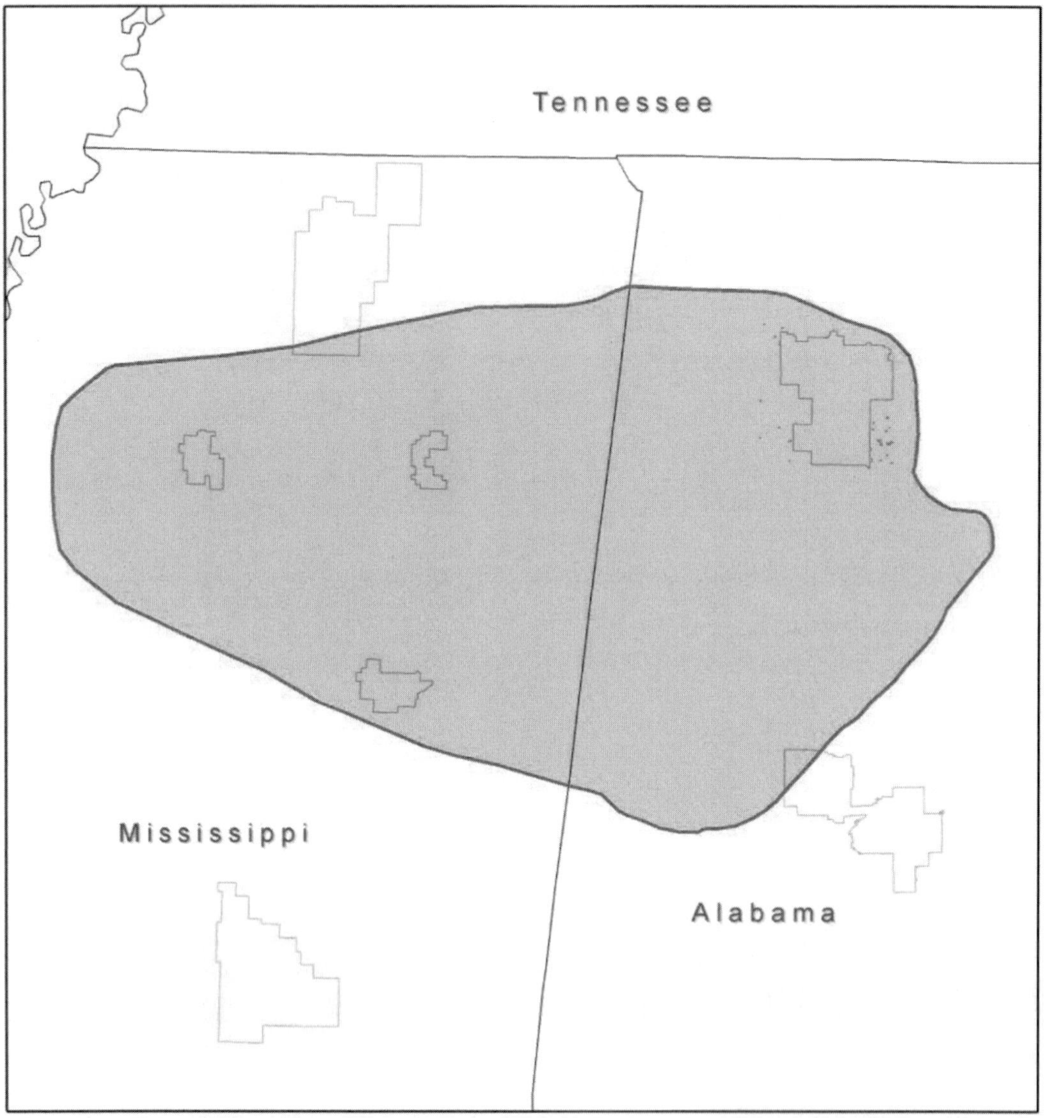

Figure 2-23. Total Oil Map, Black Warrior Basin Study Area

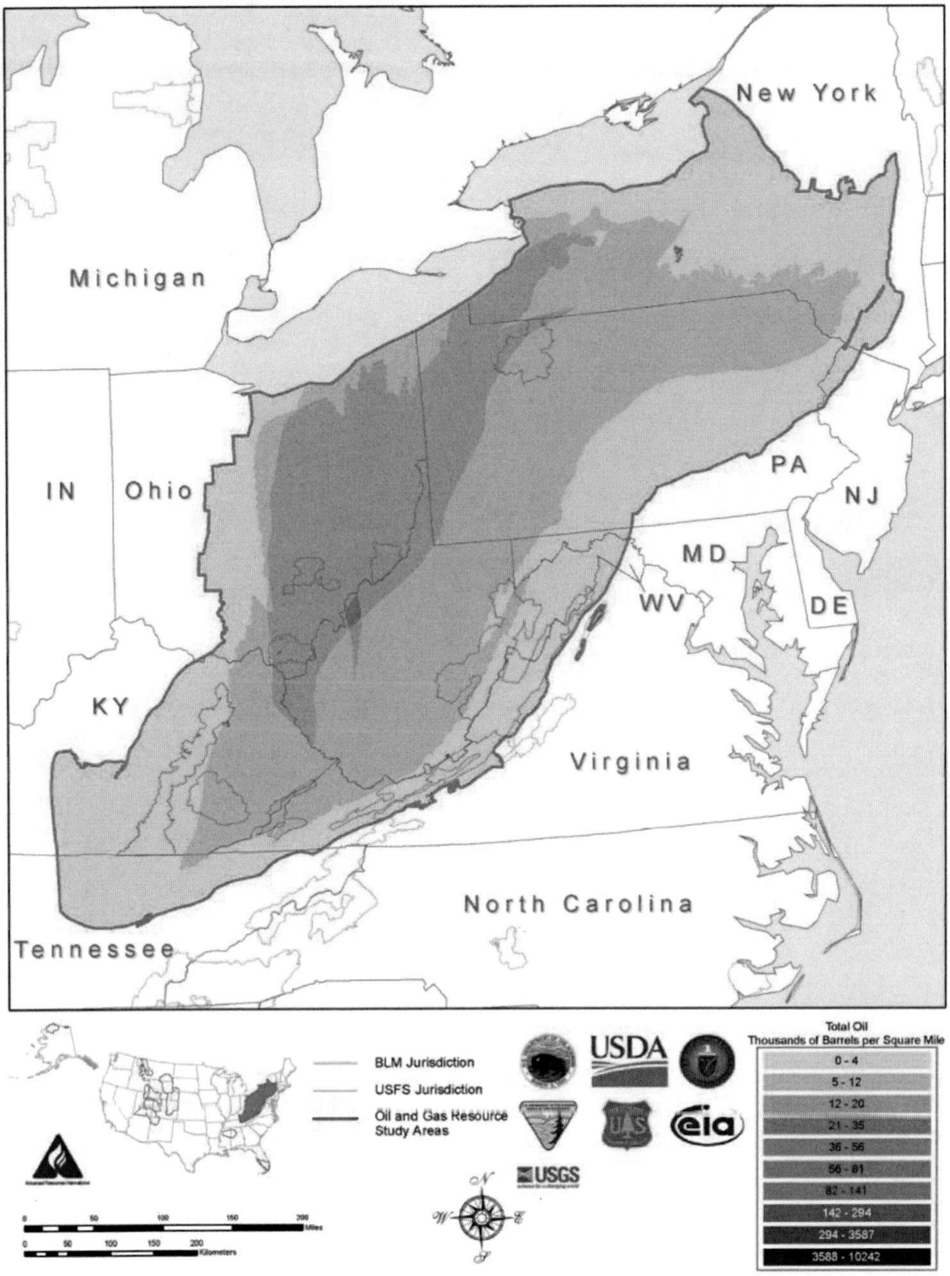

Figure 2-24. Total Oil Map, Appalachian Basin Study Area

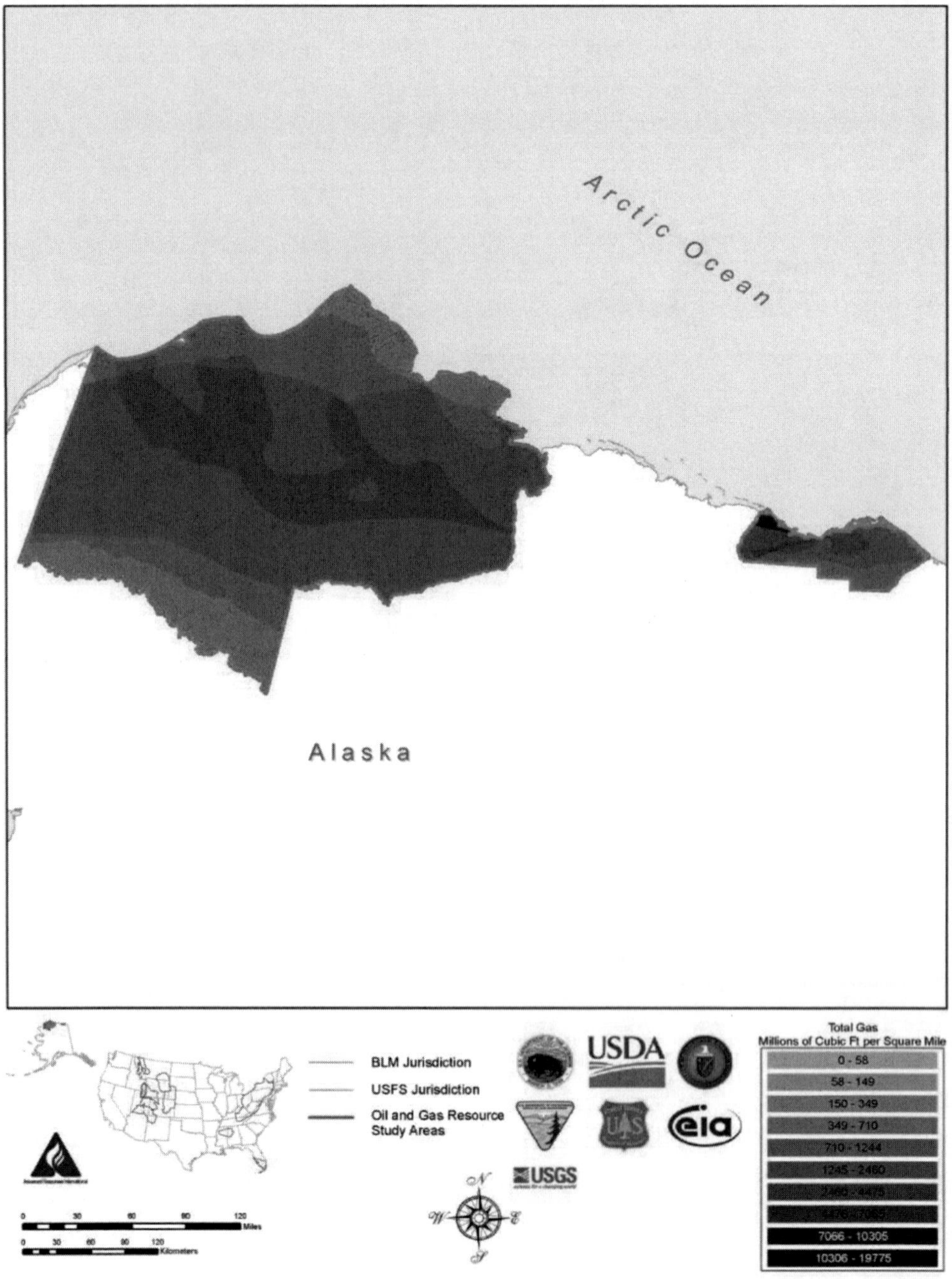

Figure 2-25. Total Natural Gas Map, Northern Alaska Study Area

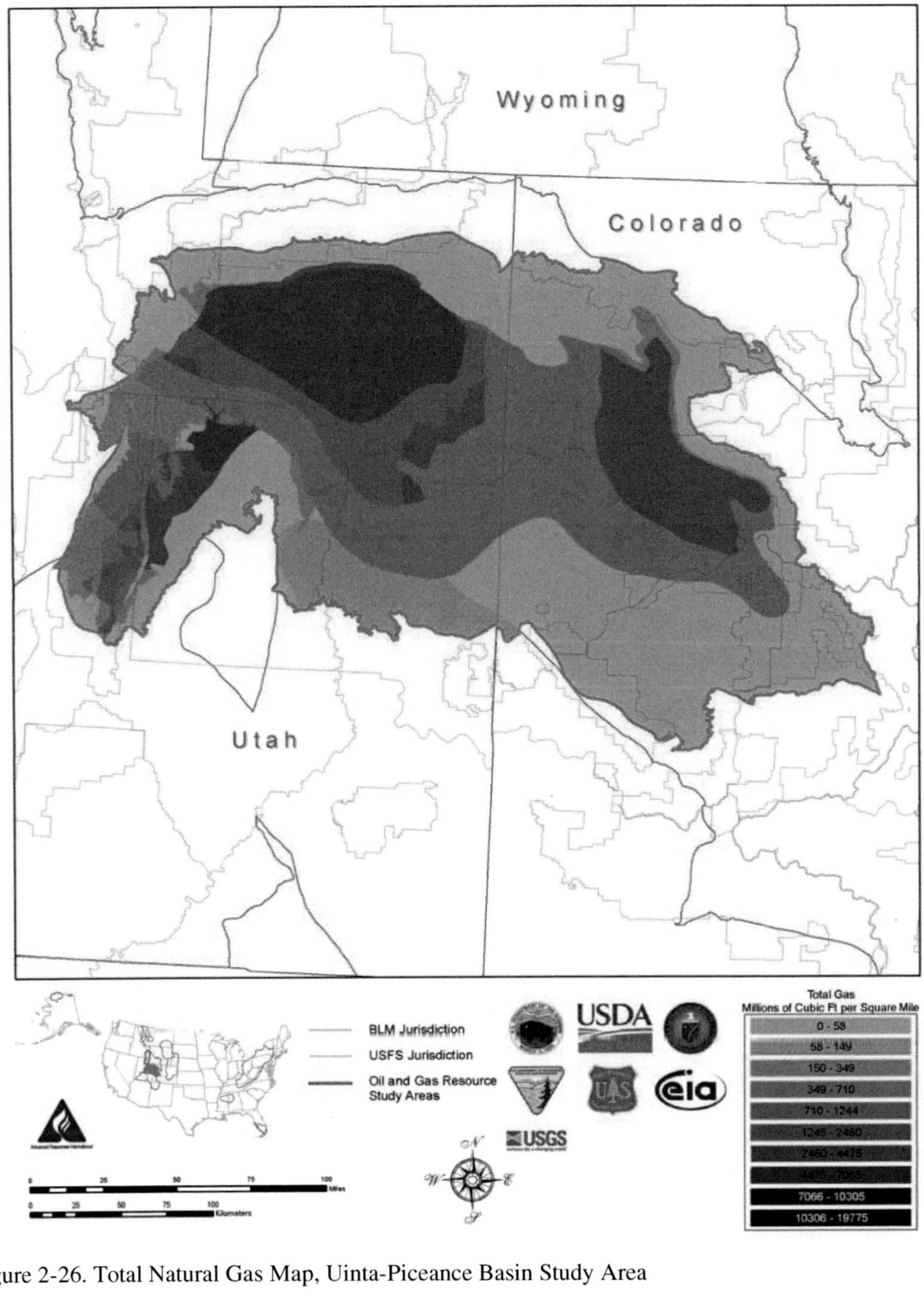

Figure 2-26. Total Natural Gas Map, Uinta-Piceance Basin Study Area

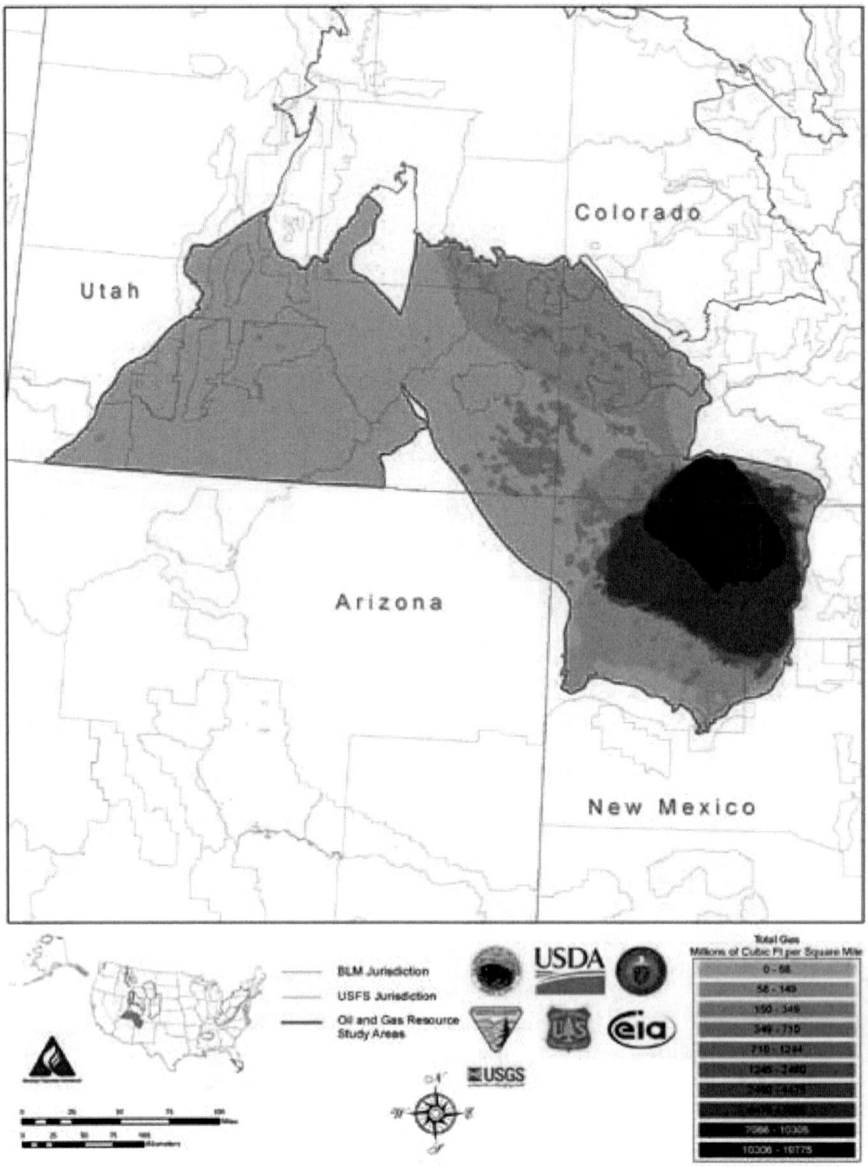

Figure 2-27. Total Natural Gas Map, Paradox/San Juan Basins Study Area

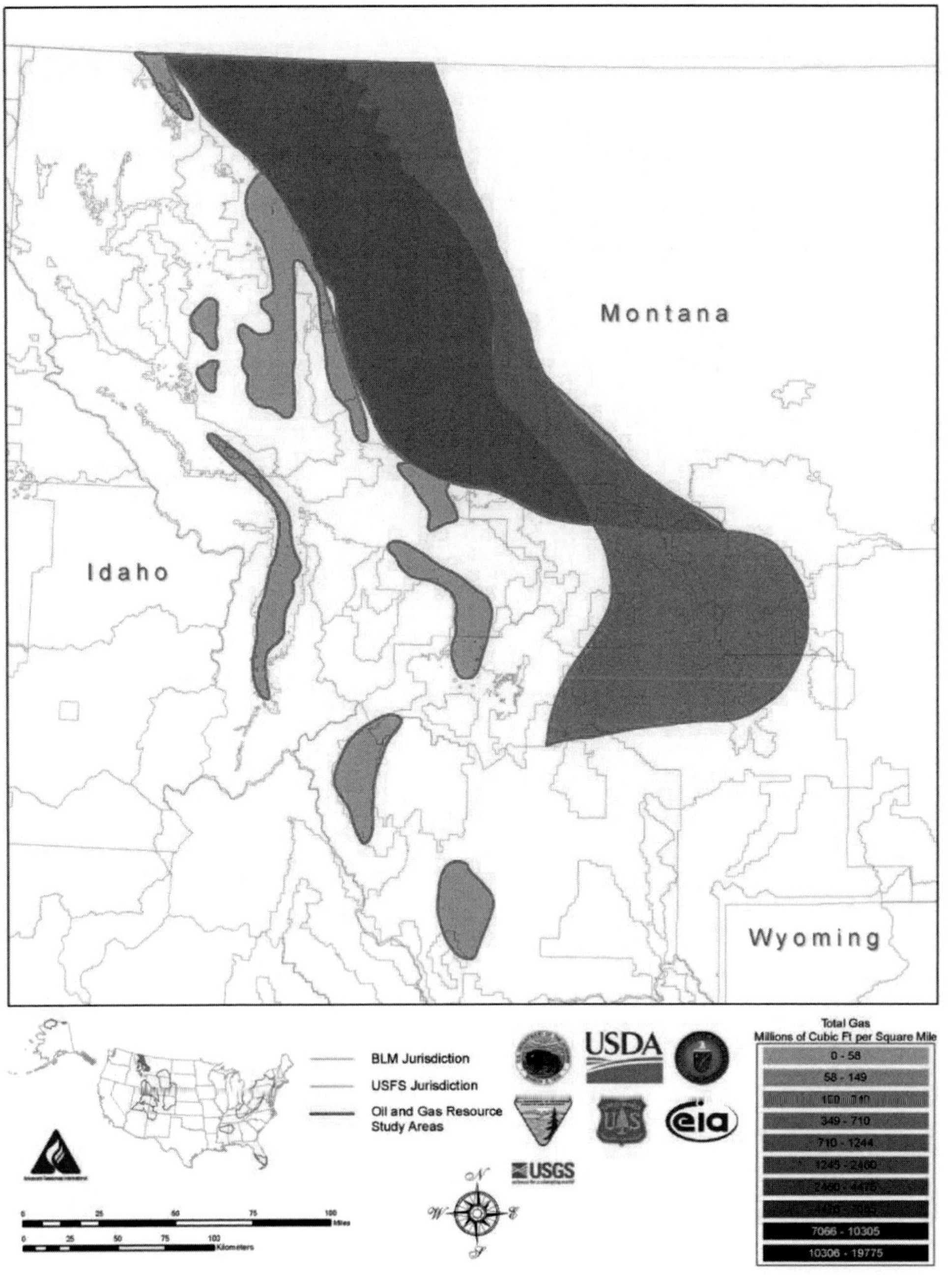

Figure 2-28. Total Natural Gas Map, Montana Thrust Belt Study Area

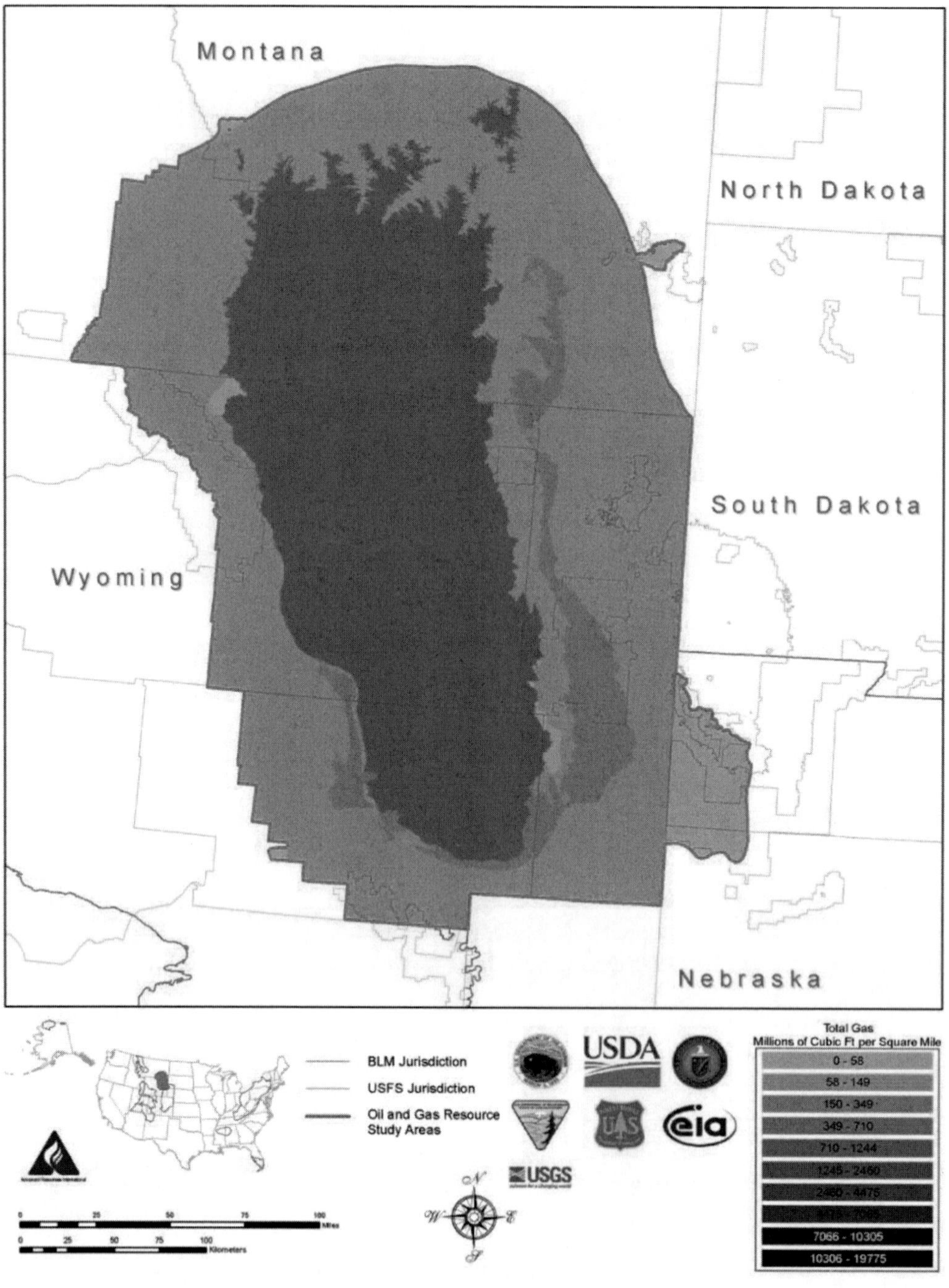

Figure 2-29. Total Natural Gas Map, Powder River Basin Study Area

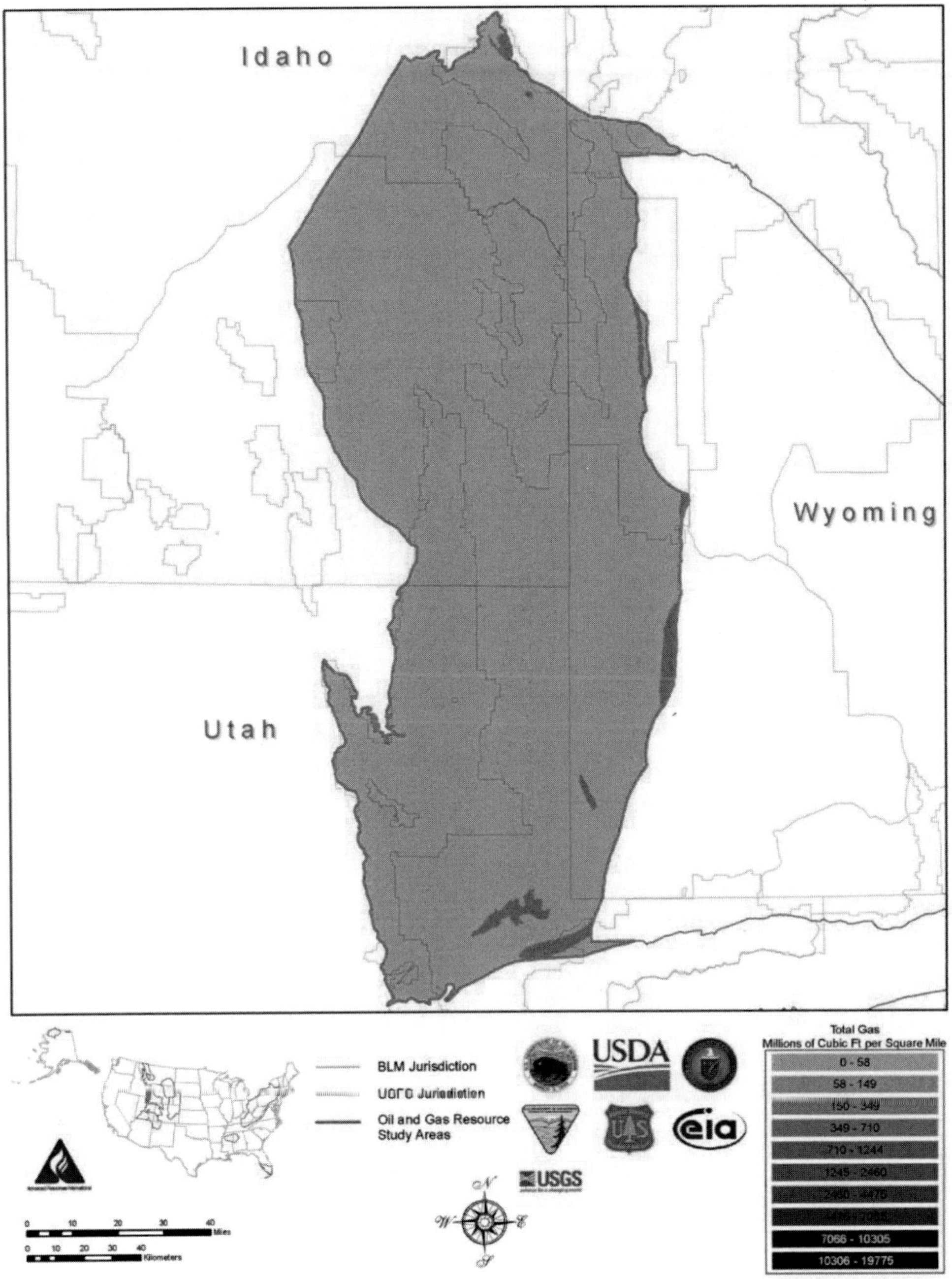

Figure 2-30. Total Natural Gas Map, Wyoming Thrust Belt Study Area

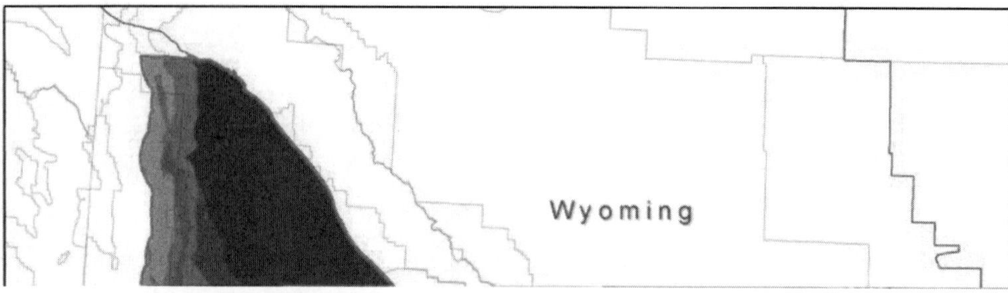

Figure 2-31. Total Natural Gas Map, Greater Green River Basin Study Area

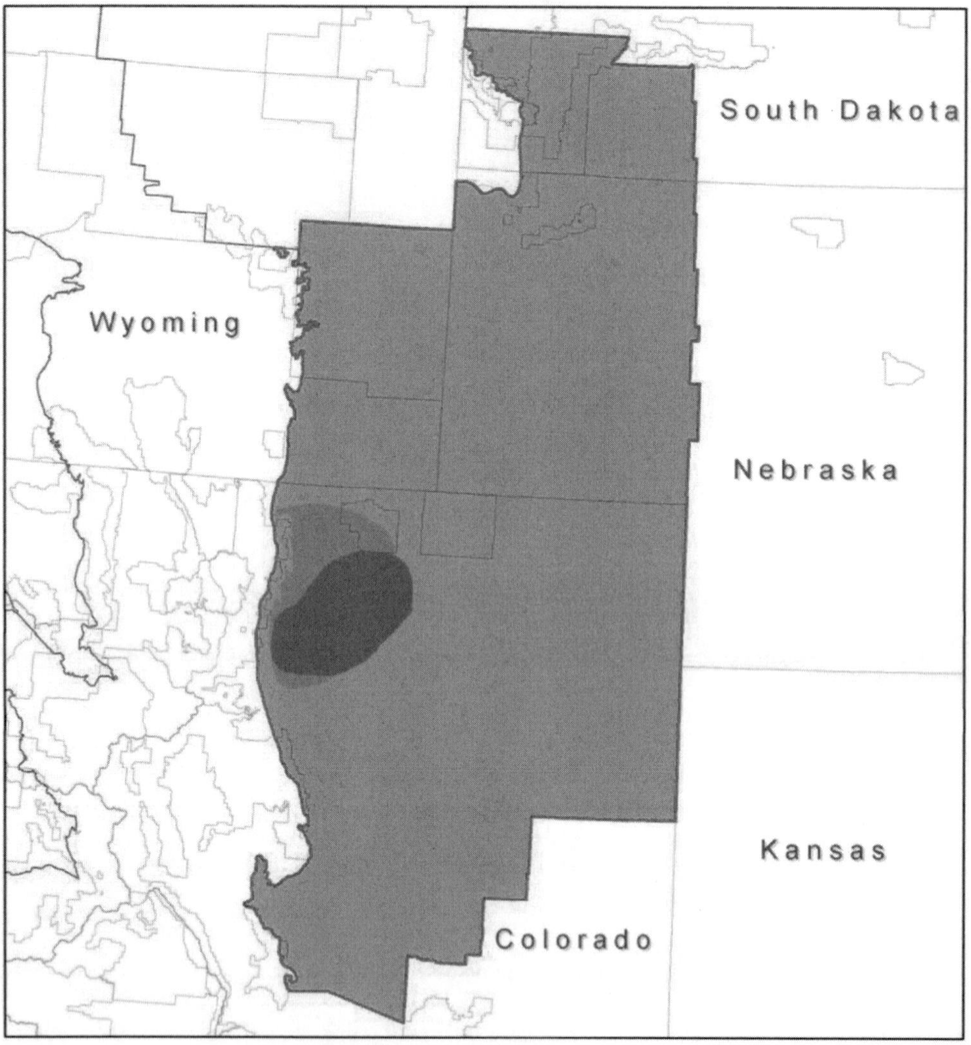

Figure 2-32. Total Natural Gas Map, Denver Basin Study Area

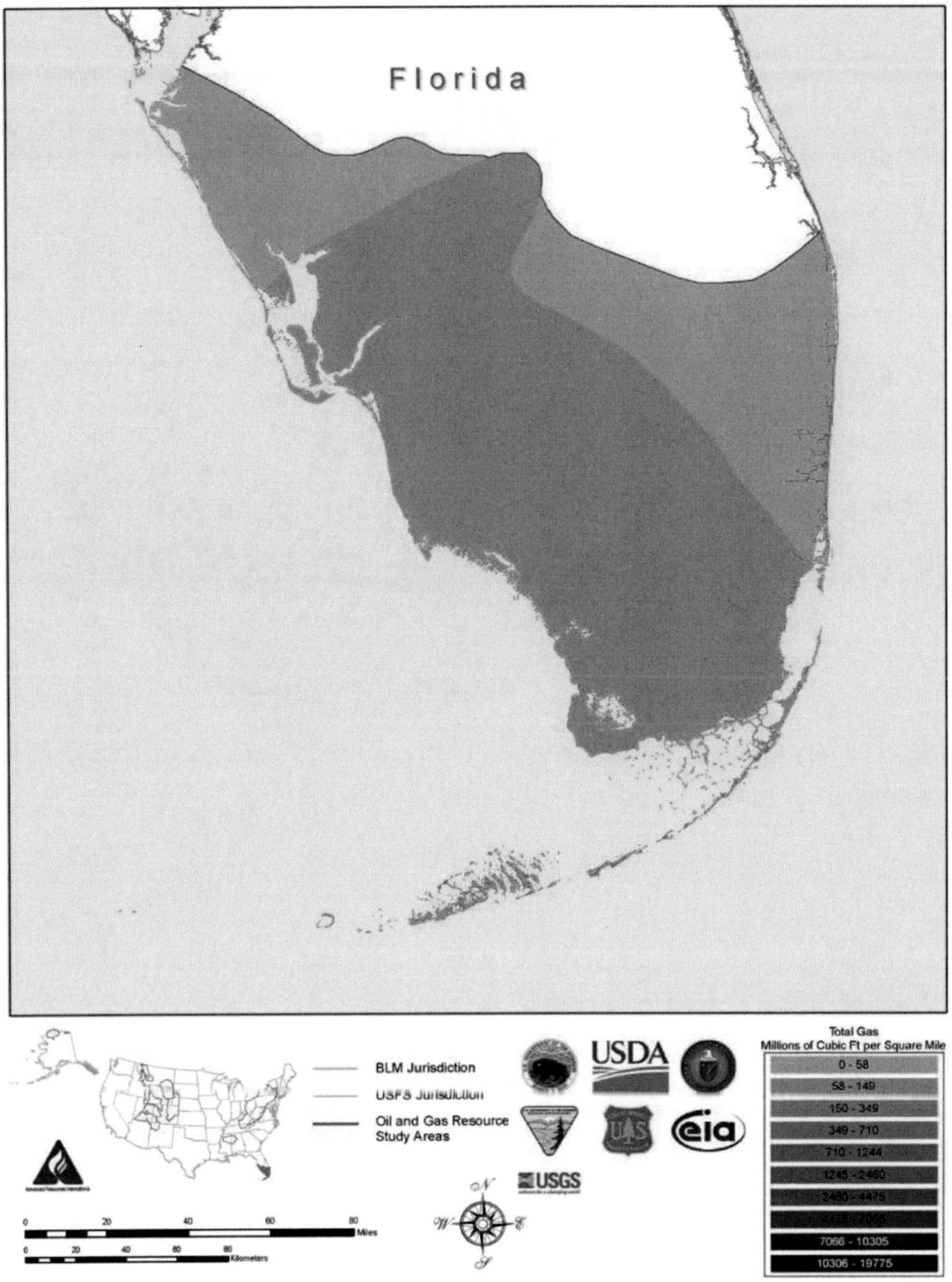

Figure 2-33. Total Natural Gas Map, Florida Peninsula Study Area

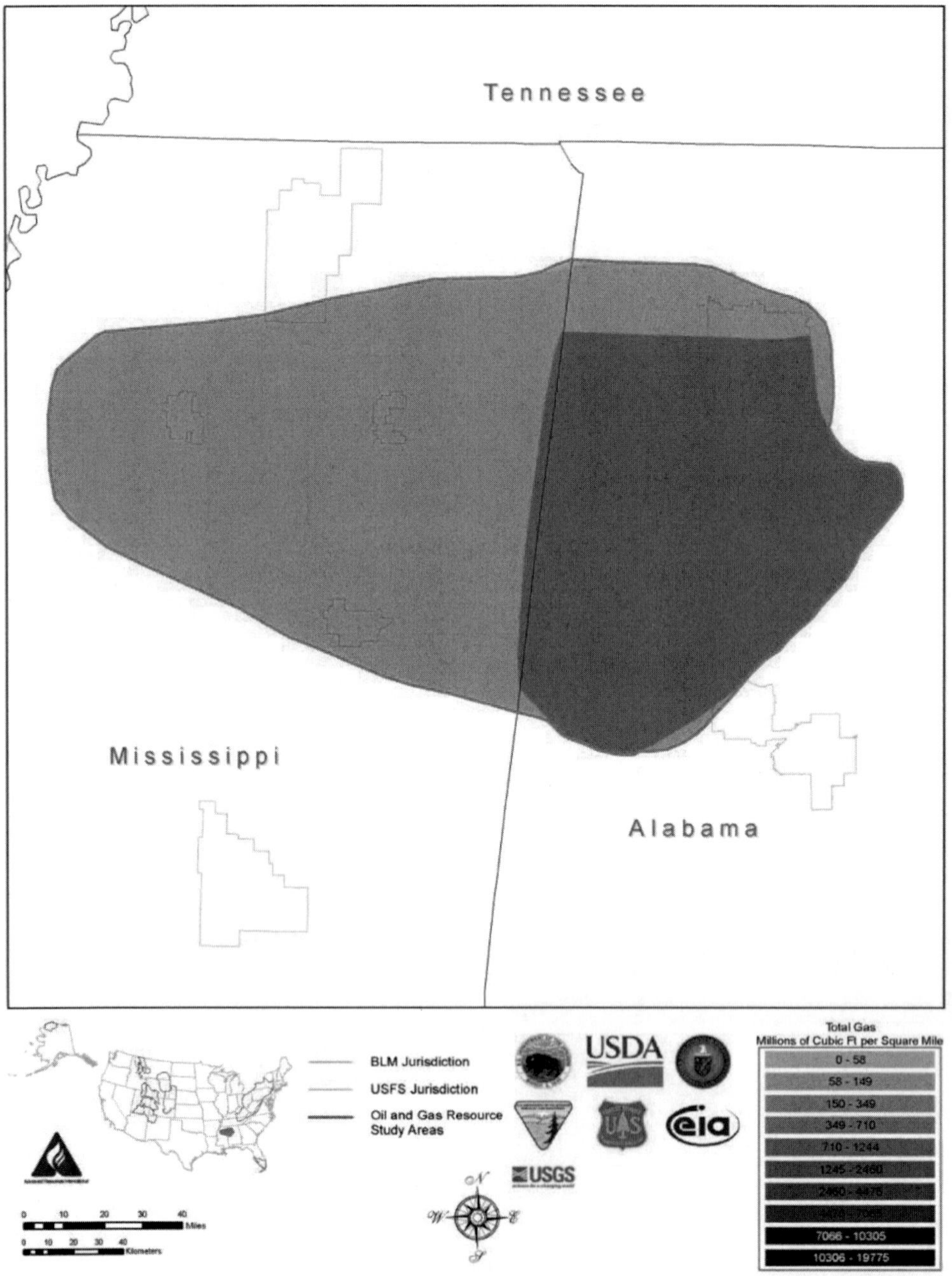

Figure 2-34. Total Natural Gas Map, Black Warrior Basin Study Area

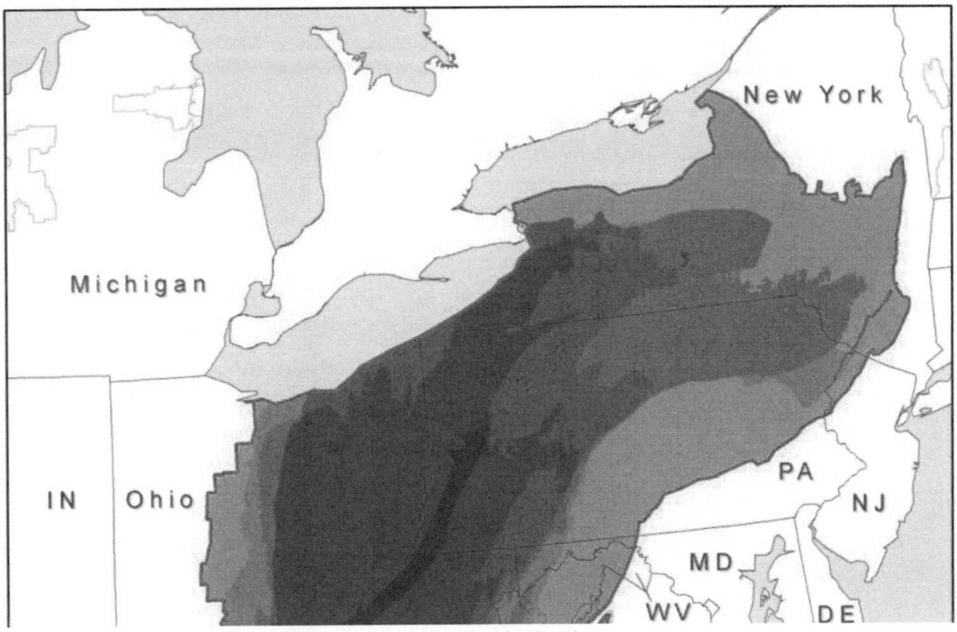

Figure 2-35. Total Natural Gas Map, Appalachian Basin Study Area

2.2.3 Oil and Natural Gas Resource Maps

The products of the oil and gas resource data preparation work are maps of hydrocarbon volumes, projected to the surface. These maps depict areas of varying potential resource richness based on often overlapping play resource volumes. The distributions of undiscovered technically recoverable resources and reserves growth are shown by study area for oil in Figures 2-14 through 2-24 and for natural gas in Figures 2-25 through 2-35.

2.2.4 Proved Reserves

Proved reserves are defined as quantities of crude oil, natural gas, or natural gas liquids that geological and engineering data demonstrate with reasonable certainty (defined as greater than 90 percent probability) to be recoverable from *known* reservoirs *under existing economic and operating conditions*. Proved reserves are, in effect, the current "inventory on-the-shelf" portion of total resource endowment.[33]

2.2.4.1 Sources of Proved Oil and Gas Reserves Data

Comprehensive estimates of the domestic proved reserves of crude oil, natural gas, and natural gas liquids are prepared annually by the EIA. These estimates are a combination of reported and statistically imputed volumes based on:

- Thousands of individual proved reserves and production estimates reported to EIA annually,[34] either at the field level or at the state level by a representative sample of the operators of domestic oil and gas wells. Of the 22,519 operators in the 2001 survey, 1,867 were included in the sample.
- All operators of active domestic natural gas processing plants who annually report their operations on Form EIA-64A "Annual Report of the Origin of Natural Gas

Liquids Production." For the 2001 survey, 525 active gas processing plants responded to the survey.

Only the largest oil and gas well operators (those producing 1.5 million barrels or more of crude oil, or 15 billion cubic feet or more of natural gas per year) are required to submit to EIA proved reserves and production estimates by field for all of their operated properties. There were 172 large operators in the 2001 survey, all of which were included in the sample. The response rate was 100 percent.

Intermediate size operators (those producing less than the largest operators but at least 400,000 barrels of crude oil, or at least 2 billion cubic feet of natural gas per year) are required to submit production estimates by field for all of their operated properties, but are only required to submit proved reserves estimates by field when they maintain them in their records. There were 439 mid-sized operators in the 2001 survey. All were included in the sample and their response rate was also 100 percent.

Small operators are those with production less than 400,000 barrels of crude oil or 2 billion cubic feet of natural gas per year. There were 21,908 small operators in the 2001 survey. Of these, 1,175 were sampled with certainty at an associated response rate of 98 percent and an additional 622 were randomly sampled at an associated response rate of 95 percent.

2.2.4.2 Proved Oil and Gas Reserves Data Preparation

The procedures used to prepare the proved oil and gas reserves data are described in Appendix 8.

2.2.4.3 Proved Reserves Data-Related Caveats

Because the EIA's proved reserves survey is expressly designed to minimize the respondents' reporting burden and yet provide reliable estimates at the state and national level of data aggregation, the EIA does not have operator-submitted, field-specific proved reserves information covering every oil or gas field in the country. However, the EIA has data reported for about 90 percent of all estimated domestic proved reserves. The EIA may have only partial reported estimates for a field that has two or more operators if one is not required to report proved reserves by field.

These deficiencies in EIA's field-specific proved reserves information were remedied for this inventory by use of additional procedures based on either publicly-available production data or reserve-to-production ratio analogs.

In addition to gaps and omissions in operator-reported estimates of proved reserves, the proved reserves data are subject to two further caveats:

1. For the EIA survey, field location is reported at the county level. The precise field locations needed for this inventory's GIS-based methodology required correlation of the EIA's reserves data files with commercial sources of field and/or well information that provide more precise location data. This process involved detailed, often well-by-well, work owing to the existence of non-standard field names and codes, or the occasional lack of a field name, in the commercial or State data sources.
2. EIA is obliged by law to ensure the confidentiality of the data submitted by each reserves survey respondent. Within the Phase II study areas, there are situations

where a field is operated by a single operator, or where a single operator is dominant. In such cases, EIA cannot disclose the proved reserves estimates for the field without a written agreement from the operator waiving the right to confidentiality. Such agreements are rare and time-consuming to obtain. To avoid the release of confidential information while still adequately supporting this inventory, EIA elected not to present field-specific proved reserves estimates even where doing so would not have compromised a respondent's identity. Instead, the fields have been grouped into a range of proved reserves categories that are broad enough to prevent extraction of the estimates for any specific field.

Table 2-7 provides a summary of proved reserves on Federal and nonfederal lands. Note that proved oil and gas reserves are not presented on Figures 2-14 through 2-35. See Appendix 8 for a more detailed explanation of proved reserves estimation and field boundary construction.

Table 2-7. Proved Reserves Summary Statistics

Study Area	Number of Fields	Total Liquid Reserves (MMbbl)	Federal Land Liquid Reserves (MMbbl)	Federal Portion of Total Liquid Reserves	Total Gas Reserves (Bcf)	Federal Land Gas Reserves (Bcf)	Federal Portion of Total Gas Reserves
Northern Alaska (NPRA and ANWR 1002 only)	3	350	0	0.0%	235	0.62	0.3%
Uinta-Piceance Basin	180	254	143	56.2%	7,182	3,794	52.8%
Paradox/San Juan Basins	250	174	53	30.4%	20,654	10,939	53.0%
Montana Thrust Belt	1	0	0	0.0%	0	0	0.0%
Powder River Basin	543	193	109	56.3%	2,399	936	39.0%
Wyoming Thrust Belt	28	35	14	39.8%	1,141	475	41.6%
Greater Green River Basin	281	177	122	69.0%	12,703	10,064	79.2%
Denver Basin	1,638	148	2.5	1.7%	2,737	30	1.1%
Florida Peninsula	21	20	0	0.0%	0.01	0	0.0%
Black Warrior Basin	235	0.55	0.00	0.4%	1,248	18	1.4%
Appalachian Basin	3,354	79	0.16	0.2%	9,550	28	0.3%
Total	6,534	1,432	444	31.0%	57,848	26,283	45.4%

Note: The smallest reserves amounts round to zero.

This inventory is designed to portray the constraints on future access to the potential oil and gas resource base. Consequently, undiscovered technically recoverable resources and reserves growth resources are included in the categorization, but not proved reserves.[35] Table 2-8 summarizes the oil and gas resource types on Federal lands for each study area.

Table 2-8. Summary of All Federal Oil and Gas Resources by Study Area and Resource Type

Study Area	Undiscovered Resources		Reserves Growth		Proved Reserves	
	Liquids (MMbbls)	Gas (BCF)	Liquids (MMbbls)	Gas (BCF)	Liquid (MMbbls)	Gas (BCF)
Northern Alaska	17,063.0	65,497.0	n/a	n/a	-	0.6
Uinta/Piceance Basin	64.3	11,866.3	65.7	827.4	142.9	3,794.1
Paradox/San Juan Basins	334.7	24,828.1	76.3	2,353.7	53.0	10,938.7
Montana Thrust Belt	170.5	6,307.4	n/a	n/a	-	-
Powder River Basin	884.0	8,781.9	14.7	8.4	109.0	935.8
Wyoming Thrust Belt	42.5	287.7	3.4	86.5	13.8	474.5
Greater Green River Basin	1,942.8	61,162.1	433.0	1,668.2	122.4	10,063.5
Denver Basin	12.8	54.2	0.3	2.3	2.5	30.4
Florida Peninsula	74.3	324.8	n/a	n/a	-	-
Black Warrior Basin	0.7	370.8	-	35.0	0.0	17.7
Appalachian Basin	33.5	2,435.1	n/a	n/a	0.2	28.0
Total	20,623.1	181,915.5	593.4	4,981.5	443.8	26,283.4

Note: The smallest reserves amounts round to zero.

Table 2-9. Federal Land Access Categorization Hierarchy

Level	Access Category	Comments
1	No Leasing (Statutory/Executive Order),	Accessibility determined by Law or Executive Order; drilling
	(NLS)	prohibited
2	No Leasing (Administrative), general	Accessibility determined by Federal surface management agency;
	category (NLA)	drilling prohibited
3	No Leasing (Administrative), Pending	Status set by Federal surface management agency; drilling
	Land Use Planning or NEPA Compliance	prohibited pending planning or NEPA compliance
	(NLA/LUP)	
4	Leasing, No Surface Occupancy (NSO)	Not accessible for drilling except for resources within an extended
	(Net NSO for O&G Resources)	drilling zone
5	Leasing, Cumulative Timing Limitations	Categorized by the cumulative effect of seasonal leasing
	(TLs) on Drilling >9 Months	stipulations during which drilling is prohibited, generally for
6	Leasing, Cumulative Timing Limitations (TLs) on Drilling >6 -≤ 9 Months	protection of wildlife
7	Leasing, Cumulative Timing Limitations (TLs) on Drilling >3 -≤ 6 Months	
8	Leasing, Controlled Surface Use (CSU)	Drilling permitted, specialized mitigation plan required (this
		category includes Cumulative Timing Limitations (TLs) on Drilling ≤ 3 Months, which are minimal)
9	Leasing, Standard Lease Terms (SLTs)	Drilling permitted, mitigation plan required

2.3 Data Integration and Spatial Analysis

2.3.1 Categorization of Oil and Gas Access Constraints

The main factors that affect access to oil and gas resources on Federal lands are land availability (Section 2.1.1) and leasing and drilling restrictions (Sections 2.1.2 and 2.1.3). To simplify the analysis and present meaningful results, these factors were categorized into a hierarchy that represents varying levels of access as shown in Table 2-8. This categorization was necessary to enable a reasonable quantitative analysis, given the fact that approximately 2,130 individual stipulations from 65 Federal land use plans (LUPs) exist for the study areas within the Phase II inventory.

The hierarchy of categories was formulated to ensure that the constraints on oil and gas development could be appropriately assessed (especially for areas of multiple, overlapping stipulations), and to ensure that the cumulative impacts on access would be examined. In addition, the hierarchy was formulated based upon the accessibility of the lands for leasing, and for areas where leasing is permitted, the impacts relative to the difficulty for conducting drilling operations.

The Federal lands categorization hierarchy is ordered from "No Leasing" (most constrained) to "Leasing with Standard Lease Terms" (least constrained) as follows:

1. **No Leasing (Statutory/Executive Order) (NLS)** are lands that cannot be leased due to Congressional or Presidential action. Examples include national parks, national monuments, and wilderness areas.
2. **No Leasing (Administrative) (NLA)** are lands that are withheld from leasing based on discretionary decisions made by the Federal land management agency. NLA areas can include endangered species habitat and historical sites.
3. **No Leasing (Administrative), Pending Land Use Planning or NEPA Compliance (NLA/LUP)** are lands that have not yet undergone or are currently undergoing land use planning or NEPA analysis, and that are generally not available for leasing. In the cases where there is no land use plan in effect, non- Federal mineral estate underlying Federal land is categorized as NLA/LUP to reflect the fact that access to mineral estate can be allowed through the NEPA process.
4. **Leasing, No Surface Occupancy (NSO) (Net NSO for Oil & Gas Resources)** are lands that can be leased but ground-disturbing oil and natural gas exploration and development activities are prohibited. These stipulations protect identified resources such as special status plant species habitat. Their surface areas are mapped as described by the land use plans. However, at least some of the resources can be accessed by directional drilling from nearby lands where surface occupancy is allowed. This is accounted for by creating an extended drilling zone (EDZ, as described in Appendix 9) that reduces the size of the NSO area. The area removed is then placed in the next most restrictive resource access category (5 through 9, below) that would otherwise apply in the absence of the NSO stipulation. Within the EDZ area the underlying resource is considered accessible even though the surface above it cannot be occupied by drilling equipment. After the EDZ is removed, the NSO area that remains is referred to as "Net NSO" (NNSO) and the resources under it are therefore considered inaccessible.

5. **Leasing, Cumulative Timing Limitations (TLs) on drilling of >9 Months**
6. **Leasing, Cumulative Timing Limitations (TLs) on drilling of >6 to ≤9 Months**
7. **Leasing, Cumulative Timing Limitations (TLs) on drilling of >3 to ≤6 Months** are lands that can be leased, but stipulations and/or COAs limit the time of the year when oil and gas exploration and drilling can take place. Timing limitation stipulations prohibit surface use during specified time intervals to protect identified resources such as sage grouse habitat or elk calving areas.
8. **Leasing, Controlled Surface Use (CSU)** are lands where stipulations and/or COAs control the surface location of natural gas and oil exploration and development activities by excluding them from portions of the lease. For example, a CSU stipulation could require an operator to develop a specialized mitigation plan based on the presence of moderately steep slopes. This category also includes the minimal areas that have timing limitations of less than three months.
9. **Leasing, Standard Lease Terms (SLTs)** areas are lands that can be leased and where no additional stipulations are added to the standard lease form. Standard lease terms, however, still dictate that the lessee must comply with many environmental standards and other requirements (see 2.1.2, above).

Categorizations were made on the basis of LUPs and discussions with Federal land management agencies. In most cases categorization is relatively straightforward; in other cases judgments were made based upon experience with stipulation datasets. For USDA-FS, FPs standards and guidelines are both included in the definition of "Management Direction" at 36 CFR 219.3 (Forest Planning), and were used synonymously without distinction in evaluating USDA-FS stipulations.

All categorizations were made available to field offices for review and comment.

2.3.1.1 Data Integration And Spatial Analysis-Related Caveats

The following precautions are advised when reviewing this study:

- A total of 2,132 stipulations in 65 LUPs were analyzed in the Phase II inventory. Substantial efforts were made to assess stipulations where no GIS data were available, either by digitizing or obtaining data from other sources. Despite these efforts, not all stipulations have corresponding GIS data. While it is impossible to assess the absolute magnitude of this issue, it is nevertheless believed to be significant. By item count, approximately 39 percent of total stipulations in the Phase II inventory do not have GIS associated with them. To the extent that this issue exists, the inventory overestimates access to lands and resources. The induced error is likely to be less than 39 percent as many of the missing stipulations are not likely to have large geographic coverage or may be outside a given study area. This issue points to a data gap to be addressed by Federal agencies.
- In NSO areas that abut non-Federal lands, no assumption was made about the availability of adjacent non-Federal lands as a base from which to drill under Federal lands. It is estimated that this situation has a minimal effect, impacting less than one half of one percent of resources in the study areas. Therefore, an Extended Drilling Zone (EDZ) was not applied to NSO lands adjacent to non-Federal lands.

2.3.2 Analytical Modeling of Federal Lands and Resources

See Appendix 9 for a detailed description of the GIS methodology used to categorize the Federal lands and resources for the inventory.

3. RESULTS

The results of the inventory are presented below, summarized by access category for land area and resources and grouped by study area. Table 3-1 shows the combined results for all 11 study areas, while Tables 3-2 through 3-12 show the results for individual study areas. Also depicted on the bottom of each table is a simplified summary showing accessibility of oil and gas resources. The tables show the results for Federal land access categorization by land area, total oil (used generically to include oil, NGLs, and liquids associated with gas reservoirs), and total natural gas (associated and non-associated with oil reservoirs). Oil and natural gas totals include undiscovered technically recoverable and reserves growth resources. Figures 3-1 through 3-57 show the corresponding pie charts depicting the simplified and the nine-category access hierarchy, the Federal land access categorization maps for each study area, and the corresponding maps showing undiscovered oil and natural gas resources on Federal lands.

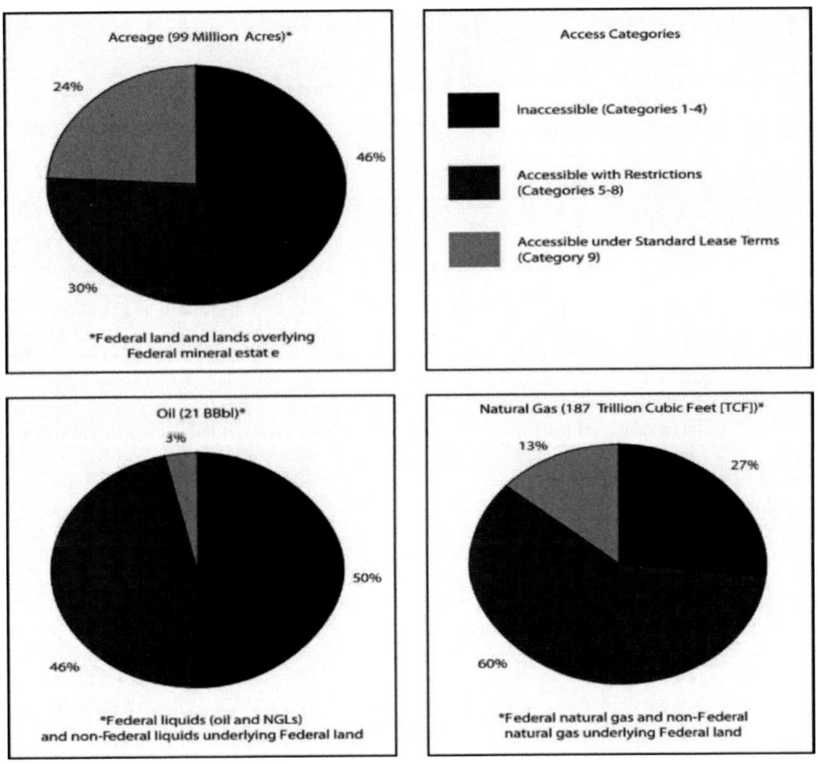

Figure 3-1. Simplified Chart of Results, Summary of All Phase II Study Areas—Federal Land and Oil and Natural Gas Resources

Table 3-1. Summary of All Phase II Study Areas—Federal Land and Oil and Natural Gas Resources by Access Category

		Area		Resources[a]			
				Total Oil[b]		Total Gas[c]	
		(acres x 1000)	Percent of Federal	(MMbbls)[d]	Percent of Federal	(BCF)[e]	Percent of Federal
1.	No Leasing (Statutory/Executive Order) (NLS)	12,601	12.7%	7,510	35.4%	14,867	8.0%
2.	No Leasing (Administrative) (NLA)	4,161	4.2%	1,405	6.6%	6,891	3.7%
3.	No Leasing (Administrative) Pending Land Use Planning or NEPA Compliance (NLA/LUP)	19,680	19.8%	1,727	8.1%	25,444	13.6%
4.	Leasing, No Surface Occupancy (NSO) (Net NSO for O&G Resources)	9,025	9.1%	135	0.6%	2,923	1.6%
5.	Leasing, Cumulative Timing Limitations (TLs) of >9 Months	88	0.1%	3	0.0%	14	0.0%
6.	Leasing, Cumulative Timing Limitations (TLs) of >6 to <9 Months	12,252	12.4%	7,059	33.3%	37,893	20.3%
7.	Leasing, Cumulative Timing Limitations (TLs) of >3 to <6 Months	9,271	9.3%	1,184	5.6%	31,188	16.7%
8.	Leasing, Controlled Surface Use (CSU)[f]	8,374	8.4%	1,451	6.8%	42,428	22.7%
9.	Leasing, Standard Lease Terms (SLTs)	23,751	23.9%	743	3.5%	25,210	13.5%
Total, Federal Lands including Split Estate		**99,203**	100%	**21,216**	100%	**186,857**	100%
Total Non-Federal		**196,204**		**4,802**		**156,603**	
Total Inventory Area		**295,406**		**26,018**		**343,460**	
Summary							
Inaccessible (Categories 1-4)		45,467	46%	10,776	51%	50,125	27%
Accessible with Restrictions (Categories 5-8)		29,985	30%	9,697	46%	111,522	60%
Accessible under Standard Lease Terms (Category 9)		23,751	24%	743	3%	25,210	13%
Total, Federal Lands Including Split Estate		**99,203**	**100%**	**21,216**	**100%**	**186,857**	**100%**

Small rounding errors may be present.

a Undiscovered technically recoverable resources and reserves growth

b Including oil, natural gas liquids (NGLs) and liquids associated with natural gas reservoirs

c Including associated dissolved and nonassociated natural gas

d Million barrels **e** Billion cubic feet **f** Includes Cumulative Timing Limitations of <3 months

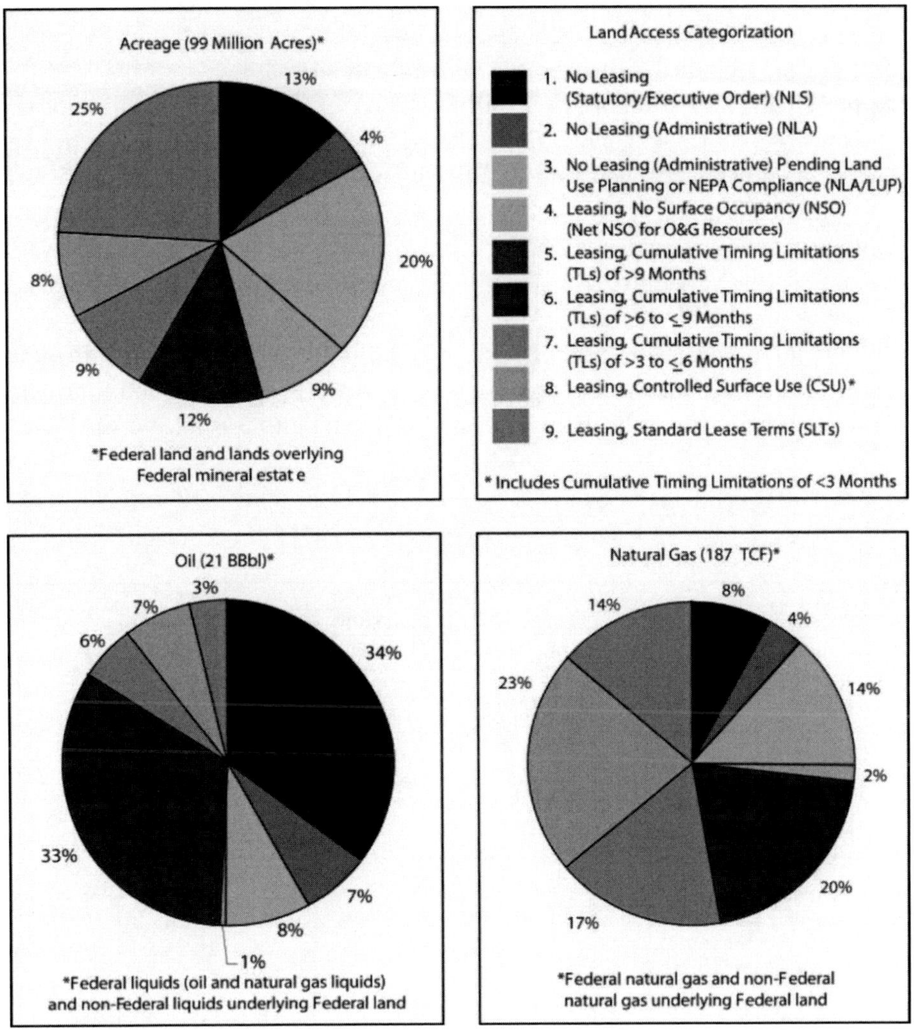

Figure 3-2. Chart of Results, Summary of All Phase II Study Areas—Federal Land and Oil and Natural Gas Resources by Access Category

3.1 Study Area Features

Each of the study areas is unique in terms of its Federal land and resources accessibility. Noteworthy features are presented below.

3.1.1 Northern Alaska (NPR-A and ANWR 1002 only)

- None of the Federal land in this study area is accessible under standard lease terms (Figures 3-3 and 3-4, Category 9).
- Approximately 43 percent (10.4 million acres) of the Federal land is accessible with restrictions on oil and gas operations beyond standard lease terms (Figures 3-3 and 3-4, Categories 5 through 8). Based on resource estimates, these lands contain 41

percent (6.9 Bbbls) of the technically recoverable Federal oil and 51 percent (33.3 TCF) of the technically recoverable Federal natural gas.

- Approximately 57 percent (13.9 million acres) of the Federal land is not accessible (Figures 3-3 and 3-4, Categories 1 through 4). Based on resource estimates, these lands contain about 59 percent (10.2 Bbbls) of the technically recoverable Federal oil and 49 percent (32.2 TCF) of the technically recoverable Federal natural gas.
- Only conventional resources have been assessed for Northern Alaska. Continuous resources (See Section 2.2.1.1) will be included in a future USGS assessment. Reserves growth has not been estimated for this study area.
- Although the Federal portion of NPR-A (22.5 million acres) is about 15 times larger in surface area than the Federal portion of ANWR 1002 (1.5 million acres), it is estimated to contain only about 1.2 times as much oil (9.3 Bbbls versus 7.7 Bbbls).

Table 3-2. Northern Alaska Study Area—Federal Land and Oil and Natural Gas Resources by Access Category

		Area		Resourcesa			
				Total Oilb		Total Gasc	
		(acres x 1000)	Percent of Federal	(MMbbls)d	Percent of Federal	(BCF)e	Percent of Federal
1.	No Leasing (Statutory/Executive Order) (NLS)	1,559	6.4%	7,217	42.3%	6,370	9.7%
2.	No Leasing (Administrative) (NLA)	1,861	7.6%	1,342	7.9%	4,857	7.4%
3.	No Leasing (Administrative) Pending Land Use Planning or NEPA Compliance (NLA/LUP)	9,159	37.6%	1,539	9.0%	20,797	31.8%
4.	Leasing, No Surface Occupancy (NSO) (Net NSO for O&G Resources)	1,368	5.6%	53	0.3%	133	0.2%
5.	Leasing, Cumulative Timing Limitations (TLs) of >9 Months	-	0.0%	-	0.0%	-	0.0%
6.	Leasing, Cumulative Timing Limitations (TLs) of >6 to <9 Months	10,182	41.7%	6,833	40.0%	33,071	50.5%
7.	Leasing, Cumulative Timing Limitations (TLs) of >3 to <6 Months	258	1.1%	78	0.5%	269	0.4%
8.	Leasing, Controlled Surface Use (CSU)f	1	0.0%	0	0.0%	1	0.0%
9.	Leasing, Standard Lease Terms (SLTs)	0	0.0%	0	0.0%	0	0.0%

Total, Federal Lands including Split Estate	**24,388**	**100.0%**	**17,063**	**100.0%**	**65,497**	**100.0%**
Total Non-Federal	**619**		**997**		**1,399**	
Total Inventory Area	**25,007**		**18,060**		**66,896**	
Summary						
Inaccessible (Categories 1-4)	13,947	57%	10,152	59%	32,156	49%
Accessible with Restrictions (Categories 5-8)	10,441	43%	6,911	41%	33,341	51%
Accessible under Standard Lease Terms (Category 9)	0	0%	0	0%	0	0%
Total, Federal Lands Including Split Estate	**24,388**	**100%**	**17,063**	**100%**	**65,497**	**100%**

Small rounding errors may be present.

a Undiscovered technically recoverable resources and reserves growth

b Including oil, natural gas liquids (NGLs) and liquids associated with natural gas reservoirs

c Including associated dissolved and nonassociated natural gas

d Million barrels e Billion cubic feet f Includes Cumulative Timing Limitations of <3 months

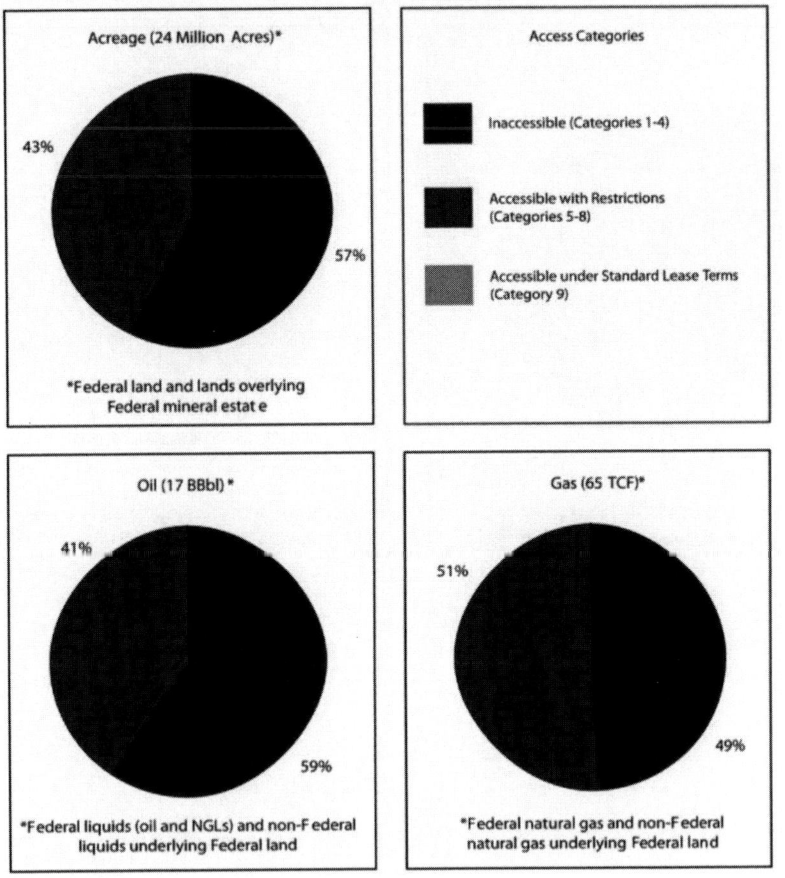

Figure 3-3. Simplified Chart of Results, Northern Alaska Study Area—Federal Land and Oil and Natural Gas Resources by Accessibility

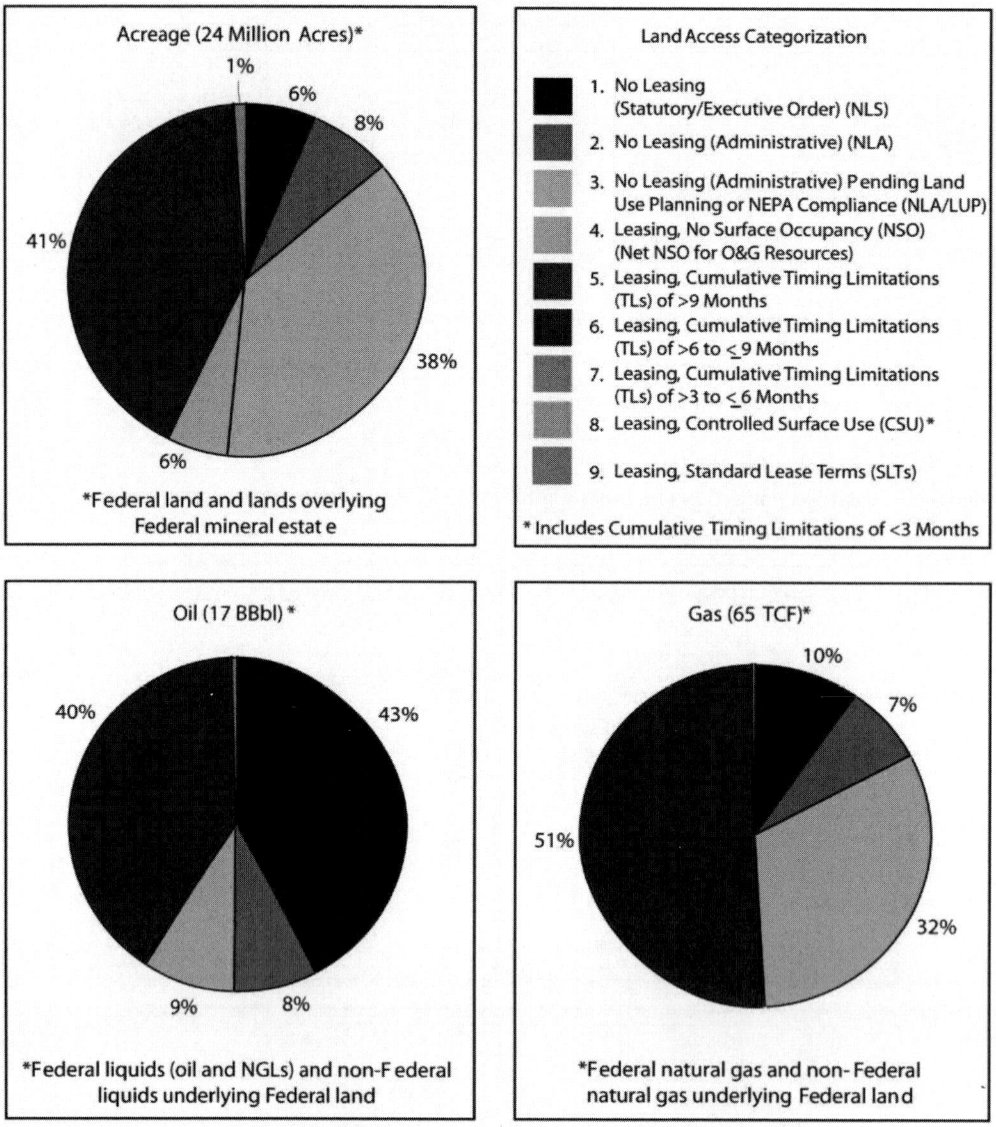

Figure 3-4. Chart of Results, Northern Alaska Study Area—Federal Land and Oil and Natural Gas Resources by Access Category

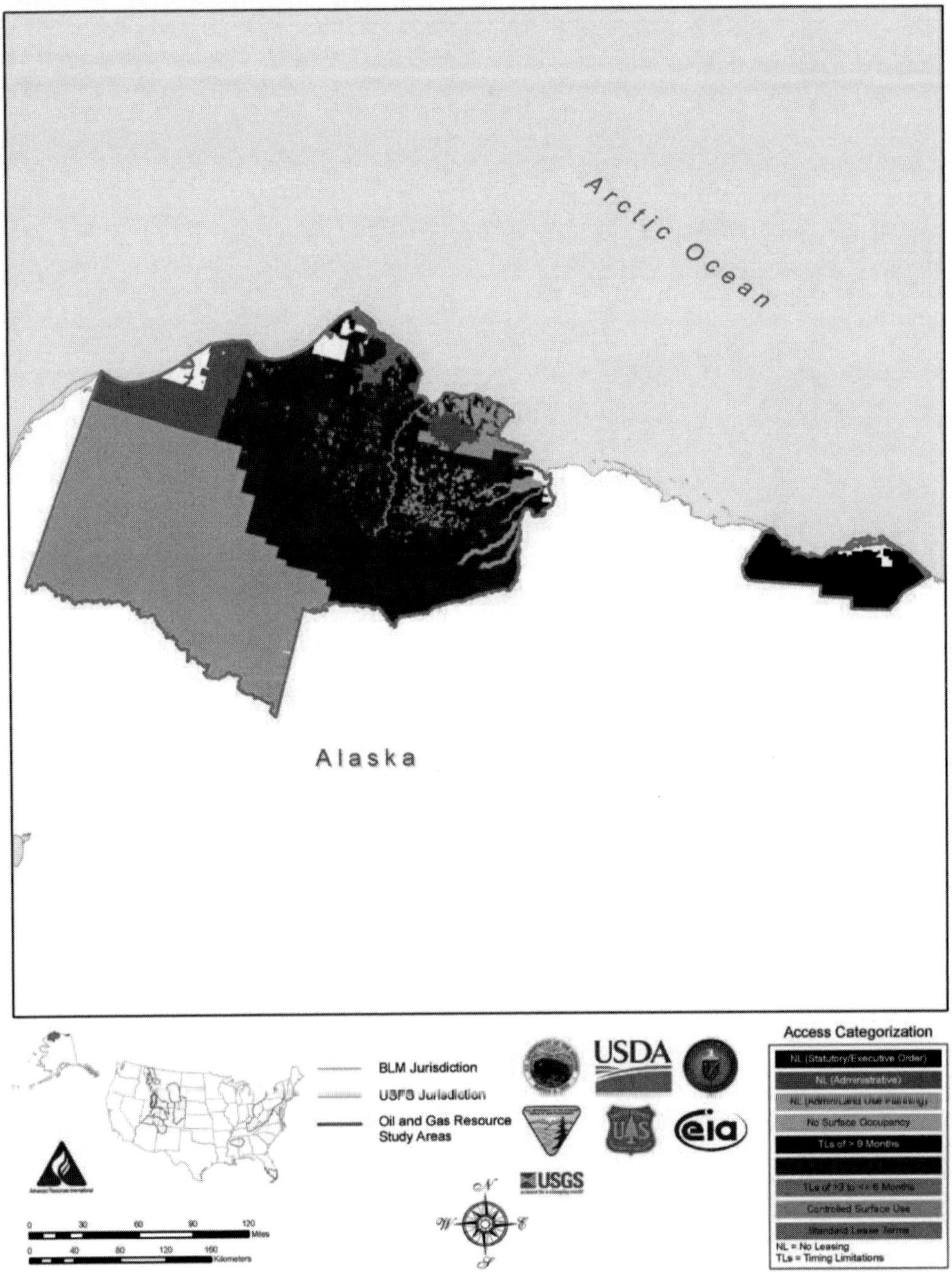

Figure 3-5. Federal Land Access Categorization Map, Northern Alaska Study Area

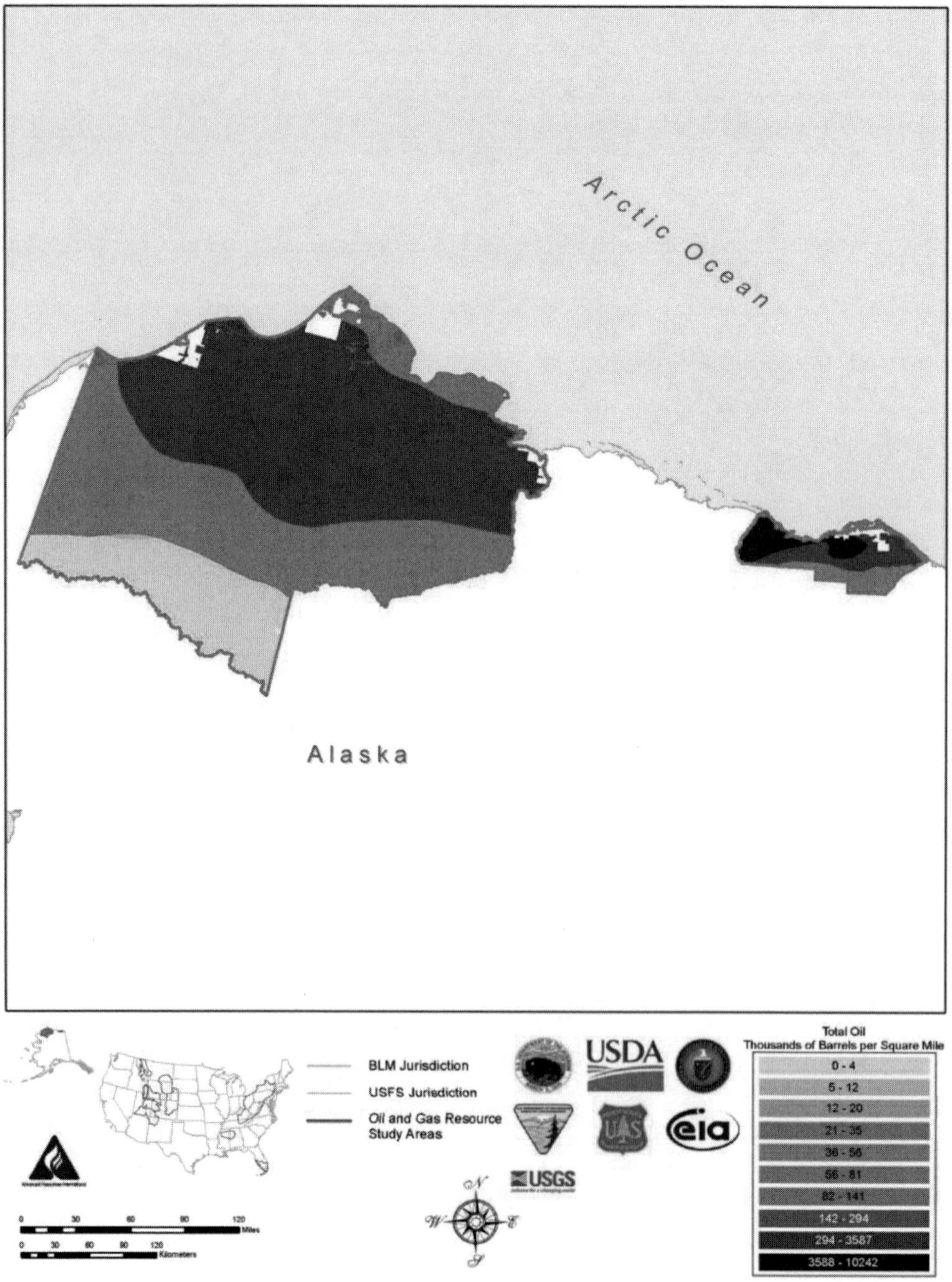

Figure 3-6. Map of Total Federal Oil, Northern Alaska Study Area

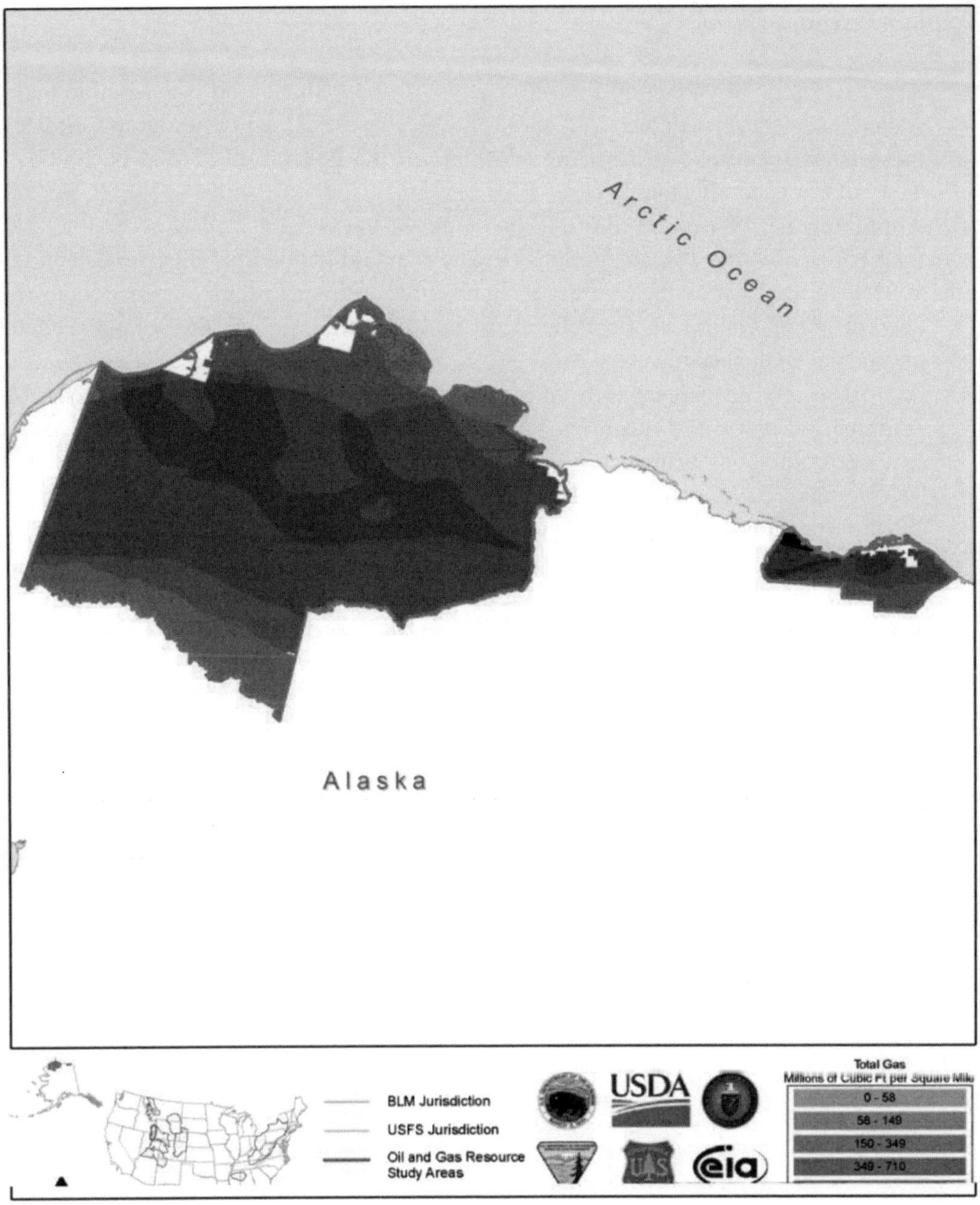

Figure 3-7. Map of Total Federal Natural Gas, Northern Alaska Study Area

3.1.2 Uinta-Piceance Basin

- Approximately 38 percent (4.9 million acres) of the Federal land is accessible under standard lease terms (Figures 3-8 and 3-9, Category 9). Based on resource estimates, these lands contain 28 percent (36 MMbbls) of the Federal oil and 24 percent (3.1 TCF) of the Federal natural gas.
- Approximately 27 percent (3.6 million acres) of the Federal land is accessible with restrictions on oil and gas operations beyond standard lease terms (Figures 3-8 and 3-9, Categories 5 through 8). Based on resource estimates, these lands contain 56 percent (72 MMbbls) of the Federal oil and 61 percent (7.8 TCF) of the Federal natural gas in the basin.
- Approximately 35 percent (4.6 million acres) of the Federal land is not accessible (Figures 3-8 and 3-9, Categories 1 through 4). Based on resource estimates, these lands contain about 17 percent (22 MMbbls) of the Federal oil and 15 percent (1 .9 TCF) of the Federal natural gas.
- Most of the undiscovered natural gas (greater than 95 percent) is expected to occur as continuous resources.

Table 3-3. Uinta-Piceance Basin Study Area—Federal Land and Oil and Natural Gas Resources by Access Category

		Area		Resourcesa			
				Total Oilb		Total Gasc	
		(acres x 1000)	Percent of Federal	(MMbbls) d	Percent of Federal	(BCF)e	Percent of Federal
1.	No Leasing (Statutory/Executive Order) (NLS)	1,644	12.6%	13	9.9%	685	5.4%
2.	No Leasing (Administrative) (NLA)	642	4.9%	2	1.9%	404	3.2%
3.	No Leasing (Administrative) Pending Land Use Planning or NEPA Compliance (NLA/LUP)	617	4.7%	1	1.1%	149	1.2%
4.	Leasing, No Surface Occupancy (NSO) (Net NSO for O&G Resources)	1,683	12.9%	5	3.9%	620	4.9%
5.	Leasing, Cumulative Timing Limitations (TLs) of >9 Months	-	0.0%	-	0.0%	-	0.0%
6.	Leasing, Cumulative Timing Limitations (TLs) of >6 to <9 Months	323	2.5%	4	3.1%	539	4.2%
7.	Leasing, Cumulative Timing Limitations (TLs) of >3 to <6 Months	1,355	10.3%	17	12.8%	2,168	17.1%

8. Leasing, Controlled Surface Use (CSU)f	1,908	14.6%	52	39.8%	5,067	39.9%
9. Leasing, Standard Lease Terms (SLTs)	4,921	37.6%	36	27.8%	3,062	24.1%
Total, Federal Lands including Split Estate	**13,092**	**100.0%**	**130**	**100.0%**	**12,694**	**100.0%**
Total Non-Federal	**5,856**		**105**		**10,224**	
Total Inventory Area	**18,948**		**235**		**22,918**	
Summary						
Inaccessible (Categories 1-4)	4,586	35%	22	17%	1,858	15%
Accessible with Restrictions (Categories 5-8)	3,586	27%	72	56%	7,774	61%
Accessible under Standard Lease Terms (Category 9)	4,921	38%	36	28%	3,062	24%
Total, Federal Lands Including Split Estate	**13,092**	**100%**	**130**	**100%**	**12,694**	**100%**

Small rounding errors may be present.

a Undiscovered technically recoverable resources and reserves growth

b Including oil, natural gas liquids (NGLs) and liquids associated with natural gas reservoirs

c Including associated dissolved and nonassociated natural gas

d Million barrels e Billion cubic feet f Includes Cumulative Timing Limitations of <3 months

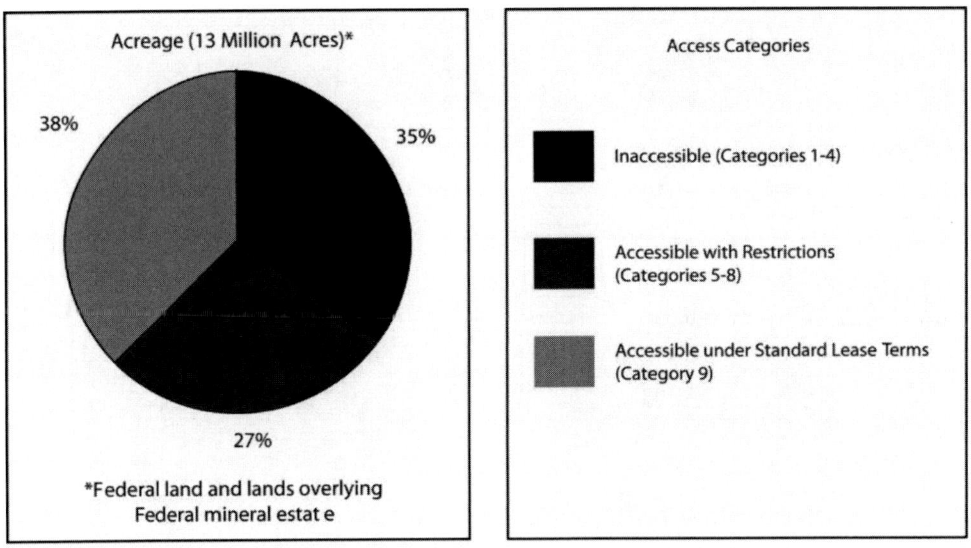

Figure 3-8. (Continued)

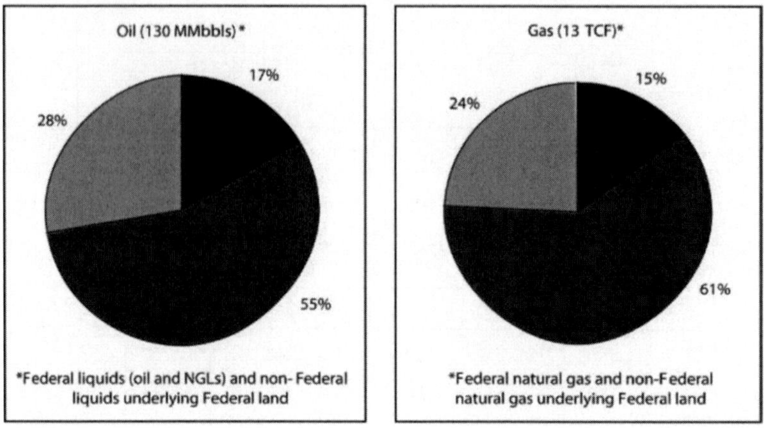

Figure 3-8. Simplified Chart of Results, Uinta-Piceance Basin Study Area—Federal Land and Oil and Natural Gas Resources by Accessibility

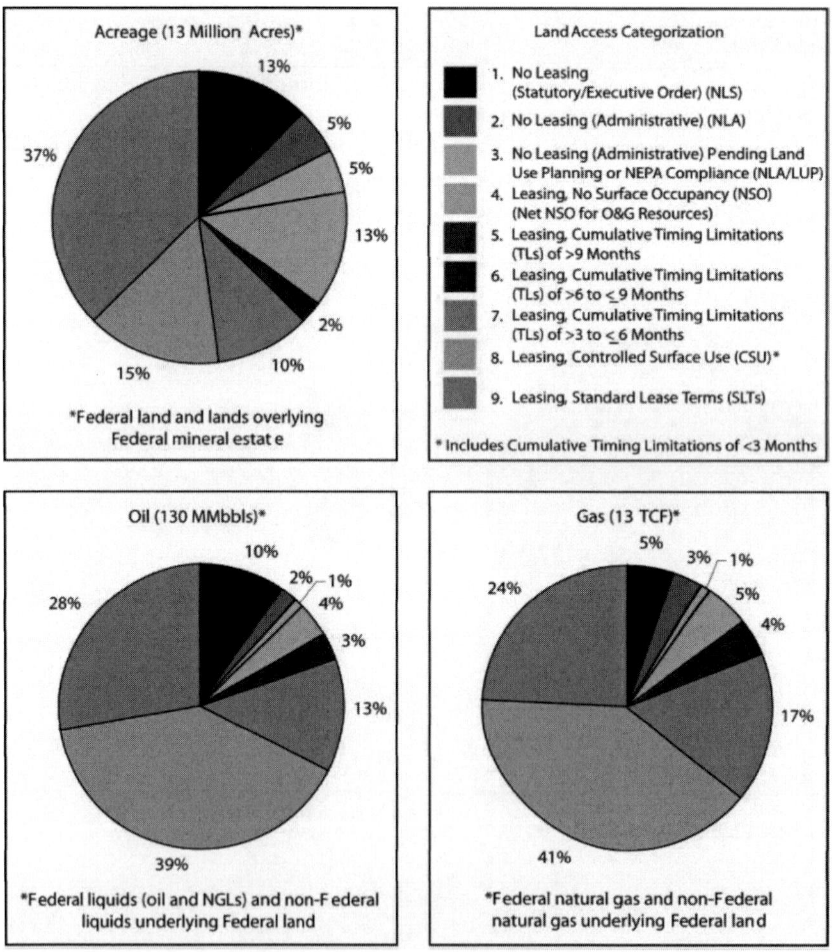

Figure 3-9. Chart of Results, Uinta-Piceance Basin Study Area—Federal Land and Oil and Natural Gas Resources by Access Category

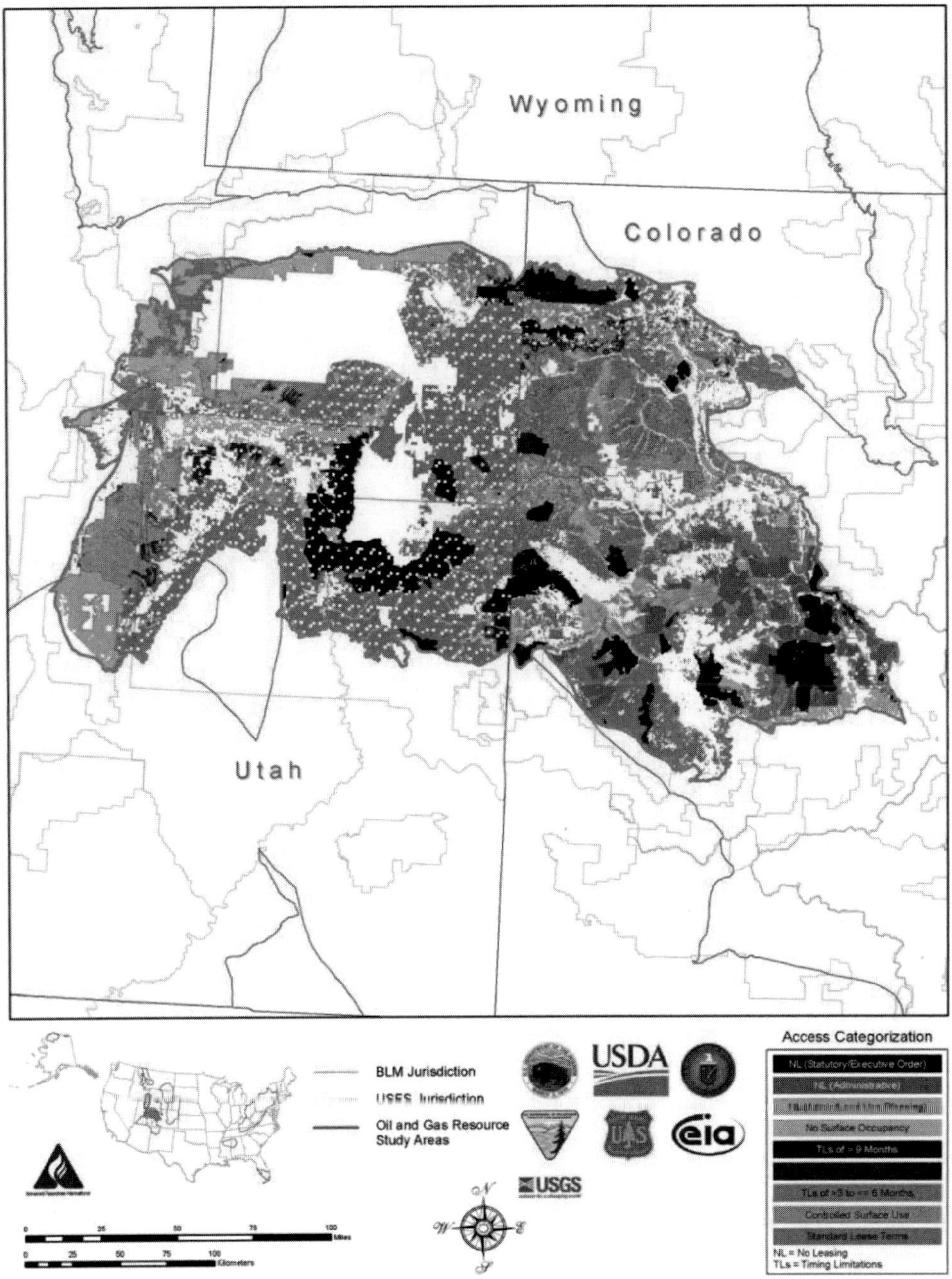

Figure 3-10. Federal Land Access Categorization Map, Uinta-Piceance Basin Study Area

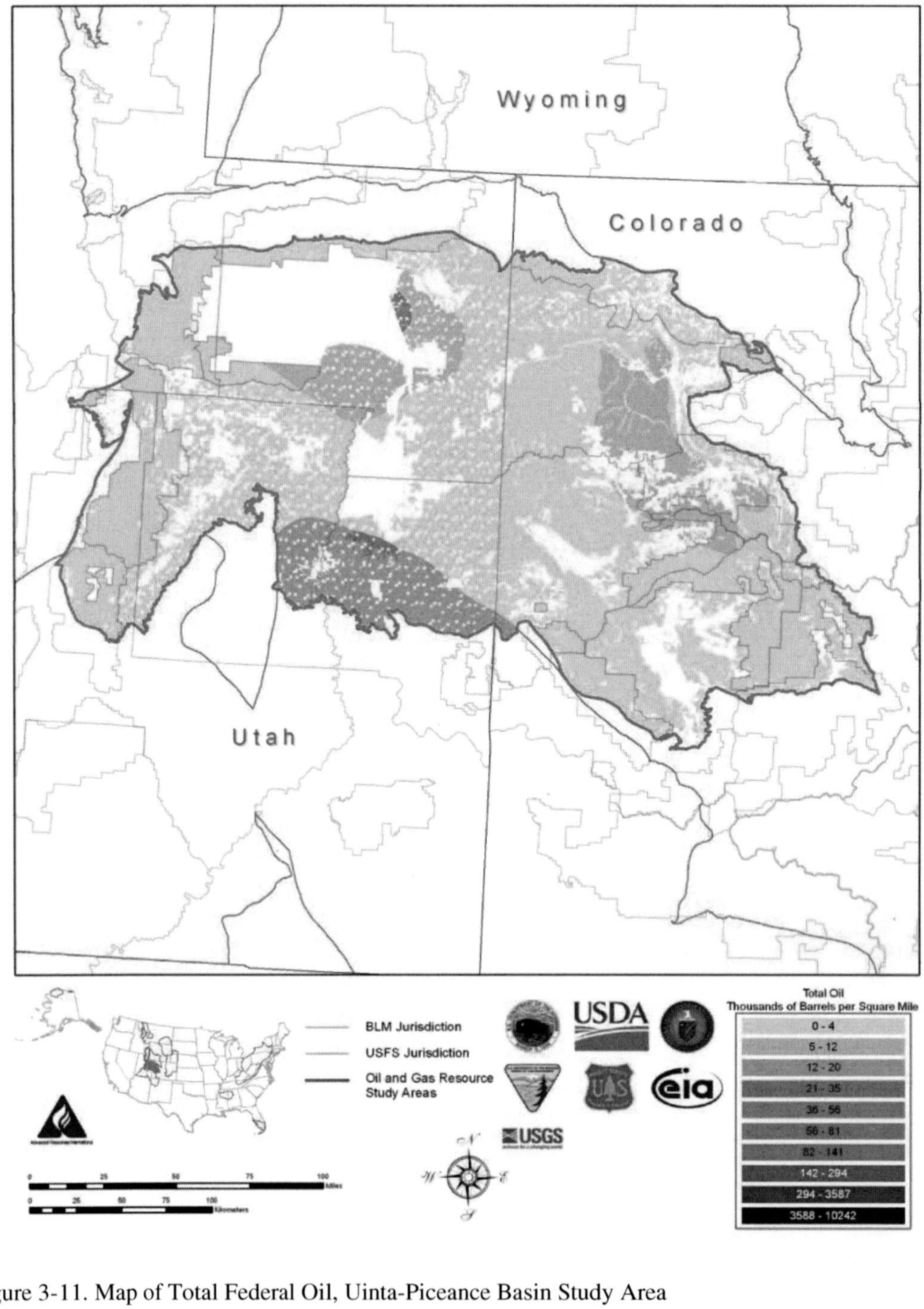

Figure 3-11. Map of Total Federal Oil, Uinta-Piceance Basin Study Area

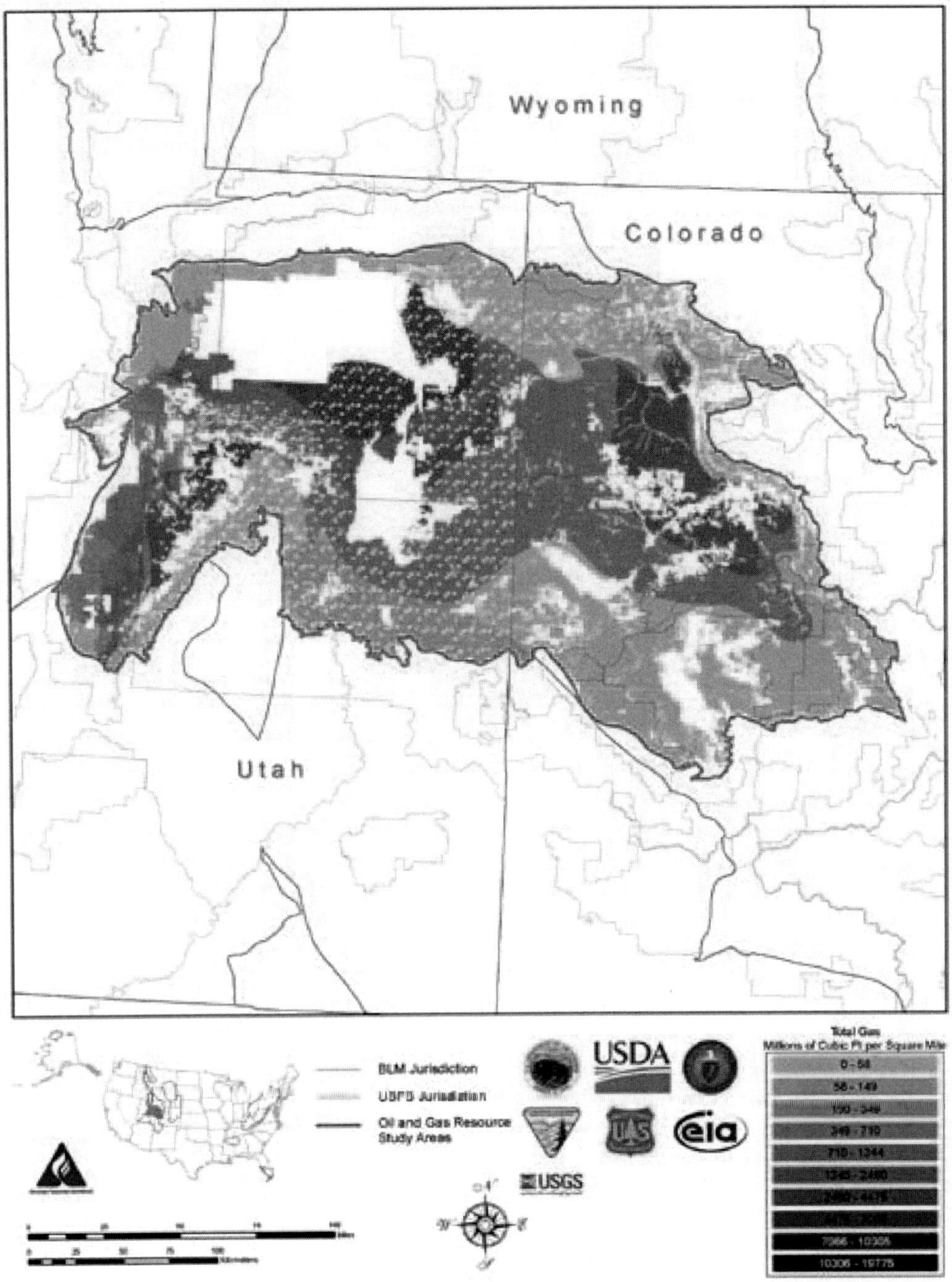

Figure 3-12. Map of Total Federal Natural Gas, Uinta-Piceance Basin Study Area

3.1.3 Paradox/San Juan Basins

- Approximately 40 percent (7.0 million acres) of the Federal land is accessible under standard lease terms (Figures 3-13 and 3-14, Category 9). Based on resource estimates, these lands contain 38 percent (156 MMbbls) of the Federal oil and 39 percent (10.5 TCF) of the Federal natural gas.

- Approximately 11 percent (1.9 million acres) of the Federal land is accessible with restrictions on oil and gas operations beyond standard lease terms (Figures 3-13 and 3-14, Categories 5 through 8). Based on resource estimates, these lands contain 39 percent (159 MMbbls) of the Federal oil and 54 percent (14.7 TCF) of the Federal natural gas.
- Approximately 49 percent (8.7 million acres) of the Federal land is not accessible (Figures 3-13 and 3-14, Categories 1 through 4). Based on resource estimates, these lands contain about 23 percent (96 MMbbls) of the Federal oil and 7 percent (2.0 TCF) of the Federal natural gas.
- Most of the undiscovered natural gas (approximately 95 percent) is expected to occur as continuous resources.

Table 3-4. Paradox/San Juan Basins Study Area—Federal Land and Oil and Natural Gas Resources by Access Category

		Area		Resourcesa			
				Total Oilb		Total Gasc	
		(acres x 1000)	Percent of Federal	(MMbbls)d	Percent of Federal	(BCF)e	Percent of Federal
1.	No Leasing (Statutory/Executiv e Order) (NLS)	5,455	30.9%	71	17.2%	547	2.0%
2.	No Leasing (Administrative) (NLA)	479	2.7%	9	2.2%	528	1.9%
3.	No Leasing (Administrative) Pending Land Use Planning or NEPA Compliance (NLA/LUP)	2,036	11.5%	5	1.2%	29	0.1%
4.	Leasing, No Surface Occupancy (NSO) (Net NSO for O&G Resources)	759	4.3%	11	2.8%	895	3.3%
5.	Leasing, Cumulative Timing Limitations (TLs) of >9 Months	50	0.3%	2	0.5%	3	0.0%
6.	Leasing, Cumulative Timing Limitations (TLs) of >6 to <9 Months	98	0.6%	4	1.0%	71	0.3%
7.	Leasing, Cumulative Timing Limitations (TLs) of >3 to <6 Months	1,033	5.8%	45	11.1%	4,659	17.1%
8.	Leasing, Controlled Surface Use (CSU)f	734	4.2%	107	26.1%	9,978	36.7%

9. Leasing, Standard Lease Terms (SLTs)	7,027	39.8%	156	38.0%	10,471	38.5%
Total, Federal Lands including Split Estate	**17,671**	**100.0%**	**411**	**100.0%**	**27,182**	**100.0%**
Total Non-Federal	**11,108**		**359**		**29,825**	
Total Inventory Area	**28,779**		**770**		**57,007**	
Summary						
Inaccessible (Categories 1-4)	8,729	49%	96	23%	2,000	7%
Accessible with Restrictions (Categories 5-8)	1,916	11%	159	39%	14,711	54%
Accessible under Standard Lease Terms (Category 9)	7,027	40%	156	38%	10,471	39%
Total, Federal Lands Including Split Estate	**17,671**	**100%**	**411**	**100%**	**27,182**	**100%**

a Undiscovered technically recoverable resources and reserves growth

b Including oil, natural gas liquids (NGLs) and liquids associated with natural gas reservoirs

c Including associated dissolved and nonassociated natural gas

d Million barrels e Billion cubic feet f Includes Cumulative Timing Limitations of <3 months

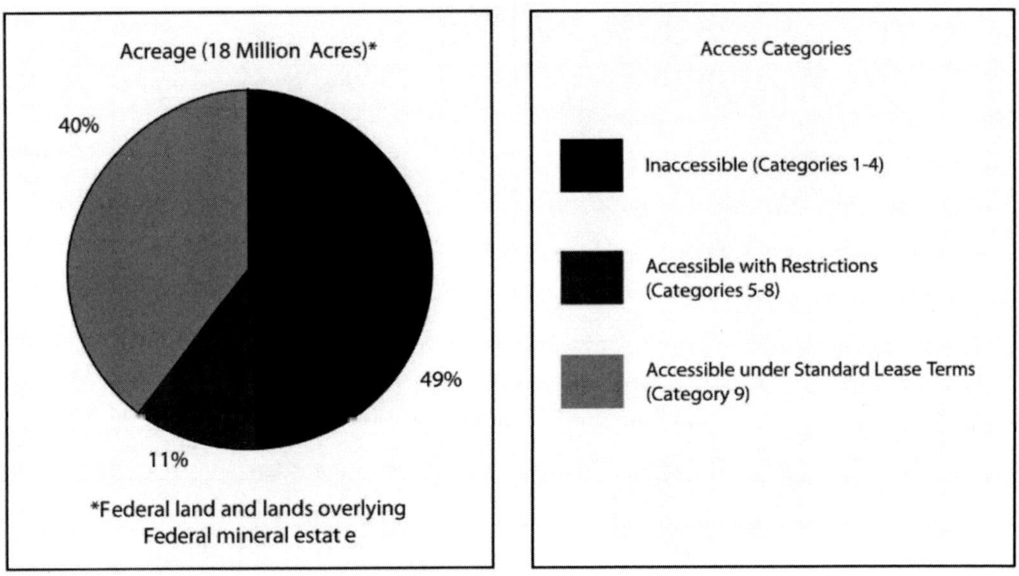

Figure 3-13. (Continued)

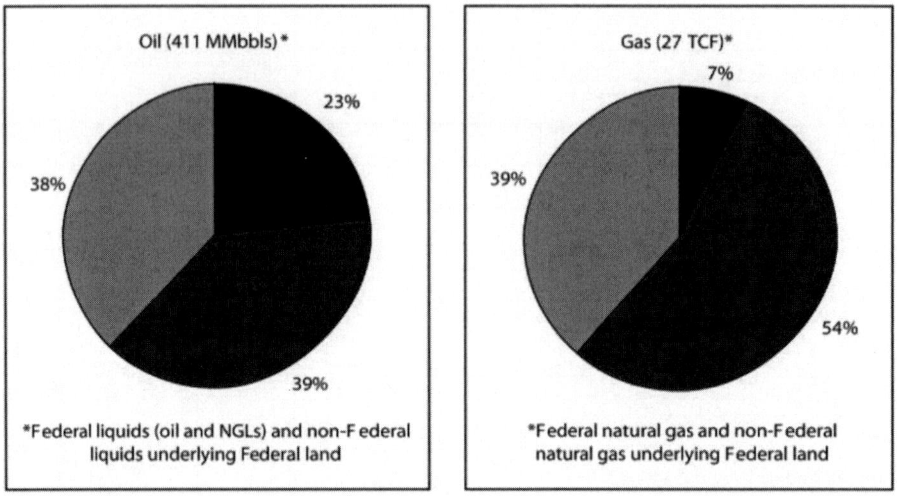

Figure 3-13. Simplified Chart of Results, Paradox/San Juan Basins Study **Area—Federal Land and Oil** and Natural Gas Resources by Accessibility

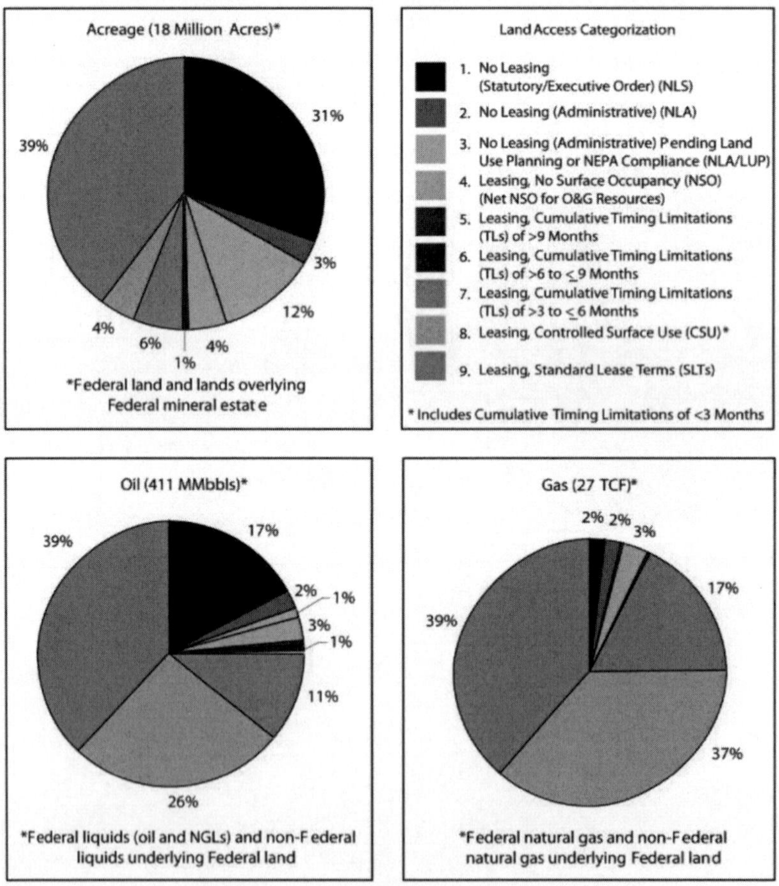

Figure 3-14. **Chart of Results, Paradox/San Juan Basins Study Area—Federal** Land and Oil and Natural Gas Resources by Access Category

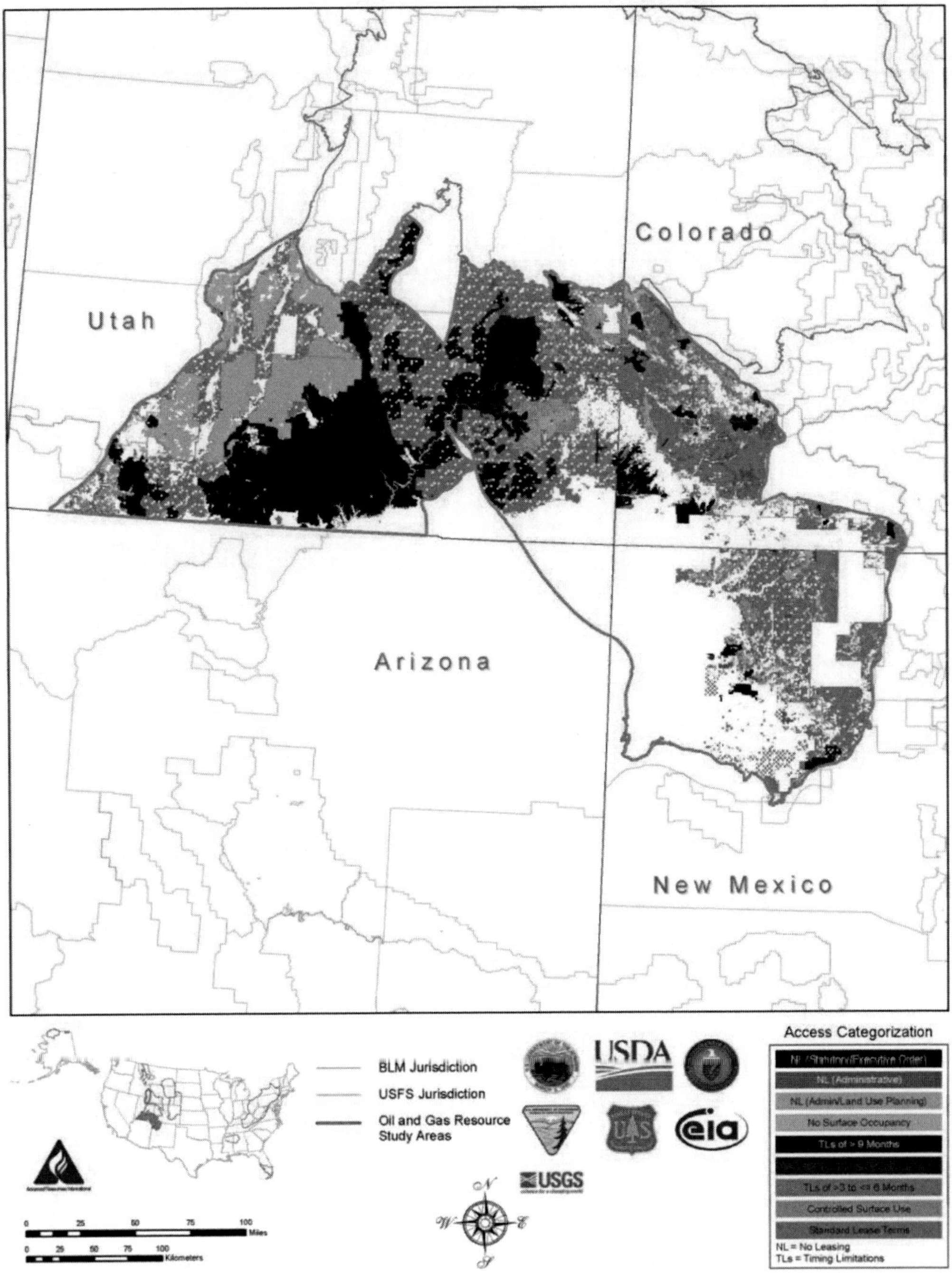

Figure 3-15. Federal Land Access Categorization Map, Paradox/San Juan Basins Study Area

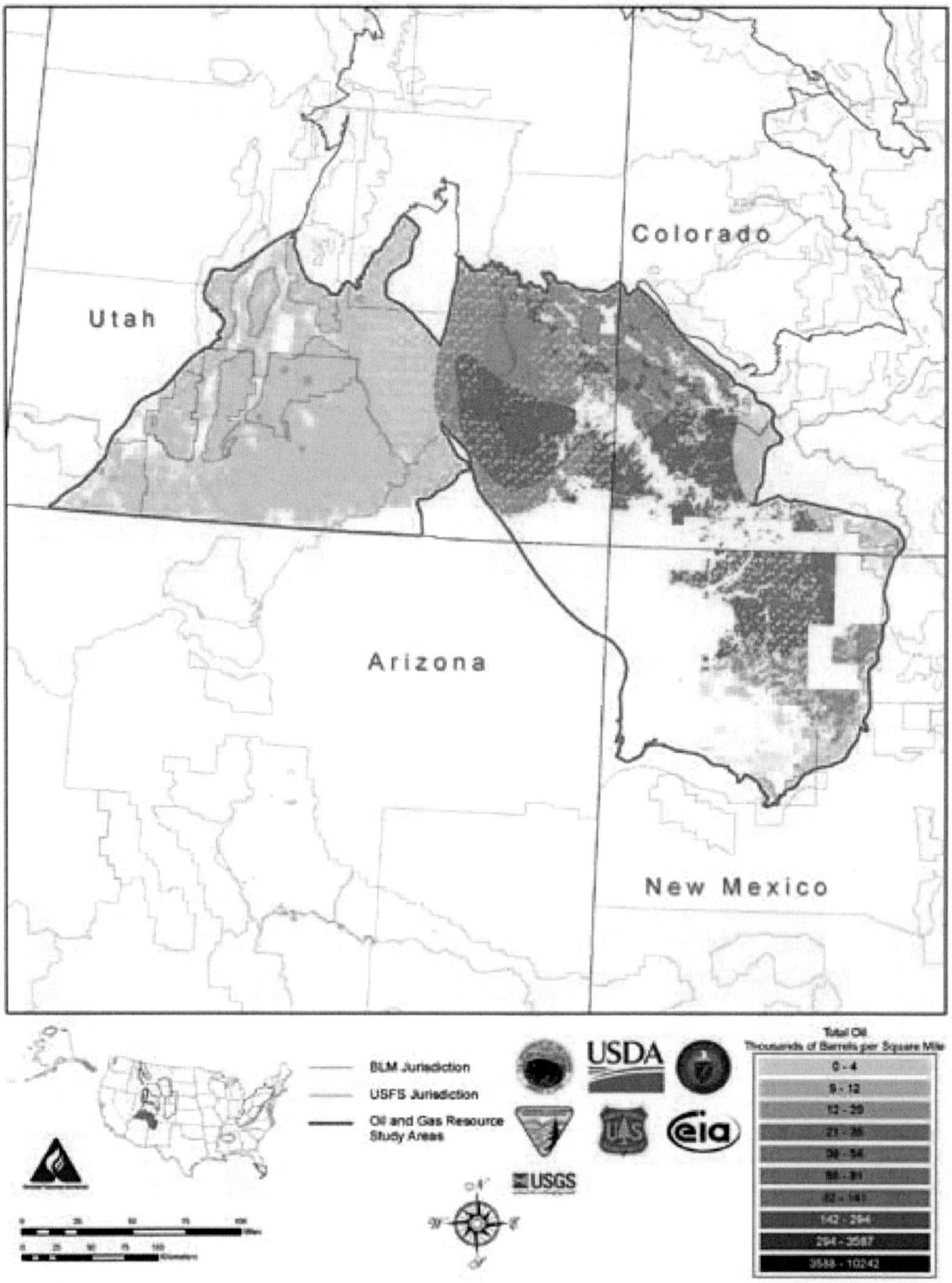

Figure 3-16. Map of Total Federal Oil, Paradox/San Juan Basins Study Area

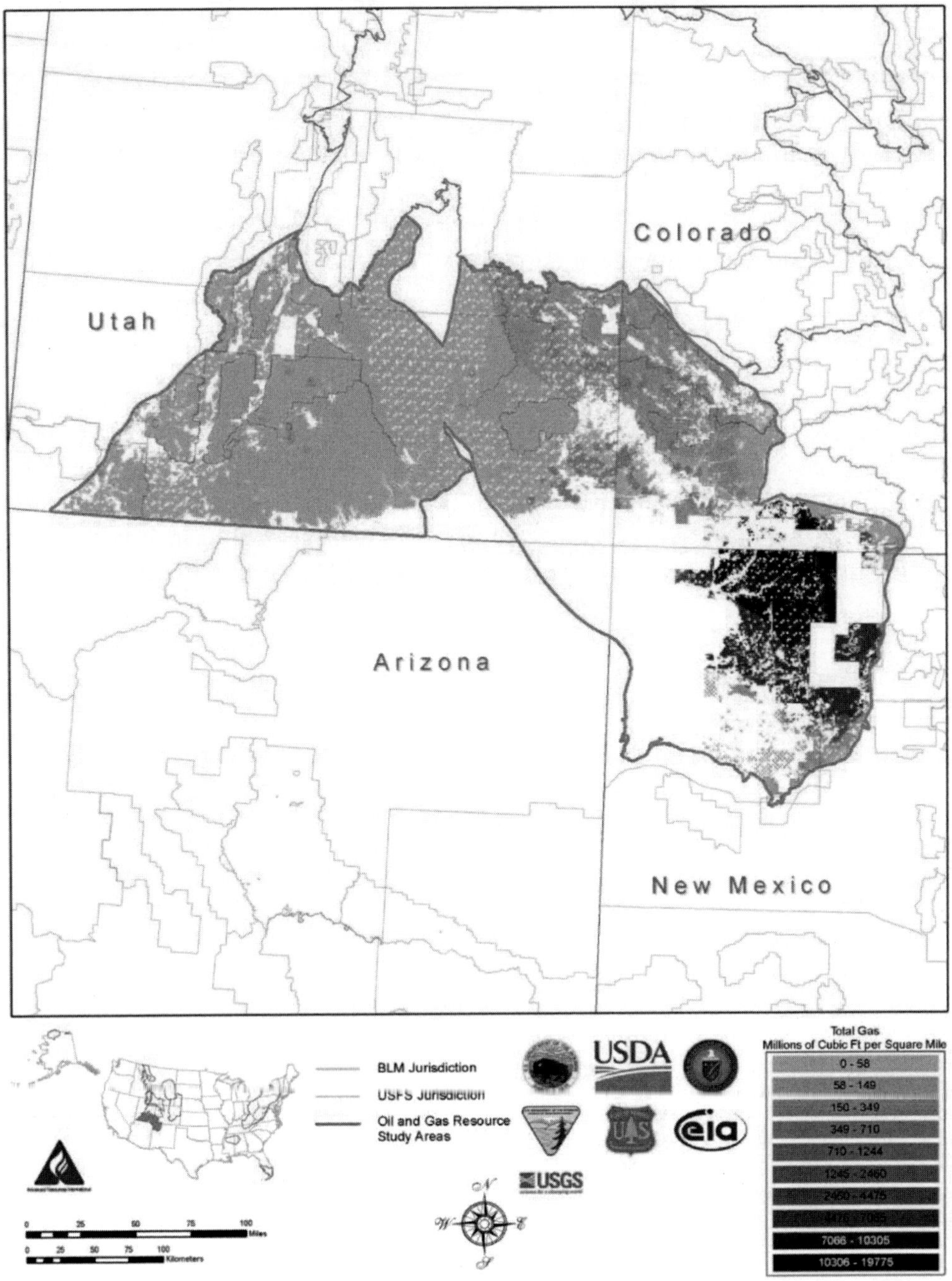

Figure 3-17. Map of Total Federal Natural Gas, Paradox/San Juan Basins Study Area

3.1.4 Montana Thrust Belt

- Approximately 3 percent (0.2 million acres) of the Federal land is accessible under standard lease terms (Figures 3-18 and 3-19, Category 9). Based on resource estimates, these lands contain 2 percent (3 MMbbls) of the Federal oil and 1 percent (0.07 TCF) of the Federal natural gas.
- Approximately 5 percent (0.3 million acres) of the Federal land is accessible with restrictions on oil and gas operations beyond standard lease terms (Figures 3-18 and 3-19, Categories 5 through 8). Based on resource estimates, these lands contain 6 percent (10 MMbbls) of the Federal oil and 4 percent (0.27 TCF) of the Federal natural gas.
- Approximately 92 percent (5.2 million acres) of the Federal land is not accessible (Figures 3-18 and 3-19, Categories 1 through 4). Based on resource estimates, these lands contain about 92 percent (158 MMbbls) of the Federal oil and 95 percent (6.0 TCF) of the Federal natural gas.
- The USDA-Forest Service is the primary land management agency in the Montana Thrust Belt, with 71 percent of the Federal lands. Almost half is currently not being leased while undergoing new land use planning.

Table 3-5. Montana Thrust Belt Study Area—Federal Land and Oil and Natural Gas Resources by Access Category

		Area		**Resourcesa**			
				Total Oilb		**Total Gasc**	
		(acres x 1000)	**Percent of Federal**	**(MMbbl s)d**	**Percent of Federal**	**(BCF)e**	**Percent of Federal**
1.	No Leasing (Statutory/Executive Order) (NLS)	2,728	48.3%	95	55.7%	3,724	59.0%
2.	No Leasing (Administrative) (NLA)	294	5.2%	6	3.5%	149	2.4%
3.	No Leasing (Administrative) Pending Land Use Planning or NEPA Compliance (NLA/LUP)	1,728	30.6%	53	31.3%	1,971	31.2%
4.	Leasing, No Surface Occupancy (NSO) (Net NSO for O&G Resources)	457	8.1%	3	1.9%	129	2.1%
5.	Leasing, Cumulative Timing Limitations (TLs) of >9 Months	3	0.1%	0	0.0%	2	0.0%
6.	Leasing, Cumulative Timing Limitations (TLs) of >6 to <9 Months	18	0.3%	1	0.5%	32	0.5%
7.	Leasing, Cumulative Timing Limitations (TLs) of >3 to <6 Months	41	0.7%	2	1.1%	50	0.8%

8.	Leasing, Controlled Surface Use (CSU)f	219	3.9%	7	4.2%	181	2.9%
9.	Leasing, Standard Lease Terms (SLTs)	164	2.9%	3	1.8%	69	1.1%
Total, Federal Lands including Split Estate		**5,651**	**100.0%**	**171**	**100.0%**	**6,307**	**100.0%**
Total Non-Federal		**5,940**		**178**		**2,331**	
Total Inventory Area		**11,591**		**349**		**8,638**	
Summary							
Inaccessible (Categories 1-4)		5,206	92%	158	92%	5,973	95%
Accessible with Restrictions (Categories 5-8)		281	5%	10	6%	265	4%
Accessible under Standard Lease Terms (Category 9)		164	3%	3	2%	69	1%
Total, Federal Lands Including Split Estate		**5,651**	**100%**	**171**	**100%**	**6,307**	**100%**

Small rounding errors may be present.

a Undiscovered technically recoverable resources and reserves growth

b Including oil, natural gas liquids (NGLs) and liquids associated with natural gas reservoirs

c Including associated dissolved and nonassociated natural gas

d Million barrels **e** Billion cubic feet **f** Includes Cumulative Timing Limitations of <3 months

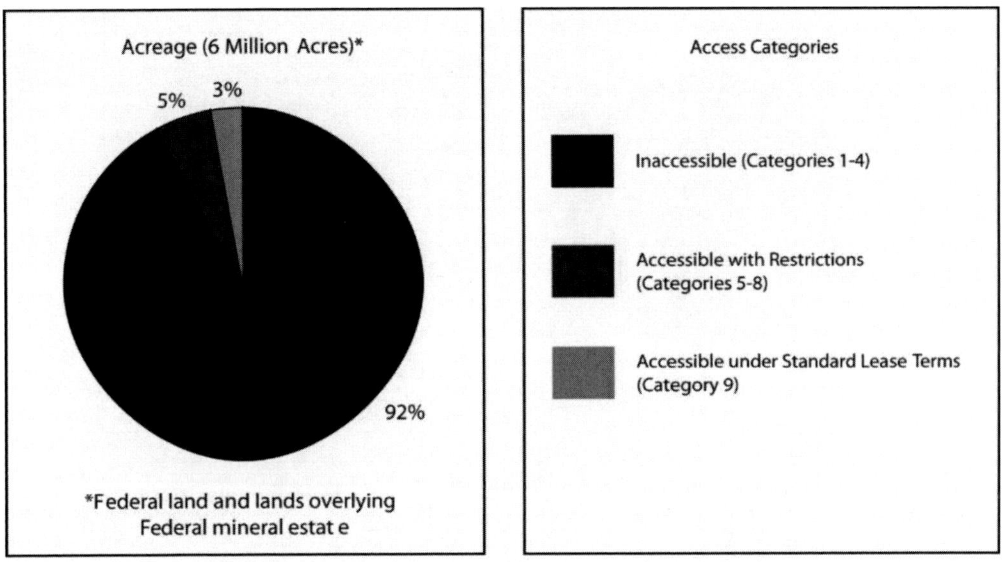

Figure 3-18. (Continued)

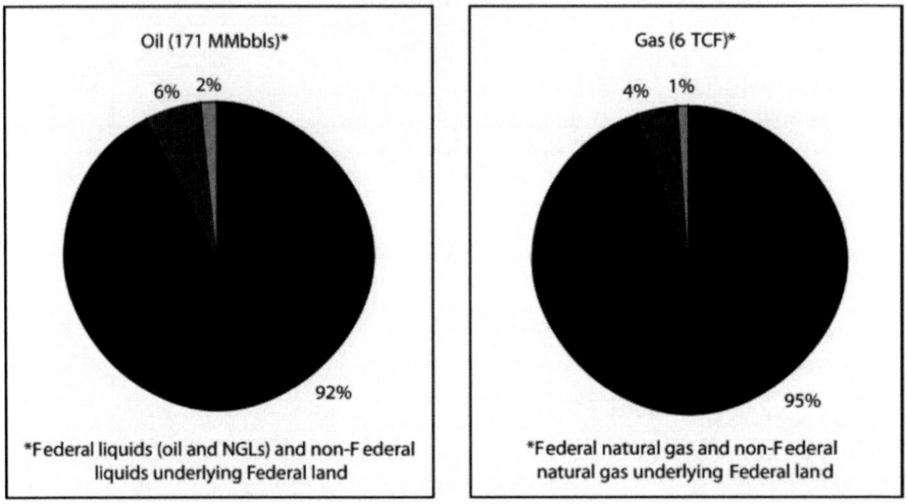

Figure 3-18. Simplified Chart of Results, Montana Thrust Belt Study Area—Federal Land and Oil and Natural Gas Resources by Accessibility

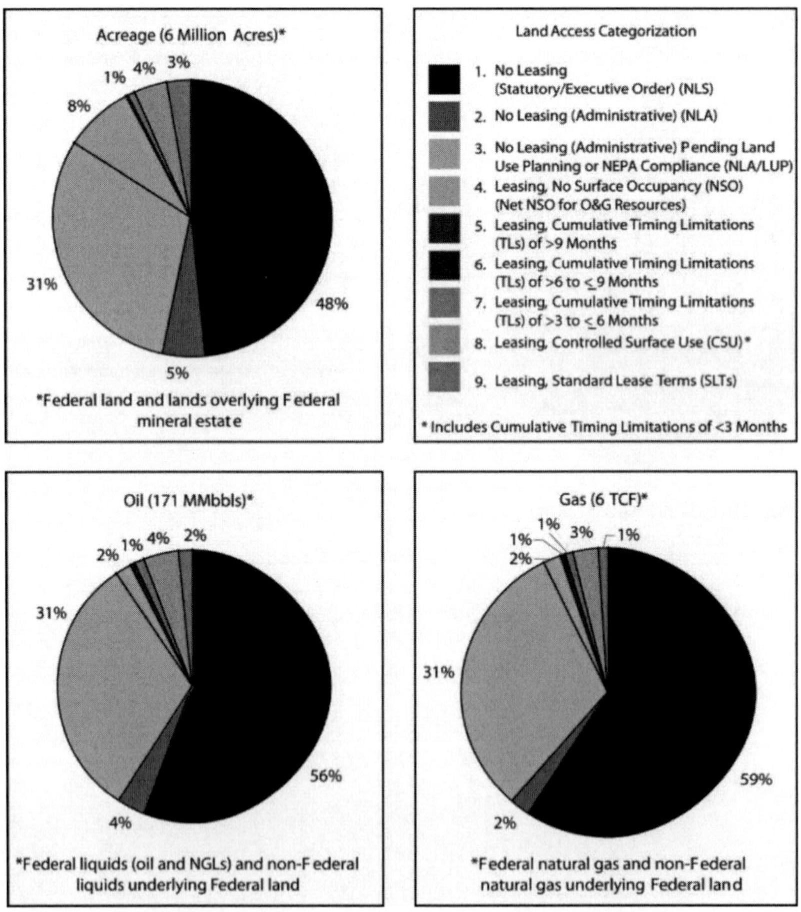

Figure 3-19. Chart of Results, Montana Thrust Belt Study Area—Federal Land and Oil and Natural Gas Resources by Access Category

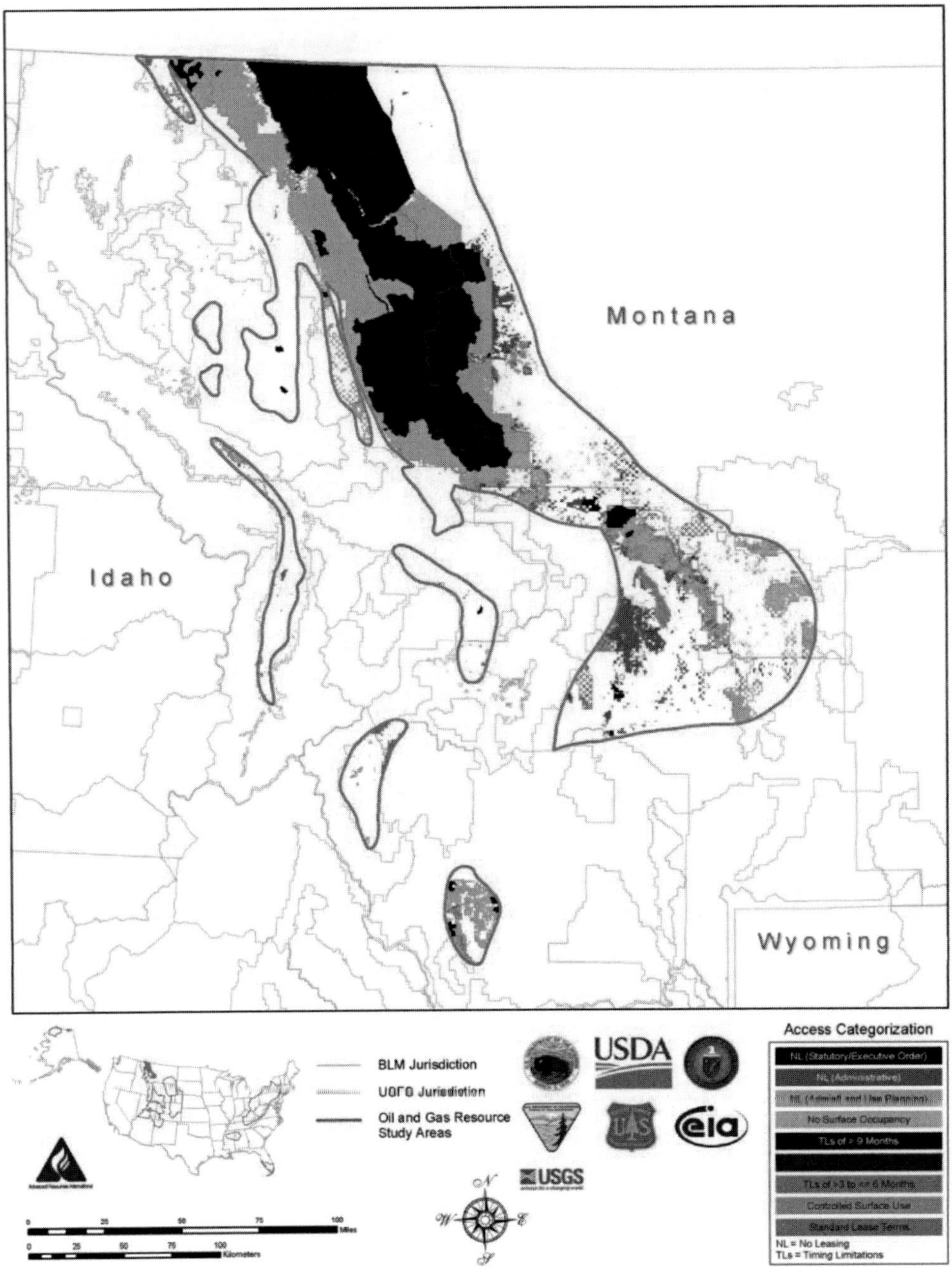

Figure 3-20. Federal Land Access Categorization Map, Montana Thrust Belt Study Area

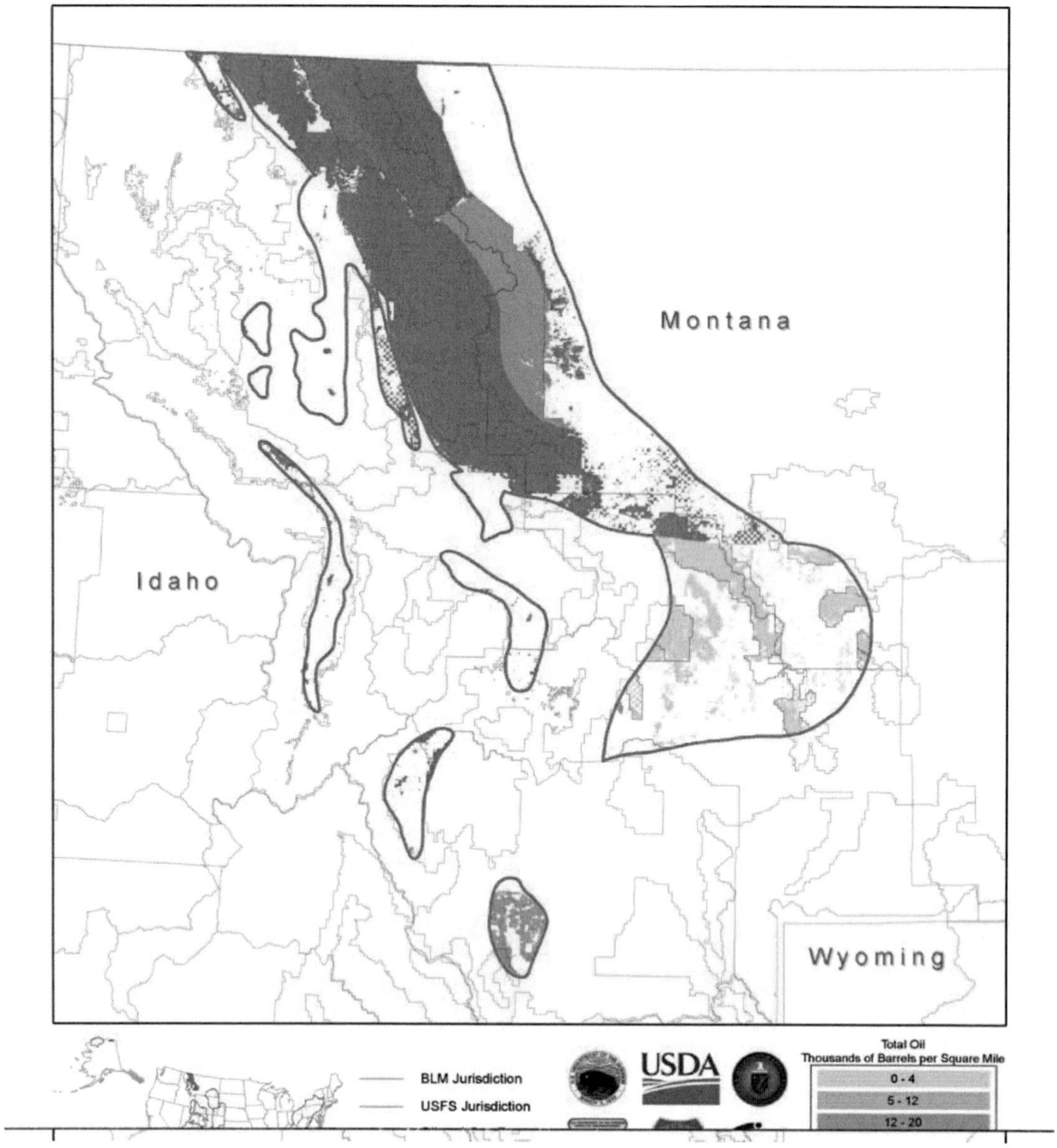

Figure 3-21. Map of Total Federal Oil, Montana Thrust Belt Study Area

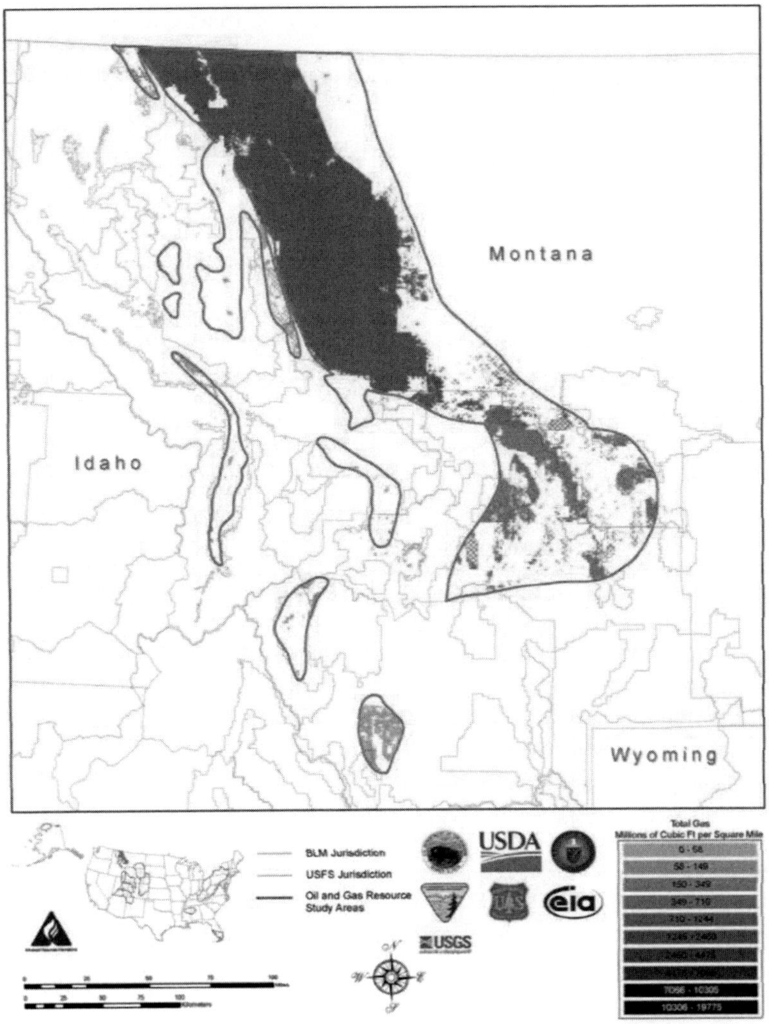

Figure 3-22. Map of Total Federal Natural Gas, Montana Thrust Belt Study Area

3.1.5 Powder River Basin

- Approximately 49 percent (5.8 million acres) of the Federal land is accessible under standard lease terms (Figures 3-23 and 3-24, Category 9). Based on resource estimates, these lands contain 22 percent (198 MMbbls) of the Federal oil and 19 percent (1.7 TCF) of the Federal natural gas.
- Approximately 32 percent (3.9 million acres) of the Federal land is accessible with restrictions on oil and gas operations beyond standard lease terms (Figures 3-23 and 3-24, Categories 5 through 8). Based on resource estimates, these lands contain 74 percent (668 MMbbls) of the Federal oil and 71 percent (6.2 TCF) of the Federal natural gas in the basin.

- Approximately 19 percent (2.3 million acres) of the Federal land is not accessible (Figures 3-23 and 3-24, Categories 1 through 4). Based on resource estimates, these lands contain about 4 percent (32 MMbbls) of the Federal oil and 10 percent (0.87 TCF) of the Federal natural gas.
- Almost all of the undiscovered natural gas is expected to be found in coalbeds (98 percent).
- Among the study areas, this area has the highest proportion of split estate lands (59 percent of the Federal oil and gas ownership is split estate).

Table 3-6. Powder River Basin Study Area—Federal Land and Oil and Natural Gas Resources by Access Category

		Area		Resourcesa			
				Total Oilb		Total Gasc	
		(acres x 1000)	Percent of Federal	(MMbbls) d	Percent of Federal	(BCF)e	Percent of Federal
1.	No Leasing (Statutory/Executive Order) (NLS)	2,728	48.3%	95	55.7%	3,724	59.0%
2.	No Leasing (Administrative) (NLA)	294	5.2%	6	3.5%	149	2.4%
3.	No Leasing (Administrative) Pending Land Use Planning or NEPA Compliance (NLA/LUP)	1,728	30.6%	53	31.3%	1,971	31.2%
4.	Leasing, No Surface Occupancy (NSO) (Net NSO for O&G Resources)	457	8.1%	3	1.9%	129	2.1%
5.	Leasing, Cumulative Timing Limitations (TLs) of >9 Months	3	0.1%	0	0.0%	2	0.0%
6.	Leasing, Cumulative Timing Limitations (TLs) of >6 to <9 Months	18	0.3%	1	0.5%	32	0.5%
7.	Leasing, Cumulative Timing Limitations (TLs) of >3 to <6 Months	41	0.7%	2	1.1%	50	0.8%
8.	Leasing, Controlled Surface Use (CSU)f	219	3.9%	7	4.2%	181	2.9%
9.	Leasing, Standard Lease Terms (SLTs)	164	2.9%	3	1.8%	69	1.1%
Total, Federal Lands including Split Estate		**5,651**	**100.0%**	**171**	**100.0%**	**6,307**	**100.0%**
Total Non-Federal		**5,940**		**178**		**2,331**	
Total Inventory Area		**11,591**		**349**		**8,638**	
Summary							
Inaccessible (Categories 1-4)		5,206	92%	158	92%	5,973	95%
Accessible with Restrictions (Categories 5-8)		281	5%	10	6%	265	4%

Accessible under Standard Lease Terms (Category 9)	164	3%	3	2%	69	1%
Total, Federal Lands Including Split Estate	**5,651**	**100%**	**171**	**100%**	**6,307**	**100%**

Small rounding errors may be present.

a Undiscovered technically recoverable resources and reserves growth

b Including oil, natural gas liquids (NGLs) and liquids associated with natural gas reservoirs

c Including associated dissolved and nonassociated natural gas

d Million barrels e Billion cubic feet f Includes Cumulative Timing Limitations of <3 months

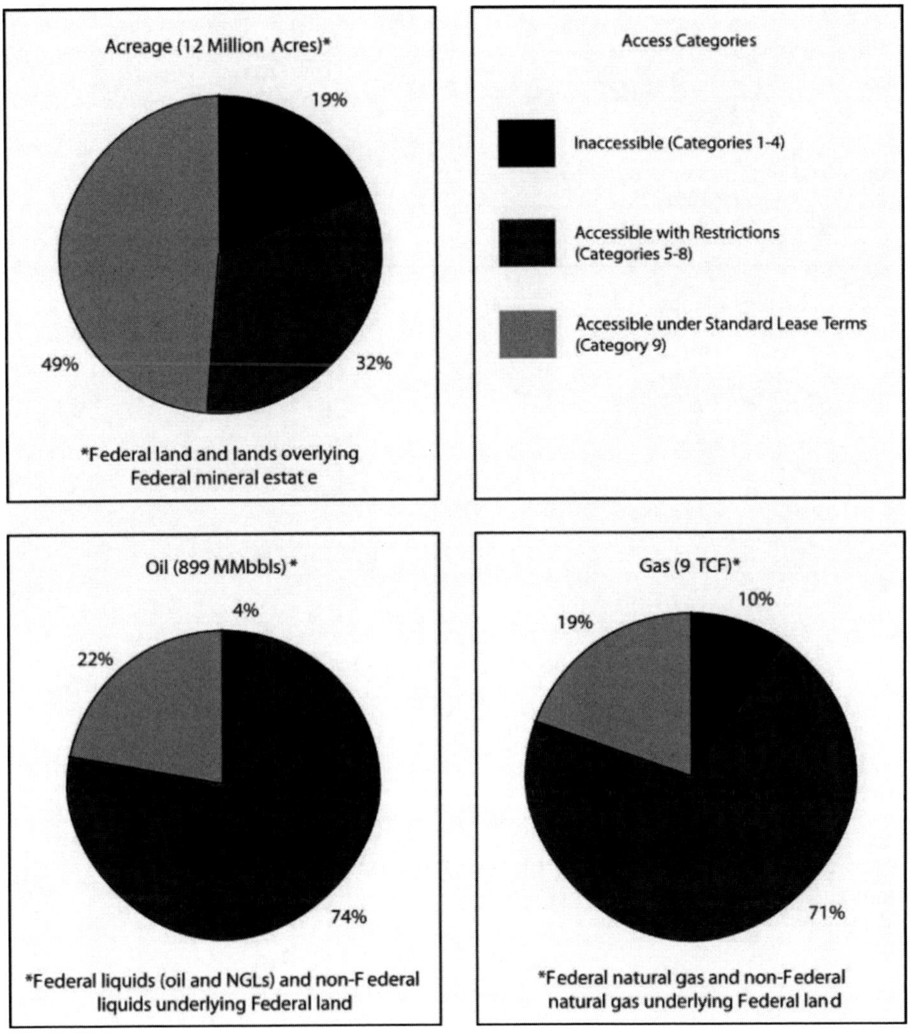

Figure 3-23. Simplified Chart of Results, Powder River Basin Study Area—Federal Land and Oil and Natural Gas Resources by Accessibility

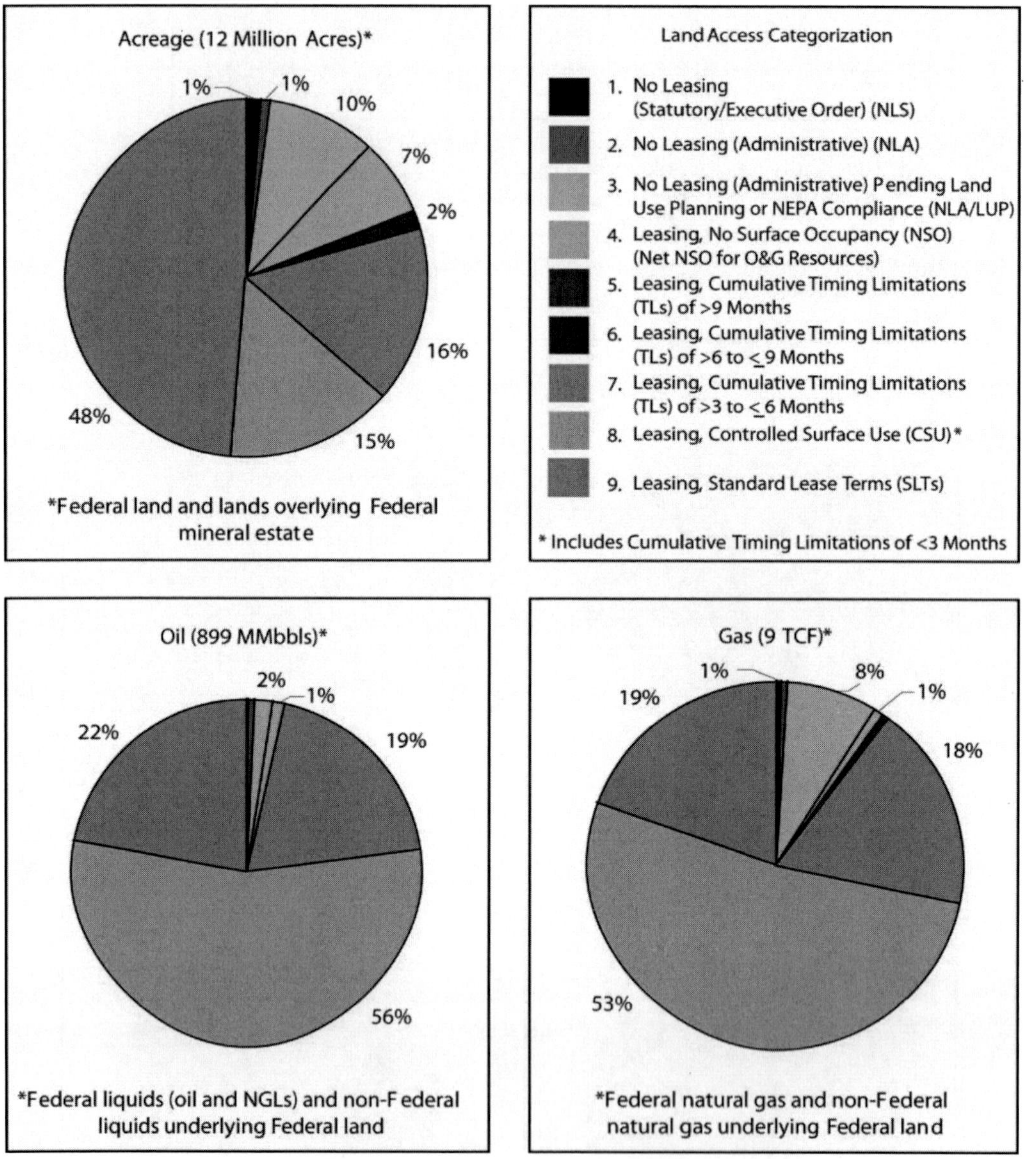

Figure 3-24. Chart of Results, Powder River Basin Study Area—Federal Land and Oil and Natural Gas Resources by Access Category

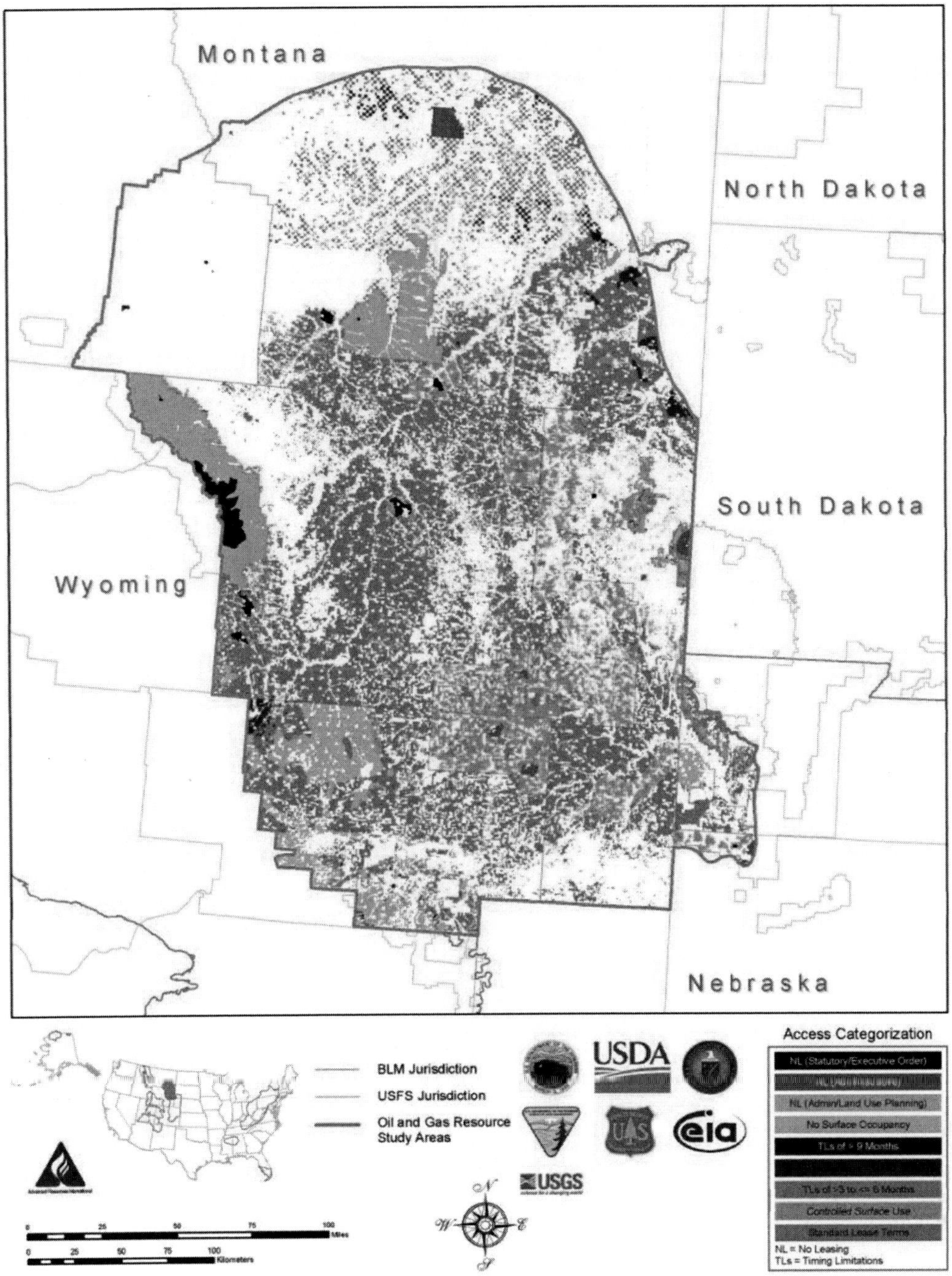

Figure 3-25. Federal Land Access Categorization Map, Powder River Basin StudyArea

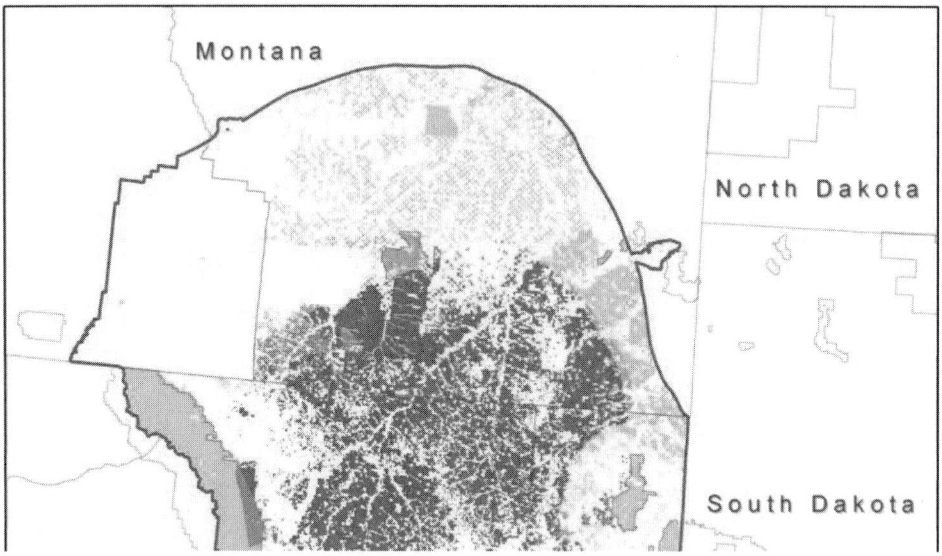

Figure 3-26. Map of Total Federal Oil, Powder River Basin Study Area

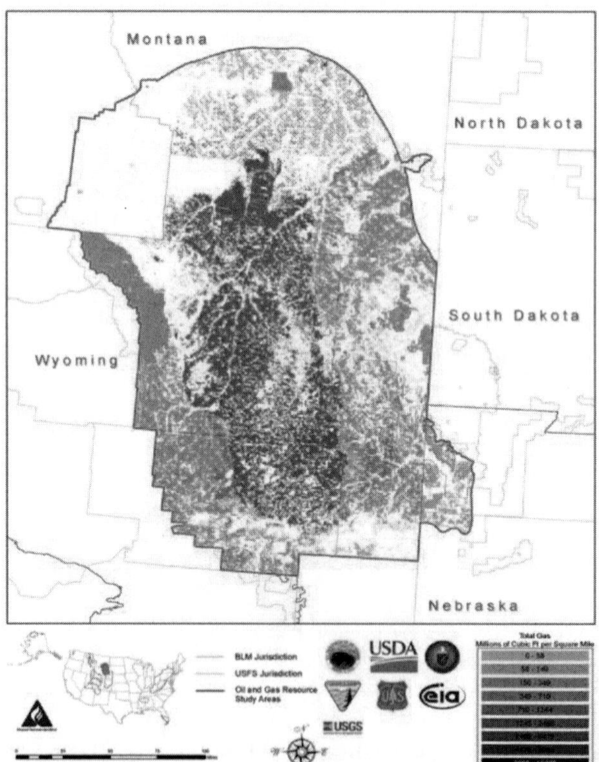

Figure 3-27. Map of Total Federal Natural Gas, Powder River Basin Study Area

3.1.6 Wyoming Thrust Belt

- Approximately 13 percent (0.6 million acres) of the Federal land is accessible under standard lease terms (Figures 3-28 and 3-29, Category 9). Based on resource estimates, these lands contain 16 percent (7 MMbbls) of the Federal oil and 14 percent (0.05 TCF) of the Federal natural gas.
- Approximately 17 percent (0.7 million acres) of the Federal land is accessible with restrictions on oil and gas operations beyond standard lease terms (Figures 3-28 and 3-29, Categories 5 through 8). Based on resource estimates, these lands contain 31 percent (14 MMbbls) of the Federal oil and 46 percent (0.17 TCF) of the Federal natural gas.
- Approximately 69 percent (2.9 million acres) of the Federal land is not accessible (Figures 3-28 and 3-29, Categories 1 through 4). Based on resource estimates, these lands contain about 53 percent (24 MMbbls) of the Federal oil and 40 percent (0.15 TCF) of the Federal natural gas.

Table 3-7. Wyoming Thrust Belt Study Area—Federal Land and Oil and Natural Gas Resources Affected by Access Category

		Area		Resourcesa			
				Total Oilb		Total Gasc	
		(acres x 1000)	Percent of Federal	(MMbbls)d	Percent of Federal	(BCF)e	Percent of Federal
1.	No Leasing (Statutory/Executive Order) (NLS)	275	6.6%	3	6.1%	17	4.5%
2.	No Leasing (Administrative) (NLA)	210	5.0%	2	4.7%	13	3.4%
3.	No Leasing (Administrative) Pending Land Use Planning or NEPA Compliance (NLA/LUP)	1,354	32.4%	14	30.0%	80	21.3%
4.	Leasing, No Surface Occupancy (NSO) (Net NSO for O&G Resources)	1,063	25.4%	6	12.4%	42	11.2%
5.	Leasing, Cumulative Timing Limitations (TLs) of >9 Months	32	0.8%	1	1.8%	7	1.8%
6.	Leasing, Cumulative Timing Limitations (TLs) of >6 to <9 Months	156	3.7%	3	5.7%	28	7.4%

Table 3-7. (Continued)

		Area		Resourcesa			
				Total Oilb		Total Gasc	
		(acres x 1000)	Percent of Federal	(MMbbls)d	Percent of Federal	(BCF)e	Percent of Federal
7.	Leasing, Cumulative Timing Limitations (TLs) of >3 to <6 Months	385	9.2%	7	14.3%	73	19.6%
8.	Leasing, Controlled Surface Use (CSU)f	150	3.6%	4	9.4%	63	16.9%
9.	Leasing, Standard Lease Terms (SLTs)	553	13.2%	7	15.7%	52	14.0%
Total, Federal Lands including Split Estate		**4,179**	**100.0%**	**46**	**100.0%**	**374**	**100.0%**
Total Non-Federal		**3,840**		**47**		**482**	
Total Inventory Area		**8,020**		**92**		**856**	
Summary							
Inaccessible (Categories 1-4)		2,904	69%	24	53%	151	40%
Accessible with Restrictions (Categories 5-8)		723	17%	14	31%	171	46%
Accessible under Standard Lease Terms (Category 9)		553	13%	7	16%	52	14%
Total, Federal Lands Including Split Estate		**4,179**	**100%**	**46**	**100%**	**374**	**100%**

Small rounding errors may be present.

a Undiscovered technically recoverable resources and reserves growth

b Including oil, natural gas liquids (NGLs) and liquids associated with natural gas reservoirs

c Including associated dissolved and nonassociated natural gas

d Million barrels e Billion cubic feet f Includes Cumulative Timing Limitations of <3 months

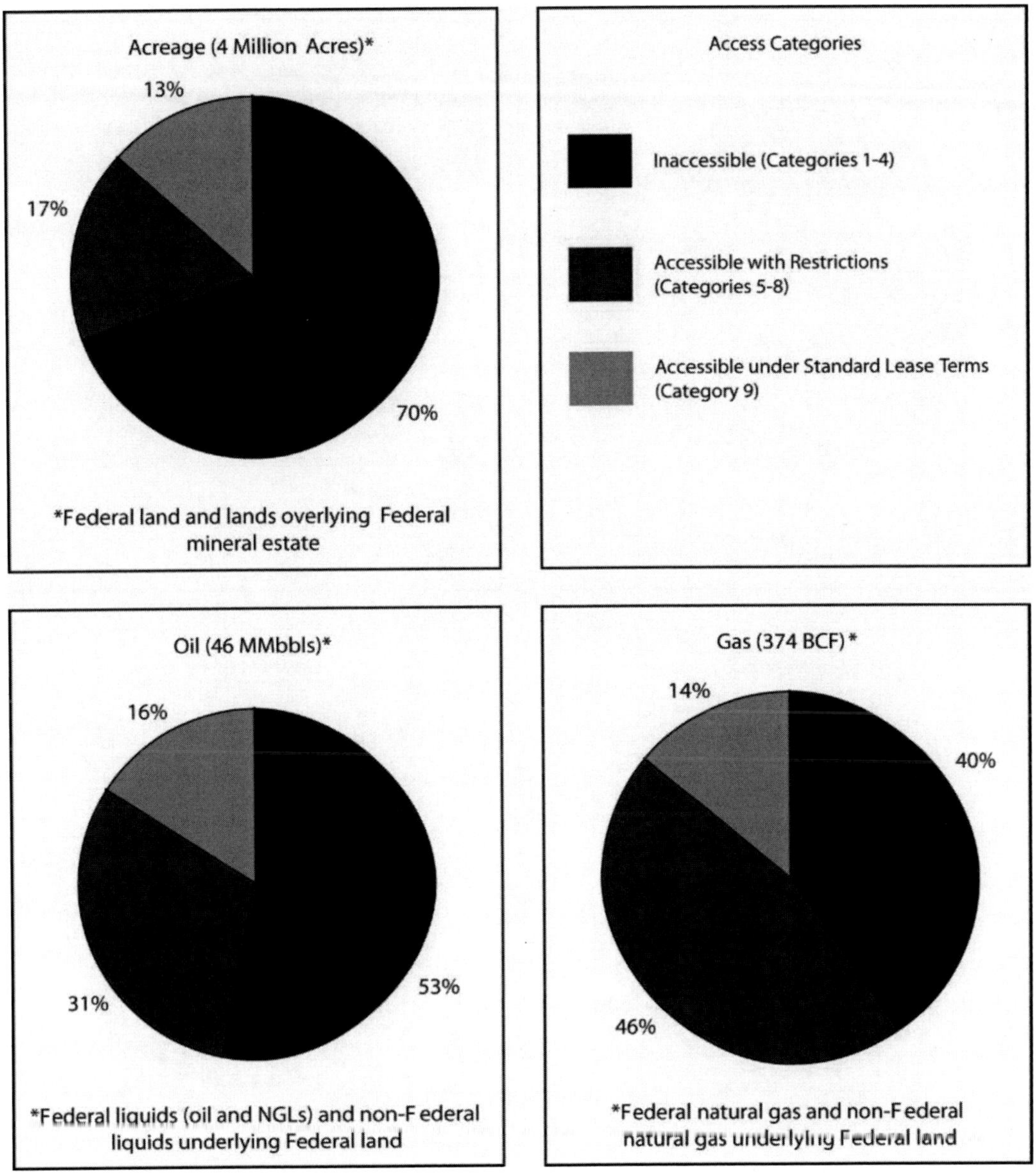

Figure 3-28. Simplified Chart of Results, Wyoming Thrust Belt Study Area—Federal Land and Oil and Natural Gas Resources by Accessibility

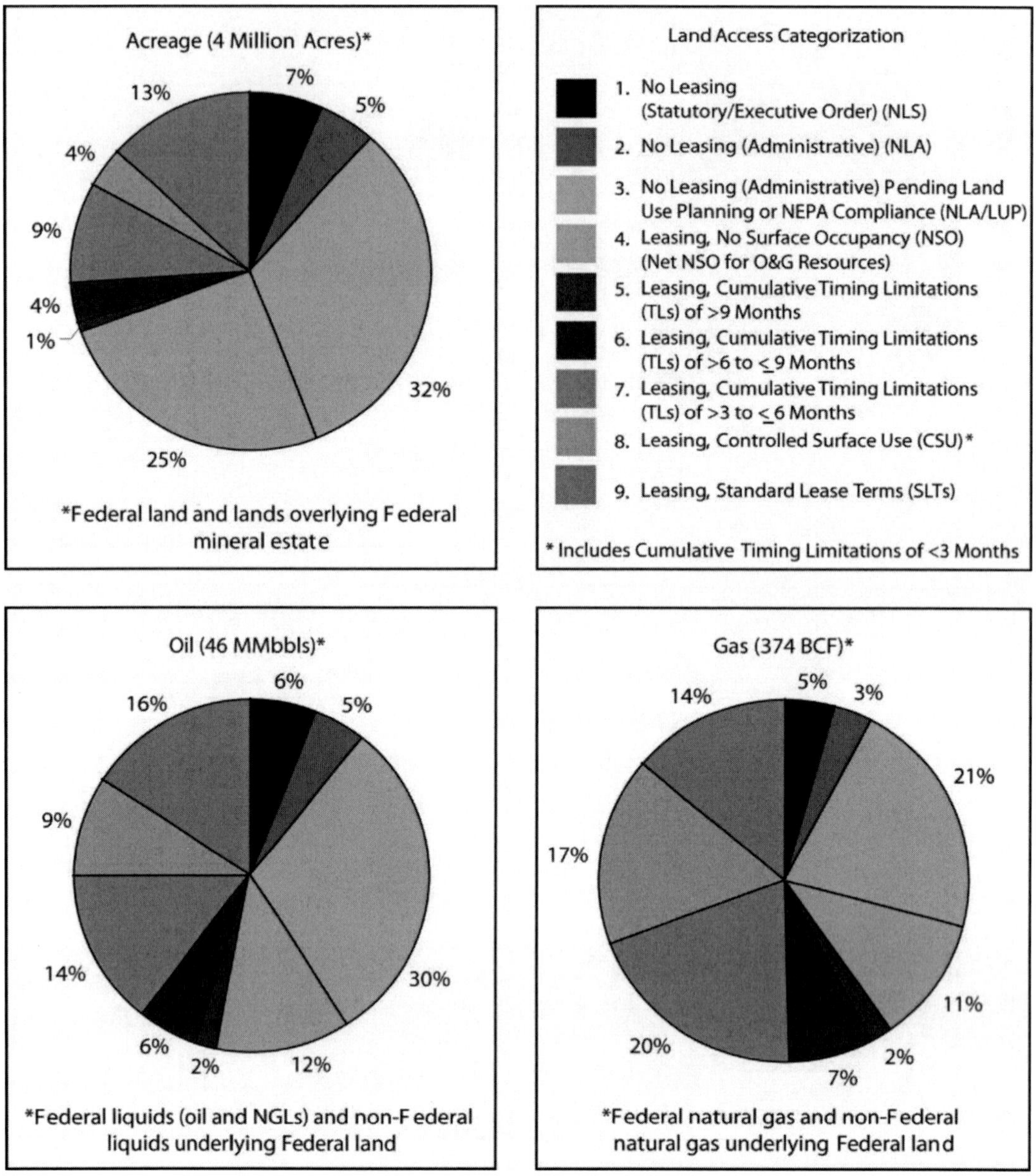

Figure 3-29. Chart of Results, Wyoming **Thrust Belt Study Area—Federal Land** and Oil and Natural Gas Resources by Access Category

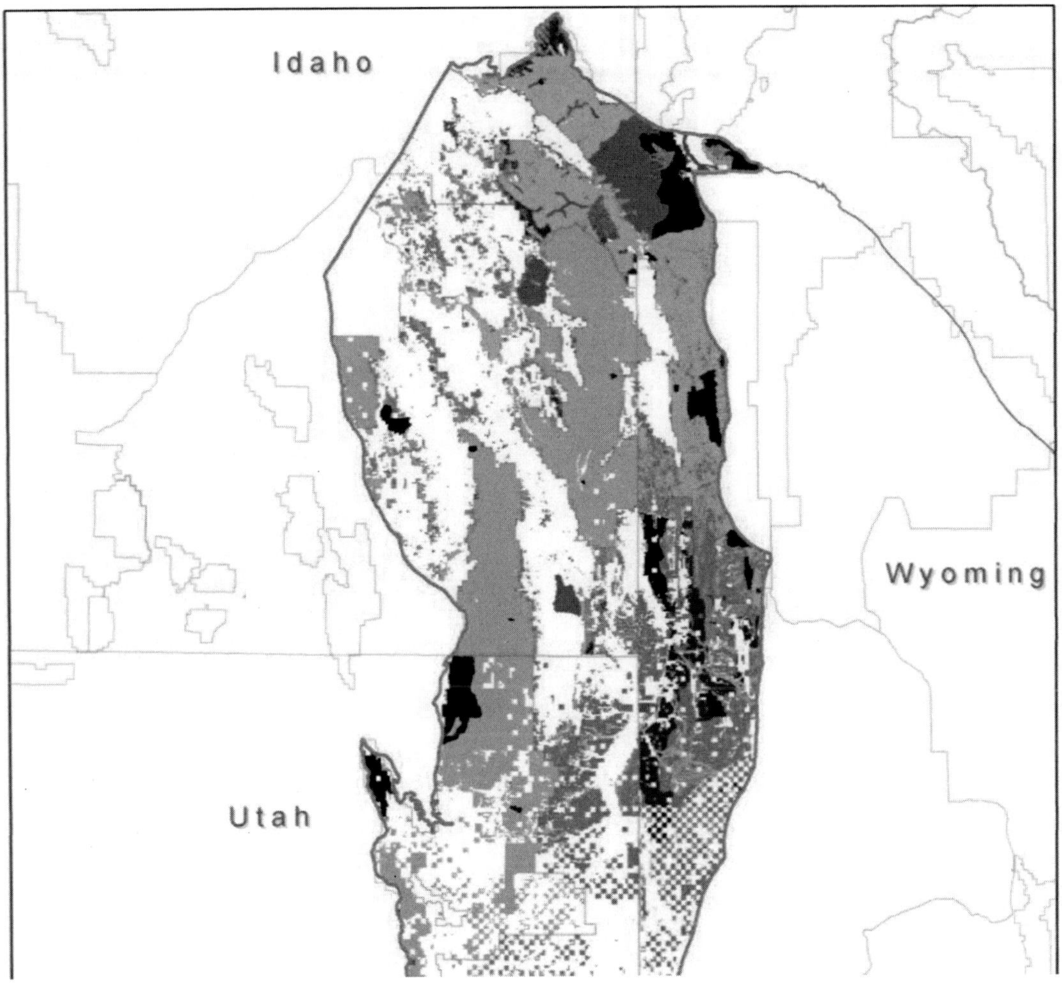

Figure 3-30. Federal Land Access Categorization Map, Wyoming Thrust Belt Study Area

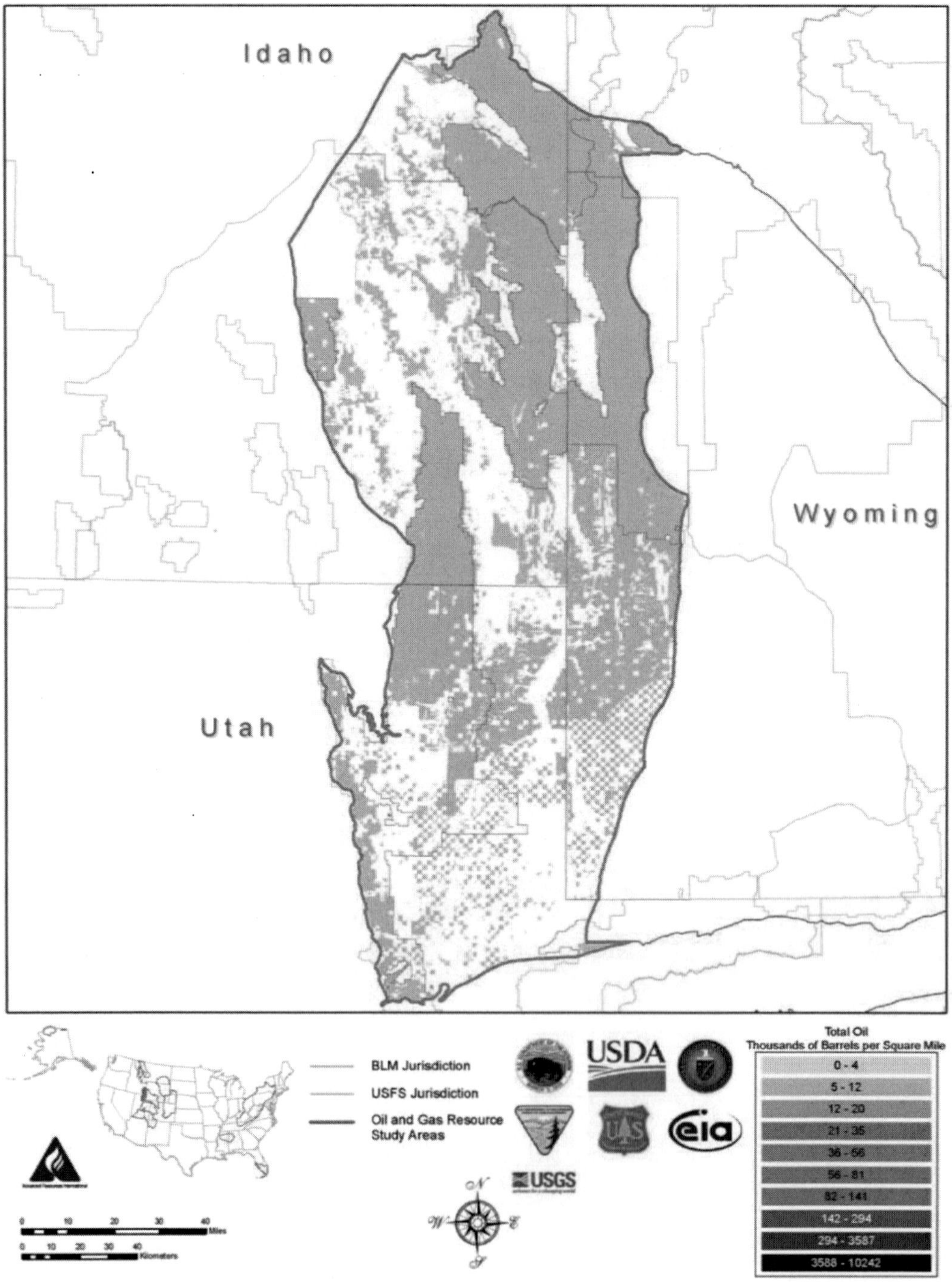

Figure 3-31. Map of Total Federal Oil, Wyoming Thrust Belt Study Area

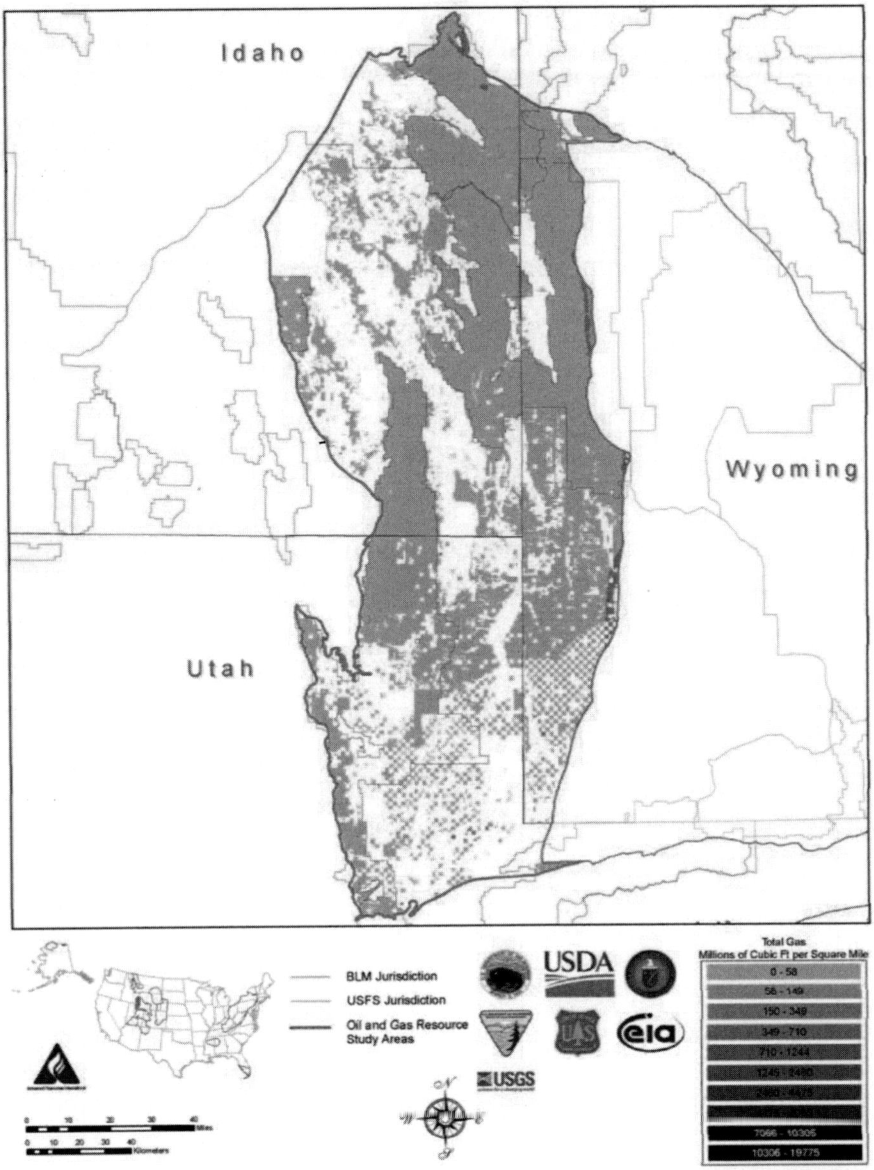

Figure 3-32. Map of Total Federal Natural Gas, Wyoming Thrust Belt Study Area

3.1.7 Greater Green River Basin (Southwestern Wyoming)

- Approximately 30 percent (3.5 million acres) of the Federal land is accessible under standard lease terms (Figures 3-33 and 3-34, Category 9). Based on resource estimates, these lands contain 14 percent (335 MMbbls) of the Federal oil and 15 percent (9.4 TCF) of the Federal natural gas.
- Approximately 50 percent (5.7 million acres) of the Federal land is accessible with restrictions on oil and gas operations beyond standard lease terms (Figures 3-33 and

3-34, Categories 5 through 8). Based on resource estimates, these lands contain 77 percent (1,828 MMbbls) of the Federal oil and 76 percent (47.8 TCF) of the Federal natural gas.

- Approximately 20 percent (2.2 million acres) of the Federal land in the basin is not accessible (Figures 3-33 and 3-34, Categories 1 through 4). Based on resource estimates, these lands contain about 9 percent (213 MMbbls) of the Federal oil and 9 percent (5.6 TCF) of the Federal natural gas.
- Almost all of the undiscovered natural gas (97 percent) is expected to occur as continuous deposits.
- A relatively large portion of the Federal land (43 percent of the surface area,) along with 44 percent of the oil and 43 percent of the natural gas, are under timing limitations of 3 to 9 months.
- The land ownership pattern is highly complex due a checkerboard pattern of ownership resulting from railroad land grants.

Table 3-8. Greater Green River Basin Study Area—Federal Land and Oil and Natural Gas Resources by Access Category

		Area		Resourcesa			
				Total Oilb		Total Gasc	
		(acres x 1000)	Percent of Federal	(MMbbls)d	Percent of Federal	(BCF)e	Percent of Federal
1.	No Leasing (Statutory/Executive Order) (NLS)	594	5.2%	108	4.5%	3,440	5.5%
2.	No Leasing (Administrative) (NLA)	139	1.2%	37	1.6%	786	1.3%
3.	No Leasing (Administrative) Pending Land Use Planning or NEPA Compliance (NLA/LUP)	363	3.2%	36	1.5%	621	1.0%
4.	Leasing, No Surface Occupancy (NSO) (Net NSO for O&G Resources)	1,131	9.9%	31	1.3%	782	1.2%
5.	Leasing, Cumulative Timing Limitations (TLs) of >9 Months	0	0.0%	0	0.0%	1	0.0%
6.	Leasing, Cumulative Timing Limitations (TLs) of >6 to <9 Months	1,046	9.2%	202	8.5%	4,058	6.5%
7.	Leasing, Cumulative Timing Limitations (TLs) of >3 to <6 Months	3,708	32.6%	863	36.3%	22,344	35.6%
8.	Leasing, Controlled Surface Use (CSU)f	948	8.3%	763	32.1%	21,426	34.1%
9.	Leasing, Standard Lease Terms (SLTs)	3,455	30.3%	335	14.1%	9,373	14.9%
Total, Federal Lands		**11,384**	**100.0%**	**2,376**	**100.0%**	**62,830**	**100.0**

including Split Estate						%
Total Non-Federal	**5,205**		**1,001**		**24,489**	
Total Inventory Area	**16,589**		**3,376**		**87,319**	
Summary						
Inaccessible (Categories 1-4)	2,227	20%	213	9%	5,629	9%
Accessible with Restrictions (Categories 5-8)	5,702	50%	1,828	77%	47,829	76%
Accessible under Standard Lease Terms (Category 9)	3,455	30%	335	14%	9,373	15%
Total, Federal Lands Including Split Estate	**11,384**	**100%**	**2,376**	**100%**	**62,830**	**100%**

Small rounding errors may be present.

a Undiscovered technically recoverable resources and reserves growth

b Including oil, natural gas liquids (NGLs) and liquids associated with natural gas reservoirs

c Including associated dissolved and nonassociated natural gas

d Million barrels e Billion cubic feet f Includes Cumulative Timing Limitations of <3 months

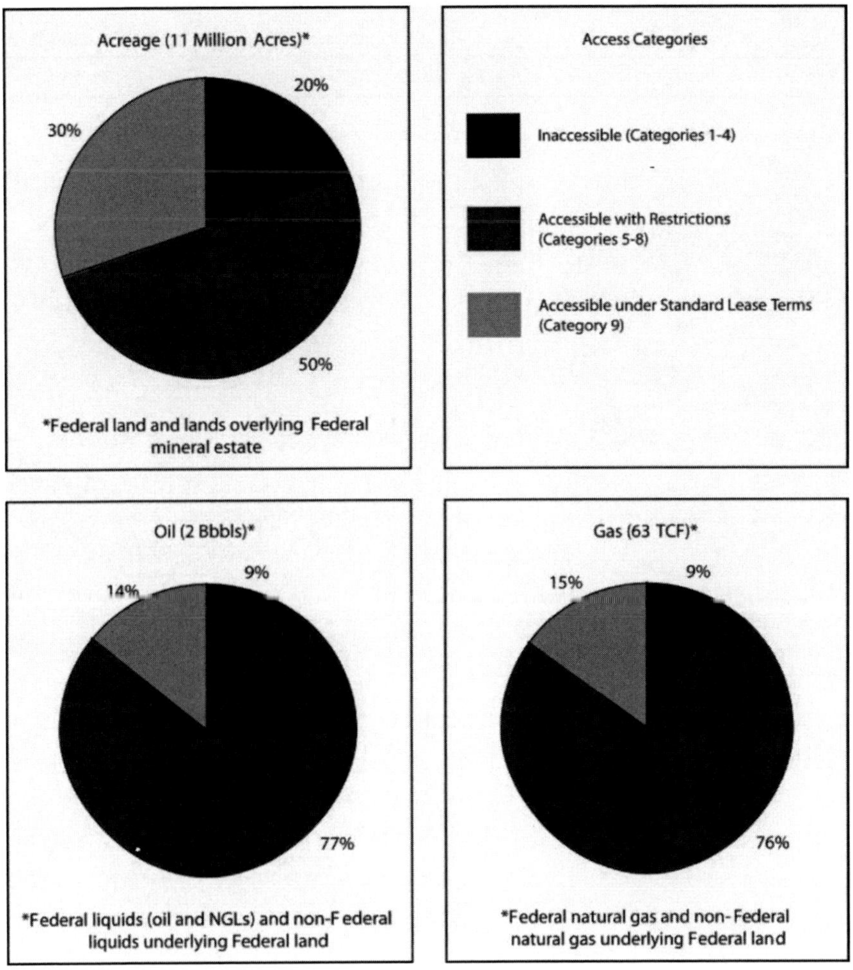

Figure 3-33. Simplified Chart of Results, Greater Green River Basin Study Area—Federal Land and Oil and Natural Gas Resources by Accessibility

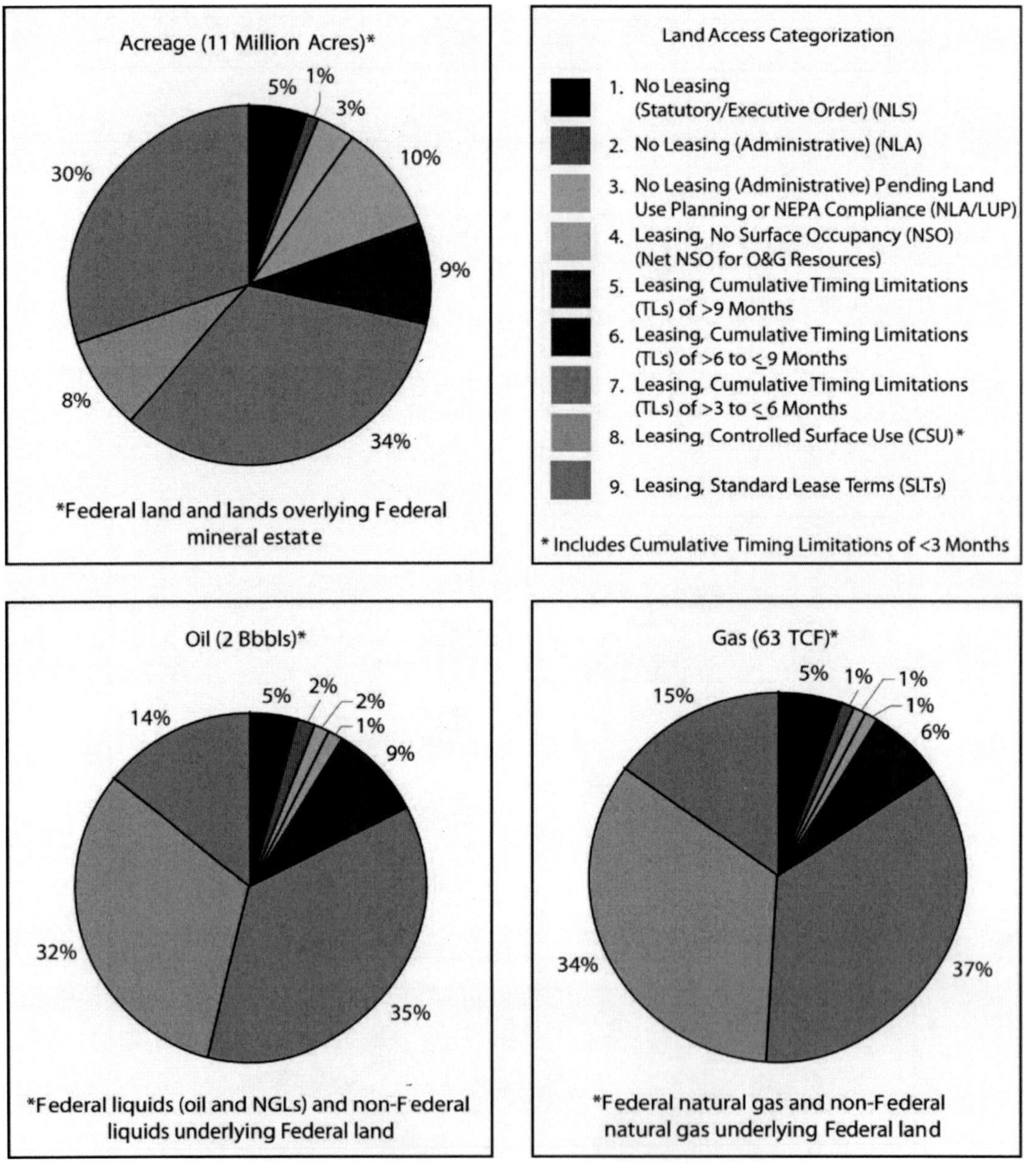

Figure 3-34. Chart of Results, Greater Green River Basin Study Area—Federal Land and Oil and Natural Gas Resources by Access Category

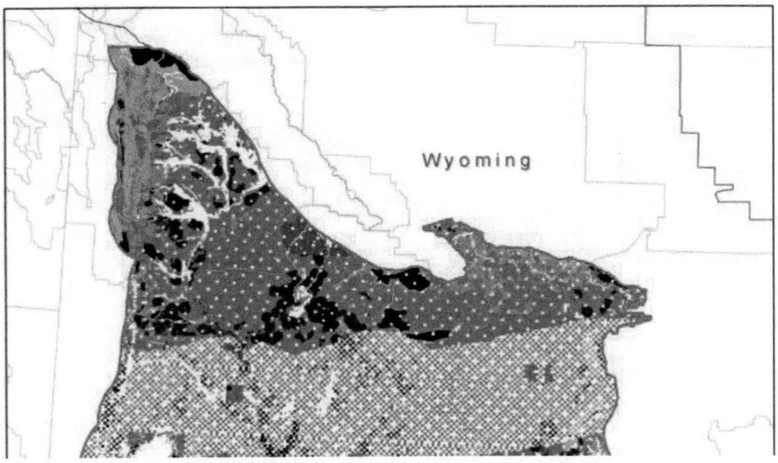

Figure 3-35. Federal Land Access Categorization Map, Greater Green River Basin Study Area

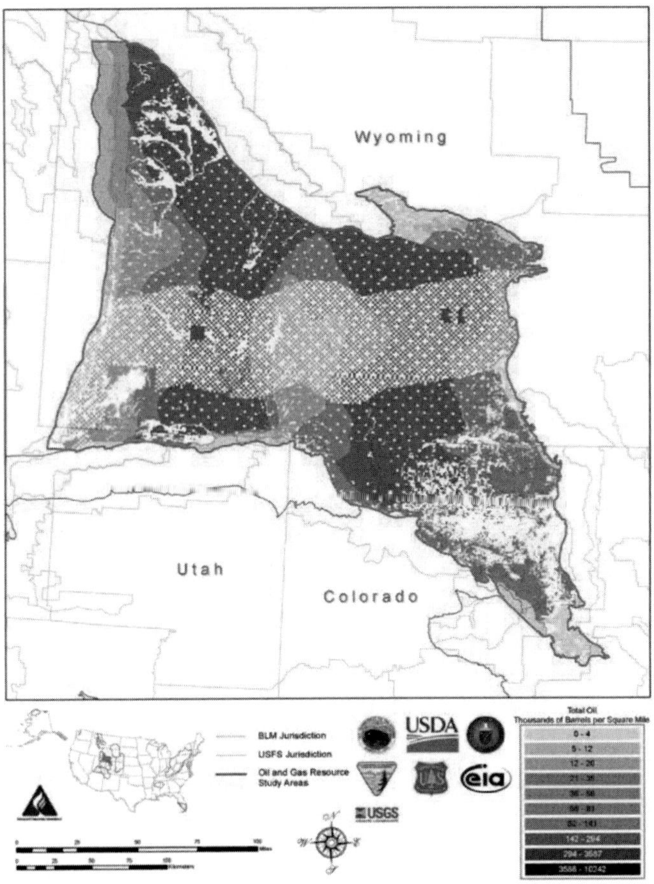

Figure 3-36. Map of Total Federal Oil, Greater Green River Basin Study Area

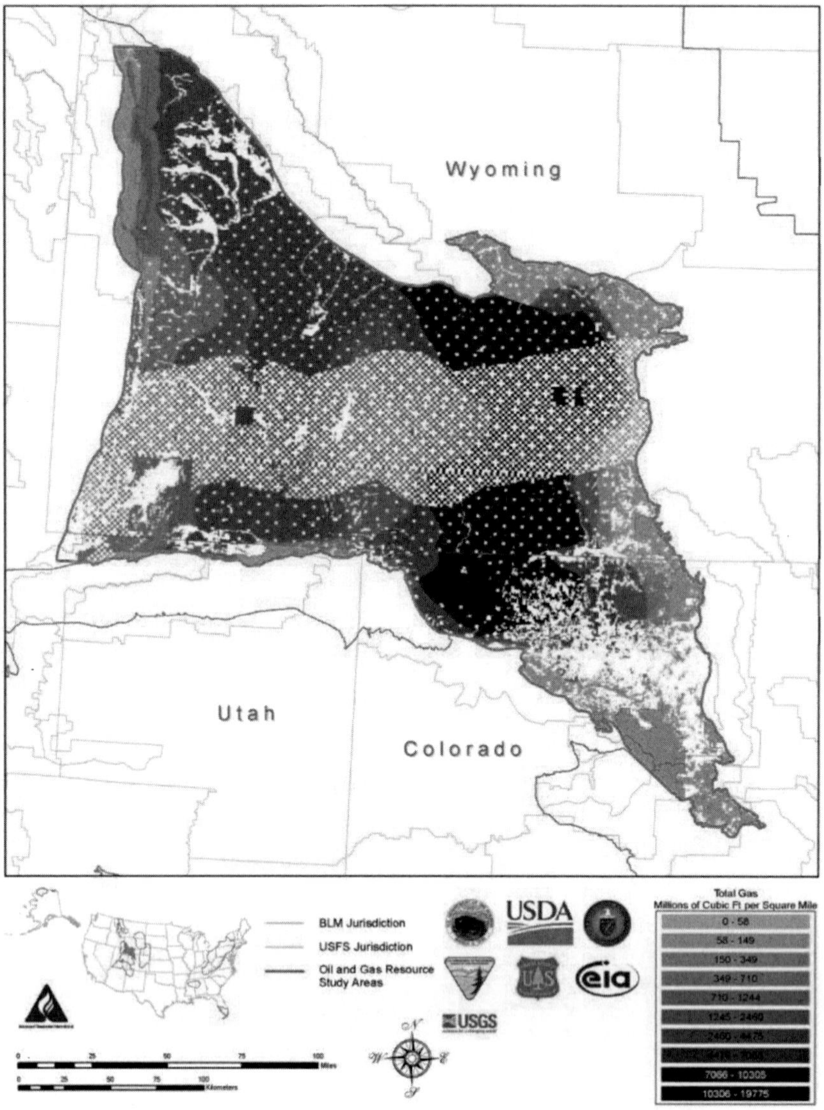

Figure 3-37. Map of Total Federal Natural Gas, Greater Green River Basin Study Area

3.1.8 Denver Basin

- Approximately 32 percent (0.9 million acres) of the Federal land is accessible under standard lease terms (Figures 3-38 and 3-39, Category 9). Based on resource estimates, these lands contain 16 percent (2 MMbbls) of the Federal oil and 11 percent (0.01 TCF) of the Federal natural gas.
- Approximately 42 percent (1.18 million acres) of the Federal land is accessible with restrictions on oil and gas operations beyond standard lease terms (Figures 3-38 and 3-39, Categories 5 through 8). Based on resource estimates, these lands contain 68

percent (9 MMbbls) of the Federal oil and 58 percent (0.03 TCF) of the Federal natural gas.

- Approximately 25 percent (0.7 million acres) of the Federal land is not accessible (Figures 3-38 and 3-39, Categories 1 through 4). Based on resource estimates, these lands contain about 16 percent (2 MMbbls) of the Federal oil and 31 percent (0.02 TCF) of the Federal natural gas.

Table 3-9. Denver Basin Study Area—Federal Land and Oil and Natural Gas Resources by Access Category

	Area		Resources[a]			
			Total Oil[b]		Total Gas[c]	
	(acres x 1000)	Percent of Federal	(MMbbls)[d]	Percent of Federal	(BCF)[e]	Percent of Federal
1. No Leasing (Statutory/Executive Order) (NLS)	68	2.5%	0	0.9%	0	0.4%
2. No Leasing (Administrative) (NLA)	299	10.8%	1	8.9%	13	23.6%
3. No Leasing (Administrative) Pending Land Use Planning or NEPA Compliance (NLA/LUP)	67	2.4%	0	2.4%	1	1.1%
4. Leasing, No Surface Occupancy (NSO) (Net NSO for O&G Resources)	273	9.8%	0	3.5%	3	6.1%
5. Leasing, Cumulative Timing Limitations (TLs) of >9 Months	2	0.1%	0	0.2%	0	0.5%
6. Leasing, Cumulative Timing Limitations (TLs) of >6 to <9 Months	33	1.2%	1	4.1%	4	6.3%
7. Leasing, Cumulative Timing Limitations (TLs) of >3 to <6 Months	281	10.1%	3	19.7%	8	15.0%
8. Leasing, Controlled Surface Use (CSU)[f]	860	31.0%	6	44.3%	20	36.1%
9. Leasing, Standard Lease Terms (SLTs)	894	32.2%	2	16.0%	6	11.1%
Total, Federal Lands including Split Estate	**2,776**	**100.0 %**	**13**	**100.0%**	**57**	**100.0%**
Total Non-Federal	**32,774**		**156**		**1,823**	
Total Inventory Area	**35,550**		**169**		**1,879**	
Summary						
Inaccessible (Categories 1-4)	707	25%	2	16%	18	31%
Accessible with Restrictions (Categories 5-8)	1,175	42%	9	68%	33	58%
Accessible under Standard Lease Terms (Category 9)	894	32%	2	16%	6	11%
Total, Federal Lands Including Split Estate	**2,776**	**100%**	**13**	**100%**	**57**	**100%**

Small rounding errors may be present.

a Undiscovered technically recoverable resources and reserves growth
b Including oil, natural gas liquids (NGLs) and liquids associated with natural gas reservoirs
c Including associated dissolved and nonassociated natural gas
d Million barrels e Billion cubic feet f Includes Cumulative Timing Limitations of <3 months

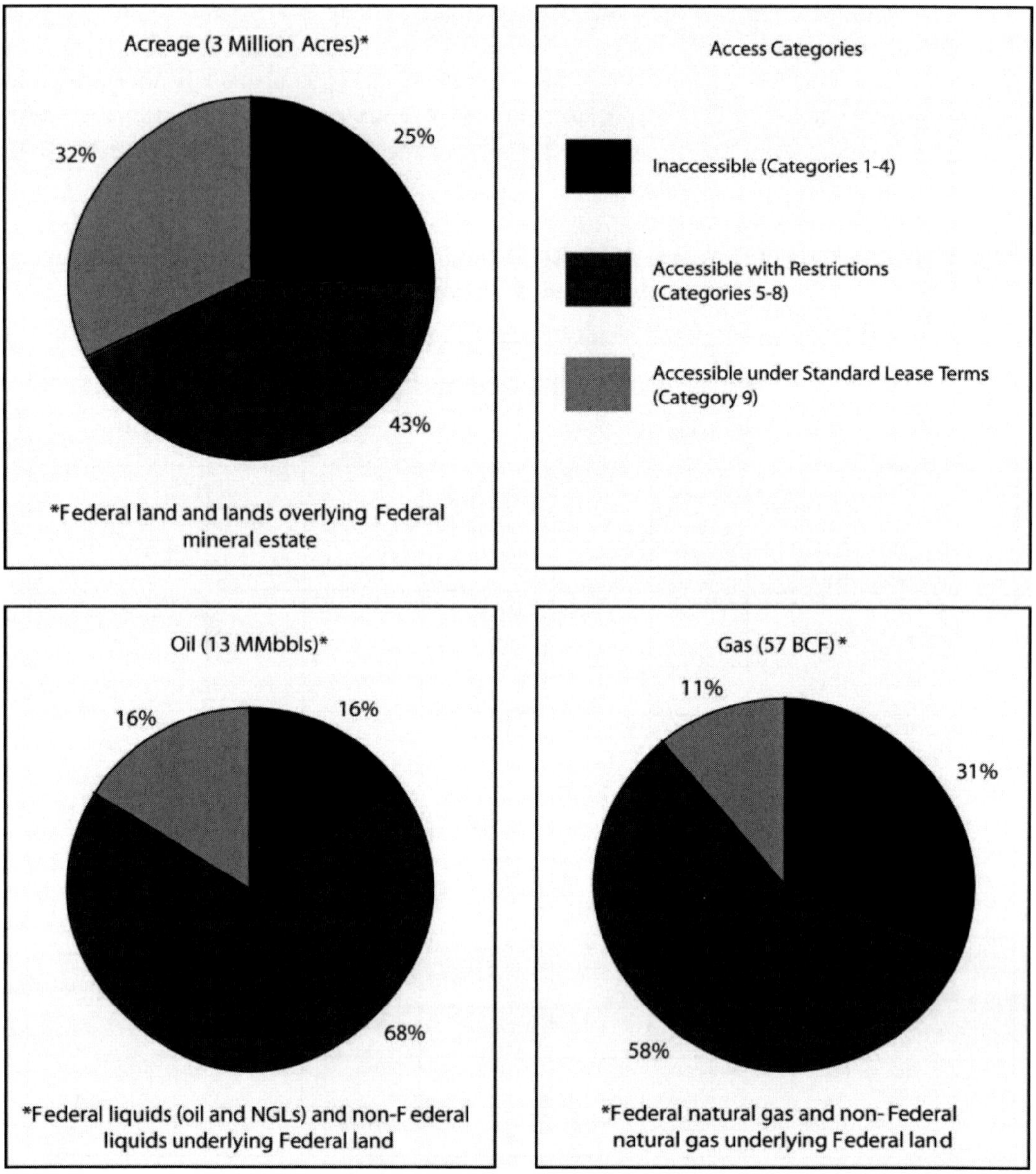

Figure 3-38. Simplified Chart of Results, Denver Basin Study Area—Federal Land and Oil and Natural Gas Resources by Accessibility

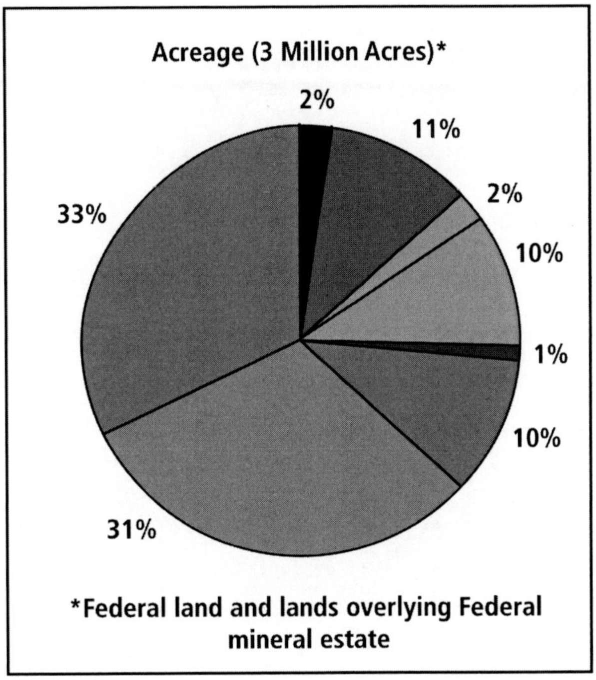

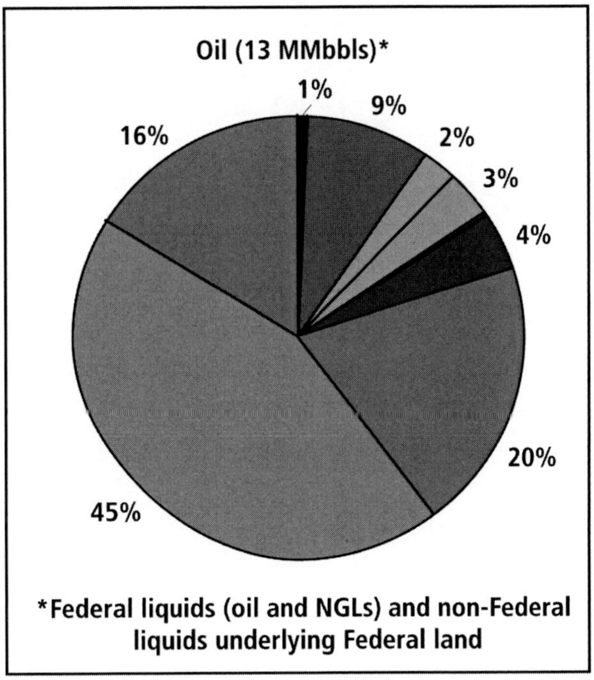

Figure 3-39. Chart of Results, Denver Basin Study Area—Federal Land and Oil and Natural Gas Resources by Access Category

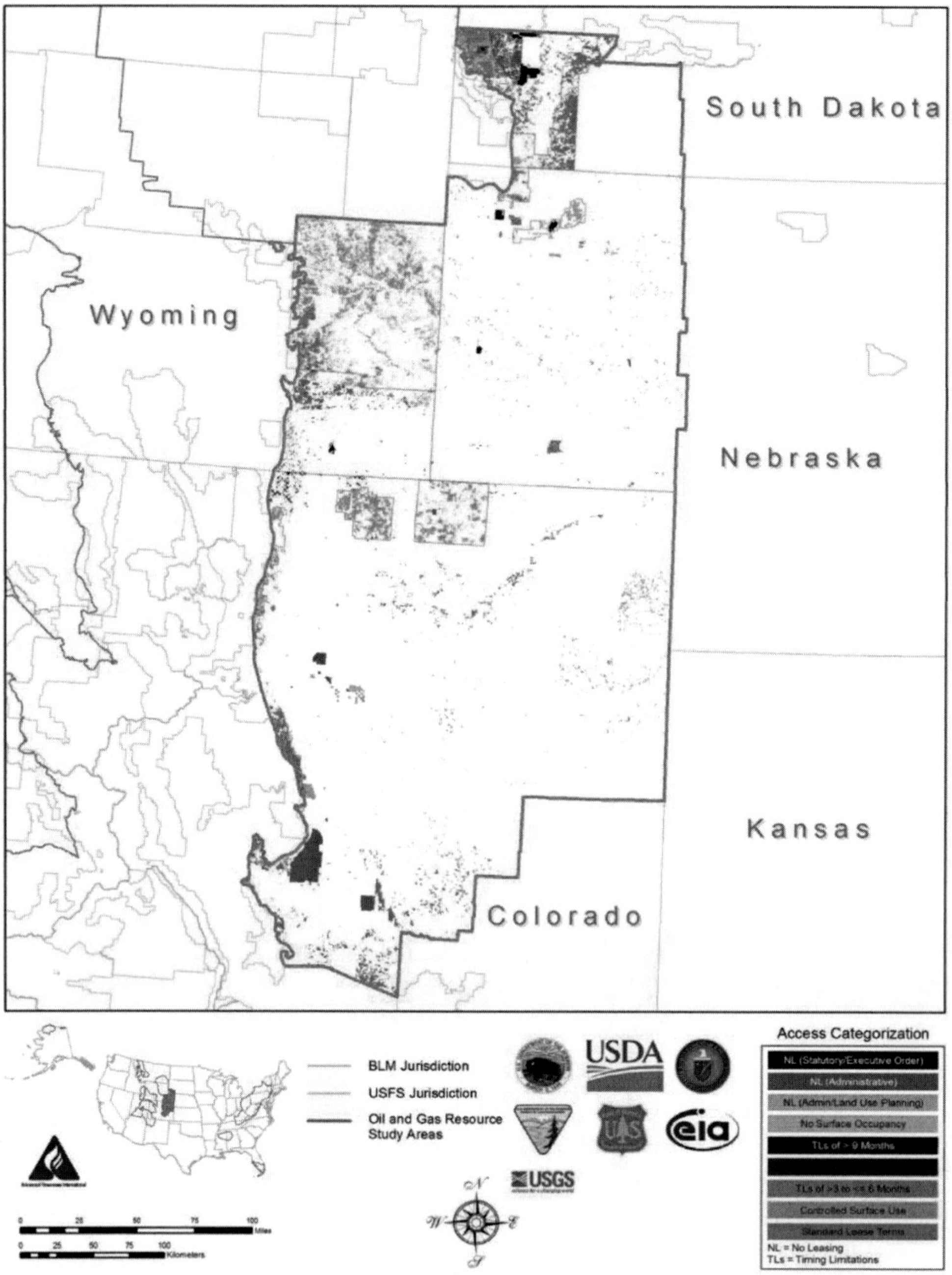

Figure 3-40. Federal Land Access Categorization Map, Denver Basin Study Area

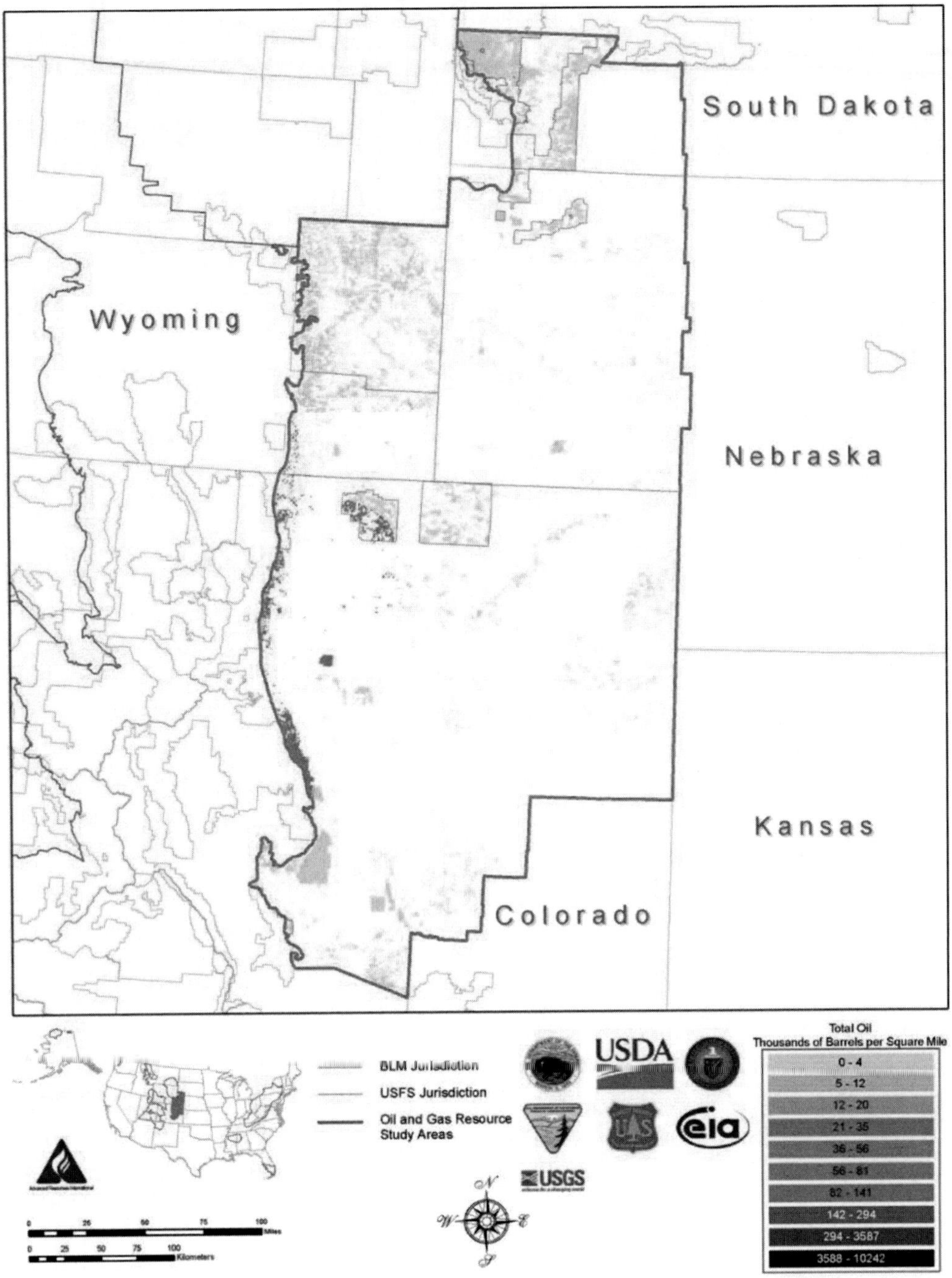

Figure 3-41. Map of Total Federal Oil, Denver Basin Study Area

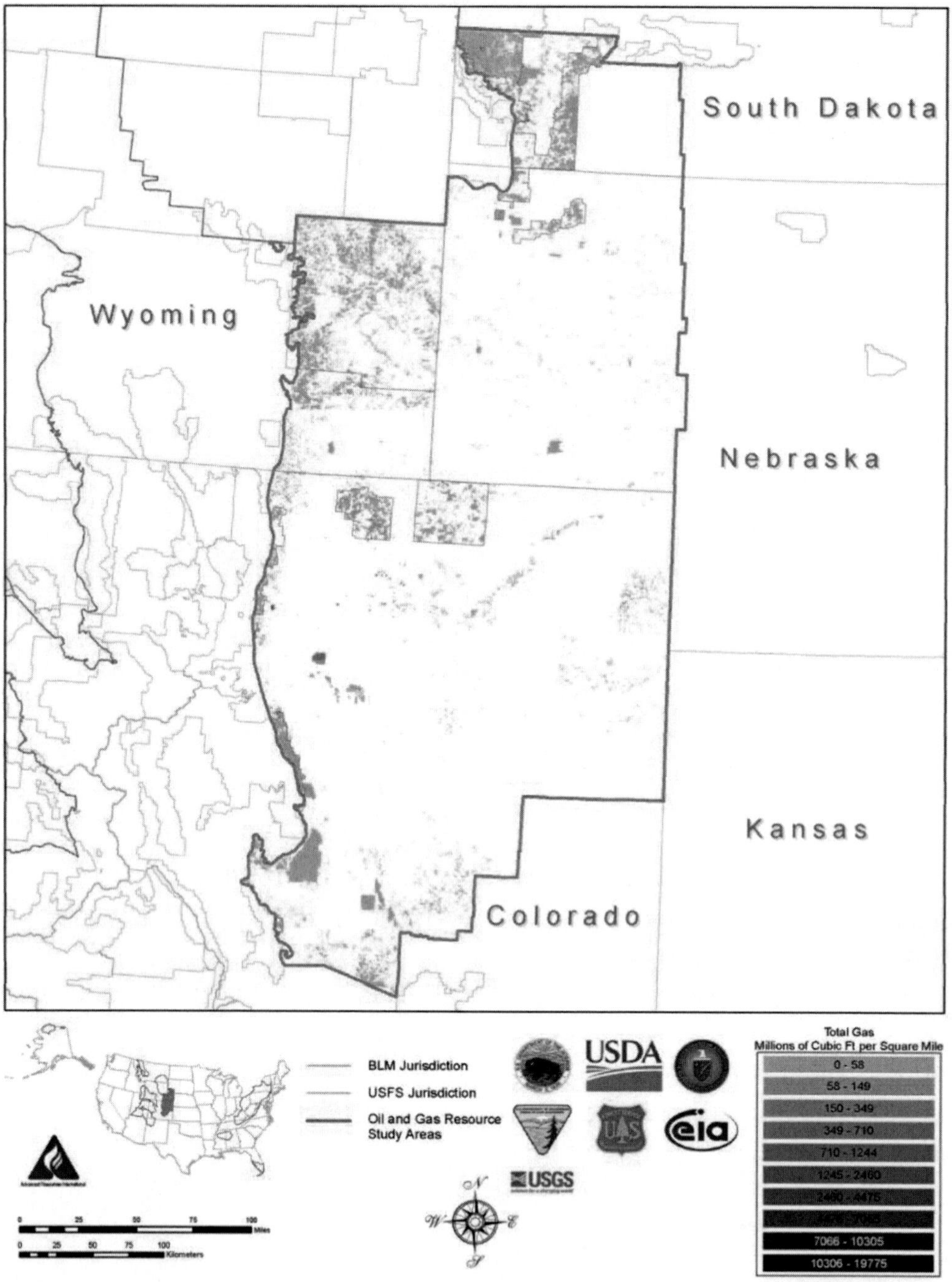

Figure 3-42. Map of Total Federal Natural Gas, Denver Basin Study Area

3.1.9 Florida Peninsula

- None of the Federal land in the study area is accessible under standard lease terms (Figures 3-43 and 3-44, Category 9).
- Approximately 6 percent (0.1 million acres) of the Federal land is accessible with restrictions on oil and gas operations beyond standard lease terms (Figures 3-43 and 3-44, Categories 5 through 8). Based on resource estimates, these lands contain 14 percent (11 MMbbls) of the Federal oil and 15 percent (0.05 TCF) of the Federal natural gas.
- Approximately 94 percent (1.88 million acres) of the Federal land is not accessible (Figures 3-43 and 3-44, Categories 1 through 4). Based on resource estimates, these lands contain about 86 percent (64 MMbbls) of the Federal oil and 85 percent (0.28 TCF) of the Federal natural gas.
- The Department of the Interior has agreed in principle to acquire the mineral rights under Big Cypress National Preserve, Florida Panther National Wildlife Refuge, and Ten Thousand Islands National Wildlife Refuge from Collier Resources Company, virtually ensuring no new oil and gas development in the three areas.[36]

Table 3-10. Florida Peninsula Study Area—Federal Land and Oil and Natural Gas Resources by Access Category

		Area		**Resources[a]**			
				Total Oil[b]		**Total Gas[c]**	
		(acres x 1000)	**Percent of Federal**	**(MMbbls)[d]**	**Percent of Federal**	**(BCF)[e]**	**Percent of Federal**
1.	No Leasing (Statutory/Executive Order) (NLS)	4	0.2%	0	0.1%	0	0.0%
2.	No Leasing (Administrative) (NLA)	4	0.2%	0	0.1%	0	0.1%
3.	No Leasing (Administrative) Pending Land Use Planning or NEPA Compliance (NLA/LUP)	1,376	69.0%	50	67.3%	217	66.8%
4.	Leasing, No Surface Occupancy (NSO) (Net NSO for O&G Resources)	497	24.9%	13	18.0%	60	18.5%
5.	Leasing, Cumulative Timing Limitations (TLs) of >9 Months	-	0.0%	-	0.0%	-	0.0%
6.	Leasing, Cumulative Timing Limitations (TLs) of >6 to <9 Months	112	5.6%	11	14.3%	47	14.5%
7.	Leasing, Cumulative Timing Limitations (TLs) of >3 to <6 Months	-	0.0%	-	0.0%	-	0.0%
8.	Leasing, Controlled Surface Use (CSU)[f]	0	0.0%	0	0.0%	0	0.0%
9.	Leasing, Standard Lease Terms (SLTs)	-	0.0%	-	0.0%	-	0.0%
Total, Federal Lands including Split Estate		**1,994**	**100.0%**	**74**	**100.0%**	**325**	**100.0%**
Total Non-Federal		**11,026**		**352**		**1,332**	
Total Inventory Area		**13,020**		**426**		**1,657**	
Summary							

Inaccessible (Categories 1-4)	1,881	94%	64	86%	278	85%
Accessible with Restrictions (Categories 5-8)	113	6%	11	14%	47	15%
Accessible under Standard Lease Terms (Category 9)	-	0%	-	0%	-	0%
Total, Federal Lands Including Split Estate	**1,994**	**100%**	**74**	**100%**	**325**	**100%**

Small rounding errors may be present.

a Undiscovered technically recoverable resources and reserves growth

b Including oil, natural gas liquids (NGLs) and liquids associated with natural gas reservoirs

c Including associated dissolved and nonassociated natural gas

d Million barrels e Billion cubic feet f Includes Cumulative Timing Limitations of <3 months

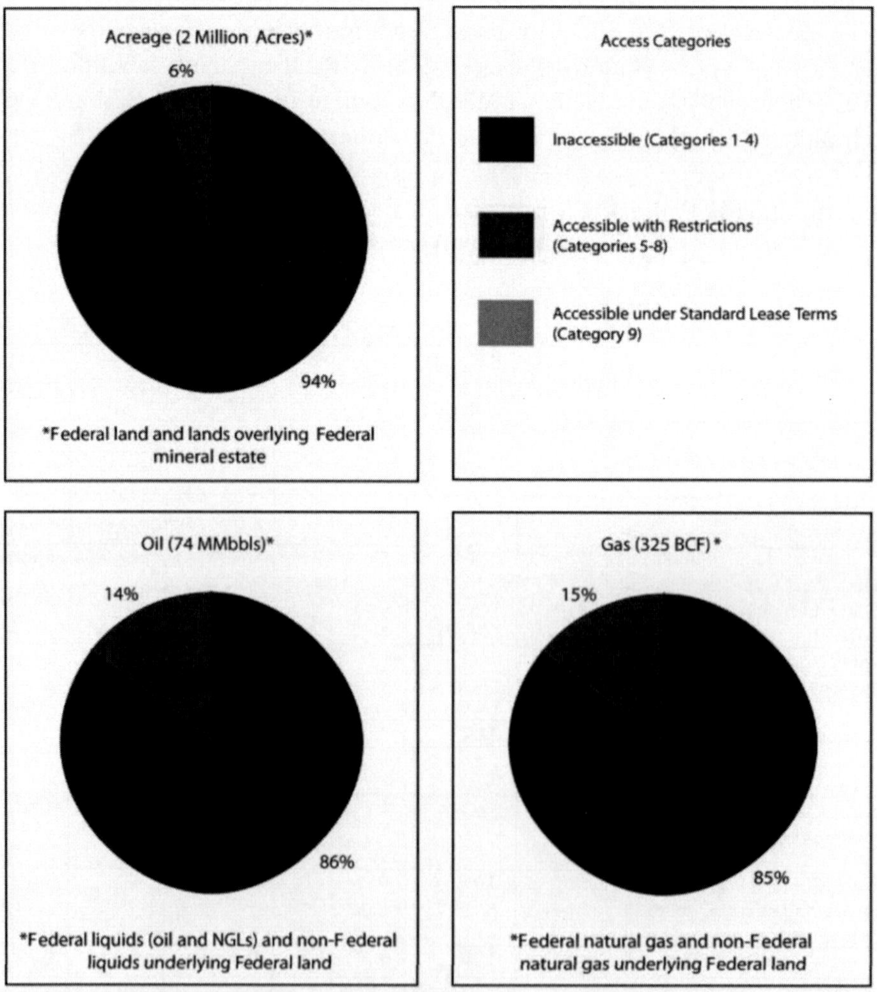

Figure 3-43. Simplified Chart of Results, Florida Peninsula Study Area—Federal Land and Oil and Natural Gas Resources by Accessibility

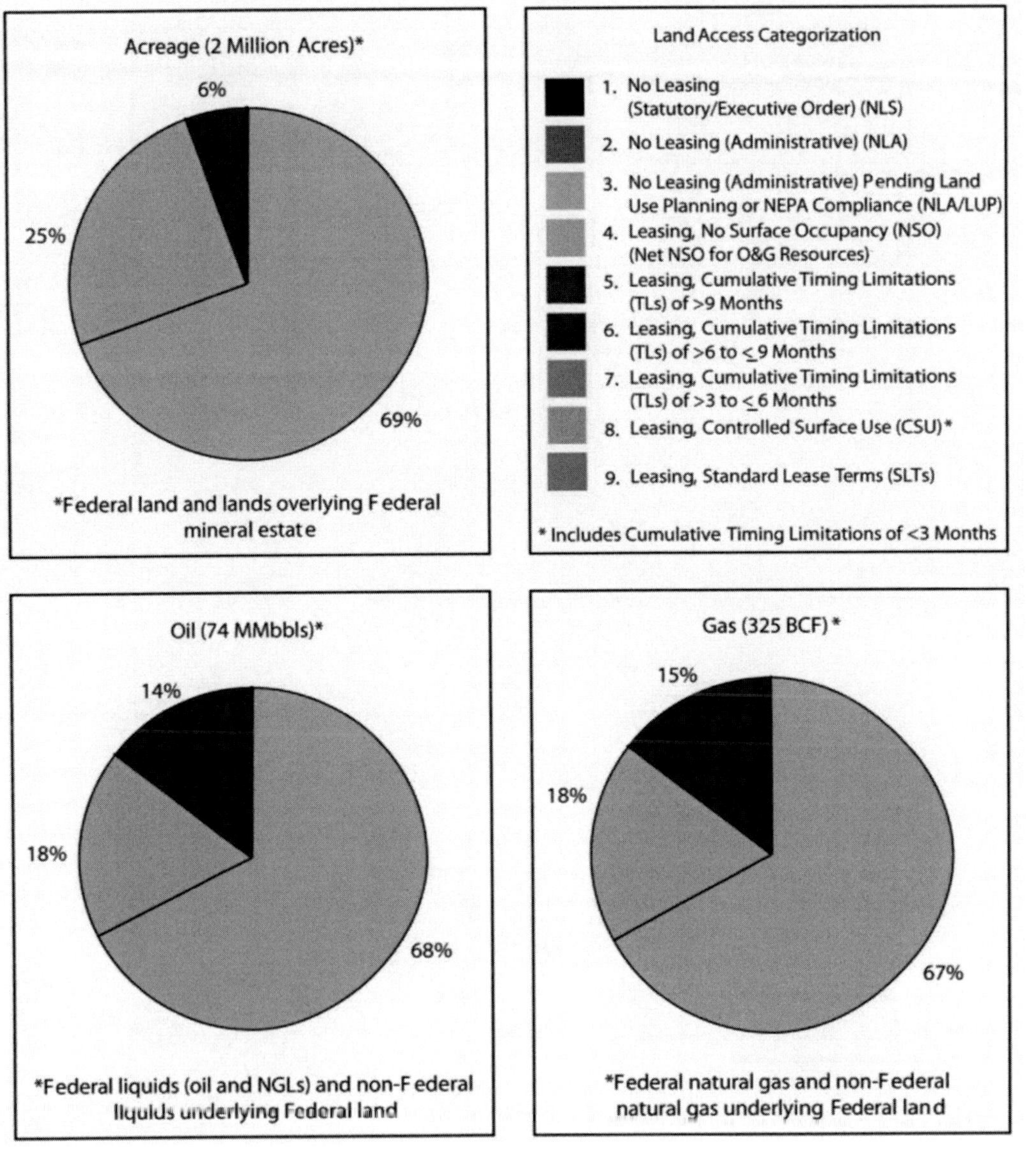

Figure 3-44. Chart of Results, Florida Peninsula Study Area—Federal Land and Oil and Natural Gas Resources by Access Category

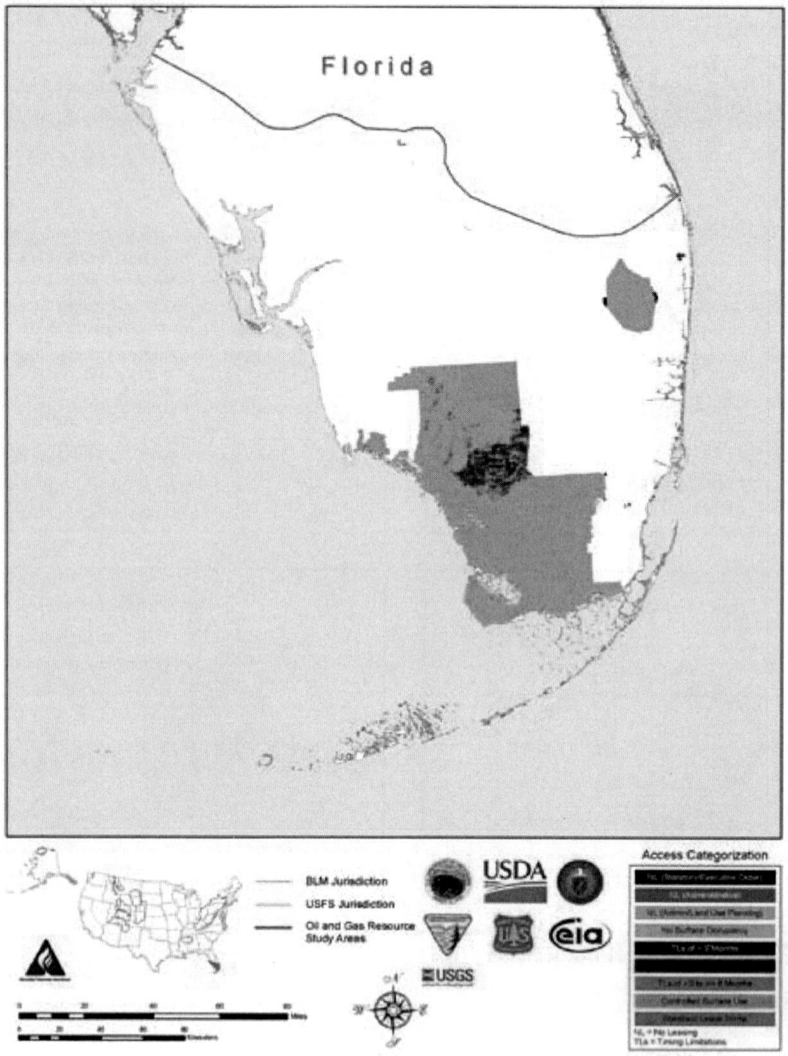

Figure 3-45. Federal Land Access Categorization Map, Florida Peninsula Study Area

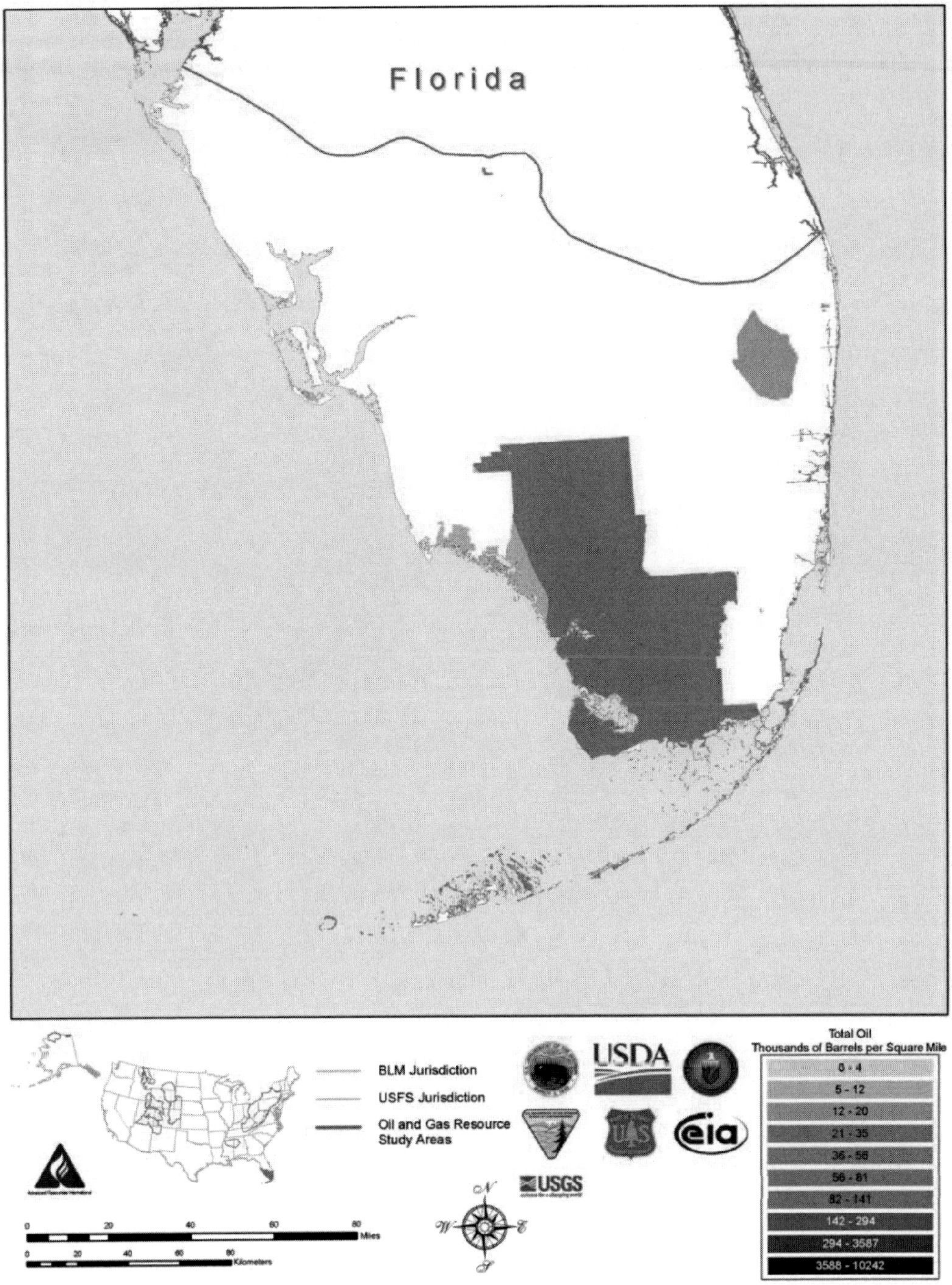

Figure 3-46. Map of Total Federal Oil, Florida Peninsula Study Area

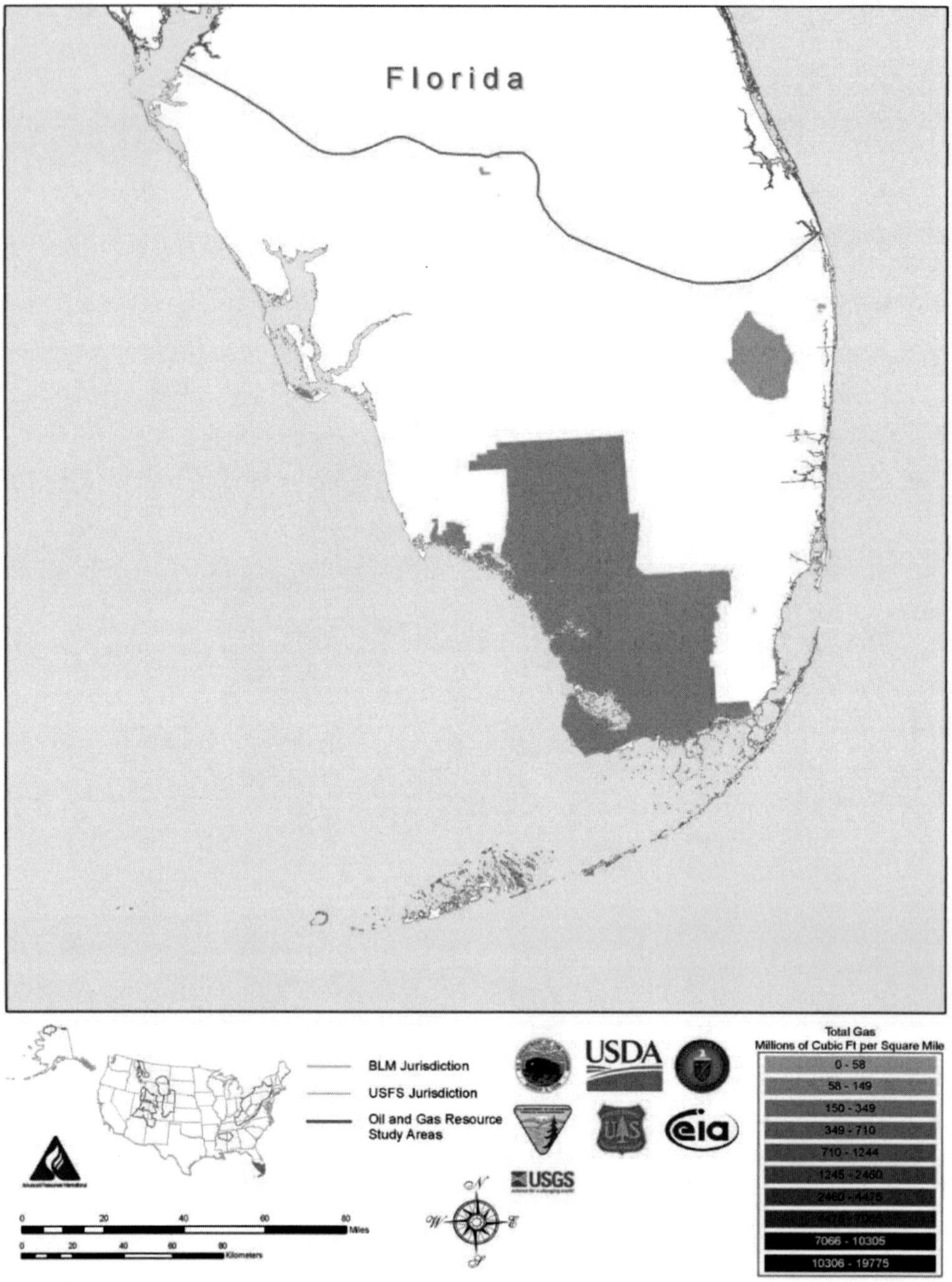

Figure 3-47. Map of Total Federal Natural Gas, Florida Peninsula Study Area

3.1.10 Black Warrior Basin

- The Federal lands in this study area contain only about 1 MMbbls of oil out of a total of 13 MMbbls for all lands.
- Approximately 3 percent (0.02 million acres) of the Federal land is accessible under standard lease terms (Figures 3-48 and 3-49, Category 9). Based on resource estimates, these lands contain 11 percent of the Federal oil (0.08 MMBbls) and 18 percent (0.07 TCF) of the Federal natural gas.
- Approximately 15 percent (0.10 million acres) of the Federal land is accessible with restrictions on oil and gas operations beyond standard lease terms (Figures 3-48 and 3-49, Categories 5 through 8). Based on resource estimates, these lands contain 32 percent of the Federal oil (0.24 MMBbls) and 35 percent (0.14 TCF) of the Federal natural gas.
- Approximately 82 percent (0.57 million acres) of the Federal land is not accessible (Figures 3-48 and 3-49, Categories 1 through 4). Based on resource estimates, these lands contain 57 percent of the Federal oil (0.43 MMBbls) and 47 percent (0.19 TCF) of the Federal natural gas.

Table 3-11. Black Warrior Basin Study Area—Federal Land and Oil and Natural Gas Resources by Access Category

		Area		Resourcesa			
				Total Oilb		Total Gasc	
		(acres x 1000)	Percent of Federal	(MMbbls)d	Percent of Federal	(BCF)e	Percent of Federal
1.	No Leasing (Statutory/Executive Order) (NLS)	1	0.2%	0	0.1%	0	0.0%
2.	No Leasing (Administrative) (NLA)	-	0.0%	-	0.0%	-	0.0%
3.	No Leasing (Administrative) Pending Land Use Planning or NEPA Compliance (NLA/LUP)	361	52.0%	0	45.8%	168	41.3%
4.	Leasing, No Surface Occupancy (NSO) (Net NSO for O&G Resources)	208	30.0%	0	11.4%	24	6.0%
5.	Leasing, Cumulative Timing Limitations (TLs) of >9 Months	-	0.0%	-	0.0%	-	0.0%
6.	Leasing, Cumulative Timing Limitations (TLs) of >6 to <9 Months	-	0.0%	-	0.0%	-	0.0%
7.	Leasing, Cumulative Timing Limitations (TLs) of >3 to <6 Months	-	0.0%	-	0.0%	-	0.0%
8.	Leasing, Controlled Surface Use (CSU)f	101	14.6%	0	31.9%	141	34.7%

Table 3-11. (Continued)

9. Leasing, Standard Lease Terms (SLTs)	23	3.3%	0	10.7%	73	17.9%
Total, Federal Lands including Split Estate	**694**	**100.0%**	**1**	**100.0%**	**406**	**100.0%**
Total Non-Federal	**10,853**		**13**		**9,484**	
Total Inventory Area	**11,547**		**13**		**9,890**	
Summary						
Inaccessible (Categories 1-4)	570	82%	0	57%	192	47%
Accessible with Restrictions (Categories 5-8)	101	15%	0	32%	141	35%
Accessible under Standard Lease Terms (Category 9)	23	3%	0	11%	73	18%
Total, Federal Lands Including Split Estate	**694**	**100%**	**1**	**100%**	**406**	**100%**

Small rounding errors may be present.

a Undiscovered technically recoverable resources and reserves growth
b Including oil, natural gas liquids (NGLs) and liquids associated with natural gas reservoirs
c Including associated dissolved and nonassociated natural gas
d Million barrels e Billion cubic feet f Includes Cumulative Timing Limitations of <3 months

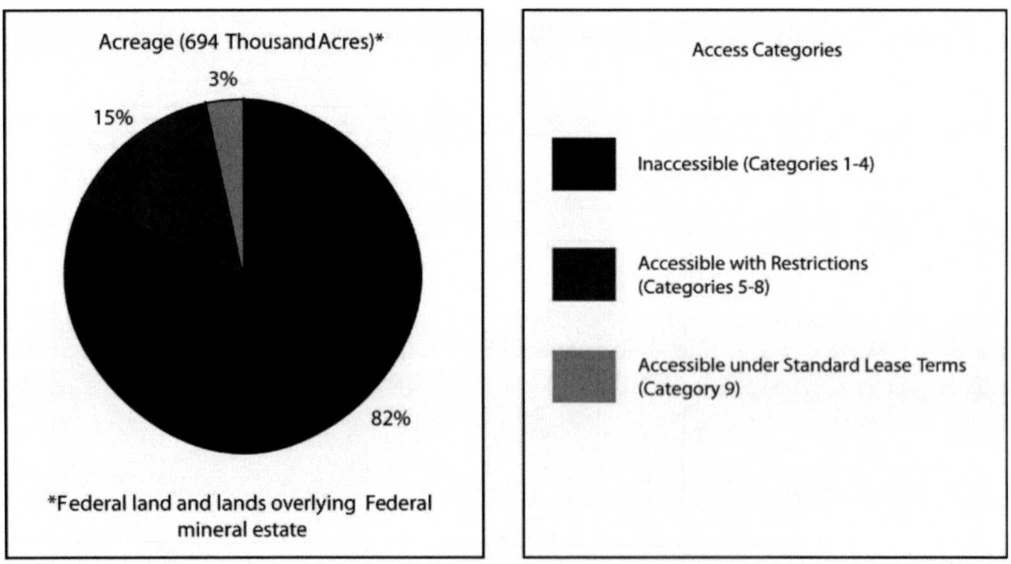

Figure 3-48. (Continued)

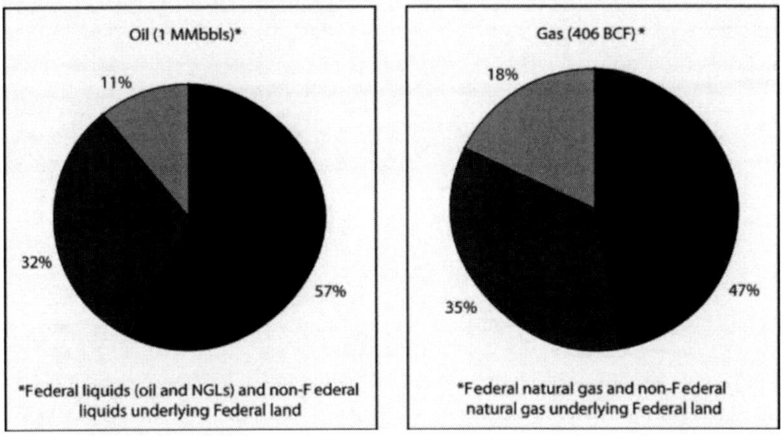

Figure 3-48. Simplified Chart of Results, Black Warrior Basin Study Area—Federal Land and Oil and Natural Gas Resources by Accessibility

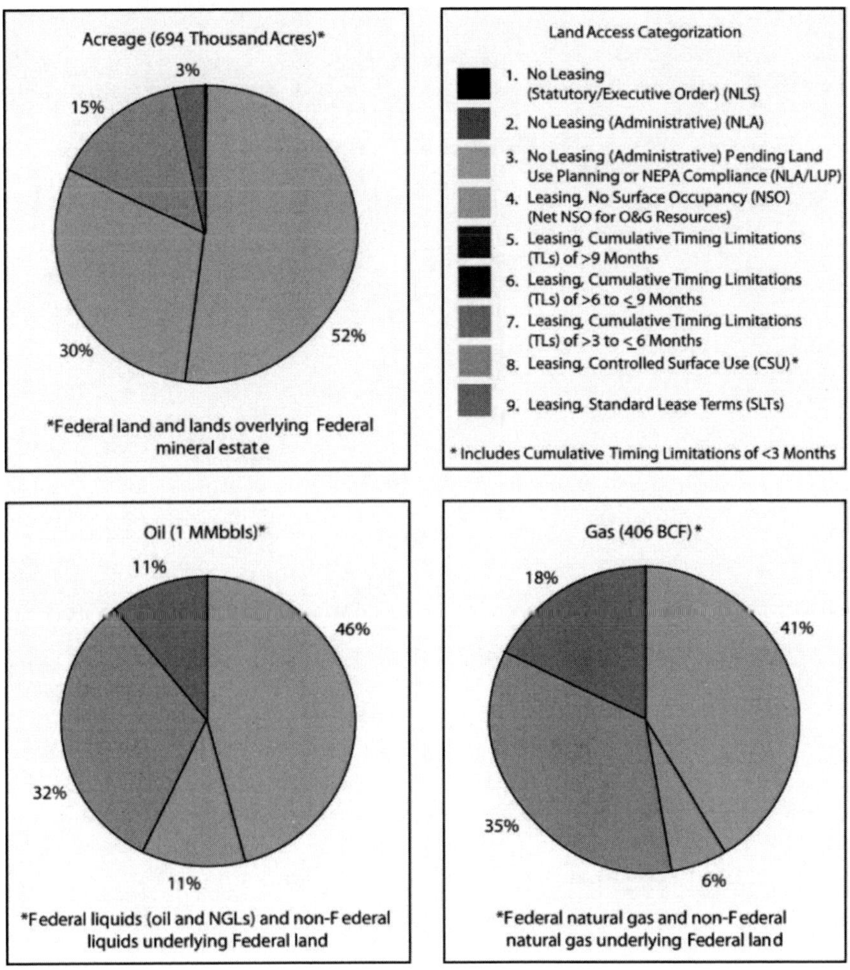

Figure 3-49. Chart of Results, Black Warrior Basin Study Area—Federal Land and Oil and Natural Gas Resources by Access Category

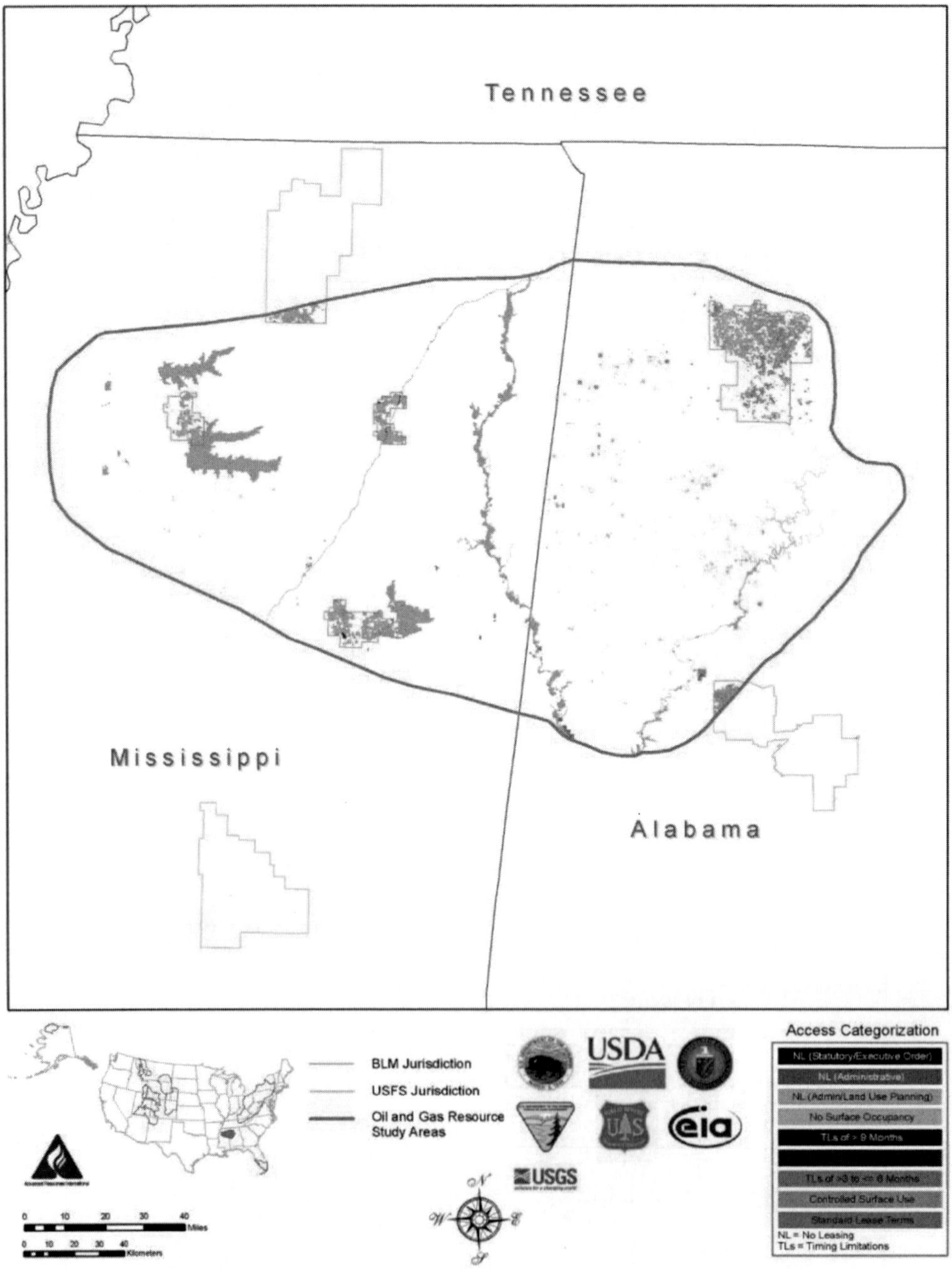

Figure 3-50. Federal Land Access Categorization Map, Black Warrior Basin Study Area

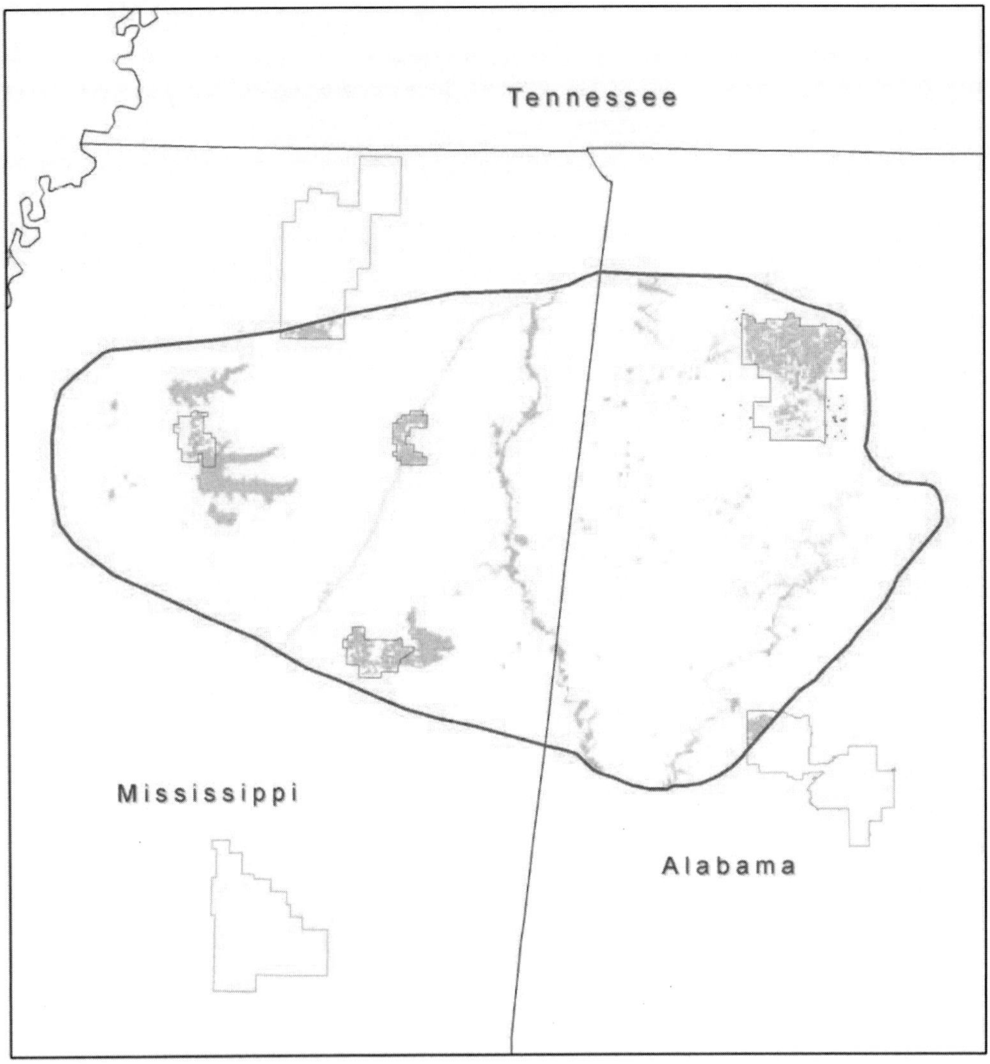

Figure 3-51. Map of Total Federal Oil, Black Warrior Basin Study Area

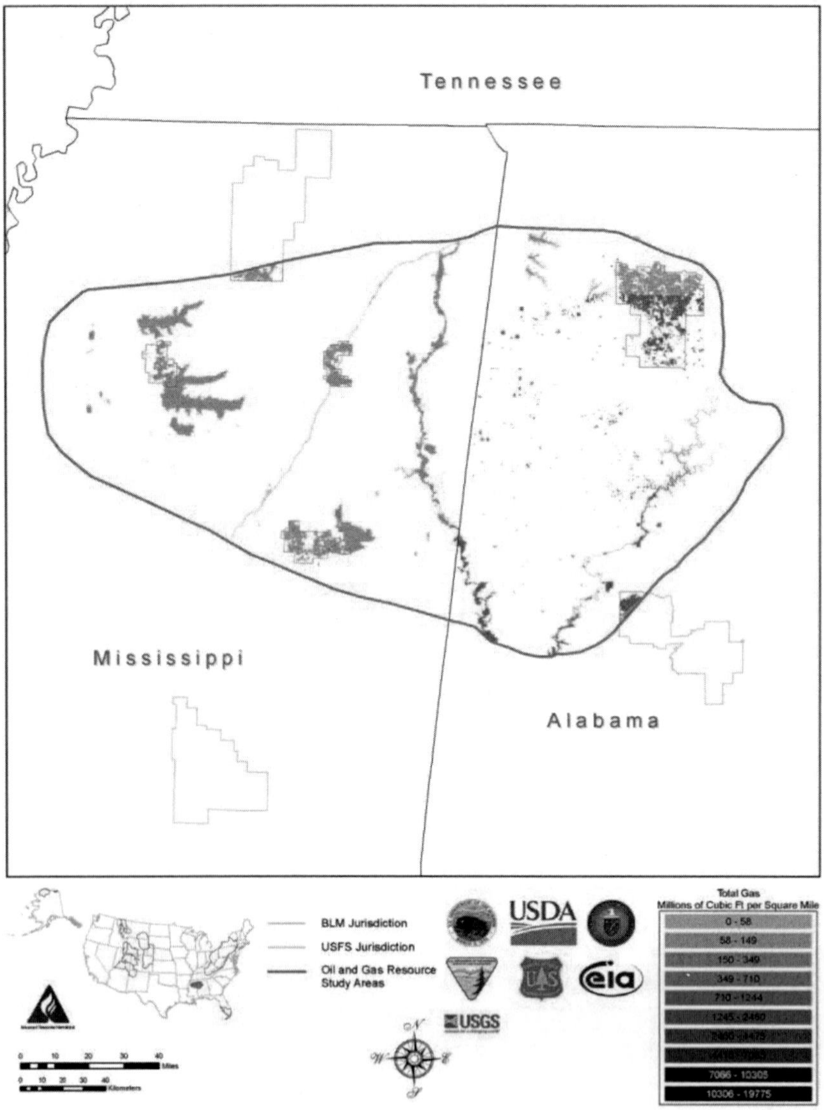

Figure 3-52. Map of Total Federal Natural Gas, Black Warrior Basin Study Area

3.1.11 Appalachian Basin

- Approximately 16 percent (0.9 million acres) of the Federal land is accessible under standard lease terms (Figures 3-53 and 3-54, Category 9). Based on resource estimates, these lands contain 15 percent (5 MMbbls) of the Federal oil and 17 percent (0.4 TCF) of the Federal natural gas.
- Approximately 39 percent (2.1 million acres) of the Federal land is accessible with restrictions on oil and gas operations beyond standard lease terms (Figures 3-53 and 3-54, Categories 5 through 8). Based on resource estimates, these lands contain 43

percent (14 MMbbls) of the Federal oil and 41 percent (1 TCF) of the Federal natural gas.

- Approximately 45 percent (2.4 million acres) of the Federal land is not accessible (Figures 3-53 and 3-54, Categories 1 through 4). Based on resource estimates, these lands contain about 41 percent (14 MMbbls) of the Federal oil and 42 percent (1.01 TCF) of the Federal natural gas.
- Most of the undiscovered gas resource (94 percent) is expected to occur in continuous deposits.
- Coalbed natural gas accounts for about 13 percent of the total undiscovered continuous gas.

Table 3-12. Appalachian Basin Study Area—Federal Land and Oil and Natural Gas Resources by Access Category

		Area		Resourcesa			
				Total Oilb		Total Gasc	
		(acres x 1000)	Percent of Federal	(MMbbls)d	Percent of Federal	(BCF)e	Percent of Federal
1.	No Leasing (Statutory/Executive Order) (NLS)	107	2.0%	0	1.2%	26	1.1%
2.	No Leasing (Administrative) (NLA)	119	2.2%	1	3.2%	99	4.1%
3.	No Leasing (Administrative) Pending Land Use Planning or NEPA Compliance (NLA/LUP)	1,477	27.4%	10	30.3%	731	30.5%
4.	Leasing, No Surface Occupancy (NSO) (Net NSO for O&G Resources)	729	13.5%	2	6.5%	151	6.3%
5.	Leasing, Cumulative Timing Limitations (TLs) of >9 Months	-	0.0%	-	0.0%	-	0.0%
6.	Leasing, Cumulative Timing Limitations (TLs) of >6 to <9 Months	96	1.8%	0	0.5%	10	0.4%
7.	Leasing, Cumulative Timing Limitations (TLs) of >3 to <6 Months	335	6.2%	0	0.5%	20	0.8%
8.	Leasing, Controlled Surface Use (CSU)f	1,651	30.6%	14	42.4%	956	39.9%
9.	Leasing, Standard Lease Terms (SLTs)	884	16.4%	5	15.4%	402	16.8%
Total, Federal Lands including Split Estate		**5,398**	**100.0%**	**33**	**100.0%**	**2,396**	**100.0%**
Total Non-Federal		**93,158**		**859**		**65,392**	
Total Inventory Area		**98,556**		**892**		**67,788**	
Summary							
Inaccessible (Categories 1-4)		2,432	45%	14	41%	1,007	42%

Table 3-12. (Continued)

Accessible with Restrictions (Categories 5-8)	2,082	39%	14	43%	987	41%
Accessible under Standard Lease Terms (Category 9)	884	16%	5	15%	402	17%
Total, Federal Lands Including Split Estate	**5,398**	**100%**	**33**	**100%**	**2,396**	**100%**

Small rounding errors may be present.

a Undiscovered technically recoverable resources and reserves growth
b Including oil, natural gas liquids (NGLs) and liquids associated with natural gas reservoirs
c Including associated dissolved and nonassociated natural gas
d Million barrels e Billion cubic feet f Includes Cumulative Timing Limitations of <3 months

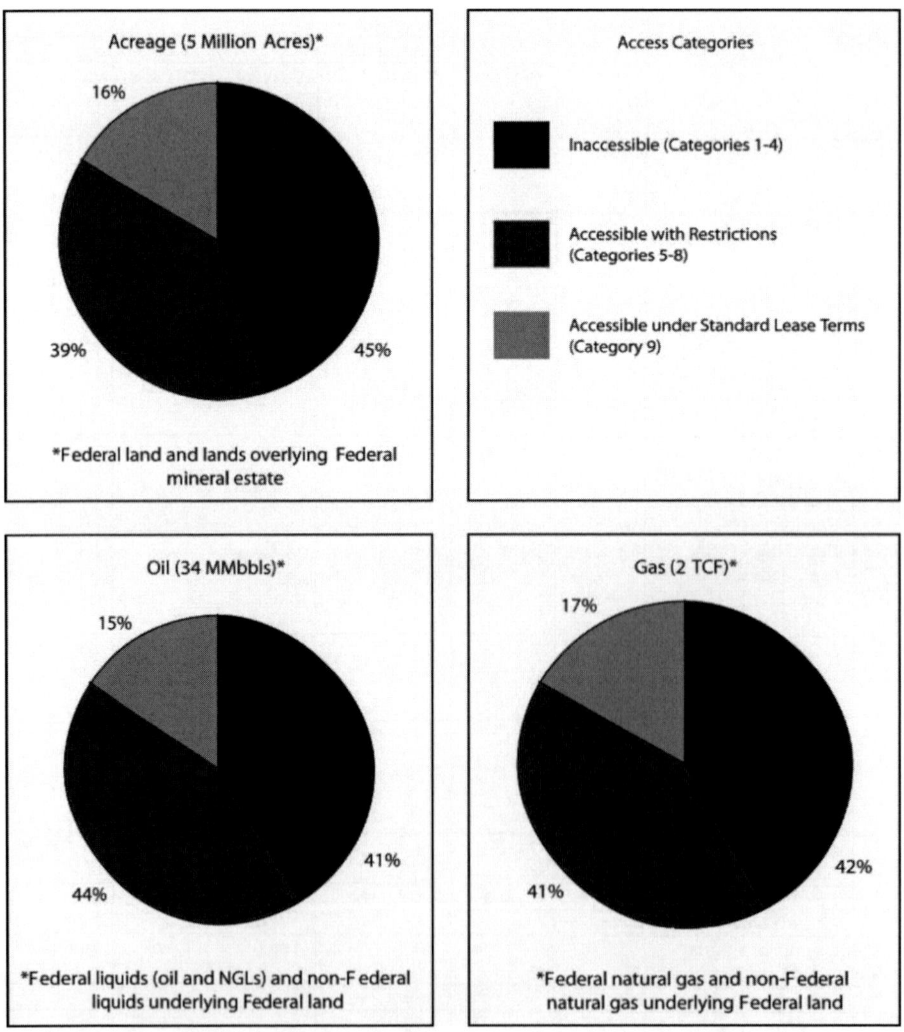

Figure 3-53. Simplified Chart of Results, Appalachian Basin Study Area—Federal Land and Oil and Natural Gas Resources by Accessibility

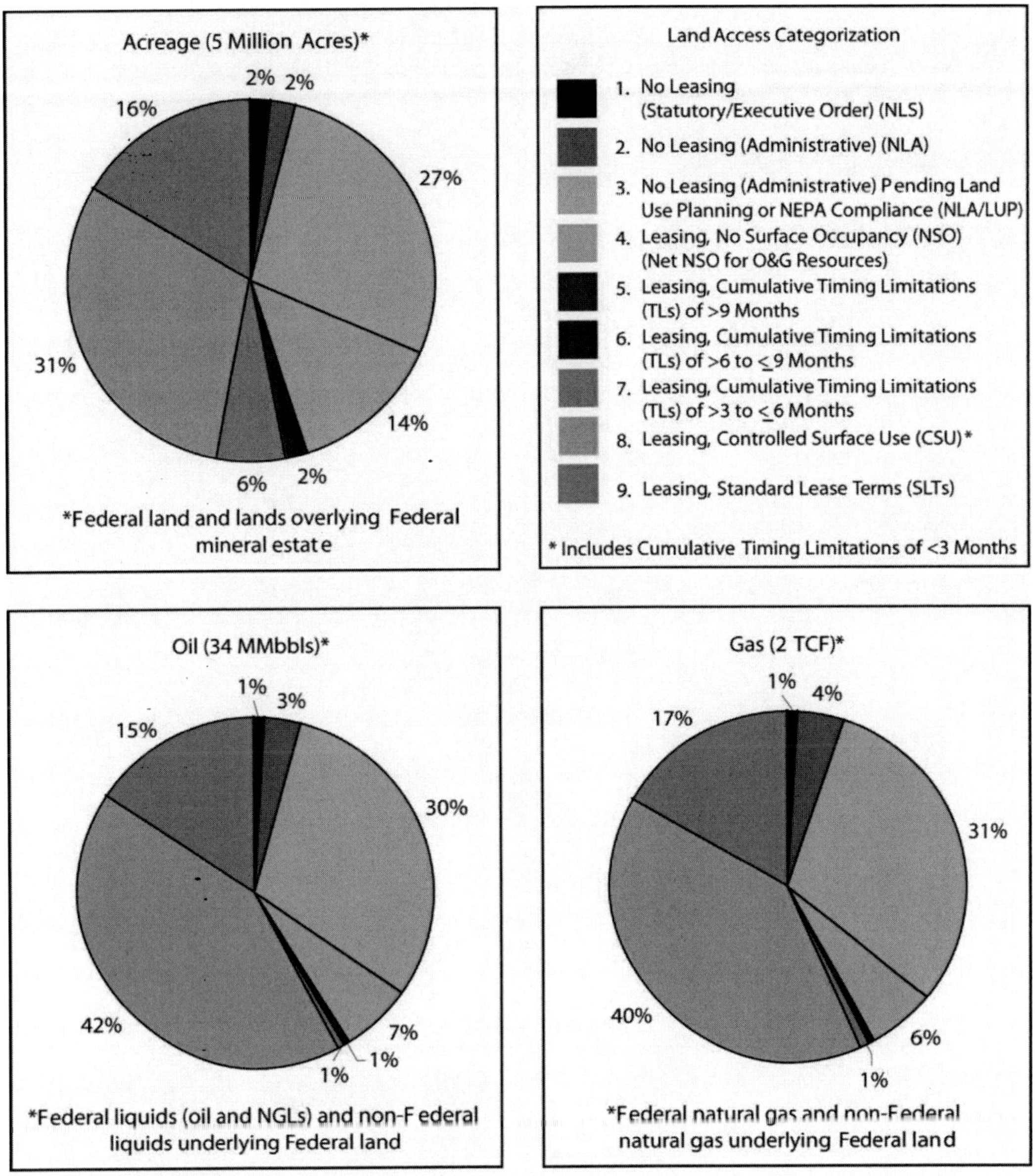

Figure 3-54. **Chart of Results, Appalachian Basin Study Area—Federal Land and** Oil and Natural Gas Resources by Access Category

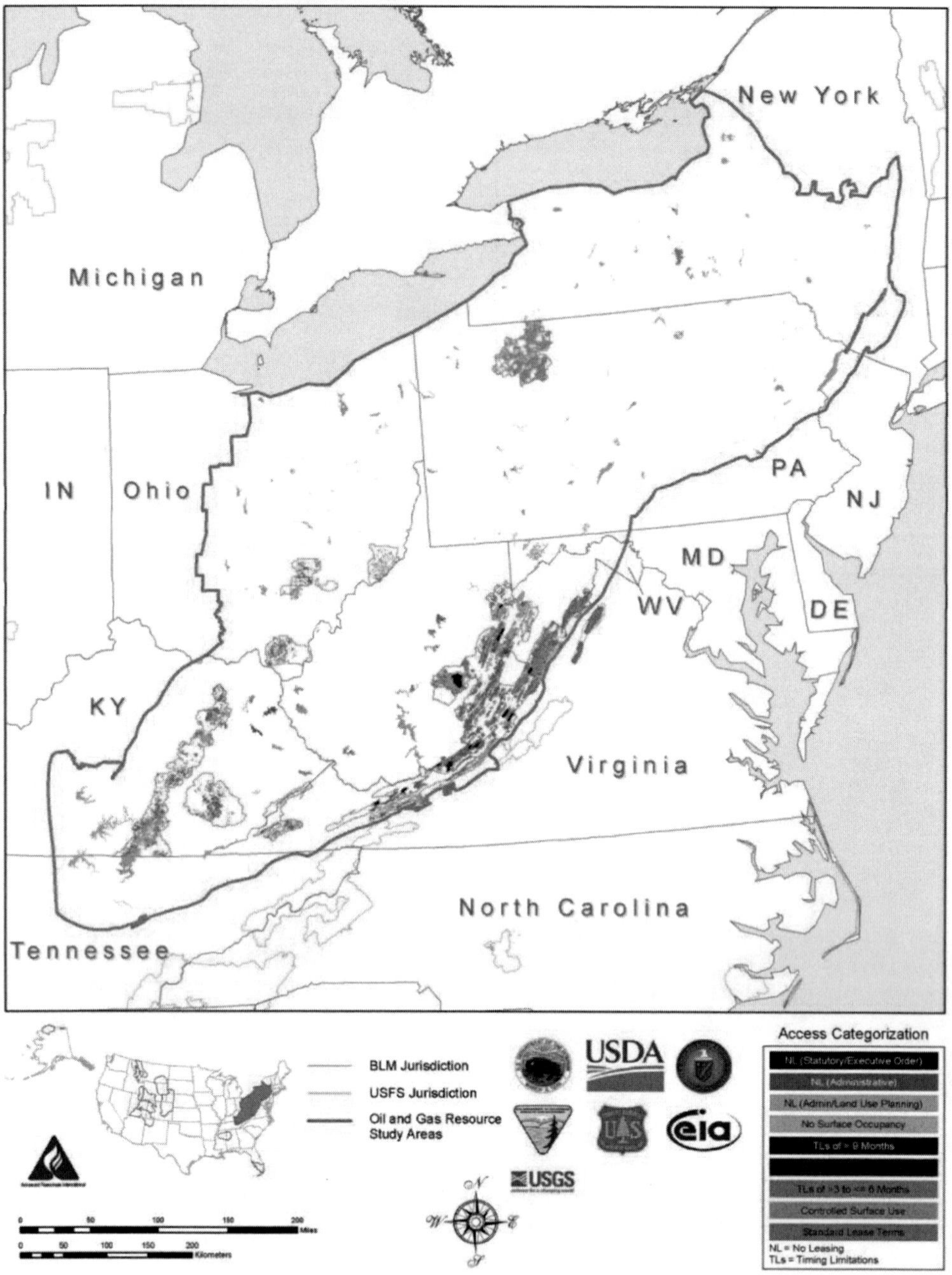

Figure 3-55. Federal Land Access Categorization Map, Appalachian Basin Study Area

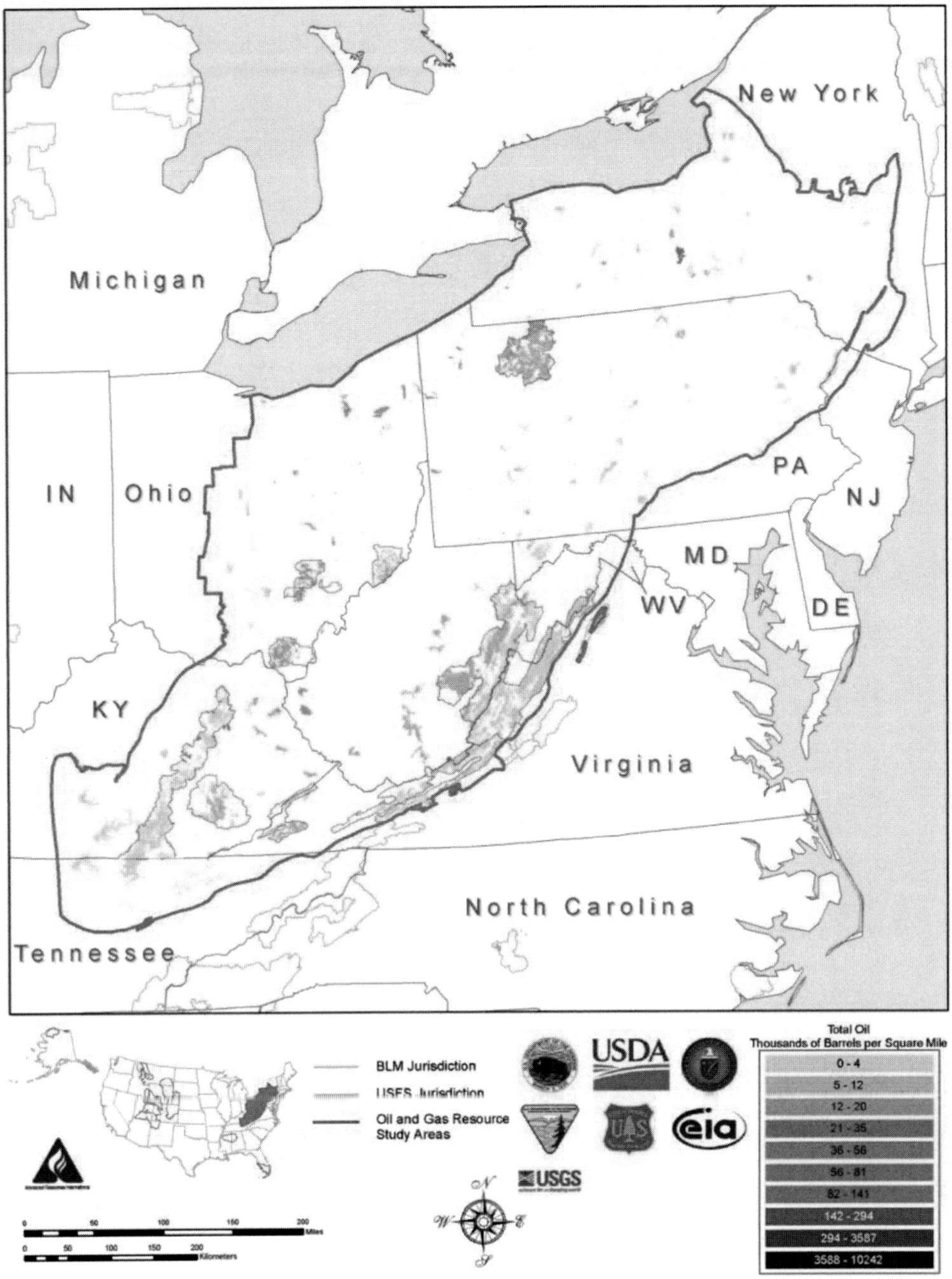

Figure 3-56. Map of Total Federal Oil, Appalachian Basin Study Area

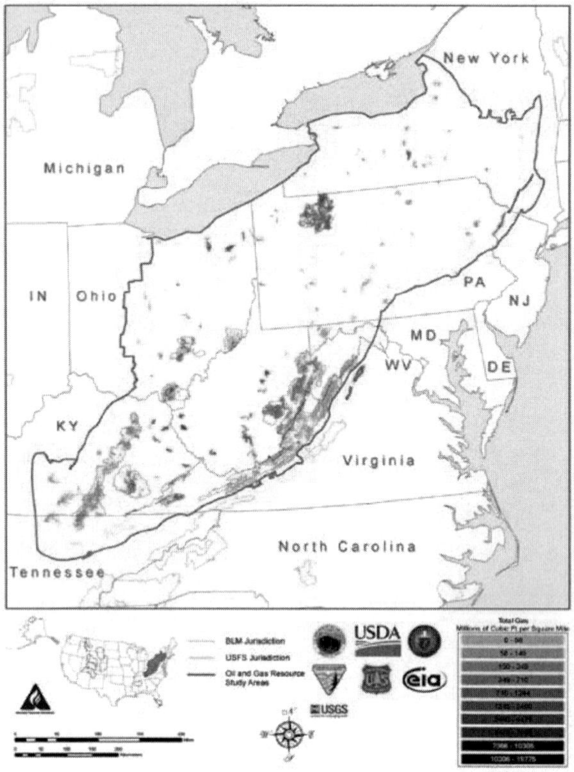

Figure 3-57. Map of Total Federal Natural Gas, Appalachian Basin Study Area

3.2 Regional Features

Figure 3-58 shows a comparison of the access charts for the top five basins in the following categories: total Federal land, total Federal oil, and total Federal natural gas. The pie charts are scaled proportionately to one another. Northern Alaska dominates both the land and the resource categories, followed by the Rocky Mountain basins.

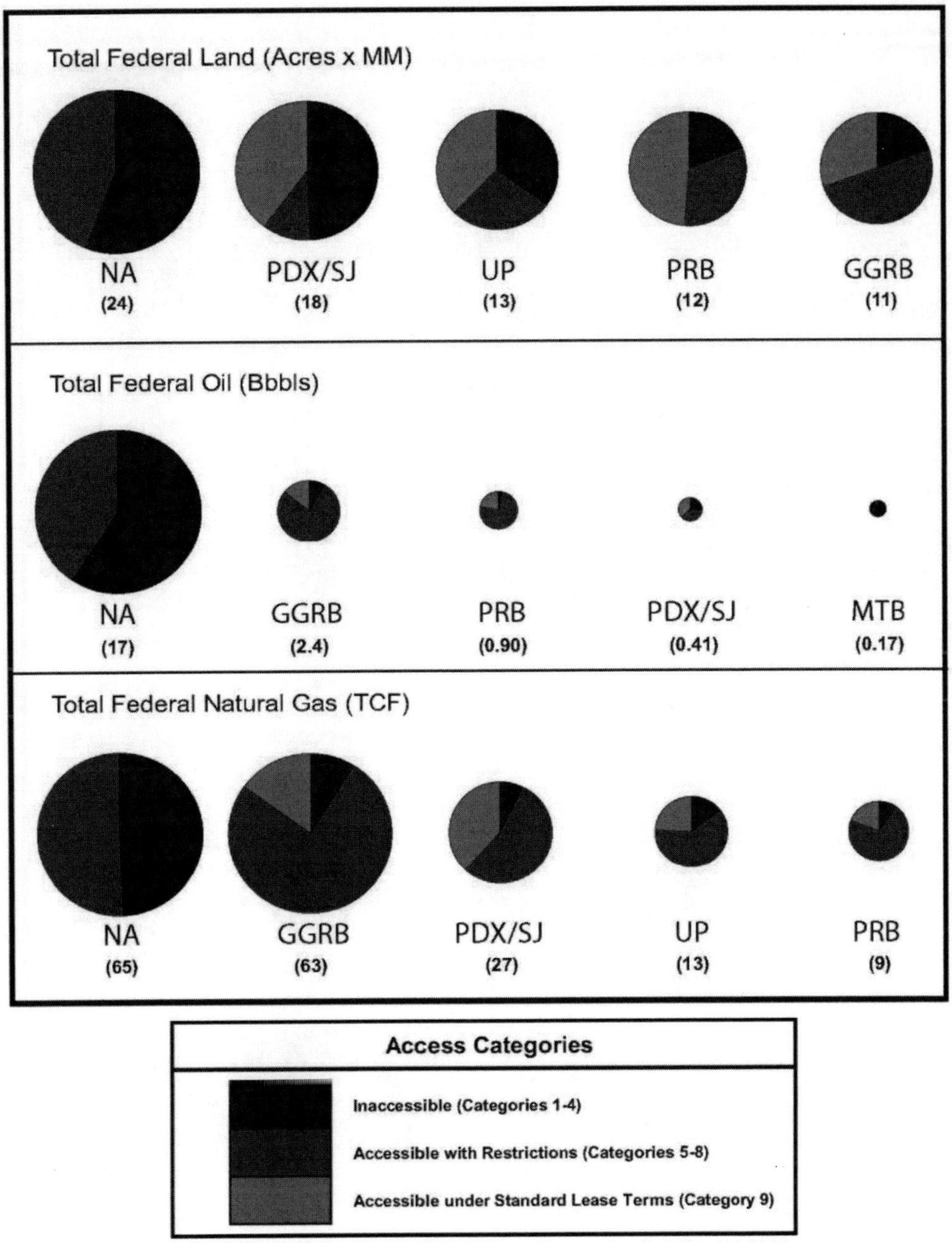

Figure 3-58. Charts of the Top Five Areas

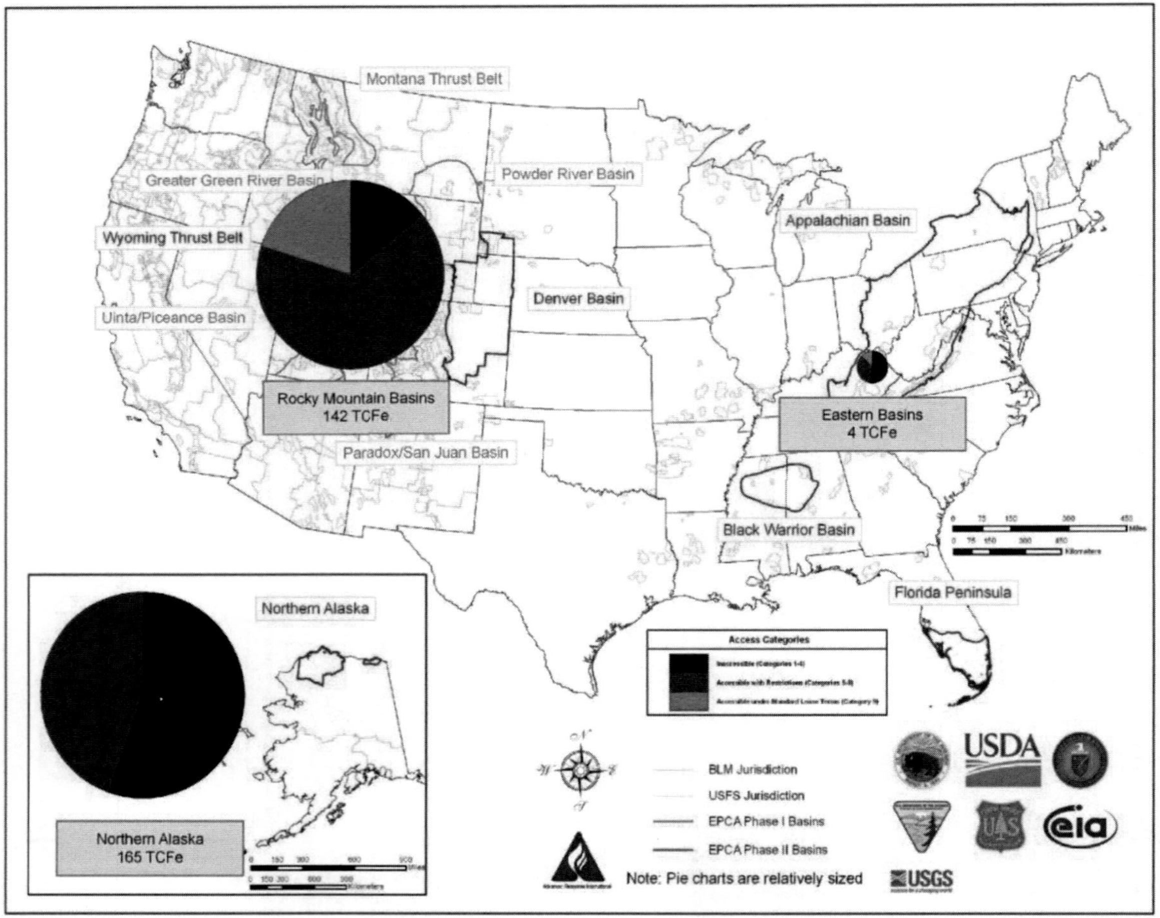

Figure 3-59. Regional Charts

Figure 3-59 is a map showing the Phase II study areas with the access category charts compiled by region, relatively sized, by total resources.[37] The largest amount of oil and gas resources are found in Northern Alaska (165 TCFe), followed closely by the Rocky Mountain region (142 TCFe), with the Eastern basins a distant third in rank (4 TCFe).

None of the resources in the two Northern Alaska study areas are accessible under standard lease terms, 45% are accessible with additional restrictions (in NPRA only, due primarily to drilling being restricted to the winter), and 55% are inaccessible.

About 20% of the resources in the seven Rocky Mountain study areas are accessible under standard lease terms, 66% are accessible with additional restrictions (primarily because of timing limitations and the impact of conditions of approval), and 14% are inaccessible.

About 13% of the resources in the three Eastern study areas are accessible under standard lease terms, 35% are accessible with additional restrictions, and 52% are inaccessible.

4. Additional Federal Land Access Issues

Additional statutory and discretionary requirements beyond lease stipulations impact Federal land access for oil and gas development. Many of these impacts were not quantified because GIS data do not exist, or they are issues that are not amenable to quantitative analysis. Many of these requirements can be considered restrictions on drilling because they have effects similar to stipulations on oil and gas development activities.

These issues can directly or indirectly impact Federal land accessibility for oil and gas development. Tables 4-1 through 4-11 present office-specific issues that were recorded from discussions with BLM and USDA-FS staff during field visits. Average APD processing time was calculated for each office using input from the offices supplemented by an analysis of BLM's Automated Fluid Minerals Support System (AFMSS).[38]

4.1 Issues Directly Impacting Access

The National Environmental Policy Act of 1969. NEPA is the nation's central environmental statute. It requires Federal agencies to consider environmental impacts before an action is taken. The NEPA process is intended to help public officials make better decisions based on an understanding of their environmental consequences.

NEPA is embedded into the fabric of Federal land management decision-making and has become the most important procedural public land management statute because it requires agencies to comply with its processes in all situations where major actions are contemplated. When an activity or action is proposed on Federal lands, an interdisciplinary review of the environmental effects of the proposal is conducted and made available to citizens and public officials. The review can take one of four forms:

- a categorical exclusion (CX)
- documentation of NEPA adequacy (DNA)
- an environmental assessment (EA)
- an environmental impact statement (EIS).

Table 4-1. Access Issues, Northern Alaska Study Area

Jurisdiction	Issue or Characteristic Noted by Office											
	Average APD Processing*	**NEPA Documents**	**Endangered Species Act and Species Generally of Concern**	**Roadless Areas**	**Tribal Consultation**	**National Historic Preservation Act**	**O&G vs Coal and other Mineral Development**	**Visual Resources**	**Air Quality**	**Clean Water**	**Infrastructure Concerns**	**Others**
Fairbanks, AK BLM (Northern Field Office)	No EA: 60 days, with EA: 30 days	NE NPRA Final Integrated Activity Plan/ EIS. NW NPRA Final Integrated Activity Plan/EIS.	Critical habitat not mapped, office takes conservative approach		Native coporations (subsistence resources), increased consultation required				Modeling required for each point source		Lack of infrastructure, ice roads	Coastal Zone Management Act, wetlands, oil spill plans, litigation, all slow down process

*Calculated based on office interviews and analysis of AFMSS data

Table 4-2. Access Issues, Paradox/San Juan Study Area (Utah)

Table 4-2. Access Issues, Paradox/San Juan Study Area (Utah)

Jurisdiction	Issue or Characteristic Noted by Office											
	Average APD Processing*	**NEPA Documents**	**Endangered Species Act and Species Generally of Concern**	**Roadless Areas**	**Tribal Consultations**	**National Historic Preservation Act**	**O&G vs Coal and other Mineral Development**	**Visual Resources**	**Air Quality**	**Clean Water**	**Infrastructure Concerns**	**Others**
Cedar City, UT BLM		Cedar Beaver Garfield Antimony RMP, 1986	Raptors			Cultural resource concerns on any area, but "can be mitigated"		Secondary issue				Steep slope issues
Dixie NF		Plan to be completed in July 2006										
Fishlake NF		Plan to be completed in July 2006										
Kanab, UT BLM	6 to 12 months	Lopez Project, Utah State BLM Statewide Stipulations	Raptors, bald eagle, Mexican spotted owl, flycatcher					Issues associated with Bryce and Zion NPs		Water disposal may be a problem in Navajo Sandstone		
Manti La Sal NF	1 year	Land and RMP – Manti-La Sal NF, 1986. New plan to be released in December 2006.	Goshawks, raptors, Mexican spotted owl, sensitive plants				Conflict with deep gas vs. coal	Retention and preservation areas near NPs (e.g., Arches, Canyonlands)			Roads used for nonsummer months require 8 inches of gravel	There exists a potential for land exchange with state such that these areas would not be leased; however, these areas have not been demarcated
Moab, UT BLM	Average 6 months, note deficient APDs from companies	Lopez Project, Utah State BLM Statewide Stipulations, Book Cliffs RMP, 1985	Mexican spotted owl, raptors, pedio, *despainii and winklerii cacti*					Can be an issue in larger field developments. RMP treats VR as an inventory process as opposed to management objective. Gas flaring would be an issue			Big flat areas-well spacing maximized and at capacity; in order for further field developments an EIS would be required.	Anticipate increased NSO due to wilderness recreation and wildlife concerns. Recreational conflicts vs APDs/geophysical surveys/oil & gas development
Monticello, UT BLM	60 days	Lopez Project, Utah State BLM Statewide Stipulations	Mexican spotted owl, raptors		McCraken Extension (50,000 acres) is split estate with Navajo lands (3 or 4 APDs per year); Navajo wants to reclaim mineral rights	High density of cultural sites, cost issue for industry but does not prohibit activity		Similar to Moab office				It would be advantageous for companies to be educated in NEPA and APD requirements
Price, UT BLM	8 months	Lopez Project, Utah State BLM Statewide Stipulations. Price RMP in draft.	*Despainii and winklerii cacti*, raptors					Last Chance field near Capital Reef NP				
Richfield, UT BLM	30 days or less	Lopez Project, Utah State BLM Statewide Stipulations										
St. George, UT BLM		St. George FO – ROD and RMP, 1999. No site specific NEPA coverage	Mexican spotted owl, southwestern willow flycatcher		MOUs with Southern Piute and Hopis					In process of assessing Clean Water Act amendment		

*Calculated based on office interviews and analysis of AFMSS data

Table 4-3. Access Issues, Paradox/San Juan Study Area (New Mexico and Colorado)

Jurisdiction	Issue or Characteristic Noted by Office											
	Average APD Processing*	NEPA Documents	Endangered Species Act and Species Generally of Concern	Roadless Areas	Tribal Consultations	National Historic Preservation Act	O&G vs Coal and other Mineral Development	Visual Resources	Air Quality	Clean Water	Infrastructure Concerns	Others
Albuquerque, NM BLM (Rio Puerco Field Office)	60 days	Rio Puerco RMP, 1992. Updated in 2001			30 days for tribes to comment	Lindrith Area-split estate with high density of cultural resources				Impaired watershed (Rio Puerco) not an issue yet but could develop; sediment loading issue		
Carson NF	6 months	Carson NF Plan, 1986	Mexican spotted owls, goshawks, bald eagles		Potential issue, esp. Gobernador	Navajo–high density of cultural resources			Centralized compression	Sediment loading, produced water	Road density	Differing motivation (Fed. vs. state) for approval of well spacing (revenue issue for NM); compliance issues influence public perception; need for cumulative effects analyses (roads, wells)
Cibola NF		Cibola NF Plan, 1985	Mexican spotted owls, goshawks, bald eagles		Pueblo and Navajo Natior sacred Mt. Taylor	High density archeological sites			Compressors	Sediment loading		Law suit in Zuni River watershed
Durango, CO BLM (San Juan Field Office)	3 months	San Juan/San Miguel RMP Amendment, October 1991. New plan to be released in 2007	Sage grouse, flycatcher, ferruginous hawk, bald eagle			Archeological sites, esp. Canyons of the Ancients (existing leases)				EIS in progress; moderate but increasing concern with surface water depletion and its effects on species	Conflicts due to increased infrastructure (public use vs. industry), esp. near Durango	
Farmington, NM BLM	60-180 days	Farmington Oil and Gas Leasing Amendment, 1991. Farmington RMP completed 01/2005	Bald eagle, Nolton's cactus, designated Mexican spotted owl habitat, razorback sucker		Split estate with Navajo surface requires 6 months to a year	High density of cultural resources	Conflict with underground mines and CBM (oil & gas rights are senior), BLM continues to issue APDs but only in center of long wall panels		Additional compression (public concern)	Endangered fish, consultation with Corp of Engineers	Centralized compression (noise concerns)	
Grand Mesa/ Uncompahgre/ Gunnison NF	25 months	GMUG - Oil and Gas Leasing File EIS ROD, April 1993	Lynx	NLA								
Montrose, CO BLM (Uncompahgre Field Office	30 to 60 days	San Juan/San Miguel RMP Amendment, October 1991. New plan to be released in December 2006								Concerned with surface water depletion		
San Juan NF	6 months	New plan to be released in December 2006	Willow flycatcher, Mexican spotted owl, Canada lynx			High density of cultural resources			Issues related to proximity to Durango	Residential concern about methane contamination	Public concerns about O&G development in general	Do not have forest-wide stipulations
Santa Fe NF		1987 Forest Plan, amended 1996	Mexican spotted owls, bald eagles		High density of cultural resources	High density of resources impacts road building		VR concerns make siting more difficult, esp. roads		Sediment loading from road construction	Aging infrastructure	Reclamation compliance and inspection

*Calculated based on office interviews and analysis of AFMSS data

Table 4-4. Access Issues, Montana Thrust Belt Study Area

Jurisdiction	Issue or Characteristic Noted by Office											
	Average APD Processing*	NEPA Documents	Endangered Species Act and Species Generally of Concern	Roadless Areas	Tribal Consultations	National Historic Preservation Act	O&G vs Coal and other Mineral Development	Visual Resources	Air Quality	Clean Water	Infrastructure Concerns	Others
Beaverhead-Deerlodge NF		1996 Beaverhead Oil and Gas EIS, 1987 FP under revision (due late 2006)	Lynx, sage grouse		Nez Pierce Trail	Lewis & Clarke Trail, Continental Divide Scenic Trail		Concerns near west side of Big Hole Valley		Sediment loading in streams	Potential concerns if development occurs in Big Hole	
Butte and Lewistown, MT BLM		1984 Headwaters RMP (revision to be completed by end of 2006), 1981 Butte District Oil & Gas environmental assessment	Grizzly bears, grey wolf, Canada lynx, reptiles, plants, raptors, fish (spawning streams, trout)	Lease sale protest decision, 1989 impacts leasing	Old North trail (historical indian migration route but with no distinct area defined)	"Sense of Place" (areas of spiritual interest to native tribes)			Sour gas production		Sour gas (only one sweetening plant), individual developments would require sweetening plants	Litigation appeals; recreation vs. wild land, infrastructure vs. vacation homes (Butte)
Dillon, MT BLM		1979 MFP, Dillon RMP awaiting ROD signature	Cutthroat trout, sage grouse, lynx, wolf reintroduction, bald eagles		Spiritual sites	Trails		Concerns near Big Hole Battlefield		Sediment loading, esp. near steep slope areas		Private access on large ranches to public lands
Gallatin NF		1987 Forest Plan scheduled for 2009 revision	Lynx									Gallatin community vehemently against development
Helena NF	1 year	Helena NF Plan and ROD, 1986	Lynx, bear		"Sense of Place", religious sites, historical sites; tribes getting more active in Dry Range and Big Belt areas	High density of cultural resources: prehistoric and historic, modern cultural resources (homesteads, mining, etc.)				Cumulative impacts for sediment loading in streams (sensitive fish, total solids in streams)		Burned areas that will need stabilization for 3 to 6 years, such that potential for high levels of restriction; geographic constraints on concurrent activity
Kootenai, Bitterroot, Flathead, and Lolo NFs		Kootenai–FP revision to be completed winter 2006/2007, Bitterroot–1987 FP, revision to be completed 10/2006, Flathead-FP revision to be completed 10/2006, Lolo–1987 FP, revision to be completed 10/2006	Bull trout, grizzly bear, lynx, wolf reintroduction		Spiritual sites	Trails (Bitterroot)				Sediment loading, esp. near steep slope areas	Flathead-FP Amendment for Grizzly Bear Habitat: 1 mile of road per square mile (limits new road construction, reclaims existing roads); road timing restrictions on roads (open only in summer)	Lolo and Flathead-900,000 acres of lease in suspension, FP 20 years out of date
Lewis and Clark NF (east)		1996 FP, 1997 Oil and Gas Leasing Decision	Lynx	NSO								Plan calls for 4 wells per year
Lewis and Clark NF (west)		1996 FP, 1997 Oil and Gas Leasing Decision	Lynx	NSO	Leases suspended due to tribal consultation	Traditional cultural district (10,000 acres) that impacts current lease suspension					H2S removal and facility location	
Missoula, MT BLM		Garnett RMP, 1986	Lynx, bull trout, grizzly bear habitat, wolf reintroduction, bald eagle, cutthroat trout			Historical mining sites and historical trails			Cumulative impacts, especially during winter; competition for discharge capacity	Sediment loading in streams	Roads and pipelines would be problematic because of local opposition and steep slopes	

*Calculated based on office interviews and analysis of AFMSS data

Table 4-5. Access Issues, Powder River Basin Study Area

Jurisdiction	Issue or Characteristic Noted by Office											
	Average APD Processing*	NEPA Documents	Endangered Species Act and Species Generally of Concern	Roadless Areas	Tribal Consultations	National Historic Preservation Act	O&G vs Coal and other Mineral Development	Visual Resources	Air Quality	Clean Water	Infrastructure Concerns	Others
Belle Fourche, SD BLM (South Dakota Field Office)		1986 South Dakota RMP, 1994 Miles City Oil and Gas Amendment, Miles City RMP draft is to be released in 2007	Raptors, grouse			High density areas in northern edge of South Dakota portion of study area					Most wells drilled 1980 or before, such that continual break downs of infrastructure has closed down wells/ production	
Black Hills NF		Black Hills NF Land and RMP, 1991										
Buffalo, WY BLM	Conventional wells–35 days/APD, CBNG (32 well permits)–60 days/APD, APDs are sometimes information deficient	Buffalo RMP 2005	Big game, sage grouse, sharp-tailed grouse		Developing routine consultation program as part of EIS, TCs can create problems in lag times common near drainages	Often Inadequate initial site investigation by companies	16 operating coal mines, but BLM addressing the issue adequately	Bozeman Trail-view shed preservation consideration	No. of vehicles results in increased road dust	In western and northern portions, sodium absorption ratios are a concern for produced water, coal aquifer being affected by drawdown.	Power requirment for submersible pumps will require small power plants that would result in surface disturbance, power line density increases and compressor noise, esp. around Gillette, increased compression	Split estate underlies over half of resources managed in the basin, requiring negotiations with surface owners, increased power lines result in increased raptor predation of sage grouse, prairie dogs, and mountain plover and raptor electrocution
Casper, WY BLM	60 days/APD	Casper RMP is currently being updated and is scheduled to be completed by 2008	Mountain plover (issue with seismic), bald eagle, golden eagle, greater sage grouse and black-tailed prairie dog (currently sensitive but potential of listing would make it an issue)		Problematic with seismic surveying	Similar to Buffalo, religious concerns	Insitu uranium development vs. shallow coal-flooding uranium sediments but taking water out of coal will result in need to monitor "hot" water production. DOE to take over remediation of mile tailings 2005-2008	Trails often result in conflicts with linear facilities that bisect (pipelines, roads, etc.), esp. for the Mormon Trail	No. of vehicles results in increased road dust, increased amount of compression		Right of way corridors at capacity	Anticipate NSO stipulations in the future due to erodable soils
Custer NF		Custer LRMP 1987, Sioux Ranger District O&G EIS 2005.			High density archeological sites, tribal sacred sites					CBNG water discharge potential issue		
Miles City, MT BLM	3 months/APD	Powder River Amendments to the Powder River RMP was completed in 01/2005. Powder River RMP will be amended by the Miles City RMP, which draft is to be released in 2007	Bald eagle, mountain plover, black footed ferret (potential), prairie dog, sage grouse		Off-reservation cultural values and historical issues Northern Cheyenne more conservative; Crow more open to development	Current approach to cultural resources is considered inadequate, "block surveys" preferred	Active coal mines near WY border (potential issue)	Remaining free stands, view sheds for Tongue, Rosebud and Rosebud rivers; major roads and Tongue River (potential issue)	Cumulative impacts from activities in WY as well as MT leading to limited discharge capacity; Northern Cheyenne is Class I air shed	CBNG ground and surface water impacts (cumulative) to be addressed in new EIS; WY uses 80% of allowable discharge capacity meaning only 20% left for MT; to the NW water quality decreasses; water quality effects on ranching		Socioeconomic-increased activity in remote areas puts ranching way of life at odds with O&G development, esp. with regard to water issues, visual intrusion, wildlife issues (migratory birds and raptor electrocution)

Table 4-5. (Continued)

Jurisdiction	Issue or Characteristic Noted by Office											
	Average APD Processing*	NEPA Documents	Endangered Species Act and Species Generally of Concern	Roadless Areas	Tribal Consultations	National Historic Preservation Act	O&G vs Coal and other Mineral Development	Visual Resources	Air Quality	Clean Water	Infrastructure Concerns	Others
Newcastle, WY BLM	30-45 days	Newcastle RMP 2000				High density of cultural resources (potential issue); dinosaur fossils in Niobrara County			Receptor area relative to coal development, which may limit further development O&G or otherwise			Much split estate, litigation common
Oglala NG, Buffalo Gap NG		Nebraska NF Revised Land and RMP, 2002	Habitat preservation is a concern			Could become an issue if development were to increase		Open grasslands often require view mitigations				
Thunder Basin NG	12 months/ APD	Thunder Basin Nat. Grassland Land and RMP, 2002	Black footed ferret reintroduction, sage grouse, mountain plover			Moderate to high vertebrate/ paleo resources ("block surveys" used to assess CBM), such that all of Thunder Basin is CSU	Substantial CBM/coal mining conflicts		Increased road dust; increased amount of compression		Aging infrastructure. Road Analysis Process (RAP), above/below ground power lines is safety issue near coal mines	

*Calculated based on office interviews and analysis of AFMSS data

Table 4-6. Access Issues, Wyoming Thrust Belt Study Area

Jurisdiction	Issue or Characteristic Noted by Office											
	Average APD Processing*	NEPA Documents	Endangered Species Act and Species Generally of Concern	Roadless Areas	Tribal Consultations	National Historic Preservation Act	O&G vs Coal and other Mineral Development	Visual Resources	Air Quality	Clean Water	Infrastructure Concerns	Others
Bridger-Teton NF	180 days	Bridger-Teton NF Land and RMP, 1990	Pygmy rabbit, white tailed prairie dog, lynx			Congressionally designated trails and cutoffs, concerns protecting viewshed (measured in miles)			Limits due to air quality in Class I areas, currently close to thresholds			
Caribou-Targhee NF	120 days	Targhee NF Revised Forest Plan, 2000	Lynx, cutthroat trout, grizzly bear, wolves, sage grouse	NSO	Ancestral area, Ft. Hill Reservation, ancestral rights to land and resources							
Idaho Falls, ID BLM (Upper Snake Field Office)	120 days	Pocatello & Medicine Lodge Resource Areas RMP, 1988	Lynx, cutthroat trout, grizzly bear, wolves, sage grouse									

Jurisdiction	Issue or Characteristic Noted by Office											
	Average APD Processing*	NEPA Documents	Endangered Species Act and Species Generally of Concern	Roadless Areas	Tribal Consultations	National Historic Preservation Act	O&G vs Coal and other Mineral Development	Visual Resources	Air Quality	Clean Water	Infrastructure Concerns	Others
Kemmerer, WY BLM	3 months	Kemmerer RMP/ROD, 1986	Pygmy rabbit, white tailed prairie dog, lynx		Tribes hesitant to state all concerns. Regional issues beyond site specific, are important.	Congressionally designated trails and cutoffs, concerns protecting viewshed (measured in miles)			An issue in SW Wyoming, compression is creating air quality problems	Change in size requirements from 5 acres to 1 acre for storm water discharge		Potential conflict with wind energy (cumulative effects and infrastructure conflicts)
Pinedale, WY BLM	3 months	Pinedale RMP, amended 2000 for oil & gas. New plan to be released 2007										No Federal land in Wyoming Thrust Belt study area
Pocatello, ID BLM	90 days	Pocatello & Medicine Lodge Resource Areas RMP, 1988	Lynx, cutthroat trout, grizzly bear, wolves, sage grouse, bald eagles, snails, Ute Ladies' Tress		Ancestral area, Ft. Hill Reservation, ancestral rights to land and resources	Lack of cultural resource inventory				Sediment and nutrient loading in streams		
Salt Lake, UT BLM	6 months	Lopez Project, Utah State BLM Statewide Stipulations, Isotract MFP, Randolph MFP, 1985	Sage grouse, lynx, pygmy rabbit, raptors									
Wasatch-Cache NF	1 year	Wasatch-Cache NF, Revised Forest Plan, 2003	Lynx									

*Calculated based on office interviews and analysis of AFMSS data

Table 4-7. Access Issues, Greater Green River Basin Study Area

Jurisdiction	Issue or Characteristic Noted by Office										
	Average APD Processing*	NEPA Documents	Endangered Species Act and Species Generally of Concern	Roadless Areas	Tribal Consultations	National Historic Preservation Act	O&G vs Coal and other Mineral Development	Visual Resources	Air Quality	Clean Water	Infrastructure Concerns	Others
Craig, CO BLM (Little Snake Field Office)	45 days	Little Snake RMP Oil and Gas Revision 1991, new plan release in 2008	White tailed prairie dog, pygmy rabbit, sage grouse are all candidate species with potential to severely impact O&G development								Largely a "wildcat" region, there is no infrastructure to transport O&G out of area	
Kremmling, CO BLM	28 days	Kremmling RMP, 1984. Revision planned for 2009	Sage Grouse		Tribes don't respond, O&G companies don't understand mandatory 3(day waiting period	O&G companies don't return complete survey with APD				Erosion and siltation issues	No pipelines, railway pulled out	
Medicine Bow-Routt NF	1 year	Medicine Bow LRMP, 2003. Routt LRMP, 1998. Thunder Basin LRMP, 2002.		Misnomer which causes conflicts with environ-mentalists					Coal mines, O&G transport, trucks, contribute to air quality issues			
Rawlins, WY BLM	6 months	Lease Stipulations, Rawlins BLM, 2001. New plan to be released late 2006			Affects timeliness	Trails are registered with NHPA, defined by rutting (which can be difficult to identify)		Looming issue, Fort Laramie, Pony Express, Oregon Trail				
Rock Springs, WY BLM	90 days	Green River RMP, 1997			Contact and scheduling of tribal representatives often precludes 30 day permitting goal. Need to define operator/ agency responsibility for tribal representative compensation.	30 day comment period for SHPO precludes meeting 30 day permitting goal. Need definitive guidance on visual impact distances and alternative mitigation regarding Historic Trails.						

*Calculated based on office interviews and analysis of AFMSS data

Table 4-8. Access Issues, Denver Basin Study Area

Jurisdiction	Issue or Characteristic Noted by Office											
	Average APD Processing*	**NEPA Documents**	**Endangered Species Act and Species Generally of Concern**	**Roadless Areas**	**Tribal Consultations**	**National Historic Preservation Act**	**O&G vs Coal and other Mineral Development**	**Visual Resources**	**Air Quality**	**Clean Water**	**Infrastructure Concerns**	**Others**
Arapaho-Roosevelt NF	5 months	Arapaho-Roosevelt NFs, Pawnee NG Revision of the Land and Resource Management Plan, 1997										
Black Hills NF	1.5 years	Black Hills NF Plan of Land and RMP, 1991			Required for all lands	Could cause activities to be limited		Could require mitigation or surface limitations	Potential issue near Rapid City	Riparian areas	Inadequate road system	
Cañon City, CO BLM (Royal Gorge Field Office)	6 months	Royal Gorge RMP and NE Royal Gorge RMP, 1991										
Casper, WY BLM	50 days	Casper RMP, 2001. Wyoming BLM Mitigation Guidelines for Surface-disturbing and Disruptive Activities				Trails are registered with NHPA, defined by rutting (which can be difficult to identify)		Looming issue, Fort Laramie, Pony Express, Oregon Trail			Surface owner/split estate surface access for roads and pipelines, urbanization conflict	
Nebraska NF	60 days	Nebraska NF Revised Land and RMP FEIS/ROD, 2002				Often locations must be modified				Easily erodable soils	Easily erodable soils	
Newcastle, WY BLM	30-45 days	Newcastle FO, ROD & Approved RMP, 2000				Trails are registered with NHPA, defined by rutting (which can be difficult to identify)		Looming issue, Fort Laramie, Pony Express, Oregon Trail			Surface owner/split estate surface access for roads and pipelines, urbanization conflict	
Pike-San Isabel NF		Pike & San Isabel NF, Cimarron & Comanche NG RMP						Recreation view sheds	Potential problem, incremental loading from O&G activity	Sedimentation concerns	Urban interface concerns, public concern about drilling, trucks	
Rawlins, WY BLM	6 months	Lease Stipulations, Rawlins BLM, 2001. New plan to be released late 2006			Affects timeliness	Trails are registered with NHPA, defined by rutting (which can be difficult to identify)		Looming issue, Fort Laramie, Pony Express, Oregon Trail				

*Calculated based on office interviews and analysis of AFMSS data

Table 4-9. Access Issues, Florida Peninsula Study Area

Jurisdiction	Issue or Characteristic Noted by Office											
	Average APD Processing*	NEPA Documents	Endangered Species Act and Species Generally of Concern	Roadless Areas	Tribal Consultations	National Historic Preservation Act	O&G vs Coal and other Mineral Development	Visual Resources	Air Quality	Clean Water	Infrastructure Concerns	Others
Big Cypress NP		Big Cypress General Management Plan/Final EIS, 1991	Florida panther, west Indian manatee, cape sable seaside sparrow, bald eagle, wood stork, red-cockaded woodpecker, snail kite, arctic peregrine falcon, American alligator, eastern indigo snake, Everglades mink, mangrove fox squirrel, Florida black bear, bachman's sparrow, swainson's hawk, reddish egret, swallow-tailed kite, southeastern kestrel, migrant loggerhead shrike, mangrove clapper rail									Office not visited
Fish and Wildlife Service in Florida												Office not visited
Jackson, MS BLM (Florida Peninsula)		Florida RMP/ROD, 1995	Red-cockaded woodpecker									

*Calculated based on office interviews and analysis of AFMSS data

Table 4-10. Access Issues, Black Warrior Basin Study Area

Jurisdiction	Issue or Characteristic Noted by Office											
	Average APD Processing*	NEPA Documents	Endangered Species Act and Species Generally of Concern	Roadless Areas	Tribal Consultations	National Historic Preservation Act	O&G vs Coal and other Mineral Development	Visual Resources	Air Quality	Clean Water	Infrastructure Concerns	Others
National Forests in Alabama	6 months	Alabama NFs – Revised Land and RMP, 2004. APD requires project-level NEPA of 3-6 months	Gopher tortoise, red cockaded woodpecker									
Jackson, MS BLM (Black Warrior Basin)	5 months	Assorted Leases	Red-cockaded woodpecker				Conflict between O&G and coal (state vs. Federal)					Hunting vs. resource conflicts in Alabama
National Forests in Mississippi	2 months	Mississippi EA report – O&G leasing on the NF's, 1976. Done at APD stage. New plan to be released in 2007										

*Calculated based on office interviews and analysis of AFMSS data

Table 4-11. Access Issues, Appalachian Basin Study Area

Jurisdiction	Issue or Characteristic Noted by Office									
	Average APD Processing*	NEPA Documents	Endangered Species Act and Species Generally of Concern	National Historic Preservation Act	O&G vs Coal and other Mineral Development	Visual Resources	Air Quality	Clean Water	Infrastructure Concerns	Others
Allegheny NF	1 year	Allegheny NF Land and RMP, 1986. New plan to be released early 2007	Bald eagle, Canada lynx, Indiana bat							
Daniel Boone NF	8-9 months (90 days for an APD on split estate lands)	Daniel Boone NF Revised Land and RMP, 2004	Black sided dace, mussels (several varieties), Indiana bat, primarily aquatic species				Becoming an issue, coal plants, O&G activity near cities	State-listed impaired streams, sedimentation concerns		
Finger Lakes NF		Finger Lakes NF O&G Leasing ROD 2001. New plan to be released 2006	Bald eagle, Canada lynx, Indiana bat							
George Washington NF	1 year	George Washington NF – Final revised Land and RMP, 1993	Indiana bat, aquatic species						Forest benefits from energy infrastructure, good maintenance	
Jackson, MS BLM (Appalachian Basin)		Assorted Leases	Red-cockaded woodpecker							
Jefferson NF	1 year	Jefferson NF – Revised Land and RMP, 2004	Indiana bat, aquatic species						Forest benefits from energy infrastructure, good maintenance	
Milwaukee, WI BLM	5 months for COE and Federal minerals (split estate)	No RMPs to cover non-FS lands, develop NEPA on project-by-project basis	Indiana bat, running buffalo clover, bald eagle	Need agreements with state historical presentation offices (SHPOs), need state protocols, opportunity for streamlining	Minor in PA					COE & NY state cooperation is limited, Fed. leases in PA are being drained losing $50 million/year royalty revenue, for most minerals Fed. have < 100% ownership (and often far less), BLM stipulations are developed on an ad hoc basis
Monongahela NF	2 months	Monongahela NF and Amendments Land and RMP, 1986. New plan to be released in 2006	Bald eagle, Canada lynx, Indiana bat							
Wayne NF	1 year	Wayne NF Land and RMP, 2006	Bald eagle, Canada lynx, Indiana bat							

*Calculated based on office interviews and analysis of AFMSS data

4.1 Issues Directly Impacting Access

The National Environmental Policy Act of 1969. NEPA is the nation's central environmental statute. It requires Federal agencies to consider environmental impacts before an action is taken. The NEPA process is intended to help public officials make better decisions based on an understanding of their environmental consequences.

NEPA is embedded into the fabric of Federal land management decision-making and has become the most important procedural public land management statute because it requires agencies to comply with its processes in all situations where major actions are contemplated. When an activity or action is proposed on Federal lands, an interdisciplinary review of the environmental effects of the proposal is conducted and made available to citizens and public officials. The review can take one of four forms:

- a categorical exclusion (CX)
- documentation of NEPA adequacy (DNA)
- an environmental assessment (EA)
- an environmental impact statement (EIS).

In its 2003 report to the Council on Environmental Quality, the NEPA Task Force published an assessment of NEPA,[39] stating that "The term 'analysis paralysis' is used to address a broad range of concerns about inefficiencies such as agency specific procedural requirements, project priority setting, project management, and Federal consultation and coordination requirements. Many respondents are concerned that the development of these analyses and documents takes too long and results in documentation that is excessive in light of the significance of the actions evaluated."

The NEPA process impacts oil and gas development in terms of cost and time delays. Typically an EIS or EA is drafted in consultation with the cooperating agencies, presented for public comment, and reviewed by multiple agencies. A simple EIS can take 24 to 36 months to complete, while those with more complex issues may require three to six years to complete. The land use planning process as a whole takes well in excess of 36 months, particularly if there is oil and gas involved. NEPA documents analyze alternatives to the proposed action and must include a "no action" alternative. Impacts are classified as direct, indirect, and cumulative, and include the evaluation of economic impacts to counties and states to be considered, as well as impacts on resources.

When considering oil and gas leasing, the BLM has identified the need to obtain additional data on such issues as air quality and clean water as a part of the cumulative impact analysis required by NEPA and land use planning processes. This has been cited as an overarching issue that affects oil and gas lease parcel nominations. This lack of data can result in leasing delays when existing documents are deemed inadequate. The net result is that potential applicants are often aware of the problem and make decisions not to develop in areas that will be or could be held up by the NEPA process.

With respect to the NEPA process itself, concern was expressed by some government officials that individual documents provide "piecemeal" information and that better environmental decisions could be made based on larger scale studies that look at the "bigger picture." For example, wildlife habitat fragmentation is better characterized when it is examined in the context of larger rather than smaller areas.

Delays can increase costs for oil and gas operations because, rather than waiting for the Federal agency to complete the work, operators frequently pay a third-party contractor to perform the necessary work.

Based on the NPC 2003 natural gas study, to conduct wildlife, cultural, and other surveys related to Federal oil and gas permitting costs between $21,000 and $330,000 and causes a delay of 3 to 26 months per exploration well. Per-well survey costs and delays for development wells range from $18,000 to $21,000 and 2 to 32 months respectively.

Section 366 of EPAct 2005 sets a deadline for the consideration of applications for permits. The permit must be issued within 30 days (if NEPA and other legal requirements have been met), or defer the decision and provide to the applicant a notice.

The Endangered Species Act of 1973. The ESA requires Federal agencies to conserve listed species. Under the ESA, species are treated as either listed, proposed, or candidate species. In BLM and USDA-FS jurisdictions, listed and proposed species are treated similarly. Candidate species are generally handled in a discretionary manner. All BLM administrative offices treat sensitive species as defined by BLM and state governments the same as endangered species.

Federal agencies are responsible for managing wildlife habitat, while state governments manage the wildlife itself. In many areas, some habitat has not yet been mapped. This can become an added delay for oil and gas development, if habitat information is required before leasing and permitting can proceed. Habitat for candidate species has been generally withheld from oil and gas leasing by Federal agencies during a consideration period of up to 21/2 years.

Inventoried Roadless Areas. A total of 8.4 million acres of National Forest Inventoried Roadless Areas (IRAs) exists within the boundaries of the Phase II study areas. Forest Service representatives recognize the complexity surrounding the issue of IRAs. In July 2004, the Forest Service published a proposed rule to revise the Roadless Area Conservation Rule published in January 2001, which had been struck down in July 2003 by the Federal District Court for the District of Wyoming.

The final roadless rule was published in May 2005. The rule allows governors to petition the Secretary of Agriculture to develop regulations to manage roadless areas in order to meet specific needs within each state. USDA-FS will accept state petitions from governors for 18 months after the effective date of the final rule. During the state- petitioning process, the Forest Service will continue to maintain interim measures to conserve inventoried roadless areas.

In spite of the controversy surrounding the issue, leasing is occurring in some roadless areas. Leases in various forests within IRAs are issued with the caveat to industry that the disposition of roadless areas is unresolved and that the areas under lease may have to remain roadless.

Visual Impacts. Concern over visual impacts is affecting oil and gas development in some areas. For example, field developments can be delayed until impacts and other issues are assessed. Visual impacts were raised as a potential issue by many BLM and USDA-FS offices.

Suburban Encroachment. Opposition to oil and gas activities is increasing as residential construction spreads into previously undeveloped areas. This has not been a significant issue until recently and has not generally been incorporated into oil and gas planning activities. NSO stipulations to maintain open space near housing developments are being considered by some offices.

Seasonal Restrictions in Alaska. The primary constraint to access in the NPRA is the restriction that limits exploratory drilling activities to the winter season, which lasts approximately five months. During that time, ice roads need to be built, a task that can take one or two months and may be limited to 25-30 miles. Coupled with timing limitations for threatened and endangered species, the cumulative effects of these limitations make drilling operations difficult and significantly impact project economics.

4.2 Issues Indirectly Impacting Access

Clean Water. In the Uinta-Piceance Basin, the issue of clean water has been raised in the context of the need for examining entire watersheds. It is increasingly recognized that an entire watershed (rather than administrative jurisdictions) must be examined in instances where activity within one jurisdiction may affect another downstream. States and counties increasingly object to drilling in municipal watersheds, often resulting in added stipulations and/or conditions of approval for protection. In addition, localized clean water issues include mitigating selenium concentrations, salinity, and sedimentation.

Air Quality. Air quality can be a contentious issue in Rocky Mountain basins such as the Greater Green River Basin. Increasingly, air quality issues are being raised, especially in Utah.

Staffing. Workload requirements are increasing and the BLM is facing challenges with respect to the timely processing of APDs, energy-related rights of ways, and monitoring compliance. The number of APDs received increased from nearly 4000 in FY 2000 to over 8000 in FY 2005. Recruitment and retention of professional oil and gas staff is challenging.

Section 365 of EPAct 2005 requires the Secretary of the Interior to establish a Federal Permit Streamlining Pilot Project to improve Federal oil and gas permit coordination. A Memorandum of Understanding establishing staffing needs and funding protocols for the pilot offices was signed on October 25, 2005, by the Department of Interior, Department of Agriculture, Environmental Protection Agency, and the Army Corps of Engineers. The seven pilot offices (Rawlins and Buffalo, Wyoming; Miles City, Montana; Farmington and Carlsbad, New Mexico; Grand Junction/Glenwood Springs, Colorado; and Vernal, Utah) have been created.

Native American Consultation. The large number of APDs and leases impacts the timeliness of completing the consultation requirements of the National Historic Preservation Act. Consultation with Tribes is increasing and can extend the time required to obtain leases and drilling permits.

Conflicts between Mineral and CBNG Developers. In the Powder River Basin, conflicts can occur between coal mining operators and coalbed natural gas producers. It is the policy of the BLM to encourage oil and gas and coal companies to resolve conflicts between themselves; when requested, the BLM will assist in facilitating agreements between the companies. The BLM will also exercise authority provided in the leases, applicable statutes, and regulations to manage federal mineral development in the public's best interest.

Infrastructure. The physical infrastructure to support oil and gas development and production is often strained. Existing pipelines may be at capacity and new pipeline construction is often a lengthy process. County roads are typically not designed for the volume of truck traffic that they can experience during oil and gas field development. Infrastructure issues can act to constrain future marketing capacity, especially for natural gas in the Piceance Basin, although new pipeline construction can relieve this bottleneck.

BLM's energy-related rights-of-way processing workload has increased along with the increase in APDs. These authorizations are required for such infrastructure as pipelines, roads, and power lines that are located outside of a lease or unit boundary.

Snow Delays. In the higher elevation areas of the Rocky Mountains, snow depths can be so great as to preclude drilling even if there are no winter drilling stipulations. This situation potentially makes for a short drilling window, especially if there are timing limitations during non-snow months.

Industry Understanding of the Leasing and Permitting Process. There is often less-than-optimal understanding and planning within some companies with respect to these processes. The BLM encourages oil and gas operators to inform and work with the permitting agencies as early in the planned development process as possible. The issuance of the recently updated *Surface Operating Standards and Guidelines for Oil and Gas Exploration and Development* (the "Gold Book," 4th edition, 2006, available at http://www.blm.gov/bmp/goldbook.htm) should enhance operators' understanding and expectations.

Appendix 1: Acronyms and Abbreviations

AAGF	Average Annual Growth Factor
AAPG	American Association of Petroleum Geologists
ACEC	Area of Critical Environmental Concern
AD	Associated Dissolved (natural gas)
AFMSS	Automated Fluid Minerals Support System
AGF	Annual Growth Factor
AK	Alaska
ANWR	Arctic National Wildlife Refuge
APB	Appalachian Basin
APD	Application for Permit to Drill
API	American Petroleum Institute
AL	Alabama
ARMP	Approved Resource Management Plan

Bbbls	Billion Barrels
BCF	Billion cubic feet (of natural gas)
BHL	Bottom-Hole Location
BLM	Bureau of Land Management
BOE	Barrels of Oil Equivalent
BOEULT	Barrels of Oil Equivalent Ultimate
BOR	Bureau of Reclamation
BWB	Black Warrior Basin
CBNG	Coalbed Natural Gas
CEQ	Council on Environmental Quality
CFR	Code of Federal Regulations
CGF	Cumulative Growth Factor
CO	Colorado
COA	Conditions of Approval
COE	Corps of Engineers
CPA	Citizens' Proposal Area
CSU	Controlled Surface Use
CWP	Citizens' Wilderness Proposals
CWR	Critical Winter Range
DEM	Digital Elevation Model
DEN	Denver Basin
DFC	Desired Future Condition
DHS	Department of Homeland Security
DNR	Department of Natural Resources
DOD	Department of Defense
DOE	Department of Energy
DOI	Department of the Interior
DOJ	Department of Justice
DOL	Department of Labor
DR	Decision Record
DVA	Department of Veterans Affairs
EA	Environmental Assessment
EDZ	Extended Drilling Zone
EF	Exception Factor
EIA	Energy Information Administration
EIS	Environmental Impact Statement
EPA	Environmental Protection Agency
EPAct	Energy Policy Act
EPCA	Energy Policy and Conservation Act
ESA	Endangered Species Act
ESRI	Environmental Systems Research Institute
EUR	Estimated Ultimate Recovery
EV	Exceptional Value
FAA	Federal Aviation Administration
FCML	Field Code Master List
FEIS	Final Environmental Impact Statement

FERC	Federal Energy Regulatory Commission
FGDC	Federal Geographic Data Committee
FL	Florida
FlorRs	Federal Lands or Resources
FLP	Florida Peninsula
FLS	Federal Land Status
FO	Field Office
FOOGLRA	Federal Onshore Oil and Gas Leasing and Reform Act
FP	Forest Plan
Ft	Feet
GCDB	Geographic Coordinate Database
GGRB	Greater Green River Basin
G IS	Geographic Information System
GNIS	Geographic Names Information System
GOR	Gas to Oil Ratio
GSA	General Services Administration
HCP	Habitat Conservation Plan
HUD	Department of Housing and Urban Development
IRAs	Inventoried Roadless Areas
ITCs	Incorporated Towns and Cities
LAC	Land Access Categorization
LGR	Liquids to Gas Ratio
LLD	Legal Land Description
LR	Legacy Rehost
LUEA	Land Use Emphasis Area
LUP	Land Use Plan
MA	Management Area
Mbbls	Thousands of Barrels
MBOE	Thousands of Barrels of Oil Equivalent
MCF	Thousand Cubic Feet
MD	Maryland
MFP	Management Framework Plan
MMbbls	Million Barrels
MMCF	Millions of Cubic Feet
MMS	Minerals Management Service
MS	Mississippi
MTB	Montana Thrust Belt
NA	Northern Alaska
NAG	Non-Associated (natural gas)
NASA	National Aeronautics and Space Administration
NE	Nebraska
NEPA	National Environmental Policy Act
NF	National Forest
NGL	National Grasslands
NGLs	Natural Gas Liquids
NHPA	National Historic Preservation Act

NIMBY	Not In My Back Yard
NLA	No Leasing, Administrative
NLA/LUP	No Leasing, Administrative/Land Use Planning
NLS	No Leasing, Statutory or Executive Order
NM	National Monument
NNSO	Net No Surface Occupancy
NPC	National Petroleum Council
NPRA	National Petroleum Reserve-Alaska
NPS	National Park Service
NRHP	National Register of Historic Places
NSF	National Science Foundation
NSO	No Surface Occupancy
O&G	Oil and Gas
OCS	Outer Continental Shelf
OGIFF	Oil and Gas Integrated Field File
OHV	Off-Highway Vehicle
P75	75th percentile
PDS	PetroDataSource
PDX/SJ	Paradox/San Juan Basins
PGC	Potential Gas Committee
PL	Public Law
PLSS	Public Land Survey System
PRB	Powder River Basin
PUR	Proved Ultimate Recovery
PURG	Proved Ultimate Recovery Growth
QC	Quality Control
RMA	Resource Management Area
RMP	Resource Management Plan
RMU	Resource Management Unit
RNA	Research Natural Area
ROD	Record of Decision
ROW	Right-of-Way
RPD	Reserves and Production Division of the EIA
RPURG	Remaining Proved Ultimate Recovery Growth
SA	Study Area
SC	Steering Committee
SHPO	State Historical Preservation Office
SLT	Standard Lease Terms
SMA	Special Management Area
SMZ	Streamside Management Zone
SOPs	Standard Operating Practices
SORs	Surface Occupancy Restrictions
SPL	Split
SPR	Semi Primitive Recreation
SRMA	Special Recreation Management Area
STI PI D	Stipulation Identification

SUPO	Surface Use Plan of Operations
T&E	Threatened and endangered (species)
TCF	Trillion cubic feet (of natural gas)
TCFe	Trillion cubic feet (of natural gas) equivalent
TIN	Triangular Irregular Network
TL	Timing Limitation
TN	Tennessee
TPS	Total Petroleum System
UP	Uinta Piceance Basin
URA	Ultimate recovery appreciation
USC	United States Code
USCG	United States Coast Guard
USDA	United States Department of Agriculture
USDA-FS	United States Department of Agriculture-Forest Service
USFS	United States Forest Service
USFWS	United States Fish and Wildlife Service
USGS	United States Geologic Survey
UT	Utah
VA	Virginia
VBA	Visual Basic for Application
VQO	Visual Quality Objective
VRM	Visual Resource Management
WRAs	Wilderness Reinventory Areas
WSA	Wilderness Study Area
WTB	Wyoming Thrust Belt
WV	West Virginia
WY	Wyoming

APPENDIX 2: GLOSSARY OF TERMS

A

Access Probability: The probability, expressed as a decimal fraction, of sufficient access (political and physical) to a particular assessment unit within a given time frame for the activities necessary to find an accumulation of minimum size and to add its volume to proved reserves. The time frame for this assessment is 30 years.

Accumulation: Consists of two types: conventional and continuous. A conventional accumulation is an individual producing unit consisting of a single pool or multiple pools of petroleum grouped on, or related to, a single structural or stratigraphic feature. A continuous accumulation is also an individual producing formation of regional extent that has among other features diffuse boundaries, no obvious oil water contact and no obvious relation to a structural or stratigraphic trap (see continuous-type accumulation).

Affected Environment: Surface or subsurface resources (including social and economic elements) within or adjacent to a geographic area that could potentially be affected by oil and gas activities; the environment of the area to be affected or created by the alternatives under consideration (40 CFR 1502.15).

Alternative: A combination of management prescriptions applied in specific amounts and locations to achieve a desired management emphasis as expressed in goals and objectives. One of several policies, plans, or projects proposed for decision-making. An alternative need not substitute for another in all respects.

Alternative, No Action: An alternative that maintains established trends or management direction and implements those actions previously analyzed and/or approved.

Application: A written request, petition, or offer to lease lands for the purpose of oil and gas exploration and/or the right of extraction.

Application for Permit to Drill (APD): An application to drill a well submitted by a lessee or operator to the BLM. The APD consists of a Drilling Plan that discusses downhole specifications and procedures (reviewed by the BLM) and a Surface Use Plan of Operations (SUPO) that examines surface uses, including access roads, well site layout, cut and fill diagrams, reclamation procedures, production facility locations, etc. (reviewed by the surface-managing agency). The approved APD is a contract between the operator and the Federal government and cannot be changed or modified unless authorized by the BLM and the surface-managing agency.

Aquifer: (1) A sand, gravel, or rock formation capable of storing or conveying water below the surface of the land (USDA, Natural Resources Conservation Services). (2) The down-dip portion of a water-drive hydrocarbon reservoir that contains predominantly water.

Archeological/historic site: A site that contains either objects of antiquity or cultural value relating to history and/or prehistory that warrant special attention.

Area of Critical Environmental Concern (ACEC): Places that receive special management attention because of potential hazards and/or to protect and prevent irreparable damage to important historic, cultural, or scenic values, fish and wildlife resources or other natural systems or processes.

Assessment Unit: A mappable volume of rock within a total petroleum system that encompasses accumulations (discovered and undiscovered) that share similar geologic traits and socio-economic factors. Accumulations within an assessment unit should constitute a sufficiently homogeneous population such that the chosen methodology of resource assessment is applicable. A total petroleum system might equate to a single assessment unit. If necessary, a total petroleum system can be subdivided into two or more assessment units in order that each unit is sufficiently homogeneous to assess individually. An assessment unit may be identified as conventional, if it contains conventional accumulations, or as continuous, if it contains continuous accumulations.

Assessment Unit Probability: Represents the likelihood, expressed as a decimal fraction, that, in a given assessment unit, at least one undiscovered accumulation of a selected minimum size exists that has the potential for its volume to be added to proved reserves in a given time frame. The assessment unit probability is the product of the probabilities of the three geologic attributes (charge, rocks, and timing) and the probability of access.

Associated/Dissolved Gas: Natural gas that occurs in an oil accumulation, either as a free gas cap or in solution; synonymous with gas in oil accumulations.

B

Barrels of Oil Equivalent (BOE): A unit of petroleum volume in which the gas portion is expressed in terms of its energy equivalent in barrels of oil. For this assessment, 6,000 cubic feet of gas equals 1 BOE.

Basin: (1) An area largely enclosed by higher lands. (2) A low in the Earth's crust of tectonic origin in which sediments have accumulated.

Big Game: Larger species of wildlife that are hunted, such as elk, deer, bighorn sheep, and pronghorn antelope.

Big Game Winter Range: An area available to and used by big game (large mammals normally managed for sport hunting) through the winter season.

Buffer Zone: (1) An area between two different land uses that is intended to resist, absorb, or otherwise preclude developments or intrusions between the two use areas. (2) A strip of undisturbed vegetation that retards the flow of runoff water, causing deposition of transported sediment.

Bureau of Land Management: An agency within the U.S. Department of the Interior that administers 261 million surface acres of America's public lands, located primarily in 12 Western States. The BLM sustains the health, diversity, and productivity of the public lands for the use and enjoyment of present and future generations. The BLM also manages 699 million subsurface acres for mineral leasing and development.

C

Candidate Species: (1) A species for which substantial biological information exists on file to support a proposal to list it as endangered or threatened, but for which no proposal has yet been published in the Federal Register. The list of candidate species is revised approximately every two years in the Notice of Review. (2) Any species not yet officially listed, but undergoing a status review or proposed for listing according to Federal Register notices published by the Secretary of the Interior or the Secretary of Commerce.

Casing: Steel pipe placed in an oil or gas well to prevent the hole from caving and to anchor well control equipment.

Cell: A subdivision or area within an assessment unit having dimensions related to the drainage areas of wells (not to be confused with finite-element cells). Three categories of cells are recognized: cells tested by drilling, untested cells, and untested cells having potential to provide additions to reserves within the forecast span of the assessment. A continuous-type assessment unit is a collection of petroleum-containing cells.

Coalbed Natural Gas: Natural gas found in coalbeds. Also termed "coalbed methane" or "coalbed gas".

Completion: The activities and methods to prepare a well for production. Includes installation of equipment for production from an oil or gas well.

Composite Total Petroleum System: A mappable entity encompassing all or a portion of two or more total petroleum systems. Composite total petroleum systems are used when accumulations within an assessment unit are assumed to be charged by more than one source rock.

Continuous-Type Accumulation: A petroleum accumulation that is pervasive throughout a large area, that is not significantly affected by hydrodynamic influences, and has no obvious seal or trap. Continuous-type accumulations lack well-defined down-dip water contacts. The terms "continuous-type accumulation" and "continuous accumulation" are used interchangeably. Example of continuous-type accumulations include basin-centered gas, coalbed methane and shale gas.

Controlled Surface Use (CSU): Allowed use and occupancy (unless restricted by another stipulation) with identified resource values requiring special operational constraints that may modify the lease rights. CSU is used as an operating guideline, not as a substitute for NSO or Timing Limitations (TLs) stipulations.

Conventional Accumulation: A discrete petroleum accumulation, commonly bounded by a down-dip water contact that is significantly affected by the buoyancy of petroleum in water. Conventional accumulations occur as the result of discrete stratigraphic or structural traps.

Council on Environmental Quality (CEQ): An advisory council to the President established by the National Environmental Policy Act of 1969. It reviews Federal programs for their effect on the environment, conducts environmental studies, and advises the President on environmental matters.

Crucial Winter Range (CWR): Winter habitat on which a wildlife species depends for survival. Because of severe weather conditions or other limiting factors, no alternative habitat would be available.

Cultural Resources: Those fragile and nonrenewable physical remains of human activity, occupation, or endeavor reflected in districts, sites, structures, buildings, objects, artifacts, ruins, works of art, architecture, burial mounds, petroglyphs, and natural features that were of importance in past human events. These resources consist of (1) physical remains; (2) areas where significant human events occurred, even though evidence of the event no longer remains; and (3) the environment immediately surrounding the resource. Cultural resources are commonly discussed in terms of prehistoric and historic values; however, each period represents a part of the full continuum of cultural values from the earliest to the most recent.

Cumulative Petroleum Production: Reported cumulative volume of petroleum that has been produced. Cumulative oil, cumulative gas, and cumulative production are sometimes used as abbreviated forms of this term.

D

Directional Drilling: The intentional deviation of a wellbore from vertical to reach subsurface targets that are not located directly below the drilling site.

E

Endangered Species: As defined in the Federal Endangered Species Act, any species that is in danger of extinction throughout all or a significant portion of its range. For terrestrial species, the U.S. Fish and Wildlife Service determines endangered status.

Environmental Assessment (EA): A public document for which a Federal agency is responsible that serves to: (1) briefly provide sufficient evidence and analysis for determining whether to prepare an Environmental Impact Statement (EIS) or a finding of no significant impact; (2) help an agency comply with the NEPA when no EIS is necessary; and (3) facilitate the preparation of an EIS when one is necessary. An EA includes brief discussions of the need for the proposal and of the environmental impacts of the proposed action and other alternatives.

Environmental Impact Statement (EIS): A written analysis of the impacts on the natural, social, and economic environment of a proposed project or resource management plan.

Estimated Ultimate Recovery (EUR): The total expected recoverable volume of oil, gas, and natural gas liquids production from a well, lease, or field under present economic and engineering conditions; synonymous with total recovery.

Extended Drilling Zone (EDZ): A buffer zone along the perimeter of NSO areas into which directional drilling can occur in a generalized (as opposed to specific) sense. An EDZ relates NSO to NNSO areas (see below).

F

Federal Land: For the purpose of this inventory, land owned by the United States, without reference to how the land was acquired or which Federal agency administers the surface; includes mineral estates underlying private surface.

Field: A production unit consisting of a collection of oil and gas pools that, when projected to the surface, form an approximately contiguous area that can be circumscribed.

Field Growth: The increases in known petroleum volume that commonly occur as oil and gas fields are developed and produced; synonymous with reserve growth.

Forecast Span: A specified future time span in which petroleum accumulations have the potential to provide additions to reserves. A 30-year forecast span is used in the USGS assessments, which affects (1) the minimum undiscovered accumulation size, (2) the number of years in the future that reserve growth is estimated, (3) economic assessments, (4) the accumulations that are chosen to be considered, and (5) the risking structure as represented by access risk.

Forest Plan (FP): A land use plan for a unit of the National Forest system.

Forest Service (USDA-FS): An agency of the U.S. Department of Agriculture that manages 193 million acres of public lands in national forests and grasslands.

G

Gas Accumulation: An accumulation with a gas to oil ratio of 20,000 cubic feet/barrel or greater.

Gas in Gas Accumulations: Gas volumes in gas accumulations.

Gas in Oil Accumulations: Gas volumes in oil accumulations.

Gas to Oil Ratio (GOR): The ratio of gas to oil (in cubic feet/barrel) in an accumulation. GOR is calculated using known gas and oil volumes at surface conditions.

Geographic Information System (GIS): A computer system capable of assembling, storing, manipulating, and displaying geographically referenced information, i.e., data identified according to their locations.

Geologic Province: A USGS-defined area having characteristic dimensions of perhaps hundreds to thousands of kilometers encompassing a natural geologic entity (for example, a sedimentary basin, thrust belt, or delta) or some combination of contiguous geologic entities.

Geospatial: Information that identifies the geographic location and characteristics of natural or constructed features and boundaries on the earth. This information may be derived from remote sensing, mapping, and surveying technologies, or from other sources.

Grown Petroleum Volume: Known petroleum volume adjusted upward to account for future reserve growth. Thirty years of reserve growth is considered for the USGS assessments.

H

Habitat: A specific set of physical conditions that surround a single species, a group of species, or a large community. In wildlife management, the major components of habitat are considered to be food, water, cover, and living space.

Hibernacula (Indiana bat): The caves and mines in which the Indiana Bat hibernates.

K

Known Petroleum Volume: The sum of cumulative production and remaining reserves as reported in the databases used in support of an assessment. Also called estimated total recoverable volume (sometimes called "ultimate recoverable reserves" or "estimated ultimate recovery").

L

Landscape: A relatively large area of land with common climate, geology, and soils containing predictably occurring terrain features such as slopes, drainage channels, rock outcrops, etc.

Lease (Oil and Gas): An authorization to use Federal lands and minerals issued under the Act of February 25, 1920, as amended (30 U.S.C. 181, et seq.); the Act of May 21, 1930 (30 U.S.C. 351-359); the Act of August 7, 1947 (30 U.S.C. 351, et seq.); or the Act of November 16, 1981 (PL 97-98, 95 Stat. 1070).

Lease Stipulations: See Stipulations.

Liquids to Gas Ratio (LGR): Ratio of total petroleum liquids (including oil, condensate, and natural gas liquids) to gas (in barrels/million cubic feet) in a gas accumulation. The LGR is calculated using known petroleum liquids and gas volumes at surface conditions. This ratio is used to assess the liquid co-products associated with undiscovered gas in gas accumulations.

M

Mineral: Organic and inorganic substances occurring naturally, with characteristics and economic uses that bring them within the purview of mineral laws; a substance that may be obtained under applicable laws from public lands by purchase, lease, or pre-emptive entry.

Minimum Accumulation Size: The smallest accumulation size (volume of oil in oil accumulations or volume of gas in gas accumulations) that is considered in the USGS assessment process for conventional accumulations.

Minimum Petroleum System: The mappable part of a total petroleum system for which the presence of essential elements has been proved by discoveries of petroleum shows, seeps, and accumulations.

Minimum Total Recovery Per Cell: The smallest total recovery per cell (volume of oil or gas) that is considered in the USGS assessment process for continuous-type accumulations.

Mitigation: Includes the following:

(1) Avoiding an impact altogether by not taking a certain action or parts of an action.
(2) Minimizing impacts by limiting the degree of magnitude of the action and its implementation.
(3) Rectifying the impact by repairing, rehabilitating, or restoring the affected environment.
(4) Reducing or eliminating the impact over time by preservation and maintenance operations during the life of the action.
(5) Compensating for the impact by replacing or providing substitute resources or environments.

Monitoring: The orderly collection, analysis, and interpretation of resource data to evaluate progress toward meeting resource management objectives.

N

National Environmental Policy Act (NEPA): An Act to establish a national policy for the environment, to provide for the establishment of a Council on Environmental Quality, and for other purposes. The law requires the assessment and documentation of the environmental and social impacts of Federal actions. (PL 91-190, 42 U.S.C. 4321- 4347, January 1, 1970, as amended by PL 94-52, July 3, 1975, PL 94-83, August 9, 1975, and PL 97-258, § 4(b), Sept. 13, 1982)

National Forest (NF): Created by an act of Congress in 1892, National Forests are Federal land reservations that are administered by the United States Department of Agriculture-Forest Service for multiple uses, including grazing, logging, minerals, and recreation.

National Register of Historic Places (NRHP): A Federal Government list of ". . .districts, sites, buildings, structures, and other objects significant in American history, architecture, archeology, and culture." The National Register is maintained by the National Park Service, U.S. Department of the Interior, and is published in its entirety in the Federal Register each year in February.

Natural Gas Liquids (NGL): Petroleum that occurs naturally as a gas in the reservoir, but that is a liquid under surface conditions. Natural gas liquids are typically reported separately from crude oil.

Natural Gas Liquids to Gas Ratio (for oil accumulations): Ratio of natural gas liquids to gas (in barrels/million cubic feet) in an oil accumulation, calculated using known natural gas liquids and gas volumes at surface conditions. This ratio is used to assess the natural gas liquids associated with undiscovered gas in oil accumulations.

Net No Surface Occupancy (NNSO): NSO areas are areas that can be leased but stipulations prohibit surface occupancy for natural gas and oil drilling activities to protect identified resources. To access O&G resources under NSO areas in the inventory, use of directional drilling technology is taken into consideration resulting in NNSO resources. The impacts of NNSO are similar to NLA areas. See also No Surface Occupancy.

Non-Associated Gas: Natural gas that occurs in a gas accumulation; synonymous with gas in gas accumulations.

No Surface Occupancy (NSO): An area where no surface-disturbing activities of any nature or for any purpose are allowed. For example, construction or the permanent or long-term placement of structures or other facilities would be prohibited. It is also used as a stipulation or mitigation requirement for controlling or prohibiting selected land uses or activities that would conflict with other activities, uses, or values in a given area. When used in this way, the NSO stipulation or mitigation requirement is applied to prohibit one or more specific types of land and resource development activities or surface uses in an area, while other—perhaps even similar— types of activities or uses (for other purposes) would be allowed. For example, protecting important rock art relics from destruction may require closing the area to the staking of mining claims and surface mining, off-road vehicle travel, construction or long-term placement of structures or pipelines, power lines, general purpose roads, and livestock grazing. Conversely, the construction of fences (to protect rock art from vandalism or from trampling or breakage by livestock), an access road or trail, and other visitor facilities to provide interpretation and opportunity for public enjoyment of the rock art would be allowed. Additionally, if there were potential and interest for leasing and consequent mineral development in the area, then leases for gas and oil, coal, etc., could be issued with a NSO stipulation or mitigation requirement for the rock art site, which would still allow access to the minerals from adjacent lands and underground. The term "no surface occupancy" has no relationship or relevance to the presence of people in an area.

In the NPRA, NSO stipulations generally apply only to permanent facilities but provide for wintertime exploration.

Notice: The communication of a pending Federal action; the notification to parties of Federal actions about to the taken. This is a part of due process.

O

Occupancy: Actual possession and use of land in something more than a slight or sporadic manner. As defined as a multiple use component, it is the management of public lands for occupancy involving the protection, regulated use, and development of lands as sites for economically and socially useful structures, either publicly or privately owned.

Oil Accumulation: An accumulation with a gas to oil ratio of less than 20,000 (in cubic feet/barrel).

Oil in Gas Accumulations: Oil volumes in gas accumulations. For the EPCA inventory, oil in gas accumulations was calculated with other liquids rather than separately.

Oil in Oil Accumulations: Oil volumes in oil accumulations.

Operator: An individual, group, association, or corporation authorized to conduct, for example, livestock grazing or oil and gas drilling on public lands.

P

Petroleum: A collective term for oil, gas, natural gas liquids, and tar.

Play: A set of known or postulated oil and gas accumulations sharing similar geologic, geographic, and temporal properties, such as source rock, migration pathway, timing, trapping mechanism, and hydrocarbon type. A play may or may not differ from an assessment unit; an assessment unit can include one or more plays.

Proposed Species: A species of plant or animal formally proposed by the U.S. Fish and Wildlife Service (USFWS) to be listed as threatened or endangered under the Endangered Species Act.

Proved Reserves: Quantities of crude oil, natural gas, or natural gas liquids that geological and engineering data demonstrate with reasonable certainty (defined as 90 percent or more probable) to be recoverable in future years from known reservoirs under existing economic and operating conditions.

Public Lands: Any land and interest in land owned by the United States that are administered by the Secretary of the Interior through the BLM, without regard to how the United States acquired ownership, except for (1) lands located on the Outer Continental Shelf and (2) lands held for the benefit of Indians, Aleuts, and Eskimos; includes public domain and acquired lands (see definitions). Vacant, unappropriated, and unreserved public lands, or public lands withdrawn by Executive Order 6910 of November 26, 1934, as amended, or by Executive Order 6964 of February 5, 1935, as amended, and not otherwise withdrawn or reserved, or public lands within grazing district established under Section 1 of the Act of June 28, 1934 (48 Stat. 1269), as amended, and not otherwise withdrawn or reserved.

R

Remaining Petroleum Reserves: Volume of petroleum in discovered accumulations that has not yet been produced. Remaining reserves is sometimes used as an abbreviated form of this term.

Reserve Growth: The increases in known petroleum volume that commonly occur as oil and gas accumulations are developed and produced; synonymous with field growth.

Resource Management Plan (RMP): A land use plan that provides the basic, general direction and guidance for BLM-administered public lands, usually within a specific administrative area.

Right-of-Way (ROW): A permit or easement which authorizes the use of public land for certain specified purposes, commonly for pipelines, roads, telephone lines, etc.; also, the lands covered by such an easement or permit. It does not grant an estate of any kind, only the right of use. May also include a site.

Riparian Areas: The vegetation along the banks of rivers and streams and around springs, bogs, wet meadows, lakes, and ponds.

Roadless: Refers to an absence of roads that have been constructed and maintained by mechanical means to ensure regular and continuous use.

Roads: Vehicle routes that have been improved and maintained by mechanical means to ensure relatively regular and continuous use. (A way maintained strictly by the passage of vehicles does not constitute a road).

S

Shapefile: GIS file format usable with ESRI (such as ArcView) and other commercial GIS software. It is a nontopological data structure that does not explicitly store topological relationships. However, unlike other simple graphic data structures, one or more rings represent shapefile polygons. A ring is a closed, non-self-intersecting loop. This structure can represent complex structures, such as polygons, that contain "islands." The vertices of a ring maintain a consistent, clockwise order so that the area to the right, as one "walks" along the ring boundary, is inside the polygon, while the area to the left is outside the polygon.

Split Estate: Federal mineral estate administered by the BLM, which is under either private lands, state lands, or lands administered by another Federal agency. On split estate lands, the surface owner or managing agency controls the surface uses but the mineral estate is the dominant estate. The BLM coordinates with surface owners on mineral leasing and development. In a few cases, the BLM administers the surface, but the minerals are owned by the state or a private entity.

Stipulations: Conditions, promises, or demands added to a lease when the environmental and planning record demonstrates the necessity for the stipulations. Stipulations, as such, are neither "standard" nor "special"; they are a necessary modification of the terms of the lease. In order to accommodate the variety of resources encountered on Federal lands, stipulations are categorized as to how the stipulation modifies the lease rights, not by the resource(s) to be protected. What, why, and how this mitigation/protection is to be accomplished is determined by the land management agency through land use planning and NEPA analysis. If, upon weighing the relative resource values, uses, and/or users, conflict with oil and gas operations is identified that cannot be adequately managed and/or accommodated on other lands, then a lease stipulation is necessary. Land use plans serve as the primary vehicle for determining the necessity for lease stipulations. Documentation of the necessity for a stipulation is disclosed in planning documents or through site-specific analysis. Land use plans and/or NEPA documents also establish the guidelines under which future waivers, exceptions, or modifications may be granted. Substantial modification or waiver of stipulations subsequent to lease issuance is subject to public review for at least a 30- day period in accordance with Section 51 02.f of the Federal Onshore Oil and Gas Leasing Reform Act of 1987. Stipulations may be necessary if the authority to control the activity on the lease does not already exist under laws, regulations, or orders. An authorized Federal officer has the authority to modify the site location and design of facilities, control the rate of development and timing of activities, and require other mitigation under standard lease terms. The necessity for individual lease stipulations is documented in the lease-file record with reference to the appropriate land use plan or other leasing analysis document. The necessity for exceptions, waivers, or modifications is documented in the lease-file record through reference to the appropriate plan or other analysis.[40]

Study Areas: Northern Alaska, Uinta-Piceance Basin, Paradox/San Juan Basins, Montana Thrust Belt, Powder River Basin, Wyoming Thrust Belt, Greater Green River Basin, Denver Basin, Florida Peninsula, Black Warrior Basin and the Appalachian Basin, which were selected as the geologic provinces for this inventory. They comprise the areas underlain by known or postulated oil and/or natural gas resources based upon USGS assessments.

Subsurface Allocation: An allocation of potential additions to reserves to land entities based on subsurface ownership of mineral rights.

Surface Allocation: An allocation of potential additions to reserves to land entities based on surface ownership.

Sweet Spot: An area within a continuous-type deposit where production characteristics are relatively more favorable.

T

Technically Recoverable Resources: In-place resources that are producible using current recovery technology but without reference to economic profitability. These resources are generally conceived as existing in accumulations of sufficient size to be amenable to the application of existing recovery technology.

Timing Limitations (TLs): Prohibit surface use during specified (usually seasonal) time periods to protect identified resource values. They do not apply to the operation and maintenance of production facilities unless there is a continued need for such mitigation and less stringent, project-specific mitigation measures would be insufficient. Also called a Seasonal Restriction.

Total Petroleum System (TPS): A mappable entity encompassing genetically related petroleum that occurs in seeps, shows, and accumulations (discovered or undiscovered) that have been generated by a pod or by closely related pods of mature source rock, together with the essential mappable geologic elements (source, reservoir, seal, and overburden rocks) that controlled fundamental processes of generation, migration, entrapment, and preservation of petroleum.

Total Recovery: The total expected recoverable volume of oil, gas, and natural gas liquids production from a well, lease, or field under present economic and engineering conditions; synonymous with estimated ultimate recovery.

U

Ultimate Recovery Appreciation (URA): The generally observed increase of Estimated Ultimate Recovery over time.

Undiscovered Petroleum Resources: Resources postulated from geologic information and theory to exist outside of known oil and gas accumulations.

USGS-Assessed Petroleum Volumes: The quantities of oil, gas, and natural gas liquids that have the potential to be added to reserves within some future time frame, which for this assessment is 30 years. The USGS assessed petroleum volumes include both those from undiscovered accumulations, whose sizes are greater than or equal to the selected minimum accumulation size, and those from the reserve growth of fields already discovered.

W

Wetlands: Permanently wet or intermittently flooded areas where the water table (fresh, saline, or brackish) is at, near, or above the soil surface for extended intervals; where hydric wet soil conditions are normally exhibited; and where water depths generally do not exceed two meters. Marshes, shallows, swamps, muskegs, lake bogs, and wet meadows are examples of wetlands.

Wilderness: A Congressionally designated area of undeveloped Federal land retaining its primeval character and influence, without permanent improvement or human habitation, that is protected and managed so as to preserve its natural conditions and that (1) generally appears to have been affected primarily by the forces of nature, with the imprint of man's work substantially unnoticeable; (2) has outstanding opportunities for solitude or a primitive and unconfined type of recreation; (3) has at least 5,000 acres of land or is of sufficient size as to make practicable its preservation and use in an unimpaired condition; and, (4) may also contain ecological, geological, or other features of scientific, educational, scenic, or historical value.

Wildlife: Animals that are neither human nor domesticated.

Withdrawal: An action that restricts the disposition of public lands and that holds them for specific public purposes; also, public lands that have been dedicated to public purposes (for example, recreation sites, office or warehouse sites, etc.).

APPENDIX 3: FEDERAL LAND STATUS PREPARATION

A3.1 Sources of Data

Federal lands mapping for Phases I and II of the inventory was completed based upon detailed research of multiple sources of information that describe the nature and extent of Federal surface and mineral interests. Spatial data themes were created that define various ownership characteristics and categories for lands within the study area boundaries. The final data sets were rendered to delineate both surface and subsurface U.S. rights. Ownership cases were extracted from the BLM's LR-2000 Database, processed, and used to create polygon themes for the project. The primary digital datasets processed and mapped include LR-2000 Status, Case Recordation, Legal Land Description, and various competitive oil and gas lease sales. In the Appalachian Basin study area, data from the "Site Log" were obtained from the BLM's Milwaukee Field Office and supplemented by other records from Federal, state and county governments. Digital land title records were supplemented with paper maps, land ownership ledgers, resource management plans and other miscellaneous real property records. The primary BLM land record databases are shown on the following schematic in Figure A3-1.[41]

In the Public Land Survey System (PLSS) states, the BLM's Geographic Coordinate Data Base (GCDB), where available, was utilized as the survey framework to create Federal land ownership and parcel boundaries. In areas where GCDB was not available, alternate sources were used to establish the positions of PLSS corners and subdivisions. In the Eastern states where only non-rectangular surveys exist, the best data available from Federal, state and county sources were used. Geographic coordinates were not available in all cases and therefore may be somewhat generalized.

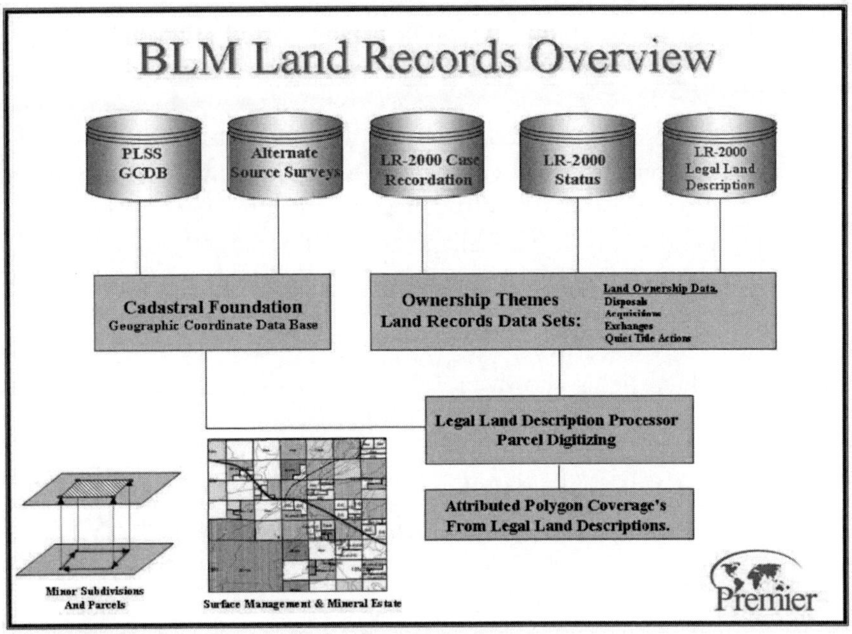

Figure A3-1. Schematic of BLM's Primary Land Records Databases

A3.2 Data Preparation

Polygon themes were created for over 180,000 individual ownership cases within the study areas that were extracted from the BLM's LR-2000 Database.

The Surface Management Agency (SMA) and ownership polygon boundaries reflect parcel geometry as described by the legal land description maintained in the electronic records. All land descriptions were processed, including minor subdivisions where available down to and including 2.5 acres or lower. Lands described by lot, tract or special surveys where GCDB was not available were processed against the BLM Legal Land Description (LLD) file to convert the lot references to nominal aliquot descriptions. Depending on the actual survey type and special survey geometry, the resulting polygon may contain a degree of generalization. Additionally, the BLM record systems do not contain individual records for public domain lands. The location of these lands was determined through various subtractive polygon-processing steps.

The primary information that defines U.S. ownership are data elements associated with various title transactions and business events recorded and maintained within the LR2000 Database. Case records that fall within the following four general categories were extracted and mapped.

1. **Land Disposals,** including patents, grants, deeds, land sales and all other transactions that conveyed ownership rights in lands from the Federal government.
2. **Acquired Lands,** including lands that were re-acquired by the United States under various legal authorities.
3. **Land Exchanges,** including lands exchanged between the Federal government and other parties.

4. **Quiet Title Cases,** including all records established to cure title and quiet adverse claims.

These four major categories formed the basis to extract the desired records from the BLM's databases. The four queries were processed against both the Status and Case Recordation datasets. Due to formatting differences between the two databases, the resulting polygon attributes contained in the GIS shape files varied slightly. Additionally, in some records extracted from the Case Recordation system, U.S. Rights were not readily available but were determined as accurately as possible through interpretation from land records obtained at BLM state and field offices.

The following attribute fields shown in Table A3-1 lists the data elements contained in the shape files produced from each of the LR-2000 datasets:

Table A3-1. Polygon Attributes from the LR-2000 Datasets

Status Attributes	Case Recordation Attributes
Shape	Meridian
Meridian	Township
Township	Range
Range	Section
Section	Surveytype
Survey Type	Aliquot
Aliquot	Serialnumb
Adminagenc County	Surveynumb Name
State	Percentint
Serialnumb	Price
Docid	Acres
Patent_num	Disposition
Case_type	Casetype
Usright1	Commodity
Usright2	Expiredate
Usright3	Expireyear
Usright4	Effectdate
Patentissu (mm/dd/yy)	Royaltyrt
Patentiss1 (year)	Geoname
Acres	Hbp
Patentee	Or
Id	Id

In the Western study areas, the data simplification process was completed through numerous steps that combined data associated with each of the four broad record categories described above.

A general discussion of the processing steps is described below:

1. The GCDB or alternate source PLSS data was used as the cadastral reference framework. The PLSS grid contains data elements and coordinates that define both townships, sections, and 1/16 subdivisions. Where legal descriptions described parcels less than 40 acres, CartéView software was used to map the minor aliquot parts down to 2.5 acres or smaller.[42]

2. After the PLSS base was loaded, a master polygon (Figure A3-2) was created to represent the original U.S. land purchases and annexations. For example, lands that fall within the geographic extent of the Denver Basin study area were acquired in 1803 through the Louisiana Purchase. All surface and subsurface rights were claimed by the United States of America.
3. The next step involved processing textual legal land descriptions against the PLSS framework file by subdividing according to the survey rules embedded in the CartéView software. The data shown in Table A3-2 shows a typical input file.

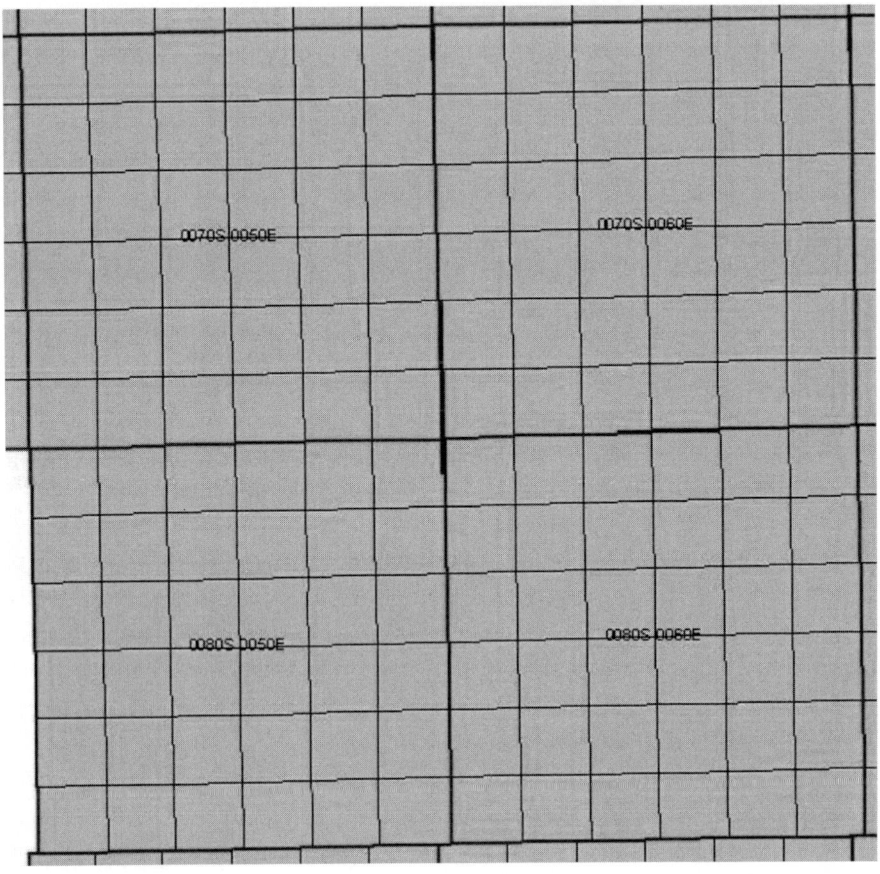

Figure A3-2. Master Polygon

4. After the records from the Status and Case Recordation datasets were processed, the resulting polygon themes were re-attributed to facilitate merging them together. These polygons were then overlaid on the Master Polygon to establish the location of lands where ownership left the Federal government by virtue of patent, grant or other title transfer authority. The resulting coverages are represented in the following graphic, Figure A3-3.

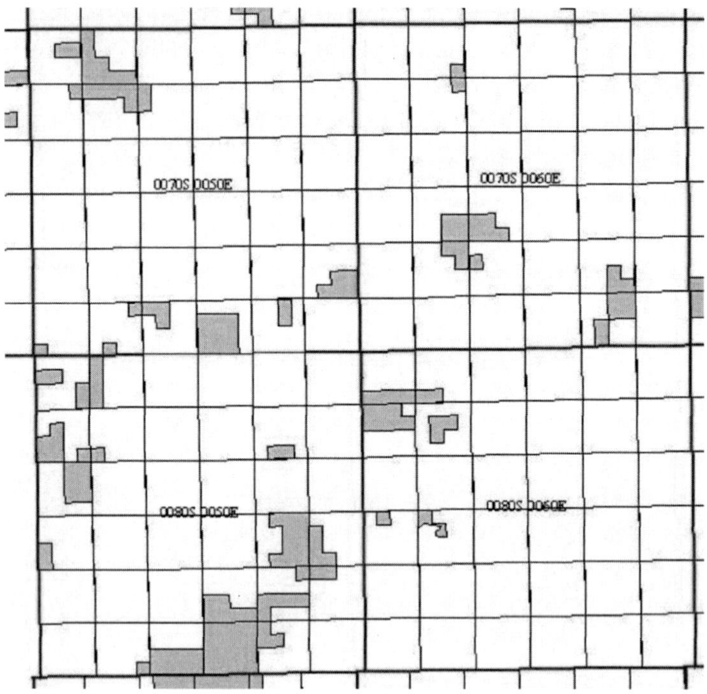

Figure A3-3. Public Domain Lands

The yellow polygons shown on the above map represent lands in the public domain where surface and subsurface rights are managed by the BLM.

5. The next step involved constructing a series of queries of the U.S. rights data associated with lands that were disposed through various title transfers. This query process, (Figure A3-4) involved a very complex analysis against the attribute tables in the spatial datasets. The results of these processes delineate all lands where subsurface oil and gas mineral rights are owned by the United States.

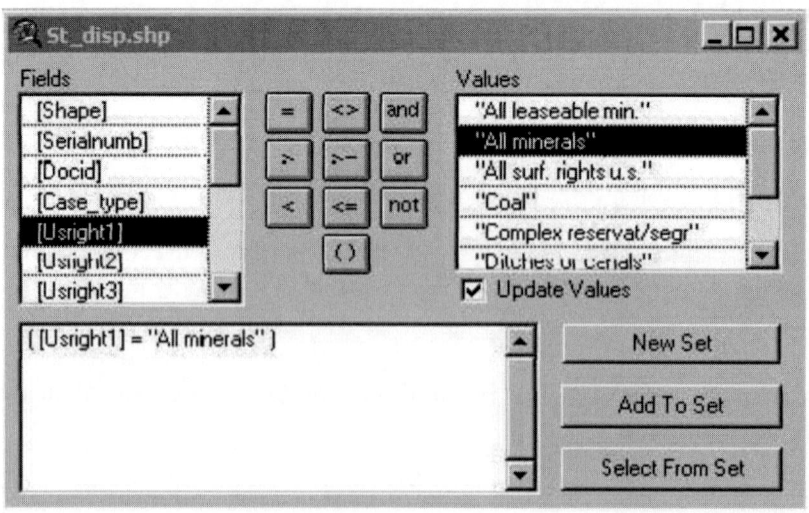

Figure A3-4. Query of U.S. Rights Data

Figure A3-5 illustrates the distribution of split estate mineral ownership within a four township area. The parcels shaded gray represent patented lands where the United States retained rights to the oil and gas mineral estate.

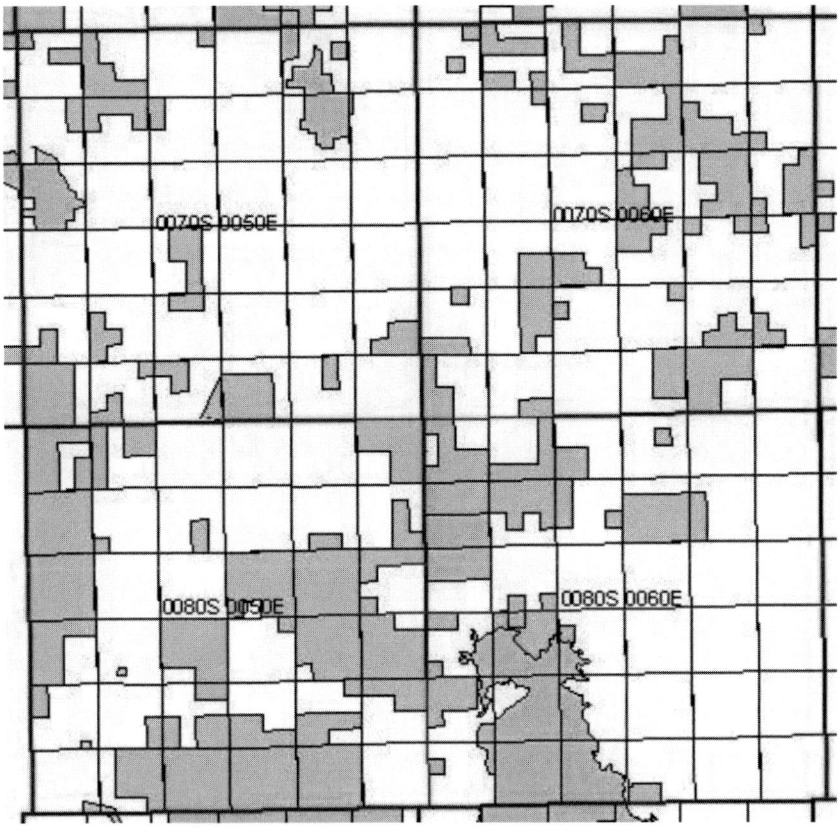

Figure A3-5. Federal Split Estate Oil and Gas Ownership

Table A3-2. Typical CarteView Input File

	A	B	C	D	E	F	G	H	I	J	K	L
1	Status	Generic	USRight1	SerialNumber								
2	Meridian	Township	Range	Section	SurveyTy	Aliquot	County	State	SerialNumber	DealID	Case_Type	USRight1
1348	6	0160N	0920W	28	T	NWNW,NWSW,SWNW;	7	WY	WYC 0001269	165770	HE ORIGINAL	Coal
1349	6	0160N	0920W	29	T	NENE,NESE,NWNE,NWSE,SENE,SW	7	WY	WYC 0001269	165770	HE ORIGINAL	Coal
1350	6	0160N	0920W	20	T	NESE,NWSE,SESE,SWSE;	7	WY	WYC 0001270	163248	HE ORIGINAL	Coal
1351	6	0160N	0920W	21	T	NWSW,SWSW;	7	WY	WYC 0001270	163248	HE ORIGINAL	Coal
1352	6	0160N	0920W	28	T	NWNW;	7	WY	WYC 0001270	163248	HE ORIGINAL	Coal
1353	6	0160N	0920W	29	T	NENE,NWNE;	7	WY	WYC 0001270	163248	HE ORIGINAL	Coal

6. The last step in the spatial query and overlay process was to define any other Federal management agencies or state surface ownership. These determinations were made by completing a series of queries against the ownership fields in the parcel base. The results of this query are shown in Figure A3-6.

   The parcels shaded blue represent lands that were granted to the State of South Dakota.

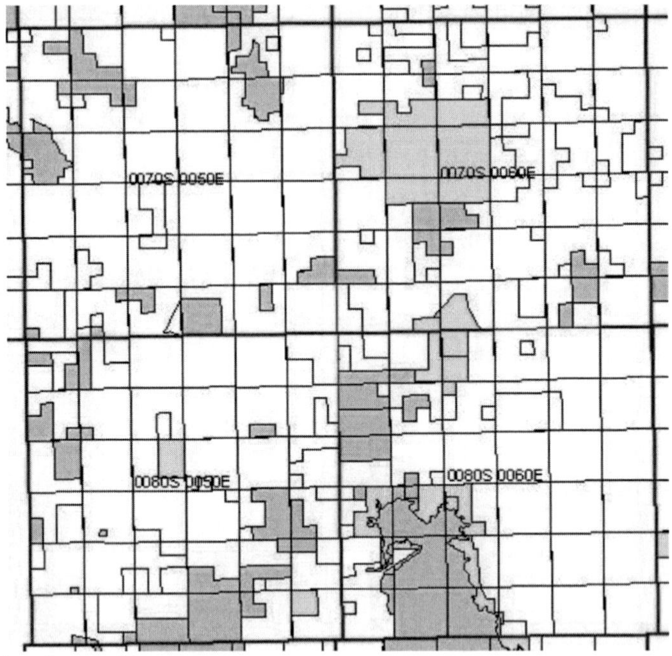

Figure A3-6. Defining Ownership

7. The final processing step was to dissolve the individual parcels into ownership categories that define the surface and mineral estates. The view in Figure A3-7 shows the surface management agencies and how land ownership is distributed within an area of the Denver Basin in South Dakota.

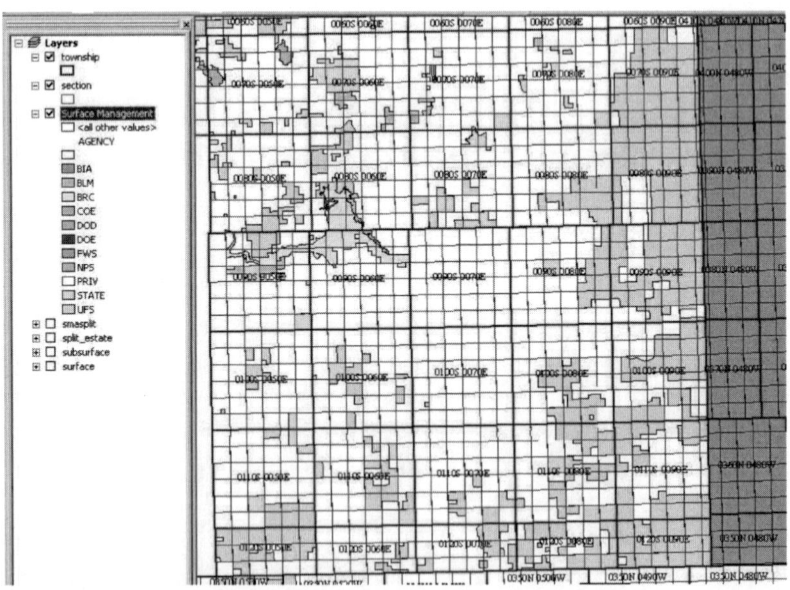

Figure A3-7. Surface Management View

In contrast to the surface management view, the mineral estate in the view shown in Figure A3-8 covers the same area and yields a much different picture. The yellow areas represent lands where the Federal government manages oil and gas rights.

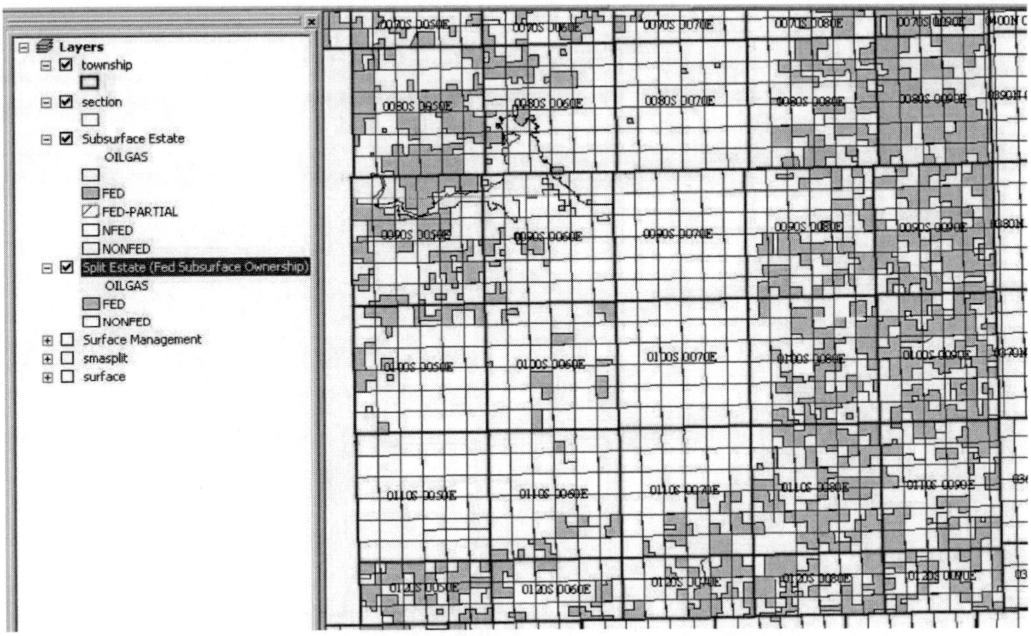

Figure A3-8. Subsurface Oil and Gas Ownership View

Eastern Study Areas Data Collection Summary

Ownership data for Eastern basins was collected by researching a range of sources that include the BLM's LR-2000 Database, Site Log, the USGS National Atlas, state and local governments and other land title records. All data sources are referenced in the metadata associated with each map theme. The data obtained from the numerous agencies varied dependant upon the knowledge base of local office personnel, technological capabilities and ability to release data. Therefore, county and state datasets were obtained when possible to support known missing Federal properties.

After the BLM records (LR-2000 and Site Log) were processed, USGS 1:24,000 quadrangle maps and the Geographic Names Information System (GNIS) provided the next level of detail for research and initial data collection. Various recreation atlases were also used to identify Federally owned lands for follow-up verification.

A3.3 Data Limitations

The data sets created from the processes described above reflect the legal land descriptions contained in the BLM databases. There was no attempt to analyze and review all of the error logs that were generated from the parcel generation process. If legal land descriptions were not properly entered and formatted according to BLM's published LR-2000 standards, an error log was generated.

In order to collect the most complete data possible, several steps were taken to determine where prior mineral activities have been recorded. The initial step was to map all of the BLM's LR-2000 mineral ownership and use authorization records and render maps that identi?ed the counties where these activities were recorded. After the records were mapped, each record was reviewed to identify the surface management agency to contact.

In areas where land ownership patterns were highly complex, parcels that contained an area of less than 40 acres were excluded.

This map shows all counties in the Appalachian Basin study area where mineral activities were recorded in the LR-2000 System. The darker colors represent higher densities of activity.

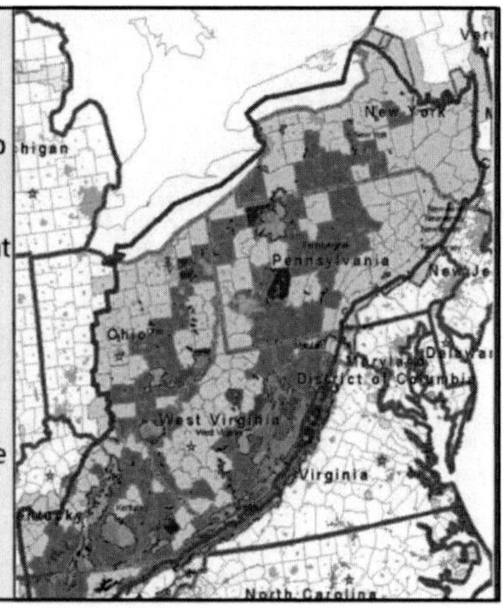

Other limitations:

- The BLM Case Recordation System is not consistently populated with U.S. Rights data. The split estate ownership generated from LR-2000 was verified by contacting BLM State and Field Offices. These data may carry a minor degree of generalization.
- The Interagency Steering Committee advised against processing certain withdrawal cases from the BLM's Status and Case Recordation datasets. This decision made it necessary to integrate Surface Management Agency information from GIS coverages obtained from multiple sources. During the spatial processing and merging of this data, sliver polygons were created. These sliver polygons were not edited and may be present in certain ownership themes.
- The PLSS data were not edge matched across state boundaries.

A3.4 Data Source by Agency

Data were provided by agencies as described below:

- **Bureau of Land Management:** Digital land records, hard copy maps and GIS shapefiles of Federal mineral ownership
- **United States Forest Service:** Hard copy maps and digital polygon files showing surface and subsurface ownership. Verbal confirmation for individual polygons overlapping other agency datasets
- **Fish and Wildlife Service:** Hard copy maps and digital shapefiles
- **National Park Service:** Digital shapefiles
- **United States Army Corps of Engineers (COE):** Hard copy maps, aerial photos, digital shapefiles of ownership polygons, county and municipal parcel datasets
- **Department of Defense:** Hard copy maps and digital shapefiles of ownership polygons. State, county and local datasets provided boundaries, verbally confirmed by direct contact with installation. BLM and COE also provided ownership boundaries by hard copy maps

- **Department of Energy:** Hard copy maps from the BLM and digital data provided by county and municipal datasets
- **Department of Homeland Security:** Digital shapefiles of ownership polygons, local county and municipal parcel datasets
- **Department of Justice:** Local tax GIS datasets. Federal prisons were verified by phone and digitized from hard copy maps
- **Department of Labor:** Local tax GIS datasets
- **Department of Veterans Affairs:** Hard copy maps from the BLM and digital polygons provided by county and municipality datasets
- **Federal Aviation Administration:** County and municipal parcel datasets
- **General Services Administration:** Local tax GIS datasets
- **National Aeronautics and Space Administration:** Hard copy maps from the BLM
- **Tennessee Valley Authority:** Digital shapefiles provided by the primary administrative and local agency offices
- **United States Department of Agriculture (other):** Local tax GIS datasets

Merging of datasets for Federal surface and subsurface ownership followed three basic rules in order of priority:

- Data extrapolated from deed records were considered have the highest confidence level
- Newer data and map publication dates were used over older sources
- Verbal verification by agency was obtained

APPENDIX 4: FEDERAL OIL AND GAS LEASE STIPULATION DATA PREPARATION

The bulk of the data preparation for lease stipulations consisted of data gathering, digitization, and compilation in a multi-layered GIS format (ESRI shapefiles). FGDC-compliant metadata for the resulting GIS layers were also created.

Where necessary, the shapefiles obtained from the Federal land management agencies were processed using ArcGIS software by matching specific leasing stipulations found in the guidance documents.

This inventory is limited to those Federal lands within the aggregate resource play boundaries of the eleven study areas, which are based on geology as defined in the USGS National Assessment of Oil and Gas Resources. The land status and stipulation shapefiles, which correspond to Federal land management agency jurisdiction boundaries, were "clipped" using the GIS to the appropriate study boundary. Some of the shapefiles fell into multiple study areas, in which case the clipping process was repeated for each area. The attribute tables of the compiled shapefiles were then queried for unique leasing stipulation values. The query results were then saved as separate polygon shapefiles. Each shapefile represents a unique stipulation value.

The following discussion of the specific data preparation steps uses the Wyoming Thrust Belt study area as an example:

1. The first step entails loading the study area (union of resource plays) boundary shapefile and the compiled stipulation shapefile into ArcGIS (Figure A4-1)

Figure A4-1. Stipulation Polygons and Study Area Boundary

The next step in this process is to "clip" or cut the compiled stipulation shapefile to the study boundary. Figure A4-2 shows the GIS coverage after it has been clipped.

Figure A4-2. Example of Polygons after Clipping to Study Area Boundary

2. The compiled stipulation shapefile is then queried for unique stipulation attributes values as shown in the ArcGIS Query Builder (Figure A4-3). For this example, all polygons covered by the leasing stipulation "Critical Big Game Habitat" were selected. The highlighted rows in the attribute table (Figure A4-5) show which records are selected.

3. Using the ArcGIS function "Create layer from Selected Features," a new shapefile is created that contains only polygons labeled with the attribute "Critical Big Game Habitat". Figure A4-5 shows the new shapefile that is created.

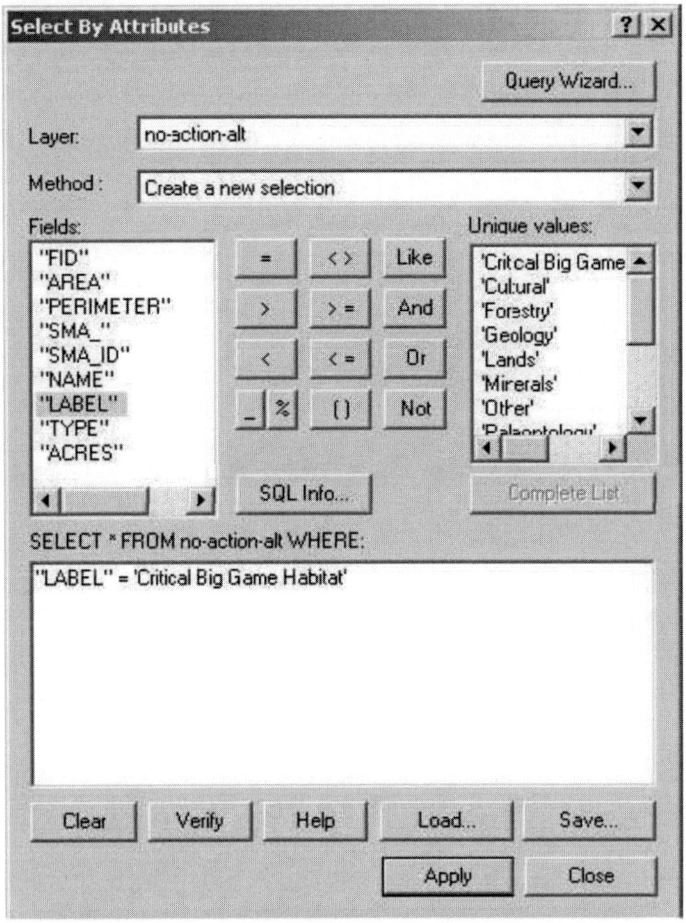

Figure A4-3. Query in ArcGIS for all "Critical Big Game Habitat" Stipulations

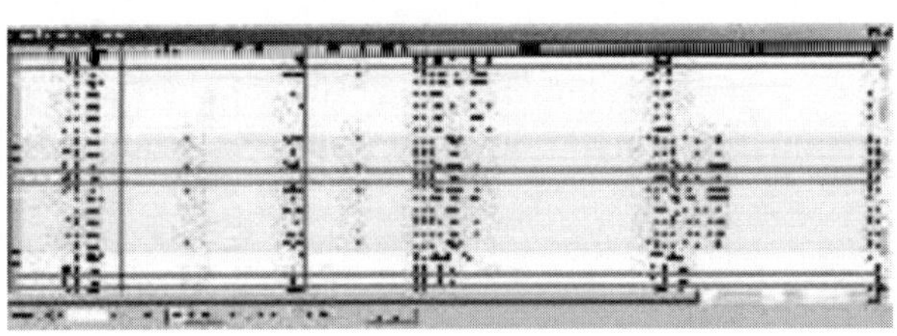

Figure A4-4. Attribute Table Showing all "Critical Big Game Habitat" Polygons

For certain stipulations, such as steep slopes, for which GIS data were not available from the BLM or Forest Service offices, shapefiles were created from available data in conformance with stipulation requirements. For example, a typical steep slope stipulation impacts leasing in areas where slopes exceed 25 percent. Polygon themes were created from slope data derived from USGS 1:24,000 Digital Elevation Models (DEMs). These raster data sets contain elevation information on a 100-meter grid spacing. The original for the Phase I inventory was a 30-meter grid spacing, which was resampled to 100 meters.

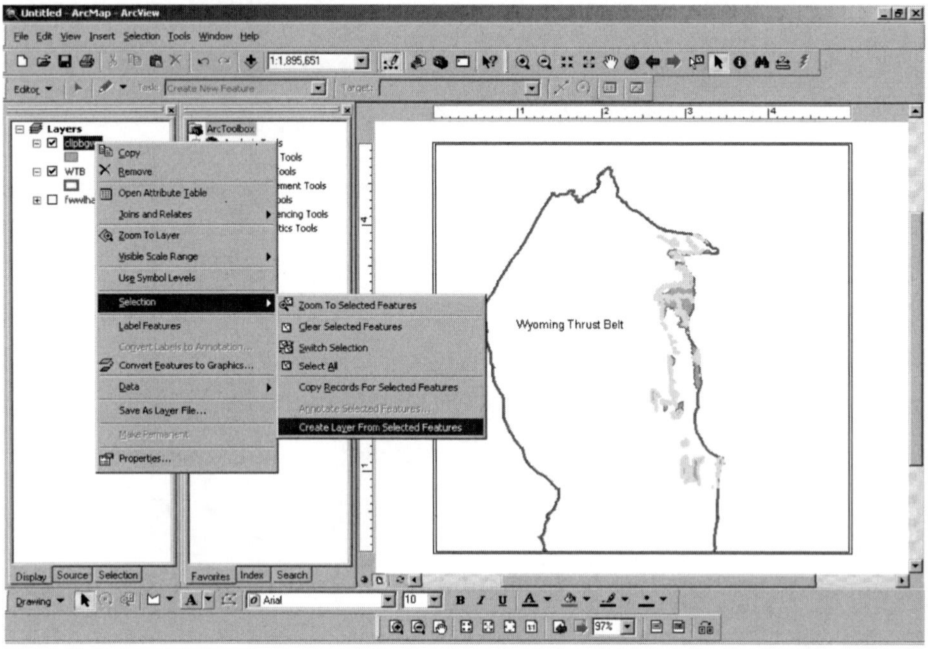

Figure A4-5. New Polygons Representing Land with Leasing Stipulation for "Critical Big Game Habitat"

The USGS DEMs were first clipped to the BLM or Forest Service jurisdictional area. In situations where more than one agency had the same stipulations, the DEM was clipped to the agencies' combined jurisdictional area. A raster coverage was then created containing slope percentage data as calculated by ArcGIS. This coverage was then queried to isolate the areas covered by the stipulation (e.g., all areas steeper than 25 percent). The selected raster data was then converted to a vector polygon coverage, and the coverage was coded and attributed as described above. Figure A4-6 shows the creation of steep slope polygons. The 100-meter USGS DEM for this portion of the Denver Basin is shown in shades of grey. The red theme represents the polygon shapefile showing areas with a greater than 25 percent slope.

Following the above procedures, the GIS shapefiles of the stipulations were coded with their respective descriptions from the various land use plans. These stipulations can be found in Appendix 11.

A4.1 Differences between the Phase II and Phase I Inventories

The Phase II inventory is a cumulative effort and incorporates data from the Phase I inventory. There are a number of differences between the two studies, some minor and some significant. These differences are divided into changes, omissions and errors as detailed below.

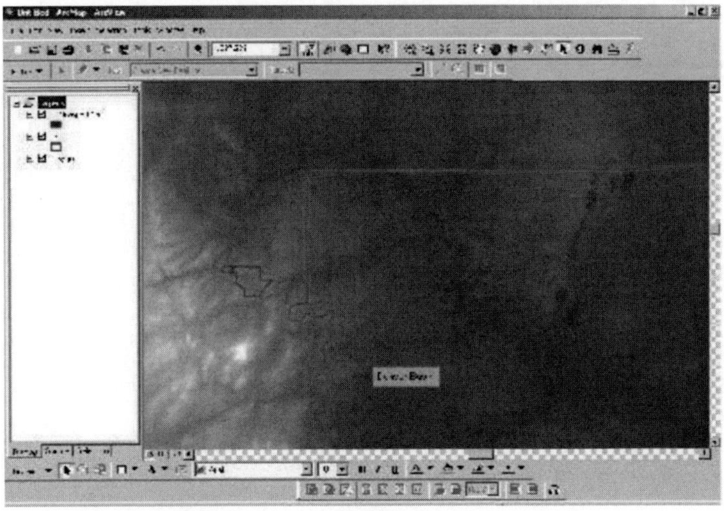

Figure A4-6. Creation of Steep Slope Restriction Polygons

Some offices inventoried in Phase I had revised their LUPs since that time. The Medicine Bow-Routt NF is an example. The Phase II inventory does not incorporate these updates. A subsequent release of this inventory will include the updated LUPs.

A4.1 .1 Methodological Changes

Categorization Hierarchy. In order to better capture the scope of the limitations on access to Federal lands, changes were made to the categorization hierarchy for the land status and the stipulations in the Phase II inventory:

- Because the purpose of the study is to identify limitations to exploration and development, proved reserves are not included in the resource categorization in the results tables (Section 3). In Phase I, proved reserves had been categorized as accessible under standard lease terms. This change was made for the Phase II inventory due to amendments to Section 604 of EPCA found in Section 364 of EPAct 2005, which strikes the term "reserves". All categories (where leasing can occur) are defined as requiring drilling for discovery and conversion into reserves. The proved reserves are listed in Section 2, Table 2-6 but are not included elsewhere in this inventory.
- The NLA/LUP and NLA categories are switched (NLA acceding to the second level in the categorization) to present a more logical progression to the hierarchy. The rationale for this decision is that the NLA category is based on a decision within the land use plan or made by the office not to lease an area. In contrast the NLA/LUP category is an area where a decision has not yet occurred and consequently the categorization may be less restrictive when the final land use plan is completed.
- Because their impacts on operators' capacities to drill are similar, stipulations for TLs ≤ 3 months and CSU were combined at level 8 as a simplification. Note that due to this change, some areas on the Phase I land access categorization maps which were pink in color will be gold on the Phase II maps. Lands stipulated with TLs ≤ 3 months cover a very small area.

- A clarification change was made to labeling for the NSO category, where the term "net" was added in reference to the oil and gas resources. Because the analytical model adjusts for directional drilling capabilities (see Appendix 7), Net NSO resource areas are effectively inaccessible.

Citizens' Proposal Areas (CPAs). CPAs, CWPs, and Wilderness Reinventory Areas (WRAs) were considered NLA in Phase I. As a result of *Utah vs Norton*[43], CPAs and WRAs are now considered leasable and subject to stipulations.

Blackleaf Study Area. The Blackleaf area in the Montana Thrust Belt study area was explicitly added due to an indefinite postponement of its EIS in 2004[44].

Additional Resources in the Phase I Study Areas. Study areas for this inventory are defined by the USGS play boundaries. Further, plays from distinct USGS oil and gas provinces can overlap, as is the case in the WTB relative to the GGRB. However, because the inventory is focused on the land surface, study areas must, by definition, be geographically unique. In the case of the WTB and the GGRB, the overlapping resources have been allocated to the GGRB, resulting in a change in the resource numbers in comparison to the originally published Phase I results. While this does not affect the land access categorization, it does affect resource access categorization to the extent that resource densities in the GGRB for the Phase II inventory are different where associated with specific stipulations. This situation also occurs at the intersection of the Powder River and Denver basins and in the Paradox and Uinta basins in Phase I inventory.

Inventoried Roadless Areas. The Phase I inventory included the IRAs as a Federal Land Use Designation and categorized them as subject to stipulations. In the Phase II inventory, the guidance from the USDA-FS was modified slightly—specifically, the accessibility of roadless areas is determined by the local Forest Plan. Roadless area stipulations exist for Ashley, Grand Mesa/Uncompahgre/Gunnison, Uinta, White River and Lewis and Clark NFs. The GIS data were not available for many of these stipulations. Instead, the national IRA GIS layer was used.

NSO Areas. In the EPCA II inventory, the geoprocessing of NSO areas was made stricter to provide greater accuracy. Specifically, if an NSO area abutted an area that cannot be leased, an "extended drilling zone" (EDZ, see Appendix 7 for a full description) was not calculated from that area based upon the fact that a drilling rig could not legally be set up. Further, within a Federal jurisdiction that contained NSO lands, buffering from non-Federal lands onto Federal lands was not performed, as it could not be assumed that the non-Federal lands are leasable.

Further, in the GGRB study area, a generalized EDZ for the basin was used in the Phase I inventory (based on a prior DOE analysis).[44] During the course of Phase II data collection, individual offices (that are also in the Phase I Study Area) were interviewed to determine specific EDZs, and those EDZ values were used in the Phase II analysis. These offices were: Kemmerer, WY, BLM FO; Rawlins, WY, BLM FO; Casper, WY, BLM FO; Wasatch-Cache NF; Bridger-Teton NF.

Stipulations for Which No GIS Data Are Available. As noted in Section 2.1.2.3., specific efforts were made to assess stipulations where no GIS data were available. By count, approximately 39 percent of the 2132 stipulations in the Phase II inventory do not have GIS associated with them. To the extent that this exists, the Inventory overestimates access to lands and resources. This quantification had not been made in the Phase I inventory.

A4.1.2 Omissions in Phase I

Additional Data Received from Offices. For some Phase I offices, especially those that are also in the Phase II study areas, some additional data was received. Offices where significant new GIS data were obtained are the Black Hills NF; Bridger-Teton NF; Casper, WY, BLM FO; Kemmerer, WY, BLM FO; Nebraska NF; Newcastle, WY, BLM FO; Rawlins, WY, BLM FO; Rock Springs, WY, BLM FO; and the Wasatch Cache NF.

In addition, an updated national GIS layer for Wilderness Areas, Inventoried Roadless Areas, Special Designated Areas, National Conservation Areas, Wilderness Reinventory Areas, Incorporated Towns and Cities, Wilderness Study Areas, Research Natural Areas, National Monuments Areas, National Wildlife Refuges, Wild and Scenic Rivers, and National Scenic and Historic Trails was provided by the BLM's National Landscape Conservation System.

Incorporated Towns and Cities (ITCs). After the Phase I inventory was published, it was determined that ITCs were not considered. These were added in Phase II because, by regulation, incorporated areas are not available for Federal mineral leasing as established in 43 CFR 3100-3(a)(2)(iii) and 3100-3(b)(2)(ii).

A4.1.3 Errors in Phase I

Analytical Errors. There were about 980 stipulations having GIS data In the Phase I inventory. Miscellaneous analytical errors were made that impacted the results presented in published version of that inventory. Without running the analytical model specifically for the stipulations in question, the absolute magnitude of these errors cannot be assessed; however their impacts are believed to be modest to minor for any individual study area. The errors are:

- In the Vernal, UT, BLM FO, Phase I results indicate larger areas of NSO than is the case. Comparison of the Phase I and Phase II model runs shows this error to make a 4 percent difference in NNSO areas in the UP study area.
- In the Rock Springs, WY, BLM FO, some sage grouse leks[45] were absent from the model runs. Based upon a comparison of the model runs for this FO, the impact of this is believed to be significant. Differences in TLs between the two runs are 13 percent, although a noteworthy portion of these differences also come from additional sage grouse stipulation data received from the Kemmerer, WY, BLM FO during Phase II. Another error in the Rock Springs FO is one stipulation that was miscategorized as NLA. It has been corrected to CSU.
- In the Lander, WY, BLM FO, a stipulation had an incorrect listing of its timing limitation resulting in a one-level higher categorization than is the case. In addition, another CSU stipulation was improperly depicted to partially cover the FO when it should have covered the portion of the FO within in the GGRB study area. The stipulation geography was corrected.

- In the Craig, CO, FO, one stipulation had been categorized as NLS and was corrected to NSO.
- In the St. George, UT, BLM FO, missing NLA and CSU stipulations were added.
- In the Richfield, UT, BLM FO some stipulations were missing from the Phase I model runs. During EPCA II a complete copy of the stipulation data was obtained and the error was corrected.
- For the Navajo Reservoir, NM, BOR, the reservoir should have been classified as NSO.
- In the Thunder Basin NG, a NSO stipulation has been deleted as it is not a USDA-FS stipulation (but does occur in the BLM RMP covering this portion of the study area).
- In the Buffalo, WY, BLM FO, a wildlife stipulation had an incorrect listing of its timing limitation resulting in a one-level higher categorization than is the case.
- In the PDX/SJ and UP study areas, an error was made in the allocation of overlapping resources resulting in changes to the results. The oil resource assessment was shown as incorrect by 30 percent (however the total amount of oil resource is modest). The gas assessment was shown as incorrect by 15 percent.
- In the PRB, an error in the land status layer resulted in a 10 percent understatement of Federal lands. At the resource level the error is $\leq$ 1.5 percent.

Table A4-1. Rendering Errors in Phase I Offices

Office	Remarks
Manti La Sal NF	Partial CSU displayed
Price, UT BLM FO	Partial NSO, TLS, CSU displayed
Moab, UT BLM FO	Partial CSU displayed
Craig, CO BLM FO	Partial TLS displayed
White River, CO BLM FO	Partial split estate, CSU displayed
GMUG NF	Partial NLA, NSO, TLS, CSU displayed
Rock Springs, WY BLM FO	Partial TLS displayed
Pinedale, WY BLM FO	Partial CSU displayed
Richfield, UT BLM FO	Partial NSO, TLS, CSU displayed
Monticello, UT BLM FO	Partial TLS displayed
PDX/SJ SA	Erroneous split estate depiction

Rendering Errors. In the presentation of some Federal land status and land access categorization (LAC) in the Phase I inventory publication, errors were made in rendering in figures within the report. These items have been checked specifically and they do not impact the analytical results presented, but are an erroneous display of the land status and categorization on maps. Table A4-1 presents listing of offices where such rendering errors occurred relative to the Phase I report figures.

To alleviate this problem, the Phase II geospatial model has been modified to explicitly produce Federal land status and LAC map presentations.

APPENDIX 5: APD CONDITIONS OF APPROVAL DATA PREPARATION

In contrast to the EPCA Phase I inventory, Phase II incorporated a large-scale statistical sampling and categorization of COAs and related data for APDs.

The data preparation consisted primarily of the creation of a Federal oil and gas permit/well GIS point data theme. This task was performed by processing legal description data from the BLM's AFMSS against the PLSS dataset collected as described in Appendix 3. Data gathering, compiling, categorizing, digitizing and analysis followed as described below.

1. The initial task consisted of a pilot study to determine more fully the nature of COAs by abstracting information from well files located in BLM's Vernal and Price FOs. The purpose of this initial task was to provide information for the subsequent design and execution of the full-scale statistical sampling in the study areas as shown on Table A5-1. The Montana Thrust Belt study area was not included because it is approximately 97 percent closed to access and has little drilling history. The Florida Peninsula was also excluded given the relative lack of drilling history.
2. Excel spreadsheets were used to collect the COA data during visits to BLM FOs. They included attributes from the AFMSS database identifying lease number, surface location legal description (including footage calls, if available), surface managing agency, operator name, well name, well number, well type, received date, approval date, spud date, and completion date.
3. All APDs approved between and including the dates of October 1, 1999 and September 30, 2004 were included. Wells on non-Federal minerals within Federal agreements and on Indian lands were excluded. The COAs and related data were collected from approved APDs issued by the BLM FOs (Table A5-2) within the Phase I and II study areas. This well/permit data theme was then spatially intersected with the study area polygons to eliminate points outside of the inventory. The distribution of the resultant APDs was then geographically mapped.
4. The above data theme was then randomly sampled to generate a new GIS point data theme. A stratified random sampling method was used with two data strata: BLM Field Office and surface managing agency. The samples from each stratum were weighted by total APDs approved for each Field Office. The resultant total sample was approximately 10 percent of the total population of permits/wells and followed the guidance presented on Table A5-3, as determined during the pilot study.

Table A5-1. Study Areas Sampled for COAs

Phase I	Uinta-Piceance Basin
	Paradox/San Juan Basins
	Powder River Basin
	Greater Green River Basin
Phase II	Northern Alaska (NPRA)
	Wyoming Thrust Belt
	Denver Basin
	Black Warrior Basin
	Appalachian Basin

Table A5-2. BLM Field Offices for which COAs Data was Abstracted

Administrative State	**BLM Field Offices**
Alaska	Northern (Fairbanks)
Colorado	Little Snake (Craig), White River (Meeker), Grand Junction, Glenwood Springs, Royal Gorge (Cañon City), Uncompahgre (Montrose), Gunnison, and San Juan (Durango)
Eastern States	Jackson, MS, and Milwaukee, WI
Montana	Miles City, Billings, North Dakota (Dickinson), and South Dakota (Belle Fourche)
New Mexico	Farmington, Rio Puerco (Albuquerque), and Taos
Utah	Salt Lake, Vernal, Richfield, Price, Moab, Cedar City, Monticello, St. George, Kanab, and Grand Staircase-Escalante National Monument (Escalante)
Wyoming	Buffalo, Newcastle, Casper, Pinedale, Kemmerer, Rock Springs, Rawlins, and Lander

Table A5-3. Stratified Random Sampling Guidance

APD Population (FY 2000-2004) within Field Office	Sample Size
0 – 30	100%
31 – 200	30 APDs
201 – 1333	15%
>1333	200 APDs

5. Contractor personnel, accompanied by BLM personnel, visited BLM FOs and abstracted COA and other related information from the hardcopy well files identified by the sampling process. Those offices whose sample count within the study areas fell below six were generally not visited. Instead, the FO was requested to transmit the COAs to the BLM Washington Office where they were examined.
   The abstracted information contained site-specific restrictions or impediments that affect the ability of the permittee and/or lessee to access the underlying lease for the purpose of exploring for and developing oil and gas resources. All abstracted information was restricted to Federal lands and limited to the 13-point surface use plan of the APD and related documents.
6. Other relevant information for the study was obtained through interviews held with FO personnel. This information was essential to determine the extent, through a qualitative analysis, of negotiations that occur prior to the submission of an APD, including adjustments at the time of well staking. This included the determination of:
   Whether applicant-funded surveys (e.g., wildlife or archeological) are a prerequisite to acceptance of an APD as administratively complete (Table A5-4a)
   The number of APDs not actually applied for because the cumulative effects of lease stipulations and probable COAs were prohibitive (Table A5-4b).
7. COA data were compiled into spreadsheets and spatial displays (GIS, etc.) that can used to assist BLM management in decisions regarding APD approvals. The compilation process consisted of grouping of COAs by class (e.g., wildlife, soils, archeological, construction, sage grouse, etc.), and subsequent assignment of a unique identifier for each type of COA within a class. Only COAs that were more restrictive than (and not merely a restatement of) the stipulations on the underlying lease were considered. A total of 175 unique COAs were identified.
8. These unique COAs were categorized as to their effect on access by the Interagency Steering Committee. The result was that COAs fell either into controlled surface use (CSU) or cumulative timing limitation (TL) categories that correspond with the leasing hierarchy described in Table 2-8. Changes in land access categorization arising from COAs were integrated into the spatial model. This recategorization methodology consisted of first computing for each unique COA the percentage of wells having that COA (% unique-COA) with respect to the total number of wells sampled within a given FO and also within the non-NSO leasable areas as represented by the equation:

$$\%uniqueCOA = \frac{(\#Wells)_{uniqueCOA}}{(\#Wells)_{Acc.Area}} = 10\%$$

Where:

$\%uniqueCOA$	:	Percentage of wells with a unique COA
$(\#Wells)_{uniqueCOA}$	:	Number of wells with a unique COA
$(\#Wells)_{Acc\,.\,Area}$	:	Total number of wells in the accessible area.

Table A5-5 is a breakdown of the COAs by BLM FO and includes the categorization, number of occurrences, and percentage of the wells in the sample that have that COA.

Table A5-4a. Findings from Interviews with BLM Field Personnel – Applicant Funded Surveys

Survey Question: Are applicant funded surveys (e.g., wildlife or archeological) a prerequisite to acceptance of an APD as administratively complete?		
Field Office	Response	Remarks
Buffalo	Yes	BLM asks companies to plan APD activities from 12 to 18 months prior to the formal
		submission. This includes meetings to plan activities, supply maps and discuss
		requirements.
Canon City	No	However, occasionally a survey is required (happened four times in the last fourteen
		years).
Casper	Yes	
Craig	No	However, without the archeological survey the archeologist usually won't finish their
		portion of the EA, so NEPA work will not be completed. Applicant funded surveys are
		encouraged to help speed up the processing of an APD, especially for archeology.
		Applicant funded wildlife surveys are rarely encouraged because usually the BLM has
		enough information. Applicant funded surveys are encouraged for special projects.
		Specialists like to have the surveys completed before the NEPA work is finished. It is
		unlikely for an APD to be approved and before the surveys are received.
Durango	Yes	
Farmington	Yes	
Glenwood Springs	Yes	
Grand Junction	No	Surveys are typically completed by a contractor. If the operator asks the BLM to
		perform the survey, long delays may occur as the archeological/cultural staff at the
		Field Office are quite busy.
Jackson	No	However, if a survey is required, it must be received prior to APD approval.
Kemmerer	Yes	

Table A5-4a. (Continued)

Survey Question: Are applicant funded surveys (e.g., wildlife or archeological) a prerequisite to acceptance of an APD as administratively complete?		
Miles City	Yes	
Lander	Yes	
Meeker	No	However, rather than waiting for the BLM to do the surveys, operators have paid a
		private consultant to perform them. Generally speaking, the survey comes in after the
		BLM has received the APD and is already processing it.
Milwaukee	No	Not automatically required. BLM tries to identify if any survey will be needed during
		the leasing process, and if so, places a notice on the lease parcel to that effect.
		Normally the required surveys are archeological.
Moab	Yes	
Newcastle	Yes	
Pinedale	Generally	Archaeological surveys can performed after permitting, but must be received before
	yes, but see	drilling (frozen ground is an issue).
	remarks	
Rawlins	No	However, lack of a cultural report will often delay approval of the APD. Except for
		a few black footed ferret surveys, wildlife surveys from the applicant are seldom
		required. These are generally done in house as part of the NEPA process
Rock Springs	Yes	Surveys are required to be in the Environmental Assessment.
Vernal	Generally	Because the specific wildlife presence may not be determined and may change over
	yes, but see	time, some APDs have COAs that call for routine wildlife surveys after the permit is
	remarks	issued.

Table A5-4b. Findings from Interviews with BLM Field Personnel – Prohibitive Lease Stipulations/COAs

Survey Question: Are there any known cases where APDs were not submitted because the cumulative effects of lease stipulations and probable COAs were deemed prohibitive by the operator		
Field Office	Response	Remarks
Buffalo	No	
Canon City	Yes	One case in the mid-nineties
Casper	No	
Craig	No	
Durango	No	
Farmington	No	
Glenwood Springs	No	

Table A5-4b. (Continued)

Survey Question: Are there any known cases where APDs were not submitted because the cumulative effects of lease stipulations and probable COAs were deemed prohibitive by the operator		
Grand Junction	No	However, there was one case where the operator chose to look for another site on
		the lease that did not have an NSO stipulation.
Jackson	Yes	Occurred rarely. The FO recalls one particular case in which an operator withdrew an
		APD after finding an archeological site (ancient cemetery) that would have required
		the well to be moved.
Kemmerer	No	
Lander	No	
Meeker	No	
Miles City	No	
Milwaukee	No	
Moab	No	
Newcastle	No	
Pinedale	No	
Rawlins	No	However, there have been some instances where APDs were withdrawn after field
		review and/or NEPA analysis indicated the need for intensive mitigation and/or
		relocation of the well site. A few APD's for coalbed natural gas were withdrawn
		because the lessee could not reach an agreement with the holder of the coal lease. In
		these instances, the holder of the coal lease had prior existing rights.
Rock Springs	No	
Vernal	No	

9. Subsequently this percentage value was extrapolated to the overall leasable area to estimate the change in accessibility. A grid composed of 400 by 400 meter grid (approximately 40 acres) was created for each FO or NF containing a study area. Cells were then randomly selected at the previously calculated percentage rate to create a potential access constraint theme. Figure A5-1 illustrates the process to extrapolate the effects of COAs on accessibility. This is an example for a case where 10 percent of the leasable area is potentially subject to a particular COA type.

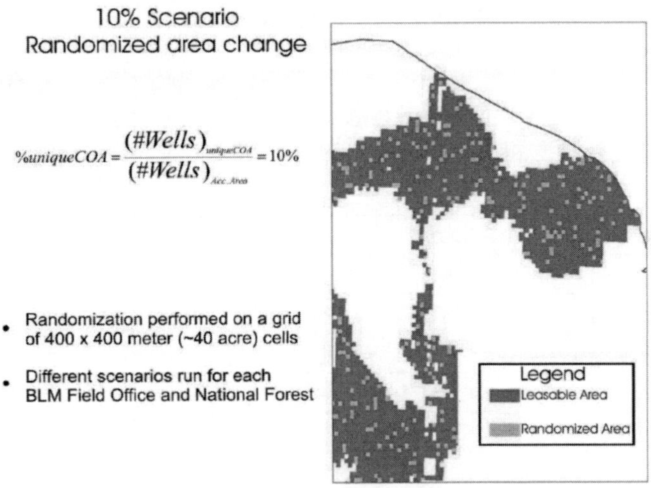

Figure A5-1. Example of Extrapolating the Effects of COAs on Accessibility

Table A5-5. COA Statistics by Field Office

BLM FO		Well Population	Sample Size	Sample Wells w/ COAs
	COA ID	COA Category	Occurrence	% of Sample
Rio Puerco		48	30	4
	archeo002	CSU	2	7%
	noise001	CSU	2	7%
Buffalo		5077	200	69
	archeo002	CSU	2	1%
	cultur001	CSU	2	1%
	cultur002	CSU	2	1%
	hydro001	CSU	4	2%
	hydro005	TLS	1	1%
	plover002	CSU	3	2%
	plover003	CSU	4	2%
	plover004	CSU	3	2%
	plover013	TLS	1	1%
	plover032	TLS	3	2%
	raptor002	CSU	15	8%
	raptor003	CSU	3	2%
	raptor004	TLS	1	1%
	raptor006	TLS	1	1%
	raptor007	TLS	17	9%

Table A5-5. (Continued)

BLM FO		Well Population	Sample Size	Sample Wells w/ COAs
	COA ID	COA Category	Occurrence	% of Sample
	raptor018	TLS	1	1%
	raptor023	CSU	1	1%
	raptor024	CSU	1	1%
	raptor027	CSU	2	1%
	raptor029	CSU	2	1%
	roads001	CSU	2	1%
	roads002	CSU	1	1%
	sagegr001	CSU	5	3%
	sagegr003	CSU	9	5%
	sagegr005	TLS	10	5%
	sagegr008	TLS	5	3%
	sagegr022	CSU	8	4%
	sagegr033	TLS	3	2%
	sagegr038	CSU	1	1%
	soils001	CSU	14	7%
	wildlf002	CSU	1	1%
	wildlf002	TLS	1	1%
	wildlf004	CSU	4	2%
	wildlf005	TLS	1	1%
	wildlf012	TLS	1	1%
	wildlf018	CSU	3	2%
Casper		170	30	25
	archeo001	CSU	1	3%
	constr001	CSU	2	7%
	constr008	CSU	18	60%
	constr014	TLS	1	3%
	cultur002	CSU	2	7%
	plover030	TLS	1	3%
	raptor003	CSU	1	3%
	raptor007	TLS	2	7%
	raptor019	TLS	1	3%
	raptor023	CSU	19	63%
	raptor029	CSU	2	7%
	sagegr005	TLS	1	3%
	soils001	CSU	21	70%

Table A5-5. (Continued)

BLM FO		Well Population	Sample Size	Sample Wells w/ COAs
	COA ID	COA Category	Occurrence	% of Sample
	sslope001	CSU	18	60%
	wildlf003	CSU	18	60%
	wildlf004	CSU	2	7%
Farmington		2713	200	74
	archeo001	CSU	1	1%
	archeo002	CSU	14	7%
	bgame008	TLS	10	5%
	bgame011	TLS	1	1%
	bgame012	TLS	1	1%
	bgame014	TLS	1	1%
	constr004	TLS	10	5%
	noise001	CSU	7	4%
	pipel002	CSU	19	10%
	pipel008	CSU	19	10%
	raptor017	TLS	1	1%
	roads001	CSU	1	1%
	soils001	CSU	64	32%
	wildlf003	CSU	1	1%
	wildlf004	CSU	3	2%
Glenwood Springs		349	53	16
	archeo002	CSU	1	2%
	bgame003	TLS	1	2%
	bgame007	TLS	3	6%
	bgame017	TLS	1	2%
	bgame019	CSU	2	4%
	constr001	CSU	1	2%
	constr003	TLS	2	4%
	constr007	TLS	1	2%
	constr009	TLS	2	4%
	pipel002	CSU	1	2%
	pipel008	CSU	1	2%
	vrm001	CSU	3	6%
	wildlf001	TLS	1	2%
	wildlf006	TLS	1	2%

Table A5-5. (Continued)

BLM FO		**Well Population**	**Sample Size**	**Sample Wells w/ COAs**
	COA ID	COA Category	Occurrence	% of Sample
Grand Junction		40	30	22
	bgame003	TLS	19	63%
	bgame017	TLS	1	3%
	pipel002	CSU	1	3%
	roads001	CSU	1	3%
	wildlf006	TLS	2	7%
	wildlf017	TLS	1	3%
Kemmerer		96	30	22
	archeo002	CSU	1	3%
	bgame002	TLS	8	27%
	bgame015	TLS	6	20%
	pipel008	CSU	2	7%
	plover009	TLS	5	17%
	plover035	TLS	7	23%
	raptor033	TLS	1	3%
	sagegr018	TLS	3	10%
	sagegr036	TLS	4	13%
	soils001	CSU	17	57%
	wildlf003	CSU	1	3%
Lander		11	11	7
	archeo002	CSU	2	18%
	bgame002	TLS	1	9%
	constr001	CSU	1	9%
	pipel004	CSU	1	9%
	plover009	TLS	1	9%
	raptor007	TLS	2	18%
	soils001	CSU	4	36%
Little Snake		63	30	23
	bgame003	TLS	1	3%
	constr002	CSU	2	7%
	erosio001	CSU	8	27%
	raptor006	TLS	10	33%
	sagegr009	TLS	7	23%
	soils001	CSU	8	27%
	sslope002	CSU	1	3%

Table A5-5. (Continued)

BLM FO		**Well Population**	**Sample Size**	**Sample Wells w/ COAs**
	COA ID	COA Category	Occurrence	% of Sample
	wildlf016	TLS	1	3%
Miles City		93	30	30
	bgame007	TLS	1	3%
	bgame008	CSU	26	87%
	bgame013	CSU	25	83%
	constr013	CSU	25	83%
	raptor003	CSU	25	83%
	raptor018	CSU	25	83%
	sagegr005	TLS	26	87%
	sagegr023	TLS	1	3%
	soils001	CSU	25	83%
	sslope003	CSU	1	3%
	wildlf001	CSU	25	83%
	wildlf008	TLS	3	10%
	wildlf011	TLS	1	3%
Milwaukee		14	14	2
	constr016	TLS	2	14%
	pipel008	CSU	2	14%
Moab		23	23	10
	bgame016	TLS	1	4%
	bgame020	TLS	4	17%
	constr001	CSU	3	13%
	pipel001	CSU	3	13%
	raptor007	TLS	1	4%
	raptor016	TLS	2	9%
	soils003	TLS	1	4%
	soils004	TLS	1	4%
Monticello		9	9	3
	paleo002	CSU	2	22%
	pipel008	CSU	1	11%
Newcastle		76	30	8
	archeo001	CSU	1	3%
	archeo002	CSU	2	7%
	constr001	CSU	1	3%

Table A5-5. (Continued)

BLM FO		**Well Population**	**Sample Size**	**Sample Wells w/ COAs**
	COA ID	COA Category	Occurrence	% of Sample
	noise001	CSU	1	3%
	sagegr031	TLS	1	3%
	soils001	CSU	2	7%
Pinedale		710	107	72
	archeo002	CSU	10	9%
	bgame002	CSU	49	46%
	bgame006	TLS	2	2%
	bgame015	TLS	7	7%
	constr001	CSU	4	4%
	cultur003	TLS	3	3%
	pipel003	CSU	5	5%
	pipel004	CSU	2	2%
	pipel008	CSU	3	3%
	raptor005	TLS	1	1%
	raptor007	TLS	14	13%
	raptor011	TLS	3	3%
	raptor021	TLS	4	4%
	raptor028	CSU	2	2%
	raptor034	TLS	2	2%
	sagegr002	TLS	12	11%
	sagegr004	TLS	3	3%
	sagegr007	TLS	5	5%
	sagegr010	TLS	4	4%
	sagegr011	TLS	3	3%
	sagegr012	TLS	13	12%
	sagegr013	TLS	25	23%
	sagegr015	TLS	1	1%
	sagegr017	TLS	7	7%
	sagegr019	TLS	1	1%
	sagegr021	TLS	2	2%
	sagegr030	CSU	15	14%
	sagegr034	TLS	2	2%
	sagegr035	TLS	9	8%
	sagegr037	TLS	1	1%
	soils001	CSU	43	40%

Table A5-5. (Continued)

BLM FO		Well Population	Sample Size	Sample Wells w/ COAs
	COA ID	COA Category	Occurrence	% of Sample
	vrm001	CSU	1	1%
	wildlf003	CSU	1	1%
Rawlins		714	107	50
	constr001	CSU	3	3%
	constr012	CSU	13	12%
	plover001	CSU	6	6%
	plover009	TLS	15	14%
	plover011	TLS	1	1%
	plover016	TLS	1	1%
	plover033	TLS	2	2%
	raptor007	TLS	2	2%
	raptor030	TLS	6	6%
	roads001	CSU	1	1%
	roads003	CSU	3	3%
	sagegr009	TLS	14	13%
	soils001	CSU	26	24%
Rock Springs		173	30	15
	archeo002	CSU	1	3%
	bgame002	TLS	5	17%
	hydro001	CSU	2	7%
	plover007	TLS	1	3%
	plover014	TLS	1	3%
	plover015	TLS	1	3%
	raptor007	TLS	3	10%
	raptor009	TLS	1	3%
	raptor014	TLS	1	3%
	raptor032	TLS	1	3%
	sagegr016	TLS	1	3%
	soils001	CSU	4	13%
	wildlf004	CSU	1	3%
	wildlf007	TLS	1	3%
	wildlf019	CSU	1	3%
Royal Gorge		39	30	23
	constr001	CSU	1	3%
	constr011	TLS	1	3%

Table A5-5. (Continued)

BLM FO		**Well Population**	**Sample Size**	**Sample Wells w/ COAs**
	COA ID	COA Category	Occurrence	% of Sample
	constr015	CSU	1	3%
	noise001	CSU	2	7%
	pipel002	CSU	5	17%
	pipel004	CSU	1	3%
	pipel008	CSU	6	20%
	plover005	TLS	7	23%
	plover006	TLS	3	10%
	plover031	TLS	1	3%
	wildlf014	TLS	5	17%
San Juan		35	30	22
	archeo002	CSU	8	27%
	bgame001	TLS	4	13%
	bgame003	TLS	4	13%
	bgame020	TLS	7	23%
	constr002	CSU	3	10%
	hydro001	CSU	1	3%
	noise001	CSU	13	43%
	pipel002	CSU	1	3%
	raptor015	TLS	1	3%
	sagegr018	TLS	1	3%
	wildlf013	TLS	1	3%
Uncompahgre		7	7	7
	archeo001	CSU	1	14%
	bgame003	TLS	1	14%
	bgame010	TLS	2	29%
	bgame020	TLS	1	14%
	constr002	CSU	1	14%
	constr013	CSU	1	14%
	noise001	CSU	2	29%
	pipel008	CSU	2	29%
	roads001	CSU	2	29%
	soils001	CSU	2	29%
Vernal		861	130	35
	archeo002	CSU	1	1%
	bgame009	TLS	2	2%
	constr001	CSU	2	2%

Table A5-5. (Continued)

BLM FO		**Well Population**	**Sample Size**	**Sample Wells w/ COAs**
	COA ID	COA Category	Occurrence	% of Sample
	archeo002	CSU	1	1%
	bgame009	TLS	2	2%
	constr001	CSU	2	2%
	noise001	CSU	10	8%
	paleo001	CSU	1	1%
	paleo002	CSU	5	4%
	pipel001	CSU	1	1%
	pipel002	CSU	7	5%
	plover007	TLS	2	2%
	plover008	TLS	2	2%
	plover010	TLS	2	2%
	plover012	TLS	3	2%
	plover034	TLS	3	2%
	raptor002	CSU	2	2%
	raptor008	TLS	2	2%
	raptor009	TLS	6	5%
	raptor010	TLS	2	2%
	raptor012	TLS	2	2%
	raptor013	TLS	4	3%
	raptor016	TLS	1	1%
	raptor020	TLS	2	2%
	raptor022	CSU	4	3%
	raptor025	CSU	2	2%
	raptor031	TLS	2	2%
	raptor032	TLS	3	2%
	sagegr009	TLS	3	2%
	sagegr020	TLS	5	4%
	sagegr033	TLS	2	2%
	soils001	CSU	5	4%
	wildlf002	CSU	4	3%
	wildlf003	CSU	2	2%
	wildlf004	CSU	2	2%
	sagegr033	TLS	2	2%

Table A5-5. (Continued)

BLM FO		**Well Population**	**Sample Size**	**Sample Wells w/ COAs**
	COA ID	COA Category	Occurrence	% of Sample
White River		320	48	22
	archeo002	CSU	1	2%
	bgame003	TLS	2	4%
	bgame005	TLS	1	2%
	constr001	CSU	1	2%
	constr002	CSU	1	2%
	paleo002	CSU	11	23%
	pipel002	CSU	1	2%
	soils001	CSU	17	35%
	wildlf008	TLS	1	2%
	wildlf009	TLS	1	2%
	wildlf010	TLS	3	6%
	wildlf015	TLS	1	2%

10. Once the recategorization was accomplished, the resulting areas and volumes of the undiscovered technically recoverable oil and gas resources and reserve growth affected by the cumulative impact of COAs was computed. The land access categorization was then performed using the method for lease stipulations described in Section 2 and Appendix 9.

Appendix 6: U.S. Geological Survey Methodology for the Assessment of Undiscovered Oil and Gas Resources

By U.S. Geological Survey National Assessment Review Team[46]

A6.1 Introduction

The USGS conducts assessments of technically recoverable undiscovered oil and gas resources of the onshore and state waters of the United States. The last comprehensive USGS oil and gas assessment was completed in 1995, and comprises the onshore and state waters portion of 71 geologic provinces (Gautier and others, 1996). In 1999, the USGS launched a new initiative to produce incremental assessments of the most significant U.S. oil and gas provinces.

To meet the requirements of Section 604 of EPCA, the USGS reorganized the priority list for the new assessments. For the Phase I inventory (released 2003), new assessments were conducted for the Uinta-Piceance Basin, San Juan Basin, Montana Thrust Belt, Powder River

Basin, and Greater Green River Basin. The 1995 assessment results were used for the Paradox Basin. For the Phase II inventory, new assessments were conducted for Northern Alaska (NPRA and ANWR-1 002), Wyoming Thrust Belt, Denver Basin, Florida Peninsula, Black Warrior Basin, and Appalachian Basin.

The general assessment methodology has not changed from the 1995 assessments; however, some refinements have been made to accommodate increased geologic understanding of the occurrence of resources and more sophisticated means of capturing the range of uncertainty inherent in these variables. For example, the assessment model for continuous resources in the 1995 assessment assumed a homogenous distribution of oil and gas resources in a play. For the new assessments, that model has been replaced with an analysis of geologically controlled sweet spots of production, which demonstrate the geologic heterogeneity common to continuous oil or gas accumulations. The recognition of production sweet spots is a major advancement in the assessment of continuous resources.

A6.2 Terminology

Terminology used in this chapter reflects standard definitions and usage of the oil and natural gas industry and the petroleum resource assessment community. Several terms have been developed by the USGS for oil and gas assessment purposes (see Glossary in Appendix 2). The 1995 USGS assessment focused on the definition and assessment of geologic *plays*. In the latest USGS assessments, the focus is on understanding total petroleum systems and defining *assessment units* within total petroleum systems. The total petroleum system approach is designed to focus the geologic studies on the hydrocarbon source rocks, processes that create hydrocarbons, migration pathways, reservoirs, and trapping mechanisms. For discussion purposes in this chapter, the term *play* will be used throughout to represent both *assessment units* and *plays*.

The USGS assesses two main categories of hydrocarbon occurrence: conventional and continuous (Figure A6-1). Conventional oil and gas accumulations are defined as discrete fields with well-defined hydrocarbon-water contacts, where the hydrocarbons are buoyant on a column of water. Conventional accumulations commonly have relatively high matrix permeabilities, have obvious seals and traps, and have high recovery factors. In contrast, continuous accumulations (also called unconventional accumulations) commonly are regional in extent, have diffuse boundaries, and are not buoyant on a column of water. Continuous accumulations have very low matrix permeabilities, do not have obvious seals and traps, are in close proximity to source rocks, are abnormally pressured, and have low recovery factors. The USGS assessment focused on understanding the geology and occurrence of continuous hydrocarbon accumulations, as the resource potential of these accumulations may be greater than that for conventional accumulations in the U.S. Included in the category of continuous accumulations are hydrocarbons that occur in tight reservoirs, shale reservoirs, unconventional reservoirs, basin-centered reservoirs, fractured reservoirs, coal beds, and oil shales.

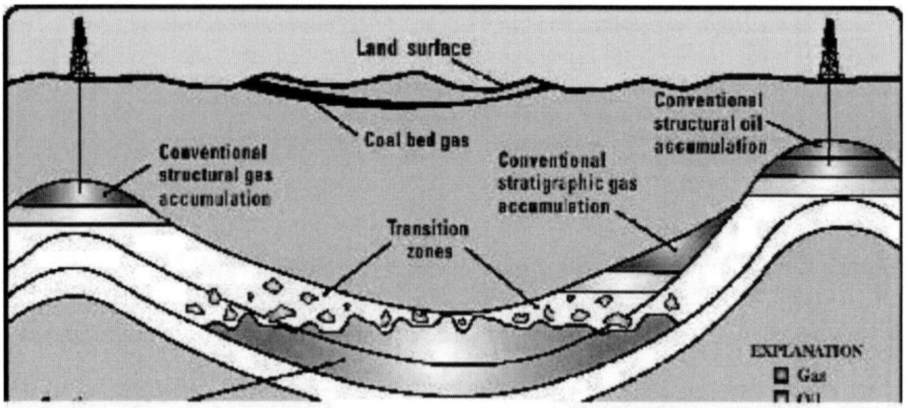

Figure A6-1. Conventional vs. Continuous Accumulations

A6.3 Overview of the Oil and Gas Assessment Procedure

The assessment process is based on the characterization of the petroleum geology of each province. The geologists define the geologic elements of the total petroleum systems, and, in conjunction with an analysis of historic oil and gas production and exploration/discovery data, define the oil and gas plays within the provinces. The geologists then develop probability distributions for sizes and numbers of undiscovered conventional accumulations, or numbers of cells and EUR for continuous accumulations, using all available geologic information and historic oil and gas data. These distributions are then used to generate probability distributions for undiscovered oil and gas resources.

A6.4 Role of Geologic Information in the Assessment

The strength of the USGS oil and gas resource assessments is the province geologists' understanding of the petroleum geology of the provinces being assessed. These fundamental geologic studies allow new concepts and hypothetical plays to be incorporated into the assessment of undiscovered resources. A purely statistical approach to an assessment such as discovery process modeling that uses only historical data will overlook any new geologic concepts, models, or hypothetical plays.

The team of geologists develops an understanding of the province petroleum geology using published, proprietary, and original research and data. Studying the total petroleum systems within a province includes: (1) identification and mapping the extent of the major hydrocarbon source rocks; (2) understanding the thermal evolution of each source rock, the extent of mature source rock, and the timing of hydrocarbon generation, expulsion, and migration; (3) estimating migration pathways and all forms of hydrocarbon trapping; (4) modeling the timing of structural development and the timing of trap formation relative to hydrocarbon migration; (5) determining the sequence stratigraphic evolution of reservoirs, and the presence of conventional or continuous reservoirs, or both; and (6) modeling the burial history of the basin and the effect burial and uplift has had on the preservation of conventional and continuous hydrocarbons.

Once the total petroleum systems of the province are known in satisfactory detail, the team of geologists defines oil and gas plays, which represent a synthesis of all geologic information, including production and exploration data. The key component of this analysis is a geologic model for the assessment of each play. The geologic model encompasses all elements of the total petroleum system, and is commonly summarized by a total petroleum system events chart.

A6.5 Sources of Oil and Gas Data

Data for domestic oil and gas fields, reservoirs, and wells are derived from commercial databases purchased annually by the USGS. With more than 2.5 million domestic oil and gas wells and 40,000 oil and gas fields, the USGS has opted to purchase the data from commercial vendors rather than attempt to generate a comprehensive database. The oil and gas wells and production databases are now purchased from the IHS Energy Group (IHS) (2000 a, b). Previous assessments used the predecessors to IHS: PetroROM Production Data (Petroleum Information/Dwights LLC, 1999a) and the Well History Control System (Petroleum Information/Dwights LLC, 1 999b). The USGS also relies on the NRG Associates, Inc. Significant Oil and Gas Fields of the United States (NRG Associates, 2001). Data from these commercial databases are subject to proprietary constraints, and the USGS cannot publish, share, or serve any data from these databases. However, derivative representations in the form of graphs and summary statistics can be prepared and presented for each play. The USGS, however, cannot verify the accuracy, completeness, or currency of data reported in commercial databases.

The IHS production database provides oil and gas production data for wells, leases, or producing units (collectively called "entities" in these databases). The IHS oil and gas wells database provides individual well data (including data for dry holes) that include well identification, locations, and information on penetrated and producing formations. Oil and gas field databases provide location, geologic characterization, and oil and gas production data for domestic oil and gas fields and reservoirs.

Additional oil and gas data are obtained, where available, from operators, state agencies, and other government sources, such as the U.S. Department of Energy's Energy Information Administration proprietary files, publications from the former Bureau of Mines, and other sources.

A6.6 Assigning Accumulations and Wells to Plays

Digital maps of plays are created using a GIS.[47] Digital play maps are used to assign oil and gas wells and accumulations to their respective plays, and these assignments are entered into the databases. Oil and gas accumulations are assigned to only one play. Wells, however, can be assigned to more than one play if they penetrate vertically stacked plays. Oil and gas accumulations and well assignments are reviewed to ensure proper assignments, identify inconsistent data, and examine the need for minor revisions of play boundaries.

Historic production and exploration/discovery data are collected for each play using oil and gas accumulations or well assignments. Types of data retrieved include: (1) known volumes (sum of cumulative production and remaining reserves) of recoverable oil, gas, and natural gas liquids (NGLs) of accumulations; (2) discovery dates of accumulations (the year the first reservoir in the accumulation was discovered); (3) monthly production and cumulative production of wells; (4) initial classification and final classification of wells (for example, new-field wildcat, development, producing, abandoned, etc.) of wells; and (5) completion dates of wells.

A6.7 Oil and Gas Production Data

The historic oil and gas production data are compiled for each play so that the data from discovered accumulations can be used as a guide for potential undiscovered accumulations. For conventional plays, these data include (1) field name, (2) field discovery year or date of completion of the discovery well, (3) known volumes of oil, gas (non-associated and associated-dissolved), and NGLs, and (4) depth to the top of each reservoir. All of the production data for conventional assessment units are arranged in terms of oil accumulations and gas accumulations and sorted by size and discovery date for statistical calculations and plotting. A list of new-field wildcat wells and their completion dates is compiled and organized into the number of wells drilled per year for conventional plays. (A new-field wildcat well is an exploratory well drilled at least two miles from a producing field to test a separate trap). Once organized, the number of wells drilled in a given year is used as a measure of exploration effort. These data are then combined with the production data using the discovery dates of the accumulations and the completion dates of the wells.

Oil and gas production data compiled for each producing well in continuous-type plays include past monthly production of liquids (oil and NGL) and gas (non-associated and associated-dissolved), from which EURs are estimated using well decline-curve analysis, the date of first production, and depth to the topmost perforation. A list of all wells and completion dates are compiled and organized. However, the number of wells drilled in a given year is not combined with production data, but analyzed separately.

Co-product ratios (GOR; NGLs to gas ratio; and LGR) are calculated and major commodities (oil or gas) are identified for each conventional accumulation. Co-product ratios are based on accumulation-level oil, gas, and NGL volumes. Oil and gas accumulations are treated separately; an oil accumulation is defined as one having a GOR less than 20,000 cubic feet/barrel whereas a gas accumulation has a GOR equal to or greater than 20,000 cubic feet/barrel.

Supplemental data from individual reservoirs within the accumulations include thickness (net and gross), average porosity, average permeability, temperature, pressure, fluid properties (for example, sulfur content of oil, API gravity of oil, non-hydrocarbon gas contents), trap type, drive type, and well spacing. These data are combined with the data from the commercial databases to help refine the geologic interpretations and assessment process.

A6.8 Graphs and Statistics for Conventional Plays

Two sets of graphs and statistics are generated for conventional plays–one set using known accumulation sizes as of the effective date of the assessment and one set using accumulation sizes that are corrected for anticipated reserve growth (grown accumulation size) within the forecast span of the assessment.

The set of graphs and statistics generated for conventional plays includes sizes and number of accumulations with respect to discovery date and exploration effort, exploration effort through time, size distributions of accumulations, reservoir depth versus discovery date and exploration effort, co-product ratios versus reservoir depth, and a histogram of the API gravity. Accumulations containing less than a specified minimum volume of oil or gas (that is, the smallest accumulation size that is considered in the assessment process) are not included in these graphs or statistics. Counts of new-field wildcat wells are used as a measure of exploration effort for finding new accumulations.

A6.9 Assessment Input for Conventional Plays

Critical input data for conventional plays are probability distributions for sizes and numbers of undiscovered oil and gas accumulations and co-product ratios. The geologists develop these distributions by synthesizing all petroleum systems information and historic oil and gas data. For hypothetical plays, the geologist may utilize an analog data set for sizes and numbers of discovered fields as a guide to the distributions of sizes and numbers of undiscovered fields in the play or assessment unit being assessed. Geologists provide information on oil and gas quality, range of drilling depths, and range of water depths for future economic analyses.

A6.10 Graphs and Statistics for Continuous-Type Plays

A set of graphs and statistics comparable to that for conventional plays is generated for continuous-type plays, but the EUR per cell and numbers of tested cells are used rather than accumulation sizes and number of discovered accumulations. Tested cells of less than the specified minimum EUR per cell are not included in these graphs or statistics, and reserve-growth adjustments for cells are not incorporated.

The set of graphs and statistics generated for continuous-type plays includes number of wells drilled through time (all wells as opposed to new-field wildcat wells), probability distributions of EUR, EUR versus production-start year and number of all wells drilled, cumulative EUR versus production-start year and number of wells drilled, cumulative EUR versus depth of the topmost perforation, and GOR versus ranked EUR. All of this information is provided to the assessor as a guide to generating distributions for the assessment of undiscovered resources.

A6.11 Assessment Input for Continuous Plays

Critical input data for the continuous play assessment model include numbers of cells that have potential to be added to reserves, the EUR distribution for these cells, and the co-product ratios. For hypothetical plays, the geologist may utilize an analog data set for distribution of cell size and for the EUR distribution as guides to the distributions of cell sizes and EUR's of undiscovered area in the play being assessed. The geologist provides information on oil and gas quality, range of drilling depths, and range of water depths for future economic analyses.

A6.12 USGS Assessment Review

The province geologist must present the geology of the play and the input data to a team of USGS personnel for a formal review. The team consists of geologists, geophysicists, and assessment methodologists with broad expertise in petroleum geology, which together promotes a consistent geological and methodological approach to the assessment. Every aspect of the geology and input data are reviewed, and any changes are incorporated into the input data at this time. Once the input data have been finalized, the input data are ready for quantitative analysis.

A6.13 Calculation of Undiscovered Conventional and Continuous Resources

The final reviewed assessment input forms are the basis of the quantitative calculations of undiscovered oil and gas resources. For conventional plays, the probability distributions for sizes and numbers of undiscovered accumulations and the co-product ratios provided by the assessor are entered into a Monte Carlo simulator and run for a specified number of iterations to provide distributions of undiscovered oil, gas, and NGL resources. In the 1995 assessment, a Truncated Shifted Pareto Distribution (Gautier and Dolton, 1996) was used for the shape of the curve for the distribution of sizes of oil and gas fields. For the present assessment, a Truncated Shifted Lognormal Distribution is used for this purpose (Charpentier and Klett, 2000).

For continuous plays, the distributions for assessment-unit area, untested percentage of assessment unit area, potential percentage of untested area, and area per cell of untested cells are combined analytically to determine the distribution for number of potential untested cells. The distribution for numbers of potential untested cells EUR per cell, and the co-product ratios are combined using an Analytic Probability Method (Crovelli, 2000) to directly calculate the probability distribution of undiscovered oil and gas resources.

A6.14 Assessment Results

The results and maps of the resource assessment of the oil and gas plays for Northern Alaska (NPRA and ANWR-1 002), Uinta-Piceance Basin, Paradox/San Juan Basins, Montana Thrust Belt, Powder River Basin, Wyoming Thrust Belt, Greater Green River Basin, Denver Basin, Florida Peninsula, Black Warrior Basin, and Appalachian Basin provinces are presented on the internet.[48]

A6.15 References Cited

Charpentier, R.R., and Klett, T.R., 2000, Monte Carlo simulation method, *in* U.S. Geological Survey World Energy Assessment Team, U.S. Geological Survey World Petroleum Assessment 2000-description and results: U.S. Geological Survey Digital Data Series DDS-60, Chapter MC.

Crovelli, R.A., 2000, Analytic resource assessment method for continuous (unconventional) oil and gas accumulations–the " ACCESS" method: U.S. Geological Survey Open-File Report 00044, 34 p.

Gautier, D.L., and Dolton, G.L., 1996, Methodology for assessment of undiscovered conventional accumulations, *in* 1995 National assessment of United States oil and gas resources-Results, methodology, and supporting data: U.S. Geological Survey Digital Data Series DDS-30, Release 2 (1 CD-ROM).

Gautier, D.L., Dolton, G.L., Takahashi, K.I., and Varnes, K.L., eds., 1996, 1995 National assessment of United States oil and gas resources-Results, methodology, and supporting data:
U.S. Geological Survey Digital Data Series DDS-30, Release 2 (1 CD-ROM).

IHS Energy Group, 2000a [includes data current as of December, 1999], PI/Dwights Plus US Production Data: Englewood, Colo., IHS Energy Group; database available from IHS Energy Group, 15 Inverness Way East, D205, Englewood, Colorado 80112, U.S.A.

IHS Energy Group, 2000b [includes data current as of December, 1999], PI/Dwights Plus US Well Data: Englewood, Colo., IHS Energy Group; database available from IHS Energy Group, 15 Inverness Way East, D205, Englewood, Colorado 80112, U.S.A.

NRG Associates, Inc., 1993, 1994, 1999, 2000, and 2001 [includes data current as of December 31, 1992, December 31, 1993, December 31, 1998, December 31, 1999, and December 31, 2000, respectively], The Significant Oil and Gas Fields of the United States: Colorado Springs, Colo., NRG Associates, Inc.; database available from NRG Associates, Inc., P.O. Box 1655, Colorado Springs, Colorado 80901, U.S.A.

Petroleum Information/Dwights LLC, 1999a [includes data current as of December, 1998], PetroROM Production Data: Englewood, Colo., Petroleum Information/Dwights LLC; database now available from IHS Energy Group, 15 Inverness Way East, D205, Englewood, Colorado 80112, U.S.A.

Petroleum Information/Dwights LLC, 1999b [includes data current as of December, 1998], Well History Control System: Englewood, Colo., Petroleum Information/Dwights LLC; database now available from IHS Energy Group, 15 Inverness Way East, D205, Englewood, Colorado 80112, U.S.A.

A6.16 General References

Uinta-Piceance Assessment: Kirschbaum, Mark A., Dubiel, Russell F., Johnson, Ronald C., Johnson, Edward A., Hettinger, Robert D., Finn, Thomas M., Anna, Lawrence O., Henry, Mitchell, Collett, Timothy S., Roberts, Laura N., Roberts, Stephen B., Lillis, Paul G., Rice, Cynthia A., Schmoker, James W., and Nuccio, Vito F.

Greater Green River Assessment: Kirschbaum, Mark A., Johnson, Ronald C., Johnson, Edward A., Hettinger, Robert D., Finn, Thomas M., Roberts, Laura N., Roberts, Stephen B., and Lillis, Paul G.

Powder River Basin Assessment: Flores, Romeo M., Anna, Lawrence O., and French, Christopher

San Juan Basin Assessment: Ridgley, Jennie L., Condon, Steven M., Dubiel, Russell F., Fishman, Neil S., and Hatch, Joseph R.

Northern Alaska Assessments–NPRA and ANWR-1 002: Bird, Kenneth J., and Houseknecht, David W.

Montana Thrust Belt Assessment: Schenk, Christopher J., Charpentier, Ronald R., Cook, Troy A., Dyman, Thaddeus S., French, Christopher D., Henry, Mitchell E., Klett, Timothy R., Perry, William J., Pollastro, Richard M., and Potter, Christopher J.

Wyoming Thrust Belt Assessment: Kirschbaum, Mark A., Charpentier, Ronald R., Crovelli, Robert A., Klett, Timothy R., Pollastro, Richard M., and Schenk, Christopher J.

Denver Basin Assessment: Higley, Debra, Charpentier, Ronald R., Cook, Troy, Klett, T. R., Pollastro, Richard, Schmoker, James W., and Schenk, Christopher J.

South Florida Basin/Florida Peninsula Assessment: Pollastro, Richard M., Schenk, Christopher J., and Charpentier, Ronald R.

Black Warrior Basin Assessment: Hatch, Josephe R., Pawlwewicz, Mark J., Charpentier, Ronald R., Cook, Troy A., Crovelli, Robert A., Klett, Timothy R., Pollastro, Richard M., and Schenk, Christopher J.

Appalachian Basin Assessment: Milici, Robert C., Ryder, Robert T., Swezey, Christopher S., Charpentier, Ronald R., Cook, Troy A., Crovelli, Robert A., Klett, Timothy R., Pollastro, Richard M., and Schenk, Christopher J.

APPENDIX 7: INITIAL ESTIMATES OF REMAINING PROVED ULTIMATE RECOVERY GROWTH

This appendix documents the methodology used by the Energy Information Administration to estimate future reserves growth, also called 'remaining proved ultimate recovery growth,' that will be associated with existing oil and gas fields in the Phase II study areas. A more complete discussion of this phenomenon and its many causes is presented in *The Intricate Puzzle of Oil and Gas "Reserves Growth."*[49] This paper is highly recommended to readers who want to fully understand the development of and rationale for current statistical approaches to estimating the future growth of existing oil and gas fields, as well as the key uncertainties and data limitations of current methods.

The Proved Ultimate Recovery (PUR) of an oil or gas field at a particular point in time is defined as the sum of its estimated proved reserves and its recorded cumulative production at that time.

Proved Ultimate Recovery Growth (PURG) is the increase in proved ultimate recovery over time that is observed for most oil and gas fields. A field's PUR estimate normally increases significantly in the early post-discovery years as a field is developed for production and its areal limits are better discerned. PUR estimates may also be conservative early in a field's life owing to the smaller knowledge base then available regarding its productive performance. A field's later years are usually characterized by slower growth arising from a variety of possible causes including the installation of improved recovery techniques, increased knowledge of the field's performance, the addition of new reservoirs to the field, and infill drilling. Growth factors calculated from most fields' ultimate recovery histories thus usually increase rapidly as initial field development occurs and then asymptotically approach a maximum value as growth slows in later years.

PURG, or *reserves growth*, and the remaining (future) portion thereof, RPURG, can be estimated from the observed historical proved ultimate recovery growth. In a given year for a group of fields of the same vintage (age) the Annual Growth Factor (AGF) is the sum of the estimated proved ultimate recovery of the fields in that year divided by the sum of estimated proved ultimate recovery of the same fields for the prior year. Going one step further, for a basin the average AGF for its multiple fields in multiple vintages is the sum of the estimated proved ultimate recoveries of all fields in all vintages at the same point in time, i.e., the same year after first production (or after field discovery), divided by the sum of estimated proved ultimate recoveries of the same fields for the prior year.

$$AAGF_n = \frac{\sum_{v=1}^{t}\sum_{f=1}^{i} PUR_n}{\sum_{v=1}^{t}\sum_{f=1}^{i} PUR_{n-1}}$$

where: AAGF = Average Annual Growth Factor
PUR = Proved Ultimate Recovery
n = Years after first production (or discovery)
t = Number of vintages at *n*
i = Number of fields in a vintage at *n*
v = Vintage
f = Field

The Cumulative Growth Factor (CGF) in a particular year is the product of the Average AGF for all fields in all vintages through that year beginning with the first production or discovery year of the first vintage.

$$CGF_n = AAGF_1 * AAGF_2 * ...AAGF_n$$

where: CGF = Cumulative Growth Factor
AAGF = Average Annual Growth Factor
n = Years since first production (or discovery)

The RPURG can be calculated as the product of the ratio of the future CGF to the current CGF and the current PUR.

$$RPURG_{t-n} = \frac{CGF_t}{CGF_n} * PUR_n$$

where: RPURG = Remaining Proved Ultimate Recovery Growth volume at time n
CGF = Cumulative Growth Factor
PUR = Proved Ultimate Recovery volume at current time (n)
N = Current time expressed as years since first production (or discovery)
t = Final time expressed as years since first production (or discovery), i.e., infinity

Equivalently, the estimate of additional ultimate recovery that may be realized in the future based on reserves growth during the future can be stated as:

$$RPURG_{t-n} = PUR_t - PUR_n$$

where: RPURG = Remaining Proved Ultimate Recovery Growth volume at time n
PUR = Proved Ultimate Recovery
N = Current time expressed as years since first production (or discovery)
t = Final time expressed as years since first production (or discovery)

A7.1 Database Preparation

A database was created containing annual oil and gas production, estimates of cumulative production for that production which occurred prior to the keeping of annual production records, annual oil and gas proved reserves, field name, and field discovery date for fields located in selected Phase II study areas (Uinta-Piceance Basin, Paradox/San Juan Basins, Montana Thrust Belt, Powder River Basin, Wyoming Thrust Belt, Greater Green River Basin, Denver Basin and Black Warrior Basin). The available data for the Appalachian Basin were insufficient for PURG analysis. Data sources included the EIA Reserves and Production Division's Oil and Gas Integrated Field File (RPD OGIFF), the EIA Field Code Master List (FCML), the EIA-23 Reserves Survey, various state web sites, and commercial sources (mainly IHS Energy Group).

Each field in a basin was assigned to a vintage year according to its date of first production or its date of discovery depending on which date was available, or which date was deemed the most reliable indicator of initial production. While the earliest field vintage was 1901, the annual proved reserves estimates and therefore the proved ultimate recovery estimates were usually available only from 1977 to present. The resulting files contained vintage year, number of fields in each vintage, annual proved ultimate recovery for each vintage (expressed in barrels of oil equivalent, BOEULT), annual natural gas proved ultimate recovery for each vintage, and annual liquid proved ultimate recovery for each vintage.

Significant effort went into quality control of the data. Many field names and codes had to be altered, corrected, and matched across the multiple data sources and time in order to properly accumulate the field data. *Quality control beyond that point was, however, deliberately conservative.* While obvious major errors had to be corrected, the desire to seek "correction" of things that were merely suspicious had to be resisted for two reasons: first they might well be correct, and second the available task resources and time frames were limited. Therefore, the reserves data were used as reported by the field operators unless very obvious errors were found. Data discontinuities and variations within vintages were for the most part accepted "as-is." Specific vintages that did not fit the trend of most of the data of a basin were excluded from the history matching and forecasting. Attempts to divide the data within a basin into conventional reservoirs, tight formation gas, and coalbed natural gas sources were largely unsuccessful because of the limited number of vintages, the short histories available for some of the fields, and frequent inability to separate the data by reservoir type within a field.

A7.2 Estimation of Remaining Proved Ultimate Recovery Growth

The remainder of this appendix describes two models that were independently used to estimate RPURG by basin and hydrocarbon type within a basin and then details the modeling results. The first model implements an exponential function having two fit parameters while the second model implements a hyperbolic function having four fit parameters. The exponential model is dependent on the annual average cumulative growth factors for the basin, whereas the hyperbolic model is dependent on incremental growth factors by vintage. Both are asymptotic functions that use time as the sole driver. Even though other potential drivers such as drilling rates or wellhead prices of oil and gas are not directly used, they have affected the historical data that feed into the models.

A7.3 Exponential Cumulative Growth Factor Model

To estimate a CGF at some time in the future a least squares fit of the historical data can be made using an exponential function. Knowing that the CGF is equal to 1.0 at discovery and that the growth rate should decrease to an asymptote of the CGF, an exponential function beginning at 1.0 at time equals zero (the time of discovery) and thereafter remaining positive as time since discovery increases was found to provide an adequate fit of the historical data, i.e.:

$$CGF = a\left(1 - e^{-bn}\right) + c$$

where: CGF = Cumulative Growth Factor
b = exponent

n = time since first production (or discovery)
c = 1.0 (constant)
a = fit parameter equal to the asymptotic CGF minus 1

Data from the Uinta/Piceance, Paradox/San Juan, Powder River, Wyoming Thrust Belt, Greater Green River, Denver, and Black Warrior basins were evaluated. Sufficient data were not available to evaluate the Montana Thrust Belt and the available coal bed natural gas data were deemed not to be analytically dependable for separate analysis.

A7.4 Hyperbolic Incremental Growth Factor Model

The RPURG for each basin can also be estimated by sorting the data by vintage within that basin and predicting the achievable PURG for the basin over time using a hyperbolic incremental model. The solely time-based model function excludes direct consideration of other factors such as drilling levels, prices, and costs. The historical estimated data were, however, subject to these factors and more. The initial dataset was limited to PUR estimates from 1977 to 2003 and there were significant data gaps in the some of the data series.

The methodology for fitting and using the hyperbolic model involves the following sequential steps:

A. Sort the field-level PUR estimates by hydrocarbon type and vintage year
B. Calculate the relative field growth factor by dividing successive PUR estimates by the “starting” 1977 estimate
C. Determine the incremental percentage increase from year to year for all vintages
D. Create a time-based hyperbolic model curve using the following formula:

$$CGF_{TBHM} = \left[1 + Tbeta1 \times \left(1 - \frac{1}{1 + Tbeta2 \times (n)}\right)\right] \times \left[1 + Tbeta4 \times \left(1 - e^{Tbeta3 \times \frac{n}{10}}\right)\right]$$

where: CGF_{TBHM} = Cumulative Growth Factor of the time-based hyperbolic model.
n = Years after first production (or discovery), a time difference factor that is the number of years between the current year and the vintage year (i.e., 1995-1901).

E. Perform a least squares fit of the incremental percentage increase per vintage year of the model with the actual incremental data, solving for Tbeta1 through Tbeta4, using the following constraints on the variables:

$$1 \leq Tbeta1 \leq 10$$
$$0.1 \leq Tbeta2 \leq 1$$
$$-1 \leq Tbeta3 \leq -0.5$$
$$0 \leq Tbeta4 \leq 5$$

F. Obtain the asymptotic limit of the model by multiplying (1+Tbeta1) x (1+Tbeta4) (note that as the time difference approaches infinity the Tbeta2 and Tbeta3 factors cancel out of the model)

G. Plot the results by basin and fuel using 50 years and 300 years as x-axis lengths to allow for quality control inspection of the results on both short and long time scales
H. Using the known PUR estimate for the basin, and the actual years after first production (or discovery) time difference, use the performance of the model curve fit to predict the RPURG volume

The results obtained using this model are presented by basin and hydrocarbon type in the "Details of Each Methodology" section of this appendix. The Montana Thrust Belt study area had just three vintages, insufficient for modeling purposes.

A7.5 Results

While at first inspection the concepts and implementations of RPURG estimation may appear to be fairly straight-forward, that's rarely the case when the mathematics meet real-world data. Each of the models described above was independently used to estimate the remaining proved ultimate recovery growth volumes for each basin and hydrocarbon type. The available data were sometimes culled differently for the two model fits, i.e., for a given basin and hydrocarbon type the exact same data may or may not have been used for both models. This was because one of the models gave reasonable results with a specific data set, whereas the other model yielded reasonable results only after certain data or vintages were eliminated. Results of the two model fits were compared for each basin and hydrocarbon type and a preferred model result was selected based on the modeling team's expert judgment and experience. The exponential model was selected the majority of the time. When selection of the preferred model fit was a toss up the exponential model was the default selection. Table A7-1 shows the results of the selection process. The preferred model associated with it is listed along with the PUR volumes by basin and hydrocarbon type for the preferred model results.

Table A7-1. Phase II Selected Models and Results

Study Area	Type	Selected Model	2003 Ultimate	Asymptote Ultimate	Remaining Ultimate
Uinta-Piceance (Bbbls)	Liquid	Hyperbolic	0.782	0.881	0.099
Paradox/San Juan (Bbbls)	Liquid	Exponential	0.903	0.938	0.035
Powder River (Bbbls)	Liquid	Exponential	3.458	3.486	0.028
Wyoming Thrust Belt (Bbbls)	Liquid	Exponential	0.351	0.362	0.011
Greater Green River (Bbbls)	Liquid	Exponential	1.059	1.718	0.659
Denver (Bbbls)	Liquid	Exponential	1.290	1.304	0.014
Black Warrior (Bbbls)	Liquid	Exponential	0.016	0.016	-
Uinta-Piceance (TCF)	Gas	Exponential	5.838	6.585	0.747

Table A7-1. (Continued)

Study Area	Type	Selected Model	2003 Ultimate	Asymptote Ultimate	Remaining Ultimate
Paradox/San Juan (TCF)	Gas	Hyperbolic	5.157	6.365	1.208
Powder River (TCF)	Gas	Exponential	3.925	3.941	0.016
Wyoming Thrust Belt (TCF)	Gas	Exponential	4.788	5.069	0.281
Greater Green River (TCF)	Gas	Hyperbolic	31.995	34.534	2.539
Denver (TCF)	Gas	Exponential	7.730	7.825	0.095
Black Warrior (TCF)	Gas	Exponential	4.756	6.136	1.379

The Energy Information Administration methodology used for the Phase II study areas and the methodology used by the U.S. Geological Survey to estimate reserves growth for the most recent National Assessment are both statistical extrapolations of historical reserves growth and are subject to the same inherent limitations,[50] although the methodologies differ in detail. These limitations introduce substantial uncertainty into the final results, which the USGS is currently addressing in an on-going review of their reserves growth estimation methodology (see below). In a recent test, the USGS found that two different statistical extrapolation methodologies produce reserves growth estimates that differed by approximately 25 percent and were as much as 60 percent higher than actual volumetric data.[51] The results shown in Table A7-1 should be interpreted with these limitations in mind:

- Inherent uncertainty in the underlying data (for example, 'reserves' are defined differently by different operators and different commercial/ private databases; fields and reservoirs are inconsistently defined)
- Current statistical methodologies rely on field age (since field discovery) as a surrogate for field development effort. Other factors such as reserves recognition practices, differential application of new technology and production monitoring practices, different operating environments and access to markets may not be adequately represented by field age alone.
- Large fields have more weight in the analysis, which may bias the results towards the development histories of the largest fields in a basin or study area. Large fields may be more likely than smaller fields to receive consistently applied development efforts and new technology applications, and be less sensitive to economic factors.
- Uncertainties are not addressed directly such as variance of the input data and uncertainties in the underlying assumed field development scenarios.

Table A7-2 compares the EIA proved ultimate recovery growth estimates shown in Table A7-1 with recent estimates of reserves growth published by the National Petroleum Council[52] and the Potential Gas Committee (PGC).[53] Table A7-2 shows that for most study areas, the reserves growth volumes estimated are significantly lower than reserves growth estimates published by other organizations. It is unlikely that there's a single cause of these differences. Most certainly there are some significant differences in methodology and input data. For example, the PGC uses a non- statistical, reservoir-specific approach that relies on expert judgment to estimate the probable resources associated with the additional development of an already discovered reservoir. Historically, in fact, the most successful estimates of reserves growth have relied on the use of reservoir level data rather than the more aggregate field level data on which the EPCA estimates are based. That is not particularly surprising since most factors that affect the reserves growth phenomenon are reservoir- specific and will not necessarily apply to an entire field when it consists of multiple reservoirs as many fields do.[54] Unfortunately, reservoir level proved reserves data are only rarely available for onshore United States fields and the EPCA RPURG estimation must therefore be done using the field level data that are available. It should also be noted that this is, insofar as we know, the first time that field level RPURG analysis has been attempted on a scale comparable to that of the EPCA project.

Table A7-2. Comparison of Estimates of Reserves Growth-Natural Gas

Study Area	EIA	NPC	PGC*
	Proved Ultimate Recovery Growth	Reserves Growth	Probable Resources
	TCF	TCF	TCF
Northern Alaska	Not Assessed	Not Assessed	6.00
Uinta-Piceance Basin	1.25	3.80	19.33
Paradox/San Juan Basins	5.00	6.40	13.51
Montana Thrust Belt	Not Assessed	-	-
Powder River Basin	0.02	1.00	8.11
Wyoming Thrust Belt	0.28	1.40	0.80
Greater Green River Basin	2.54	7.30	10.95
Denver Basin	0.10	2.00	1.48
Florida Peninsula	Not Assessed	Not Assessed	-
Black Warrior Basin	1.38	0.10	1.30
Appalachian Basin	Not Assessed	2.00	22.80
Total	10.56	24.00	84.28
Total for EIA Assessed Study Areas	10.56	22.00	55.48

* Potential Gas Committee estimates include tight plus conventional (not differentiated) and coalbed natural gas (differentiated)

Recognizing that the oil and gas constraints analysis is cumulative and ongoing, subsequent phases in the inventory may provide opportunities to use new input data or an improved methodology to investigate and adjust the estimates of proved ultimate recovery growth.

Recognizing the inherent uncertainties and limitations of recent USGS reserves growth estimation methods, the USGS has undertaken a scoping project to review current extrapolation methods and develop feasible improvements to the existing reserve growth methodologies.[55] The USGS "FY 2006 Reserves Growth Scoping Project" will result in various products which could potentially inform and improve the estimates of remaining proved ultimate recovery growth for future inventory releases. These include USGS recommendations for reserves growth estimation methodologies, updates to the USGS database, an evaluation of the use of field "age" or field development effort to estimate reserves growth, and evaluation of "cell-based" estimation approaches.

EIA is investigating whether it will be possible to develop improved, less labor-intensive means of cleansing the field level data of its apparent anomalies and errors. Another EIA goal is improvement of the RPURG estimation methodology via multi-parameter modeling.

A7.6 Detailed Results by Model Type

The detailed results of each model are presented in this section. The preferred results previously shown in Table A7-1 were selected after comparing the model results described in this section.

A7.6.1 Exponential Cumulative Growth Factor Model Runs

The exponential cumulative growth factor estimation results for Phase II are reported in Table A7-3. Charts of the exponential model curve fit of the oil equivalent, total liquids, and natural gas are included as Figures A7-1 through A7-26. Separate estimates for gas in tight reservoirs and coal bed methane could not be relied on for most basins owing to a combination of data anomalies and data interpretation concerns. For purposes of consistency, the results for the three instances in which such estimates could be made were not carried forward.

For each type of production any obviously anomalous vintages may not have been used in the analysis and forecast but are nevertheless shown in Figures A7-1 through A7-26. Because some forecasts did not show the expected asymptotic behavior, a CGF calculated for the distant, arbitrarily selected year 2303 was used (t-n = 300) for the CGF in lieu of a model-derived asymptote (as listed in Table A7-3).

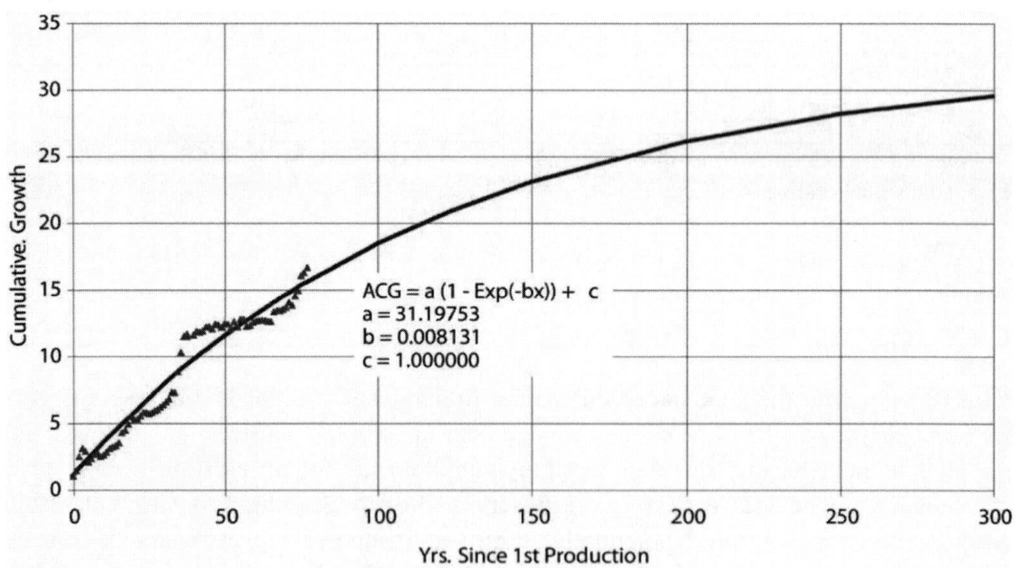

Figure A7-1. Uinta-Piceance Basin Exponential Curve Fit of Equivalent Oil Cumulative Growth Factor

Table A7-3. Exponential Method Ultimate Recovery Growth from 2003 to 2303

Study Area	Type	Cumulative Growth Factor		Future Growth Factor Ratio	2003 Ultimate	2303 Ultimate	Remaining Ultimate (Reserves Growth)
		2003	2303	2303/2003			
Uinta-Piceance	Liquids (TCF)	15.364	28.219	1.837	0.782	1.436	0.654
	Gas (selected data) (TCF)	18.244	20.575	1.128	5.838	6.584	0.746
	Tight - Gas (TCF)	7.595	7.817	1.029	1.700	1.750	0.050
Paradox/ San Juan	Liquids (selected data) (Bbbls)	3.567	3.706	1.039	0.903	0.938	0.035
	Tight - Liquids (selected data) (Bbbls)	3.164	6.394	2.021	0.124	0.251	0.127
	Gas (selected data) (TCF)	2.494	6.803	2.728	5.157	14.067	8.910
	Tight - Gas (selected data) (TCF)	8.072	9.700	1.202	18.783	22.571	3.788
Montana Thrust Belt	Insufficient Data (3 Vintages)						
Powder River	Liquids (selected data) (TCF)	7.394	7.455	1.008	3.458	3.487	0.029
	Gas (selected data) (TCF)	32.383	32.514	1.004	3.925	3.941	0.016
Wyoming Thrust Belt	Liquid - fit years 15 - 24 (Bbbls)	3.919	4.046	1.032	0.351	0.362	0.011
	Gas - fit years 15 - 24 (TCF)	8.203	8.684	1.059	4.788	5.069	0.281
Greater Green River	Liquids w/o '01, '03 vintages (TCF)	30.491	39.766	1.304	1.059	1.381	0.322
	Gas (TCF)	51.878	83.146	1.603	31.995	51.279	19.284
Denver	Liquid w/o 1901 data (Bbbls)	5.081	5.136	1.011	1.290	1.304	0.014
	Gas - fit after year 30 (TCF)	11.970	12.117	1.012	7.730	7.825	0.095
Black Warrior	Liquid fit after 10 years (Bbbls)	11.941	11.969	1.002	0.016	0.016	0.000
	Gas (TCF)	29.361	37.876	1.290	4.756	6.135	1.379

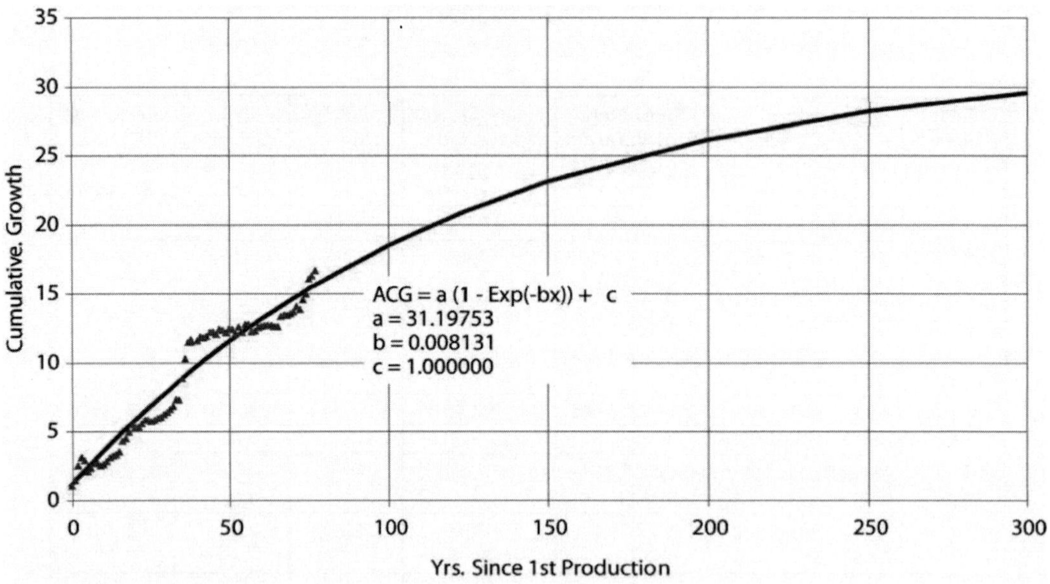

Figure A7-1. Uinta-Piceance Basin Exponential Curve Fit of Equivalent Oil Cumulative Growth Factor

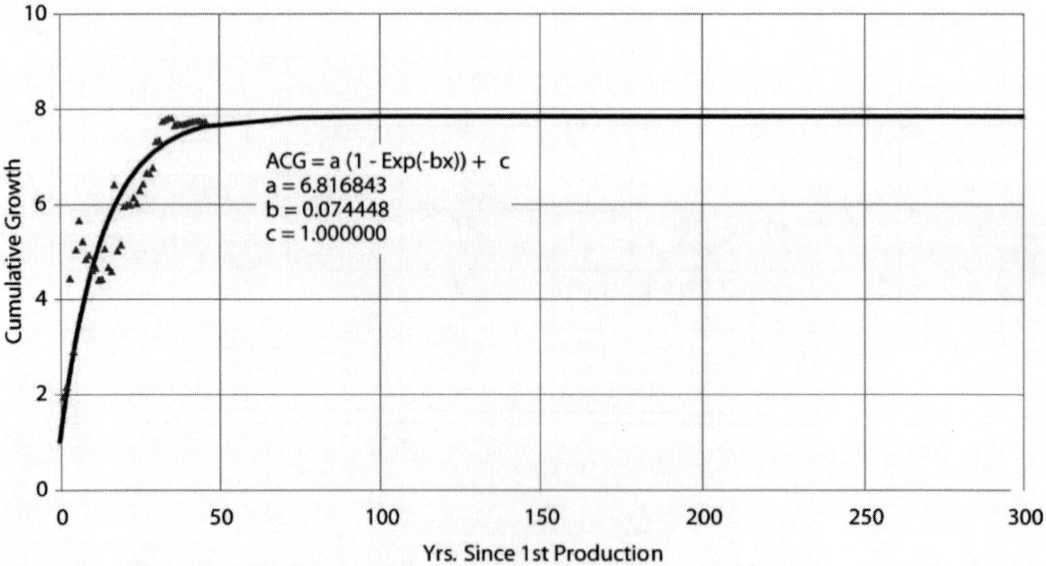

Figure A7-2. Uinta-Piceance Basin Exponential Curve Fit of Tight Formation Equivalent Oil Cumulative Growth Factor

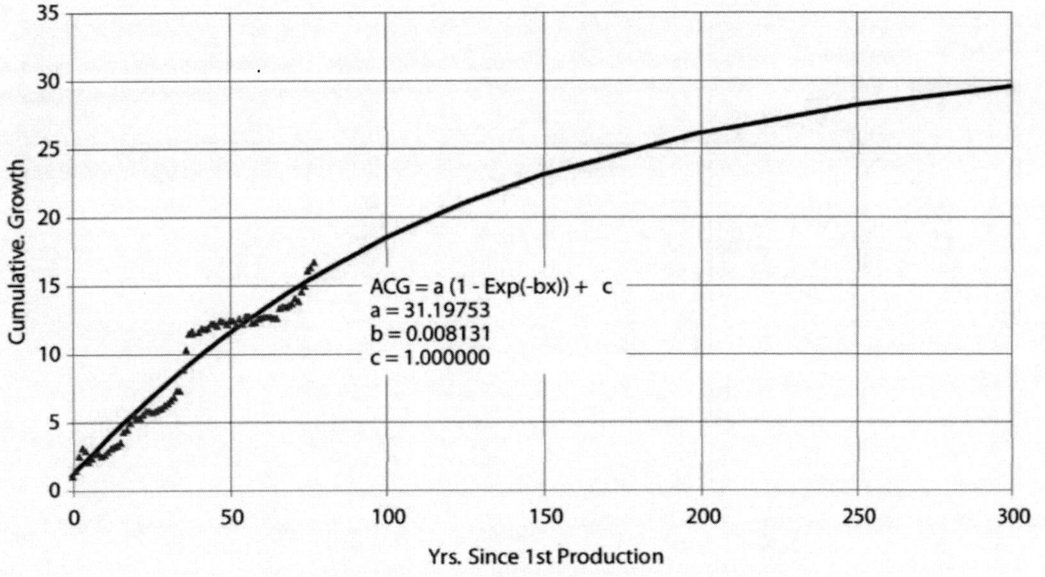

Figure A7-3. Uinta-Piceance Basin Exponential Curve Fit of Liquids Cumulative Growth Factor

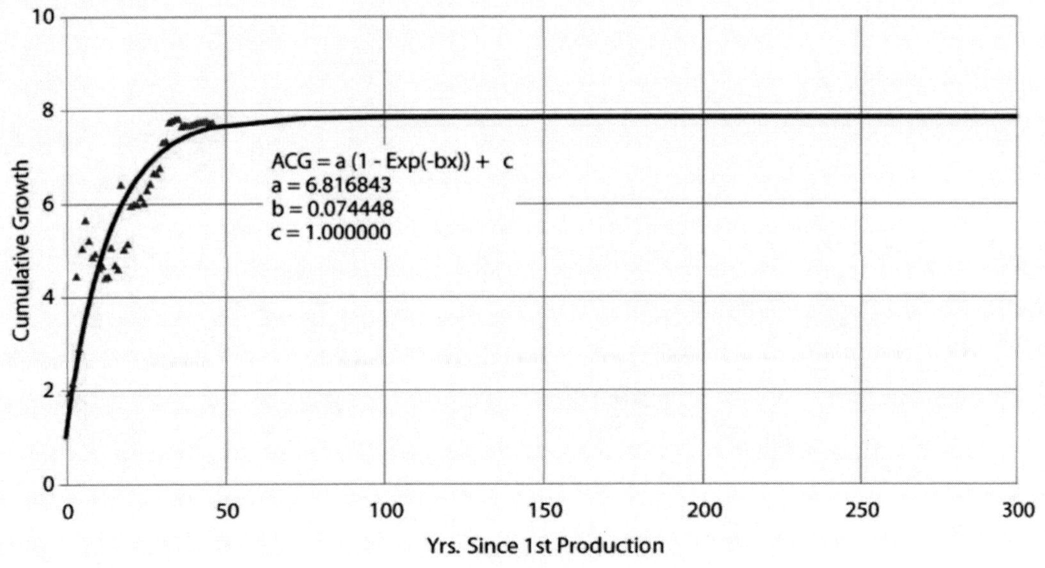

Figure A7-4. Uinta-Piceance Basin Exponential Curve Fit of Gas Cumulative Growth Factor

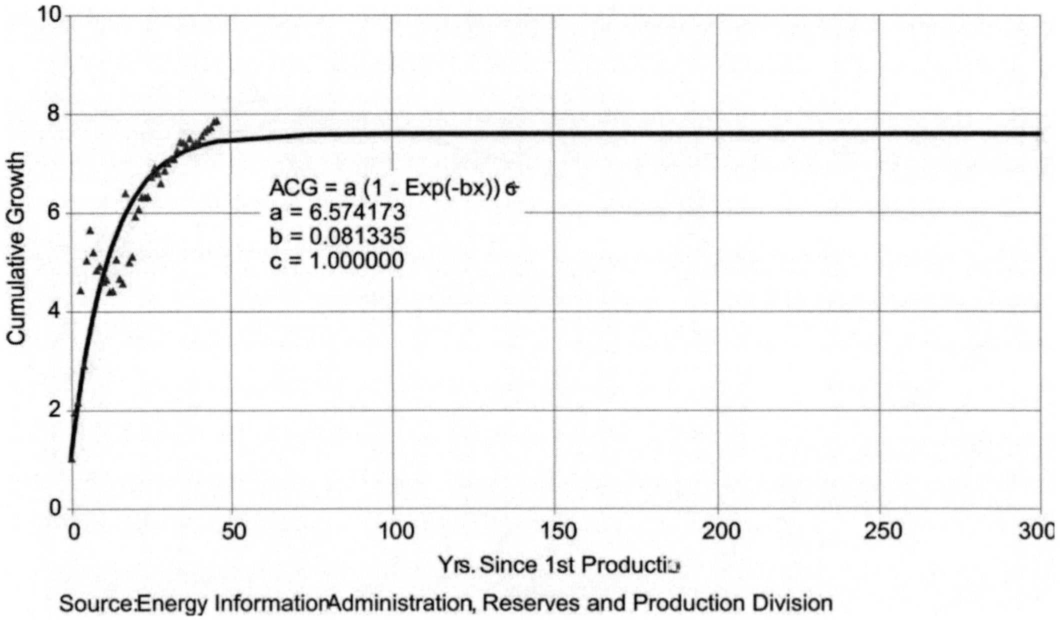

Figure A7-5. Uinta-Piceance Basin Exponential Curve Fit of Tight Formation Gas Cumulative Growth Factor

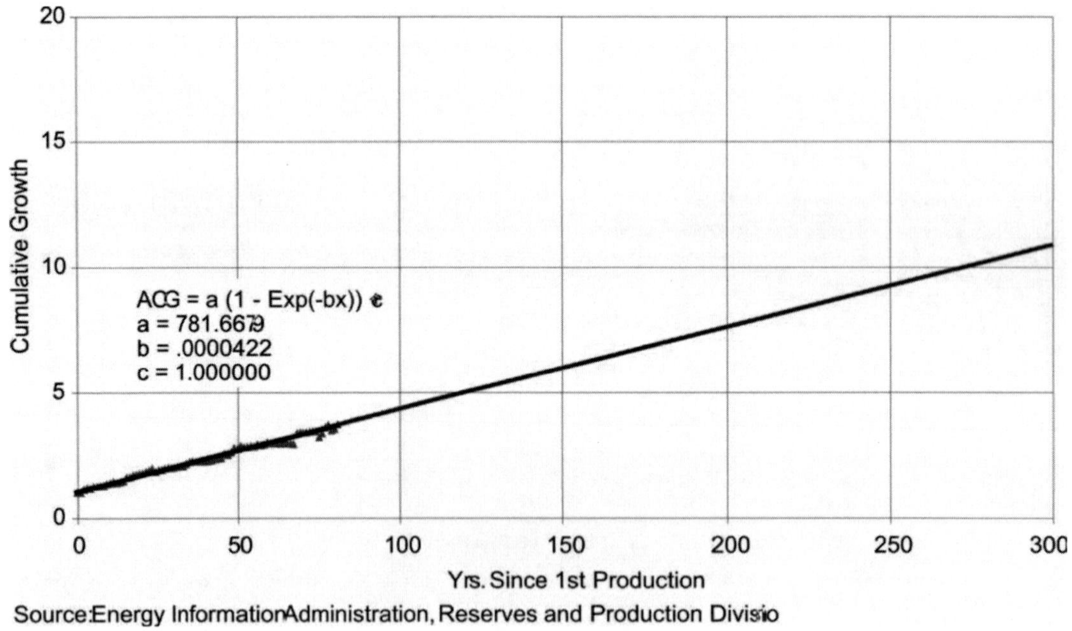

Figure A7-6. Paradox/San Juan Basins Exponential Curve Fit of Equivalent Oil Cumulative Growth Factor

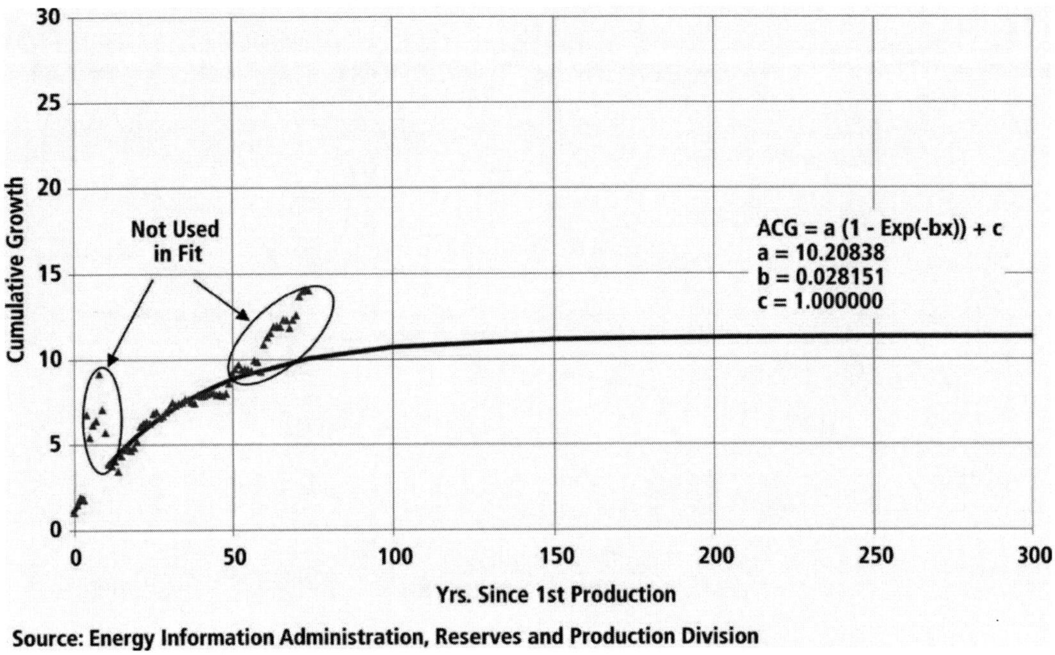

Figure A7-7. Paradox/San Juan Basins Exponential Curve Fit of Tight Formation Equivalent Oil Cumulative Growth Factor

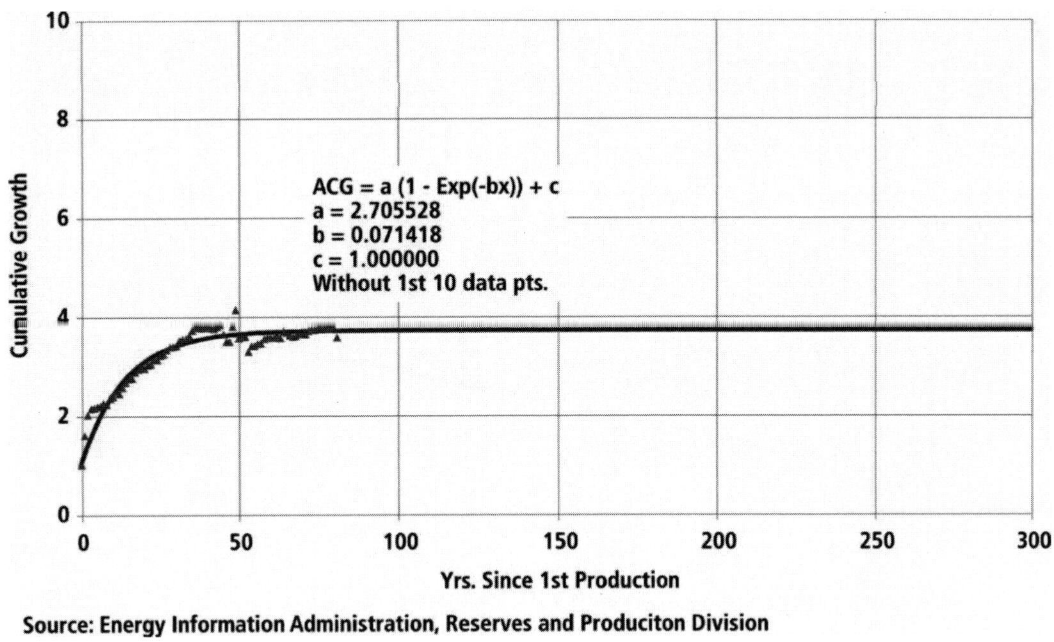

Figure A7-8. Paradox/San Juan Basins Exponential Curve Fit of Liquids Cumulative Growth Factor

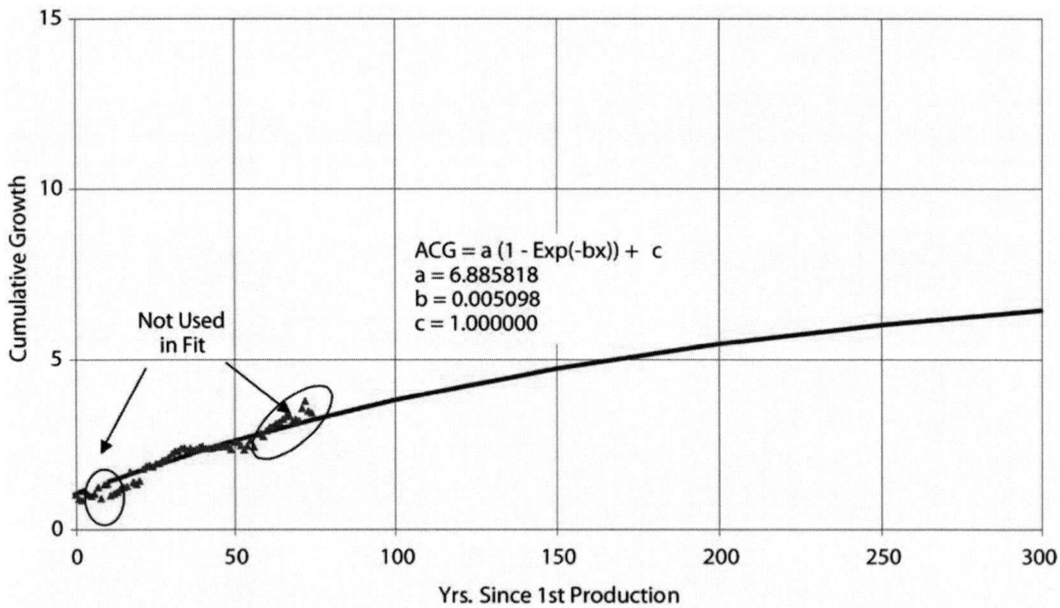

Source: Energy Information Administration, Reserves and Production Division

Figure A7-9. Paradox/San Juan Basins Exponential Curve Fit of Tight Formation Liquids Cumulative Growth Factor

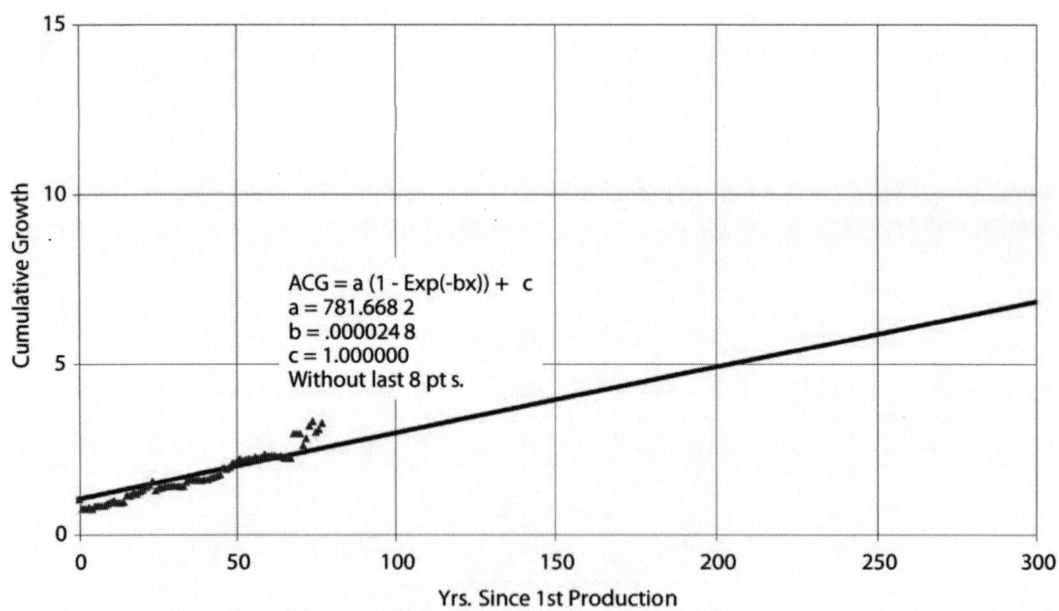

Source: Energy Information Administration, Reserves and Production Division

Figure A7-10. Paradox/San Juan Basins Exponential Curve Fit of Gas Cumulative Growth Factor

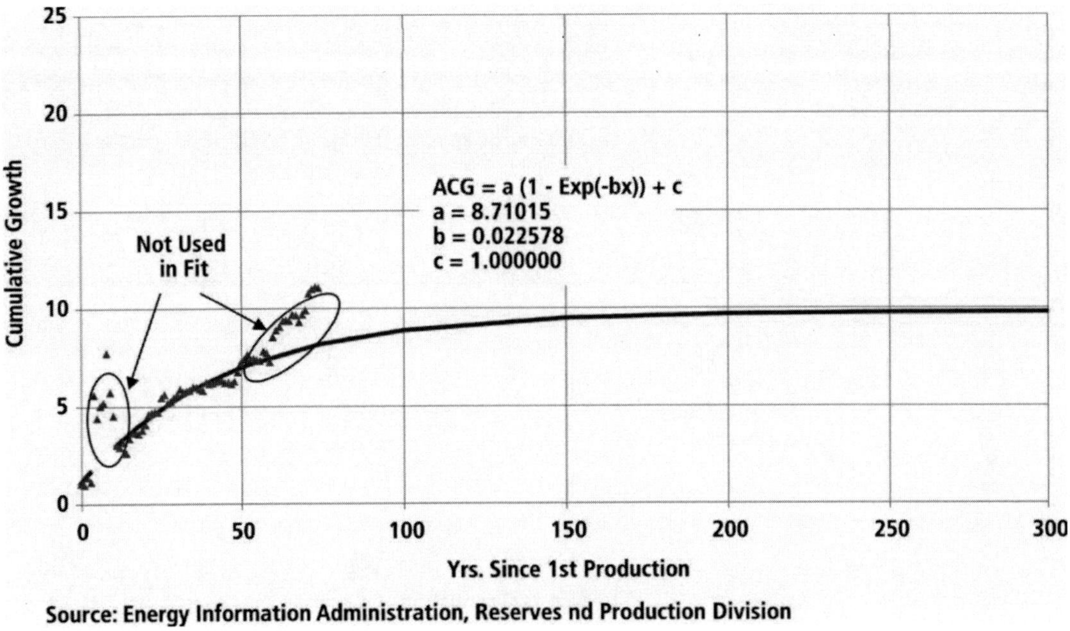

Figure A7-11. Paradox/San Juan Basins Exponential Curve Fit of Tight Formation Gas Cumulative

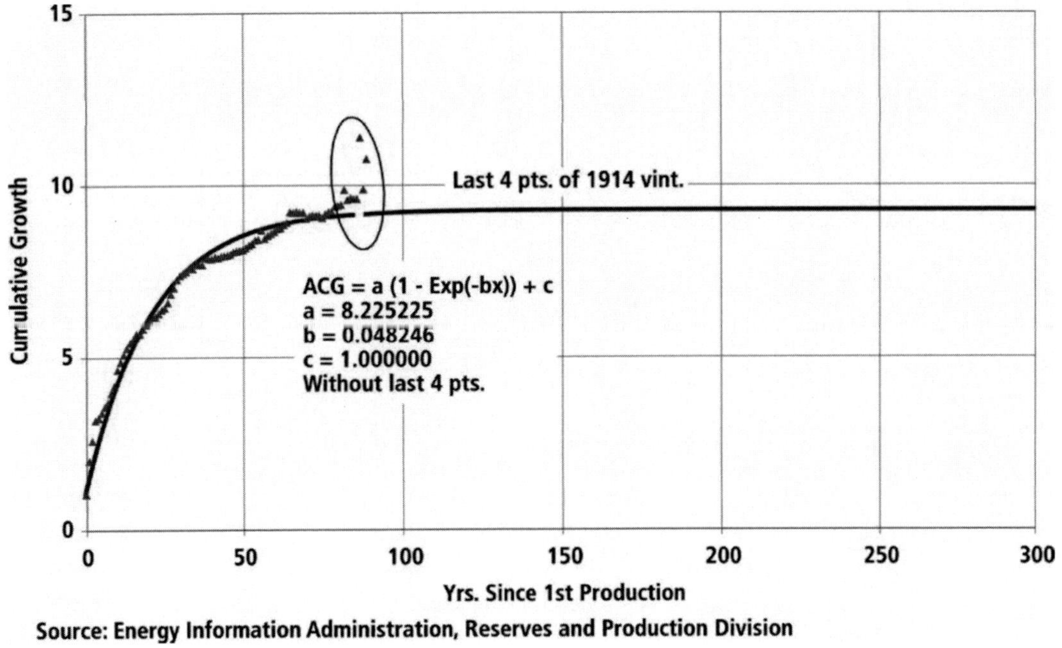

Figure A7-12. Powder River Basin Exponential Curve Fit of Equivalent Oil Cumulative Growth Factor

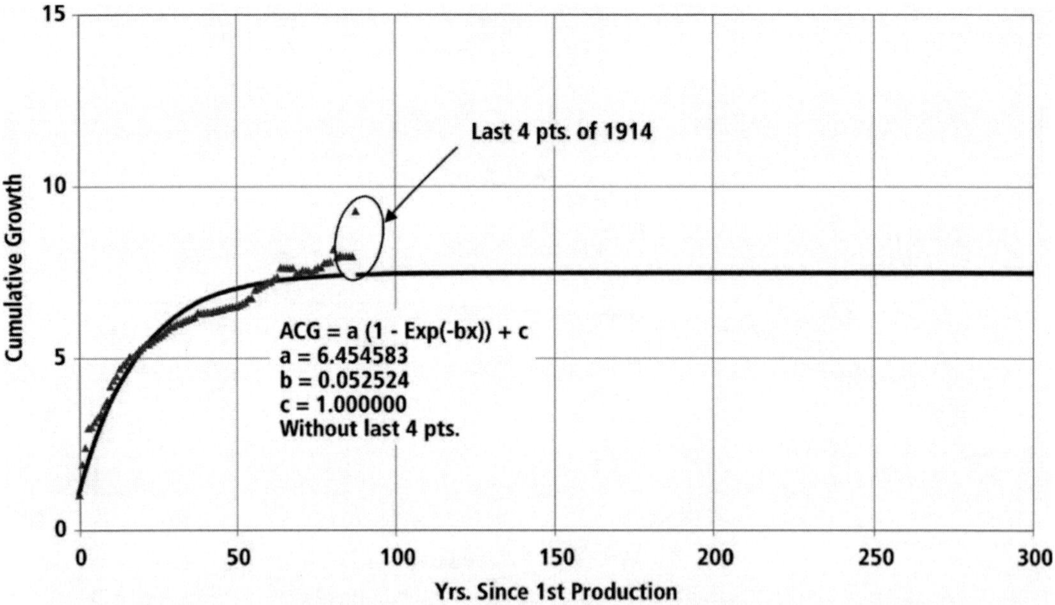

Source: Energy Information Administration, Reserves and Production Division

Figure A7-13. Powder River Basin Exponential Curve Fit of Liquids Cumulative Growth Factor

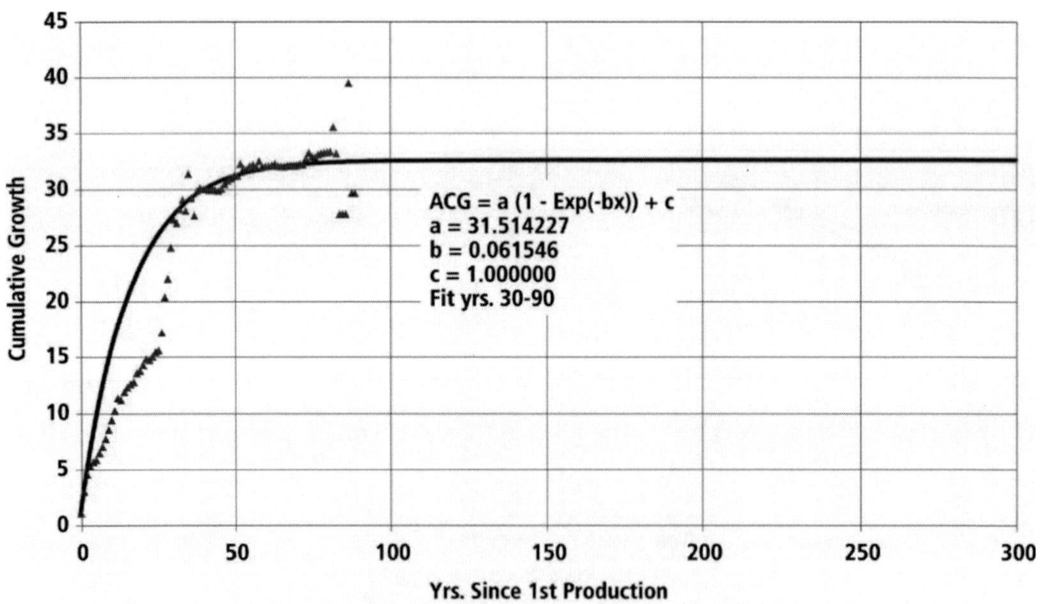

Source: Energy Information Administration, Reserves and Production Division

Figure A7-14. Powder River Basin Exponential Curve Fit of Gas Cumulative Growth Factor

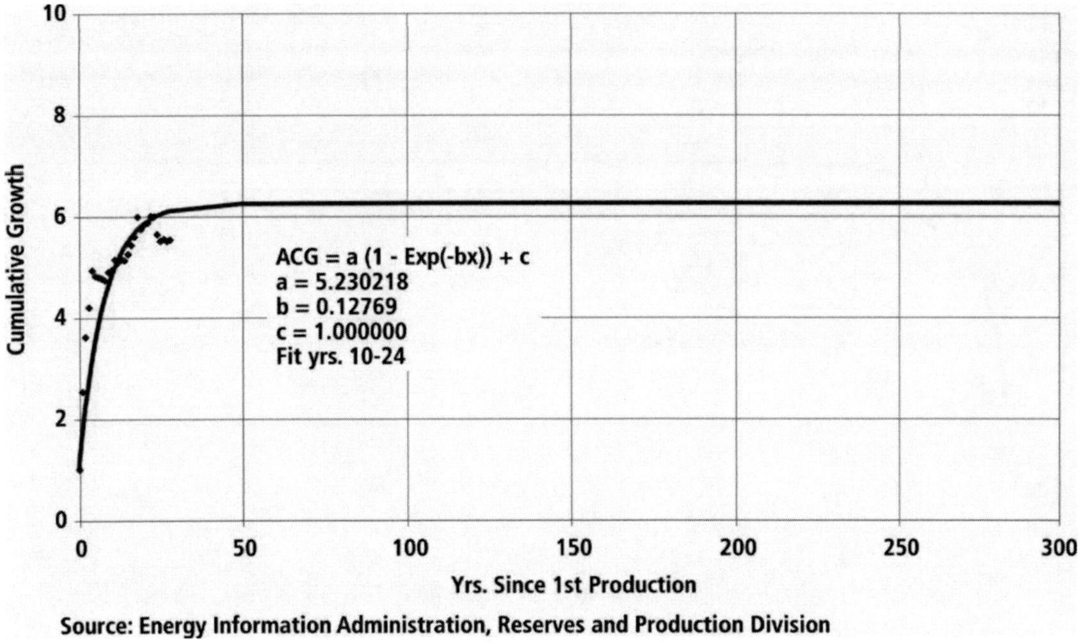

Figure A7-15. Wyoming Thrust Belt Exponential Curve Fit of Oil Equivalent Cumulative Growth Factor

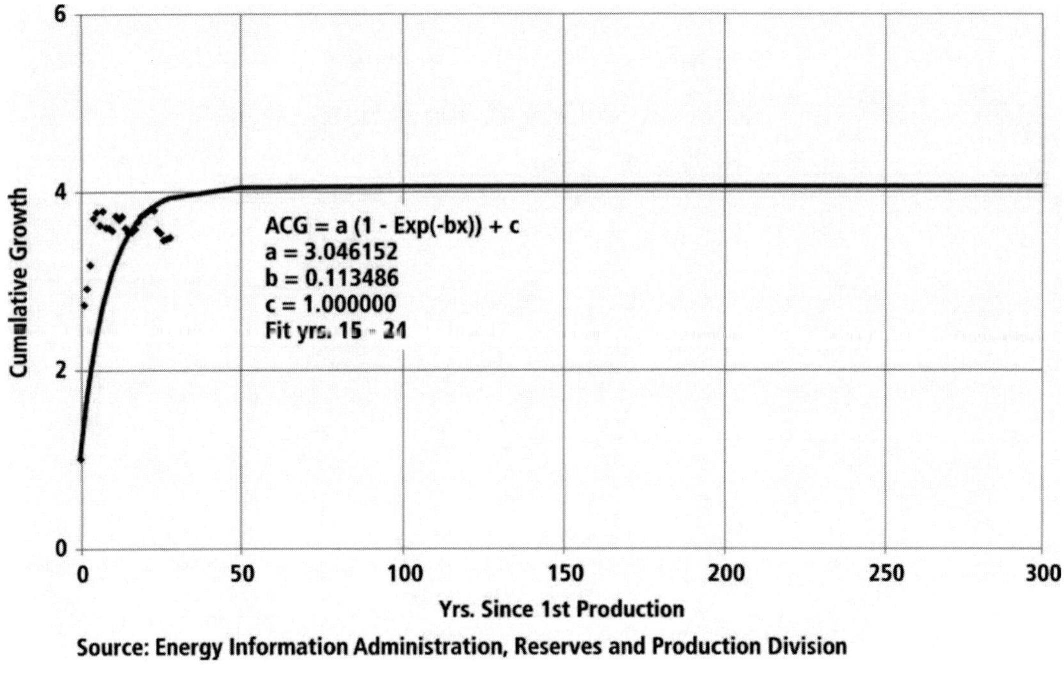

Figure A7-16. Wyoming Thrust Belt Exponential Curve Fit of Liquids Cumulative Growth Factor

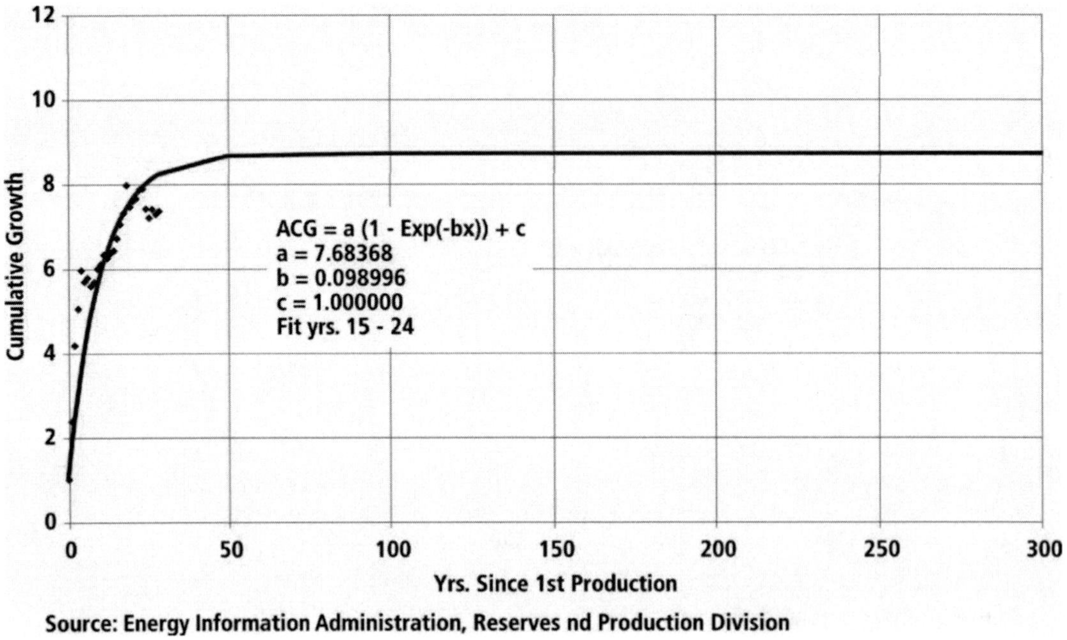

Figure A7-1 7. Wyoming Thrust Belt Exponential Curve Fit of Gas Cumulative Growth Factor

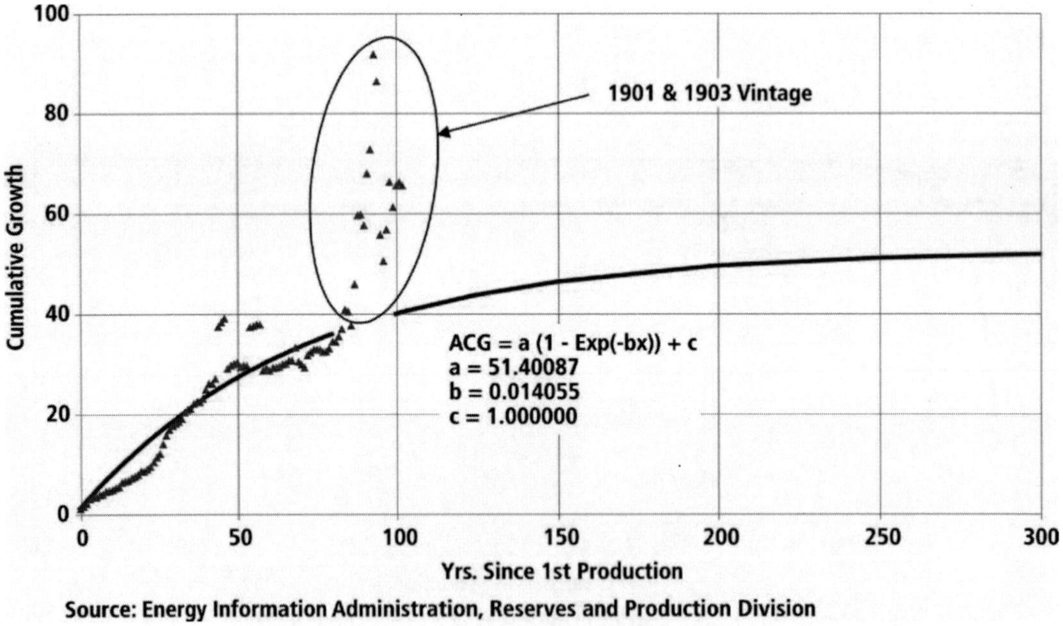

Figure A7-18. Greater Green River Basin Exponential Curve Fit of Equivalent Oil Cumulative Growth Factor

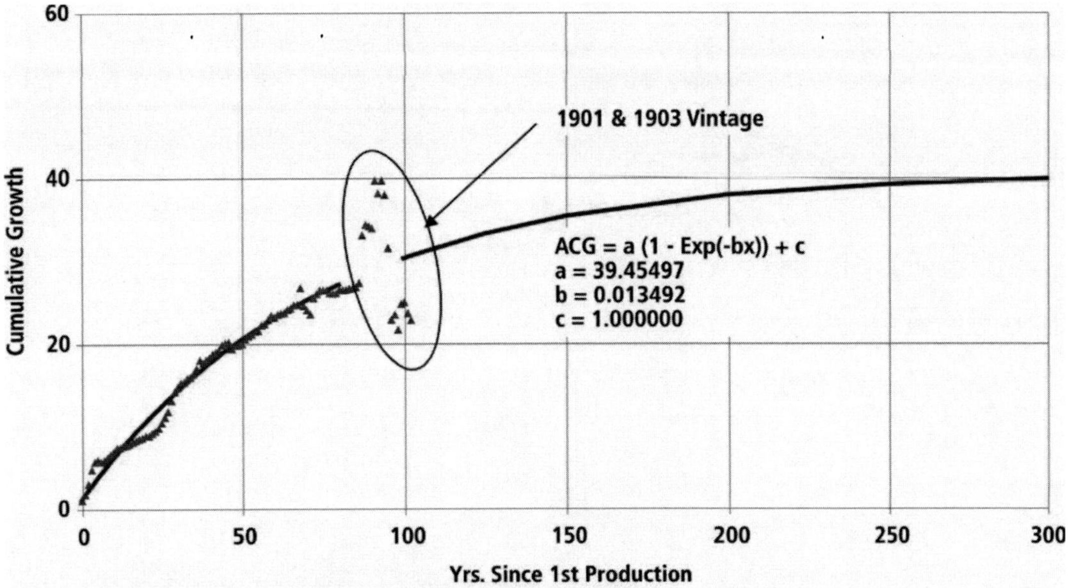

Source: Energy Information Administration, Reserves and Production Division

Figure A7-19. Greater Green River Basin Exponential Curve Fit of Liquids Cumulative Growth Factor

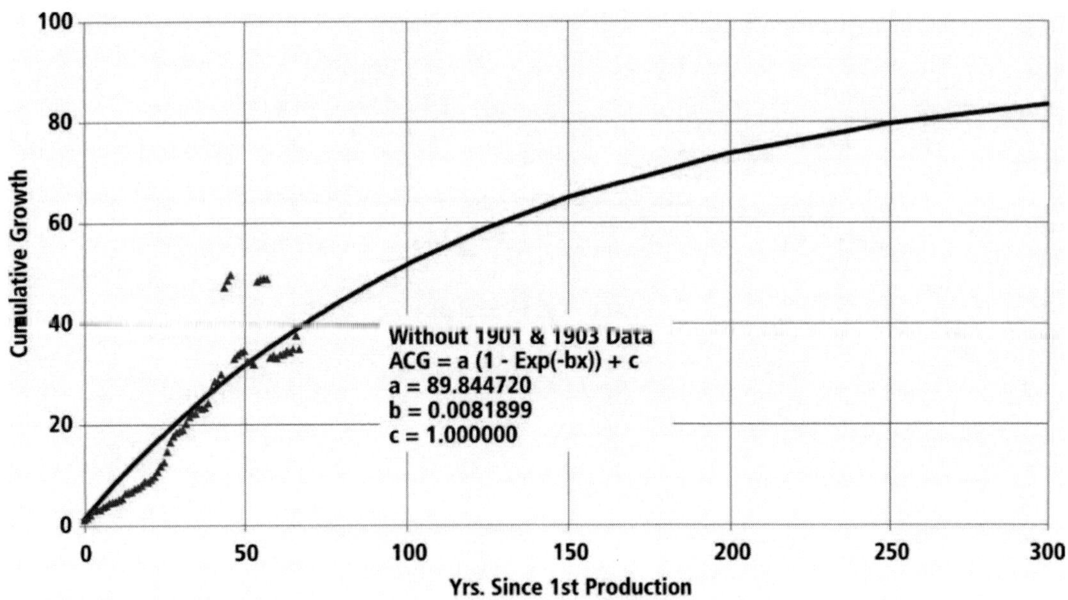

Source: Energy Information Administration, Reserves and Production Division

Figure A7-20. Greater Green River Basin Exponential Curve Fit of Gas Cumulative Growth Factor

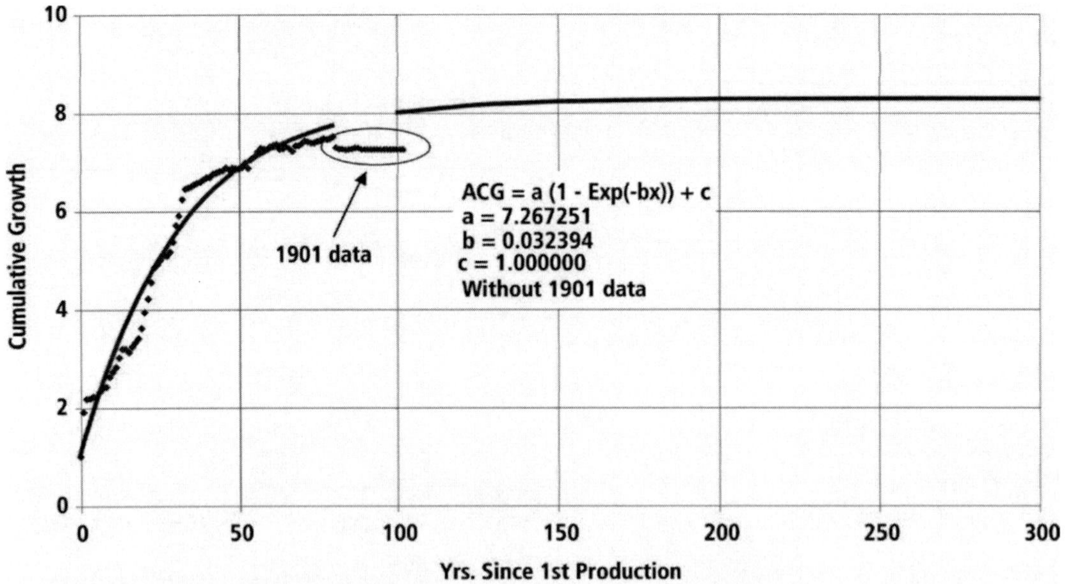

Source: Energy Information Administration, Reserves and Production Division

Figure A7-21. Denver Basin Exponential Curve Fit of Equivalent Oil Cumulative Growth Factor

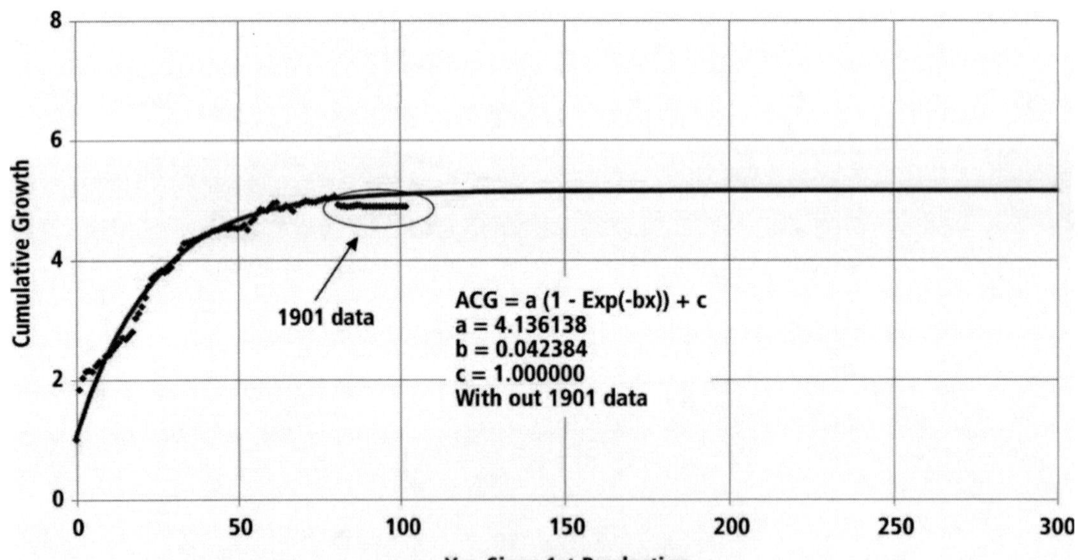

Source: Energy Information Administration, Reserves and Production Division

Figure A7-22. Denver Basin Exponential Curve Fit of Liquids Cumulative Growth Factor

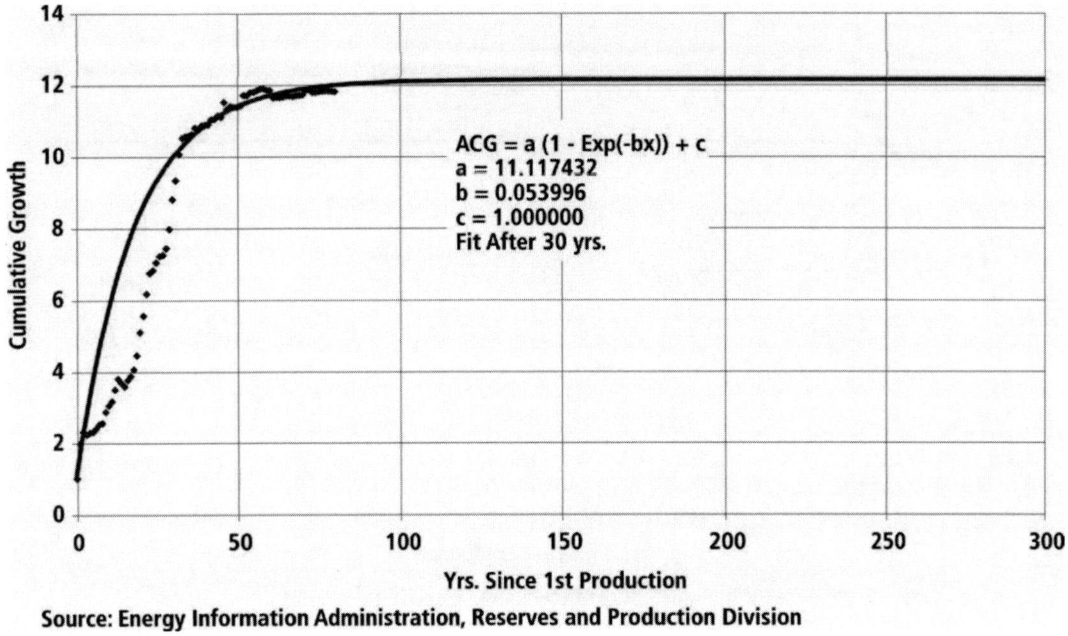

Figure A7-23. Denver Basin Exponential Curve Fit of Gas Cumulative Growth Factor

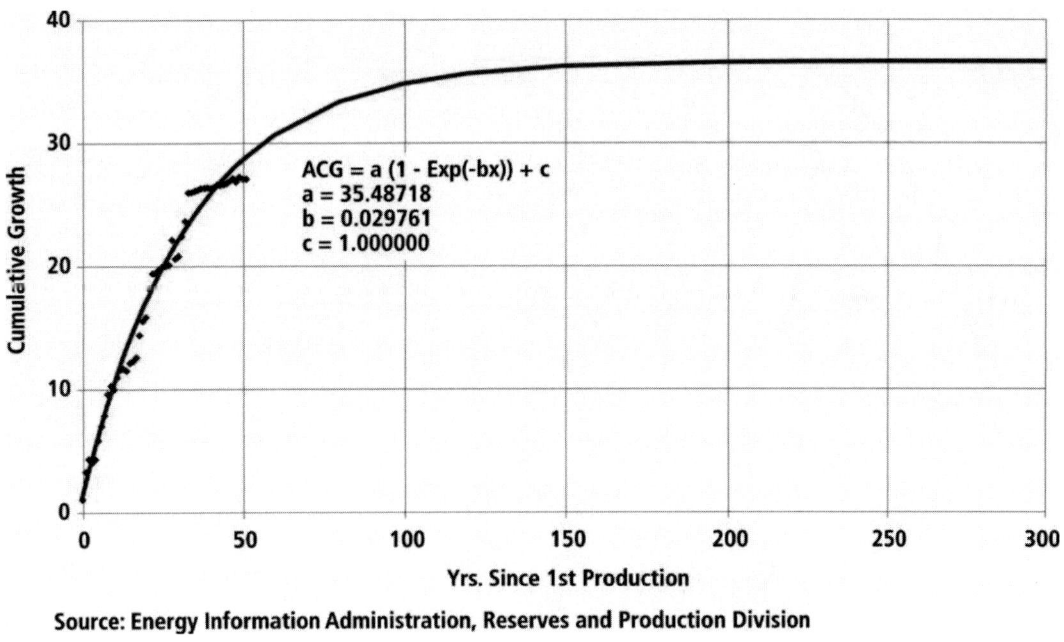

Figure A7-24. Black Warrior Basin Exponential Curve Fit of Oil Equivalent Cumulative Growth

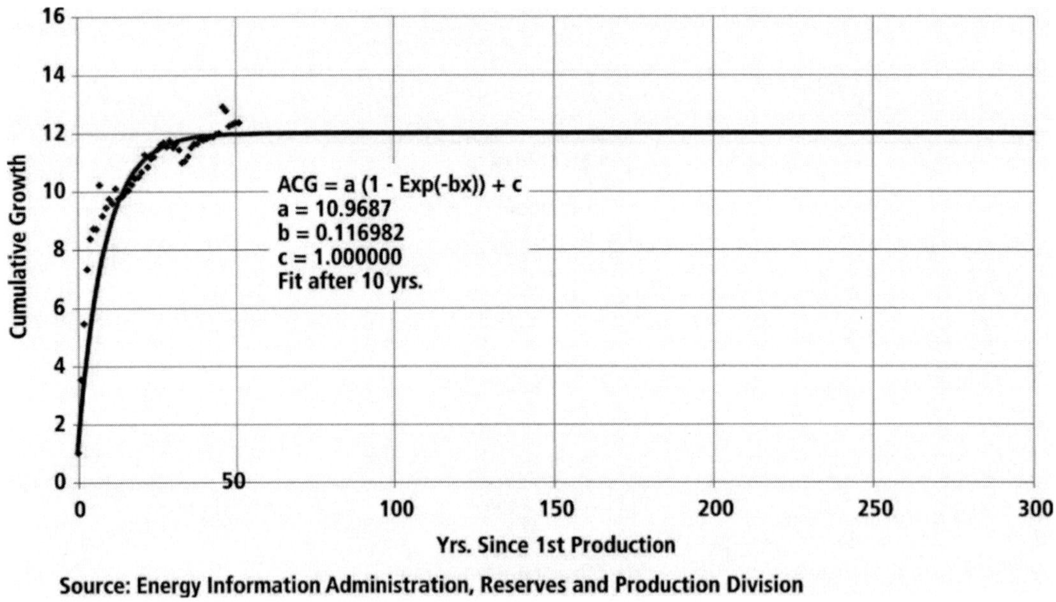

Figure A7-25. Black Warrior Basin Exponential Curve Fit of Liquids Cumulative Growth Factor

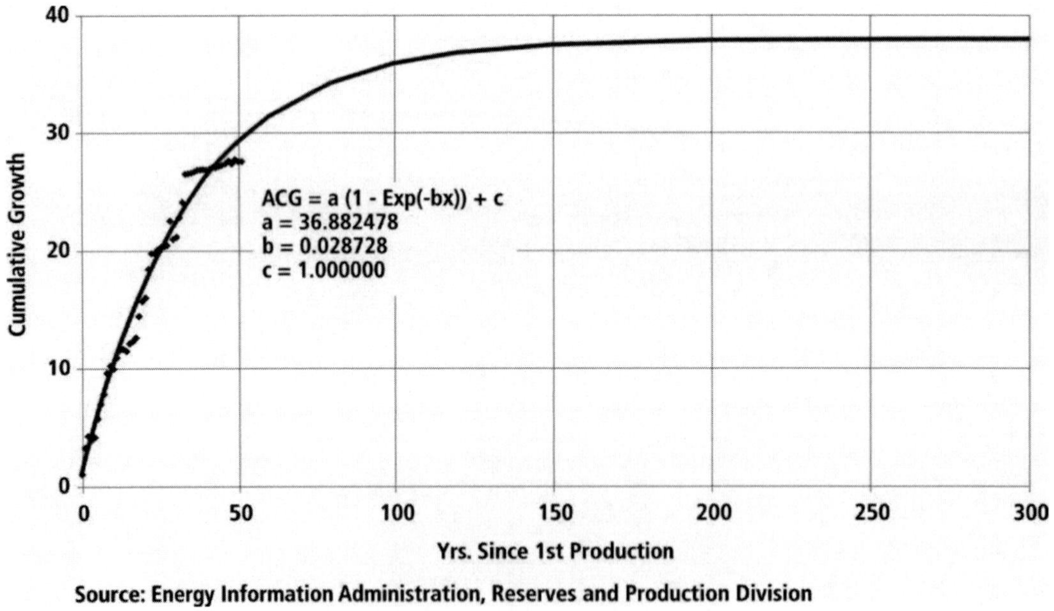

Figure A7-26. Black Warrior Basin Exponential Curve Fit of Gas Cumulative Growth Factor

A7.6.2 Hyperbolic Incremental Growth Factor Model Runs

The following Table A7-4 and Figures A7-27 through A7-40 show the detailed results of the hyperbolic incremental growth factor model as applied to the Phase II basins.

Table A7-4. Hyperbolic Incremental Growth Factor Model Results

Study Area	Type	Model Cumulative Growth Factor	Asymptote	Asymptote Growth Factor Ratio	2003 Ultimate	Asymptote Ultimate	Remaining Ultimate (Reserves Growth)
Uinta-Piceance	Liquid (Bbbls)	16.511	18.602	1.127	0.782	0.881	0.099
Paradox/ San Juan	Liquid (Bbbls)	10.754	16.155	1.502	0.903	1.356	0.453
Powder River	Liquid (Bbbls)	9.558	10.214	1.069	3.458	3.695	0.237
Wyoming Thrust Belt	Liquid (Bbbls)	6.211	6.471	1.042	0.351	0.366	0.015
Greater Green River	Liquid (Bbbls)	31.369	32.950	1.050	1.059	1.112	0.053
Denver	Liquid (Bbbls)	4.964	5.012	1.010	1.290	1.302	0.012
Black Warrior	Liquid (Bbbls)	10.137	10.316	1.018	0.016	0.016	0.000
Uinta/ Piceance	Gas (TCF)	17.042	21.803	1.279	5.838	7.469	1.631
Paradox/ San Juan	Gas (TCF)	8.275	10.214	1.234	5.157	6.365	1.208
Powder River	Gas (TCF)	25.412	28.665	1.128	3.925	4.427	0.502
Wyoming Thrust Belt	Gas (TCF)	4.839	5.161	1.067	4.788	5.107	0.319
Greater Green River	Gas (TCF)	46.343	50.021	1.079	31.995	34.534	2.539
Denver	Gas (TCF)	4.894	4.948	1.011	7.730	7.815	0.085
Black Warrior	Gas (TCF)	18.109	19.430	1.073	4.756	5.103	0.347

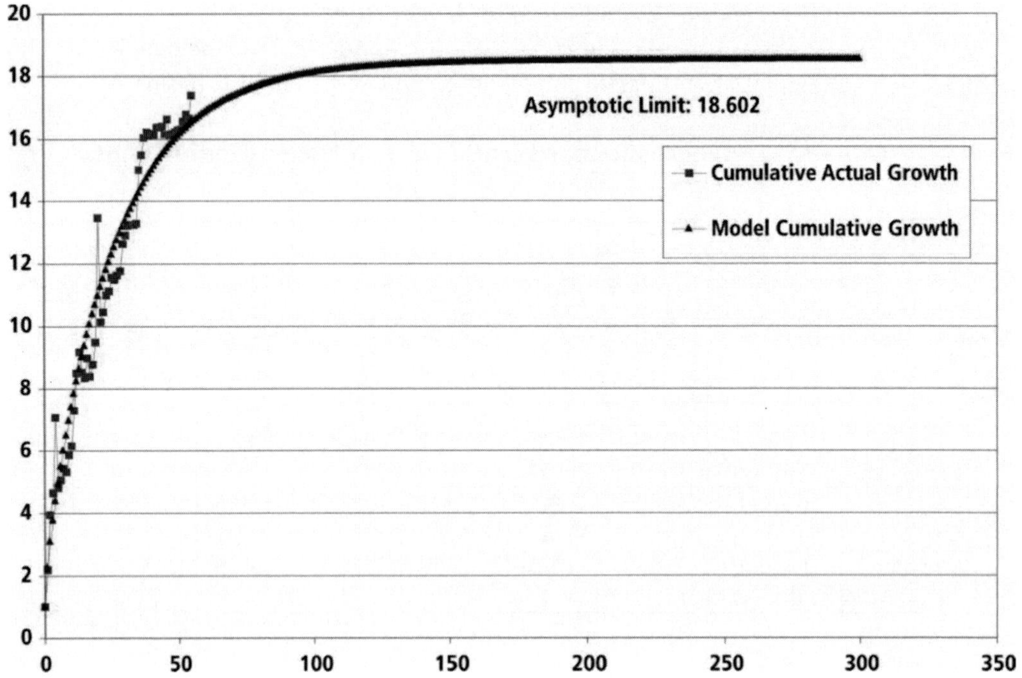

Figure A7-27. Uinta/Piceance Basin Liquids Fields Model Fit

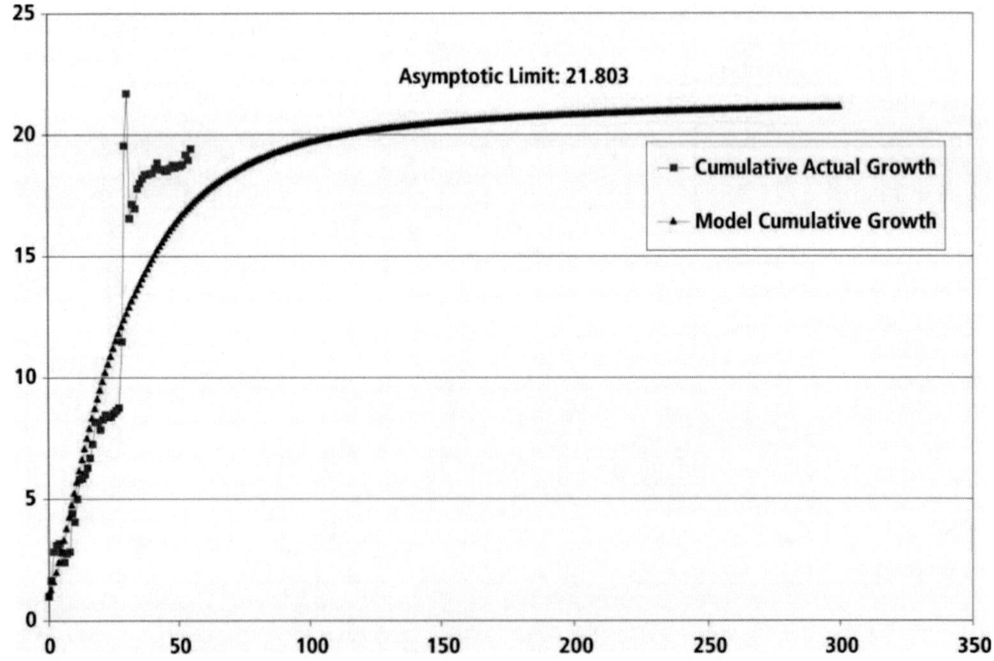

Figure A7-28. Uinta/Piceance Basin Gas Fields Model Fit

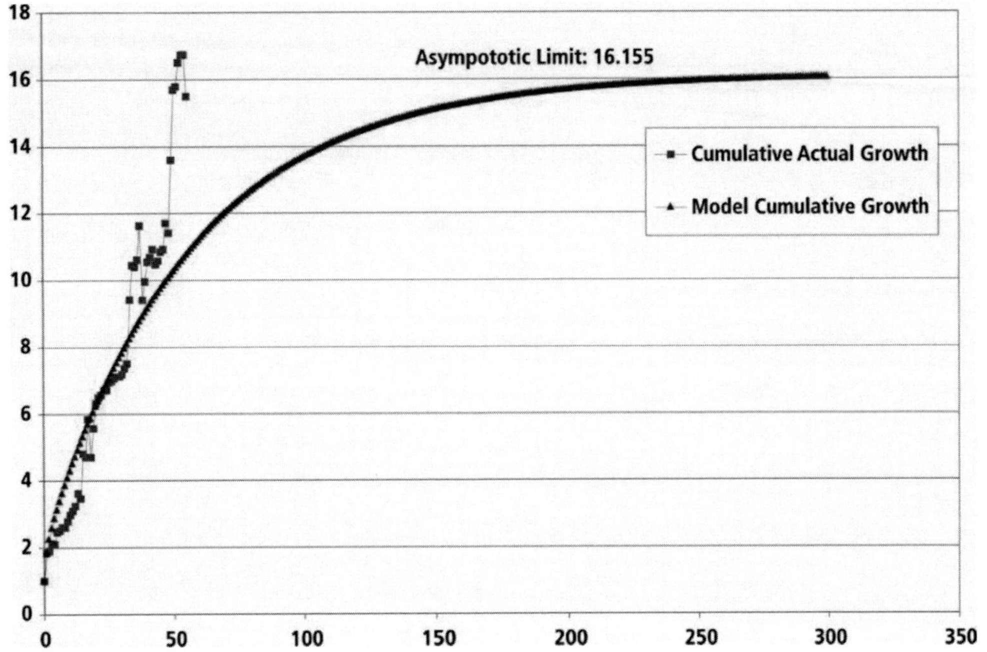

Figure A7-29. Paradox/San Juan Basins Liquids Fields Model Fit

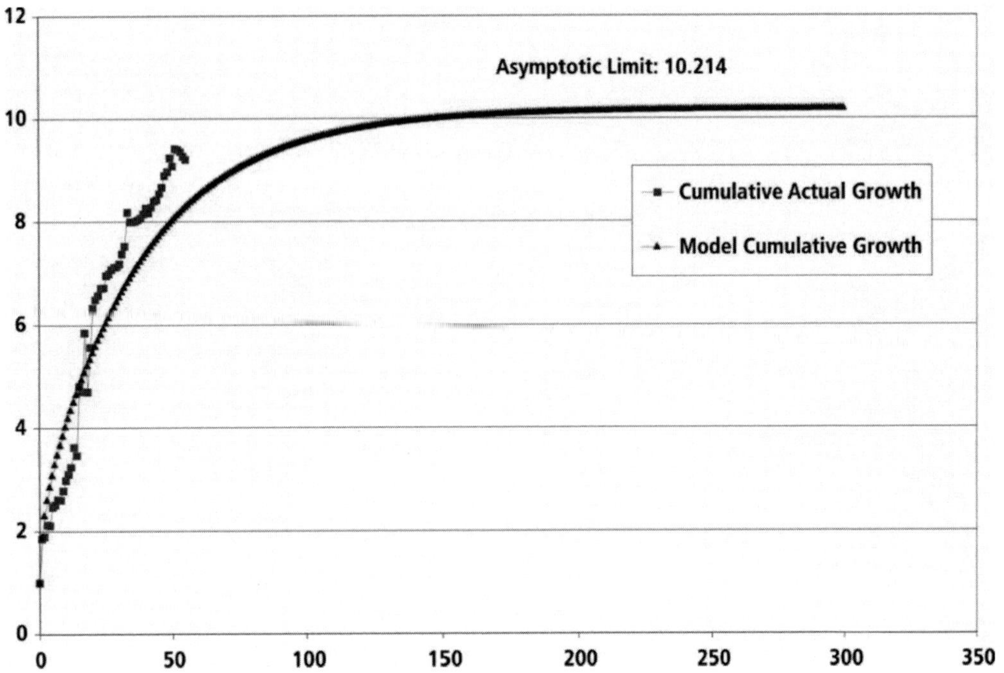

Figure A7-30. Paradox/San Juan Basins Gas Fields Model Fit (Coalbed Natural Gas Not Included)

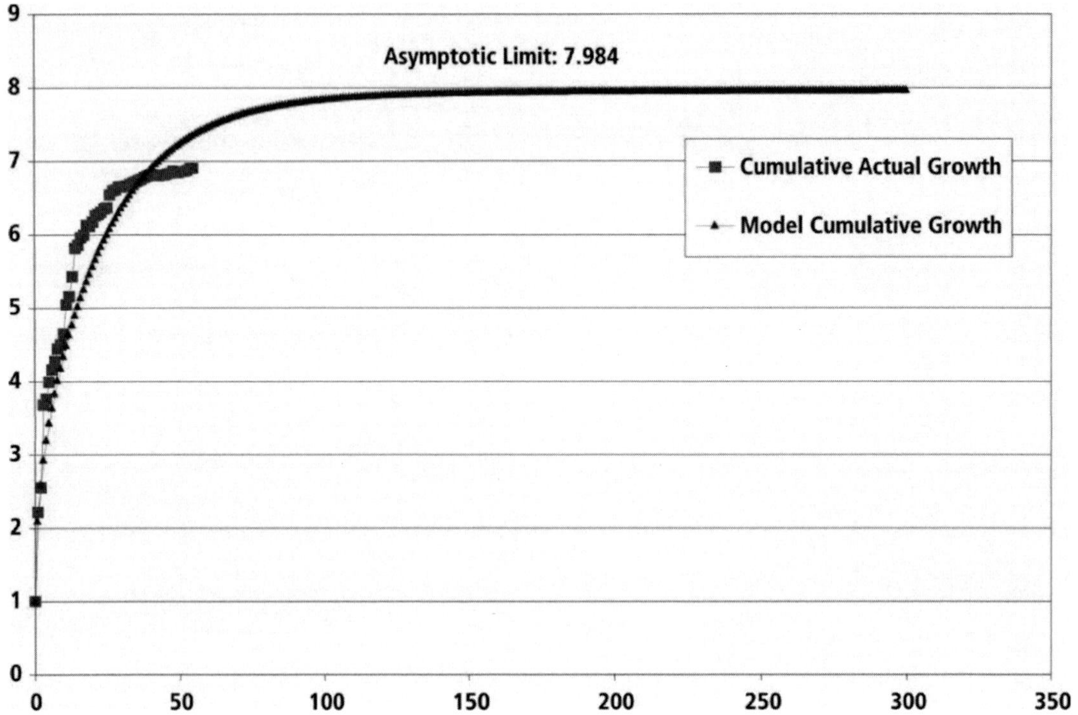

Figure A7-31. Powder River Basin Liquids Fields Model Fit

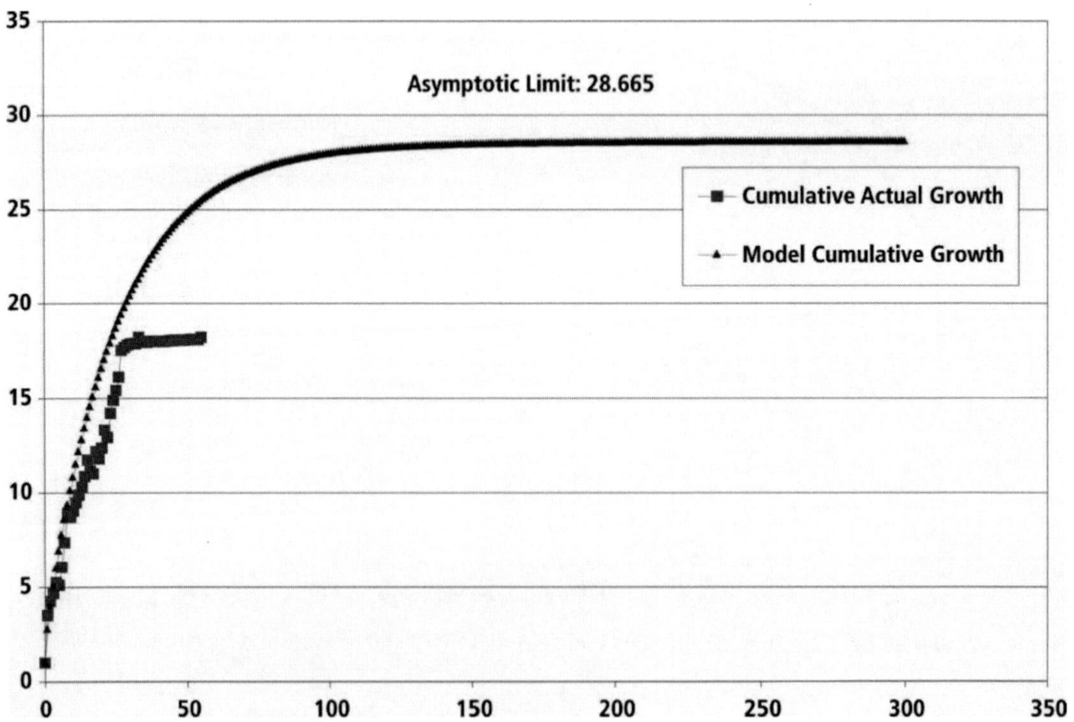

Figure A7-32. Powder River Basin Gas Fields Model Fit

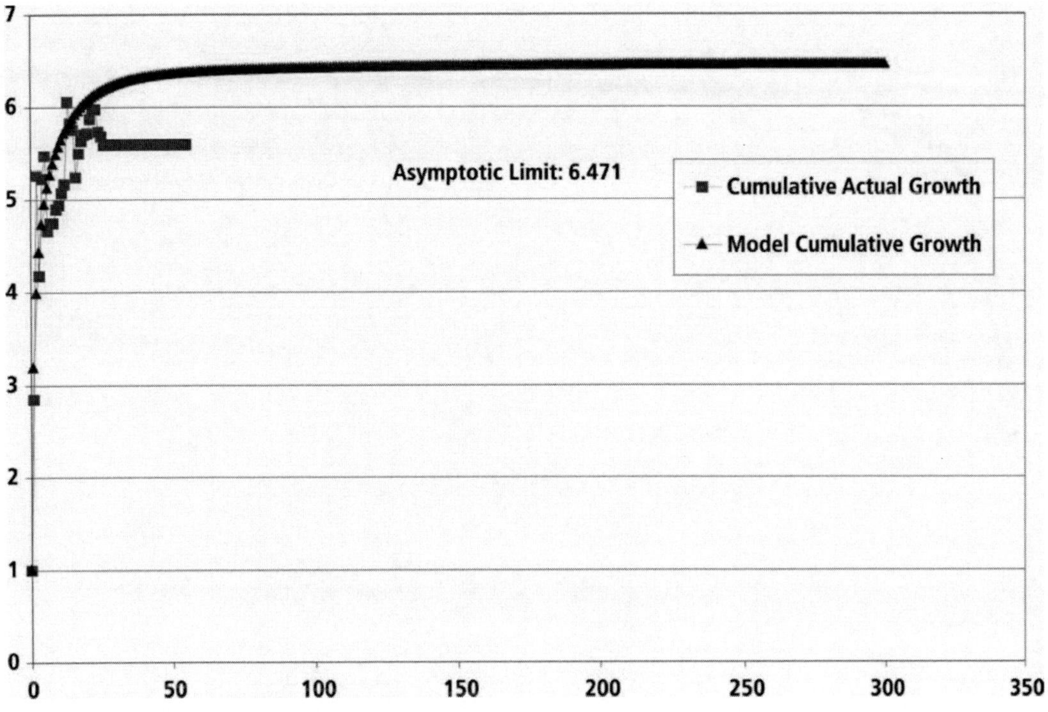

Figure A7-33. Wyoming Thrust Belt Liquids Fields Model Fit

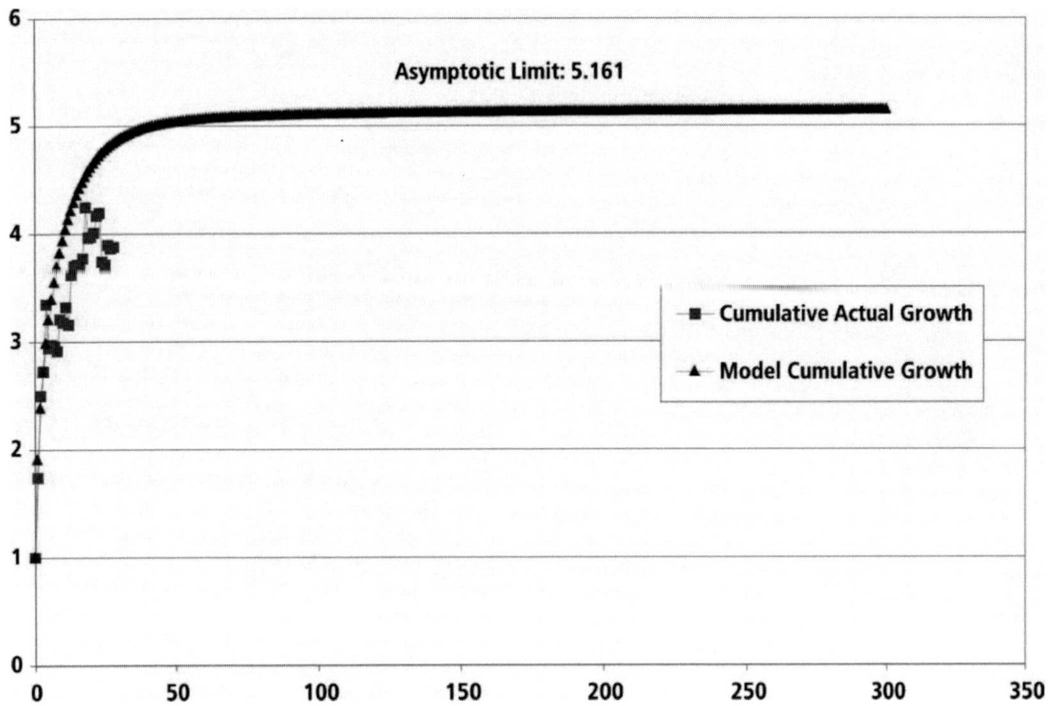

Figure A7-34. Wyoming Thrust Belt Gas Fields Model Fit

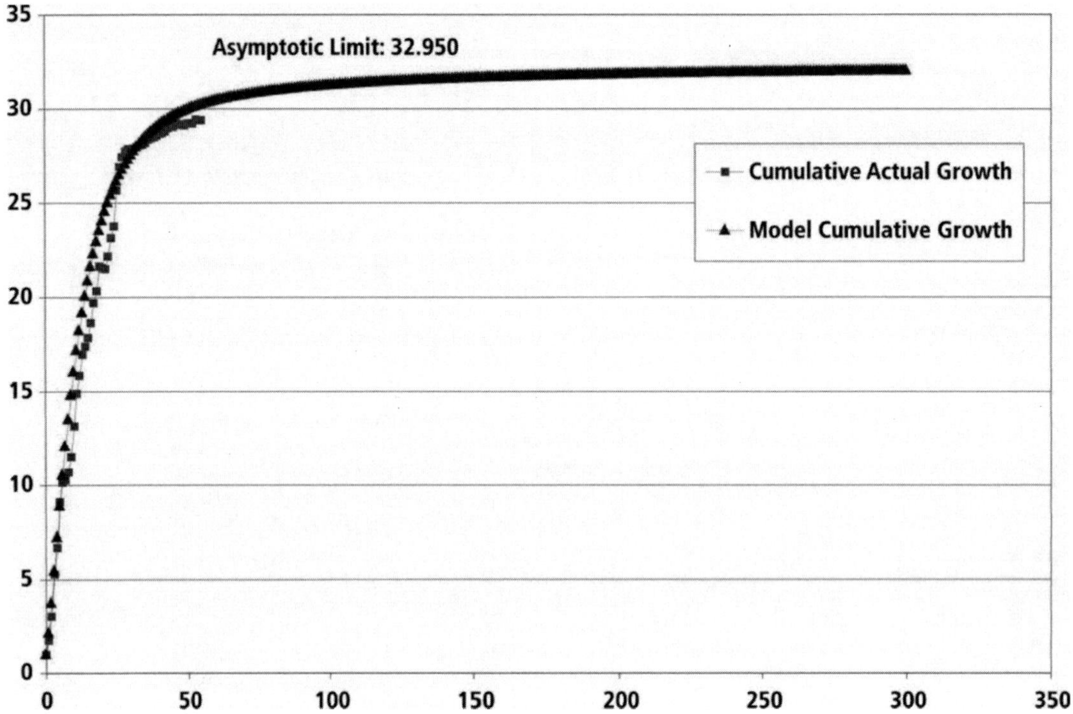

Figure A7-35. Greater Green River Basin Liquids Fields Model Fit

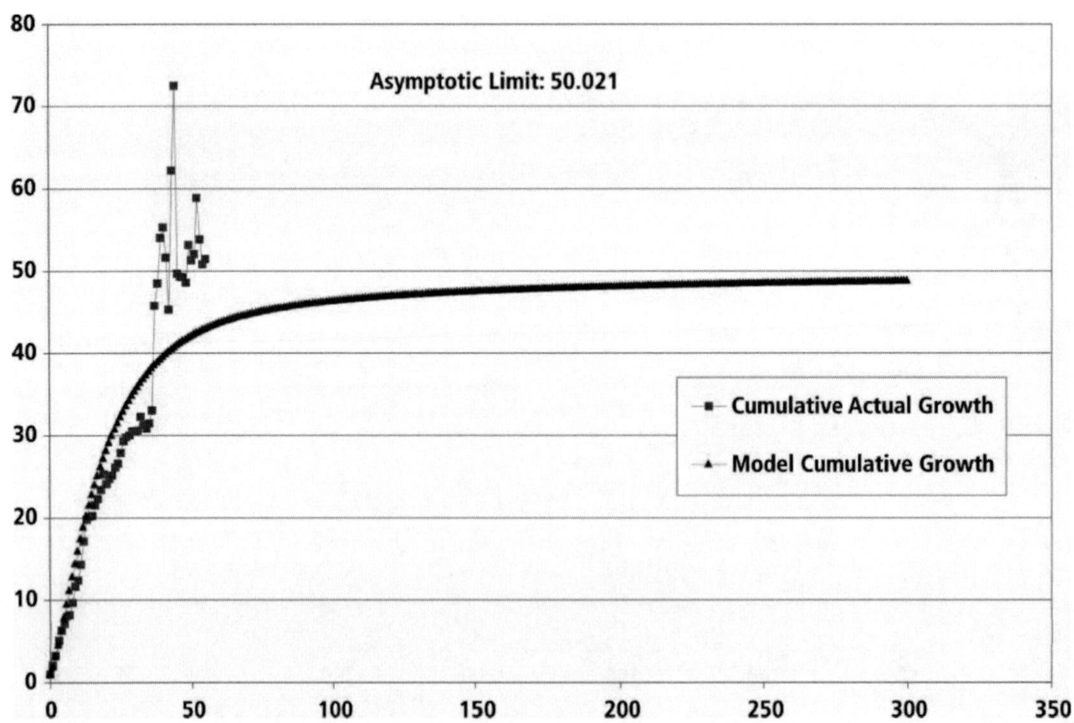

Figure A7-36. Greater Green River Basin Gas Fields Model Fit

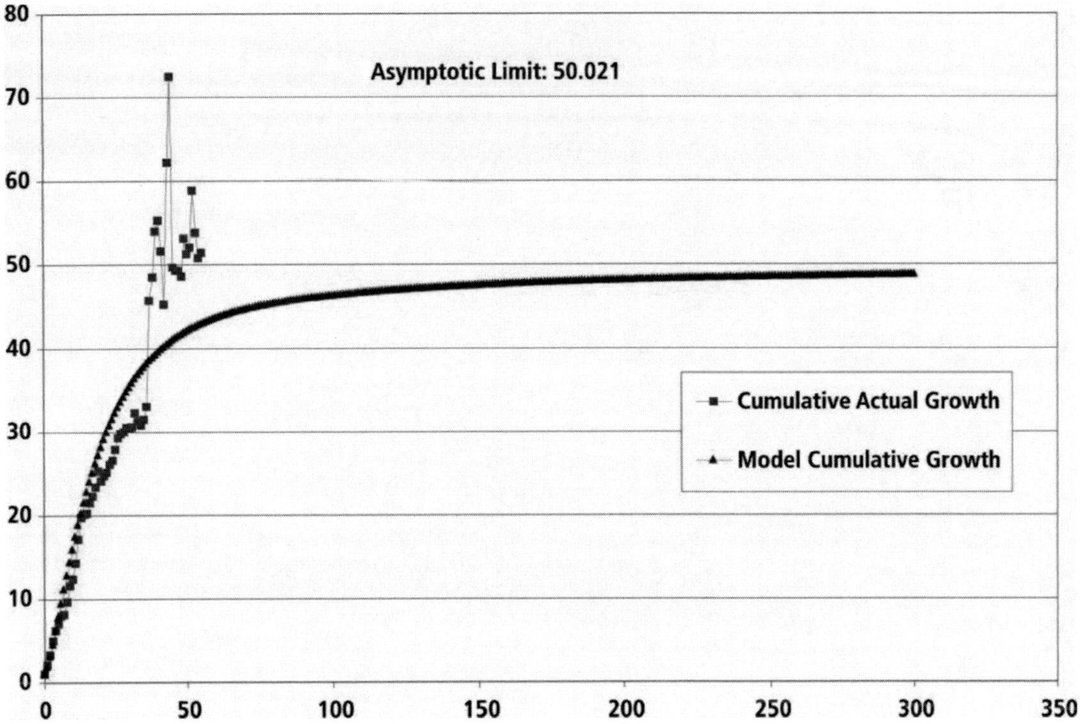

Figure A7-37. Denver Basin Liquids Fields Model Fit

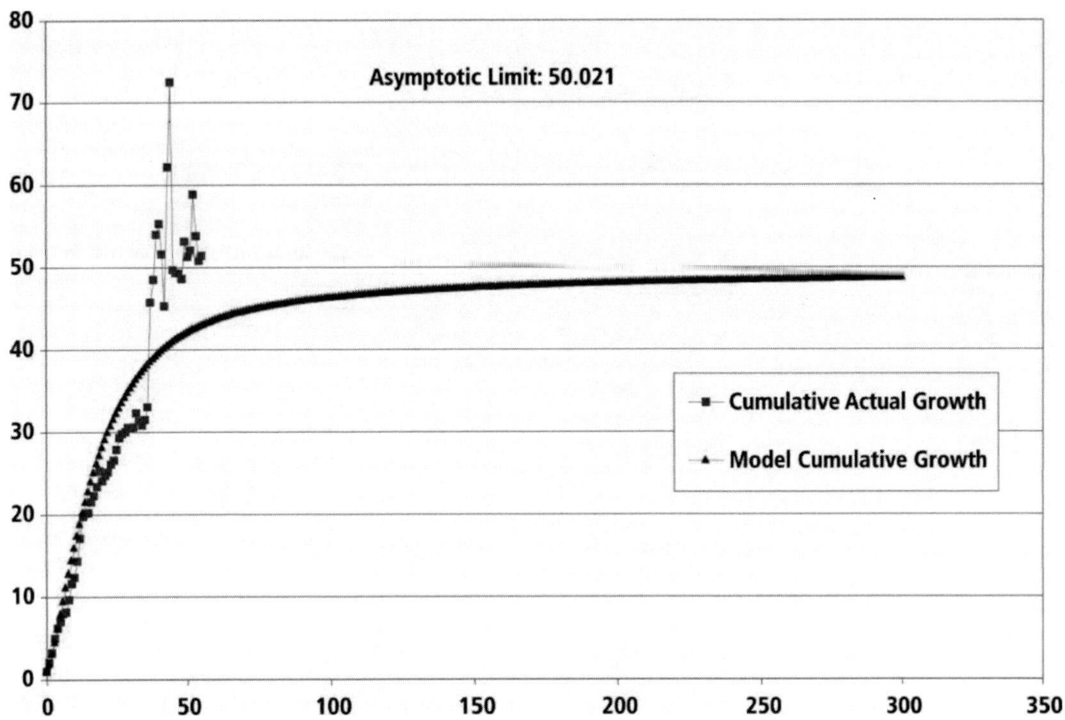

Figure A7-38. Denver Basin Gas Fields Model Fit

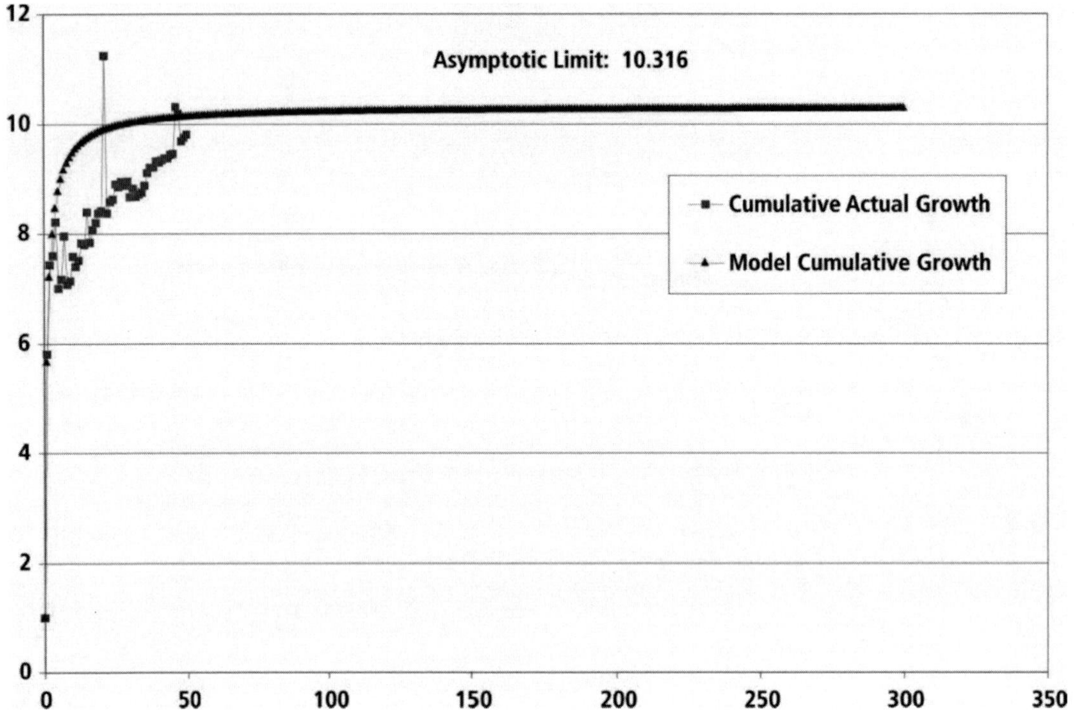

Figure A7-39. Black Warrior Basin Liquids Fields Model Fit

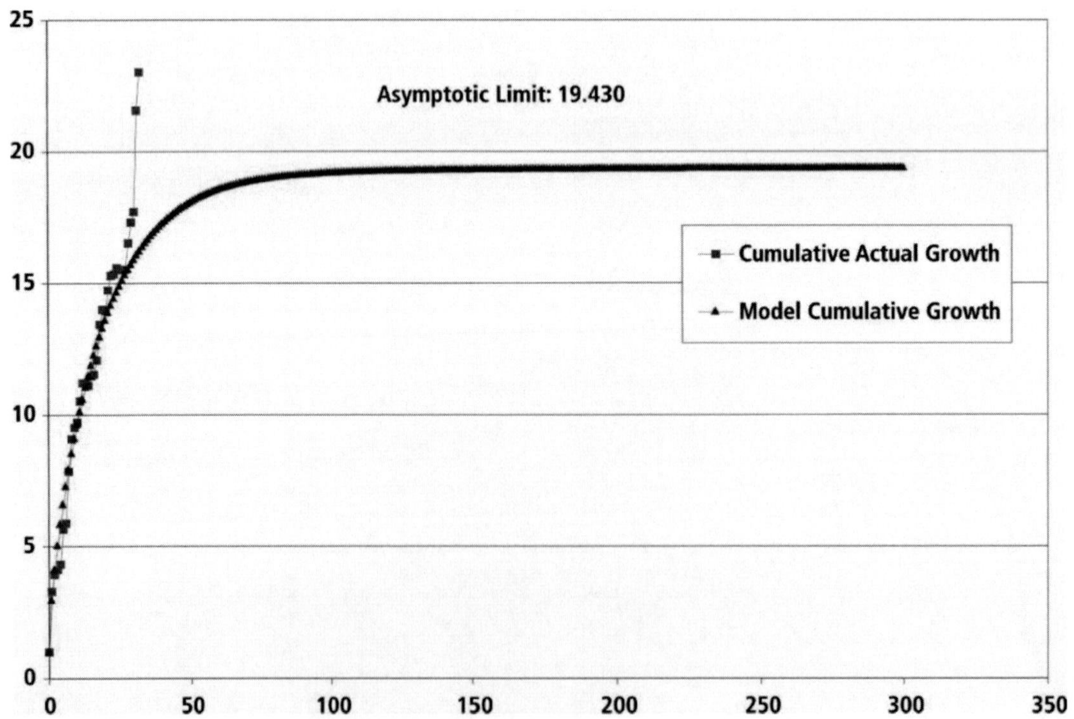

Figure A7-40. Black Warrior Basin Gas Fields Model Fit

APPENDIX 8: PROVED RESERVES ESTIMATION AND FIELD BOUNDARY CONSTRUCTION

A8.1 Summary

The Reserves and Production Division (RPD), Office of Oil and Gas, of the Energy Information Administration, estimated proved reserves of crude oil, natural gas and natural gas liquids on Federal lands located in selected geologic basins of the Rocky Mountain, Appalachian, Alaska, and Southeastern United States regions. This task involved attributing reported and imputed proved reserves to individual fields, developing field boundaries, and allocating these to Federal lands. The primary results are presented in a multi-layered GIS format accompanied by metadata compliant with the Federal Geographic Data Committee Metadata Standard. Most of the methods used were modified from those developed for the Phase I inventory in 2002. Some modifications were made to accommodate geological differences between the Phase I and Phase II basins, whereas other modifications represent the implementation of planned improvements.

To provide a fully consistent set of estimates the Phase I study areas were reprocessed using the modified methods. The updated Phase I results, which slightly differ from those previously published, are provided at the end of this appendix.

Four types of data obtained from a variety of sources were used for the project:

- Federal agencies
  The 2001 Form EIA-23 Reserves Survey was the source for the bulk of the proved reserves estimates
  The USGS was the source of well data for the state of Virginia (VA)
  The Federal lands boundary data were provided by the Bureau of Land Management, Department of the Interior.
- State agencies (oil and gas regulatory agencies and geological surveys) provided well and production data either directly or via their websites.
- Commercial vendors
  The IHS Energy Group Production Data set was a source of field names, reservoir names and 2001 production data for the states of Wyoming (WY), Utah (UT), Colorado (CO), Nebraska (NE), Mississippi (MS), Alabama (AL), Florida (FL) and Alaska (AK)
  The IHS Well History Data set was a source of well locations for the states of WY, UT, NE and CO
  PetroDataSource (PDS) was a source of well data for the states of FL, MS and Tennessee (TN)
  HPDI was a source of well data for the states of West Virginia (WV) and Maryland (MD).

Several steps were involved in the collection and preparation phase:

- Identification of all wells, reservoirs and fields in the study areas

- Standardization of reservoir and field names to make them consistent from source to source
- Assigning field names to wells where they were missing
- Identification and standardization of well types
- Merging of the state, vendor, and Form EIA-23 survey data
- Identification and name editing of those fields that had wells located both inside and outside of the defined Phase II study areas and fields that crossed state boundaries.

To compare the fields and their proved reserves to Federal lands it was necessary to construct a boundary or outline for each field. Field boundaries were determined by placing reasonable and appropriate buffers around individual wells, followed by their union. Buffer size was based on well spacing as determined by measuring the distances between wells in a reservoir or field using the latitude and longitude of each well's spud point or surface location relative to those of neighboring wells (with the exception of Northern AK, where bottom-hole locations were used). For the Eastern states, wells within the same field were used to determine the appropriate buffer size because reservoir information was frequently absent or incomplete. Rules were developed on the basis of these measurements to determine which standard well spacing (buffer) should be used for each reservoir or field. After assigning the appropriate standard well spacing-based buffers to each field or reservoir, field boundary polygons were then generated using ESRI's ArcGIS Version 8.3 software. A Visual Basic application was written to automate this process. The GIS mapping software performed these main steps:

- Selection of all wells with a specific field name
- Creation of a buffer around each well in the field using the assigned "buffer distance" (standard well spacing)
- Unioning of the buffers in each field to dissolve the inner boundaries of overlapping buffers
- Outputting of a boundary polygon (sometimes more than one polygon if one or more wells are located far from the other field wells) for each field.

Portions of field boundaries that extended outside of the defined Phase II study areas were clipped at the basin boundary and removed. For each field the fraction of total field area that was within the study area boundary was then calculated. This fraction was used to reduce the proved reserves for the field portion inside the study area boundary.

The outer margins of resultant multi-well field polygons often have a scalloped appearance. The polygons also often have small internal non-field "islands." Numerous alternative methods were tested to identify and develop an algorithm which would adequately automate smoothing of scalloped-appearing field boundaries and fill in the small "islands" while acceptably limiting the polygon area increase. The resultant smoothing algorithm, automated by a Visual Basic application in ArcGIS, was applied to all field boundary polygons. Ninety-nine percent of the resultant smoothed outlines have areas that are less than 108 percent of the unsmoothed polygon areas.

Geographic comparison of the smoothed field boundary polygons to the Federal lands polygons was then performed, resulting in output of a Federal lands fraction for each field.

Proved reserves estimates submitted on the 2001 Form EIA-23 survey were used in the estimation process. For those fields in which only some of the operators reported on Form EIA-23, the minimum reserves-to-production ratio of those that had reported was multiplied by the production of non-reporting operators to impute the latter's proved reserves. For those fields (which were usually small) in which no operator had reported on Form EIA-23, regression equations were developed from other reported observations in the basin that were used to estimate proved reserves. The portion associated with Federal lands within the field was then computed using the Federal lands fraction. Each field was then assigned to a proved reserves size class sufficiently narrow to be useful for this inventory's purposes while at the same time broad enough to ensure confidentiality of each Form EIA-23 respondent's proprietary estimates.

For the combined study areas proved Federal lands liquid reserves (crude oil plus condensate) were estimated to be 23.0 percent of total proved reserves with the individual percentages for ranging from 0.0 to 85.9 percent. Similarly, the proved Federal lands gas reserves were estimated to be 22.1 percent of total proved reserves with the individual percentages ranging from 0.0 to 96.1 percent. Also for the combined basins, Federal lands proved barrel-of-oil equivalent (BOE) reserves were estimated to be 22.3 percent of total proved reserves with the percentage for individual basins ranging from 0.0 to 93.6 percent.

A8.2 Study Areas

The Phase II study areas and the states and counties pertinent to them are listed in Table A8-1. Their boundaries were provided by the USGS. All wells in the listed states and counties for which location information (in the form of latitude and longitude coordinates or projected coordinates) were available were selected if within the study area boundaries. Wells not located within the study area boundaries were discarded unless they were in a field that had wells located both inside and outside of the boundaries.

Table A8-1. Phase II Study Areas and Their State and County Affiliations

Study Area	State	Counties
Northern Alaska	Alaska	North Slope Borough (part)
Wyoming Thrust Belt	Idaho	Bannock (part), Bear Lake, Bingham (part), Bonneville (part), Caribou, Franklin (part), Jefferson (part), Madison (part), Teton (part)
	Utah	Box Elder (part), Cache (part), Davis (part), Morgan, Rich, Salt Lake (part), Summit (part), Weber (part)
	Wyoming	Lincoln (part), Teton (part), Uinta (part)
Denver Basin	Colorado	Adams, Arapahoe, Boulder (part), Broomfield, Crowley, Custer (part), Denver, Douglas (part), El Paso (part), Elbert, Freemont (part), Jefferson (part), Kit Carson, Larimer (part), Lincoln, Logan, Morgan, Phillips, Pueblo (part), Sedgwick, Teller (part), Washington, Weld, Yuma
	Nebraska	Banner, Box Butte, Cheyenne, Dawes, Deuel, Garden, Kimball, Morrill, Scotts Bluff, Sheridan, Sioux (part)
	South Dakota	Custer (part), Shannon, Fall River (part)
	Wyoming	Albany (part), Converse (part), Goshen, Laramie (part), Platte (part)

Table A8-1. (Continued)

Study Area	State	Counties
Appalachian Basin	Kentucky	Adair, Bath, Bell, Bourbon (part), Boyd, Boyle (part), Breathitt, Carter, Casey, Clark, Clay, Clinton, Cumberland, Elliot, Estill, Fayette (part), Fleming, Floyd, Garrard (part), Green, Greenup, Harlan, Hart (part), Jackson, Jessamine (part), Johnson, Knott, Knox, Larue, Laurel, Lawrence, Lee, Leslie, Letcher, Lewis, Lincoln, Madison, Magoffin, Marion, Martin, Mason, McCreary, Menifee, Metcalfe, Monroe, Montgomery, Morgan, Nelson, Nicholas, Owsley, Perry, Pike Powell, Pulaski, Robertson, Rockcastle, Rowan, Russell, Taylor, Wayne, Whitley, Wolfe
	Maryland	Allegany, Garrett, Washington (part)
	New Jersey	Sussex (part), Warren (part)
	New York	Albany (part), Allegany, Broome, Cattaraugus, Cayuga, Chautauqua, Chemung, Chenango, Cortland, Delaware, Dutchess (part), Erie, Fulton (part), Genesee, Greene (part), Herkimer (part), Jefferson (part), Lewis (part), Livingston, Madison, Monroe, Montgomery, Niagara, Oneida, Onondaga, Ontario, Orange, Orleans, Oswego, Otsego, Rensselaer, Saratoga, Schenectady, Schoharie, Schuyler, Seneca, Steuben, Sullivan, Tioga, Tompkins, Ulster, Wayne, Wyoming, Yates
	Ohio	Adams (part), Ashland, Ashtabula, Athens, Belmont, Brown (part), Carroll, Columbiana, Coshocton, Crawford, Cuyahoga, Delaware, Erie, Fairfield, Fayette, Franklin, Gallia, Geauga, Guernsey, Harrison, Highland (part), Hocking, Holmes, Huron, Jackson, Jefferson, Knox, Lake, Lawrence, Licking, Lorain, Madison, Mahoning, Marion, Median, Meigs, Monroe, Morgan, Morrow, Muskingum, Noble, Perry, Picaway, Pike, Portage, Richland, Ross, Sandusky, Scioto, Seneca, Stark, Summit, Trumbull, Tuscarawas, Union, Vinton, Washington, Wayne
	Pennsylvania	Allegheny, Armstrong, Beaver, Bedford, Berks (part), Blair, Bradford, Butler, Cambria, Cameron, Carbon, Centre, Clarion, Clearfield, Clinton, Columbia, Crawford, Cumberland (part), Dauphin (part), Elk, Erie, Fayette, Forest, Franklin (part), Fulton, Green, Huntingdon, Indiana, Jefferson, Juniata, Lackawanna, Lawrence, Lebanon, Lehigh, Lezerne, Lycoming, McKean, Mercer, Mifflin, Monroe, Montour, Northampton, Northumberland, Perry, Pike, Potter, Schuylkill, Snyder, Somerset, Sullivan, Susquehanna, Tioga, Union, Venango, Warren, Washington, Wayne, Westmorland, Wyoming
	Tennessee	Anderson (part), Campbell, Claiborne, Clay (part), Cumberland (part), Fentress, Grainger (part), Hamblen (part), Hancock, Hawkins (part), Jackson (part), Knox (part), Morgan, Overton, Pickett, Putnam (part), Roane (part), Scott, Sullivan (part), Union, White
	Virginia	Alleghany, Augusta (part), Bath, Bland, Botetourt (part), Bristol (part), Buchanan, Clifton Forge, Covington, Craig, Dickenson, Frederick (part), Giles, Highland, Lee, Montgomery (part), Norton, Page (part), Pulaski (part), Radford (part), Roanoke (part), Rockbridge, Rockingham, Russell, Salem, Scott, Shenandoah, Smyth, Tazewell, Washington, Wise, Wythe

Table A8-1. (Continued)

Study Area	State	Counties
	West Virginia	Barbour, Berkeley (part), Boone, Braxton, Brooke, Cabell, Calhoun, Clay, Doddridge, Fayette, Gilmer, Grant, Greenbrier, Hampshire, Hancock, Hardy, Harrison, Jackson, Kanawha, Lewis, Lincoln, Logan, Marion, Marshall, Mason, McDowell, Mercer, Mineral, Mingo, Monongalia, Monroe, Morgan, Nicholas, Ohio, Pendleton, Pleasants, Pocahontas, Preston, Putnam, Raleigh, Randolph, Ritchie, Roane, Summers, Taylor, Tucker, Tyler, Upshur, Wayne, Webster, Wetzel, Wirt, Wood, Wyoming
Black Warrior Basin	Alabama	Blount (part), Cullman (part), Fayette, Franklin, Greene (part), Hale (part), Jefferson (part), Lamar, Lawrence (part), Marion, Morgan (part), Pickens, Sumter (part), Tuscaloosa (part), Walker, Winston
	Mississippi	Attala (part), Calhoun, Carroll (part), Chickasaw, Choctaw (part), Clay, Grenada, Itawamba, Lafayette (part), Lee, Leflore (part), Lowndes, Monroe, Montgomery (part), Noxubee (part), Oktibbeha, Panola (part), Pontotoc, Prentiss (part), Quitman (part), Tallahatchie, Tishomingo, Union, Webster, Winston, Yalobusha
Southern Florida Peninsula	Florida	Broward, Charlotte, Collier, Dade, DeSoto (part), Glades (part), Hardee (part), Hendry, Highlands (part), Lee, Manatee (part), Monroe, Palm Beach (part), Pinellas (part), Sarasota

Note: "(part)" indicates that a portion of a county's area is in the basin

A8.3 Data Sources

Three principal sources of data were used for this study:

- Federal Agency Data
  The 2001 Form EIA-23 Survey files which contain field-by-field proved reserves estimates and production data as reported by large operators
  A well data table with well spud point location (latitude and longitude), field name, and well type at time of completion for VA was obtained from the USGS (Robert Milici)
  Federal lands boundary data were provided by the Bureau of Land Management, Department of the Interior.
- State Agency Data
  Many of the oil and gas regulatory entities and the geological surveys of the producing US states have official websites where tables with the following data can be downloaded and/or queried: well spud point location (latitude and longitude), field name, and well type at time of completion. Several states also have online interactive web-mapping (webmapper) applications where wells can be viewed on a map and queries about them can be made. A few states have constructed their own oil and gas field boundary or outline files; these were used, where available, to check the reasonableness of the field boundaries constructed for this project. Oil and gas production data, usually annual by well, is available to download or query for some states. Links to the websites used in this study are listed in Table A8-2.

Some data can't be downloaded from the state websites even though they can be queried online and must therefore be obtained directly from a state agency. Certain data were obtained from the listed state agencies (and contact persons) in Table A8-3.

Table A8-2. Links to Websites Used in Phase II

State Data	Website
AK well data	*http://www.state.ak.us/local/akpages/ADMIN/ogc/publicdb.htm*
AK web mapper	*http://www.state.ak.us/local/akpages/ADMIN/ogc/publicdb.htm*
AK production	*http://www.state.ak.us/local/akpages/ADMIN/ogc/publicdb.htm*
AL well data	*http://www.ogb.state.al.us/*
AL production	*http://www.ogb.state.al.us/*
CO well data	*http://www.oil-gas.state.co.us/*
CO web mapper	*http://www.oil-gas.state.co.us/*
CO field outlines	*http://www.oil-gas.state.co.us/*
CO production	*http://www.oil-gas.state.co.us/*
FL well data	*http://www.dep.state.fl.us/geology/gisdatamaps/oil_gas_permit_data.htm*
FL production	*http://www.dep.state.fl.us/geology/programs/oil_gas/prod_report/oil_gas_production.htm*
KY well data	*http://www.uky.edu/KGS/emsweb/data/ogdata.html*
KY field outlines	*http://www.uky.edu/KGS/emsweb/ogmap/ogmaps.html*
KY production	*http://www.uky.edu/KGS/emsweb/data/ogdata.html*
MS well data	*http://www.ogb.state.ms.us/welldatamenu.php*
MS field outlines	*http://library.geology.deq.state.ms.us/energy/maps/production/*
MT web mapper	*http://www.bogc.dnrc.state.mt.us/website/mtcbm/webmapper_intro.htm*
MT data	*http://bogc.dnrc.state.mt.us/jdpIntro.htm*
NE well data	*http://www.nogcc.ne.gov/NOGCCPublications.htm*
NM web mapper	http://geoinfo.nmt.edu/resources/petroleum/poolmaps.html
NM data	http://octane.nmt.edu/data/, http://www.emnrd.state.nm.us/ocd/data.htm
NY well data download	http://www.dec.state.ny.us/website/dmn/ogdata.htm
NY well data search	http://www.nysm.nysed.gov/esogis/
NY field outlines	http://www.nysm.nysed.gov/esogis/mapField.cfm
NY production	http://www.nysm.nysed.gov/esogis/productionSearch.cfm
OH well data	http://www.ohiodnr.com/geosurvey/ogcim/petrol/digmaps.htm
OH well data	ftp://ftp.dnr.state.oh.us/OilGas/Download/RBDMSTransferDatabase/
OH production data	http://www.ohiodnr.com/geosurvey/ogcim/petrol/digddf.htm#ddf4
OH field outlines	http://www.ohiodnr.com/geosurvey/pdf/map_pg1.pdf
PA well data & web mapper	http://www.dcnr.state.pa.us/topogeo/oilandgas/pa_iris_home.aspx

Table A8-2. (Continued)

State Data	Website
SD maps (not interactive)	http://www.sdgs.usd.edu/digitalpubmaps/testholewells/testholewellsmapne.html
SD data	http://www.state.sd.us/denr/DES/Mining/Oil&Gas/producti.htm
UT well data & production	http://ogm.utah.gov/oilgas/DOWNLOAD/downpage.htm
UT web mapper	http://atlas.utah.gov/oilgaswells2/viewer.htm
UT field outlines	http://ogm.utah.gov/oilgas/MAP_SEARCH/Utah_map.htm
WV well data & production	http://www.dep.state.wv.us/item.cfm?ssid=23&ss1id=97
WV well data & production	http://www.wvgs.wvnet.edu/www/datastat/datastat.htm#ogwelldata
WY well data	http://wogcc.state.wy.us/ >download
WY web mapper	http://wogra.wygisc.uwyo.edu/misc/wograindex.html
WY field outlines	http://www.wsgs.uwyo.edu/sids/OGsid.aspx
WY production	http://wogcc.state.wy.us/ > production

- Commercial Data
  Well data tables with spud point location (latitude and longitude), field name, and well type at time of completion for the states of FL, MS, and TN were purchased from vendor PetroDataSource
  Well data tables with spud point location (latitude and longitude), field name, and well type at time of completion for the states of WV and MD were purchased from vendor HPDI
  IHS Production CDs were the source of production data at the well (for gas) or the lease (for oil) for crude oil, associated-dissolved gas, nonassociated gas, and condensate production in the Rocky Mountain states (CO, NE, UT, WY), the Black Warrior Basin states (AL, MS), FL, and AK
  IHS Well History CDs were the source of spud point location (latitude and longitude thereof generated by Tobin International, Ltd.), field names, producing formation(s), and well type at the time of completion for the Rocky Mountain states (CO, NE, UT, WY) and Alaska.

A8.4 Limitations Imposed by the Available Data Sources

A variety of shortcomings and flaws in the available data impose unavoidable limitations either on what can be done or on the achievable level of accuracy. Chief among these are:

- Field and reservoir names are frequently non-standard as concerns their content and/or spelling. This makes accurate automated—and often even manual— matching of field and well records across data sources difficult and sometimes impossible. While standardized field codes are assigned and supported by EIA, most field names and their spellings are assigned by State agencies. When reporting well or production information for a field on which the state has not yet given an official name, the field operator is free to use any name or spelling.

An additional factor was the demise of the American Association of Petroleum Geologists' (AAPG) Committee on Statistics of Drilling, which for many years performed an essential quality control function relative to U.S. well statistics and field and reservoir names. Staffed by industry volunteers the Committee was disbanded in 1986 and its files were turned over to the American Petroleum Institute (API), which that for many years maintained them absent the "in-the-field" quality control that the AAPG Committee had provided. Eventually this task was transferred to two competing commercial data vendors for continued maintenance and updating. Both recipient firms were subsumed into IHS Energy Group.

- Related to the field name problem is the problem of unknown and/or unassigned field names. This was most prevalent in the Appalachian Basin where thousands of wells exist that are not associated with field names. Such wells were assigned field names by proximity to existing fields and by determining producing formations in common with existing fields. This process involved viewing of mapped well locations and the use of automated programs that calculated distances from unknown wells to nearby wells associated with field names. After this there were still, especially in the Appalachian basin, wells that could not be assigned field names. These were assigned temporary names with Reserves and Production Division and county name as part of the name.
- Well misclassification is a perennial problem. For the most part it is caused by insufficient recursive quality control. For example, a new well may initially be classified as a wildcat well, which by definition has discovered a new field. Subsequent drilling of extension wells in this or an adjacent field may, over time connect the two adjacent fields. At this point both fields will shift to the field name of the earliest discovered of the two. This and other similar reclassifications occur frequently, but that fact often never filters backward, i.e., in this case to re-classification of the wildcat well type to extension or even development status.
- With the notable exception of fields located on the Outer Continental Shelf, the Federal government has access to subsurface data other than the well data available in state or vendor well files and state well log files. Because seismic data and interpretations, surface and subsurface geologic maps, and many well logs are proprietary data, in the context of this inventory, this limits what can be done concerning the construction of field boundaries to a purely geometric approach based on the buffering of well locations around their surface spud points (or bottom- hole locations for AK only).
- Many wells located in the Appalachian Basin were drilled and completed in the 1800's, long before there were laws to regulate them or any government or commercial organization tracking them. Digital records do not exist for many of the oldest wells and these are not represented in the field boundaries that resulted from this study unless they were producing relatively recently or were replaced with newer wells. The state geological surveys of OH, PA and KY are addressing this issue to varying extents by digitizing older field boundary maps and integrating them with digital well records in a GIS.

For these reasons, the resultant field boundaries are approximations, the accuracy of which, in the absence of adequate subsurface information, depends to a greater or lesser extent, on the professional judgment of the EIA RPD's petroleum geologists and engineers. *Collectively the field boundaries provided here are likely to be of sufficient accuracy for policy formulation concerning access to Federal onshore lands. In specific instances they may not be accurate enough for the application of policy and regulation.*

A8.5 Process Overview

Figure A8-1 is a flow chart of the major steps followed in estimation of field-level proved reserves (on the left-hand side) and the construction of field boundaries (on the right- hand side), plus their merger into the final principal reserves product. The following discussion provides details for each of the indicated steps.

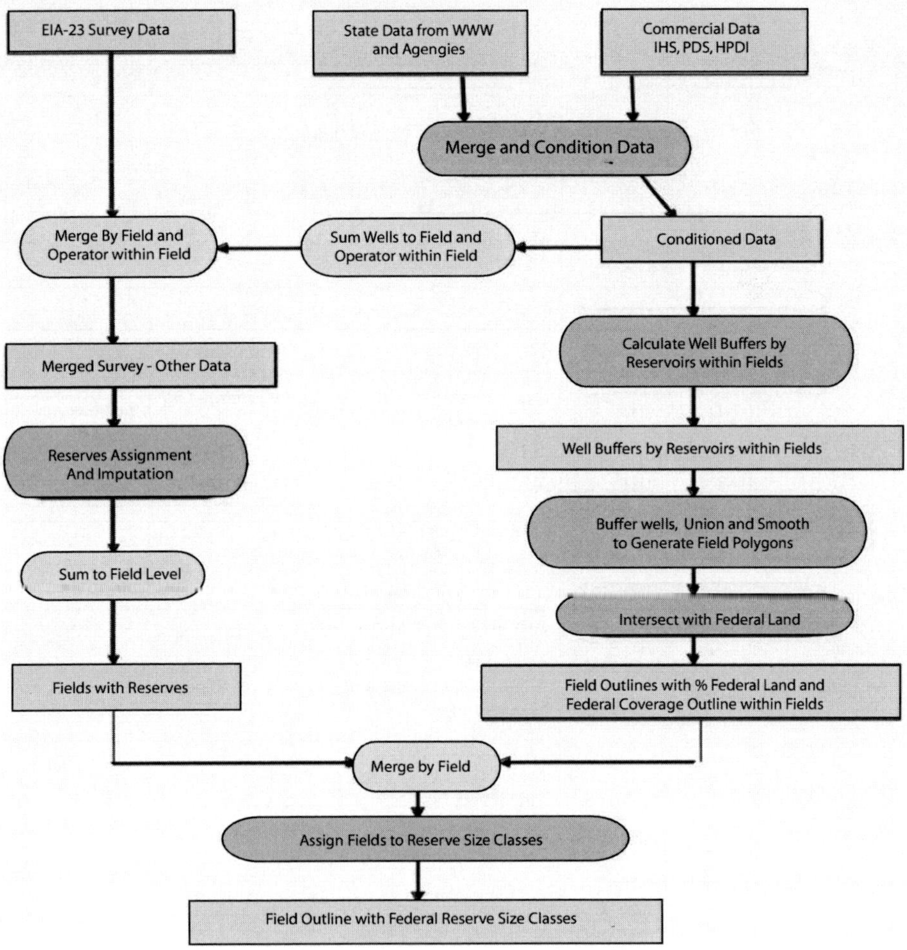

Figure A8-1. Phase II Process Flows

A8.6 Quality Checking and Combination of Data Sources for Each State

Owing to different histories of tracking of oil and gas industry activity and to non-standardization, each state's data posed unique challenges relative to assembling the most complete and accurate well data set possible for use in constructing field boundaries. State agencies were a primary source of well data for all 16 of the producing states involved in the Phase II basins. These data were augmented with vendor well data in 11 of the 16 states (see Table A8-4).

Table A8-4. Well Data Sources by State for Phase II

WELL DATA SOURCES FOR THE PHASE II INVENTORY				
Study Area	**State**	**Vendor**	**State or Federal Agencies**	**Comments**
N. Alaska NPRA	AK	IHS	AK Oil & Gas Conservation Commission	Bottom-hole locations used
N. Alaska ANWR	AK		AK Oil & Gas Conservation Commission	No producers in ANWR
Wyoming Thrust	WY	IHS	WY Oil & Gas Conservation Commission	State wells for 3 cos. only
Belt	UT	IHS	UT Division of Oil, Gas & Mining	
	ID		ID Department of Lands- Surface & Mineral Resources Bureau	No production in ID
Denver Basin	CO	IHS	CO Oil & Gas Conservation Commission	
	NE	IHS	NE Oil & Gas Conservation Commission	
	SD	IHS	SD Dept of Envir & Natural Resources- Oil & Gas Section	No SD production in basin
	WY	IHS	WY Oil & Gas Conservation Commission	State wells for 8 cos. only
Florida Peninsula	FL	PDS, IHS	FL Department of Environmental Protection- Oil & Gas Section	
Black Warrior Basin	AL	IHS	AL State Oil & Gas Board	
	MS	IHS/PDS	MS State Oil & Gas Board	
Appalachian Basin	NY		NY State Dept of Environmental Conservation-	
			Division of Mineral Resources	
	PA		PA Dept of Conservation & Natural Resources	Subscription required
	OH		OH Geological Survey; OH Dept of Natural Resources	No field names in well
	MD	HPDI	MD Department of the Interior- Minerals, Oil & Gas Division	
	WV	HPDI, IHS	WV Geological & Economic Survey; WV Dept.of Environmental Protection	Survey wells for 20 cos. only

Table A8-4. (Continued)

WELL DATA SOURCES FOR THE PHASE II INVENTORY				
Study Area	**State**	**Vendor**	**State or Federal Agencies**	**Comments**
	VA		US Geological Survey; VA Department of Mines,	
			Minerals & Energy	
	KY		KY Geological Survey; KY Division of Mines & Minerals- Division of Oil & Gas	
	TN	PDS	TN Department of Environment & Conservation- Geology Division	
	NJ			No production in NJ

IHS = IHS Energy
PDS = PetroDataSource
HPDI = HPDI, LLC

A8.7 Merging of Well Data Files

For Colorado, Wyoming, Utah, Nebraska, and Alaska, a well data set with locations was available from both a state agency and the vendor IHS. For those states an initial step was added that combined the IHS Annual Production data file (includes well location and type) with the IHS Well History file location and well type. The API well number, present in both files, was the common key for this merging process.

The IHS Well History records that did not match with IHS Production records were most often dry holes, injection wells or storage wells. If these did not match well records in other state or vendor files for that state, they were discarded. To create valid field boundaries only oil and gas wells were retained, whether or not they had recorded 2001 production data, excepting in Alaska where the injection wells were retained. The spud point location data in the IHS Well History file are Tobin International, Ltd's, most accurate coordinates and were used when available. If location information was not available in the IHS Well History file, the information in the IHS Production file was used.

For the states with multiple state and/or vendor sources, the available well data sets were merged using the API number of the well (or the state permit number if the API number was not available) as the common data field. The following rules and procedures were developed and used to merge the files:

A8.7.1 Preparation of Spud Point Location Information (Well Latitude and Longitude at the Surface)

For each state with multiple well data, the wells from each source were plotted on a map using the ArcGIS software. Location quality of the data sets was checked by looking for wells located far from a field's core location, wells with locations out of state, and wells located in the wrong county. This information was used to determine which source of location coordinates was the best one to use as the primary source. If location information was not available from any source the well record was deleted from the data used for field boundary construction but was retained for merger with the Form EIA-23 database and subsequent use in the determination of production and reserve volumes.

Because more horizontal or highly deviated wells are increasingly being drilled in the U.S. onshore, it is better to use the latitude and longitude of a bottom-hole location (BHL) to locate wells rather than the surface spud-point location. Only the state of Alaska data had sufficient BHLs, so for all other states the spud point (surface) location was used.

West Virginia was one of the most problematic states for the data combination process, as EIA had four well data sources from two vendors and two state agencies. Unfortunately, the data considered most reliable (from the WV Geologic and Economic Survey) were not complete inasmuch as the Survey would only provide EIA with well data for the 20 counties where Federal Land was believed to exist. It was therefore necessary to "mosaic" a well data set using the data deemed best from all four sources.

Some states such as Virginia provided spud point locations in a projected coordinate system such as state plane. For these data the latitude and longitude values were calculated in ArcGIS because the buffer calculation program required location coordinates in that format.

A8.7.2 Field and Reservoir Name Respelling and Renaming

Variation in field and reservoir names and spellings is common among the commercial data files and state sources. Names were altered as necessary to make them as consistent as possible across sources. To achieve better field boundaries it was assumed that the buffers created for wells should be calculated on a reservoir level where possible (otherwise on a field level) and that the field boundary would then be constructed by unioning of the reservoirs in the field. Reservoir names were only consistently available for the states of WY, CO, UT, NE, AK, MS, AL and FL.

Names carried on the IHS Production file were used when available because they were most consistent with the names in the EIA Field Code Master List. Otherwise names from the state files, non-IHS vendor files, or the IHS Well History file were used.

If a well did not have a legitimate *field* name associated with it, (e.g., the associated name was 'UNDESIGNATED', 'UNKNOWN', 'WILDCAT'), an RPD-assigned name incorporating identification of the well's county location was used to replace it (e.g. a new field name like "RPD_Washington_Cnty-1" was created). When records appeared not to have a legitimate *reservoir* name, (e.g., 'UNKNOWN', 'UNKNWN', 'WILDCAT'), "UNNAMED" was used as the reservoir name.

If a reservoir name was abbreviated, the full reservoir name was assigned. If a reservoir name was augmented by a layer/zone/horizon modifier (e.g. "11250 A Washita-Freder," "11300 Washita-Freder") the modifier was removed (e.g. all were changed to "Washita-Freder"). Most records did not contain horizon information so the zone name was used instead as the best available data for reservoir naming.

Some field names were changed based on information obtained from state data sets, state websites, and conversations with state agency personnel. A few states such as CO, UT, WY and MS have developed their own spatial data files of field boundaries. These are often digitized versions of geologic outlines originally drawn by hand on paper. When these outlines were overlaid on the field boundaries created in the present study some discrepancies were noted and investigated. The comparison resulted in additional field name edits in some instances.

A8.7.3 Missing Field Names

Well files for every state had records where the field name was missing or that contained values such as 'UNKNOWN,' 'UNKNWN' or 'WILDCAT.' For all areas except the Black Warrior and Appalachian Basins the field name data field for these wells was populated manually. Wells with missing field names were plotted on a map showing the outlines of all named fields. Unnamed field wells located within or in close proximity to a named field boundary were given the name of that field. Unnamed wells judged to be too far from named field outlines to be considered part of that field were given RPD field names as described in section (b) above.

A very large number of unnamed field wells existed in the Appalachian and Black Warrior basins, so a SAS program was created to automatically assign field names to wells depending on their distance from wells located in the nearest named fields. An interwell distance of 2700 feet for oil wells and 5300 feet for gas wells was used for a first pass assignment of such field names. If a well without a field name was within these distances to a well with a field name, it was assigned that field name. Second and third passes were made at 2 and 3 times these distances to assign field names and 'grow' a field from assigned wells to unassigned wells. Wells that did not meet these proximity criteria after the third pass were assigned an RPD field name as described in section (b) above.

A special edit was made for one KY field name. The KY Division of Oil and Gas assigns the field name CATRON CREEK to all wells in unnamed fields. CATRON CREEK is defined as only being a valid field name in Harlan Co., KY. So all CATRON CREEK wells not located in Harlan County, KY had to be reassigned new/substitute names via the SAS program.

The state of Ohio presented a particularly unique challenge because the state well files do not yet include field name as an attribute. The OH Geological Survey, however, has constructed a field boundary polygon layer incorporating older development areas that lack digital well control (as described in the Limitations section, item (4) above). A Visual Basic program was written to place each well in a field boundary polygon and write the polygon field name as a well file attribute. Due to overlapping of the polygons many wells fell into two or more polygons and were assigned from 2 to 5 field names. The 2 to 5 field names were then ordered by the distance between the well and each polygon center, the first having the shortest distance, the second the next shortest, etc. Since completion formation data was available for the OH well records, a series of programs was written that used the completion formation name to pick the most probable field name out of these 2 to 5 possible fields.

A8.7.4 Identification of Well Types for Later Buffering

Deciding which wells to include in the buffering process is critically important in the construction of field boundaries. All wells where type = oil or type = gas in at least one of the source datasets were retained and classified as oil or gas. Wells which were not of type = oil or type = gas in at least one source were classified as a dry hole, a CO_2 producer, or an injection well. Some states such as CO and WY have interactive online webmapping sites. These were used extensively to arbitrate well type discrepancies between data sets. Following final assignment of the well type only the positively identified oil and gas wells were retained for input to the well buffering process, with the exception of wells located in Northern AK. Since the wells drilled there as injectors had a significant impact on the field outlines, they were retained and buffered in Northern AK.

Some of the state well files mix dry holes which never produced (usually typed as "drilled and abandoned" or "D&A") with former oil or gas producing wells that are now plugged and abandoned (typed as "P&A"). This makes the task of separating present and former producers from wells that never produced difficult and, emphasizes the importance of having good historical production data records.

A8.7.5 Merging of Non-IHS Production Data

Well-level production data from state or vendor sources other than IHS were merged to the well files by API number or by drilling permit number. Some states have incomplete production data. For example, NY only has gas production data at the individual well level; oil production data are at the lease level.

A8.8 Construction of Well Buffers

The procedure used to generate well buffers consisted of several development and application steps. Creation of oil and gas field boundaries was accomplished using ArcGIS 8.3 software and the methodologies developed by EIA for Phase I of the inventory which are documented in detail in the original Phase I report.

The basic method used to construct field boundaries was to buffer each well in a reservoir or a field with a circle. The radius of the circle was determined by analysis of the spacing pattern for the wells in each reservoir in a field if reservoir names were consistently available, or for the wells in each field if they were not. The resulting circular buffer polygons were then unioned into a single field boundary polygon set (note that if wells are far enough apart there can be more than one non-contiguous polygon per resultant single field boundary). Given the large volume of data involved this method was used because it most effectively utilizes the available information on the different reservoir spacing patterns present within a field and is relatively easy to perform on a large data set.

A8.8.1 Determination of Nominal Well Spacing and the Assignment of Buffer Radii

An analysis of the distances between wells in a reservoir or a field, calculated from their spud point locations (or their bottom-hole locations in Northern Alaska), was used to assign a standard well spacing unit to each reservoir or field. The same technique was used in Phase I of the inventory. Nearest neighbor inter-well separation distances were calculated separately for oil wells and gas wells. The upper and lower bounds of the observed spacing ranges are shown in the two left-hand columns of Table A8-5. The corresponding nominal standard well spacings (a geometric distribution) and buffer radii are shown in the two right-hand columns. The 75th percentile (P75) of the observed inter-well distance distribution was taken to be the observed inter-well distance. This statistic was selected because, as judged by the RPD project team, it yielded the best match to nominal well spacings in an extensive set of map trials done for Phase I. If the P75 distance fell within the corresponding interval shown in the two left-hand columns of the table then the corresponding nominal spacing was selected and its buffer size was initially assigned to every well in the reservoir (or field).

Table A8-5. Inter-Well Distance Ranges, Nominal Standard Well Spacings, and Buffer Radii

Inter-Well Distance		Nominal	Corresponding
Lower Bound (feet)	Upper Bound (feet)	Spacing Unit (acres)	Buffer Radius (feet)
0	277	1.3	233.0
277	392	2.5	330.0
392	555	5.0	467.0
555	785	10.0	660.0
785	1110	20.0	933.0
1110	1570	40.0	1,320.0
1570	2220	80.0	1,867.0
2220	3140	160.0	2,640.0
3140	4440	320.0	3,734.0
>4440		640.0	5,280.0

A8.8.2 Well Buffer Construction Rules

Rules for the assignment of buffers were created to handle reservoirs (or fields if no reservoir names were available) that did not, for whatever reason, readily conform to a nominal spacing. The rules are based on well types and well counts

- For oil reservoirs the maximum spacing allowed was 160 acres, i.e. a buffer radius of 2,640 feet.
- If the reservoir had between 1 and 10 oil wells or the reservoir name was 'UNNAMED' a spacing of 160 acres was assigned.
- For gas reservoirs the maximum spacing allowed was 640 acres, i.e. a buffer radius of 5,280 feet.
- If the reservoir had only 1 gas well or the reservoir was named 'UNNAMED' a spacing of 640 acres was assigned.
- If a gas reservoir located in the Black Warrior Basin or a field located in the Appalachian Basin had 3 or fewer wells a spacing of 160 acres was assigned. If it had more than 3 wells and less than 10 wells the nominal spacing unit was used per Table A8-5 up to a maximum spacing of 160 acres.
- For coalbed methane wells a maximum spacing of 160 acres was assigned, i.e. a buffer radius of 2,640 feet.
- If the oil well count divided by the sum of the oil well count and the gas well count was less than or equal to 0.05 *and* if the oil well spacing was greater than the gas well spacing, the oil well spacing was set to the gas well spacing; otherwise, the original oil well spacing was retained.
- If the ratio of gas well count to the sum of the oil well count and the gas well count was less than or equal to 0.05 the gas well spacing was set to the oil well spacing for the field or reservoir; otherwise, the original gas well spacing was retained.

A8.9 Construction of Field Boundaries

A SAS file containing the oil and gas well data with field name attribute "Field" (and reservoir name attribute "Reservoir" if that data was available) was imported into ArcGIS as a dBase (.dbf) file. The wells were then plotted using the latitude/longitude information in the file and converted to a geodatabase point feature class file. The coordinate system used was UTM NAD27 with the following UTM zones for each study area: Denver Basin–Zone 14, Wyoming Thrust Belt–Zone 12, Florida Peninsula, Black Warrior Basin, and Appalachian Basin–Zone 16, and Northern Alaska–Zone 7.

Before field boundary construction the following procedure was performed to ensure that all wells in the fields of interest lay entirely inside the study area boundaries. Two dbf files were made for each state, one of all wells inside the study area and another of all wells outside the study area. SAS queries were performed on those files to identify, for each state, all field names that had wells both inside and outside the study areas. These fields were then researched to determine if they were fields that actually extended across the study area boundaries (e.g. Colville River Field in AK NPR-A, Speaker Field in CO Denver Basin) or if they were geographically separate fields (not in reservoir communication) with the same name in the same state. The latter situation is, for example, especially common in KY and TN. In instances of the latter case, county names were appended to the field names (e.g. CACTUS_Morgan vs. CACTUS_Garfield) so that they would be put into different fields when the field boundaries were constructed.

Well files for each state were built that included only those wells located inside the study area/basin boundaries and all well records for fields that extended across the study area boundaries (e.g. Colville River Field, AK as mentioned above). These files were then used to construct the field boundary polygons.

The Visual Basic for Applications (VBA) code implemented within ArcGIS for Phase I of the inventory was used to automatically create polygonal field boundaries from the buffered wells. The principal steps performed were:

- Select the "field name" attribute and "buffer distance" attribute from the well file. Select all wells with the first "field name" encountered.
- Create a buffer around each selected well using "buffer distance" (see Figure A8-2)
- Union the buffers.
- Dissolve the barriers between overlapping buffers.
- Iteratively perform the above steps for each unique "field name".
- Output a polygon feature class with one polygon (often consisting of multiple polygon rings) for each field.
- Convert to a shapefile.

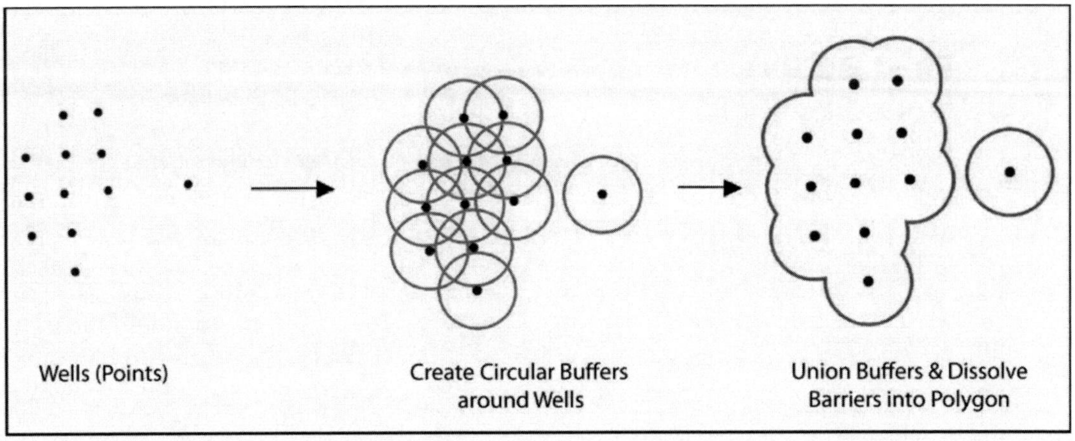

Figure A8-2. Buffering Process

Figures A8-3 and A8-4 show the buffered field boundary of a field with two reservoirs. Figure A8-3 displays buffers by reservoir: Reservoir A is composed of oil wells with 80 acre buffers while reservoir B contains oil wells with 160 acre buffers and gas wells with 640 acre buffers. The final product of the field boundary creation process with buffers for both reservoirs unioned into one polygon record is shown on Figure A8-4.

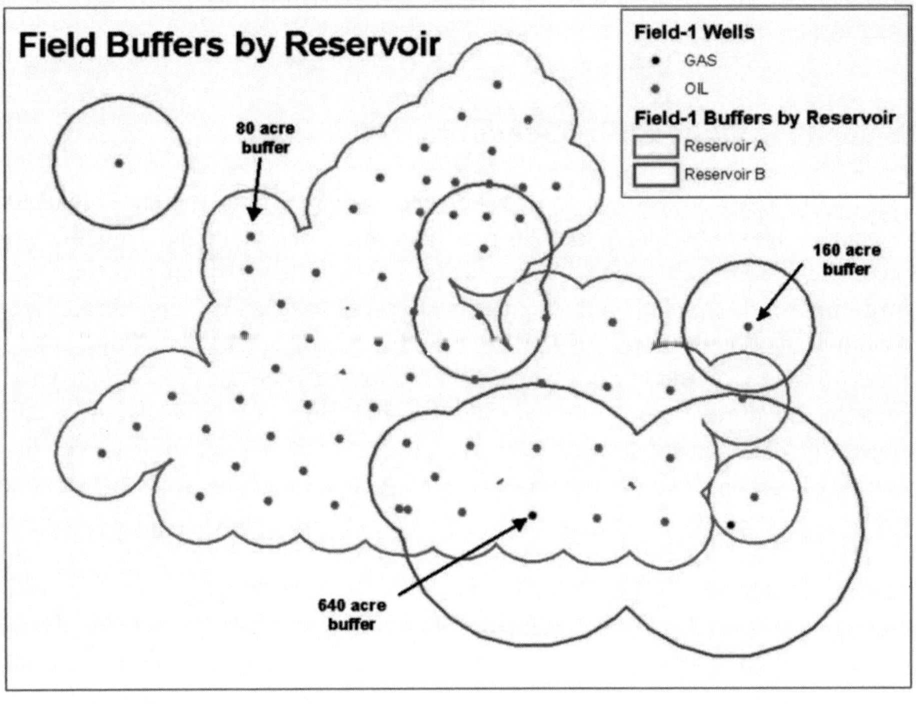

Figure A8-3. Field Buffers by Reservoir

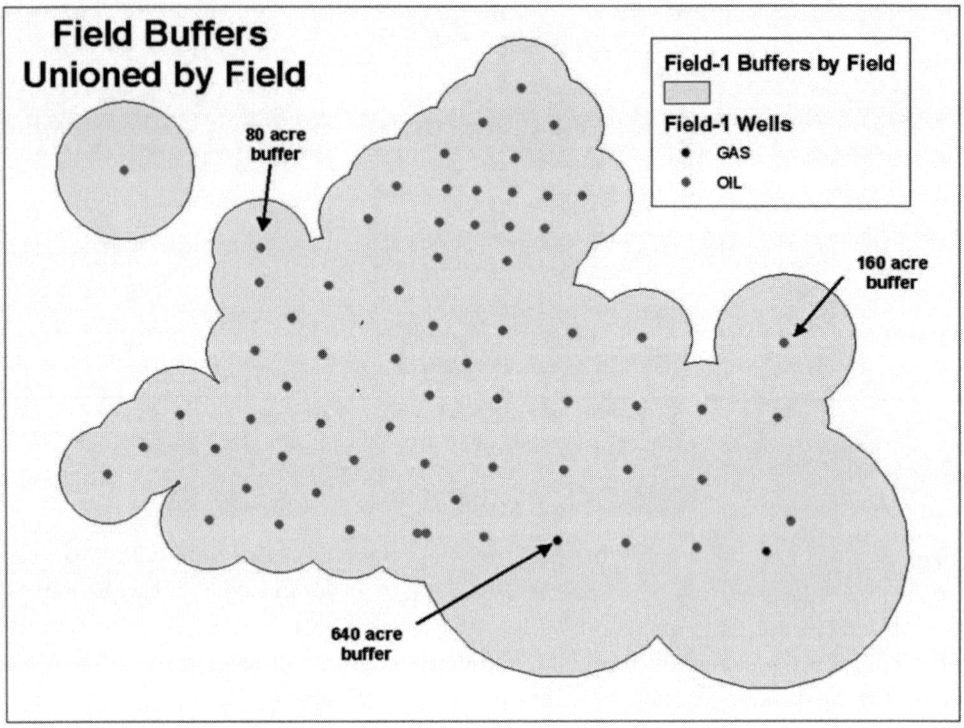

Figure A8-4. Field Buffers by Field

A8.10 Smoothing of the Field Boundaries

An artifact of the well buffer approach to field boundary construction is that multi-well field boundaries inevitably have an irregularly scalloped, botryoidal (grape cluster-like) appearance. Field boundaries tend to be much smoother than that in their natural reality. Other artificial results include small interior non-field "islands" and small separations between multiple polygon "rings" of a single field boundary (see Figure A8-5). It is probable that in most instances (1) the interior islands are legitimately part of the field area and should therefore be included in it, and (2) that the "outlier" polygons of a field should be joined with (i.e., bridged into) the main field boundary when the separation distance is sufficiently small. That is the way a geologist or petroleum engineer would subjectively draw the field boundary by hand based on only the well spud point location and well spacing information available (i.e., absent subsurface information). For Phase II the field boundary construction effort was therefore enhanced by development and inclusion of a methodological extension that both automatically and more closely approximates what a geologist or petroleum engineer would draw as the field boundary. To have a consistent set of field boundaries for all of the inventory phases this extended methodology was also applied to upgrade the Phase I study area/basin field boundaries.

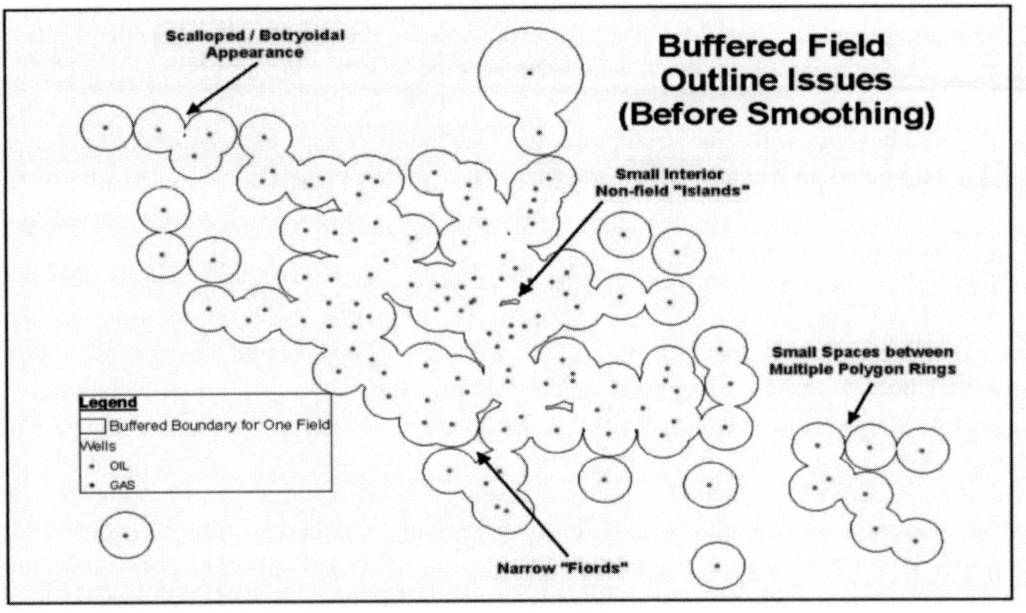

Figure A8-5. Buffered Field Outline Issues

A Visual Basic application that could be implemented within ArcGIS to smooth the irregular boundaries and fill in the smaller spaces in an automatic, quick, systematic, consistent, and repeatable manner was developed. The guiding principles adhered to in development of the smoothing application were to (1) add field area to the concave indented portions to smooth the scalloped look, (2) not add or subtract area from the convex portions in order to maintain the well buffer spacing, (3) fill in the interior non- field "islands" that are smaller than the buffer size as these are very likely part of the actual field area, (4) join separated polygon "rings" of the same field by a "bridge" if they are sufficiently close together, and (5) minimize the concomitant increase in the field's area. A number of alternative smoothing techniques were considered, tested, and rejected before the implemented technique was selected. These included:

- Raster Filters: Buffered field boundaries were converted from vector (point-line polygon) format to raster (pixel) format. A variety of neighborhood statistical operators (filters) were applied to the raster and then converted back to vector format. This approach was not satisfactory because it always added field area to the convex portions of boundaries.
- *Generalize* and *Smooth* methods: These two vector-based methods are built into the ArcGIS software. The *Generalize* method was not chosen because it consistently subtracts area from the convex portions of field boundaries. The *Smooth* method results in inconsistent addition and subtraction of field area in the convex and concave portions of a field boundary, also not acceptable.
- Maximum angle technique: This technique first filled in and merged all interior non-field islands smaller in area than the maximum field buffer size. It then stepped along each vertex in a polygon and moved the vertex out until the angle formed by that vertex and the two vertices on either side of it was less than a maximum specified

angle. Because moving one vertex out affects the angles of adjacent vertices, it required many iterations to get all angles to be less than the maximum allowed angle. Also, narrow fiord-like indentations in the field boundaries were particularly problematic with this technique and needed to be manually addressed prior to automated movement of the vertices. The increased complexity, human resource needs, longer processing time, and inconsistent handling of problems made this technique undesirable.

A technique based on tangent trapezoids was ultimately selected for field boundary smoothing because it focuses on how close wells in a field should be in order for their associated buffers to be unioned and is also simpler than the other tested techniques. It's begins by comparing the distance between each pair of wells within a field boundary to the average of the two wells' calculated buffer sizes. Three cases for the tangent trapezoid technique based on that relative distance are summarized in Figure A8-6. If the inter-well distance is less than or equal to two times the average buffer size, the buffers are either tangent (just touching) or overlapping (Figure A8-6a). When that is the case a trapezoid is constructed through both wells that extends to the full diameter of the buffers and is then unioned to the boundary polygon for that field. If the inter-well distance is between 2 to 2.5 times the average buffer size a trapezoid of one-half the buffer diameter is constructed and unioned to the boundary polygon for that field (Figure A8-6b). This thinner union of the well buffers reflects a higher uncertainty that the field is hydraulically connected in the subsurface within the space between the wells. If the inter-well distance is greater than 2.5 times the average buffer size no trapezoid is drawn and the field outline remains segmented (Figure A8-6c).

In addition to filling in the concave boundary areas, the tangent trapezoid technique aptly handles the matter of interior non-field "islands," fiord-like indentations in the field boundary, and spaces between multiple polygon "rings" belonging to the same field. Figure A8-7 shows an example of a field boundary before and after smoothing via the tangent trapezoid technique. The ratio of smoothed boundary area to unsmoothed boundary area was calculated in each instance to ensure that field area additions were sufficiently minimized. The mean increase in field area from unsmoothed to smoothed boundaries was 4.2 percent for all basins combined. Less than 1 percent of all fields exceeded an 8 percent change, and only 0.02 percent of all fields had a 10 to 14 percent change.

Field boundary polygons that crossed study area boundaries were exported as a separate file, and were then clipped to the study area boundary polygon files. For each of these fields the ratio of field area after clipping (area inside basin) to total field area (area inside + area outside basin) was calculated as the attribute INBAS_FRC (in-basin fraction). The value of this attribute is 1 for fields located entirely inside a study area/basin and ranges from greater than zero to less than 1 for those fields that cross a study area/basin boundary. It was necessary to clip these fields before calculating the Federal land fraction because the BLM-provided Federal land coverages do not always extend far enough outside the study area to permit its calculation for the entire unclipped field boundaries. The attribute INBAS_FRC is later multiplied by the field reserves to derive field reserves located inside the study area/basin boundary.

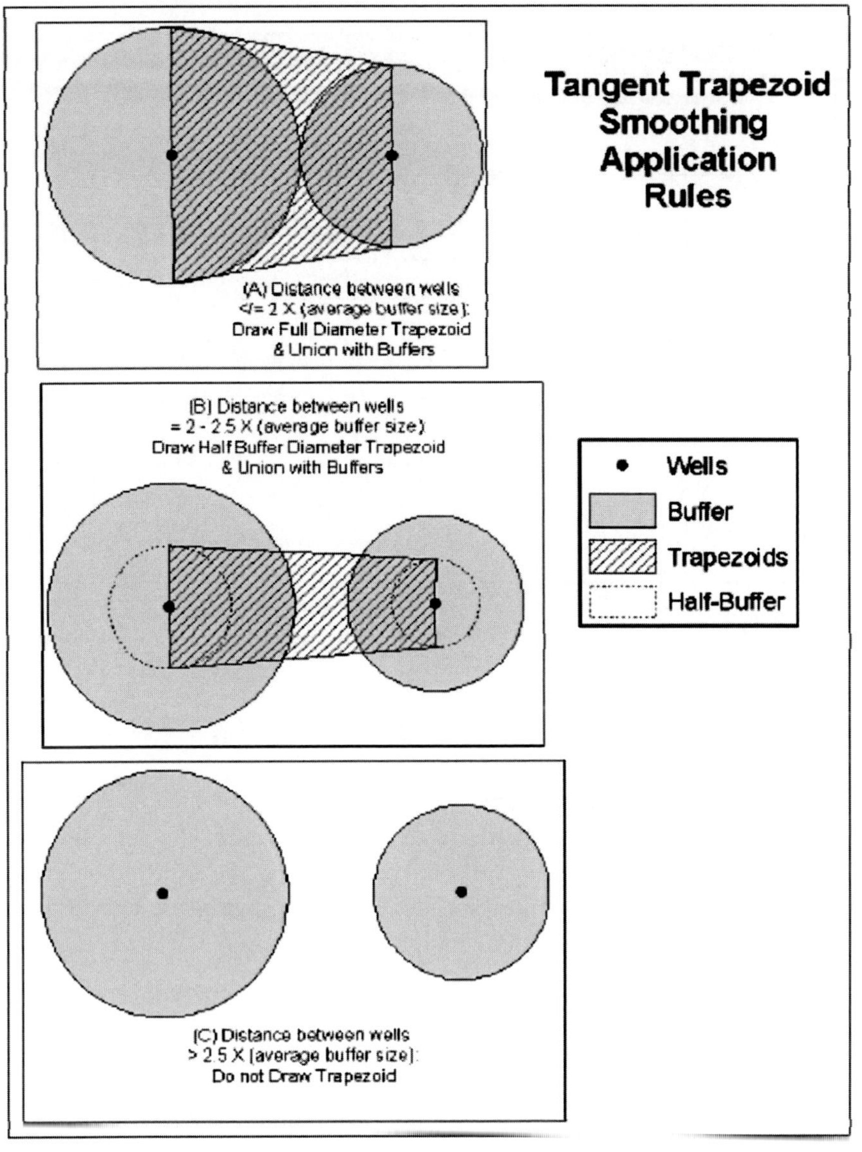

Figure A8-6. Tangent Trapezoid Smoothing Rules

Figure A8-6. Tangent Trapezoid Smoothing Rules

A8.11 Calculation of the Federal Lands Fraction within a Field's Boundary

The Federal land ownership coverages provided by the BLM, (one coverage per study area) were intersected with the field boundary outlines to ascertain the land ownership aspect of each field's area. A definition query was used to exclude land with private and state mineral ownership and then an automated procedure (developed for Phase I) was used to calculate the fraction of Federal land within each oil and gas field polygon. The procedure intersected the Federal land coverages with the field polygons and then populated a column in the field boundary polygon table "PctFedLand."

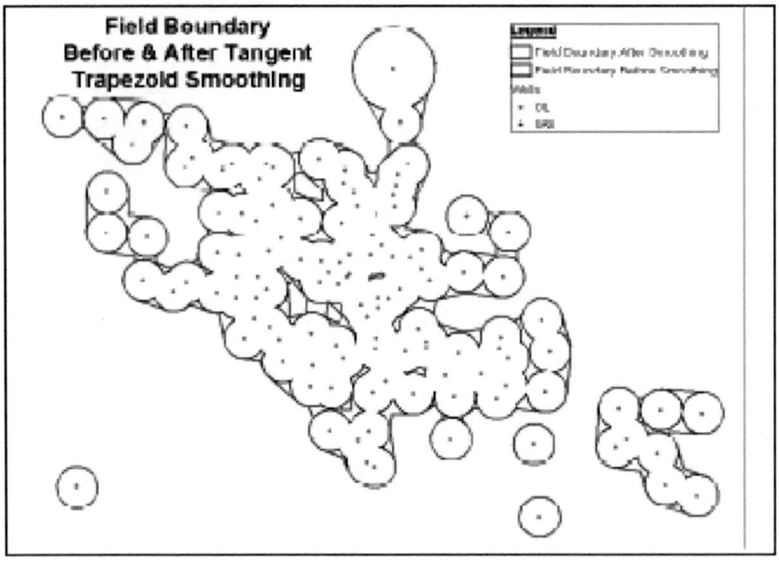

Figure A8-7. Field Boundary Before and after Smoothing with Tangent Trapezoid Technique

A8.12 Review and Quality Control of the Resulting Maps

Maps were printed at an appropriate scale for each study area to facilitate quality checking of the constructed field boundaries both before and after the smoothing algorithm was applied. These maps displayed the wells in the field and the field boundary polygons. They also showed selected field attributes such as state, county, basin, and percent Federal land. Figure A8-8 provides an example of a quality control map.

A8.13 Field-Level Proved Reserves Estimation

The conditioned state/vendor well history and production data were summed to the field/operator level and then merged with the field proved reserves estimates reported on Form EIA-23 by the largest operators. Fields were classified into four types for the purpose of reserves estimation:

- Fields with no 2001 production data or reserves estimate data
- Fields that were completely reported by both IHS and the EIA survey, with 2001 production and all operators in the fields being surveyed by EIA. The proved reserves estimates submitted by the operators for these fields were used as reported.
- Fields that were partially reported and partially imputed. These fields are represented in both the IHS and EIA survey data by 2001 production volumes, but only part of the total field reserves estimate was reported to EIA because some operators in the field were not required to report proved reserves on Form EIA-23. The remainder of the field's proved reserves were therefore imputed by RPD by assigning the weighted average reserves-to-production ratio of the reporting operators to the non-reporting

operators and multiplying it by the non-reporting operators' reported production volumes as taken from state/vendor data.

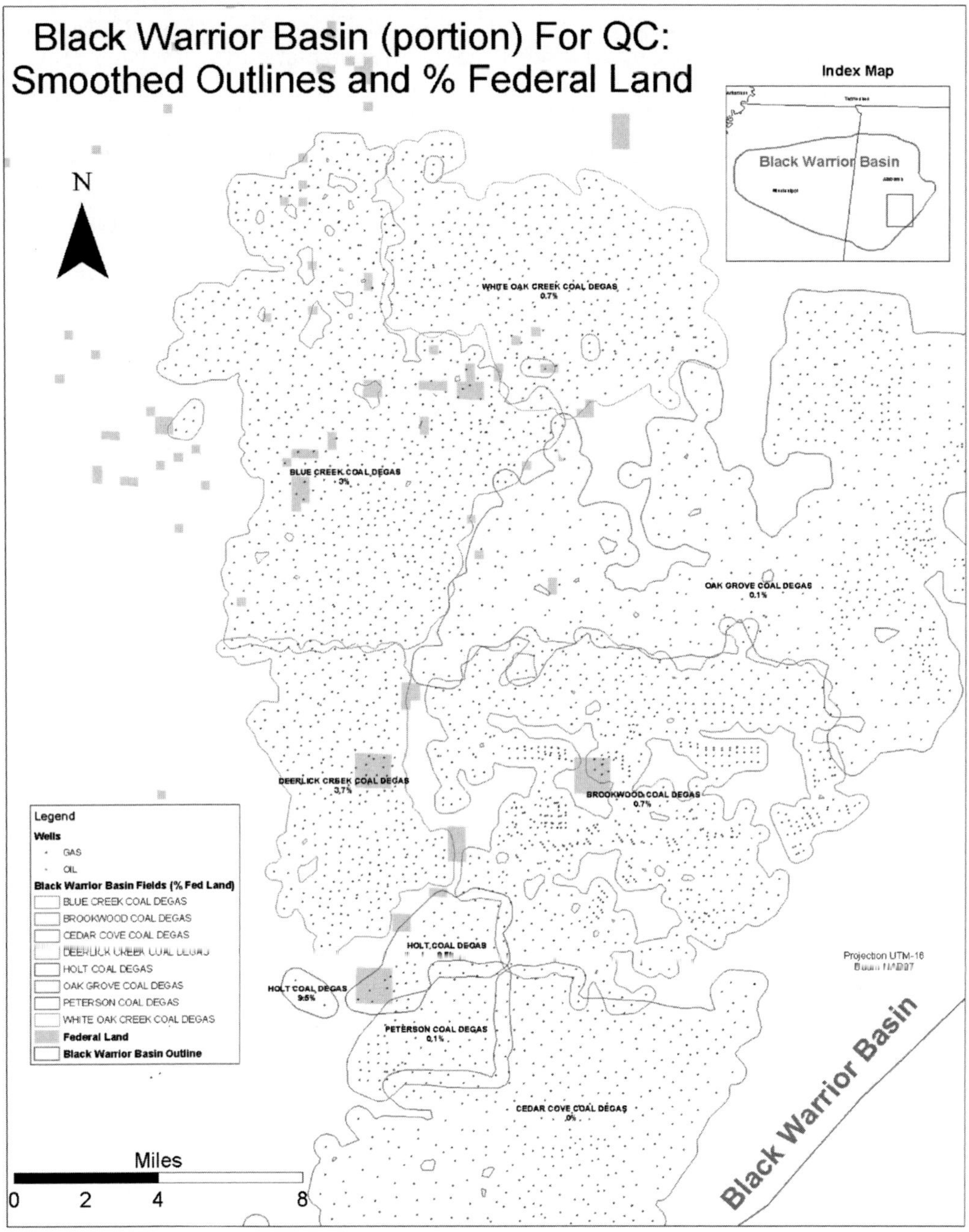

Figure A8-8. Black Warrior Basin Quality Check Map Showing Smoothed Field Outlines and Percent Federal Land

- Fields that were completely estimated based on vendor/state 2001 production data because the operators of these fields were not required to submit a Form EIA-23. Although these fields constitute a sizeable fraction of the total number of fields in the study areas, their aggregate proved reserves represent only a small portion of total proved reserves. The proved reserves and corresponding production data reported on the 2001 Form EIA-23 were used to develop predictive least squares regression equations quantitatively descriptive of their relationship. These equations were then used to estimate proved reserves for this class of fields based on the vendor/state production data available for them. The estimation equations were developed using SAS statistical software, one each for oil, associated-dissolved gas, non-associated gas, and condensate, for each basin, state (including fields both in-basin and outside-basin) and the United States as a whole. The form of the equation is:

$$\log_e(\text{Proved Reserves}) = a + b \log_e(\text{Production})$$

Table A8-6 lists the resulting regression parameters. For any field where reserves were imputed, the basin-level parameters were used if available, followed in their absence by state-level parameters if available, followed in the absence of both by US-level parameters. Where no parameter is listed in the table there was not sufficient data available for that basin or state to validly estimate the parameter.

The resultant crude oil proved reserves estimates were then summed with the proved condensate reserves estimates to yield the proved liquid reserves estimates. Similarly, the proved associated-dissolved gas reserves estimates and the proved non-associated gas reserves estimates were summed to yield the total proved gas reserves estimates. Lastly, a gas-to-oil ratio of 6000 cubic feet per barrel was used to convert the total proved gas reserves to their oil equivalent, which was then summed with the proved liquid reserves estimates to yield the proved barrel-of-oil-equivalent reserves estimates.

For each of the four reserve types Table A8-7 summarizes by study area the number of fields, the basin field count, the barrel-of-oil-equivalent production, and the barrel-of-oil-equivalent proved reserves. The percentage of each reserve type in the study area/basin is also shown.

A8.14 Calculation of Federal Reserves

The Federal reserves for each field were estimated by multiplying the fraction of Federal land for each field (derived by GIS analysis as described above) by the proved reserves estimates for each product. This procedure assumes that the distribution of proved reserves per unit area within a field boundary is uniform. While that is never precisely the case, this procedure is sufficiently precise for a regional study such as this one.

Table A8-6. Regression Equation Parameters for the Estimation of Non-Reported Reserves

		Regression Parameters							
		Crude		Assoc		Non-A		Conde	
		a	b	a	b	a	b	a	b
Study Area	NORTHERN AK (NPRA)								
Equations	WYOMING THRUST BELT					1.98	1.00		
	DENVER BASIN	1.26	1.14	1.67	1.04	1.68	1.05	1.55	1.01
	FLORIDA PENINSULA								
	BLACK WARRIOR BASIN					0.51	1.13		
	APPALACHIAN BASIN	2.04	1.00			2.26	1.05		
State	AK	2.25	0.99						
Equations	AL	0.48	1.13	1.15	0.93	0.68	1.11		
	CO	1.26	1.12	1.72	1.00	1.53	1.07	1.65	1.00
	FL	0.48	1.13	1.15	0.93	0.68	1.11		
	KY	2.02	1.01			2.24	1.05		
	MD	2.02	1.01			2.24	1.05		
	MS	1.24	1.00	1.18	0.94	0.25	1.15	1.06	1.06
	NE	1.26	1.12	1.72	1.00	1.53	1.07	1.65	1.00
	NY	2.02	1.01			2.24	1.05		
	OH	1.77	1.02			2.00	1.06		
	PA	2.02	1.01			2.24	1.05		
	TN	2.02	1.01			2.24	1.05		
	UT	1.30	1.11	1.94	0.97	1.49	1.07		
	VA	2.02	1.01			2.24	1.05		
	WV	2.02	1.01			2.24	1.05		
	WY	1.57	1.04	1.67	0.96	1.69	1.03	1.86	1.00
Country Equation	USA	1.47	1.03	1.52	0.99	1.86	0.94	1.45	0.86

Table A8-7. Field count, BOE Production & BOE Reserves for Four Reserve Types in Each Study Area

Study Area	Reserve Type	Field Count	% Basin Field Count	BOE Production	% Basin BOE Production	BOE Reserves	% Basin Boe Reserves
Northern Ak (NPRA)	Completely Reported	3.0	100.0	32,162.0	100.0	388,672	100.0
Wyoming Thrust Belt	No 2001 Production/ Reserves	12.0	42.9	-	-	-	-
Wyoming Thrust Belt	Completely Reported	16.0	57.1	32,091.0	100.0	224,850	100.0
Denver Basin	No 2001 Production/ Reserves	916.0	55.9	-	-	-	-
Denver Basin	Completely Estimated	541.0	33.0	4,693.0	10.5	27,214	4.5
Denver Basin	Completely Reported	82.0	5.0	2,376.0	5.3	21,578	3.6
Denver Basin	Partially Reported/ Imputed	99.0	6.0	37,458.0	84.2	555,719	91.9
Florida Peninsula	No 2001 Production/ Reserves	14.0	66.7	-	-	-	-
Florida Peninsula	Completely Estimated	2.0	9.5	61.0	5.2	166	0.8
Florida Peninsula	Completely Reported	5.0	23.8	1,116.0	94.8	20,282	99.2
Black Warrior Basin	No 2001 Production/ Reserves	101.0	43.0	-	-	-	-
Black Warrior Basin	Completely Estimated	61.0	26.0	677.0	3.1	2,009	1.0
Black Warrior Basin	Completely Reported	37.0	15.7	16,623.0	76.5	162,414	77.9
Black Warrior Basin	Partially Reported/ Imputed	36.0	15.3	5,117.0	23.5	46,184	22.1
Appalachian Basin	No 2001 Production/ Reserves	1,185	35.3	-	-	-	-
Appalachian Basin	Completely Estimated	1,567	46.7	22,180.0	19.7	252,747	15.1
Appalachian Basin	Completely Reported	160	4.8	6,528.0	5.8	123,111	7.4
Appalachian Basin	Partially Reported/ Imputed	442	13.2	84,128.0	74.5	1,294,977	77.5

A8.15 Reserves Classification

In order to sufficiently protect the proprietary proved reserves data submitted to EIA, each field was then assigned to a gross reserves size class and a Federal reserves size class, by product, per the following classification scheme:

Class Number Proved Liquid Reserves
0 Zero reserves (i.e., no recorded 2001 production)
1 Greater than zero but less than 10 Mbbls liquid
2 Greater than 10 but less than 100 Mbbls liquid
3 Greater than 100 but less than 1000 Mbbls liquid
4 Greater than 1000 but less than 10,000 Mbbls liquid
5 Greater than 10,000 Mbbls liquid

Class Number Proved Gas Reserves
0 Zero reserves (i.e., no recorded 2001 production)
1 Greater than zero but less than 10 MMCF gas
4 Greater than 10 but less than 100 MMCF gas
5 Greater than 100 but less than 1000 MMCF gas
4 Greater than 1000 but less than 10,000 MMCF gas
5 Greater than 10,000 but less than 100,000 MMCF gas
Greater than 100,000 MMcf gas
Class Number Proved Barrel-of-Oil Equivalent Reserves
0 Zero reserves (i.e., no recorded 2001 production)
1 Greater than zero but less than 10 MBOE
2 Greater than 10 but less than 100 MBOE
3 Greater than 100 but less than 1000 MBOE
4 Greater than 1000 but less than 10,000 MBOE
5 Greater than 10,000 but less than 10,0000 MBOE
6 Greater than 10,0000 MBOE
Note: M=1 ,000; MM=1 ,000,000; bbls=barrel; cf=cubic feet

A8.16 Merging of Proved Reserves Classes with Field Boundaries and Fraction of Federal Land

A GIS file was produced that contains the intersection of the Federal land coverages with the field boundaries. Owing to the existence of multiple federal land parcels within each field boundary, the resultant boundary polygons were then dissolved on the attribute "field" to union the data into one polygon record per field. A table with the reserves classes by field (range 0 to 6) and the field name was then joined to the shapefile associated with the field boundary shapefile. The latter was then converted to coverage format and thence to interchange file format (.e00).

For all study areas except the Appalachian Basin there was good correspondence between the production file and the map file with Federal land percentages. Owing to the poor condition of field names in the Appalachian Basin there was less correspondence between these files; there were approximately 1200 Appalachian Basin fields that had map locations but no 2001 production data. All of these fields were assigned to reserve class zero although because of faulty or incomplete field names some of them might properly belong to other fields for which there were 2001 production data. Approximately 130 fields appeared to have 2001 production but there were no available location data. These fields, which together accounted for less than 1 percent of the liquids production and approximately 1.5 percent of the gas production in the Appalachian Basin, were assumed not to be on Federal land because that was more likely to be the case in this basin.

A8.17 Summary of Results

GIS is clearly the information conveyance method of choice where both analysis of Federal lands policy and regulations and their application are concerned. The primary proved reserves result is therefore a GIS layer containing field boundary polygons attributed with field name and a proved reserves size class for each field product. Unfortunately, none of this very detailed information can be usefully conveyed on a piece of paper this size. You have to use a GIS workstation to view it and a wide-format printer to print it at a size where the detail can be distinguished. Therefore, in lieu of a close look at the reserves results, summary statistics are provided by study area in Table A8-8.

Table A8-8. Summary of 2001 Federal Lands Proved Reserves by Study Area

Study Area	Number of Fields	Total Liquid Reserves (Mbbls)	Federal Land Liquid Reserves (Mbbls)	Federal	Total Gas Reserves (MMcf)	Federal Land Gas Reserves (MMcf)	Federal
Northern Alaska NPRA	3	349,563	-	0.0%	234,654	618	0.3%
Uinta/ Piceance Basin	180	254,329	142,921	56.2%	7,181,669	3,794,133	52.8%
Paradox/ San Juan Basins	250	174,193	53,024	30.4%	20,653,622	10,938,741	53.0%
Montana Thrust Belt	1	1	-	-	-	-	-
Powder River Basin	543	193,456	108,971	56.3%	2,398,604	935,773	39.0%
Wyoming Thrust Belt	28	34,634	13,791	39.8%	1,141,293	474,545	41.6%

Table A8-8. (Continued)

Study Area	Number of Fields	Total Liquid Reserves (Mbbls)	Federal Land Liquid Reserves (Mbbls)	Federal	Total Gas Reserves (MMcf)	Federal Land Gas Reserves (MMcf)	Federal
Greater Green River Basin	281	177,362	122,433	69.0%	12,703,038	10,063,526	79.2%
Denver Basin	1,638	148,342	2,537	1.7 %	2,736,689	30,373	1.1%
Florida Peninsula	21	20,446	-	-	14	-	-
Black Warrior Basin	235	552	2	0.4 %	1,248,250	17,693	1.4%
Appalachian Basin	3,354	79,141	159	0.2 %	9,550,156	27,961	0.3%
Total	6,534	1,432,019	443,838	31.0%	57,847,989	26,283,363	45.4%

A8.18 Summary of Updated Phase 1 Results

The land status files provided by the Department of the Interior for the Phase I study areas have been updated since the original work was done in 2002 and EIA has incrementally improved its field boundary construction process. For the purpose of maintaining a consistent set of estimates, the Phase I study areas were reprocessed to reflect these changes. Specifically:

The field outlines were smoothed using the algorithm described in the appendix documentation for Phase II.

Portions of field outlines that extended outside of the defined basin boundary were clipped to the basin boundary.

The projection for the GIS files of all basins except the Montana Thrust Belt were changed from UTM-12/NAD27 to UTM-13/NAD27.

Taken together these changes only very slightly impacted the Federal reserves totals and percentages, the updated version of which is shown in Table A8-9.

Table A8-9. Summary of Updated 2001 Federal Lands Proved Reserves by Phase I Study Area

Study Area	Number of Fields	Total Liquid Reserves (Mbbl)	Federal Land Liquid Reserves (Mbbl)	%	Total Gas Reserves (MMcf)	Federal Land Gas Reserves (MMcf)	%	Total BOE Reserves (Mbbl)	Federal Land BOE Reserves (Mbbl)	%
Greater	281	177,362	122,433	69	12,703,038	10,063,526	79.2	2,294,535	1,799,688	78.4
Green										
River										
Montana	1		0					1	0	
Thrust										
Belt										
Paradox-	250	174,193	53,024	30.4	20,653,622	10,938,741	53	3,616,464	1,876,147	51.9
San Juan										
Powder	543	193,456	108,971	56.3	2,398,604	935,773	39	593,223	264,933	44.7
River										
Uinta-	180	254,329	142,921	56.2	7,181,669	3,794,133	52.8	1,451,274	775,276	53.4
Piceance										
Total	1,255	799,341	427,349	53.5	42,936,933	25,732,174	59.9	7,955,497	4,716,044	59.3

Appendix 9: GIS Methodology

Following are further descriptions of how Federal lands were placed into the nine categories referred to in Table 2-8 and a detailed description of the GIS methodology used.

Based upon guidance from BLM and USDA-FS offices, Table A9-1 shows the NLA/LUP jurisdictions within the inventory area.

Table A9-1. Jurisdictions Classified as NLA/LUP

Jurisdiction	Comments
Arapaho-Roosevelt NF	Select areas
Ashley NF	Northern unit only
Big Cypress NPS	Select areas
Big Horn NF	
Bitterroot NF	
Bridger-Teton NF	Areas east of of Highway 189
Caribou-Targhee NF	Caribou NF
Corps of Engineers	Black Warrior Basin
Custer NF	
Department of Defense	Selected areas in the Denver Basin
Dillon, MT, BLM Field Office	
Dixie NF	
Fairbanks BLM Field Office	Southern NPRA only
Fish Lake NF	
Flathead NF	
Florida Panther FWS	
Gallatin NF	
Gunnison, CO, BLM Field Office	
Kootenai NF	
Lewis and Clark NF	Western portion only
Lolo NF	
Milwaukee BLM Field Office	All Federal subsurface interests
Nebraska NF	Pine Ridge Ranger District
Routt-Medicine Bow NF	Medicine Bow portion only
Ten Thousand Islands FWS	
Uinta NF	Unmapped western portions only
Wasatch-Cache NF	Western portion only

Table A9-2 shows how agency jurisdictions were used to categorize lands for this inventory.

GIS files were available to define most of the access categories; however, for the NLA/LUP category, they had to be created. In these situations, the administrative boundary (such as a National Forest) was extracted from the surface ownership data and the resultant polygon was then attributed as NLA/LUP. For example in Figure A9-1, the Wasatch-Cache National Forest boundary in the Wyoming Thrust Belt is shown in green. The grey represents the area within the forest that is undergoing land use planning, which is categorized as NLA/LUP.

Table A9-2. Federal Land Categorization

Federal Land Management		Categorization	Level
Bureau of Land Management	BLM	Subject to stipulations	
Bureau of Reclamation	BOR	Subject to stipulations	
Department of Agriculture*	USDA	No Leasing (Administrative), general category (NLA)*	2
Department of Defense**	DOD	No Leasing (Administrative), general category (NLA)**	2
Federal Split Estate	SPLIT	Subject to stipulations	
Fish and Wildlife Service	FWS	No Leasing (Administrative), general category (NLA)	2
United States Forest Service	UFS	Subject to stipulations	
Miscellaneous Federal Land Managers (DOE, DOJ, DHS, etc.)		On Advisement from Office	
National Park Service	NPS	No Leasing (Statutory/Executive Order), (NLS)	1
Federal Land Use Designations			
Inventoried Roadless Areas	IRA	Subject to stipulations	
National Conservation Areas	NCA	No Leasing (Statutory/Executive Order), (NLS)	1
National Monuments	NM	No Leasing (Statutory/Executive Order), (NLS)	1
National Recreation Areas	NRA	No Leasing (Statutory/Executive Order), (NLS)	1
National Wildlife Refuges	NWR	No Leasing (Statutory/Executive Order), (NLS)	1
Special Designated Areas	SDA	No Leasing (Statutory/Executive Order), (NLS)	1
Wilderness Areas	WILD	No Leasing (Statutory/Executive Order), (NLS)	1
Wilderness Reinventory Areas	WRA	Subject to stipulations	
Incorporated Towns and Cities	ITC	No Leasing (Statutory/Executive Order), (NLS)	1
Wilderness Study Areas	WSA	No Leasing (Statutory/Executive Order), (NLS)	1

* Ft. Keo Agricultural Experimental Station, MT, only

** Except for the Naval Petroleum Reserve, Casper Field Office, which is subject to stipulations

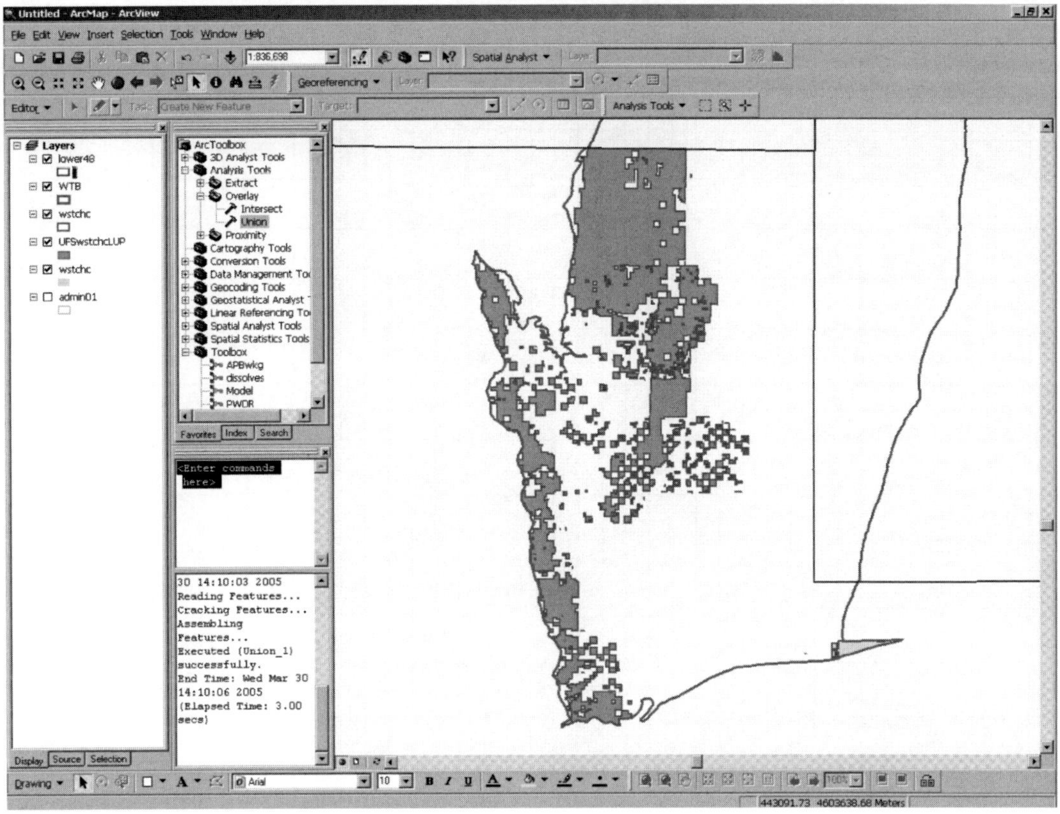

Figure A9-1. Creation of NLA/LUP Polygons

A9.1 Stipulation Exceptions

Exceptions to stipulations are sometimes granted. For example, a crucial elk winter range timing limitation exception may be granted if seasonal conditions (e.g., an early spring and snowmelt) are such that the elk have moved out of and are not using the general areas during a particular year. Because records of exceptions to lease stipulations were not available, BLM and USDA-FS field personnel were asked to determine, based on their experience, which lease stipulations were granted exceptions for drilling and how often. The exception factors thus determined are shown by jurisdiction in Table A9-3.

Lease stipulations, particularly timing limitations, can overlap. Where exception factors overlap, the cumulative effect is calculated by multiplying the overlapping factors (from Table A9-3). This calculation implicitly assumes that exceptions for multiple stipulations would likely not be obtained for a given area. For example, cumulative effects of excepted stipulations for the Wyoming Thrust Belt study area are determined as shown in Table A9-4. The application of these exception factors is described below in Section A9.3.

Table A9-3. Stipulation Exception Factors by USDA-FS and BLM Office

Jurisdiction	Study Area	Exception Factors										Exception Factors												
		Big Game Winter Range	Indiana Bat	Steep slopes	Raptors	Scenic Landscapes	Designated Non-motor Sites	Calving and Fawning	Visual Resources Management	Designated Historic Sites	Spotted owl, Lynx (T&E)	Sharp-tailed Grouse and Sage Grouse Display Grounds	Sage Grouse	Birds	Recreation Sites	Riparian/flood Areas	Sedimentation (roads)	Bald Eagle Winter Roost	City of Rifle Watershed	Sensitive Resources	Antelope Fawning	Soils, Watershed	Marshes	Mangrove Forests
Allegheny NF	APB		10%																					
Arapaho Roosevelt NF	DEN				10%									10%										
Big Cypress NP	FLP																						5%	5%
Black Hills NF	DEN					60%	40%			25%														
Bridger-Teton NF	WTB	10%		10%				10%																
Buffalo, WY, BLM Field Office	PRB				25%								25%											
Caribou-Targhee NF	WTB	10%																						
Carson NF	PDX/SJ	10%															10%							
Casper, WY, BLM Field Office	PRB	25%			25%																			
Glenwood Springs, CO, BLM Field Office	UP																		100%					
Glenwood Springs, CO, BLM Field Office	GGRB	20%			30%								20%											
Grand Junction, CO, BLM Field Office	UP, PDX/SJ	70%		15%																30%				
Idaho Falls, ID, BLM Field Office	WTB	10%																						
Kemmerer, WY, BLM Field Office	WTB	10%			10%								10%											
Kemmerer, WY, BLM Field Office	GGRB	20%			30%								20%											
Lander, WY, BLM Field Office	GGRB	20%			30%								20%											
Little Snake, CO, BLM Field Office	GGRB	20%			30%								20%											
Manti La Sal NF	UP, PDX/SJ			50%				80%																
Medicine Bow-Routt NF Thunder Basin NG	GGRB	20%			30%								20%											
Miles City, MT, BLM Field Office	PRB	50%			50%								10%											
Milwaukee, WI, BLM Field Office	APB		10%																					
Missoula, MT, BLM Field Office	MTB	20%		15%	20%																			
Moab, UT, BLM Field Office	UP, PDX/SJ	70%																			70%	70%		
Monongahela NF	APB		10%																					
Nebraska NF	DEN											15%			5%	5%								
Pinedale, WY, BLM Field Office	GGRB	20%			30%								20%											
Pocatello, ID, BLM Field Office	WTB	20%																						
Rawlins, WY, BLM Field Office	GGRB	20%			30%								20%											
Rock Springs, WY, BLM Field Office	GGRB	20%			30%								20%											
Royal Gorge, CO, BLM Field Office	DEN			15%					20%		20%													
San Juan, CO, BLM Field Office	PDX/SJ	50%			50%													50%						
Uncompahgre, CO, BLM Field Office	UP	10%			10%																			
Uncompahgre, CO, BLM Field Office	PDX/SJ	50%			50%													50%						
White River, CO, BLM Field Office	UP	80%			25%																			
White River NF	UP, GGRB							50%																

Table A9-4. Exception Factors Example for Overlapping Stipulations (WTB Study Area)

Stipulation	Exception Factor (EF)
Big Game	10%
Sage Grouse	10%
Raptors	10%
Big Game and Sage Grouse	1%
Big Game/Raptors	1%
Sage Grouse/Raptors	1%
Big Game, Sage Grouse and Raptors	0.10%

A9.2 Treatment of NSO Areas

Directional drilling (or "extended reach drilling") is technology that can be employed to reach subsurface targets not located directly underneath the drilling rig. In this inventory resources beyond a certain EDZ are assumed to not be technically recoverable (Figure A9-2). While it is true that directional drilling horizontally out to distances of 5 or 6 miles is possible in production settings such as Alaska, this type of drilling is not the general case in the lower 48 and is impracticable for exploration.

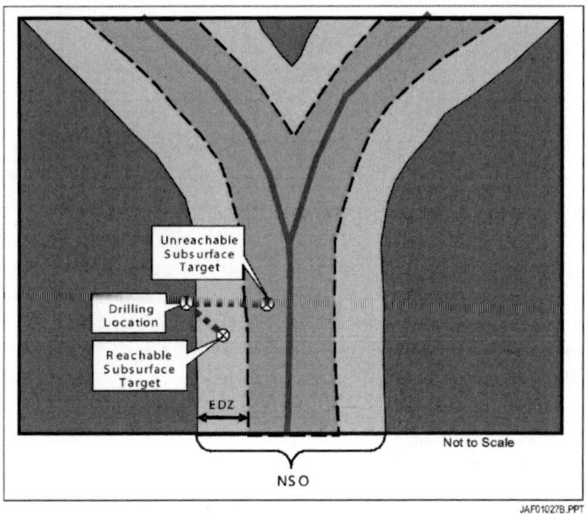

Figure A9-2. Extended Drilling Zone Conceptual Diagram

Directional drilling for exploratory purposes occurs in some areas but is much more limited in scope. As in the case of stipulation exceptions, BLM and USDA-FS field personnel were interviewed to determine the practicable width of the EDZ. The width of the EDZ is partially a function of the depth to the drilling objective—generally the deeper the objective, the larger the EDZ. The EDZ distances supplied by the offices and used in this inventory are shown in Table A9-5.

Table A9-5. Extended Drilling Zones by Jurisdiction

Jurisdiction	Study Area	EDZ (miles)
Alabama NF	BWB	0.25
Albuquerque, NM, BLM Field Office	PDX/SJ	0.25
Allegheny NF	APB	0.13
Arapaho Roosevelt NF	DEN	0.25
Ashley NF	UP, GGRB	0.25
Beaverhead-Deerlodge NF	MTB	0.50
Big Cypress NP	FLP	0.25
Black Hills NF	PRB, DEN	0.25
Bridger-Teton NF	WTB, GGRB	0.50
Buffalo, WY, BLM Field Office	PRB	0.25
Butte, MT, BLM Field Office	MTB	0.25
Caribou-Targhee NF	WTB	0.50
Carson NF	PDX/SJ	0.25
Casper, WY, BLM Field Office	PRB, DEN	0.25
Cedar City, UT, BLM Field Office	PDX/SJ	0.00
Cibola NF	PDX/SJ	0.25
Daniel Boone NF	APB	0.00
Fairbanks, AK, BLM Field Office–AK NPR-A NE	NA	3.00
Fairbanks, AK, BLM Field Office–AK NPR-A NW	NA	1.00
Fairbanks, AK, BLM Field Office–AK NPR-A S	NA	N/A (NLA/ LUP)
Fairbanks, AK, BLM Field Office–ANWR	NA	N/A (NLS)
Farmington, NM, BLM Field Office	PDX/SJ	0.25
Finger Lakes NF	APB	0.25
George Washinton NF	APB	0.25
Glenwood Springs, CO, BLM Field Office	UP, GGRB	0.25
Grand Junction, CO, BLM Field Office	UP, PDX/SJ	0.25
Grand Mesa Uncompahgre/ Gunnison NF	UP	0.25
Grand Mesa Uncompahgre/ Gunnison NF	PDX/SJ	0.00
Gunnison, CO, BLM Field Office	UP	0.25
Helena NF	MTB	0.25
Idaho Falls, ID, BLM Field Office	WTB	0.50
Jackson, MS, BLM Field Office	FLP, BWB	0.50
Jackson, MS, BLM Field Office	APB	0.00
Jefferson NF	APB	0.25
Kanab, UT, BLM Field Office	PDX/SJ	0.00
Kemmerer, WY, BLM Field Office	WTB	0.50
Kemmerer, WY, BLM Field Office	GGRB	0.25

Table A9-5. (Continued)

Jurisdiction	Study Area	EDZ (miles)
Lander, WY, BLM Field Office	GGRB	0.25
Lewis and Clark NF	MTB, eastern portions	0.25
Lewistown, MT, BLM Field Office	MTB	0.25
Little Snake, CO, BLM Field Office	UP, GGRB	0.25
Manti La Sal NF	UP	0.50
Manti La Sal NF	PDX/SJ	0.25
Medicine Bow-Routt NF	UP, PRB,	0.25
Thunder Basin NG	GGRB	
Miles City, MT, BLM Field Office	PRB	0.25
Milwaukee, WI, BLM Field Office	APB	N/A (NLA/ LUP)
Mississippi NF	BWB	0.13
Missoula, MT, BLM Field Office	MTB	0.50
Moab, UT, BLM Field Office	UP, PDX/SJ	0.25
Monongahela NF	APB	0.25
Monticello, UT, BLM Field Office	PDX/SJ	0.25
Nebraska, Oglala, Buffalo Gap NF	PRB	0.13
Nebraska, Oglala, Buffalo Gap NF	DEN	0.00
Newcastle, WY, BLM Field Office	PRB	0.00
Newcastle, WY, BLM Field Office	DEN	0.25
Pike-San Isabel NF	DEN	0.25
Pinedale, WY, BLM Field Office	GGRB	0.25
Pinedale, WY, BLM Field Office	WTB	N/A (NLA/ LUP)
Pocatello, ID, BLM Field Office	WTB	0.50
Price, UT, BLM Field Office	UP	0.25
Price, UT, BLM Field Office	PDX/SJ	0.00
Rawlins, WY, BLM Field Office	GGRB, DEN	0.25
Richfield, UT, BLM Field Office	UP	0.25
Richfield, UT, BLM Field Office	PDX/SJ	0.00
Rock Springs, WY, BLM Field Office	GGRB	0.25
Royal Gorge, CO, BLM Field Office	DEN	0.25
Salt Lake, UT, BLM Field Office	UP	0.25
Salt Lake, UT, BLM Field Office	WTB	0.50
San Juan, CO, BLM Field Office	SJ portion	0.00
San Juan, CO, BLM Field Office	PDX portion	0.50
Santa Fe NF	PDX/SJ	0.25

Table A9-5. (Continued)

Jurisdiction	Study Area	EDZ (miles)
South Dakota BLM Field Office	PRB, DEN	0.25
St. George, UT, BLM Field Office	PDX/SJ	0.00
Tennessee Valley Authority	BWB	0.50
Tennessee Valley Authority	APB	0.00
Uinta NF	UP	0.25
Uncompahgre, CO, BLM Field Office	UP	0.25
Uncompahgre, CO, BLM Field Office	PDX/SJ	0.50
Vernal, UT, BLM Field Office	UP	0.00
Wasatch-Cache NF	WTB	0.50
Wayne NF	APB	0.13
White River, CO, BLM Field Office	UP	0.25
White River NF	UP, GGRB	0.25

The effect of the inclusion of the EDZs in the analysis is to remove an area of land from the perimeters of NSO polygons. The width of this area removed via GIS processing is determined by Federal jurisdiction (Table A9-5) as determined by each field office. The area removed then defaults to the resource access category that would otherwise apply in the absence of the NSO stipulation. The net effect is that the underlying resource is no longer considered inaccessible even though the surface above it cannot be occupied by drilling equipment.

Figure A9-3 shows an actual example from the Wyoming Thrust Belt. Areas shown in light blue represent a 1/2-mile extended drilling zone removed from the NSO areas for the resource categorization. Areas shown in blue represent the resource Net NSO. The black area depicts an area of no leasing; as such the EDZ was not applied to these lands as a rig cannot be sited in no lease areas.

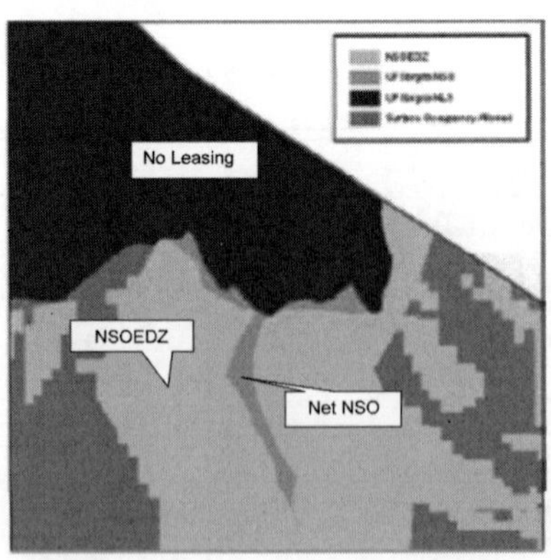

Figure A9-3. Removal of the Extended Drilling Zone from NSO Areas

A9.3 Analytical Modeling of Federal Lands and Resources

The analytical goal of the inventory is to calculate the area of Federal lands (including non-Federal lands overlying federally owned oil and gas estate [split estate]) in each access category in the hierarchy and the volume of oil and gas resources underlying the Federal lands in each access category, while at the same time accounting for stipulation exceptions and the accessibility of the EDZ.

One of the primary objectives for the development of the categorization is to achieve geographic independence for a given parcel of land subject to overlapping stipulations (hence, the use of the categorization hierarchy where that parcel of land would be subject to only one category). The following discussion illustrates the application of the land access categorization for an area of multiple stipulations from the Kemmerer, WY, BLM FO in the Wyoming Thrust Belt, where sage grouse leks and nesting habitat and big game winter range define an access category. These types of stipulations are among the most common found in the study areas.

Figure A9-4 shows a selected point where the stipulations overlap and the resultant categorization is "Timing Limitation Stipulations >6 to <9". A query at that point brings up a dialog box which lists the stipulations in effect. Table A9-6 contains the corresponding stipulation data extracted from a corresponding master stipulations list.

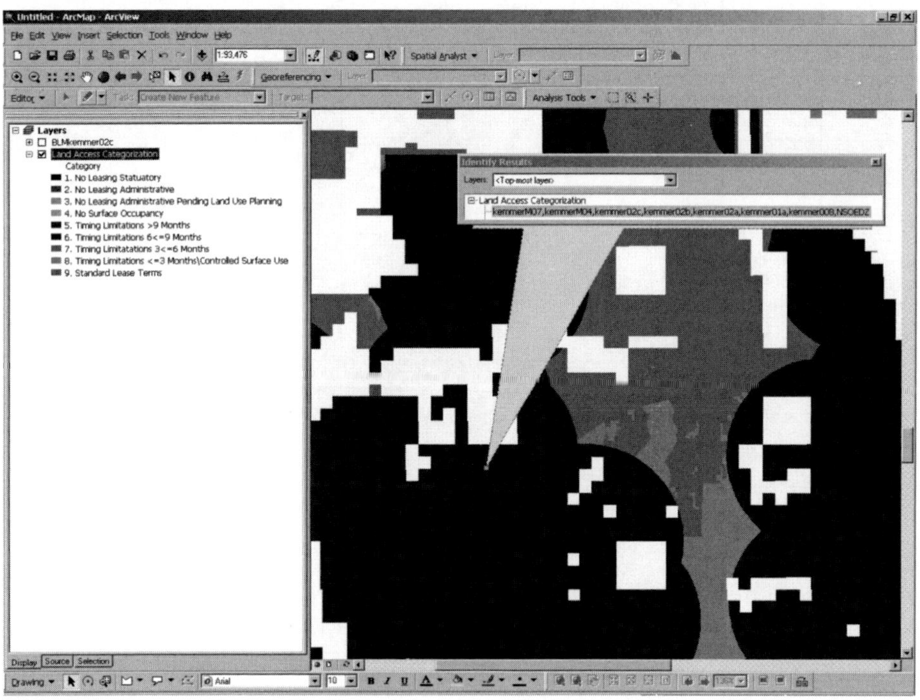

Figure A9-4. Display of Overlapping Timing Limitations (WTB Study Area)

Table A9-6. Sample Master Stipulations List for a Selected Area

Agency	STIPID	Description	LUP Source	Category	TLS months	Exception Factor	EDZ (mi)	Study Area	
								WTB	GGRB
BLM	kemmer 008	Green River formation paleontologic survey	p. 11	CSU				X	X
BLM	kemmer 01a	Slopes >25%	p. 55	CSU				X	X
BLM	kemmer M04	Sage and sharp-tailed grouse strutting grounds	WY SO	CSU				X	X
BLM	kemmer M07	Big game winter range	WY SO	CSU				X	X
BLM	kemmer 02c	Wildlife habit protection — grouse leks and other important habitat	p. 55	NSO			WTB - 0.5, GGRB- 0.25	X	X
BLM	kemmer 02a	Big game winter range	p. 55	TLS	_AB0123	10 %		X	X
BLM	kemmer 02b	Sage and sharp-tailed grouse nesting habitat	p. 55	TLS	123456	10 %		X	X

Figure A9-5 shows the land categorization as determined by the stipulations listed in the relevant land use plan. Note that the core nesting habitat of the sage grouse (shown in blue), is designated a "no surface occupancy" area. The remaining area is under various timing limitations (colored in shades of red), controlled surface use (gold) or standard lease terms (green).

Note that in the inventory, with regard to NSO areas, lands and resources are treated differently due to the application of EDZs. Figure A9-6 shows the effect where the EDZ is applied to NSO areas to determine the resource categorization. Note that the application of the EDZ in this example renders the resources under the sage grouse nest area accessible. While the acreage figures for each access category faithfully reflect the management prescriptions contained in the land use plans, the oil and gas volumes are calculated using this adjustment. The net result is that more oil and gas resources are accessible than would be assumed if NSO stipulations were taken at face value.

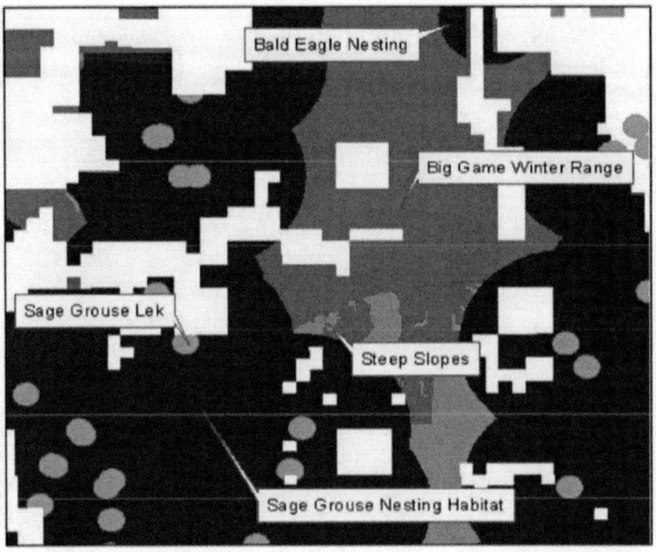

Figure A9-5. Display of Federal Land Access Categorization (WTB Study Area)

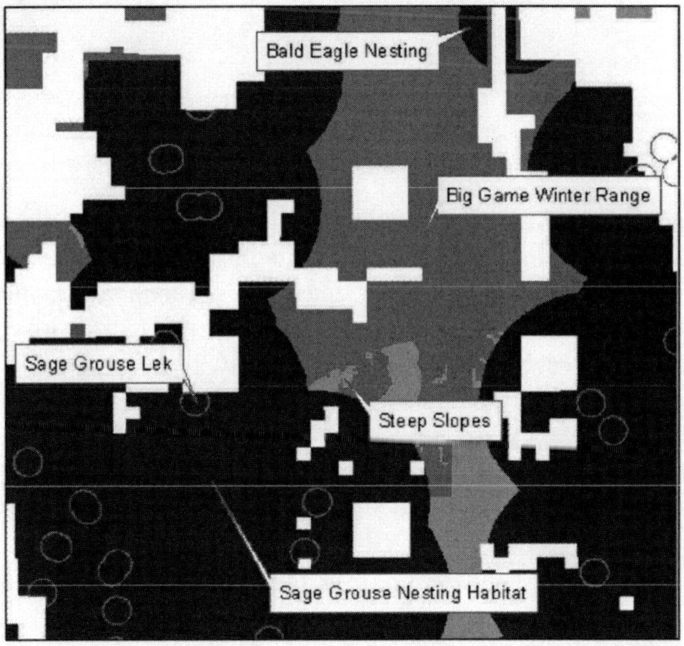

Figure A9-6. Display of Resource Access Categorization with Extended Drilling Zone Applied (WTB Study Area)

In addition, to account for stipulation exceptions, the GIS model determined the effects due to the presence or absence of the stipulations by selectively removing excepted stipulations in the computer. This is illustrated by Figure A9-7, which shows an example for the Wyoming Thrust Belt where the sage grouse nesting habitat stipulation has been removed.

Note that in the case of an excepted stipulation, the analysis defaults to the underlying stipulation or standard lease terms, as appropriate.

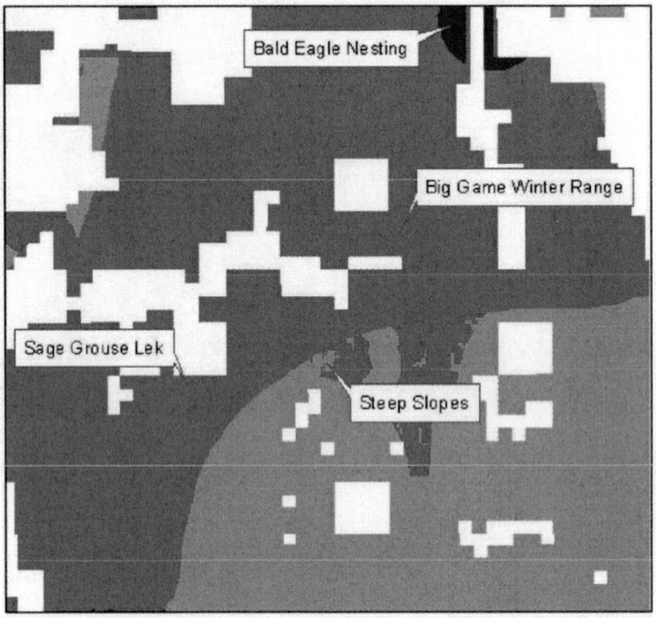

Figure A9-7. Display of Federal Land Access Categorization with Extended Drilling Zone Removed and with Sage Grouse Nesting Habitat Stipulation Excepted (WTB Study Area)

For example, if sage grouse nesting stipulations are excepted 10 percent of the time (as shown on Table A9-6), then, for an area represented by the sage grouse polygon (where sage grouse stipulations do not overlap other excepted stipulations), 90 percent of the resources is categorized according to the stipulation and 10 percent is categorized according to the underlying stipulation category next in the hierarchy. This calculation is performed accordingly for all of the exception factors within a given office jurisdiction (see Table A9-3) or where combinations of these exceptions exist (see Table A9-4).

Access categorization of the Federal lands and resources was determined in aggregate based upon discrete examination of individual GIS polygons using the following equation:

$$FLorRs = \sum((1\text{-}EF) * FLorRs_{(EDZ)} + (EF * FLorRs_{(EDZ\ w/\ Excepted)}))$$

Where FlorRs = Federal Lands or Resources

EF = Exception Factor (e.g., see Table A9-4)

$FLorRs_{(EDZ)}$ = FLorRs determined using the Extended Drilling Zone

$FLorRs_{(EDZ\ w/\ Excepted)}$ = FLorRs determined using the EDZ plus removal of stipulations for which exceptions are granted

This equation accounts for the occurrence of the extended drilling zone and stipulation exceptions. For excepted stipulations the model defaults to the underlying stipulation category in the hierarchy.

This process results in the generation of numerous individual GIS polygons for each study area. These data are then summed and reported by access category and Federal management agency. For oil and gas resources, categorization is provided by specific resource type (see folder "Detailed Spreadsheets" on accompanying DVD).

A9.4 Quality Control of Modeling Results

A rigorous quality control (QC) check was instituted for the Phase II model. During processing a typical study area will generate more than one million discrete GIS polygons, each with unique characteristics in terms of land status, oil and gas resources, stipulations and exception factors. Complex study areas generate two to three million polygons each. As such, imprecision in GIS mapping data that are insignificant for individual polygons can be amplified in the aggregate. Such imprecision is a direct function of the quality of the data received from the various sources contributing to the inventory.

For all study areas, the quality of the model output is high. For QC purposes, input oil and gas resource volumes and land areas were compared to outputs. A comparison of the study areas revealed percentage differences ranging from zero to 1.32 percent, with most well below 0.5 percent. For a limited number of offices (e.g., Monongahela NF, Vernal, UT, BLM FO, and Allegheny NF) corrections were made to bring errors down to within two percent of input values. Corrections entailed removal of topological errors occurring in the GIS source data.

The model's land output data differs by 0.26 percent from the input data on an aggregate basis. For oil and gas resources, model output data differs by 0.34 percent from the input data on an aggregate basis.

The QC logs for the study area lands areas and resources are presented on spreadsheets on the accompanying DVD.

Appendix 10 : Federal Land Use Planning Documents Used for the Phase II Inventory

Alabama NFs Revised Land and RMP, 2004
Allegheny NF Land and RMP, 1986
Arapaho-Roosevelt NFs, Pawnee NG Revision of the Land and RMP, 1997
Ashley NF Stipulation for Lands of the NF System, 1992
Beaverhead NF EIS, 1996
Berlin Lake Project DR, 1990
Big Cypress General Management Plan/ Final EIS, 1991
Black Hills NF Plan of Land and RMP, 1991
Book Cliffs RMP/ROD and Rangeland Program Summary, 1985
Bridger-Teton NF Land and RMP, 1990
Bureau of Reclamation in Wyoming Special Stipulations

Bureau of Reclamation in New Mexico–Navajo Reservoir Stipulations Carson NF Plan, 1986

Cedar/Beaver/Garfield/Antimony RMP, 1986

Cibola NF Plan, 1985

Conemaugh River Lake Project EA, 1985

Daniel Boone NF Revised Land and RMP, 2004

Diamond Mountain Recreation Area RMP/ROD, 1994

Farmington Oil and Gas Leasing Amendment, 1991

Florida RMP/ROD, 1995

Garnet RMP, 1986

George Washington NF Final revised Land and RMP, 1993

Glenwood Springs Resource Area Plan Amendment, 1999

GMUG NFs Oil and Gas Leasing File EIS ROD, April 1993

Grand Junction Resource Area Management Plan and ROD, 1987 Headwaters RMP/EIS, 1983

Helena NF Plan and ROD, 1986

Isotract MFP, 1985

Jefferson NF Revised Land and RMP, 2004

Kemmerer RMP/ROD, 1986

La Sal NF Land and RMP–Manti, 1986

Lander RMP, 1987

Lewis and Clark NF, Oil and Gas Leasing Final EIS, 1997

Little Snake BLM Leasing Stipulations

Miles City BLM Oil and Gas Amendment, 1994

Mississippi EA Report–O&G leasing on the NFs, 1976

Monongahela NF and Amendments Land and RMP, 1986

Montana State Office, BLM–Bi llings

Mosquito Creek Lake DR, 2000

Nebraska NF Revised Land and RMP, 2000

Nebraska RMP, 1992

Newcastle FO, ROD & Approved RMP, 2000

Northeast NPRA Final Integrated Activity Plan/EIS Amendment, 2006

Northwest NPRA Final Integrated Activity Plan/EIS, 2003

Pike & San Isabel NF, Cimarron & Comanche NG, O&G Leasing Final EIS, 1992

Pinedale RMP, 1988, Amended 2000

Platte River RMP Revised & Updated Decisions, 2001

Pocatello & Medicine Lodge Resource Areas RMP, 1988

Randolph MFP, 1980

Rawlins BLM Lease Stipulations, 2001

Rock Springs BLM Lease Stipulations

Rio Puerco RMP, 1992

Routt NF Land and RMP 1997 Revision

Royal Gorge RMP and NE Royal Gorge RMP, 1991

San Juan/San Miguel RMP Amendment, October 1991

Santa Fe NF Plan 1987, 1996 Amendment, O&G EA NM 85795

Seneca Army Depot and Sampson State Park, 1993

St. George FO–ROD and RMP, 1999
Targhee NF Revised Forest Plan, 2000
Thunder Basin Nat. Grassland Land and RMP, 2002
Uinta NF Land and RMP Revision, 2003
Utah BLM Lopez Project, Statewide Stipulations for Fillmore
Utah BLM Lopez Project, Statewide Stipulations for Kanab
Utah BLM Lopez Project, Statewide Stipulations for Moab
Utah BLM Lopez Project, Statewide Stipulations for Monticello
Utah BLM Lopez Project, Statewide Stipulations for Price
Utah BLM Lopez Project, Statewide Stipulations for Richfield
Utah BLM Lopez Project, Statewide Stipulations for Salt Lake
Wasatch-Cache NF, Revised Forest Plan, 2003
Wayne NF Land and RMP, 1988
White River NF, Oil and Gas Final EIS/ROD, 1993
White River Resource Area RMP
Wyoming BLM Mitigation Guidelines for Surface-disturbing and Disruptive Activities

APPENDIX 11: FEDERAL OIL AND GAS SURFACE MANAGEMENT PRESCRIPTIONS

This appendix contains the text of stipulations applicable to the Phase II inventory. Note that only the pages of the land use plans that contain stipulations used in the inventory are reproduced. The stipulations used are annotated with an EPCA code, e.g., [EPCA Code: UFSashley003] for a stipulation in the Ashley National Forest.

Note also that the various jurisdictions are presented by study area. They are presented only once in the study area in which they dominantly occur even though they may be present in more than one.

End Notes

[1] Federal lands are defined as not including Indian lands.
[2] EPAct 2005 amends the inventory requirements at 42 USC 6217. The updates have been reflected in the text of this document.
[3] In recognition of the increased emphasis on the development of alternative energy resources in the National Energy Policy, the Department of Energy, in coordination with the Department of the Interior, has released a report, analogous to the present report, on the potential of Federal lands to support alternative energy technologies such as wind, solar, and biomass. See http://www.nrel.gov/docs/fy03osti/33530.pdf
[4] Available on the EIA website: http://www.eia.doe.gov/oiaf/aeo/key.html
[5] Available on the USGS website: http://energy
[6] Assessment of Undiscovered Technically Recoverable Oil and Gas Resources of the Nation's Outer Continental Shelf, 2006 Update, available on the MMS website: http://www.mms.gov/revaldiv/PDFs/2006NationalAssessmentBrochure.pdf
[7] See the "Undiscovered Petroleum Resources" definition in Appendix 2.
[8] Advanced Resources International estimate
[9] Meeting the Challenges of the Nation's Growing Natural Gas Demand, December 1999, available on the NPC website: http://www.npc.org/reports/ng.html
[10] "Federal Lands Analysis, Natural Gas Assessment, Southern Wyoming and Northwestern Colorado, Study Methodology and Results," May 2001, available on the DOE website: http://fossil
[11] Section 604 of EPCA was amended by Section 364 of EPAct 2005 (42 USC 6217).
[12] Congressional Record, October 11, 2001, House, p. H6526.

[13] National Energy Policy, Report of the National Energy Policy Development Group, May 2001, available on the White House website: http://www.whitehouse.gov/energy

[14] Scientific Inventory of Onshore Federal Lands' Oil and Gas Resources and Reserves and the Extent and Nature of Restrictions or Impediments to Their Development, January 2003, available on the BLM website: http://www.blm.gov/energy

[15] Balancing Natural Gas Policy: Fueling the Demands of a Growing Economy, National Petroleum Council, September 2003, available on the NPC website: http://www.npc.org/reports/ng.html

[16] The contractor is Advanced Resources International of Arlington, VA. They have engaged Premier Data Services of Englewood, CO as a subcontractor.

[17] The study areas in this document are referenced in USGS Oil and Gas province order.

[18] "Plays," more recently referred to as "assessment units," are a set of known or postulated oil and gas accumulations having similar geologic origins. The term plays is used generically in this document (see section 2.2.1 for further explanation).

[19] The form is available at https://www.blm.gov/FormsCentral/show-form.do?nodeId=687#

[20] The stipulation list for each Study Area exists as a Microsoft Access Table within its respective ESRI geodatabase on the DVD. It can either be imported into an ArcMap project or viewed directly in Access.

[21] Federal Lands Analysis, Natural Gas Assessment, Southern Wyoming and Northwestern Colorado, Study Methodology and Results, June 2001, available on the DOE website: http://fossil

[22] GIS layers for surface management agency land status, stipulations, and the analyses, as well as the associated metadata, are available on the DVD and the web site.

[23] Energy Information Administration, U.S. Crude Oil, Natural Gas, and Natural Gas Liquids Reserves 2004 Annual Report, November 2005, available online at http://www.eia.doe.gov/oil

[24] Data sources included the EIA Reserves and Production Division's Oil and Gas Integrated Field File (RPD OGIFF), the EIA Field Code Master List (FCML), the EIA-23 Reserves Survey, various state web sites, and commercial sources (mainly IHS Energy Group).

[25] Root, D.H. and others, 1995, Estimates of inferred reserves for the 1995 USGS national oil and gas resource assessment, U.S. Geological Survey Open-File Report 95-75L.

[26] National Petroleum Council, 2003, *Balancing Natural Gas Policy-Fueling Demands of a Growing Economy*, September 2003. The Supply Task Group estimated reserves growth for natural gas.

[27] Potential Gas Committee, 2005, *Potential Supply of Natural Gas in the United States as of December 31, 2004*, September 2005. The PGC estimates "Probable Resources" for natural gas. PGC defines Probable Resources as resources associated with known fields including supply from future extensions of existing pools in known productive reservoirs, infill drilling, and future new pool discoveries within existing fields.

[28] For example, EnCana reports significant reserves growth in Jonah and Mamm Creek fields.

[29] *The Intricate Puzzle of Oil and Gas "Reserves Growth,"* available online at http://www.eia.doe.gov/pub/oilgas/petroleum

[30] From Klett, Timothy, *One-Year Reserve-Growth Scoping Project, Fiscal Year 2006*, presentation to American Association of Petroleum Geologists, Committee on Resource Evaluation, February 9, 2006.

[31] Ibid; slide titled "Test of Modified Arrington and USGS Least Squares/Monotonic Methods"

[32] Brenda S. Pierce, USGS, personal communication to Jeffrey Eppink, Advanced Resources International, regarding USGS Energy Resources Team Reserves Growth Scoping Project, project number 8930C1K.

[33] The full technical definition of proved reserves is at the Society of Petroleum Engineers website at http://www.spe.org/spe/jsp/basic/0,,110412169,00.html

[34] Form EIA-23 "Annual Survey of Domestic Oil and Gas Reserves."

[35] Proved reserves were incorporated into the EPCA Phase I inventory. Due to the revision of inventory requirements by the Energy Policy Act of 2005, proved reserves volumes are reported in this Phase II inventory but are excluded from the access categorization.

[36] *Interior Reaches Agreement to Acquire Mineral Rights in Everglades, Settles Litigation on Offshore Oil and Gas Leases in Destin Dome.*. See the website: http://www.fws.gov/southeast/news/2002/n02-002.html

[37] On a TCF-equivalent (TCFe) basis

[38] These tables include only offices that were visited or specifically contacted during EPCA Phase I and Phase II data collection. Not all offices responded.

[39] See the website http://ceq.eh.doe.gov/ntf/report/finalreport.pdf for the "Modernizing NEPA Implementation" report.

[40] Taken from the booklet, "Uniform Format for Oil and Gas Lease Stipulations," prepared by the Rocky Mountain Regional Coordinating Committee in March 1989. These guidelines were developed by the BLM and USDA-FS.

[41] Information is available at http://www.geocommunicator.gov which provides searching, accessing and dynamic mapping of data for Federal land stewardship, land and mineral use records, and land survey information. It also provides spatial display for land and mineral cases from BLM's LR2000 system.

[42] CartéView is the proprietary software of Premier Data Services, Englewood, CO.

[43] See http://www.blm.gov/nhp/efoia/wo/fy03/im2003-274.htm

[44] See http://www.doi.gov/news/041005a

[45] The Greater Green River Basin Study. See website http://www.fossil

[46] Sage grouse have a lek mating system in which males defend display territories but provide no resources such as nesting or forage to females.

[47] EPCA Geology and Assessment Review Team: Schenk, Christopher J., Charpentier, Ronald R., Klett, Timothy R., Pollastro, Richard M., Cook, Troy A., and Crovelli, Robert A.

[48] The oil and gas play boundaries are available at http://energy

[49] They can be downloaded from http://energy

[50] Available online at http://www.eia.doe.gov/pub/oil_gas/petroleum/feature_articles/1997/intricate_puzzle_reserves_growth/m07fa.pdf .

[51] From Klett, Timothy, *One-Year Reserve-Growth Scoping Project, Fiscal Year 2006*, presentation to American Association of Petroleum Geologists, Committee on Resource Evaluation, February 9, 2006.

[52] **Ibid; slide titled "Test of Modified Arrington and USGS Least Squares/Monotonic Methods"**

[53] National Petroleum Council, 2003, *Balancing Natural Gas Policy*, Supply Task Group Report.

[54] Potential Gas Committee, 2005, *Potential Supply of Natural Gas in the United States as of December 31, 2004*, September 2005

[55] U.S. Geological Survey, Energy Resources Team, *Reserves Growth Scoping Project*, Project No. 8930C1K, October 1, 2005 to September 30, 2006, Timothy Klett, project chief. Also, Klett, Timothy, *One-Year Reserve-Growth Scoping Project, Fiscal Year 2006*, presentation to American Association of Petroleum Geologists, Committee on Resource Evaluation, February 9, 2006.

In: Federal Land Resources
Editors: Quintin R. Telles
ISBN: 978-1-60692-130-2

Chapter 2

OIL SHALE: HISTORY, INCENTIVES AND POLICY*

Anthony Andrews

SUMMARY

Oil shale is prevalent in the western states of Colorado, Utah, and Wyoming. The resource potential of these shales is estimated to be the equivalent of 1.8 trillion barrels of oil in place. Retorted oil shale yields liquid hydrocarbons in the range of middle-distillate fuels, such as jet and diesel fuel. However, because oil shales have not proved to be economically recoverable, they are considered a contingent resource and not true reserves. It remains to be demonstrated whether an economically significant oil volume can be extracted under existing operating conditions. In comparison, Saudi Arabia reportedly holds proved reserves of 267 billion barrels.

Federal interest in oil shale dates back to the early 20th Century, when the Naval Petroleum and Oil Shale Reserves were set aside. Out of World War II concerns for a secure oil supply, a Bureau of Mines program began research into exploiting the resource. Commercial interest followed during the 1960s. After a second oil embargo in the 1970s, Congress created a synthetic fuels program to stimulate large- scale commercial development of oil shale and other unconventional resources. The federal program proved short-lived, and commercially backed oil shale projects ended in the early 1980s when oil prices began declining.

The current high oil prices have revived the interest in oil shale. The Energy Policy Act of 2005 (EPACT) identified oil shale as a strategically important domestic resource, among others, that should be developed. EPACT also directed the Secretary of Defense to develop a separate strategy to use oil shale in meeting Department of Defense (DOD) requirements when doing so is in the national interest. Tapping unconventional resources, such as oil shale, has been promoted as a means of reducing dependence on foreign oil and improving national security.

Opponents of federal subsidies for oil shale argue that the price and demand for crude oil should act as sufficient incentives to stimulate development. Projections of increased demand

---

* This is an edited, reformatted and augmented edition of a Congressional Research Service publication, Report RL33359, dated April 13, 2006.

and peaking petroleum production in the coming decades tend to support the price-and-supply incentive argument in the long term.

The failure of oil shale has been tied to the perennially lower price of crude oil, a much less risky conventional resource. Proponents of renewing commercial oil shale development might also weigh whether other factors detract from the resource's potential. Refining industry profitability is overwhelmingly driven by light passenger vehicle demand for motor gasoline, and oil-shale distillate does not make ideal feedstock for gasoline production. Policies that discourage the wider use of middle- distillates as transportation fuels indirectly discourage oil shale development. Because the largest oil shale resources reside on federal lands, the federal government would have a direct interest and role in the development of this resource.

INTRODUCTION

Projections that peak petroleum production may occur in the coming decades, along with increasing global demand, underscore the United States' dependence on imported petroleum. After Hurricanes Katrina and Rita, the spike in crude oil price and the temporary shutdown of some Gulf Coast refineries exacerbated that dependency. With imports making up 65% of the United States' crude oil supply and the expectation that the percentage will rise, proponents of greater energy independence see the nations's huge but undeveloped oil shale resources as a promising alternative.[1]

Oil shales are prevalent throughout the United States. Their kerogen content is the geologic precursor to petroleum. The most promising oil shale resources occur in the Green River formation that underlies 16,000 square miles of northwestern Colorado, northeastern Utah, and southwestern Wyoming (**Figure 1**). Approximately 72% of the land overlying the Green River Formation is federally held.[2] The formation is estimated to contain more than 8 trillion barrels of shale oil in place; however, much of the formation has been considered too thin, too deep, or too low in yield to economically develop using older technology. The former Office of Technology Assessment (OTA) estimated in 1980 that 1.8 trillion barrels appeared marginally attractive to production, based on deposits that would yield 15 gallons per ton and were at least 15 feet thick.[3] In a more recent analysis, the portion of the formation yielding greater than 10 gallons per ton was estimated to contain 1.5 trillion barrels.[4] Because oil shales have not been proven economically recoverable, they are considered contingent resources and not true reserves.[5] By comparison, the conventional proved oil reserves of the United States are less than 22 billion barrels, and Saudi Arabia's are reportedly 267 billion barrels.[6]

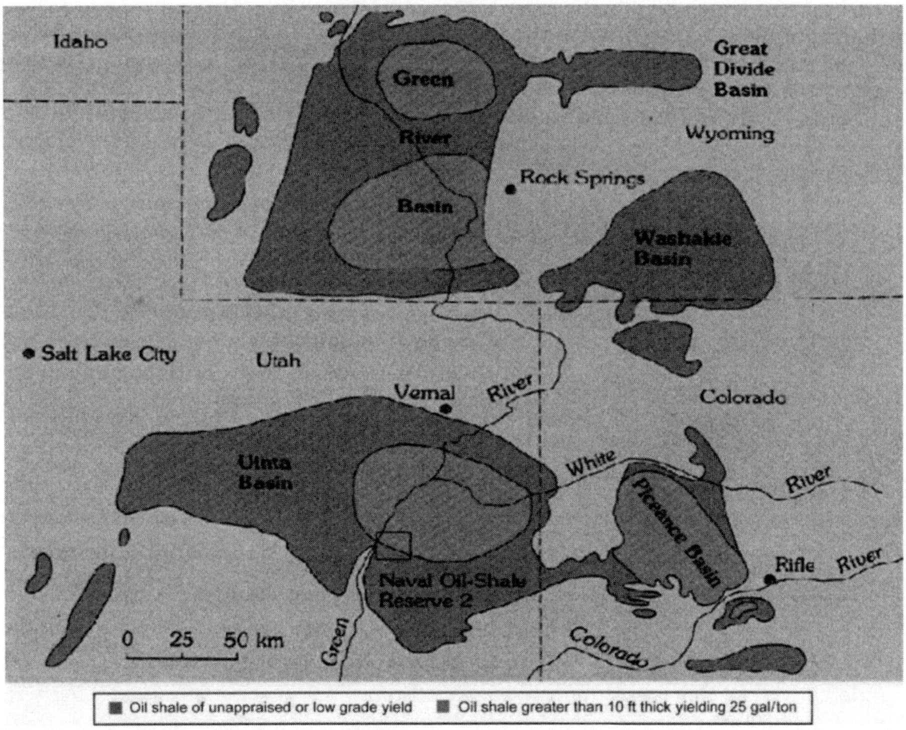

Source: U.S. Geologic Survey, Circular 523 (1965), as reproduced by the U.S. Department of Energy in *Strategic Significance of America's Oil Shale Resources*, Mar. 14, 2005.

Note: The Green River formation may contain more than 8 trillion barrels of shale oil in place, with an estimated 1.8 trillion barrels marginally attractive to production. The United States holds proved reserves of less than 22 billion barrels of conventional crude oil, compared with Saudi Arabia's reported 267 billion barrels.

Figure 1. Distribution of Oil Shale in the Green River Formation of Colorado, Utah, and Wyoming

In the early 20th century, three oil shale reserves were set aside on federal lands out of concern for the Navy's petroleum supply. Naval Oil Shale Reserves (NOSRs) Nos. 1 (36,406 acres) and 3 (20,171 acres) are located 8 miles west of Rifle, Colorado, in Garfield County. Reserve No. 2 (88,890 acres) in Carbon and Uintah Counties, Utah, has been transferred to the Ute Indian Tribe. NOSR No.1 has been estimated to contain more than 18 billion barrels of shale oil in place.[7] As much as 2.5 billion barrels of oil may be recoverable from shale yielding 30 gallons of oil or more per ton. NOSR No. 3 is not considered to have commercial value.

Oil shale production has faced unique technological and environmental challenges. The hydrocarbon resource is bound up in the shale and is not free to flow like petroleum. In previous attempts at production, conventional subsurface and strip mining methods were combined with high-temperature processing (*retorting*) to extract petroleum-like distillates. Not only was a plentiful water supply required, but certain processing methods had associated groundwater contamination issues. Unlike conventional petroleum production, wherein crude oil is shipped or piped to an established refining and distribution center, oil shale production would have required the vertical integration of resource extraction, processing, and upgrading to a finished product ready for blending and distribution. Recent interests in oil shale look to overcoming the past technical challenges associated with mining by adapting oil field production methods. Unlike conventional crude oil, oil-shale distillates make poor feedstock for gasoline production and thus may be better suited to making distillate- based fuels such as diesel and jet fuel. The cost of producing oil shale remains uncertain, especially when compared with the economic fundamentals of extracting conventional petroleum reserves.

GEOLOGY AND PRODUCTION TECHNOLOGY OF OIL SHALE

Kerogen

The first phase in organic matter's geologic transformation to petroleum is intermediate conversion to kerogen. During this low-temperature transformation — referred to as *diagenesis* — organically bound oxygen, nitrogen, and sulfur are released.[8] Complete transformation to petroleum occurs during *catagenesis* — the prolonged exposure to temperatures in the range of 122° to 392°F, generally occurring at depths of 4,000 to 9,800 feet. The catalytic properties of the shale binding the kerogen contribute to the transformation. The threshold for intense oil generation begins at 149°F, equivalent to depths of 4,500 feet or more. Temperatures above 392°F mark the *metamorphic* end-state of transformation — ultimate conversion to methane gas and graphite (pure carbon).

Oil shales have not thermally matured beyond the diagenesis stage due to their relatively shallow depth of burial. Some degree of maturation has taken place, but not enough to fully convert the kerogen to petroleum hydrocarbons. The Green River oil shale of Colorado has matured to the stage that heterocyclic (ring-like) hydrocarbons have formed and predominate, with up to 10% normal- and isoparaffins (the range of hydrocarbons that includes natural gasoline).[9] In comparison, conventional crude oil may contain as much as 40% natural gasoline. The kerogen's rich hydrogen/carbon ratio (1.6) is a significant factor in terms of yielding high-quality fuels. Its 1%-3% nitrogen content, however, may be problematic in terms of producing stable fuels (petroleum typically contains less than 0.5% nitrogen), as well as producing environmentally detrimental nitrogen oxides during combustion.[10] To assess kerogen's potential for yielding hydrocarbon-like fuels, the processes of conventional petroleum refining, synthetic fuel production, and oil shale retorting are compared below.

Conventional Refining

A conventional refinery distills crude oil into various fractions, according to boiling point range, before further processing.[11] In order of their increasing boiling range and density, the distilled fractions are fuel gases, light and heavy straight-run naphtha (90°-380°F), kerosene (380°-520°F), gas-oil (520°-1,050°F), and residuum (1,050°F +). Gasoline's molecular range is C_5-C_{10}; middle-distillate fuels (kerosene, jet, and diesel) range C_{11}-C_{18}. Crude oil may contain 10%-40% gasoline, and early refineries directly distilled a straight-run gasoline (light naphtha) of low-octane rating.[12] A hypothetical refinery may "crack" a barrel of crude oil into two-thirds gasoline and one-third distillate fuel (kerosene, jet, and diesel), depending on the refinery's configuration, the slate of crude oils refined, and the seasonal product demands of the market.[13]

Just as natural clay catalysts help transform kerogen to petroleum through catagenesis, metallic catalysts help transform complex hydrocarbons to lighter molecular chains in modern refining processes. The *catalytic-cracking* process developed during the World War II era enabled refineries to produce high-octane gasolines needed for the war effort. *Hydrocracking*, which entered commercial operation in 1958, improved on catalytic-cracking by adding hydrogen to convert residuum into high-quality motor gasoline and naphtha-based jet fuel. U.S. refineries rely heavily on *hydroprocessing* to convert low-value gas oils residuum to high-value transportation fuel demanded by the market. Middle-distillate range fuels (diesel and jet) can be blended from a variety of refinery processing streams.[14] To blend jet fuel, refineries use desulfurized straight-run kerosene, kerosene boiling range hydrocarbons from a hydrocracking unit, and light coker gas-oil (cracked residuum). Diesel fuel can be blended from naphtha, kerosene, and light cracked-oils from coker and fluid catalytic cracking units. From the standard 42-gallon barrel of crude oil, U.S. refineries may actually produce more than 44 gallons of refined products through the catalytic reaction with hydrogen.[15]

From a simple crude distillation unit, a typical U.S. refinery has grown to a complex of 10 to 15 types of processes.[16] The Nelson Complexity Index, a measure of a refinery's complexity, assigns factors to the capacities of various processing units and compares them to the refinery's crude distillation unit capacity. U.S. refineries rank highest in complexity index, averaging 9.5 compared with Europe's at 6.5. The difference in complexity index reflects the 2-times greater catalytic cracking and 11/2-times greater reformation capacities of U.S. refineries.[17] Although U.S. refineries have optimized to produce reformulated gasoline, European refineries yield more middle-distillate diesel fuel to meet the greater European demand for that fuel.

Synthetic Fuel Production

Synthetic fuel technology was developed in prewar Germany to address its scarce petroleum resources. An early process developed by Friedrich Bergius used a catalyst to promote the reaction of hydrogen with coal liquids to produce low- quality gasoline. During the 1960s, the Department of the Interior's Office of Coal Research sponsored research to directly liquefy Eastern coal into substitutes for natural gas and oil (synthetic liquid fuels).[18]

In a competing process developed by German scientists Fischer and Tropsch, low-temperature catalysts were used to promote hydrogen's reaction with coal gas and produce gasoline. The South African oil company Sasol later developed this technology further. Modern "gas-to-liquids" (GTL) technology based on the Fischer-Tropsch process converts natural gas to liquid fuels.

Essentially, both the Bergius and Fisher-Tropsch synthetic fuel processes build up longer chain hydrocarbons from smaller molecules. This is the opposite of hydrocracking, the refining process that breaks heavier-weight molecular chains and rings into lighter-weight molecules using hydrogen and catalysts.

Oil Shale Retorting

Oil derived from shale has been referred to as a synthetic crude oil and thus closely associated with synthetic fuel production. However, the process of retorting shale oil bears more similarities to conventional refining than to synthetic fuel processes. For the purpose of this chapter, the term *oil-shale distillate* is used to refer to middle-distillate range hydrocarbons produced by retorting oil shale. Two basic retorting processes were developed early on — aboveground retorting and underground, or *in situ*, retorting. The retort is typically a large cylindrical vessel, and early retorts were based on rotary kiln ovens used in cement manufacturing. In situ technology involves mining an underground chamber that functions as a retort. A number of design concepts were tested from the 1960s through the 1980s.

Retorting essentially involves destructive distillation (*pyrolysis*) of oil shale in the absence of oxygen. Pyrolysis (temperatures above 900°F) thermally breaks down (*cracks*) the kerogen to release the hydrocarbons and then cracks the hydrocarbons into lower-weight hydrocarbon molecules. Conventional refining uses a similar thermal cracking process, termed *coking*, to break down high-molecular weight residuum.

OTA compiled properties of oil-shale distillates produced by various retorting processes (**Table 1**). In general, oil-shale distillates have a much higher concentration of high boiling-point compounds that would favor production of middle-distillates (such as diesel and jet fuels) rather than naphtha.[19] Oil-shale distillates also had a higher content of olefins, oxygen, and nitrogen than crude oil, as well as higher pour points and viscosities. Above-ground retorting processes tended to yield a lower API gravity oil than the in situ processes (a 25° API gravity was the highest produced).[20] Additional processing equivalent to hydrocracking would be required to convert oil-shale distillates to a lighter range hydrocarbon (gasoline). Removal of sulfur and nitrogen would, however, require hydrotreating.

Table 1. Properties of Oil-Shale Distillates Compared with Benchmark Crude Oils

	° API	% Sulfur
OTA Reported Oil-Shale Distillates Properties[a]	19.4-28.4	0.59-0.92
Shell ICP Oil-Shale Distillate[b]	34	0.8
Oil Tech Oil-Shale Distillate[c]	30	no report
West Texas Intermediate Crude Oil[d]	40	0.30
NYMEX Deliverable Grade Sweet Crude Oil Specification[e]	37-42	<0.42
Alaska North Slope Crude Oil[d]	29-29.5	1.10

a. OTA, *An Assessment of Oil Shale Technologies*, Table 19, 1980.
b. Energy Washington Week, "Shell Successfully Tests Pilot of New In Situ Oil Shale Technology," Oct. 12, 2005.
c. Jack Savage, Testimony Before the Subcommittee on Energy and Mineral Resources, June 23, 2005.
d. *Platt's Oil Guide to Specifications*, 1999.
e. NYMEX, *Exchange Rulebook*, Light "Sweet" Crude Oil Futures Contract.

By comparison, a typical 35° API-gravity crude oil may be composed of up to 50% of gasoline and middle-distillate range hydrocarbons. West Texas Intermediate crude (a benchmark crude for trade in the commodity futures market) has a 0.3% sulfur content, and

Alaska North Slope crude has a 1.1% sulfur content.[21] The New York Mercantile Exchange (NYMEX) specifications for light "sweet" crude limits sulfur content to 0.42% or less (A.S.T.M. Standard D-4294) and an API gravity between 37 and 42 degrees (A.S.T.M. Standard D-287).[22]

Oil-shale distillate has been considered a synthetic substitute for crude oil; however, its fungibility may be limited in modern refining operations. Because the *kerogen* contained by the shale is only a petroleum precursor, it lacks the full range of hydrocarbons used by refineries in maximizing gasoline production. Also, because of technology limitations, only hydrocarbons in the range of middle- distillates (kerosene, jet fuel, diesel fuel) appear extractable.

Both in situ and above-ground retorting processes have been plagued with technical and environmental problems. Apart from the problem of sustaining controlled combustion underground, in situ retorting suffered from the environmental drawback of causing groundwater contamination. Above-ground retorting required underground or open-pit mining to excavate the shale first. While either mining method is well-practiced, the expended shale that remained after retorting presented a disposal problem, not to mention the overburden rock that had to be removed in the case of open-pit mining. Above-ground retorts also faced frequent problems from caked-up shale, which led them to shut down. Some recent approaches have aimed to avoid these drawbacks altogether.

Shell in situ Conversion Process

For the past five years, the Shell Exploration and Production Company has been conducting research into directly extracting oil-shale distillates on its 20,000-acre Cathedral Bluffs property near Parachute (Rio Blanco County), Colorado.[23] Unlike previously attempted in situ retorting, Shell's *in situ conversion process* (ICP) involves drilling holes up to 2,000 feet deep, inserting electrical resistance heaters, and heating the shale to 650-700°F over a period of months. The ICP converts the kerogen to gas and petroleum-like liquids. The process not only consumes high amounts of energy to operate the heaters, it also requires freezing the perimeter of the production zone to restrict groundwater flow. Shell Oil Company reports extracting a 34°API product consisting of 1/3 gas (propane and butane) and 2/3 liquids split 30% naphtha, 30% jet fuel, 30% diesel, and 10% slightly heavier oil. Sulfur content was 0.8% by weight.

Oil Tech above-Ground Retorting

Oil Tech, Inc., has been developing a new above-ground retort, which it reports as having the capacity of extracting one barrel of shale-oil per ton of shale per hour.[24] The company has reported producing a low-sulfur 30° API-gravity oil consisting of 10% naphtha, 40% kerosene, 40% diesel, and 10% heavy residual oil. Starting off where past retorting attempts ended, Oil Tech intends to use previously mined oil shale that had been stockpiled.

HISTORY OF OIL SHALE DEVELOPMENT

Oil shale was originally considered as a reserve supply of crude oil to fuel U.S. naval vessels in times of short supply or emergencies. Because the largest oil shale resources reside on federal lands, the federal government historically has had a direct interest and role in encouraging the development of this resource. Potential oil-bearing lands in California and Wyoming were first set aside for withdrawal as sources of fuel for the Navy under the Pickett Act of 1910. Later, presidential executive orders created NOSR Nos. 1 and 3 in Colorado and NOSR No. 2 in Utah.

Early Synthetic Liquid Fuels Efforts

During World War II, Congress's concern for conserving and increasing the nation's oil resources prompted passage of the Synthetic Liquid Fuels Act of 1944 (30 U.S.C. Secs. 321 to 325), which authorized funds for the Interior Department's Bureau of Mines to construct and operate demonstration plants to produce synthetic liquid fuel from oil shales, among other substances.

Congress passed the Defense Production Act of 1950 (Ch. 932, 64 Stat. 798) during the Korean War to develop and maintain whatever military and economic strength was necessary to support collective action through the United Nations. The Title III program authorized governmental requisition of property for national defense and expansion of productive capacity, among other authorities. Between 1949 and 1955, the U.S. Bureau of Mines received $18 million to operate three above-ground gas combustion retorts at Anvil Points, Colorado, the site of NOSR No. 1.

Long before the United States' increasing dependence on imported crude oil become apparent, oil shale began attracting the interest of some major petroleum companies: Exxon, Occidental Petroleum, and Union Oil, among others. In 1961, the Union Oil Company began testing its "Union A" retort at Parachute Creek, Colorado. Though producing 800 barrels per day (bpd), Union shut the retort down after 18 months due to cost. In 1964, The Oil Shale Company (Tosco), Standard Oil of Ohio (Sohio), and Cleveland Cliffs Mining formed a consortium to operate the Colony Oil Shale mine. Despite producing 270,000 barrels, Tosco shut down production in 1972. Occidental Petroleum also began oil shale retorting experiments in 1972 near Rifle, Colorado, and ultimately evaluated six retorts.

Defense Department Programs

The Defense Department had become interested in oil shale as an alternative resource for producing quality jet fuel as early as 1951.[25] The U.S. Navy and the Naval Petroleum and Oil Shale Reserves Office (NPSRO) started large-scale evaluations of oil shale's suitability for military fuels in the early 1970s. Tosco was contracted to produce and process 10,000 barrels of oil-shale distillates. Development Engineering, Inc., leased the federal Anvil Points site (Naval Oil Shale Reserve 3) in 1972 and formed the Paraho Development Corporation in 1973 (a consortium of 17 energy companies). Paraho's plans included a five-year program to develop two pilot scale retorts and produce oil-shale distillates for the Navy fuel testing. Paraho initially produced 10,000 barrels of oil-shale distillates that Sohio processed into gasoline, JP-4 and JP-5 jet fuel, diesel fuel marine (DFM), and a heavy fuel oil at the Gary Western Refinery in Fruita, Colorado. Though the fuels produced were off-specification, analysis indicated that the refining process could be optimized to produce specification fuels.

Paraho was awarded a follow-on contract to produce 100,000 barrels of oil-shale distillates for processing specification fuels in Sohio's Toledo Refinery. The Navy conducted extensive tests with the fuels in military and commercial equipment.

In the late 1 970s, the Air Force became interested in evaluating oil shale's suitability for producing JP-4 jet fuel. Under Project Rivet Shale, in 1979, the Air Force awarded contracts to Ashland Research and Development, Suntech, Inc., and UOP, Inc., to develop technology to produce oil shale-derived JP-4 jet fuel. In 1982, over 10,000 gallons of JP-4 were processed at the Caribou Four Corners Refinery in Woods Cross, Utah, from crude oil-shale distillates produced by Geokinetics. JP-4 specification fuel was produced from other oil shale retorting techniques pioneered by Occidental, Paraho, and Union Oil. Unocal (formerly Union Oil Company) operated the Parachute Creek oil shale plant and reportedly produced 4.6 million barrels of oil-shale distillates from 1985 to 1990 for Air Force evaluation under Project Rivet Shale.[26] The Air Force generally phased out JP-4 in the early 1990s in favor of kerosene-based JP-8.

Department of Energy Synthetic Fuels Program

The Department of Energy (DOE) encouraged interest in large-scale oil shale development through its Synthetic Fuels Program. DOE initially promoted two prototype lease tracts in the Piceance Basin of Rio Blanco County, Colorado (NOSR tracts C-a and C-b).[27] Amoco later produced 1,900 barrels using in situ retorting in tract C-a, and Occidental Petroleum planned a similar effort for tract C-b.

The Interior Department Appropriations Act (P.L. 96-126) and the Supplemental Appropriations Act of 1980 (P.L. 96-304) appropriated $1 7.522 billion to the Energy Security Reserve fund in the Treasury Department. Of that amount, $2.6 16 billion was committed by the Department of Energy to three synthetic fuels projects. Two of the projects were approved under the Defense Production Act: Union Oil Company's Parachute Creek project in Garfield County, Colorado, and ExxonTosco's Colony oil shale project, also in Garfield County. Union Oil Company received a $0.4 billion price guarantee for the Parachute Creek Shale Oil Project, and the Exxon-Tosco Colony Oil Shale Project received a loan guarantee of $1.15 billion (applied to the 40% owned by Tosco).[28] Union Oil was expected to produce 10,400 bpd at $42.50/bbl, which, adjusted for inflation, equaled $51.20/bbl by March 1, 1985.

As an additional stimulus to producing alternative fuels — for which oil shale, among others, qualified — Congress provided a $3.00 /bbl production tax credit provision in the Crude Oil Windfall Profit Tax Act of 1980 (P.L. 96-223). The credit would take full effect when crude oil prices fell below $23.50 /bbl (in 1979 dollars) and would gradually phase out as prices rose above to $29.50/bbl.

Tosco's interest in the Colony project was sold in 1979, and again in 1980, to Exxon Company for the Colony II development. Exxon planned to invest up to $5 billion in a planned 47,000 bpd plant using a Tosco retort design. After spending more than $1 billion, Exxon announced on May 2, 1982, that it was closing the project and laying off 2,200 workers.

U.S. Synthetic Fuels Corporation

The Energy Security Act of 1980 (P.L. 96-294, Title I, Part B) established the United States Synthetic Fuels Corporation (SFC) with the authority to provide financial assistance to qualified projects that produced synthetic fuel from coal, oil shale, tar sands, and heavy oils. The SFC's loan commitments would be paid from the Energy Security Reserve fund. Executive Order 12346 (Synthetic Fuels) later provided for an orderly transition of DOE's earlier synthetic fuel program to the SFC.

Between 1981 and 1984, the SFC received 34 proposals for oil shale projects in three rounds of solicitations. Only three letters of intent were ever issued. Union Oil's Parachute Creek Phase II 80,000 bpd plant was to receive a $2.7 billion funding commitment and a guarantee of $60/bbl, escalated up to $67 /bbl; another $0.5 billion in price and loan guarantees was added in October 1985 to Union's Parachute Creek Phase I. Cathedral Bluffs, a 14,300 bpd plant based on a Union Oil design, was to receive a $2.19 billion loan guarantee and a $60/bbl price guarantee. Seep Ridge Oil Shale's 1,000 bpd plant was to receive $45 million in price and loan guarantees. None of the oil shale projects that received SFC loan guarantees ever received actual funding, as Congress rescinded $2 billion originally appropriated for the Energy Security Reserve fund in the Deficit Reduction Act of 1984 (P.L. 98-369) and later abolished the SFC.

In 1984, Congress asked the General Accounting Office (GAO) to report on the progress of synthetic fuels development and to specifically respond to the question "Why have project sponsors dropped synthetic fuels projects?" GAO answered that oil had become plentiful, with about 8 to 10 million barrels per day in excess worldwide capacity, and the trend in rising oil prices had reversed after early 1981.

President Reagan's Executive Order 12287 had removed price and allocation controls on crude oil and refined petroleum products in 1981. For the first time since the early 1970s, market forces replaced regulatory programs and domestic crude oil prices were allowed to rise to a market-clearing level. Decontrol also set the stage for the relaxation of export restrictions on refined petroleum products. Oil demand had also declined, due in part to energy conservation measures and a worldwide economic recession. A more fundamental change had taken place in the way that oil commodities were traded. Prior to 1980, the price of crude oil was determined by long-term contracts, with 10% or so of internationally traded oil exchanged on the spot market.[29] By the end of 1982, more than half of the internationally traded oil was exchanged on the spot market or tied to the spot market price. The most significant change occurred in 1983, with the introduction of crude oil futures by the New York Mercantile Exchange (NYMEX). All served to undermine price setting by the Organization of Petroleum Exporting Countries (OPEC).

Tax incentives for oil shale projects had also been reduced. Some of the generous oil depreciation allowances under the 1981 Economic Recovery Tax Act (P.L. 97-48) were rescinded in 1982 by the Tax Equity and Fiscal Responsibility Act (P.L. 97-248), reducing potential project sponsors' after-tax rates of return.

The House began considering a bill to abolish the SFC in 1985, and Congress terminated the Corporation the following year under the Consolidated Omnibus Budget Reconciliation Act of 1985 (P.L. 99-272). The **Appendix** to this chapter provides a more complete legislative history of the Synthetic Fuels program.

Renewed Interest in Oil Shale

In 2005, Congress conducted hearings on oil shale to discuss opportunities for advancing technology that would facilitate "environmentally friendly" development of oil shale and oil sands resources.[30] The hearings also addressed legislative and administrative actions necessary to provide incentives for industry investment, as well as exploring concerns and experiences of other governments and organizations and the interests of industry. The Energy Policy Act of 2005 included provisions under Section 369 (Oil Shale, Tar Sands, and Other Strategic Unconventional Fuels[31]) that direct the Secretary of the Interior to begin leasing oil shale tracts on public lands and to cooperate with the Secretary of Defense in developing a program to commercially develop oil shale, among other strategic unconventional fuels.

The Bureau of Land Management (BLM) established the Oil Shale Task Force in 2005 to address oil shale access on public lands and impediments to oil shale development on public lands. Title 30, Section 24 1(a) of the Mineral Lands Leasing Act formerly restricted leases to 5,120 acres. Advocates of oil shale development claimed that restrictions on lease size hindered economic development. The Energy Policy Act amended Section 241(a) by raising the lease size to 5,760 acres and restricting total lease holdings to no more than 50,000 acres in any one state.[32]

On September 20, 2005, the Bureau of Land Management announced it had received 19 nominations for 160-acre parcels of public land to be leased in Colorado, Utah, and Wyoming for oil shale research, development, and demonstration (RD&D). On January 17, 2006, BLM announced that it accepted eight proposals from six companies to develop oil shale technologies; the companies selected were Chevron Shale Oil Co., EGL Resources Inc., ExxonMobil Corp., Oil-Tech Exploration LLC, and Shell Frontier Oil & Gas.[33] Six of the proposals will look at in situ extraction to minimize surface disturbance. Each proposal will be evaluated under the National Environmental Policy Act (NEPA). In addition to the 160 acres allowed in the call for RD&D proposals, a contiguous area of 4,960 acres is reserved for the preferential right for each project sponsor to convert to a future commercial lease after additional BLM reviews.

The Energy Policy Act also identified oil shale as a strategically important domestic resource and directed DOE to coordinate and accelerate its commercial development. Section 369(q) (Procurement of Unconventional Fuels by the Department of Defense) of the act directs the Secretaries of Defense and Energy to develop a strategy to use fuel produced from oil shale to help meet the fuel requirements of the Defense Department when the Defense Secretary determines that doing so is in the national interest. The Defense Department had worked jointly with Energy on a Clean Fuels Initiative to develop, test, certify, and use zero-sulfur jet fuels from alternative resources (oil shale, among others). By eliminating sulfur, the fuels would be suitable for use in fuel cells to generate electricity and in turbine engines used in aircraft and ground vehicles. A synthetic fuel process based on Fischer-Tropsch had been considered. At the time of the President's FY2007 budget request, DOE proposed terminating oil technology research, and the Defense Department left Clean Fuels unfunded.[34]

Since 1910, several legislation-based initiatives have attempted to promote oil shale development. (Legislation establishing the oil shale reserves and related federal programs is summarized in the **Appendix** of this chapter.) However, more recent regulatory policies (see below) appear adverse to oil shale development, at least to the wider use of middle-distillate fuels producible from oil shale.

INCENTIVES AND DISINCENTIVES TO DEVELOPMENT

The economic incentive for producing oil shale has long been tied to the price of crude oil. The highest price that crude oil ever reached — $87/bbl (2005 dollars) — occurred in January 1981 (**Figure 2**).[35] Exxon's decision to cancel its Colony oil shale project came a year and half later, after prices began to decline and newly discovered, less-costly-to-produce reserves came online. The price of crude oil spiked to nearly $70/bbl after Hurricanes Katrina and Rita, and the recent climb to above $67 /bbl has led to some speculation that prices may remain high indefinitely. In the Energy Information Administration's (EIA' s) reference case projection, though, "the average world crude oil price continues to rise through 2006 and then declines to $46.90/bbl in 2014 (2004 dollars) as new supplies enter the market. It then rises slowly to $54.08/bbl in 2025."[36] Near-record gasoline prices have led to similar speculation, as the average price of gasoline has stayed consistently above $2 per gallon since May of 2005, and the on-highway diesel price has stayed even higher.[37] However, oil company investment decisions may be more conservatively based on making profits at the $20-$30/barrel range of just a few years ago than on projected prices. That is, high prices may not be enough of an incentive for risky developments in conventional oil, let alone oil shale.

Crude oil production costs vary widely by geography and reservoir conditions, and they may be more important factors now than 25 years ago as aging reservoirs decline in production. Production involves lifting the oil to the surface and the gathering, treating, and field processing and storage of the oil. The cost of production, sometimes referred to as *lifting cost*, includes labor to operate the wells and related equipment; repair and maintenance of the wells and equipment; and materials, supplies, and energy required to operate the wells and related equipment. In the Persian Gulf region, where a single well may produce thousands of barrels per day, production costs may be as little as a few dollars per barrel. Production costs in the United States had approached $15/bbl by 2004.[38] ExxonMobil reported production costs increases from $41/2 to $51/2 /bbl for its U.S. operations over the past several years.[39] In older, far less productive wells in the United States, production costs may reach more than $25/bbl.[40]

In 1998, a supply glut forced the price of crude oil down to almost $10/barrel and gasoline sold for less than $0.80/gallon in some markets. Some domestic producers charged, in a U.S. Court of International Trade suit, that oil imports had been dumped on the American market.[41] Though unsuccessful, the suit does say something further about bottom-line production costs (the crude oil price equivalent that producers could not compete below) and the production costs that oil shale may need to compete against. For several years preceding the price drop, crude oil ranged from $20 to $30/bbl.

The perception that oil shale serves as a crude oil substitute overlooks the limited fungibility of the middle distillates that are extractable — they make poor feedstock for gasoline production. That does not necessarily prevent oil-shale distillates from being used as gasoline feedstock, but additional energy and hydrogen are needed to crack them. The loss may be even greater considering the lower fuel efficiency of spark-ignition engines that use gasoline, compared with compression ignition engines that use diesel distillate fuels.

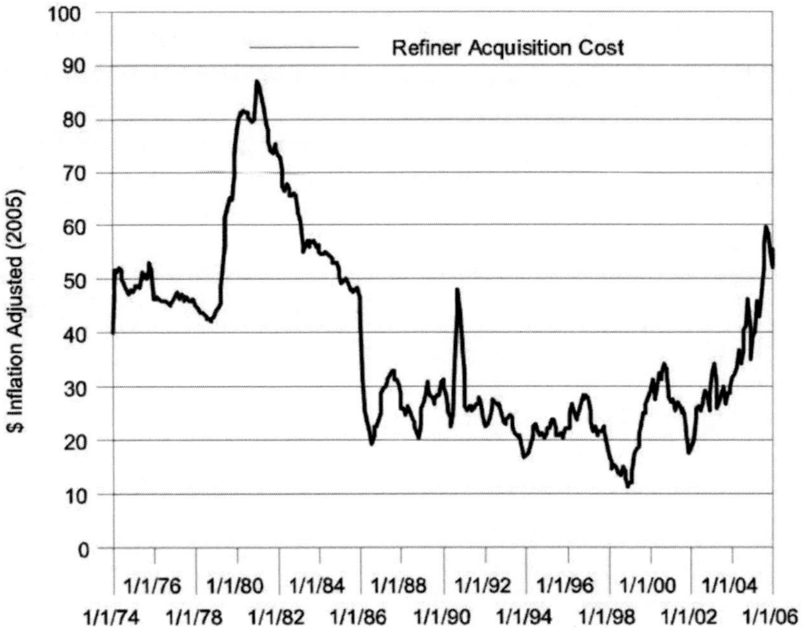

Source: U.S. DOE EIA, *World Oil Market and Oil Price Chronologies 1970-2004*, Mar. 2005, at [http://www.eia.doe.gov/cabs/chron.html]; EIA Refiner Acquisition Cost of Crude Oil (for July 2005 to Jan. 2006), at [http://tonto.eia.doe.gov/dnav/ pet/pet_pri_rac2_dcu_nus_m.htm].

Figure 2. Refiner Acquisition Cost of Imported Crude Oil

Other incentives or disincentives may include the cost and size of an oil shale processing facility, conventional refining profitability, and the cost and availability of refined commodities. Certain environmental and tax regulations that act as incentives to using gasoline in light-duty vehicles discourage middle-distillate diesel fuel use, and thus oil-shale distillates as substitute motor fuels.

The Cost of Constructing an Oil Shale Facility

A reliable cost estimate for producing oil shale has proved challenging, if not controversial. The cost of resources extraction had depended on whether conventional underground or strip-mining methods were employed. Because there was a considerable experience in mining, reliable cost estimates could be developed. A second variable — the cost of constructing and operating an oil shale facility — had to be accounted for separately. The former OTA estimated in 1979 that a 50,000 bpd oil shale facility (based on above-ground retorting technology) would have required an investment of $1.5 billion and operating costs of $8 to $13/bbl. Using the Nelson-Farrar Cost Indexes to adjust refinery construction and operation costs to 2004 dollars, the investment would be equivalent to $3.5 billion, with operating costs of $13 to $2 1/bbl.[42] This excludes the cost of shale extraction.

In comparison, the cost of building a new conventional refinery has been estimated to range between $2 and $4 billion as recently as 2001.[43] The cost of operating a refinery (marketing, energy, and other costs) averaged nearly $6/bbl during 2003-2004, as reflected in the difference between gross and net margins (where the gross margin reflects the refiner's revenue minus the cost of crude oil).[44]

An oil shale facility may not be directly comparable to a refinery in terms of construction costs, though some processes, such as hydrotreating, may be common to both. If oil field-based technologies such as Shell's proposed ICP are successfully adapted to resource extraction, facility costs could be reduced, but operating costs could increase given the energy-intensive aspect of the technology.

Under the U.S. Air Force Project Rivet Shale, Union Oil's Parachute Creek Phase I project produced 4.6 million barrels of oil-shale distillates from 1985 to 1990 at a cost of $650 million; roughly the equivalent of $141/bbl, or $3.52/gal. (wholesale). Since Rivet Shale produced a jet fuel equivalent, a comparison might be made with the price of jet fuel at the time. In comparison, a refiner's crude oil acquisition costs ranged from a less $15/bbl to $27/bbl in nominal dollars over that same time period.[45] The spot market price for kerosene-based jet fuel rose from less than $0.40/gal in 1985 to more than $1.10/gal by 1990.

The Rand Corporation recently estimated that a "first-of-kind" surface retort facility might cost $5-$7 billion, with operating costs of $17 to $23/bbl in 2005 dollars. Rand projects that a crude oil equivalent of West Texas Intermediate would need to be at least $70 to $95/bbl for such an operation to be profitable.[46] Shell Oil believes that in situ conversion can be profitable, producing oil-shale distillates at $25/bbl once steady-state production is reached.[47] The disparity in estimates demonstrates the controversy over the issue. It should be noted that Rand refers to the older retorting technology that relied on mining methods for resource extraction, whereas Shell's estimate is based on oil field-based technology for resource extraction.

The Ideal Size for an Oil Shale Facility

As domestic crude oil production declined through the 1970s, many marginally profitable and often smaller refineries were closed or idled.[48] Of the 324 refineries operating 1981, 142 refineries currently remain operating. However, they represent a crude distillation capacity of approximately 17.5 million bpd, compared with 14.5 million bpd in the mid 1980s, and range in size from 557,000 bpd (ExxonMobil's Baytown, Texas refinery) to 1,707 bpd (Foreland Refining Corp's refinery in Eagle Springs, Nevada).[49] The median capacity (half above and half below) of all operating refineries is approximately 80,000 bpd (**Figure 3**). The 71 refineries above the median capacity are responsible for 85% of the current overall U.S. production (14.8 million bpd). The trend toward larger refineries reflects the economic efficiency gained by increased scale. (For further information on refining, refer to CRS Report RL32248, *Petroleum Refining: Economic Performance and Challenges for the Future*, by Robert L. Pirog.)

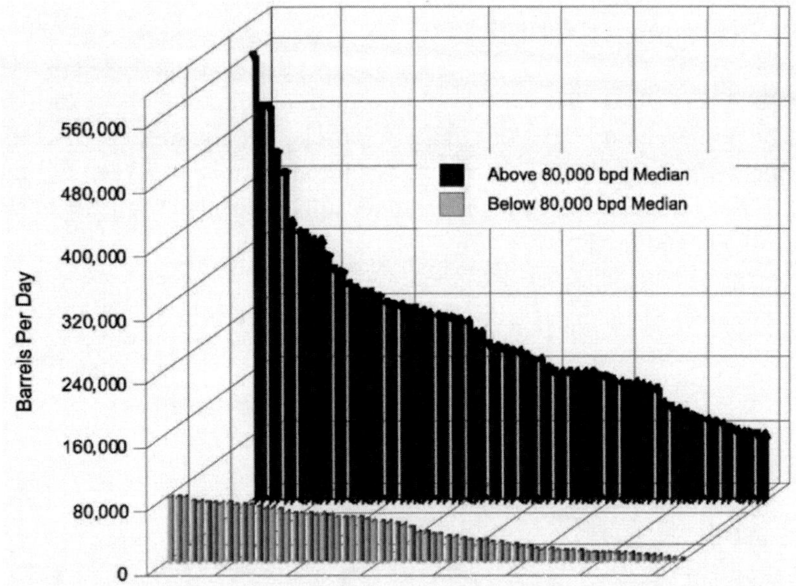

Source: EIA Annual Energy Outlook, Table 38, Capacity of Operable Petroleum Refineries by State, 2005.

Figure 3. Refinery Capacity Distribution Above and Below Median 80,000 BPD Size

OTA's reference case 50,000 bpd oil shale facility would have been typical for refinery capacities in the late 1970s, but compared with current capacities, it might appear undersized. However, in terms of matching middle-distillate output, an oil shale facility requires ºf½ the capacity of a conventional refinery. Since U.S. refineries yield at most 47% motor gasoline vs. 33% middle-distillates, a 50,000 bpd oil shale facility today (producing middle distillates exclusively) would match the distillate output of a 150,000 bpd conventional refinery.[50] This suggests that relatively smaller oil shale production facilities could be as effective as a larger conventional refinery when it comes to producing middle distillates.

The complicated permitting process has been an argument against building a new refinery and for expanding an existing refinery's capacity instead. The approval process for new refinery construction has been estimated to require up to 800 different permits.[51] An oil shale facility's considerably less complexity would appear to have an inherent advantage over a conventional refinery when it comes to permitting. Congress recognized that increasing petroleum refining capacity serves the national interest and included provisions in the Energy Policy Act of 2005 (Title III, Subtitle H — Refinery Revitalization) to streamline the environmental permitting process. A refiner can now submit a consolidated application for all permits required by the Environmental Protection Agency (EPA). To further speed the permit's review, the EPA is authorized to coordinate with other federal agencies, enter into agreements with states on the conditions of the review process, and provide states with financial aid to hire expert assistance in reviewing the permits. Additional provisions under Title XVII (Incentives for Innovative Technologies) of the act guarantee loans for refineries that avoid, reduce, or sequester air pollutants and greenhouse gases if they employ new or significantly improved technology. Permitting would be a secondary consideration for new construction, if refining was an unfavorable investment.

Competing with Imported Distillates

Between 1993 and 2005, low-sulfur middle distillate production in the United States tripled from 328 million barrels to 1,058 million barrels, but some imports were still needed to satisfy demand (**Figure 4**). The current 55 million barrels per year of imports is the equivalent of 150,000 bpd in production, or three oil shale plants on the scale of OTA's reference case 50,000 bpd facility.

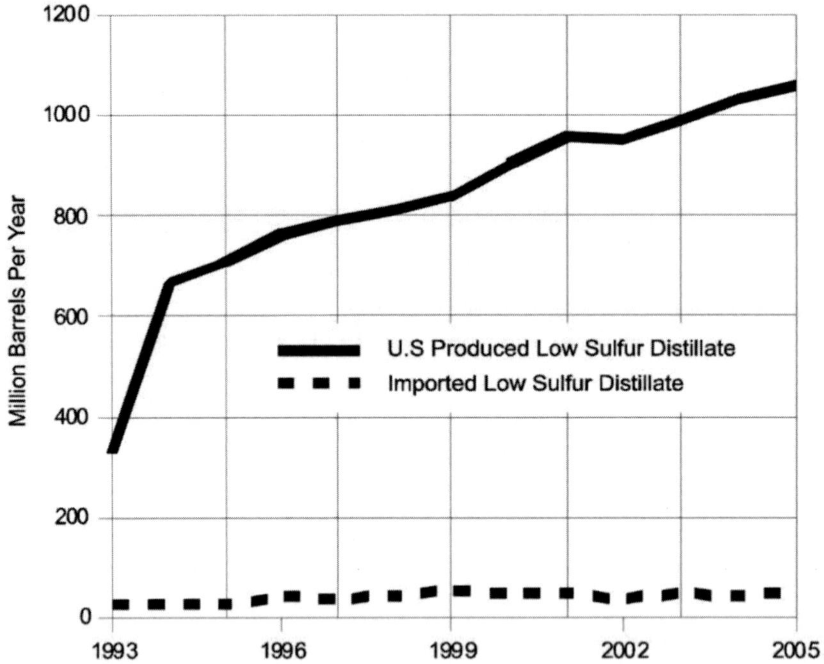

Source: EIA Petroleum Navigator, U.S. Refinery Production of Distillates 15-500 ppm Sulfur, and U.S. Distillates 15-500 ppm Sulfur Imports, at [http://tonto.eia.doe.gov/dnav/pet/hist].

Figure 4. Imported Crude Oil and Refined Products

Like U.S. refineries, European refineries also began to optimize for gasoline production in the early 1990s, only to see the European demand shift toward middle- distillate diesel fuel due largely to European tax incentives (discussed below) that favor diesel fuel use. Excess gasoline now produced by these refineries is exported to the U.S. market. Diesel fuel is forecast to make up 68% percent of European consumption by 2010.[52] How European refineries respond to an increased diesel fuel demand will likely affect gasoline exports to the United States, particularly if the refineries shift their optimization more toward diesel than investing capital in additional diesel capacity. Both diesel and gasoline exports to the U.S. market could be reduced. U.S. refineries appear to have little excess capacity to make up both the gasoline and diesel loss, leaving some opportunity for oil shale to make up the distillate loss.

Assuming that U.S. refineries yield 1/3 middle-distillates, actual refining capacity on the order of 1 million bpd would have been required. In terms of oil shale production, three 50,000-bpd plants processing 1,867 million tons of oil shale (yielding 15 to 30 gallons per ton) could be required to fill the possible gap in domestic supply.

Regulatory Disincentives

Apart from economic reasons, some regulatory policies may discourage the production and use of oil-shale distillate fuels. Both gasoline and diesel fuel are subject to Clean Air Act regulations and federal motor fuel taxes. Both regulations and taxes are more lenient towards gasoline use. In comparison, European Union (EU) environmental standards and tax regulations are more lenient towards diesel fuel and consequently have stimulated its broader consumption. Since oil-shale distillates could substitute for diesel fuel, any regulatory bias toward gasoline could act as a disincentive to oil shale production.

Diesel Vehicle Demand

Passenger vehicles and light-duty trucks (under 8,500 lbs. gross vehicle weight) create the primary demand for transportation fuel in the United States. However, nearly 22% of the transportation fuel demand is for diesel, primarily in heavy-duty on- and off-road vehicles (semi-tractor trucks, earthmoving equipment, and railroad locomotives). Light-duty diesel trucks and passenger vehicles make up a smaller (but uncertain) percentage of the diesel demand, based on the lower number of miles private vehicles drive annually compared with commercial vehicles. Light-duty vehicles do, however, make up slightly more than half of the on-road diesel vehicles sold. Though overall, light-duty diesel vehicles have made up only 5% of the total light-duty vehicles sold recently (~349,000 light-duty diesel trucks and ~30,000 diesel passenger vehicles versus 16.9 million total light-duty vehicles sold in 2004).[53] The EIA sees a slower growth of light-duty diesel vehicles in the United States than in Europe.[54] In contrast to U.S. sales of light-duty diesel vehicles, new diesel passenger vehicle registration in Europe rose from 22.3% in 1998 to 48.25% in 2004.[55] The effect of increased diesel registration can be seen in the increased refinery output and net deliveries of diesel reported for European members of the Organization of Economic Co-operation and Development (OECD) by the International Energy Agency (IEA).[56] (See **Figure 5**.)

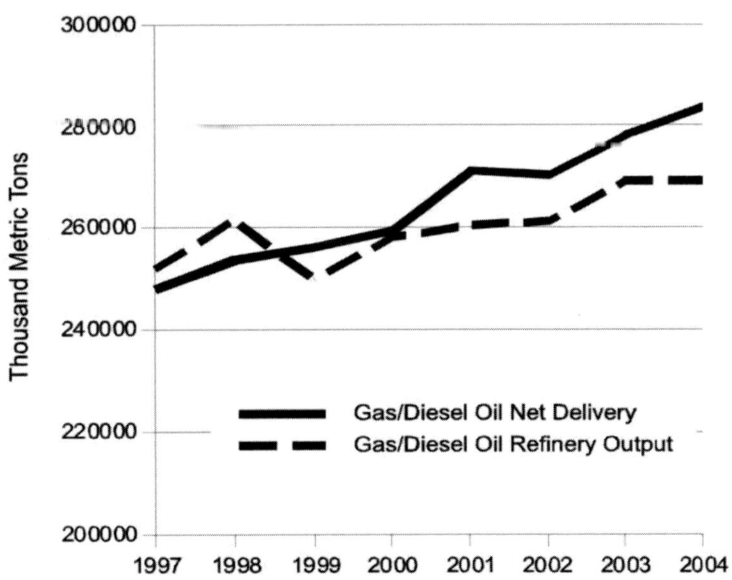

Source: International Energy Agency, *Monthly Oil Survey*, 2000 through 2005.

Figure 5. Net Deliveries vs. Refinery Output of Gas/Diesel Oil for OECD Europe

Assuming that a separate diesel fuel for light-duty diesel vehicles will not be created, the EIA projects that U.S. refiners are unlikely to see the impact of a developing light-duty diesel vehicle market in the next decade. Given EIA's projection, the opportunity for oil-shale distillates as diesel substitutes would appear similarly limited in the United States.

CO, NOx, and PM Emissions

Compared with spark-ignition (gasoline) engines, compression-ignition (diesel) engines characteristically emit lower amounts of carbon monoxide (CO) and carbon dioxide (CO_2), but they emit higher amounts of nitrogen oxides (NOx) and particulate matter (PM). NOx is the primary cause of ground-level ozone pollution (smog) and presents a greater problem, technically, to reduce in diesel engines than PM.

The CO, NOx, and PM emissions for gasoline and diesel engines are regulated by the 1990 Clean Air Act amendments (42 U.S.C. 7401-7671q) Tier 1 and 2 Emission Standards. Under Tier 1, the NOx standard had been 1.0 gram/mile for diesel passenger and light-duty trucks, versus 0.4 grams/mile for gasoline vehicles. The Tier 2 standards that started taking effect in 2004 are fuel-neutral. Regardless of the fuel, a fleet of vehicle models manufactured in a given year must average 0.07 grams/mile for NOx emissions. A particular vehicle model may qualify in a unique emission "bin" (the maximum allowable is 0.2 grams/mile), as long as the fleet of models meets the average NOx emission standard. Other pollutants are similarly regulated.

Since diesel engines inherently produce more NOx and PM than gasoline engines, producing more diesel vehicles raises the fleet emission average and thus limits the total number of vehicles a manufacturer can sell in the United States. This in turn limits the demand for diesel vehicles, which thus limits the opportunity for oil-shale distillates. The U.S. Tier 2 NOx emissions standards are more stringent than the EU's current Euro 4 standards of 0.4 grams/mile for diesel cars and 0.6 grams/mile for light-duty diesel trucks. Tier 2 PM-emission standards of 0.01 to 0.02 grams/mile are also more stringent than Euro 4 PM-emissions of 0.04 grams/mile.

The Tier 2 CO-standard of 4.2 grams/mile is significantly less stringent than the Euro 4 standard of 0.8 grams/mile for diesel passenger cars and 1.2 grams/mile for light-duty diesel trucks. Tier 2 favors gasoline over diesel in this case.

The EU is moving toward taxing cars on the basis of CO_2 emissions (which favors diesel).[57] This move is in response to the Kyoto Protocol on climate change, which seeks to limit CO_2 emissions, a treaty that the United States signed but did not ratify.

Should oil-shale distillates substitute for diesel, Tier 2 limits on CO, NOx, and PM emissions would continue to apply, as the standard is fuel-neutral. However, the emission characteristics of oil-shale distillates (similar to diesel) have not been the subject of documented research.

Ultra-Low Sulfur Diesel

By mid-2006, new U.S. standards for ultra-low sulfur diesel (ULSD) take effect under a 2001 rule issued by the EPA.[58] Diesel fuel sulfur content must be reduced to no more than 15 parts-per-million (ppm) from the current 500 ppm (established by a 1993 rule that reduced the level from 5,000 ppm). However, to account for pipeline contamination, refiners may have to produce diesel fuel with a sulfur content as low as 7 ppm; a four-year phase-in period allows for 20% of the highway diesel produced to meet the current limit.

The EIA estimates the marginal cost of producing ultra-low sulfur diesel to range from 2.5¢ to 6.8¢ per gallon, depending on whether supply falls short of demand or consumers bid up the price.[59] EIA projects the ULSD rule to require total refinery investments ranging from $6.3 to $9.3 billion. As the energy content of ULSD is somewhat less than 500 ppm diesel, fuel efficiency may be affected (increasing fuel consumption and therefore demand).

The sulfur content of oil-shale distillates is comparable in weight percentage to crude oil (**Table 1**). U.S. refiners were able to meet the current 500 ppm requirement by increasing the existing capacity of their hydrotreatment units and adding new units. However, refineries may face difficulty in treating diesel to below 500 ppm. The remaining sulfur is bound in non-hydrocarbon, multi-ring thiophene-type compounds that prove difficult to hydrotreat because the molecular ring structure attaches the sulfur on two sides. Although these compounds occur throughout the range of petroleum distillates, they are more concentrated toward the residuum end.

So, the problem is compounded when residuum is cracked to increase gasoline production. Improved hydrotreatment technology since the 1980s has increased sulfur removal and provided a means to removing oil-shale distillate's excessive nitrogen content (desirable in terms of producing stable fuels with low NOx emissions).

Whereas conventional refineries may be able to further upgrade hydrotreatment capacity by retrofitting, an oil shale processing plant would be designed and built from the ground up with necessary capacity. However, many refineries either produce the hydrogen needed for hydrotreating or purchase it from vendors that operate near established refining centers. An oil shale facility may require the addition of a steam reforming process to convert natural gas to the hydrogen needed.

Refiners' response to the ULSD rule ultimately affects diesel supply and thus price. As increased diesel fuel prices are likely to erode the lower operating-cost advantage of diesel engines over gasoline, the incentive for purchasing light-duty diesel vehicles would be less, in keeping with EIA's projection of a slow growth in light-duty diesel vehicles over the next decade. On the other hand, a decline in diesel demand would offer even less incentive to produce oil-shale distillates for light-duty vehicles.

Fuel Tax

The U.S. federal tax rate on motor fuel currently favors gasoline over diesel fuel by 6¢ per gallon (18.4¢ and 24.4¢, respectively).[60] Both gasoline and diesel tax rates began increasing after the mid-1980s, but diesel increased at a faster rate (**Figure 6**). The higher diesel fuel tax is essentially a user fee paid by heavy-duty trucks to offset the higher road damage they cause than lighter duty vehicles. Where motor fuel taxes are applied to transportation infrastructure improvements in the United States, they are a source of general revenue for the 15 EU member states.

Overall, motor fuel taxes are significantly higher in the EU, ranging from the equivalent of $3.28/gallon (€ 742/1,000 liters at an exchange rate of $1.17: € 1) for diesel and gas in the United Kingdom, to as low as €253/1,000 liters) ($1.12/gallon) for diesel in Luxemburg. Except for the United Kingdom, diesel fuel is taxed on average 62¢/gallon(€140/1,000 liters) less than gasoline.[61] In December 2005, the average end-use prices of gasoline in France and Germany were $5.26/gallon and $6.08/gallon, respectively (€1.170/liter and €1.226/liter), compared with $2.17/gallon in the United States — with automotive diesel averaging

$3.89/gallon and $4.23/gallon in France and Germany, respectively (€0.865/liter and €0.941/liter), compared with $2.45/gallon in the United States.[62] The end-use price difference in the two fuels appears to correlate with the increasing registration of diesel cars in the EU. With higher crude oil prices, the fuel savings advantage of diesel cars should become even more compelling.

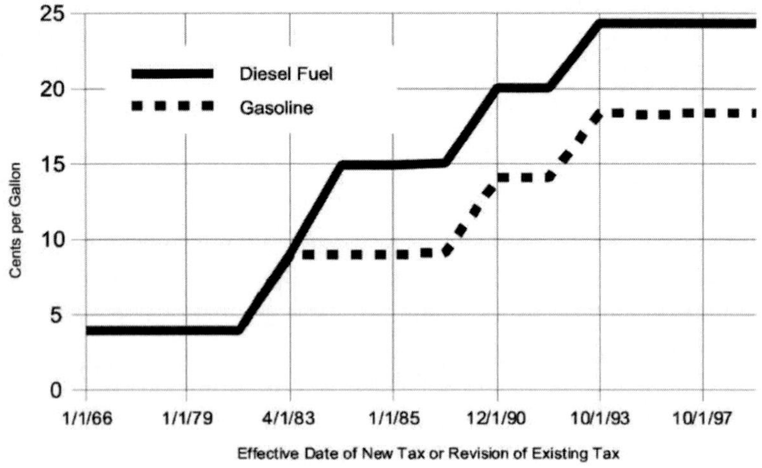

Source: U.S. DOT, "Federal Tax Rates on Motor Fuels and Lubricating Oil," Table Fe-101a.
Note: The U.S. federal tax rate on motor fuel currently favors gasoline over diesel fuel by 6¢ per gallon. European Union states (except UK) tax diesel fuel on average (62¢/gallon less than gasoline).
Figure 6. Diesel vs Gasoline Fuel Tax

Diesel fuel demand is "regulatory driven" to an extent. Motor fuel taxes that favor diesel over gasoline offer one means of redirecting demand, but the tax differential may need to be significantly higher than the current 6¢ per gallon differential favoring gasoline. Raising motor fuel taxes above the current federal level runs counter to current policy. In the aftermath of Hurricane Katrina, when gasoline prices surged above $3 per gallon, some states suspended or considered suspending taxes on gasoline. However, advocates of energy conservation argued that the higher gasoline prices conserved fuel by discouraging driving, thus the motor fuel tax should have remained or even increased. If higher motor fuel tax stimulates the demand for more fuel-efficient vehicles, as the European experience suggests, the inherent fuel efficiency offered by a diesel passenger vehicle becomes more apparent, if not desirable. This in turn could act as an additional incentive for producing diesel or alternatives such as oil-shale distillates.

Policy Perspective and Consideration

Federally sponsored research to develop fuel substitutes from oil shale dates back the U.S. Synthetic Liquid Fuels Act of 1944 out of World War II concerns for oil supplies. Later, in response to the oil embargos of the 1970s, Congress created the Synthetic Fuels Corporation. National security had been a motivating concern (i.e., to aid the prosecution of the war and to contend with foreign actions that interrupt energy supplies). As newly discovered, less-costly-to-produce petroleum reserves entered production in the early 1980s, the economic and operating conditions of oil shale production became unfavorable. As commercial interests backed out of projects, Congress terminated synthetic fuel development. Various commercial attempts to exploit the resource met with limited success. Technological developments that transformed petroleum refining efficiency, and the discovery of new petroleum reserves, shifted private sector interest away from oil shale resources.

The global demand-driven petroleum supply cycle, if true to history, is likely to exhibit periods of surplus and shortage. Periods of surplus fit well with the just-intime supply model that seeks to hold down inventory costs by minimizing stocks on hand. Proponents of the self-correcting petroleum market theory may argue that supply interruptions are temporary and that price spikes signal customers to reduce consumption. Opponents may argue that reduced consumption is not an option during a national security crisis and that there ought to be a "just-in-case" contingency in place, such as oil shale. While the threat from future OPEC-like embargoes appears unlikely, the President's goal "to replace more than 75 percent of our oil imports from the Middle East by 2025" indicates continuing concern.[63]

Recent high crude oil prices renewed interest in oil shale, prompting Congress to include provisions in the Energy Policy Act of 2005 promoting the lease and development of federal oil shale holdings. The Act also identified oil shale as a strategically important domestic resource and directed the Energy Department to coordinate and accelerate its commercial development.

The misconception persists, however, regarding oil shale's fungibility as a crude oil substitute. It doesn't effectively replace crude oil as a gasoline feedstock. Thus, policies that attempt to foster oil shale development come into conflict with regulatory policies that favor gasoline as transportation fuel. The best use of the resource appears to be as feedstock for producing middle-distillate fuels. Regulatory policies that are acting to discourage wider use of middle-distillate fuels thus may be acting as a disincentive to oil shale production. Congress may wish to consider whether a special case should be made for oil shale, and whether to exempt the middle-distillate fuels produced from regulatory policies that restrict their wider use as transportation fuels.

The President's FY2007 budget request would terminate the Energy Department's oil technology research, and the Defense Department's initiative to develop clean fuels from oil shale (among other resources) appears unfunded.[64]

Whether oil shale can be economically produced, even given the current high cost of conventionally recovered petroleum, remains unclear. However, without a long-term concerted effort to produce oil shale, either through a federal- or private sector-sponsored enterprise, the economic viability will remain questionable. The expectation of initial high unit costs should be weighed against the offset in demand for imported products and the effect on lowering price that competition brings.

APPENDIX: LEGISLATIVE HISTORY

The Pickett Act of 1910 initially authorized withdrawal of potential oil-bearing lands in California and Wyoming as sources of fuel for the Navy. Executive orders later created three

Naval Petroleum and Oil Shale Reserves between 1912 and 1927 by setting aside federal lands believed to contain oil as an emergency reserve.

The U.S. Synthetic Liquid Fuels Act of 1944 (30 USC Secs. 321 to 325) authorized $30 million over five years for "the construction and operation of demonstration plants to produce synthetic liquid fuels from coal, oil shales, agricultural and forestry products, and other substances, in order to aid the prosecution of the war, to conserve and increase the oil resources of the Nation, and for other purposes." The act also authorized the Interior Secretary to construct, maintain, and operate plants producing synthetic liquid fuel from coal, oil shale, and agricultural and forestry products. The Bureau of Mines received $87.6 million for an 11-year demonstration plant program.

The Defense Production Act of 1950 (Ch. 932, 64 Stat. 798), enacted during the Korean War, was intended to develop and maintain whatever military and economic strength necessary to support collective action through the United Nations. The diversion of certain materials and facilities from civilian to military use required expansion of production facilities beyond the levels needed to meet civilian demand. Section 303 of Title III (Expansion of Production Capacity and Supply) authorized the President "extraordinary" procurement power to have liquid fuels processed and refined for government use or resale, and to make improvements to government or privately owned facilities engaged in processing and refining liquid fuels when it would aid the national defense. In 1980, Congress added provisions (P.L. 96-294) that related to preparing for terminated or reduced availability of energy supplies for national defense needs. Section 305 of the act authorized the President to purchase synthetic fuels for the purpose of national defense. Executive Order 12242 then directed the Secretary of Defense to determine the quantity and quality of synthetic fuel needed to meet national defense needs for procurement.

The Naval Petroleum Reserves Production Act of 1976 (P.L. 94-258), in reference to Naval Petroleum Reserve No. 4 in Alaska, defined petroleum to include crude oil, gases (including natural gas), natural gasoline, and other related hydrocarbons, oil shale, and the products of such sources.

The Department of Energy Organization Act of 1977 (P.L. 95-9 1) transferred control of the Naval Petroleum and Oil Shale Reserves from the Navy to the Department of Energy.

The United States Synthetic Fuels Corporation Act of 1980 (P.L. 96-294)[65] amended the Defense Production Act by establishing the U.S. Synthetic Fuels Corporation (SFC) "to improve the Nation's balance of payments, reduce the threat of economic disruption from oil supply interruptions, and increase the Nation's security by reducing its dependence on foreign oil." The corporation was authorized to provide financial assistance to qualified projects that produced synthetic fuel from coal, oil shale, tar sands, and heavy oils. Financial assistance could be awarded as loans, loan guarantees, price guarantees, purchase agreements, joint ventures, or combinations of those types of assistance. An Energy Security Reserve fund was also established in the U.S. Treasury and appropriated $19 billion to stimulate alternative fuel production. Executive Order 12242 (1980) directed the Secretary of Defense to determine the quantity and quality of synthetic fuel needed to meet national defense needs for procurement under the Defense Production Act. Executive Order 12346 (Synthetic Fuels) of 1982 revoked EO 12242 and provided for an orderly transition of synthetic fuel responsibilities from the Department of Energy to the United States Synthetic Fuels Corporation.

The Crude Oil Windfall Profit Tax Act of 1980 (P.L. 96-223) ostensibly provided revenue to maintain the Energy Security Reserve fund. The Internal Revenue Code was amended to impose an excise tax on windfall profits of domestic producers of taxable crude oil. A production tax credit of $3.00 (1979 dollars) per barrel of oil equivalent was provided to stimulate oil shale development. The House conference report (H. Rept 96-8 17) projected $227.3 billion in total revenue from the tax after 1988. In the Windfall Profit Tax Account established to hold the revenue, 15% had been allocated for energy and transportation. In 1983, the Congressional Budget Office estimated that the revenue would only reach 40% of the conference report's projection and only 20% by 1988, as the price of crude oil had been lower than projected. Congress repealed the windfall profit tax in 1988 (P.L. 100-418).

The House began considering a bill to abolish the SFC with the Synthetic Fuels Fiscal Responsibility Act of 1985 (H.R. 935). The Energy and Commerce Committee debate of the bill (Rept. 99-196) linked abolishing the Corporation to reducing the federal deficit and viewed purchasing oil for the Strategic Petroleum Reserve as a far more cost effective defense against another embargo by OPEC than subsidizing synthetic fuels. The minority view noted that as late as 1983, the Department of Defense had certified that synthetic fuel was needed to meet national defense needs under Executive Order 12242. In September 1985, the Senate Committee on Appropriations report (S.Rept. 99-14 1) recommended increasing the Department of Energy Oil Shale Program budget and reaffirmed the goal of oil shale reserves supplying petroleum during a national emergency. Support for the SFC could not be sustained, and Congress terminated it under the Consolidated Omnibus Reconciliation Act of 1985 (P.L. 99-272). Remaining obligations were transferred to the Treasury Department, and the duties of the Chairman of the SFC Board were transferred to the Secretary of the Treasury.

The Department of Energy Organization Act of 1977 (P.L. 95-9 1) transferred Navy control of the NOSRs to the Department of Energy. The National Defense Authorization Act of 1998 (P.L. 105-85) transferred NOSR Nos. 1 and 3, located near Rifle, Colorado, from the Department of Energy to the Bureau of Land Management. The National Defense Authorization Act of 2000 (P.L. 106-398) transferred NOSR No. 2 in Utah to the Ute Indian Tribe.

The Oil Shale, Tar Sands, and Other Strategic Unconventional Fuels Act of 2005[66] declares the strategic importance of domestic oil shale resources and their development. The act directs the Secretary of the Interior to commence commercial leasing of oil shale on public lands and to establish a task force in cooperation with the Secretary of Defense to develop a program for commercially developing strategic unconventional fuels, including but not limited to oil shale. Section 2398a. (Procurement of Fuel Derived from Coal, Oil Shale, and Tar Sands) directs the Secretary of Defense to develop a strategy to use fuel produced from oil shale to help meet the fuel requirements of the Department of Defense when the Secretary determines that doing so is in the national interest

End Notes

[1] U.S. DOE Energy Information Administration (EIA), *Monthly Energy Review January 2006*, Table 1.7, Overview of U.S. Petroleum Trade, at [http://www.eia.doe.gov/ emeu/mer/pdf/pages/sec 1_15.pdf], visited Feb. 17, 2006.

[2] Thomas Lonnie, Bureau of Land Management, Testimony before the Senate Energy and Natural Resources Committee, Oversight Hearing on Oil Shale Development Effort, Apr. 12, 2005.

[3] Office of Technology Assessment, *An Assessment of Oil Shale Technologies*, 1980, pp. 89- 91, NTIS order #PB80-210115.

[4] James W. Bunger and Peter M. Crawford, "Is oil shale America's answer to peak-oil challenge?" *Oil & Gas Journal*, Aug. 9, 2004.

[5] The Society of Petroleum Engineers defines true reserves as "those quantities of petroleum which are anticipated to be commercially recoverable from known accumulations from a given date forward." See [http://www.spe.org/spe/j sp/basic/0,, 1 104_1575_1 040460, 00.html] (viewed Feb. 17, 2006).

[6] U.S. DOE EIA, *International Petroleum (Oil) Reserves and Resources*, at [http://www.eia.doe.gov/emeu/international/oilreserves.html], visited Feb. 17, 2006.

[7] U.S. DOE, *Naval Petroleum & Oil Shale Reserves, Annual Report of Operations Fiscal Year 1995* (DOE/FE-0342).

[8] John M. Hunt, *Petroleum Geochemistry and Geology*, W.H. Freeman and Co., 1979.

[9] C_n is shorthand notation for the number of carbon atoms. John M. Hunt, *Petroleum Geochemistry and Geology*, W.H. Freeman and Co., 1979

[10] Exxon Research and Engineering Co., *Fundamental Synthetic Fuel Stability Study, First Annual Report for May 1, 1979 to April 30, 1981.*

[11] James H. Gary and Glenn E. Handwerk, *Petroleum Refining, Technology and Economics* 4th ed., 2001. (Hereafter cited as Gary and Handwerk, Petroleum Refining: Technology and Economics.)

[12] *Octane* number refers to the gasoline property that reduces detrimental knocking in a spark-ignition engine. In early research, iso-octane (C_8-length branched hydrocarbon molecules) caused the least knock and was rated 100. Cetane number refers to a similar property for diesel fuel, for which normal hexadecane ($C_{16}H_{34}$) is the standard molecule.

[13] The term "crack spread" refers to the 3-2-1 ratio of crude-gasoline-distillate. The crack spread and the 3-2-1 crack is a hypothetical calculation used by the New York Mercantile Exchange for trading purposes.

[14] Gary and Handwerk, *Petroleum Refining: Technology and Economics.*

[15] Hydroprocessing describes all the processes that react hydrocarbons with hydrogen to synthesize high-value fuels. Hydrocracking reduces denser molecular weight hydrocarbons to lower boiling range products (predominantly gasoline). Impurities such as sulfur are removed by hydrotreating. Refineries produce the hydrogen needed for hydrotreating either by steam reformation of methane (liberated during the atmospheric distillation) or from a vendor who similarly converts natural gas (methane) to hydrogen. Alan G. Bridge "Hydrogen Processing," Chapter 14.1, in *Handbook of Petroleum Refining Processes*, 2nd ed., McGraw-Hill, 1996.

[16] Robert E. Maples, *Petroleum Refinery Process Economics*, 2nd ed., Penwell Corp., 2000.

[17] Ibid., Table 4-1.

[18] Cohen, Linda R. and Roger G. Noll, "The Technology Pork Barrel," Chapter 10, in *Synthetics from Coal*, Washington, DC: The Brookings Institution, 1991.

[19] OTA, Ch. 5 — Technology, p. 157.

[20] API gravity refers to the American Petroleum Institute measure of crude oil density — the higher the API gravity, the lighter the crude oil's density. Light crudes exceed 38° API, intermediate crudes range 22° to 38° API, and heavy crudes fall below 22° API.

[21] Platt's *Oil Guide to Specifications*, 1999 [http://www.emis.platts.com/thezone/guides/platts/oil/crudeoilspecs.html], viewed Apr. 5, 2006.

[22] New York Mercantile Exchange, *Exchange Rulebook*, Light "Sweet" Crude Oil Futures Contract, at [http://www.nymex.com/rule_main.aspx], visited Aug. 25, 2005.

[23] Testimony of Stephen Mut, Shell Unconventional Resources Energy Oil, *Shale and Oil Sands Resources Hearing*, Senate Energy and Natural Resources Committee, Tuesday, Apr. 12, 2005.

[24] Jack S. Savage, Oil Tech, Inc., Testimony before the *Hearing on The Vast North American Resource Potential of Oil Shale, Oil Sands, and Heavy Oils — Part 1*, House Subcommittee on Energy and Mineral Resources, June 23, 2005.

[25] Personal communication with William E. Harrison III, Office of Deputy Under Secretary of Defense for Advanced Systems and Concepts, Oct. 25, 2005.

[26] The Center for Land Use Integration, *Unocal Oil Shale Plant*, at [http://ludb.clui.org/ ex/i/CO3191/], visited Mar. 28, 2006.

[27] Garfield County, Colorado, *Garfield County Comprehensive Plan Revision, Study Area Five*, adopted version, Apr. 24, 2002, at [http://garfield-county.com/home/index.asp?page =664], visited Mar. 28, 2006.

[28] H.Rept. 99-196, Part 1, July 11, 1985.

[29] Daniel Yergin, *The Prize*, Touchstone, 1991, pp. 722-725.

[30] The Senate Energy and Natural Resources Committee, *Oversight Hearing on Oil Shale Development Effort*, Apr. 12, 2005.

[31] Also cited as the Oil Shale, Tar Sands, and Other Strategic Unconventional Fuels Act of 2005.

[32] 30 USC 241 (4) "For the privilege of mining, extracting, and disposing of oil or other minerals covered by a lease under this section ... no one person, association, or corporation shall acquire or hold more than 50,000 acres of oil shale leases in any one State."

[33] Bureau of Land Management, *BLM Announces Results of Review of Oil Shale Research Nominations*, Jan. 17, 2006, at [http://www.blm.gov/nhp/news/releases/pages/2006/ pr0601 17_oilshale.htm], visited Mar. 29, 2006.

[34] Personal communication with Dr. Theodore K. Barna, Feb. 8, 2006.

[35] U.S. DOE EIA, *Imported Crude Oil Prices: Nominal and Real*, at [http://www.eia.doe.gov/emeu/ steo/pub/fsheets/petroleumprices.xls], visited Apr. 5, 2006.

[36] U.S. DOE EIA, *Annual Energy Outlook 2006 with Projections to 2030 (Early Release) — Overview*, December 2005, at[http://www.eia.doe.gov/oiaf/aeo/key.html], visited Apr. 5, 2006.

[37] U.S. DOE EIA, *Gasoline and Diesel Fuel Update*, at [http://tonto.eia.doe.gov/oog/ info/gdu/gasdiesel.asp], visited Apr. 5, 2006.

[38] U.S. DOE EIA, *Performance Profiles of Major Energy Producers 2004*,Table 11, Income Components and Financial Ratios in Oil and Natural Gas Production for FRS Companies, 2003 and 2004, at [http://www.eia.doe.gov/emeu/perfpro/], visited Apr. 12, 2006.

[39] Exxon Mobil Corp, *Form 10-K*, Average sales prices and production costs per unit of production — consolidated subsidiaries Feb. 28, 2006.

[40] Thomas R. Stauffer, "Trends In Oil Production Costs In The Middle East, Elsewhere," *Oil & Gas Journal*, Mar. 21, 1994.

[41] "U.S. Oil Dumping Case Wins Investigation By Commerce," *Oil & Gas Journal*, Oct. 2, 2000.

[42] *1980 vs. 2004 Refinery Inflation Index* and *1980 vs. 2004 Refinery Operating Index* from the Nelson-Farrar Cost Indexes, *Oil & Gas Journal* (published first issue each month).

[43] "U.S. appears to have built last refinery," *Alexander's Gas & Oil Connections*, vol. 6, issue 13, Jul. 17, 2001.

[44] U.S. DOE EIA, *Performance Profiles of Major Energy Producers 2004*, Table 15, U.S. Refined Product Margins and Costs per Barrel Sold and Product Sales Volume for FRSCompanies, 2003-2004, at [http://www.eia.doe.gov/emeu/perfpro/], visited Apr. 12, 2006.

[45] U.S. DOE EIA, *Crude Oil Refiner Acquisitions Costs*, Table 5.21, 1968-2004, at [http://www.eia.doe.gov/emeu/aer/txt/ptb052 1 .html], visited Feb. 21, 2006.

[46] Bartis, James, T., et al., *Oil Shale Development in the United States*, The Rand Corporation, 2005.

[47] "Is Oil Shale America's Answer to Peak-Oil Challenge?" *Oil & Gas Journal*, Aug. 9, 2004.

[48] The last new U.S. refinery was built in 1976 by Marathon Ashland in Garyville, Louisiana. U.S. DOE EIA, *Country Analysis Briefs — United States of America January, 2005*, at [http://www.eia.doe.gov/emeu/cabs/usa.html], visited Apr. 5, 2006.

[49] U.S. DOE EIA, *Refinery Utilization and Capacity*, at [http://tonto.eia.doe.gov/ dnav/pet/pet_pnp_top.asp.], visited Feb. 22, 2006.

[50] U.S. DOE EIA, *Petroleum Supply Annual 2004*, vol. 1, Table 19, Percent Refinery Yield of Petroleum Products by PAD and Refining Districts, 2004, at [http://www.eia.doe.gov/ oil_gas/petroleum/ data_publications/petroleum_supply_annual/psa_volume 1/ps a_volum e1.html], visited Apr. 5, 2006.

[51] "Crude Awakening," *Investor's Business Daily*, Mar. 28, 2005.

[52] Energy Intelligence Group, "European Refiners Need to Bite Bullet of Downstream Investment," Mar. 14, 2005, at [http://www.energyintel.com/].

[53] Ward's Automotive Yearbook 2005, *U.S. Diesel Car Market Share*, p. 36.

[54] U.S. DOE EIA, *Can U.S. Supply Accommodate Shifts to Diesel-Fueled Light-Duty Vehicles?*, Oct. 7, 2005.

[55] "The Changing Face of Europe's Car Industry,"*The Economist Newspaper Ltd*, Mar. 24, 2005.

[56] International Energy Agency, IEA Energy Statistics, *Monthly Oil Survey*, at [http://www.iea.org/ Textbase/stats/oilresult.asp], visited Apr. 12, 2006.

[57] "Emission Taxes Could Displace Registration Taxes," *The Economist Newspaper Ltd.*, Mar. 24, 2005.

[58] U.S. EPA, "Control of Air Pollution from Motor Vehicles: Heavy-Duty Engine and Vehicle Standards and Highway Diesel Fuel Sulfur Control Requirements: Final Rule," *Federal Register*, 40 CFR, Parts 69, 80, and 86.

[59] U.S. DOE EIA, *The Transition to Ultra-Low-Sulfur Diesel Fuel: Effects on Prices and Supply*, May 2001.

[60] U.S. DOT, "Federal Tax Rates on Motor Fuels and Lubricating Oil," Table Fe-101a., at [http://www.fhwa.dot.gov/policy/ohim/hs03/htm/fe 10 1a.htm]. The effective tax rate on gasoline and diesel terminated Oct. 1, 2005; new rates have not yet been published.

[61] EurActive, *Fuel Taxation*, Nov. 25, 2003, at [http://www.euractiv.com/Article? tcmuri=tcm:29-1 17495-16&type=LinksDossier], visited Apr. 5, 2006.

[62] International Energy Agency, *End-user Petroleum Product Prices and Average Crude Oil Import Costs, December 2005*, Jan. 6, 2006.

[63] President George W. Bush, *State of the Union*, Jan. 31, 2006.

[64] Personal communication with Dr. Theodore K. Barna, Feb. 8, 2006.

[65] Title I, Part B of the Energy Security Act of 1980.

[66] Section 369 of the Energy Policy Act of 2005.

In: Federal Land Resources
Editors: Quintin R. Telles

ISBN: 978-1-60692-130-2

Chapter 3

OFFSHORE OIL AND GAS DEVELOPMENT: LEGAL FRAMEWORK*

Adam Vann

SUMMARY

The development of offshore oil, gas, and other mineral resources in the United States is impacted by a number of interrelated legal regimes, including international, federal, and state laws. International law provides a framework for establishing national ownership or control of offshore areas, and domestic federal law mirrors and supplements these standards.

Governance of offshore minerals and regulation of development activities are bifurcated between state and federal law. Generally, states have primary authority in the three geographical mile area extending from their coasts. The federal government and its comprehensive regulatory regime governs those minerals located in federal waters, which extend from the states' offshore boundaries out to at least 200 nautical miles from the shore. The basis for most federal regulation is the Outer Continental Shelf Lands Act (OCSLA), which provides a system for offshore oil and gas development planning, leasing, exploration, and ultimate development. Regulations run the gamut from health, safety, and environmental standards to requirements for production based royalties and, when appropriate, royalty relief and other development incentives.

Several contentious legal issues remain the subject of national debate and legislative proposals. Before adjournment, the 109th Congress passed a bill that would allow new offshore drilling in the Gulf of Mexico in an area known as Lease Area 181. This measure was incorporated into H.R. 6111, a broad bill passed in the final days of the 109th Congress. President Bush signed the bill into law (P.L. 109- 432) on December 20, 2006.

At the same time, the role of the coastal states in deciding whether to lease in areas adjacent to their shores has also received recent attention, with some legislative proposals granting significant decisional authority to state governments while others would direct the Secretary of the Interior to lease specific areas, limiting the state role to what is provided under existing statutes.

* This is an edited, reformatted and augmented edition of a Congressional Research Service publication, Report RL33404, dated January 30, 2008

In addition to these legislative efforts, there has also been significant litigation related to offshore oil and gas development. Cases handed down over a number of years have clarified the extent of the Secretary's discretion in deciding how leasing and development are to be conducted.

The development of offshore oil, gas, and other mineral resources in the United States is impacted by a number of interrelated legal regimes, including international, federal, and state laws. International law provides a framework for establishing national ownership or control of offshore areas, and United States domestic law has, in substance, adopted these internationally recognized principles. U.S. domestic law further defines U.S. ocean resource jurisdiction and ownership of offshore minerals, dividing regulatory authority and ownership between the states and the federal government based on the resource's proximity to the shore. This chapter[1] explains the nature of U.S. authority over offshore areas pursuant to international and domestic law. It also describes the laws, at both the state and federal levels, governing the development of offshore oil and gas and the litigation that has flowed from development under the current legal regimes. Also included is an outline of the recent changes to the authorities regulating offshore development wrought by the Energy Policy Act of 2005 and subsequent legislation enacted by the 109th Congress prior to adjournment. Finally, this chapter discusses legislation under consideration by the 1 10th Congress that might also amend existing law in this area.

Ocean Resource Jurisdiction

Under the United Nations Convention on the Law of the Sea,[2] coastal nations are entitled to exercise varying levels of authority over a series of adjacent offshore zones. Nations may claim a twelve nautical mile territorial sea, over which they may exercise rights comparable to, in most significant respects, sovereignty. An additional area, termed the contiguous zone and extending 24 nautical miles from the coast (or baseline), may also be claimed. In this area, coastal nations may regulate in so far as necessary to protect the territorial sea and to enforce their customs, fiscal, immigration, and sanitary laws. Further, in the contiguous zone and an additional area, the exclusive economic zone (EEZ), coastal nations have sovereign rights to explore, exploit, conserve, and manage marine resources and jurisdiction over:

(i) the establishment and use of artificial islands, installations and structures;
(ii) marine scientific research; and
(iii) the protection and preservation of the marine environment.[3]

The EEZ extends 200 nautical miles from a nation's recognized coastline. This area overlaps substantially with another offshore area designation, the continental shelf. International law defines a nation's continental shelf as the seabed and subsoil of the submarine areas that extend beyond either "the natural prolongation of [a coastal nation's] land territory to the outer edge of the continental margin, or to a distance of 200 nautical miles from the baselines from which the breadth of the territorial sea is measured where the outer edge of the continental margin does not extend up to that distance."[4] In general, however, a nation's continental shelf cannot extend beyond 350 nautical miles from its recognized coastline regardless of submarine geology.[5] In this area, as in the EEZ, a coastal nation may claim "sovereign rights" for the purpose of exploring and exploiting the natural resources of its continental shelf.[6]

Federal Jurisdiction

While a signatory to UNCLOS, the United States has not ratified the treaty. Regardless, many of its provisions are now generally accepted principles of customary international law and, through a series of Executive Orders, the United States has claimed offshore zones for itself that are virtually identical to those described in the treaty.[7] In a series of related cases, the U.S. Supreme Court confirmed federal control of these offshore areas.[8] Federal statutes also regularly refer to these areas and, in some instances, define them as well. Of particular relevance, the primary federal law governing offshore oil and gas development indicates that it applies to the "outer Continental Shelf," which it defines as "all submerged lands lying seaward and outside of the areas ... [under state control] and of which the subsoil and seabed appertain to the United States and are subject to its jurisdiction and control...."[9] Thus, the U.S. Outer Continental Shelf (OCS) would appear to comprise an area extending at least 200 nautical miles from the official U.S. coastline and possibly further where the geological continental shelf extends beyond that point. The federal government's legal authority to provide for and to regulate offshore oil and gas development therefore applies to seemingly all areas under U.S. control except where U.S. waters have been placed under the primary jurisdiction of the states.

State Jurisdiction

In accordance with the federal Submerged Lands Act of 1953 (SLA),[10] coastal states are generally entitled to an area extending three geographical miles[11] from their officially recognized coast (or baseline).[12] In order to accommodate the claims of certain states, the SLA provides for an extended three marine league[13] seaward boundary in the Gulf of Mexico if a state can show such a boundary was provided for by the state's "constitution or laws prior to or at the time such State became a member of the Union, or if it has been heretofore approved by Congress."[14] After enactment of the SLA, the Supreme Court of the United States held that the Gulf coast boundaries of Florida and Texas do extend to the three marine league limit; other Gulf coast states were unsuccessful in their challenges.[15]

Within their offshore boundaries, coastal states have "(1) title to and ownership of the lands beneath navigable waters within the boundaries of the respective states, and (2) the right and power to manage, administer, lease, develop and use the said lands and natural resources...."[16] Accordingly, coastal states have the option of developing offshore oil and gas within their waters; if they choose to develop, they may regulate that development.

Coastal State Regulation

State laws governing oil and gas development in state waters vary significantly from jurisdiction to jurisdiction. Some state laws are limited to a single paragraph and do not differentiate between onshore and offshore state resources; other states do not distinguish between oil and gas and other types of minerals. In addition to regulation aimed specifically at oil and gas development, it should be noted that a variety of other laws could impact offshore development, such as environmental and wildlife protection laws and coastal zone management regulation. Finally, in states that authorize offshore oil and gas leasing, they decide which lands will be opened for development. Appendix A of this chapter contains a table of state laws banning or otherwise regulating offshore mineral development. The table indicates which state agency is primarily responsible for authorizing oil and gas development and if state oil and gas leasing is limited to specific areas by statute.

Federal Resources

The primary federal law governing development of oil and gas in federal waters is the Outer Continental Shelf Lands Act (OCSLA).[17] As stated above, the OCSLA codifies federal control of the OCS, declaring that the submerged lands seaward of the state's offshore boundaries appertain to the U.S. federal government. More than simply declaring federal control, the OCSLA has as its primary purpose "expeditious and orderly development [of OCS resources], subject to environmental safeguards, in a manner which is consistent with the maintenance of competition and other national needs...."[18] To effectuate this purpose, the OCSLA extends application of federal laws to certain structures and devices located on the OCS,[19] provides that the law of adjacent states will apply to the OCS when it does not conflict with federal law,[20] and, significantly, provides a comprehensive leasing process for certain OCS mineral resources and a system for collecting and distributing royalties from the sale of these federal mineral resources.[21] The OCSLA thus provides comprehensive regulation of the development of OCS oil and gas resources.

Moratoria

Although in general the OCSLA requires the federal government to prepare, revise and maintain an oil and gas leasing program, many offshore areas are withdrawn from disposition under the OCSLA. There are currently two broad categories of OCS moratoria, those imposed by the President under authority granted by the Outer Continental Shelf Lands Act[22] and those imposed directly by Congress, which have most often taken the form of limitations on the use of appropriated funds.[23] Congressionally imposed moratoria have been imposed since the early 1980s and have been approved annually thereafter. In 1990, President Bush issued a directive essentially paralleling the congressionally mandated moratoria, prohibiting most oil and gas development outside of the offshore areas associated with (though not belonging to) Texas, Louisiana, and Alabama.[24] This presidential withdrawal was to be effective until after the year 2000. In 1998, President Clinton issued a new executive branch moratorium, lasting until June 30, 2012.[25] The Clinton order refers to the 1997 congressional moratorium[26] and adopts the substance of that enactment expressly, which itself included by reference those areas covered by the 1990 presidential withdrawal. The provisions of the moratorium state the following:

SEC. 108. No funds provided in this title may be expended by the Department of the Interior for the conduct of offshore leasing and related activities placed under restriction in the **President's moratorium** statement of June 26, 1990, in the areas of northern, central, and southern California; the North Atlantic; Washington and Oregon; and the eastern Gulf of Mexico south of 26 degrees north latitude and east of 86 degrees west longitude.

SEC. 109. No funds provided in this title may be expended by the Department of the Interior for the conduct of offshore oil and natural gas preleasing, leasing, and related activities, on lands within the North Aleutian Basin planning area.

SEC. 110. No funds provided in this title may be expended by the Department of the Interior to conduct offshore oil and natural gas preleasing, leasing and related activities in the eastern Gulf of Mexico planning area for any lands located outside Sale 181, as identified in the final Outer Continental Shelf 5- Year Oil and Gas Leasing Program, 1997-2002.

SEC. 111. No funds provided in this title may be expended by the Department of the Interior to conduct oil and natural gas preleasing, leasing and related activities in the Mid-Atlantic and South Atlantic planning areas.[27]

In addition, the President also withdrew from disposition by leasing all areas on the OCS designated as Marine Sanctuaries at the time. Areas under moratoria as of March 2006 are depicted in **Figure 1**.[28]

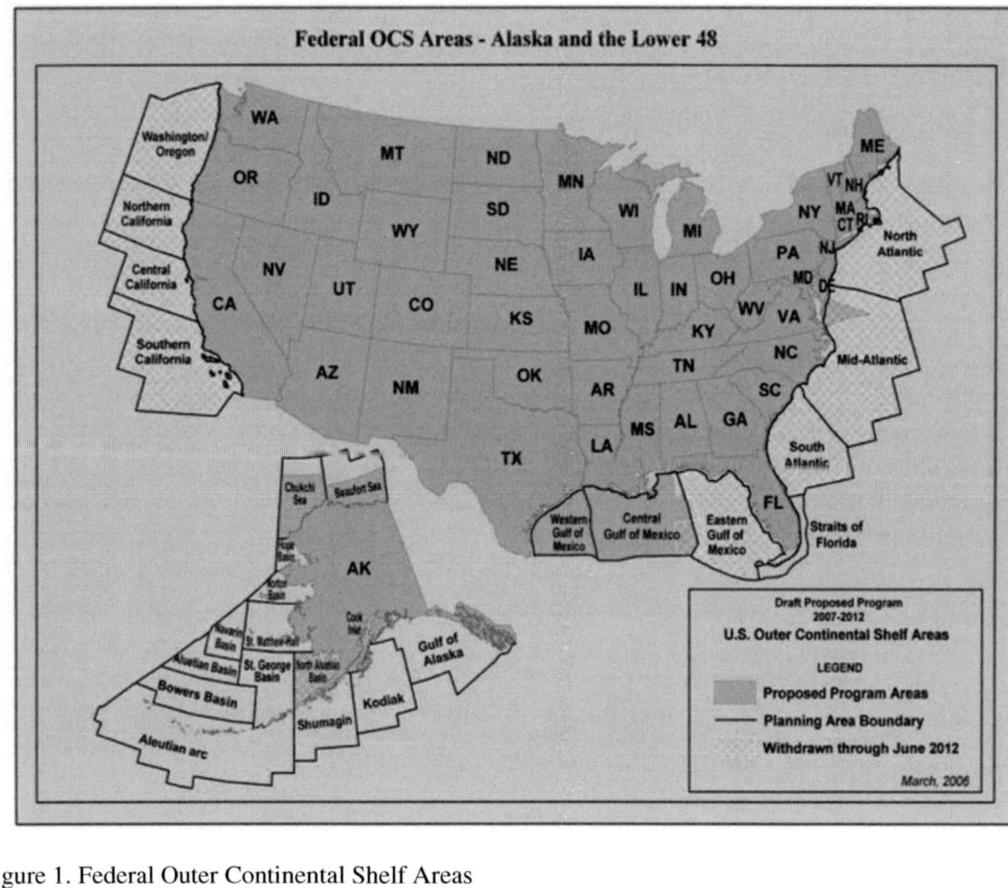

Figure 1. Federal Outer Continental Shelf Areas

Congressionally imposed moratoria have closely paralleled the structure and the substance of the Clinton-era withdrawal order discussed above. However, one significant legal difference does exist. The presidential withdrawal only prevents the "disposition by leasing" of the OCS areas it references. Thus, other activities authorized by the OCSLA, such as planning for lease sales or initial oil and gas exploration, might still be carried on in the absence of additional prohibitions. The congressional moratoria have consistently contained broader restrictions. These enactments typically preclude the expenditure of appropriated funds "for the conduct of offshore leasing and related activities" or, even more specifically, "for the conduct of offshore oil and natural gas preleasing, leasing, and related activities."[29] Thus, congressionally imposed moratoria would generally appear to have the effect of prohibiting leasing, exploration, planning for lease sales and other OCS oil and gas related activities authorized by the OCSLA. The enactment of the Energy Policy Act of 2005 does appear to alter this, however. Section 357 of that act requires the Secretary of the Interior to conduct an inventory and analysis of oil and natural gas resources beneath all of the waters of the U.S. OCS.[30] The law permits some forms of exploration, including 3-D seismic technology, but prohibits drilling. The inventory is to include analysis of the existing regulatory structure, including the moratoria, and assess the extent to which relevant laws and policies "restrict or impede the development of identified resources and the extent that they affect domestic supply...."[31]

Bills are often introduced to amend or alter existing prohibitions on OCS development. For example, the Gulf of Mexico Energy Security Act of 2006 was enacted just before adjournment of the 109th Congress as part of H.R. 6111, the omnibus Tax Relief and Health Care Act of 2006.[32] This measure provides for the oil and gas leasing in an area in the Gulf of Mexico known as "181 Area." Large portions of this Area are to be offered for oil or gas leasing pursuant to the leasing terms of the OCSLA as soon as practicable after enactment of the act.[33] Leasing in this area had been prohibited under P.L. 105-83.

Leasing and Development

The Secretary of the Interior oversees OCS mineral leasing, with the leasing of tracts and royalty collection performed by the Minerals Management Service (MMS), a bureau of the Department of Interior (DOI).[34] In 1978, the OCSLA was significantly amended so as to increase the role of the affected coastal states in the leasing process.[35] The amendments also revised the bidding process and leasing procedures, set stricter criteria to guide the DOI environmental review process, and established new safety and environmental standards to govern drilling operations.

The OCS leasing process consists of four distinct stages: (1) the five-year planning program,[36] (2) the lease sale,[37] (3) exploration,[38] and (4) development and production.[39]

The Five-Year Plan

The Secretary of the Interior is required to prepare a five-year leasing plan, subject to annual revisions, that governs any offshore leasing that takes place during the period of plan coverage.[40] Each five-year plan establishes a schedule of proposed lease sales, providing the timing, size, and general location of the leasing activities. This plan is to be based on multiple considerations, including the Secretary's determination as to what will best meet national energy needs for the five-year period and the extent of potential economic, social, and environmental impacts associated with development.[41]

During the development of the plan, the Secretary must solicit and consider comments from the Governors of affected states, and at least sixty days prior to publication of the plan in the *Federal Register*, the plan is to be submitted to the Governor of each affected state for further comments.[42] After publication, the Attorney General is also authorized to submit comments regarding potential effects on competition.[43] Subsequently, at least sixty days prior to its approval, the plan is to be submitted to Congress and the President, along with any received comments and an explanation for the rejection of any comment.[44] Once the leasing plan is approved, tracts included in the plan will be available for leasing, consistent with the terms of the plan.[45]

The development of the five-year plan is considered a major federal action significantly affecting the quality of the human environment and as such requires preparation of an environmental impact statement (EIS) under the National Environmental Policy Act (NEPA).[46] Thus, the NEPA review process complements and informs the preparation of a five-year plan under the OCSLA.[47]

Leasing

The lease sale process involves multiple steps as well. Leasing decisions are impacted by a variety of federal laws; however, it is section 8 of the OCSLA and its implementing regulations that establish the mechanics of the leasing process.[48]

The process begins when the Director of MMS publishes a call for information and nominations regarding potential lease areas. The Director is authorized to receive and consider these various expressions of interest in lease areas and comments on which areas should receive special concern and analysis.[49] The Director is then to consider all available information and perform environmental analysis under NEPA in crafting both a list of areas recommended for leasing and any proposed lease stipulations.[50] This list is submitted to the Secretary of the Interior and, upon the Secretary's approval, published in the *Federal Register* and submitted to the Governors of potentially affected states.[51]

The OCSLA and its regulations authorize the Governor of an affected state and the executive of any local government within an affected state to submit to the Secretary any recommendations concerning the size, time, or location[52] of a proposed lease sale within sixty days after notice of the lease sale.[53] The Secretary must accept the Governor's recommendations (and has discretion to accept a local government executive's recommendations) if the Secretary determines that the recommendations reasonably balance the national interest and the well-being of the citizens of an affected state.[54]

The Director of MMS publishes the approved list of lease sale offerings in the *Federal Register* (and other publications) at least thirty days prior to the date of the sale.[55] This notice must describe the areas subject to the sale and any stipulations, terms, and conditions of the sale.[56] The bidding is to occur under conditions described in the notice and must be consistent with certain baseline requirements established in the OCSLA.[57]

Although the statute establishes base requirements for the competitive bidding process and sets forth a variety of bid formats,[58] many of these requirements are subject to significant modification at the discretion of the Secretary.[59] Before the acceptance of bids, the Attorney General is also authorized to review proposed lease sales to analyze any potential effects on competition, and may subsequently recommend action to the Secretary of the Interior as may be necessary to prevent violation of antitrust laws.[60] The Secretary is not bound by the Attorney General's recommendation, and likewise, the antitrust review process does not affect private rights of action under antitrust laws or otherwise restrict the powers of the Attorney General or any other federal agency under other law.[61] Assuming compliance with these bidding requirements, the Secretary may grant a lease to the highest bidder, although deviation from this standard may occur under a variety of circumstances.[62]

In addition, the OCSLA prescribes many minimum conditions that all leases must contain. The statute supplies generally applicable minimum royalty or net profit share rates, as necessitated by the bidding format adopted, subject, under certain conditions, to Secretarial modification. Indeed, several provisions authorize royalty reductions or suspensions. Royalty rates or net profit shares may be reduced below the general minimums or eliminated to promote increased production.[63] For leases located in "the Western and Central Planning Areas of the Gulf of Mexico and the portion of the Eastern Planning Area of the Gulf of Mexico encompassing whole lease blocks lying west of 87 degrees, 30 minutes West longitude and in the Planning Areas offshore Alaska," a broader authority is also provided, allowing the Secretary, with the lessee's consent, to make "other modifications" to royalty or profit share requirements to encourage increased production.[64] Additionally, the 2005 Energy Policy Act also authorizes royalty relief in the form of reduced payments if 44 cents for every dollar owed to the federal government is paid to the state of Louisiana instead.[65] The lease generating these royalty payments does not necessarily have to be located adjacent to Louisiana waters. Indeed, all OCS leases are covered by the provision. However, in order to take advantage of the reduction, the lessee must have had "an ownership interest in State of Louisiana leases SL10087, SL10088 or SL10187, or ownership interests in the production or proceeds therefrom, as established by assignment, contract or otherwise" as of August 18, 1990.[66] Royalties may also be suspended pursuant to the Outer Continental Shelf Deep Water Royalty Relief Act.

The OCSLA also generally requires successful bidders to furnish a variety of up-front payments and performance bonds upon being granted a lease.[67] Additional provisions require that leases provide that certain amounts of production be sold to small or independent refiners. Further, leases must contain the conditions stated in the sale notice and provide for suspension or cancellation of the lease pursuant to section 1334.[68] Finally, the law indicates that a lease entitles the lessee to explore, develop and produce oil and gas, conditioned on applicable due diligence requirements and the approval of a development and production plan, discussed below.[69]

Exploration

Exploration for oil and gas pursuant to an OCSLA lease must comply with an approved exploration plan.[70] Detailed information and analysis must accompany the submission of an exploration plan, and, upon receipt of a complete proposed plan, the relevant MMS Regional Supervisor is required to submit the plan to the Governor of an affected state and the state's Coastal Zone Management agency.[71]

Under the federal Coastal Zone Management Act (CZMA), federal actions and federally permitted projects, even in federal waters, must be submitted for state review.[72] The purpose of this review is to ensure consistency with state Coastal Zone Management Programs as contemplated by the federal law. When a state determines that a lessee's plan is inconsistent with its Coastal Zone Management Program, the lessee must either reform its plan to accommodate those objections and resubmit it for MMS and state approval or succeed in appealing the state's determination to the Secretary of Commerce.[73] Simultaneously, the MMS Regional Supervisor is to analyze the environmental impacts of the proposed exploration activities under NEPA; however, it should be noted that regulations prescribe that MMS complete its action on the plan review within thirty days. Hence, extensive environmental review at this stage may be constrained or rely heavily upon previously prepared NEPA documents.[74] If the Regional Supervisor disapproves the proposed exploration plan, the lessee is entitled to a list of necessary modifications and may resubmit the plan to address those issues.[75] Once a plan has been approved, drilling associated with exploration remains subject to the relevant MMS District Supervisor's approval of an Application for a Permit to Drill, which involves analysis of even more specific drilling plans.

Development and Production

While exploration will regularly involve drilling wells, the scale of such activities will significantly increase during the development and production phase. Accordingly, additional regulatory review and environmental analysis are required by the OCSLA before this stage begins.[76] Operators are required to submit a Development and Production Plan for areas where significant development has not occurred before[77] or a less extensive Development Operations Coordination Document for those areas, such as certain portions of the Western Gulf of Mexico, where significant activities have already taken place.[78] The information required to accompany submission of these documents is similar to that required at the exploration phase, but must address the larger scale of operations.[79] As with the processes outlined above, the submission of these documents complements the Department's and MMS's environmental analysis under NEPA. As with the exploration plan review process, it may not always be necessary that a new EIS be prepared at this stage, and environmental analysis may be tied to previously prepared NEPA documents.[80] In addition, affected states are allowed, under the OCSLA, to submit comments on proposed Development and Production Plans and to review these plans for consistency with state Coastal Zone Management Programs.[81] Additionally, if the drilling project involves "non-conventional production or completion technology, regardless of water depth" applicants must also submit a Deepwater Operations Plan (DWOP) and a Conceptual Plan.[82] These additional documents allow MMS to adequately review the engineering, safety, and environmental impacts associated with these technologies.[83]

As with the exploration stage, actual drilling cannot take place without approval of an Application for Permit to Drill (APD).[84] An APD focuses on the specifics of particular wells and associated machinery. Thus, an application must include a plat indicating the well's proposed location, information regarding the various design elements of the proposed well, and a drilling prognosis, among other things.[85]

Lease Suspension and Cancellation

The OCSLA authorizes the Secretary of the Interior to promulgate regulations on lease suspension and cancellation.[86] The Secretary's discretion over the use of these authorities is specifically limited to a set number of circumstances established by the OCSLA. These authorities are described below.

Suspension of otherwise authorized OCS activities may generally occur at the request of a lessee or at the direction of the relevant MMS Regional Supervisor, given appropriate justification.[87] Under the statute, a lease may be suspended (1) when it is in the national interest, (2) to facilitate proper development of a lease, (3) to allow for the construction or negotiation for use of transportation facilities, or (4) when there is "a threat of serious, irreparable, or immediate harm or damage to life (including fish and other aquatic life), to property, to any mineral deposits (in areas leased or not leased), or to the marine, coastal, or human environment...."[88] The regulations also indicate that leases may be suspended for other reasons, including (1) when necessary to comply with judicial decrees, (2) to allow for the installation of safety or environmental protection equipment, (3) to carry out NEPA or other environmental review requirements, or (4) to allow for "inordinate delays encountered in obtaining required permits or consents...."[89] Whenever suspension occurs, the OCSLA generally requires that the term of an affected lease or permit be extended by a length of time equal to the period of suspension.[90] This extension requirement does not apply when the suspension results from a lessee's "gross negligence or willful violation of such lease or permit, or of regulations issued with respect to such lease or permit...."[91]

After a suspension period of, in general, five years,[92] the Secretary may cancel a lease upon holding a hearing and finding that (1) continued activity pursuant to a lease or permit would "probably cause serious harm or damage to life (including fish and other aquatic life), to property, to any mineral (in areas leased or not leased), to the national security or defense, or to the marine, coastal, or human environment" (2) "the threat of harm or damage will not disappear or decrease to an acceptable extent within a reasonable period of time" and (3) "the advantages of cancellation outweigh the advantages of continuing such lease or permit in force...."[93]

Upon cancellation, the OCSLA entitles lessees to certain damages. The statute calculates damages at the lesser of (1) the fair value of the canceled rights on the date of cancellation[94] or (2) the excess of the consideration paid for the lease, plus all of the lessee's exploration- or development-related expenditures, plus interest, over the lessee's revenues from the lease.[95]

The OCSLA also indicates that the "continuance in effect" of any lease is subject to a lessee's compliance with the regulations issued pursuant to the OCSLA, and failure to comply with the provisions of the OCSLA, an applicable lease, or the regulations may authorize the Secretary to cancel a lease as well.[96] Under these circumstances, a nonproducing lease can be canceled if the Secretary sends notice by registered mail to the lease owner and the noncompliance with the statute lease or regulations continues for a period of thirty days after the mailing.[97] Similar noncompliance by the owner of a producing lease can result in cancellation after an appropriate proceeding in any United States district court with jurisdiction as provided for under the OCSLA.[98]

LEGAL CHALLENGES TO OFFSHORE LEASING

Multiple statutes govern aspects of offshore oil and gas development and therefore may give rise to legal challenges. Certainly, violations of the Clean Water Act,[99] Endangered Species Act,[100] and other environmental laws have provided mechanisms for challenging actions associated with offshore oil and gas production in the past.[101] Of primary interest here, however, are legal challenges to agency action with respect to the planning, leasing, exploration, and development phases under the procedures mandated by the OCSLA itself and the related environmental review required by the National Environmental Policy Act. An overview of the relevant case law follows.

Suits under the Outer Continental Shelf Lands Act

The OCSLA provides for judicial review of agency action alleged to be in violation of federal law, including the OCSLA, its implementing regulations, and the terms of any permit or lease.[102] The following paragraphs provide an overview of the existing case law and address the limitations applicable to relief at each phase of the leasing and development process.

Jurisdiction to review agency actions taken in approving the five-year plan is vested in the U.S. Court of Appeals for the D.C. Circuit, subject to appellate review by writ of certiorari to the U.S. Supreme Court.[103] It appears that only three challenges to the five-year plan have been brought to court. The first, *California ex. rel. Brown v. Watt,*[104] involved a variety of challenges to the 1980 — 1985 plan, and, while the court ultimately found that the Secretary had failed to comply with certain procedural requirements in making determinations, the court established a relatively deferential standard of review, which it has continued to apply in later challenges. When reviewing "findings of ascertainable fact made by the Secretary," the court will require the Secretary's decisions to be supported by "substantial evidence."[105] However, the court noted that many of the decisions required in the formulation of the five-year plan will involve the determination of policy in the face of disputed facts, and that such determinations should be subject to a less searching standard. In such instances, a court will examine agency action and determine whether "the decision is based on a consideration of the relevant factors and whether there has been a clear error of judgment."[106]

The standards for review outlined in *Watt* have been upheld in subsequent litigation related to the five-year plan.[107] In these subsequent cases, the Court of Appeals for the D.C. Circuit applied a deferential standard in reviewing the Secretary's decisions, particularly in reviewing the Secretary's environmental impact determinations, such that the Secretary could perform environmental analysis using "any methodology so long as it is not irrational."[108] Further, these cases indicate that the Secretary is vested with significant discretion in determining which areas are to be offered for leasing and which areas will not. Thus, while the Secretary must receive and consider comments related to excluding areas from leasing, the court has clearly stated that the Secretary need only identify the legal or factual basis for leasing determinations at this stage and explain those determinations; more searching judicial review of the Secretary's analysis is not required.[109]

Litigation under the OCSLA has also challenged actions taken during the leasing phase. As described above, the OCSLA authorizes states to submit comments during the notice of lease sale stage and directs the Secretary to accept a state's recommendations if they "provide for a reasonable balance between the national interest and the well-being of the citizens of the affected State."[110] Courts have typically applied the deferential "arbitrary and capricious" standard to Secretary decisions with respect to these recommendations. According to the cases from the Ninth Circuit Court of Appeals, because the OCSLA does not provide clear guidance as to how balancing of national interest and a state's considerations is to be performed, agency action will generally be upheld so long as "some consideration of the relevant factors ..." takes place.[111] Cases from the federal courts in Massachusetts, including a decision affirmed by the First Circuit Court of Appeals, have, while embracing the arbitrary and capricious standard, found the Secretary's balancing of interests insufficient.[112] However, it should be noted that the Massachusetts cases reviewed agency action that was not supported by explicit analysis of the sort challenged in the Ninth Circuit. Thus, it is possible that, given a more thorough record of the Secretary's decision, these courts may afford more significant deference to the Secretary's determination.

Apart from matters relating primarily to the authority of the Secretary to authorize the various stages of leasing, recent litigation has focused on the authority of MMS to require royalty payments on certain offshore leases allegedly subject to mandatory royalty relief provisions. In *Kerr-McGee Oil & Gas Corp. v. Burton*, the plaintiff, an oil and gas company operating offshore wells in the Gulf of Mexico pursuant to federal leases, is challenging actions by the Department to collect royalties on deepwater oil and gas production.[113] The plaintiff alleged the Department does not have authority to assess royalties based on an interpretation of the 1995 Outer Continental Shelf Deepwater Royalty Relief Act (DWRRA) that the act requires royalty-free production until a statutorily prescribed threshold volume of oil or gas production has been reached, and does not permit a price-based threshold for this royalty relief.[114]

The DWRRA separates leases into three categories based on date of issuance. These categories are (1) leases in existence on November 28, 1995, (2) leases issued after November 28, 2000, and (3) leases issued in between those periods, during the first five years after the act's enactment. The third category of leases is the current source of controversy. According to Kerr-McGee, its leases, which were issued during the initial five year period after the DWRRA's enactment, are subject to different legal requirements than those applicable to the other two categories. Kerr- McGee argues that the Department has a nondiscretionary duty under the DWRRA to provide royalty relief on its deepwater leases, and that the statute does not provide a exception to this obligation based on any preset price threshold. To the extent any price threshold has been included in these leases, Kerr-McGee argued that such provisions are contrary to DOI's statutory authority and unenforceable.

Section 304 of the DWRRA, which addresses deepwater leases[115] issued within five years after the DWRRA's enactment, directs that such leases use the bidding system authorized in section 8(a)(1)(H) of the OCSLA, as amended by the DWRRA. Section 304 of the DWRRA also stipulates that leases issued during the five-year post-enactment time frame must provide for royalty suspension on the basis of volume. Specifically, section 304 states

> [A]ny lease sale within five years of the date of enactment of this title, shall use the bidding system authorized in section 8(a)(1)(H) of the Outer Continental Shelf Lands Act, as amended by this title, except that the suspension of royalties shall be set at a volume of not less than the following:
>
> (1) 17.5 million barrels of oil equivalent for leases in water depths of 200 to 400 meters;
> (2) 52.5 million barrels of oil equivalent for leases in 400 to 800 meters of water; and
> (3) 87.5 million barrels of oil equivalent for leases in water depths greater than 800 meters.[116]

It is possible to interpret this provision as authorizing leases issued during the five-year period to contain *only* royalty suspension provisions that are based on production volume with no allowance at all for a price-related threshold in addition. Such an intent might be gleaned from the language of the quoted section alone; indeed, in this provision, Congress provides for a specific royalty suspension method and does not clearly authorize the Secretary to alter or supplement it. Kerr-McGee's challenge to the Secretary's authority to impose price-based thresholds on royalty suspension was based on this interpretation of the statutory language above.

The U.S. District Court for the Western District of Louisiana agreed with Kerr- McGee' s interpretation of the language discussed above. The court found that the DWRRA allowed only for volumetric thresholds on royalty suspension for leases issued between 1996 and 2000, and that the Secretary did not have authority under the DWRRA to attach price-based thresholds to royalty suspension for those leases.[117] The U.S. government has filed notice of appeal of this decision, and so this decision may be reversed.

Suits under the National Environmental Policy Act

In the context of proposed OCS development, NEPA generally requires publication of notice of an intent to prepare an Environmental Impact Statement (EIS), acceptance of comments on what should be addressed in the EIS, agency preparation of a draft EIS, a comment period on the draft EIS, and publication of a final EIS addressing all comments at each stage of the leasing process where government action will significantly affect the environment.[118] As described above, NEPA figures heavily in the OCS planning and leasing process and requires various levels of environmental analysis prior to agency decisions at each phase in the leasing and development process.[119] Lawsuits brought under NEPA are thus indirect challenges to agency decisions in that they typically question the adequacy of the environmental analysis performed prior to a final decision.

There has only been one NEPA-based challenge to a five-year plan, *Natural Resources Defense Council v. Hodel*.[120] The plaintiff challenged the adequacy of the alternatives examined in the EIS and the level of consideration paid to cumulative effects of offshore drilling activities. The court held that not every possible alternative needed to be examined, and that the determination as to adequacy was subject to the "rule of reason."[121] This standard appears to afford some level of deference to the Secretary, and his choice of alternatives was found to be sufficient by the court in this instance.[122] However, without significant explanation of the standard of review to be applied, the court did find that the Secretary's failure to analyze certain cumulative impacts was a violation of NEPA.[123] Thus, the Secretary was required to include this analysis, although final decisions based on that analysis remained subject to the Secretary's discretion, with review only under the arbitrary and capricious standard.[124]

As mentioned above, NEPA plays a role in the leasing phase as well. MMS often uses NEPA and its tiering option to evaluate lease sales.[125] The NEPA procedures and standard of review remain the same at this phase; however, due to the structure of the OCSLA process, more specific information is generally required.[126] Still, courts are deferential at the lease sale phase. In challenges to the adequacy of environmental review, courts have stressed that inaccuracies and more stringent NEPA analysis will be available at later phases.[127] Thus, because there will be an opportunity to cure any defects in the analysis as the OCSLA process continues, challenges under NEPA at this phase are often unsuccessful.[128]

It also appears possible to challenge exploration and development plans under NEPA, although a search of the relevant case law has revealed only one NEPA-based challenge to a development and production plan and no challenges to exploration plans.[129] In *Edwardsen v. U.S. Department of the Interior*, the Ninth Circuit Court of Appeals applied the typical "rule of reason" to determine if the EIS adequately addressed the probable environmental consequences of the development and production plan, and held that, despite certain omissions in the analysis and despite an MMS decision to tier its NEPA analysis to an EIS prepared for a similar lease sale, the requirements of NEPA were satisfied.[130] Thus, while additional analysis was required to account for the greater specificity of the plans and to accommodate the "hard look" at environmental impacts NEPA mandates, the reasonableness standard applied to what must be examined in an EIS did not allow for a successful challenge to agency action.

APPENDIX

Table 1. State Laws That Ban or Regulate Offshore Mineral Development

State	Policy	Statutes
AL	Drilling is authorized in Alabama's state waters. The State Lands Division of the Department of Conservation & Land Resources is charged with leasing offshore oil and gas in state waters. In addition, the Alabama State Oil and Gas Board regulates oil and gas production to ensure the conser-vation and proper development of oil and gas resources.	**Authorization:** Ala. Code § § 9- 15-18; 9-17-1 *et seq.*; 40-20-1 *et seq.*
AK	The Alaska Department of Natural Resour-ces is responsible for leasing oil and gas on state lands, including offshore areas. Certain areas are specifically designated as off limits to oil and gas leasing, and administra-tive decisions not to offer leases in offshore areas may further restrict access.	**Ban:** Alaska Stat. §§ 38.05.140(f); 38.05.184. **Authorization:** Alaska Stat. §§ 38.05.13 1 *et seq.*; 38.05.135 *et seq.*
CA	The State Lands Commission is generally responsible for oil and gas leasing. Califor-nia issued offshore oil and gas leases in the past, while banning development in multi-ple areas within state waters at both the sta-tutory and administrative levels. California currently has a general ban in place restrict-ing any state agency from issuing new off-shore leases, unless the President of the United States determines that there is a "severe energy supply inter-ruption and has ordered distribution of the Strategic Petro-leum Reserve ..., the Gover-nor finds that the energy resources of the sanctuary will contribute significantly to the alleviation of that interruption, and the Legislature subse-quently acts to amend... [the law] to allow that extraction." The ban is limited to areas that are not currently subject to a lease.	**Ban:** Cal. Pub. Res. Code § § 6871.1-.2 (repealed 1994); 6870 (Santa Barbara limitations); 6243 (general ban). **Authorization:** Cal. Pub. Res. Code §§ 6870 *et. seq.*; 6240 *et seq.*

Table 1. (Continued)

State	Policy	Statutes
CT	Connecticut does not appear to have laws addressing oil and gas development in state waters.	
DE	The Governor and the Secretary of the Department of Natural Resources and Environmental Control are authorized to lease oil and gas in state waters. Lands "administered by the Department of Natural Resources and Environmental Control" may not be leased by the Secretary.	**Ban:** Del. Code Ann. tit. 7 ch. 61 § 6102(e). **Authorization:** Del. Code. Ann. tit. 7 ch. 61.
FL	In general, the Department of Natural Resources is vested with the authority to permit oil and gas development on state lands and submerged lands; however, in 1990 Florida enacted a broad ban on offshore oil and gas development by prohibiting oil and gas drilling structures in a variety of locations, including Florida's territorial waters. The development ban provides an exception for valid existing rights.	**Ban:** Fla. Stat. Ann. §377.242. **Authorization:** Fla. Stat. Ann. §§ 377.01 et seq.; 253.001 et seq.
GA	The State Properties Commission is authorized to issue leases for state owned oil and gas. The statute does not distinguish between onshore and offshore minerals.	**Authorization:** Ga. Stat. § 50- 16-43.
HI	The Board of Land and Natural Resources is authorized to lease oil and gas on state lands, including submerged lands. There would not appear to be a statutory ban in place.	**Authorization:** Hawaii Rev. Stat. §§ 182-1 et seq.
LA	The state Mineral Board is responsible for leasing oil and gas in Louisiana and its offshore territory. There does not appear to be a statutory ban on oil and gas drilling in offshore areas, although development is limited to areas offered by the Board for leasing.	**Authorization:** La. Rev. Stat. § § 30:121 et seq.
ME	The Bureau of Geology and Natural Areas has primary authority over oil and gas development on state lands, including tidal and submerged lands. The Bureau is authorized to issue exploration permits and mineral leases.	**Authorization:** Me. Rev. Stat. tit. 12 §§ 549 et seq.
MD	The Department of the Environment regu lates oil and gas development. The areas underlying Chesapeake Bay, its tributaries, and the Chesapeake Bay Critical Area are unavailable for oil and gas development.	**Ban:** Md. Code, Envt. § 14-107. **Authorization:** Md. Code, Envt. §§ 14-101 *et seq*.
MA	The Division of Mineral Resources is char-ged with administering the leasing of oil and gas on state lands. The law requires a public hearing before any license to explore or lease for extraction is issued for mineral resources located in coastal waters. Further, many of the state's offshore areas are desig-nated as ocean sanctuaries in which oil and gas development is prohibited.	**Authorization:** Mass. Gen. Laws Ann. Ch. 21 §§ 54 *et seq.* **Ban:** Mass. Gen. Laws Ann. Ch. 132A § 15.

Table 1. (Continued)

State	Policy	Statutes
MS	The Mississippi Major Economic Impact Authority is responsible for administering oil and gas leases on state lands. Offshore oil and gas development is generally permi-ssible. However, specific areas are not available for leasing. No development may occur in areas north of the coastal barrier islands, except in Blocks 40, 41, 42, 43, 63, 64 and 66 through 98. Further, "surface offshore drilling operations" may not be conducted within one mile of Cat Island.	**Authorization:** Miss. Code. Ann. §§ 29-7-1 *et seq.* **Ban:** Miss. Code. Ann. § 29-7-3.
NH	No statute appears to address offshore oil and gas development.	
NJ	State law authorizes the removal of sand and "other materials" from lands under tide-waters and below the high water mark if approved by the Tidelands Resource Council. Offshore oil and gas development is not expressly addressed.	**Authorization:** N.J. Stat. Ann. §§ 12:3-12-1 *et seq.*
NY	Leases and permits for the right to use state owned submerged lands for navigation, commerce, fishing, bathing, and recreation are authorized for specified submerged areas. General authority for issuing oil and gas leases is vested in the Department of Environmental Conservation. Certain sub- merged lands underlying specified lakes are excluded from exploration and leasing, but offshore areas would not appear to be sub-ject to a similar ban.	**Authorization:** N.Y. Pub. Lands. Law § 75; N.Y. Envt'l & Conserv. Law §§ 23-0101 *et seq.*
NC	State law authorizes the sale or lease of any state owned mineral underlying the bottoms of any sounds, rivers, creeks, or other waters of the State. The state is authorized to dispose of oil and gas "at the request of the Department of Environment and Natural Resources."	**Authorization:** N.C. Gen. Stat. § 146-8.
OR	The Department of State Lands is generally responsible for leasing state owned mine-rals, including oil and gas. Leasing of tidal and submerged lands is governed by sepa-rate provisions of law. There would not appear to be a ban in place.	**Authorization:** Or. Rev. Stat. §§ 274.705 *et seq.*; 273.551 (for submerged lands seaward more than 10 miles easterly of the 124th West Meridian).
RI	The Coastal Resources Management Council is charged with identifying, evalua-ting, and determining which uses are appro-priate for the state's coastal resources and submerged lands.	**Authorization:** R.I. Gen. Laws. §§ 46-23-1 *et seq.*
SC	The state Budget and Control Board is authorized to "negotiate for leases of oil, gas and other mineral rights upon all of the lands and waters of the State, including offshore marginal and submerged lands."	**Authorization:** S.C. Code. Ann. § § 10-9-10 *et seq.*
TX	The School Land Board is authorized to lease those portions of the Gulf of Mexico under the state's jurisdiction for oil and gas development.	**Authorization:** Tex. Nat. Res. Code §§ 52.011 *et seq.*

Table 1. (Continued)

State	Policy	Statutes
VA	The Marine Resources Commission is authorized to grant easements or to lease "the beds of the waters of the Common-wealth outside of the Baylor Survey" for oil and gas development.	**Authorization:** Va. Code Ann. § 28.2-1208.
WA	In general, the Department of Natural Resources is responsible for mineral deve-lopment on state lands. State law prohibits leasing of tidal or submerged lands "exten-ding from mean high tide seaward three miles along the Washington coast from Cape Flattery south to Cape Disappointment, nor in Grays Harbor, Willapa Bay, and the Columbia river downstream from the Longview bridge, for purposes of oil or gas exploration, development, or production."	**Ban:** Wash. Rev. Code Ann. § § 43.143.005 *et seq.*

End Notes

[1] This chapter was authored originally by Aaron M. Flynn.

[2] United Nations Convention on the Law of the Sea III (entered into force November 16, 1994) (hereinafter UNCLOS).

[3] Id. at Art. 56.1

[4] Id. at Art. 76.1.

[5] Id. at Art. 76.4-76.7.

[6] Id. at Art. 77.1.

[7] Policy of the United States with Respect to the Natural Resources of the Subsoil and Sea Bed of the Continental Shelf, Proclamation No. 2667, 10 *Fed. Reg.* 12,303 (September 28, 1945); Exclusive Economic Zone of the United States of America, Proclamation No. 5030, 48 Fed. Reg. 10,605 (March 14, 1983); Territorial Sea of the United States of America, Proclamation No. 5928, 54 *Fed. Reg.* 777 (December 27, 1988); Contiguous Zone of the United States, Proclamation No. 7219, 64 *Fed. Reg.* 48,701 (August 2, 1999).

[8] *See* United States v. Texas, 339 U.S. 707 (1950); United States v. Louisiana, 339 U.S. 699 (1950); United States v. California, 332 U.S. 19 (1947). In accordance with the Submerged Lands Act, states generally own an offshore area extending three geographical miles from the shore. Florida (Gulf coast) and Texas, by virtue of their offshore boundaries prior to admission to the Union, have an extended three marine league offshore boundary. *See* United States v. Louisiana, 363 U.S. 1, 36-64 (1960); United States v. Florida, 363 U.S. 121, 121-29 (1960).

[9] 43 U.S.C. § 133 1(a).

[10] 43 U.S.C. §§ 1301 *et seq.*

[11] A geographical or nautical mile is equal to 6,080.20 feet, as opposed to the typical land mile, which is equal to 5,280 feet.

[12] 43 U.S.C. §1301(b).

[13] A marine league is equal to 18,228.3 feet.

[14] 43 U.S.C. §§ 1312, 1301(b).

[15] United States v. Louisiana, 363 U.S. 1, 66 (1960) ("[P]ursuant to the Annexation Resolution of 1845, Texas' maritime boundary was established at three leagues from its coast for domestic purposes .... Accordingly, Texas is entitled to a grant of three leagues from her coast under the Submerged Lands Act."); United States v. Florida, 363 U.S. 121, 129 (1960) ("We hold that the Submerged Lands Act grants Florida a three-marine-league belt of land under the Gulf, seaward from its coastline, as described in Florida's 1868 Constitution.").

[16] 43 U.S.C. § 1311.

[17] 43 U.S.C. §§ 1331-1356.

[18] 43 U.S.C. § 1332(3).

[19] 43 U.S.C. § 1333. The provision also expressly makes the Longshore and Harbor Workers' Compensation Act, the National Labor Relations Act, and the Rivers and Harbors Act applicable on the OCS, although application is limited in some instances.

[20] Id.

[21] 43 U.S.C. §§ 1331(a), 1332, 1333(a)(1).

[22] 43 U.S.C. § 134 1(a) ("The President of the United States may, from time to time, withdraw from disposition any of the unleased lands of the outer Continental Shelf."). The President's Memorandum on Withdrawal asserts that the presidential authority for imposing the OCS moratorium is contained in section 12(a) of the OCSLA. The statement also indicates that withdrawal from leasing is also authorized under those portions of the Marine Protection, Research, and Sanctuaries Act of 1972 authorizing the President, under certain circumstances, to establish marine sanctuaries and to impose certain levels of environmental protection within those sanctuaries. Notably, this presidential statement does not cite any inherent, constitutionally-based executive authority for executive control of OCS resources, and none is immediately apparent. In general, Congress, acting pursuant to its constitutional authority over federal property and U.S. territories and its authority over foreign and interstate commerce, has sufficient constitutional authority to regulate OCS resources.

[23] *See, e.g.*, P.L. 108-447, §§ 107-109.

[24] Statement on Outer Continental Shelf Oil and Gas Development, 26 WEEKLY COMP. PRES. DOC. 1006 (June 26, 1990).

[25] Memorandum on Withdrawal of Certain Areas of the United States Outer Continental Shelf from Leasing Disposition, 34 WEEKLY COMP. PRES. DOC. 1111 (June 12, 1998).

[26] P.L. 105-83.

[27] Id.

[28] **Figure 1** does not account for the recent legislation that made the so-called "181 Area" in the Gulf of Mexico available for leasing. This legislation is discussed *infra.*

[29] *See, e.g.*, P.L. 106-291.

[30] 42 U.S.C. § 15912.

[31] Id.

[32] P.L. 109-432.

[33] Id. at Division C, § 103 .

[34] 43 U.S.C. §§ 1331(b), 1334; 30 C.F.R. § 250.101.

[35] P.L. 95-372.

[36] 43 U.S.C. § 1344.

[37] 43 U.S.C. §§ 1337, 1345.

[38] 43 U.S.C. § 1340.

[39] 43 U.S.C. § 1351.

[40] 43 U.S.C. § 1344(a), (e).

[41] Id.

[42] "Affected state" is defined in the act as any state:

(1) the laws of which are declared, pursuant to section 1333(a)(2) of this title, to be the law of the United States for the portion of the outer Continental Shelf on which such activity is, or is proposed to be, conducted;

(2) which is, or is proposed to be, directly connected by transportation facilities to any artificial island or structure referred to in section 1333(a)(1) of this title;

(3) which is receiving, or in accordnace [sic] with the proposed activity will receive, oil for processing, refining, or transshipment which was extracted from the outer Continental Shelf and transported directly to such State by means of vessels or by a combination of means including vessels;

(4) which is designated by the Secretary as a State in which there is a substantial probability of significant impact on or damage to the coastal, marine, or human environment, or a State in which there will be significant changes in the social, governmental, or economic infrastructure, resulting from the exploration, development, and production of oil and gas anywhere on the outer Continental Shelf; or

(5) in which the Secretary finds that because of such activity there is, or will be, a significant risk of serious damage, due to factors such as prevailing winds and currents, to the marine or coastal environment in the event of any oilspill, blowout, or release of oil or gas from vessels, pipelines, or other transshipment facilities....

43 U.S.C. § 1331(f).

[43] 43 U.S.C. § 1344(d).

[44] Id.; *see also* 30 C.F.R. §§ 256.16-. 17.

[45] 43 U.S.C. § 1344(d).

[46] 42 U.S.C. § 4332(2)(C). In general, NEPA and its CEQ regulations require various levels of environmental analysis depending on the circumstances and the type of Federal action contemplated. Certain actions that have been determined to have little or no environmental effect are exempted from preparation of NEPA documents entirely and are commonly referred to as "categorical exclusions." In situations where a categorical exclusion does not apply, an intermediate level of review, an environmental assessment (EA), may be required. If, based on the EA, the agency finds that an action will not have a significant effect on the environment, the agency issues a "finding of no significant impact" (FONSI), thus terminating the NEPA review process. On the other hand, major Federal actions that are found to significantly affect the environment

require the preparation of an environmental impact statement (EIS), a document offering detailed analysis of the project as proposed as well as other options, including taking no action at all. NEPA does not direct an agency to choose any particular course of action; the only purpose of an EIS is to ensure that environmental consequences are considered. For additional information, see CRS Report RS20621, *Overview of NEPA Requirements*, by Kristina Alexander.

[47] *See* Natural Resources Defense Council v. Hodel, 865 F.2d 288, 310 (D.C. Cir.1988).

[48] 43 U.S.C. § 1337.

[49] 30 C.F.R. §§ 256.23, 256.25.

[50] 30 C.F.R. § 256.26.

[51] 30 C.F.R. § 256.29.

[52] It should be noted that the OCSLA establishes certain minimum requirements applicable to these subjects. For instance, lease tracts are, in general, to be limited to 5,760 acres, unless the Secretary determines that a larger area is necessary to comprise a "reasonable economic production unit...." *Id.* § 1337(b). The law and its implementing regulations also set the range of initial lease terms and baseline conditions for lease renewal.

[53] 43 U.S.C. § 1345(a); *see also* 30 C.F.R. § 256.31.

[54] 43 U.S.C. § 1345(c).

[55] 43 U.S.C. § 1337(*l*).

[56] 30 C.F.R. § 256.32(1).

[57] 43 U.S.C. § 1337.

[58] 43 U.S.C § 1337(a)(1)(A)-(H). For example, bids may be on the basis of "cash bonus bid with a royalty at not less than 12 1/2 per centum fixed by the Secretary in amount or value of the production saved, removed, or sold ...." *See also* 30 C.F.R. §§ 256.35 - 256.47.

[59] 43 U.S.C 1337(a)(1)-(3), (8)-(9). It should be noted that the OCSLA also provides for a legislative veto of the bidding system selected by the Secretary and that a similar provision was declared unconstitutional by the U.S. Supreme Court. *See* Immigration and Naturalization Service v. Chadha, 462 U.S. 919 (1983).

[60] 43 U.S.C. § 1337(c); 30 C.F.R. § 256.47(d).

[61] 43 U.S.C § 1337(c), (f).

[62] Restrictions include a statutory prohibition on issuance of a new lease to a bidder that is not meeting applicable due diligence requirements with respect to the bidder's other leases. *See* 43 U.S.C § 1337(d).

[63] Id. § 1337(a)(3).

[64] 43 U.S.C. § 1337(a)(3)(B)

[65] P.L. 109-58 (codified at 43 U.S.C. § 1334 note).

[66] Id.

[67] 43 U.S.C § 1337(a)(7); 30 C.F.R. §§ 256.52 - 256.59.

[68] 43 U.S.C § 1337(b). Leases may also be cancelled at any time if obtained by fraud or misrepresentation. 43 U.S.C § 1337(o).

[69] 43 U.S.C § 1337(b)(4).

[70] 43 U.S.C § 1340(b), (c).

[71] 30 C.F.R. §§ 250.226, 250.227, 250.232, 250.235.

[72] 16 U.S.C. § 1456(c).

[73] 30 C.F.R. § 250.235.

[74] 30 C.F.R. § 250.232(c).

[75] 30 C.F.R. §§ 250.23 1 - 250.233.

[76] 43 U.S.C. § 1351.

[77] 30 C.F.R. § 250.201.

[78] Id.

[79] 30 C.F.R. §§ 250.24 - 250.262.

[80] The regulations indicate that "at least once in each planning area (other than the western and central Gulf of Mexico planning areas) we [MMS] will prepare an environmental impact statement (EIS) ...." 30 C.F.R.§ 250.269.

[81] 30 C.F.R. § 250.267.

[82] 30 C.F.R. §§ 250.286, 250.287.

[83] 30 C.F.R.§§ 250.289, 250.292.

[84] 30 C.F.R. §§ 250.4 10 - 250.469.

[85] 30 C.F.R. § 250.411.

[86] 43 U.S.C. § 1334; *see also* 30 C.F.R. §§ 250.168 - 250.185.

[87] 30 C.F.R. §§ 250.168, 250.171-250.175.

[88] 43 U.S.C.§ 1334(a)(1).

[89] 30 C.F.R. § 250. 173 - 250. 175.

[90] 43 U.S.C.§ 1334(a)(1).

[91] Id.

[92] The requisite suspension period may be reduced upon the request of the lessee. 43 U.S.C. § 1334(a)(2)(B).

93 43 U.S.C. § 1334(a)(2)(A)(i)-(iii). For regulations implementing the cancellation provisions, see 30 C.F.R. §§ 250.180 - 250.185.

94 The statute requires "fair value" to take account of "anticipated revenues from the lease and anticipated costs, including costs of compliance with all applicable regulations and operating orders, liability for cleanup costs or damages, or both, in the case of an oilspill, and all other costs reasonably anticipated on the lease ...." 43 U.S.C. § 1334(a)(2)(C).

95 Exceptions from this method of calculation are carved out for leases issued before September 18, 1978, and for joint leases that are canceled due to the failure of one or more partners to exercise due diligence. 43 U.S.C. § 1334(a)(2)(C)(ii)(I), (II); *see also* 30 C.F.R. §§ 250.184 - 250.185.

96 43 U.S.C. § 1334(b).

97 43 U.S.C. § 1334(c).

98 43 U.S.C. § 1334(d).

99 33 U.S.C. §§ 125 1-1387.

100 16 U.S.C. §§ 153 1-1544.

101 Village of Akutan v. Hodel, 869 F.2d 1185 (9th Cir. 1988); Village of False Pass v. Clark, 733 F.2d 605 (9th Cir. 1984); North Slope Borough v. Andrus, 642 F.2d 589 (D.C. Cir. 1980); Conservation Law Foundation v. Andrus, 623 F.2d 712 (1st Cir.1979).

102 43 U.S.C. § 1349.

103 43 U.S.C. § 1349(c).

104 668 F.2d 1290 (D.C. Cir.1981).

105 Watt, 668 F.2d at 1302; *see also* 43 U.S.C. § 1349(c)(6).

106 Watt, 668 F.2d at 1301-1302 (*quoting* Citizens to Preserve Overton Park v. Volpe, 401 U.S. 402, 416 (1971) (internal quotations omitted)).

107 *See* California v. Watt, 712 F.2d 584 (D.C. Cir.1983); Natural Resources Defense Council v. Hodel, 865 F.2d 288 (D.C. Cir. 1988).

108 California, 715 F.2d at 96 (internal quotations omitted).

109 Hodel, 865 F.2d at 305.

110 43 U.S.C. § 1345(d).

111 California v. Watt, 683 F.2d 1253, 1269 (9th Cir. 1982); *see also* Tribal Village of Akutan v. Hodel, 869 F.2d 1185 (9th Cir.1988).

112 Conservation Law Foundation v. Watt, 560 F.Supp. 561 (D.Mass. 1983), aff'd sub nom. Massachusetts v. Watt, 716 F.2d 946 (1st Cir.1983); Massachusetts v. Clark, 594 F.Supp. 1373 (D.Mass. 1984).

113 Kerr-McGee Oil & Gas Corp. v. Burton, No. CV06-0439 LC (W.D. La. March 17, 2006).

114 P.L. 104-58.

115 This term refers to "tracts located in water depths of 200 meters or greater in the Western and Central Planning Area of the Gulf of Mexico, including that portion of the Eastern Planning Area of the Gulf of Mexico encompassing whole lease blocks lying west of 87 degrees, 30 minutes West longitude ...." 43 U.S.C. § 1337 note.

116 P.L. 104-58.

117 CITE.

118 40 C.F.R. §§ 1501.7, 1503.1, 1503.4, 1506.10.

119 42 U.S.C. § 4332.

120 Natural Resources Defense Council, Inc. v. Hodel, 865 F.2d 288 (D.C. Cir. 1988).

121 Id. at 294.

122 Id. at 296.

123 Id. at 297-300.

124 *See* California ex. rel. Brown v. Watt, 668 F.2d 1290, 1301-1302 (D.C. Cir.1981).

125 *See* 30 C.F.R. § 256.26(b); 40 C.F.R. § 1508.28.

126 Tribal Village of Akutan v. Hodel, 869 F.2d 1185, 1191 (9th Cir.1988).

127 Id. at 1192; Alaska v. Andrus, 580 F.2d 465, 473 (D.C. Cir. 1978); Village of False Pass v. Clark, 733 F.2d 605, 612-16 (9th Cir.1984); North Slope Borough v. Andrus, 642 F.2d 589, 594-905 (D.C. Cir.1980).

128 *But see* Conservation Law Foundation v. Clark, 560 F.Supp. 561 (D. Mass. 1983).

129 Edwardsen v. U.S. Department fo the Interior, 268 F.3d 781 (9th Cir. 2001).

130 *Id.* at 784-790.

In: Federal Land Resources
Editors: Quintin R. Telles
ISBN: 978-1-60692-130-2

Chapter 4

BLM-Alaska Releases Supplemental Final Plan for Northeast National Petroleum Reserve-Alaska*

U.S. Department of the Interior Bureau of Land Management

In a plan released today, the Bureau of Land Management (BLM) announced that it would make land available for leasing in the Northeast portion of the National Petroleum Reserve in Alaska (NPR-A) that could yield nearly 3 billion barrels of oil, equaling one quarter of the oil produced over the last 31 years by North America's largest oilfield in Prudhoe Bay. The lands could also provide trillions of cubic feet of gas for shipment to North American markets through gas pipelines currently in the planning stages.

The BLM would not open 219,000 acres of Teshekpuk Lake and its islands to oil and gas leasing according to the preferred alternative selected by the agency in its Supplemental Final Integrated Activity Plan/Environment Impact Statement (IAP/EIS). The plan's preferred alternative would also defer leasing for 10 years on 430,000 acres north and east of Teshekpuk Lake that are currently unavailable for leasing.

"This plan provides a balanced approach to energy development and wildlife protection, and forms a solid basis for the Bureau of Land Management to proceed with an oil and gas lease sale later this year," said Secretary of the Interior Dirk Kempthorne.

The BLM expects to hold a lease sale this fall for available portions of the Northeast area, as well as portions of the Northwest planning area.

North Slope Borough Mayor Edward Itta expressed support for the plan's deferral of acreage near Teshekpuk Lake. "BLM listened to local communities and it made the plan better," Itta said. "The lease sale can proceed while one of the region's most sensitive wildlife habitats will be protected. It's a win-win." BLM-Alaska State Director Tom Lonnie agreed, saying, "We appreciate the collaboration of Mayor Itta and the North Slope Borough in the development of this plan. Their input will assist the BLM in the management of these important lands."

---

* This is an edited, reformatted and augmented edition of a United States Department of the Interior, Bureau of Land Management National News Report, dated May 16, 2008.

"The strength of this improved and updated plan is its ability to adapt new information and new technology through its performance-based requirements," said Lonnie. "We know that the Northeast area has significant oil and gas reserves that are important to our country, but we also recognize the importance of protecting the area's wildlife values."

The plan includes protections for the polar bear, including requirements to consider impacts on areas used by the polar bears for denning. Additionally, with the listing of the polar bear earlier this week, the agency will continue to work closely with the U.S. Fish and Wildlife Service on future oil and gas activities.

The supplemental final plan for Northeast NPR-A updates information in the 2005 Northeast NPR-A Amended Environmental Impact Statement. The BLM began developing the supplement in December 2006 in response to a September 25, 2006, U.S. District Court for the District of Alaska decision that the 2005 Northeast NPR-A Amended Integrated Activity Plan/Environmental Impact Statement (IAP/EIS) failed to adequately address cumulative impacts. The Notice of Availability announcing the release of the plan will be published in the *Federal Register* later this month.

The Northeast Draft Supplement, released for public comment in August 2007, presented essentially the same alternatives as the Amended IAP/EIS. After considering public comments on the draft Supplement, the BLM modified and selected Alternative D as the preferred alternative in its final plan. The BLM expects to issue a Record of Decision by mid-summer. The Supplemental Final IAP/EIS for the Northeast NPR-A can be reached through a link on the BLM-Alaska's home page at www.blm.gov/ak.

The BLM, an agency of the U.S. Department of the Interior, manages more land – 258 million surface acres – than any other Federal agency. Most of this public land is in 12 Western states, including 80.8 million surface acres in Alaska. The Bureau also administers 700 million acres of sub-surface mineral estate throughout the nation. The BLM's multiple-use mission is to sustain the health and productivity of the public lands for the use and enjoyment of present and future generations. The Bureau accomplishes this by managing such activities as outdoor recreation, livestock grazing, mineral development, and energy production, and by conserving natural, historical, cultural, and other resources on the public lands.

INDEX

A

B

C

D

E

F

G

H

I

J

K

L

P

Q

R

S

T

U

V

W

Y

Z